D0142629

Routledge History of Philosophy
Volume II

This volume provides a comprehensive survey of the work of philosophers who wrote in Greek and Latin from the mid-fourth century BC to the fifth century AD – from the death of Plato to the beginning of Christian philosophy.

Five chapters are devoted to Aristotle and the Peripatetic school, three to the major Hellenistic schools – the Epicurean, Stoic and the Sceptic – two to the arguments of mathematicians and biologists, and one each to Neo-Platonism and Augustine.

Supplemented with a chronology, a glossary of technical terms and an extensive bibliography, Volume II of the *Routledge History of Philosophy* provides a comprehensive and user-friendly survey and analysis of the methods and achievements of post-Platonic Classical philosophers.

David Furley is Professor of Classics, Emeritus, at Princeton University, and an Honorary Fellow of Jesus College Cambridge. He is the author of *Cosmic Problems: Essays on Greek and Roman Philosophy of Nature* (1989). He was Editor of *Phronesis* (1968–72) and he was elected Corresponding Fellow of the British Academy in 1990.

Routledge History of Philosophy
General Editors – G. H. R. Parkinson and S. G. Shanker

The *Routledge History of Philosophy* provides a chronological survey of the history of Western philosophy, from its beginnings in the sixth century BC to the present time. It discusses all major philosophical developments in depth. Most space is allocated to those individuals who, by common consent, are regarded as great philosophers. But lesser figures have not been neglected, and together the ten volumes of the *History* include basic and critical information about every significant philosopher of the past and present. These philosophers are clearly situated within the cultural and, in particular, the scientific context of their time.

The *History* is intended not only for the specialist, but also for the student and the general reader. Each chapter is by an acknowledged authority in the field. The chapters are written in an accessible style and a glossary of technical terms is provided in each volume.

Each volume contains 10–15 chapters by different contributors

Routledge History of Philosophy
Volume II

From Aristotle to Augustine

EDITED BY
David Furley

London and New York

Mohawk Valley Community College Library

First published 1999
by Routledge
11 New Fetter Lane, London EC4P 4EE

Simultaneously published in the USA and Canada
by Routledge
29 West 35th Street, New York, NY 10001

© 1999 Selection and editorial matter David Furley;
individual contributions, the contributors

The right of David Furley to be identified as the Author of this
Work has been asserted by him in accordance with the Copyright,
Designs and Patents Act 1988

Typeset in Stempel Garamond by
Keystroke, Jacaranda Lodge, Wolverhampton
Printed and bound in Great Britain by
TJ International Ltd, Padstow, Cornwall

All rights reserved. No part of this book may be reprinted or
reproduced or utilised in any form or by any electronic,
mechanical, or other means, now known or hereafter
invented, including photocopying and recording, or in any
information storage or retrieval system, without permission in
writing from the publishers.

British Library Cataloguing in Publication Data
A catalogue record for this book is available from the British Library

Library of Congress Cataloging in Publication Data
From Aristotle to Augustine / edited by David Furley.
p.   cm. — (Routledge history of philosophy ; v. 2)
Includes bibliographical references and index.
ISBN 0–415–06002–8 (HB)
1. Philosophy, Ancient. 2. Aristotle. 3. Augustine, Saint,
Bishop of Hippo. I. Furley, David J. II. Series.
B505.F76 1999
180—dc21   98–8543
CIP

ISBN 0–415–06002–8

Ref
B
72
.R68
1993
v. 2

Contents

General editors' preface

The history of philosophy, as its name implies, represents a union of two very different disciplines, each of which imposes severe constraints upon the other. As an exercise in the history of ideas, it demands that one acquire a 'period eye': a thorough understanding of how the thinkers whom it studies viewed the problems which they sought to resolve, the conceptual frameworks in which they addressed these issues, their assumptions and objectives, their blind spots and miscues. But as an exercise in philosophy, we are engaged in much more than simply a descriptive task. There is a crucial critical aspect to our efforts: we are looking for the cogency as much as the development of an argument, for its bearing on questions which continue to preoccupy us as much as the impact which it may have had on the evolution of philosophical thought.

The history of philosophy thus requires a delicate balancing act from its practitioners. We read these writings with the full benefit of historical hindsight. We can see why the minor contributions remained minor and where the grand systems broke down: sometimes as a result of internal pressures, sometimes because of a failure to overcome an insuperable obstacle, sometimes because of a dramatic technological or sociological change and, quite often, because of nothing more than a shift in intellectual fashion or interests. Yet, because of our continuing philosophical concern with many of the same problems, we cannot afford to look dispassionately at these works. We want to know what lessons are to be learnt from the inconsequential or the glorious failures; many times we want to plead for a contemporary relevance in the overlooked theory or to reconsider whether the 'glorious failure' was indeed such or simply ahead of its time: perhaps even ahead of its author.

We find ourselves, therefore, much like the mythical 'radical translator' who has so fascinated modern philosophers, trying to understand an author's ideas in his and his culture's eyes, and at the same time, in our own. It can be a formidable task. Many times we fail in the historical undertaking because our philosophical interests are so strong, or lose sight of the latter because we are so enthralled by the former. But the nature of philosophy is such that we are compelled to master both techniques. For learning about the history of philosophy is not just a challenging and engaging pastime: it is an essential element in learning about the nature of philosophy – in grasping how philosophy is intimately connected with and yet distinct from both history and science.

The *Routledge History of Philosophy* provides a chronological survey of the history of Western philosophy, from its beginnings up to the present time. Its aim is to discuss all major philosophical developments in depth, and with this in mind, most space has been allocated to those individuals who, by common consent, are regarded as great philosophers. But lesser figures have not been neglected, and it is hoped that the reader will be able to find, in the ten volumes of the *History*, at least basic information about any significant philosopher of the past or present.

Philosophical thinking does not occur in isolation from other human activities, and this *History* tries to situate philosophers within the cultural, and in particular the scientific, context of their time. Some philosophers, indeed, would regard philosophy as merely ancillary to the natural sciences; but even if this view is rejected, it can hardly be denied that the sciences have had a great influence on what is now regarded as philosophy, and it is important that this influence should be set forth clearly. Not that these volumes are intended to provide a mere record of the factors that influenced philosophical thinking; philosophy is a discipline with its own standards of argument, and the presentation of the ways in which these arguments have developed is the main concern of this *History*.

In speaking of 'what is now regarded as philosophy', we may have given the impression that there now exists a single view of what philosophy is. This is certainly not the case; on the contrary, there exist serious differences of opinion, among those who call themselves philosophers, about the nature of their subject. These differences are reflected in the existence at the present time of two main schools of thought, usually described as 'analytic' and 'continental' philosophy. It is not our intention, as general editors of this *History*, to take sides in this dispute. Our attitude is one of tolerance, and our hope is that these volumes will contribute to an understanding of how philosophers have reached the positions which they now occupy.

One final comment. Philosophy has long been a highly technical subject, with its own specialized vocabulary. This *History* is intended not only for the specialist but also for the general reader. To this end, we have tried to ensure that each chapter is written in an accessible style; and since technicalities are unavoidable, a glossary of technical terms is provided in each volume. In this way these volumes will, we hope, contribute to a wider understanding of a subject which is of the highest importance to all thinking people.

G. H. R. Parkinson
S. G. Shanker

Notes on contributors

Alan C. Bowen is the Director of the Institute for Research in Classical Philosophy and Science (Princeton). He has published numerous articles on the history of ancient science and is currently writing a book, *Greco-Latin Planetary Theory before Ptolemy: History and Historiography*.

Alan Code is Nicholas C. Petris Professor of Greek Studies at the University of California at Berkeley. Until recently he was O'Donnell Professor of Philosophy at the Ohio State University. He is the author of many articles on Aristotle's metaphysics, logic, philosophy of mind and philosophy of nature.

Roger Crisp is Fellow and Tutor in Philosophy at St Anne's College Oxford. He is the editor of *Utilitas*. In addition to articles on Aristotle, and contributions to modern problems in moral philosophy, he has published *Mill on Utilitarianism* (Routledge, 1997), and is translating Aristotle's *Nicomachean Ethics* for Cambridge University Press's History of Philosophy series.

Eyjólfur K. Emilsson received his PhD degree from Princeton University, and then became a Fellow in the Institute of Philosophy at the University of Iceland. He now teaches in the Philosophy Department of the University of Oslo. His book *Plotinus on Sense-Perception: A Philosophical Study* was published by Cambridge University Press in 1988.

Stephen Everson is the author of *Aristotle on Perception* (1997), as well as articles on Aristotle and Epicurus. He is currently a member of the Department of Philosophy at the University of Michigan.

Michael Frede is Professor of Ancient Philosophy at the University of Oxford. He is the author of *Die stoische Logik* (1974), *Galen: Three Treatises on the Nature of Science* (1985) and *Essays in Ancient Philosophy* (1987), and has published many other papers on ancient philosophy and medicine.

David Furley is Professor of Classics, Emeritus, at Princeton University, and an Honorary Fellow of Jesus College Cambridge. He is the author of *Two Studies in the Greek Atomists* (1967), *The Greek Cosmologists* vol. 1 (1987), and *Cosmic Problems: Essays on Greek and Roman Philosophy of Nature* (1989). He was Editor of *Phronesis* (1968–72), and Joint Editor with R.E. Allen of *Studies in Presocratic Philosophy* I (1970) and II (1975). He was elected Corresponding Fellow of the British Academy in 1990.

David Gallop is Professor of Philosophy, Emeritus, at Trent University, Ontario, where he taught from 1969 to 1989. His publications include numerous articles on philosophical and literary subjects. He has translated and edited Plato's *Phaedo* for the Clarendon Press series (1975), as well as *Euthyphro, Defence of Socrates, Crito*, and *Phaedo* for World's Classics (1993, 1997). He has also published *Parmenides of Elea* (Toronto, 1984) and *Aristotle on Sleep and Dreams* (Warminster, 1996).

R.J. Hankinson is Professor of Philosophy at the University of Texas at Austin. He is the author of many articles on the philosophical thought of Hellenistic and later Greek biologists. His book *Galen on Antecedent Causes* was published by Cambridge University Press in 1994.

Brad Inwood is Professor of Classics, University of Toronto. He is the author of *Ethics and Human Action in Early Stoicism* (1985), *Hellenistic Philosophy: Introductory Readings* with L.P. Gerson (1988, 2nd, expanded edition, 1997), and *The Poem of Parmenides* (1992). He is co-editor, with Jaap Mansfeld, of *Assent and Argument in Cicero's Academic Books* (1997), and has contributed articles to two volumes on Hellenistic philosophy, *Passions and Perceptions* (1993), and *Justice and Generosity* (1995).

Gerard O'Daly is Professor of Latin at University College London. His chief publications are *Plotinus' Philosophy of the Self* (1973), *Augustine's Philosophy of Mind* (1987), and *The Poetry of Boethius* (1991). He is co-editor of the *Augustinus-Lexikon* (1986–).

Trevor J. Saunders is Professor of Greek at the University of Newcastle upon Tyne. His chief interests are in Greek political, social, and legal theory. He has produced three volumes in the Penguin Classics series: a translation of Plato's *Laws* (1970), a revision of T.A. Sinclair's translation of Aristotle's *Politics* (1981), and (as contributing editor) *Plato: Early Socratic Dialogues* (1987). He has written numerous articles on the political philosophy of Plato and Aristotle, and his latest books are *Plato's Penal Code: Controversy and Reform in Greek Penology* (Oxford: Clarendon Press, 1991), and *Aristotle, Politics Book I and II* (1995), in the Clarendon Aristotle series.

Robert W. Sharples is Professor of Classics and Head of the Department of Greek and Latin at University College London. His publications include English translations of Alexander Aphrodisias, *On Fate* (1983), *Ethical Problems* (1990), and *Quaestiones* (1992 and 1994). He is a member of the team for *Theophrastus of Eresus*, eds W.W. Fortenbaugh and others (Leiden, Brill, 1992), and contributor to two commentary volumes (1995 and forthcoming). He is currently editor of *Phronesis*.

Chronology

Politics and religion	The arts
BC	BC
338 Athenians defeated by Macedonians at Chaeronea	
336 Alexander succeeds to the throne of Macedon	
323 Alexander dies. Empire partitioned among Generals	c.324–292 Menander's comedies
	320–250 Life of Theocritus
322 Demosthenes dies	307 Museum and Library of Alexandria begun under Ptolemy Soter
285 Ptolemy II Philadelphus King of Egypt (dies 247)	285–46 Callimachus active (Alexandria)
280 Pyrrhus of Epirus invades Italy, withdraws 275	
264–241 First Punic War	

Science and technology	Philosophy
BC	BC

Science and technology BC		Philosophy BC	
c.340	Eudoxus of Cnidos (astronomer) dies	347	Plato dies. Speusippus heads Academy: Aristotle leaves Athens for Atarneus, Assos, Lesbos
c.330	Callimachus (astronomer) active		
		342	Aristotle tutors Alexander, crown prince of Macedon
		341	Epicurus born in Samos
		339	Xenocrates heads Academy
		335	Zeno born in Citium (Cyprus). Aristotle returns to Athens, founds Peripatetic School in Lyceum
?325–250	Life of Euclid	c.325–275	Pyrrhon of Elis active (founder of Greek Sceptics)
c.315–?240	Life of Aratus (author of astronomical poem *Phainomena*)	322	Aristotle dies. Theophrastus heads Peripatetic School
		314	Xenocrates dies. Polemo heads Academy.
		313	Zeno of Citium comes to Athens, later founds Stoic School
		c.307	Epicurus founds school in Athens ('The Garden')
c.290	Herophilus *fl.* (anatomy and physiology)	287	Theophrastus dies. Strato of Lampsacus heads Peripatetic School
c.280	Erasistratus *fl.* (anatomy and physiology)	270	Epicurus dies. Hermarchus heads Epicurean School
280–c.232	Aristarchus of Samos active (astronomer, heliocentric hypothesis)	269	Strato dies. Lyco heads Peripatetic School until 225
		268	Arcesilaus head of Academy until 242
		263	Zeno dies. Cleanthes of Assos head of Stoic School

Politics and religion		The arts	
		c.250	Apollonius of Rhodes active (Argonautica)
247	Ptolemy III Euergetes King of Egypt	c.230	Temple of Horus at Edfu
c.219–201	Second Punic War: Rome defeats Hannibal of Carthage	c.205–184	Comedies of Plautus
		c.200–170	Ennius active
		c.170–159	Comedies of Terence
147	Greece ruled by Romans	106–43	Life of Cicero
146	Romans destroy Carthage	87–54	Life of Catullus
85	Sack of Athens by Sulla	86–35	Life of Sallust
60	Julius Caesar consul in Rome. First Triumvirate (Caesar, Pompey, Crassus)	70–19	Life of Vergil
		65–8	Life of Horace
44	Caesar murdered. Second Triumvirate (Antony, Lepidus, Octavian)	59–AD17	Life of Livy
		47	Alexandrian Library destroyed by fire
31	Battle of Actium: Antony and Cleopatra defeated by Octavian	43–AD18	Life of Ovid
30	Octavian virtual Emperor, renamed Augustus		
AD		AD	
14	Tiberius Emperor.	43–120	Life of Martial
37	Caligula Emperor.	58–138	Life of Juvenal
42	Claudius Emperor.		
54	Nero Emperor.		
60	Trial of St Paul in Rome		

Science and technology		Philosophy	
c.247–212	Archimedes of Syracuse active (mathematician and inventor)	232	Cleanthes dies. Chrysippus of Soli head of Stoic School
c.245	Eratosthenes (astronomer) head of Alexandrian library	c.225	Ariston of Ceos head of Peripatetic School
c.200	Apollonius of Perge fl. (epicyclic/eccentric theory of planetary motion)	207	Chrysippus dies. Zeno of Tarsus head of Stoic School
		c.185–c.110	Life of Stoic Panaetius of Rhodes
		c.160–137	Carneades head of Academy
		159–84	Life of (Academic) Philo of Larissa
		155	Philosophical embassy to Rome: Carneades, Diogenes (Stoic), Critolaus (Peripatetic School)
c.147–127	Hipparchus (astronomer) active in Rhodes	c.135–c.50	Life of (Stoic) Posidonius of Apamea in Syria (later Rhodes)
?c.100–50	Life of Asclepiades of Bithynia (corpuscular theory of physiology)	c.130–69	Life of (Academic) Antiochus of Ascalon
?c.62	Heron of Alexandria fl. (mathematician and inventor)	c.95–55 or 51	Life of Lucretius
?c.50	Vitruvius fl. (Roman architect, engineer, historian)	c.50	Andronicus of Rhodes fl. (Peripatetic)
		55–54	Cicero De oratore, De republica
		54	Lucretius' poem mentioned by Cicero
		45–44	Most of Cicero's philosophical works
		4–AD65	Life of Seneca the Younger
		AD Early 1st century	Philo Judaeus fl. (in Alexandria)

Politics and religion		The arts	
69	Vespasian Emperor	68	Josephus' *History of Jewish War*
70	Destruction of Jerusalem. First diaspora	c.60–230	'Second Sophistic' (Greek rhetoric)
117–138	Hadrian Emperor	c.117	Tacitus' *Histories*
121–180	Life of Marcus Aurelius, Emperor 161–180		
135	Expulsion of Jews from Jerusalem	?c.150	Apollonius Dyscolus (Alexandrian grammarian)
286	Emperor Diocletian divides Roman Empire		
306–37	Constantine proclaimed Caesar: overcomes rivals; promotes Christianity		
325	Nicene Creed formulated by ecumenical council	314–c.393	Life of Libanius (rhetorician)
330	Foundation of Constantinople by Constantine	330–395	Life of Ammianus Marcellinus (Roman historian)
361–63	Julian 'the Apostate' Emperor in Constantinople	c.370–c.404	Life of Claudian (Latin poet)
410	Sack of Rome by Alaric the Visigoth		
452	Huns under Attila invade N. Italy		
527–65	Justinian Roman Emperor in the East	c.500–542+	Life of Procopius (Greek historian)

Science and technology	Philosophy
	65 Suicide of Seneca
	Late 1st century Epictetus *fl.* (Stoic)
AD	*c.*100–150 Life of Aspasius (Peripatetic)
146–*c.*170 Ptolemy (mathematician) active in Alexandria	
	205– 269/70 Life of Plotinus (first Neoplatonist)
129–199/216 Life of Galen of Pergamum, court physician in Rome	*c.*200–? Alexander of Aphrodisias *fl.* (commentator on Aristotle)
	234–*c.*305 Life of Porphyry (Neoplatonist)
*c.*260–339 Eusebius of Caesarea (Christian apologist and historian)	
*c.*320 Pappus *fl.* (mathematician)	*c.*245–*c.*325 Life of Iamblichus (Neoplatonist)
	354–430 Life of Augustine: Bishop of Hippo 396
	*c.*410–485 Life of Proclus (Neoplatonist)
	*c.*480–525 Life of Boethius
	6th century Simplicius (Neoplatonist) and Philoponus (Christian Neoplatonist) commentators on Aristotle
	529 Emperor Julian closes Aristotle's school in Athens

List of Sources

The following are those ancient authors and works most frequently cited as sources in this volume. This list mentions English translations whenever possible. 'Loeb' indicates that a Greek (Latin)/English edition is available in the Loeb Classical Library published by Harvard University Press.

More detailed information in given in the bibliographies attached to individual chapters. Each bibliographic entry is given a number for reference. The twelve chapters of this volume can be seen as divided into four sections: books relevant to all chapters of the section are listed in its first chapter, or in the individual chapters in the case of sections (c) and (d).

(a) Aristotle and the Peripatetic School: chapters 1–5. See the bibliography of chapter 1: [1.1] to [1.59], pp. 34–7.
(b) Hellenistic Philosophy: chapters 6–8. See the bibliography of chapter 6: [6.1] to [6.24], pp. 218–20.
(c) Mathematics and Biology: chapters 9–10. See the bibliographies of both these chapters, pp. 315–19 and pp. 353–5.
(d) From the Classical to the Christian Age: chapters 11–12. See the bibliographies of both these chapters, pp. 385–7 and pp. 421–8.

Alexander of Aphrodisias. See Aristotelian Commentators.
Aristotelian Commentators. In Greek, *Commentaria in Aristotelem Graeca*, Berlin, Reimer, 1822–1909, with *Supplementum Aristotelicum*, 1882–1903. Some commentaries are now available in English translation: *Ancient Commentators on Aristotle*, General Editor Richard Sorabji, London, Duckworth, 1989 and continuing.
Aristotle. *The Complete Works of Aristotle*, ed. Jonathan Barnes, Princeton University Press, Bollingen Series LXXI, 1984. Also Loeb.
Augustine. Theologian and philosopher, AD 354–430. See [12.1] to [12.29].
Aurelius, Marcus. Roman Emperor and Stoic, AD 121–80. *Meditations* (Loeb).

Cicero. Roman statesman and orator; 1st c. BC. Philosophical essays: *De republica, De legibus, De finibus, De natura deorum, Academica, De fato, Tusculan Disputations.* Loeb.

Diogenes Laertius (abbr. DL). Probably 3rd c. AD. *Lives of the Philosophers.* Loeb.

Diogenes of Oenoanda. Eccentric author of an inscription on the stone walls of the agora of Oenoanda summarizing Epicurean philosophy; probably 2nd c. AD. See [6.28].

Epictetus. Stoic philosopher; mid-1st to mid-2nd *c.* AD. *Discourses.* Loeb.

Epicurus. 341–270 BC. Three Letters and *Principal Doctrines* in Diogenes Laertius book 10 (Loeb). Also (with *Vatican Sayings*) in Greek and English in Cyril Bailey, *Epicurus*, Oxford, Clarendon Press, 1926. Also with papyrus fragments of *On Nature* in Greek with Italian translation in G. Arrighetti, ed., *Epicuro, Opere*, Turin, Einaudi, 1960.

Eusebius. Biblical scholar and apologist; *c.* AD 260–339. *Ecclesiastical History* (Loeb).

Galen of Pergamum. 2nd c. A.D. Physician and prolific writer (in Greek) on medical theory and practice as well as logic and philosophy.

Heraclides of Pontus. Philosopher of Plato's Academy; later 4th c. BC. English translation of some texts in H.B. Gottschalk, *Heraclides of Pontus*, Oxford, Clarendon Press, 1980.

Iamblichus. Neo-Platonist philosopher; *c.* AD 245–c.325. See [11.38] to [11.40].

Lucretius. Latin poet, author of *De rerum natura*; early 1st c. BC. Major source for Epicureanism. Loeb, and many other English translations, for example C. Bailey [6.27].

Philo (Judaeus) of Alexandria. Philosopher; 1st c.AD. Some works in Loeb.

Philodemus. Epicurean philosopher; *c.*110–c.40 BC. Fragments survive on papyri at Herculaneum: *On Methods of Inference*, ed. with English translation by P.H. and E.A. De Lacy, Naples, Bibliopolis, 1978; *On Choices and Avoidances*, ed. with English translation by V. Tsouna-McKirahan, ibid. 1995.

Philoponus, John. 6th c. AD. See Aristotelian Commentators.

Plotinus. Neo-Platonist philosopher; 3rd. c. AD. *Enneads* (Loeb).

Plutarch of Chaeronea. Philosopher, biographer, essayist. Before AD 50 to after 120. *Moralia* (Loeb).

Porphyry. Disciple of Plotinus; AD 234 to *c.*305. See [11.29] to [11.33].

Posidonius. Stoic philosopher; 1st c. BC. *Fragments*, ed. L. Edelstein and I.G. Kidd, with English translation and commentary, Cambridge University Press, 1988.

Proclus. Neo-Platonist philosopher; 5th c. AD. See [11.41] to [11.45].

Seneca (the younger). Roman statesman and Stoic philosopher, *c.*4 BC to AD 65. *Natural Questions, Moral Essays, Letters.* Loeb.

Sextus Empiricus. (Some time in the early centuries AD). *Outlines of Pyrrhonism* (abbr. *PH*), and *Adversus mathematicos* (abbr. *M*) (sometimes subdivided into four: *Against the Professors, Against the Logicians, Against the Physicists, Against the Ethicists*). Loeb.

Simplicius. 6th c. AD. Commentaries on Aristotle's *Physics* and *On the Heavens*. See Aristotelian Commentators.

Stobaeus (John of Stobi). Anthologist; 6th c. AD. *Eclogae*, ed. Wachsmuth and Hense, Berlin, Weidmann, 1884.

Stoics (early). No complete works survive. See *Stoicorum veterum fragmenta* (abbr. SVF), ed. J. von Arnim, Leipzig, Teubner, 1921.

Strato of Lampsacus. Aristotelian philosopher; 3rd c. BC. Texts with German translation in vol. 5 of [5.57] F. Wehrli, *Die Schule des Aristoteles*. Some English translations in [5.58] H.B. Gottschalk, *Strato of Lampsacus: Some Texts*.

Themistius. Philosopher and rhetorician; AD 317–c.378. See Aristotelian Commentators. *Orationes* (Greek only), ed. Dindorf, Leipzig, 1832.

Theophrastus. Aristotle's successor; c.371–c.287 BC. *Metaphysics*, see [5.15]. Minor works, see [5.5] to [5.14]. *Historia plantarum* and *De causis plantarum* in Loeb. *Theophrastus of Eresus: Sources for his Life, Writings, Thought and Influence*, ed. Wm. W. Fortenbaugh and others (abbr. FHS&G), Leiden, Brill, 1992.

Introduction
David Furley

ᴥ◆⟨⟩◆ᴥ

This volume aims to discuss the most significant works of classical philosophy written during the period from the mid-fourth century BC to the early fifth century AD. We begin with Aristotle, whose intellectual power and influence extend over the whole of this period, and beyond. We end with Augustine, who stands near the end of Hellenism and the beginning of Christianity as the dominant mode of thought in the Western world. In between is the Hellenistic period, when Alexander's conquests spread Greek culture through most of the Middle Eastern lands that after centuries of political turmoil were united in the Roman Empire.

The concept of philosophy during this period has variable boundaries. There were schools of philosophy, designated as such at the time of their existence, and much of what was taught there is recognizably similar to what is taught in the Departments of Philosophy in twentieth-century universities. On the other hand, philosophy then sometimes included much more than it does now – theology, astronomy, physics, physiology, zoology, literary criticism, and more. If this book included nothing but what is now recognized as philosophy, it would seriously falsify the achievements of the thinkers of the period. There were very great advances in mathematics, astronomy, biology and others of the special sciences, and something must be said about them here, though this is not the place for an attempt at a full summary. In chapters 9 and 10 below we find samples of Hellenistic contributions to mathematics and biology.[1] The Hellenistic period has sometimes been underestimated because its philosophers could hardly compare with the creative genius of Plato and Aristotle in metaphysics or moral philosophy. But it was very far from being a period of intellectual decline or stagnation.

First, however, comes Aristotle, the pupil of Plato. Aristotle himself was not an Athenian. He was born in 384 BC in Stagira in Chalcidice – a region

1

colonized by Greeks from further south but much influenced throughout its history by close contacts, sometimes friendly, sometimes hostile, with its neighbour to the north-east, Macedonia. Aristotle's father, Nicomachus, was court physician to Amyntas II of Macedonia. When he was 17, Aristotle went to Athens to join Plato's school in the Academy, where he stayed for twenty years.

His personal relationship with Plato is obscure. Unquestionably he learnt more of philosophical method from Plato and his associates than from any other source: many of the most important questions addressed in his own surviving works can be traced to Platonic sources. On the other hand, he disagreed with Plato on crucial issues, and expressed his disagreement freely and at length. On the subject of Plato's conception of the Form of the Good, he remarked (*NE* 1.6, 1096a12) that to discuss it 'is an uphill task, because the Forms have been introduced by friends of our own. Yet it would perhaps be thought better, indeed to be our duty, for the sake of maintaining the truth, even to destroy what touches us closely, especially as we are philosophers; for while both are dear, piety requires us to honour truth above our friends.' *Amicus Plato, sed magis amica veritas.*[2] Aristotle quotes or refers to many of Plato's dialogues: the continuity of the philosophical tradition is unquestionable.

After Plato's death in 367, perhaps because he found it hard to work with Plato's successor Speusippus, Aristotle crossed the Aegean to Assos, where the ruler Hermeias (whose niece he married) supported a group of resident philosophers. Later he went across the strait to the island of Lesbos, the home of his student Theophrastus. His *History of Animals* shows detailed knowledge of the fauna of Lesbos.

After four years in these eastern regions, he was summoned by Philip of Macedon to his court in Pella to act as tutor to his son Alexander; his association for two or three years with the most powerful military figure of the fourth century has always stimulated the imagination of historians of philosophy – but the evidence for the influence of teacher on pupil, or vice versa, is very slender.

In 335 Aristotle returned to Athens to set up his own school there. As a non-citizen he could not own property, but he established himself as a teacher in the public sanctuary and gymnasium on the outskirts of the city, dedicated to Apollo Lyceius and called the Lyceum.[3] (The Academy, the site of Plato's school, was a similar place.) The school became known as 'the Peripatos' ('The Walk') because its main location for teaching was the covered walkway or cloister contained in its buildings. Aristotle remained there until the death of Alexander in 323, when anti-Macedonian sentiments grew powerful in Athens. A charge of 'impiety' was brought against him, as it had been many decades before against Socrates; he left, according to the biographers, 'lest Athens should sin twice against philosophy', leaving the school to Theophrastus. He died a year later in Chalcis.[4]

His writings can be divided into three kinds. First were the 'popular' works, mainly dialogues modelled to some uncertain extent on Plato's dialogues. These were famous in the period of his lifetime and for many years after his death; not one of them survives now, although there are fairly substantial quotations and translations into Latin from some of them, and many smaller references.[5]

Second, there were collections of research materials, by himself and others: his *Constitution of Athens* is the only surviving example.

In the the third group are almost all the works that survive. 'School-treatises' is the usual modern name for them. Except for some segments which show signs of more elaborate literary form, they are evidently designed as working materials for serious students of their subject. Sometimes they are called 'lecture-notes', but it seems unlikely that they could have been exactly that. It is more likely that they were read and re-read in privacy or in groups – perhaps after the manner of seminar papers for graduate students today. Some of them were probably collected under their present titles by editors rather than by Aristotle himself. Unlike Plato's dialogues, they are divided into chapters by subject-matter, often with clear opening and closing statements; sometimes there are duplicate versions, presumably composed at different times and not intended to co-exist in the same 'book'. Their history during the three centuries after Aristotle's death is obscure and controversial; for some years it seems that the 'published' works, now lost, were much better known than the school treatises. The latter were not published, in anything like the modern sense, until they were collected by Andronicus of Rhodes in the late first century BC, having been brought to Rome from Athens by the conquering army of Sulla.[6]

'Everyone by nature desires to know.' These are the famous opening words of Aristotle's *Metaphysics*, and the extraordinary range of his own inquiries testifies to the power of his own desire. The greatest pleasure, he claims, comes from knowledge of whatever in nature is eternal – that is to say, the cosmos itself, and especially the heavenly regions. But living nature also, not eternal but liable to generation and corruption, 'offers immeasurable pleasures to those who are philosophers by nature and are able to recognize causes'.[7] He himself wrote systematic studies in the fields of astronomy, meteorology, the structure of matter and material change, motion, zoology, embryology, botany (but this does not survive), perception, memory, sleep, life and death, ethics, politics, rhetoric and poetics. He was, as he claims,[8] the first to write about the logic of argument (as opposed to rhetoric). And he followed Plato in exploring the most fundamental concepts of language and thought in his *Metaphysics*.

Aristotle was the first in the Western world to set up an institution for teaching and research in which the subjects were systematically distributed into specialist branches. Each of his own surviving writings is devoted to a single subject-matter, unlike the dialogues of his teacher Plato. Some branches of knowledge were covered not by himself but by his students: for example Theophrastus wrote the major work on botany, Eudemus wrote on the history of mathematics, Menon on the history of medicine.[9] Moreover, the school founded by Aristotle in the Lyceum was the first to compile a systematic library; it was handed on after the founder's death to his successor Theophrastus (though its later history is confused).

It can rightly be claimed that he began the process of dividing the realm of intellectual research into specialized segments. But there is nevertheless a marked degree of unity in his own modes of thought: he did not, as it were, hold a number of different and separate Chairs. His own metaphysical concepts pervade the rest of his studies. His notion of an individual substance – something that *is* what it is in its own right, without dependence on some other being, distinguished thus from its subordinate properties, such as its qualities, quantities, relations with other things – serves as the primary metaphysical frame for all or most of his thought. Much of the technical vocabulary of later philosophy is derived from Latin versions of Aristotle's metaphysical terms: for example, 'substance', 'essence', 'quality', 'quantity' and 'category.'

The Aristotelian tradition continued for many centuries. From the first century AD the richest kind of philosophical writing took the form of commentary on the works of Aristotle. The famous German edition of the Greek commentaries on Aristotle occupies twenty-three heavy volumes, dating from Aspasius in the first century AD to Sophonias at the turn of the thirteenth to fourteenth centuries. It is only recently that a systematic effort to make the most important commentaries available in English has been undertaken, by Richard Sorabji and an impressive team of translators and interpreters.[10]

In chapter 5 of the present volume, R.W. Sharples reviews the work of the immediate successors of Aristotle in the Peripatetic School, especially Theophrastus, and discusses one of the earliest of the Greek commentators, Alexander of Aphrodisias. Later commentators fall outside the period covered by this volume; within the given limits, it is not possible to discuss the work of the Neoplatonist commentators such as Ammonius, Simplicius, and Olympiodorus, or of Christians such as Philoponus.

In the Hellenistic period, from the end of the fourth century to the first century BC, the most important schools of philosophy were the Epicureans and the Stoics (chapters 6 and 7 below), and Plato's Academy (chapter 8). There is a marked change of direction in the first two, in that emphasis is now laid more strongly on moral philosophy. It is not more than a change of emphasis, in that both schools continued the debate with earlier philosophers, as well as with each other, about the nature of the physical world, and indeed about fundamental metaphysical problems. The Stoics, too, from Chrysippus onwards, made vitally important contributions in the field of logic – though their importance was not fully appreciated until the twentieth century. But the historical importance of both schools was concentrated rather on their reasoning about the right way for human beings to live. The words 'Epicurean' and 'Stoic' have entered into ordinary language as descriptions of attitudes to human experience. The sense in which they are now used is something of a travesty of the original sense – especially in the case of the Epicureans – but it is not accidental that they are used with this kind of application.

It is interesting that they adopted opposite positions in the fields of physics and cosmology – Epicurus following the Atomist tradition of Democritus, the Stoics following Plato and Aristotle.

To study Plato and Aristotle, the modern reader has access to original works – to everything that Plato wrote, so far as we know, and the most important of Aristotle's writings. Things are very different with regard to Epicurus, the early Stoics, and the Sceptics of the Academy. 'Epicurus', says Diogenes Laertius (10.26), 'was a most prolific writer, and outdid everyone in the number of his books, which numbered up to three hundred rolls.' All that survives of them amounts to three open letters (rather similar in form to the letters of St Paul), two collections of brief 'thoughts', and the ruins of his great *Physics* on papyrus rolls at Herculaneum.

We are heavily dependent on other classical writers for knowledge of Epicureanism. Fortunately one of these is an outstandingly brilliant writer, and a devoted disciple of Epicurus – the Latin poet Lucretius. More than two centuries after Epicurus, Lucretius wrote his epic poem *De rerum natura*, which still survives to give us a comprehensive view of Epicurus' cosmology, and to provide reliable confirmation and expansion of our understanding of his epistemology and moral doctrines.

The Stoics are less fortunate. No work by an acknowledged Stoic survives before Seneca in the Roman Empire: for knowledge of Zeno the founder, Cleanthes and Chrysippus, we depend on second-hand reports. This is perhaps especially grievous in the case of Chrysippus, who was astonishingly prolific, and from all accounts much the most systematic and wide ranging philosopher among the early Stoics. The Stoic world picture was much less well known than Aristotle's in the medieval and early modern periods; the Roman Stoic writers who were relatively well known (especially Seneca and the Emperor Marcus Aurelius) wrote mainly about ethical subjects.

During the Hellenistic period the Platonic tradition took a somewhat surprising turn. The Academy under Arcesilaus, following the example of Socrates, perhaps, rather than that of Plato in his later life, concentrated its attention on criticizing claims to knowledge. The Stoics were apparently the most obvious targets, but the sceptical arguments were universal in their application. The development of different forms of scepticism is examined by Frede in chapter 8.

The most notable of the Academic Sceptics were Carneades, who became head of the school before the middle of the second century BC, and in the first century Philo of Larissa. After Philo, the sceptical Academy was criticized and abandoned by Antiochus of Ascalon, who reclaimed the more positive stance of Plato himself, adopted much from the Stoics, and also began the tendency, which later became much stronger, to emphasize the agreements rather than the differences between Plato and Aristotle.

With Antiochus there began the intermediate phase known as 'Middle Platonism', best represented by the many surviving works of Philo of Alexandria (known also as Philo Judaeus) and the philosophical essays of Plutarch of Chaeronea (author of the more famous *Lives*).[11]

A very different interpretation of the Platonic tradition began in the third century AD, and proved to be a powerful influence on European philosophy for many centuries, through the Renaissance and into the early modern period. Neo-Platonism began with Plotinus, who studied in Alexandria, then moved to Rome, but wrote in Greek. His work survives, in the form of six sets of nine treatises (the *Enneads*). The tradition continued prolifically in Greek. The inspiration of Plato was always in the forefront, but that by no means entailed neglect of Aristotle.

Perhaps the most important mode of philosophizing in the centuries after Plotinus consisted of commentaries on Aristotle. The unity of Platonism and Aristotelianism was declared and defended by Plotinus' pupil, Porphyry, whose Introduction to Aristotle's *Categories*, known as the *Isagoge*, survives; and the unity thesis was defended and qualified through the following centuries.

Most of the philosophy and science studied in this volume was written in Greek. The Latin contribution begins in the first century BC with Lucretius and Cicero. The inestimable contribution of Lucretius to Epicureanism has already been mentioned. Epicurus' hedonism, his materialism, his denial of the immortality of the soul, and his rejection of divine providence, all combined to set the Christian tradition against him, and little of it survived, as we noted above. But Lucretius wrote an epic poem in Latin hexameters; Vergil referred to him with respect, and something of the high value attached to Vergil through the centuries was transferred to Lucretius. Even so, he only just survived: he was little known in the Christian Middle Ages until a manuscript of *De rerum natura* was found by Poggio in the early fifteenth century, copied, and thus made known to the scholars of Florence.

Cicero, a contemporary of Lucretius, is a different matter. His work was always regarded as an essential educational tool, and copies of many of his numerous books were not in short supply. His value in the history of philosophy is unquestionable, but it arises not from his own originality or a philosophical system of his own, but from his wide range of knowledge of earlier philosophers and the astonishing fluency of his Latin translations and commentaries. He is particularly valuable for his comments on Epicureanism (which he does not value highly) and Stoicism, and most of all for his account of post-Platonic Academic philosophy.[12]

Many of Cicero's philosophical works take the form of a dialogue, with representatives of the various schools as spokesmen. He wrote on logic and epistemology (two versions of *Academica*, extant only in part), on political philosophy (*De republica*, extant in part, and *De legibus*), on ethics (*De finibus*, *Tusculan Disputations*, and *De officiis*), and on philosophy of nature, especially on the relation of the gods to the natural world – a topic on which Epicureans and Stoics were most sharply divided (*De natura deorum*, *De divinatione*, and *De fato*).

Seneca (early first century AD) is the first avowed Stoic represented by works that have survived intact. Like Cicero, he was not a teacher or philosopher but wrote most of his works after retirement from politics – he was an adviser to the Emperor Nero. He was an essayist, rather than a writer of dialogues, treatises or textbooks. His *Moral Essays* present practical interpretations of Stoic ethics, and treat some subjects that are not so well represented elsewhere in classical philosophy (for example *On Anger*).

But the best known philosophical works of the early Roman period were written in Greek – the books of the Neoplatonists Plotinus, Porphyry, Proclus, the Commentaries on Aristotle, even the *Meditations* of the Roman Emperor Marcus Aurelius. It was the Latin language, however, that provided the crucial bridge between classical philosophy and Christianity. St Augustine, who represents the beginning of Christian philosophy in this volume (chapter 12), was a reader of Greek but learnt more from Cicero and from Latin translations of Greek classics. Boethius, in the sixth century, began a translation of Aristotle's books into Latin with the aim of adding these vital works to the content of Christian education, but died after completing the logical works (see chapter 11).

The classical Greek contribution to philosophy was in the main passed on without interruption to the culture of Western Europe, with the notable exception of Epicureanism. The hedonism that was the basis of Epicurus' morality was in fundamental conflict with Christian ethics; the mortality of the soul, and the denial of providential intervention in the world by God were of course equally unacceptable. Only the poetry of Lucretius, preserved in one manuscript in a monastic library, eventually caught the attention of literary men, and revived interest in the letters of Epicurus that had been transcribed in the tenth book of Diogenes Laertius. The 'one world' cosmology of Plato, Aristotle and the Stoics was thus left for several centuries without a competitor. The natural philosophy of the ancient

Atomists, including Epicurus, was hardly taken seriously until the time of Gassendi, in the early seventeenth century.

 NOTES

1 For more extensive treatment, see the bibliographies attached to these chapters.
2 This is a medieval Latin version, of uncertain origin; the same thought is also attributed to Plato with regard to Socrates. See [1.40] Guthrie, p.25, n.2.
3 The discovery of its site by archaeologists was announced in *The Times* of London in January 1998.
4 For textual evidence on the life of Aristotle, see [5.73] I. Düring, *Aristotle in the Biographical Tradition*, and for the history of the Lyceum see [5.3] J.P. Lynch, *Aristotle's School*.
5 They are collected in the Oxford Classical Text *Aristotelis Fragmenta*, and translated in the 12th volume of the Oxford translation, both by Sir David Ross. The most important are the *Protrepticus, On Philosophy, On the Good, On Ideas, On Justice*.
6 But the role of Andronicus has been questioned recently by J. Barnes, in [6.14] *Philosophia Togata* II, 1997.
7 *Parts of Animals* 1.5, 645a9.
8 In the last chapter of *Sophistici Elenchi*.
9 See chapter 5, 'The Peripatetic school'.
10 *Ancient Commentators on Aristotle*, London, Duckworth, 1987, in progress.
11 In the history of philosophy, the Middle Platonists are perhaps more valuable for the light shed by their surviving works on other philosophers than for their own positive contributions. For an accessible account of them, see [11.3] John Dillon, *The Middle Platonists*.
12 See chapter 8, below.

CHAPTER 1

Aristotle the philosopher of nature

David Furley

❧◆❧

❧ 1 THE TREATISES ON NATURE ❧

The subject-matter of the present chapter is what Aristotle has to say about the natural world – the subject that in classical Greek is most accurately rendered as *ta physika*. But of course this includes many topics that would not now count as natural science – indeed Aristotle's own book called *Physics* contains discussions that according to twentieth-century categories belong rather to philosophy or metaphysics. Book 1 criticizes the views of Aristotle's predecessors on the first principles of natural objects, and defends his own view that they are three – matter, form, and privation. Book 2 analyses the kind of explanation that is to be expected of the natural philosopher, introducing the doctrine of 'the four causes'. The third book deals with motion and change, and infinity; the fourth with place, void and time. The second quartet of books seems to form a separate entity – or perhaps two. Books 5, 6 and 8 are sometimes referred to by commentators under a separate title: *On Change* (*kinêsis* – the word may denote motion or change in general). Book 5 analyses concepts essential to the study of motion, book 6 deals with continuity, Book 8 argues for the eternity of motion and an eternal mover. Book 7 (part of which has been transmitted in two versions) perhaps contains a preliminary version of Book 8.

In the traditional ordering of Aristotle's works, *Physics* is followed by three theoretical treatises concerned with different aspects of the cosmos: *On the Heavens*, *On Generation and Corruption*, and *Meteorologica*. After a short essay *On the Cosmos*, generally and rightly held to be spurious, these are followed by a sequence of works on biology, which constitutes one fourth of the surviving Corpus Aristotelicum. First comes the treatise *On the Soul* (the principle of life), and a collection of related short essays concerning sensation, memory, sleep, dreams, etc., known as the *Parva Naturalia*. Then

9

follow the three principal works of zoology: *History of Animals* (*Zoological Researches* would be a more appropriate modern title), *Parts of Animals*, and *Generation of Animals*. (The traditional Corpus contains also a number of works on the natural world now held to be spurious: *On Colours*, *On Things Heard*, *Physiognomonics*, *On Plants*, *On Marvellous Things Heard*, *Mechanics*, and *Problems*.)

2 ARISTOTLE'S SCIENTIFIC METHODS IN *POSTERIOR ANALYTICS* AND ELSEWHERE

Before entering upon a discussion of Aristotle's researches into the natural world, something must be said about the book in which he theorizes about scientific proof – the *Posterior Analytics*.[1]

The book sets out a system of proof by syllogisms. We have scientific understanding of something, says Aristotle, 'when we believe we know the cause (the *aitia*)[2] of the thing's being the case – know that it *is* the cause of it – and that it could not be otherwise' (1.2, 71b10–12). From premisses that are known to be true, the scientific theorist draws a conclusion that is then also known to be true because it follows necessarily from the premisses. If the argument is to qualify as part of a science (*epistêmê*), its premisses must have certain qualities: they must be 'true and primitive and immediate and more familiar than and prior to and explanatory of the conclusion' (1.2, 71b22–24, tr. Barnes).

Now when one turns to the treatises in which Aristotle sets out his philosophy of nature (the treatises listed above in section 1), it is at once obvious that they do not even attempt to meet these conditions. They are, in general, inquiries, or the records of inquiries, rather than proofs. They do not confine themselves to necessary truths, which cannot be otherwise. In many cases, particularly in the biological works, they start from propositions based on observation. They do not proceed by syllogistic proofs alone.

It is clear that we are dealing with two different phases in the presentation of science, and it is important that this be recognized if the reader is not to be disappointed by the apparent difference between the ideal set out in the *Analytics* and the more dialectical nature of the other treatises. The *Posterior Analytics* are generally held to describe the way in which a completed science should ideally be presented; the treatises on the natural world present the inquiries or researches that are preliminary to the finished product. 'In a perfect Aristotelian world, the material gathered in the *Corpus* will be systematically presented; and the logical pattern will follow the pattern of the *Posterior Analytics*' (Barnes [1.28], p. x).

It should be added that the pattern of the Analytics evidently suits the mathematical sciences rather than biology, and Aristotle would be in difficulties if he confined his biology to the knowledge that could satisfy exacting demands for necessary truths and syllogistic proof.

In the two treatises (*Physics* and *Generation and Corruption*) that deal with the concepts most fundamental to our study of the natural world, Aristotle uses methods that are based neither on the scientific syllogism nor directly on empirical studies of natural phenomena. Most typically, he starts from the views expressed by others – by his philosophical predecessors, or by educated and thoughtful ordinary men in general.[3]

For example, in book 4 of the *Physics* he analyses the concept of place. We should assume, he says (4.4, 210a32), whatever is rightly believed to belong to it essentially: i.e. that it is the first thing surrounding that whose place it is, that it is not a part of the thing, that it is neither bigger nor smaller than it; and that it is detachable from its content when the latter changes place. It is only because of locomotion, he adds, that we enquire about place. The object of the enquiry is to determine what place is in such a way that the problems are solved and the beliefs about its properties are shown to be true, and to show the reasons for the difficult problems about it.

The first of Aristotle's statements about place – namely that it 'surrounds' (*periechein*) its contents – turns out to be highly significant. This at once distinguishes 'place' from 'space'; Aristotle's place is a surface – the inner surface of a container that is in contact with the outer surface of the contents. Thus place is not measured by its volume, as space is, or as space would be measured if Aristotle allowed its existence. In fact, he denies it: it is not necessary, he claims, for the analysis of locomotion, because the concept of place will supply all that is needed (and he finds other problems with the idea of space).

It follows, in Aristotle's view, that there can be no such thing as the void. The void could only be an empty place: but place is a container, and a container is nothing if it contains nothing. When something changes place, its former place is occupied *pari passu* by something else, or else the former container collapses on to itself as an empty bag does.

In this analysis there are no experiments, no measurements, and no observations other than those of ordinary everyday experience. What we have is a study of descriptions of motion, and of the assumptions underlying these descriptions. We have also an exhibition of the problems arising from alternative and incompatible descriptions in terms of space rather than place.

There is a somewhat similar but more far-reaching conceptual analysis in book 1 of the *Physics*. It begins by asking: what are the *principles* of nature? That is to say, what are the things that are essential to the existence of any natural object? To find the principles, we have to start with what is familiar to us, because the principles themselves are not accessible directly to our minds, nor universally agreed. It is not principles that we are directly acquainted with, but the changing compounds of the natural world.

11

After a criticism of the ideas of earlier philosophers of nature about the principles, Aristotle continues with reflections on our common notions about the essential features of *change*, since change is a necessary feature of everything in the sublunary natural world. Change takes place between opposites: things are said to change from hot to cold, for example, or from dry to wet, or from unmusical to musical. So opposites must be among the principles. But it is false to say that *hot* changes to *cold*: it is not the opposites themselves that change, but something that is characterized first by one opposite, then the other (or if not from one extreme to the other, from one position on the continuum between the two to another position *in the direction of* the other). What, then, is the 'something', the substratum, presupposed by such change?

Aristotle's answer is 'matter' (*hylê*). His concept of matter is one that would be thought of now as belonging to metaphysics rather than to physics. Matter is an abstraction: it is arrived at, in thought only, by stripping away from a physical object all the attributes that belong to its form. It never exists in separation from all attributes. The simplest kind of object with substantial existence in Aristotle's hierarchy of existent things is a piece of one of the four elements: but any such piece is analysable in theory into matter and certain qualities that give it form.

In the sublunary world, as opposed to the heavens, everything that exists is liable to change, from a quality to its opposite, from a given size to a larger or smaller one, or from being what it is to being something else (for example from being a table to being a heap of firewood, from being firewood to being smoke and ash, etc.). What underlies physical change is matter: matter has the *potentiality* for losing one form and taking on another.

A favourite example of physical change in Aristotle's works is the making of a piece of sculpture. An amount of bronze or stone is the matter: it has the potentiality for becoming an image of a man, and the sculptor gives it that form in actuality. But this is rather too static an analysis: at each stage of the process of making the statue, the material in its penultimate state is matter (potentiality) for the actuality of the next stage. Matter and form, and potentiality and actuality, are pairs of relative terms.

The elements themselves, better named 'the primary bodies' – earth, water, air, and fire – have the potentiality for changing into each other. For example water has the potentiality for vaporizing into 'air' or for solidifying into 'earth' – the names themselves in Aristotelian usage each denote a range of solid, liquid, gaseous, and fiery substances.[4]

❧ 3 ARISTOTLE'S WORLD PICTURE ❧

We shall begin with an outline of Aristotle's picture of the natural world as a whole, contrasting it with others of the classical period, and continue with comments on his contribution to each of the major fields, from astronomy to biology.

The general character of Aristotle's interpretation of the natural world is determined primarily by two theses: that the cosmos had no beginning and will have no end in time, and that it is a finite whole that exhausts the contents of the universe.

The first main point – that the cosmos is sempiternal – is argued in book 8 of the *Physics*. The first premiss is that there can be no time without change: change is necessary, if parts of time are to be distinguished from each other. But according to Aristotle's analysis of change, there can be no *first* change, and correspondingly no *last* change. It follows that both change and time are eternal (*Physics* 8.1). Further argument (in *Physics* 8.6) shows that if change is to be eternal, there must be both something eternal that causes change (we shall return to this all-important being in section 7), and something eternal in which this change occurs. This latter being is the 'first heaven', the sphere of the fixed stars. Since the rest of the cosmos is determined in its essentials by the motions of the heavens, the whole cosmic order is also eternal.

These claims (defended, of course, by arguments to which this bare summary does no justice) distinguish Aristotle from all major philosophers of the classical period, with the possible exception of Heraclitus. Anaxagoras held that the cosmos emerged from a primitive mixture of all its contents; Empedocles that it grows from unity, passes through a period of plurality, and returns to unity, in repeating cycles; the Atomists argued for a plurality of cosmoi, each with a finite lifetime; Plato maintained that the single cosmos is indeed eternal, but he wrote (in the *Timaeus*) a description of its creation at a particular point in time, which Aristotle at least believed was to be taken literally; the Stoics returned to a cyclic theory.

The second of these claims – that the universe is finite – follows from a set of prior assumptions and arguments. In *Physics* book 4, Aristotle argues that there can be no such thing as a vacuum anywhere in the universe, and hence that there cannot be an infinitely extended vacuum. What people mean when they talk about a vacuum or void, as Leucippus and Democritus did, is an empty *place*. But Aristotle produced arguments to show that there can be no such thing. The place of a thing is its *container*, or rather the inner boundaries of its container. According to our experience, when we try to empty a container, either the contents are replaced instantly by something else (usually air), or the container collapses upon itself. In either case we have no empty place. A place is always the place of something or other. It follows from this that there can be no void place within the cosmos, and it follows from Aristotle's theory of the motions of the elements (which we shall examine shortly) that there can be no place outside the cosmos, since all of the body in the universe is concentrated in the cosmos.

In order to show that the universe is finite, then, it remains to show that there cannot be an infinitely extended *body* or plurality of bodies. This

Aristotle aims to do in *On the Heavens* 1.5–7. He begins with an argument concerned with the 'first body' – i.e. the body of which the sphere of the fixed stars is composed (for which see section 5). Like most Greeks of the classical period Aristotle believed the earth to be stationary at the centre of the spherical heavens. The fact that it was stationary seemed to be given by experience: once that thesis was accepted, it followed that the heavenly bodies move around the earth. Before Aristotle's time, it had been established that there was a difference in the motions of the heavenly bodies: the stars appear to move in concert without changing their relative positions, while the sun, moon, and five 'wanderers' (*planêtai*) move around the earth in orbits different from each other and from the 'fixed' stars.

The appearance of the fixed stars suggests that they are placed on a sphere that rotates as a whole on its axis, with the earth at its centre. We observe that this sphere completes one revolution in a day. If it were infinite in radius, each radius drawn from the centre would sweep an infinitely large distance in every segment traversed. But that is impossible: it is not possible to traverse an infinite distance, since the infinite is 'that of which there is always more beyond' (*Physics* 3.6, 207a1).

In dealing with the four sublunary elements – earth, water, air, and fire – Aristotle takes as given his theory of their natural places and natural motions. *All* earth tends to move towards a single centre, *all* fire to a single circumference, and the other two to intermediate positions. Consequently there cannot be any portion of the four elements, either simple or in compounds, outside the boundary of the sphere of the stars. But neither can there be any empty place outside this sphere, since, as Aristotle has argued, all place must be the place of something. Hence the universe (not merely the cosmos bounded by the starry sphere) is finite.

⟫⟫ 4 THE NATURAL MOTIONS OF THE ⟪⟪ ELEMENTS

Aristotle's theory of the elements is defended in detail in his *On the Heavens*; books 3 and 4 deal with the four elements that had become traditional since the time of Empedocles – earth, water, air, and fire – while books 1 and 2 introduce what Aristotle calls 'the first element' or 'the first body' and subsequent writers called 'aether', the element of which the heavens are composed.

Observation of the natural world suggests a distinction between forced and natural motions: a stone can be thrown upwards, but falls downwards if not prevented; fire and hot vapours rise upwards unless confined by something above them. Aristotle systematizes these simple observations with the help of the geometrical picture of the cosmos described in the last section. 'Downwards' is defined as 'in a straight line towards the centre of the universe'; 'upwards' is the contrary direction, away from the centre. These two rectilinear movements are contrasted with motion in a circle around the centre of the universe.

The rectilinear motions are natural to the elements contained within the sphere of the heavens – commonly called the 'sublunary' elements, since the moon is the innermost of the heavenly bodies. These motions are defined according to the 'natural place' of each element. Each element has a natural tendency to seek its natural place, if displaced from it. Earth and water move naturally downwards, towards the centre; fire and air upwards. The tendency to move in these directions is what is meant by 'weight' and 'lightness' respectively – thus lightness is not a relative property but an absolute one. Earth has more weight than water, and fire has more lightness than air.

It is important to note that Aristotle takes the centre, and therefore the elementary motions, to be defined by the spherical shape of the universe as a whole, not by the shape of the cosmos. Later philosophers abandoned Aristotle's notion that the sphere of the stars has nothing whatever outside it, and posited an infinite volume of empty space around the cosmos. In such a cosmology no centre of the universe as such could be defined, and Aristotle's theory of natural motion had to be changed. To deal with this problem, the Stoics made the highly significant claim that the body of the cosmos is naturally attracted towards *its own* centre. This theory of attraction began to make clear what Aristotle never elucidated: what is the *cause* of the natural motions of the elements? We shall discuss this problem later (section 7).

5 THE STRUCTURE OF THE HEAVENS

The natural motions of the four sublunary elements were rectilinear. But the heavenly bodies move in circular orbits, carried around on the surfaces of rotating spheres (we shall describe the arrangement of the spheres in the next sections). But physical spheres must have physical *body*. So Aristotle is faced with the question: what are the heavenly spheres made of? They can hardly be made of any of the four elements which have rectilinear motions. The motion of the heavens, according to Aristotle's view in the *On the Heavens*, requires us to posit a fifth element whose natural motion is not rectilinear but circular. Since he regards it as superior, in more than one sense, to the other four elements, he names it 'the first body'. But although he made a technical term out of it, the idea of a special element in the heavens was not his alone, and others referred to it with the old word 'aether' – originally used for the bright sky above the misty air. For convenience I shall adopt this term for Aristotle's 'first body'.

We can distinguish more than one argument for the existence of aether.[5] The main argument in Aristotle's *On the Heavens* is the argument from motion that we have just described. A second argument is also found there: it may be called the argument from incorruptibility. Earth, water, air, and fire are perishable in that they are all liable to change into each other. But the heavens are eternal: they must therefore be made of a different element. This argument can be found, in rather disguised form, in Aristotle's *On the Heavens* 1.3 (there is a very similar statement of it in *Meteorologica* 1.3). It is disguised in this sense. Aristotle first states the argument for the existence of what he calls 'the first body' from the need for a body endowed with natural circular motion. He then *deduces* that it must be ungenerated, indestructible, and unchangeable. His reasoning is that all generation takes place between opposites, opposites have opposed motions, and there is no opposite to circular motion (it is not clear why he dismisses the notion that clockwise has its opposite in anticlockwise – if we may use such modern terms). Hence, the body that moves in a circle is not liable to generation and destruction. He continues the chapter with some less technical thoughts about this element. These include the idea that 'according to the records handed down from generation to generation, we find no trace of change either in the whole of the outermost heaven or in any of its proper parts'. Moreover, he says, the name 'aether' was given to the first body 'by the ancients . . . choosing its title from the fact that it "runs *always*" (*aei thein*) and eternally' (270b13–24). It is not, in other words, *circular* motion that is the primary characteristic of this element, but *eternal* motion. These ideas at least produce the materials out of which the incorruptibility argument for the existence of the fifth body can be constructed, and the etymology suggests that in Aristotle's view this might have been the earliest argument for its existence.

There are indications that Aristotle rather tentatively gave a role to aether in the sublunary world as well as in the heavens. Cicero knew something to this effect, from his acquaintance with some of the works of Aristotle that are now lost:

> He [sc. Aristotle] thinks there is a certain fifth nature, of which mind is made; for thinking, foreseeing, learning, teaching, making a discovery, holding so much in the memory – all these and more, loving, hating, feeling pain and joy – such things as these, he believes, do not belong to any one of the four elements. He introduces a fifth kind, without a name, and thus calls the mind itself '*endelecheia*', using a new name – as it were, a certain continual, eternal motion.
> (Cicero *Tusculan Disputations* 1.10.22)

It is hardly likely that Aristotle *identified* the mind with aether, but it is possible that at some time he wrote of the soul, or some of its faculties, as being based in an element different from the usual four. There is some confirmation of this in his own more cautious words:

> Now it is true that the power of all kinds of soul seems to have a connexion with a matter different from and more divine than the so-called elements; but as one soul differs from another in honour and

16

dishonour, so also the nature of the corresponding matter differs. All have in their semen that which causes it to be productive; I mean what is called vital heat. This is not fire or any such power, but it is the breath included in the semen and the foam-like, and the natural principle in breath, being analogous to the element of the stars.

(Aristotle *Generation of Animals* 2.3, 736b29–737a1)

The evaluative strain in this quotation is significant. The extra element is called 'divine' and is associated with the ranking in 'honour' of the soul that is based on it – this refers, no doubt, to a *scala naturae* which puts man, the rational animal, at the top and grades the lower animals according to their faculties.[6] Aether is not merely the element endowed with the natural faculty of moving in a circle, which is the main emphasis in the *On the Heavens*. It is also eternal, and therefore divine, and free from the corruption of the earthly elements.

Aristotle was committed to a dualism as sharp as Plato's distinction between the intelligible and unchanging Forms and the perceptible and perishable material world. The heavens are the realm of a matter that moves eternally in circles, is incorruptible, unmixed, divine. With the possible limited exception of the material base of the animal soul, everything in the cosmos inside the sphere of the moon – the sublunary world – is made of different materials, all of them rectilinear and therefore finite in motion, perishable, liable to mixture and interchange among themselves. This was a dualism that lasted, notoriously, until the time of Galileo and Kepler, when the telescope revealed the moon to be not so very different from the earth, and the idea of circular motion at last released its powerful grip on the astronomers' imagination.

6 THE BORROWED ASTRONOMY

Plato (said Sosigenes) set this problem for students of astronomy: 'By the assumption of what uniform and ordered motions can the phenomena concerning the motions of the planets be saved?'

(Simplicius *De caelo* 488.21)

Aristotle followed Plato in analysing the motions of the heavenly bodies entirely into circles with the earth as centre. The motions of the 'fixed' stars, during the time they are visible at night to an observer on the earth, are arcs of circles, and they are assumed to complete their circular paths in the daytime, when they are invisible. But the planetary bodies, including the sun and the moon, appear to 'wander' (in Greek, *planân*) with reference to the fixed stars in the course of a year. In fact, however, they do not *wander*, Plato had said; Aristotle agreed that their paths could be analysed as being circular, but adopted a much more complex account of the circles than Plato's.

17

Mohawk Valley Community College Library

The basis for his account of the heavens was the work of two contemporary astronomers: Eudoxus of Cnidos and Callippus of Cyzicus.[7] They worked out what was basically a geometrical model of the paths of the heavenly bodies. Aristotle added what he considered to be necessary for a physical model (to be described in the next section).

The essence of the geometrical model is as follows. The fixed stars are assumed to be set rigidly in the outermost sphere of the heavens, which turns at a constant speed about its north/south axis once a day. Inside the outermost sphere are seven sets of concentric spheres, one set for each of the five known planets and the sun and the moon. The innermost sphere of each set carries the planetary body on its equator (this applies to the geometrical account: the physical model is still more complex). The outermost sphere of each set moves on the same axis and with the same direction and speed as the sphere of the fixed stars. It carries with it the poles of a second sphere, concentric with the first, rotating about its own, different axis at its own constant speed. The axis of the second sphere is inclined to that of the first so that its equator, as it rotates, passes through the middle of the signs of the zodiac (i.e. along the ecliptic circle). The second sphere of each of the planetary bodies has the same orientation relative to the fixed stars and the same direction of rotation as each other; they differ in the time taken to complete a rotation.

But the planetary bodies are observed to deviate from regular motion on the ecliptic circle: they do not keep to the same path. To account for the differences, Eudoxus posited a third and fourth sphere for each planet, nested inside the first two, rotating on different axes and completing their rotation in different times. The planet is assumed to lie on the equator of the fourth, innermost sphere. The third and fourth spheres are so arranged that the planet follows a path (relative to the ecliptic) known as a 'hippopede' or 'horse-fetter', roughly equivalent to a figure 8.[8]

All that is visible to the observer, of course, is the light of the heavenly bodies: the spheres are invisible. The visible heavenly bodies themselves do not move at all; they are carried around by the motion of the sphere in which they are set.

The seven sets of spheres are nested inside each other, in the order Saturn, Jupiter, Mars, Venus, Mercury, sun, moon.[9] In Eudoxus' scheme, there are no eccentric spheres and no epicycles, as in later astronomical theories. Consequently it was assumed that all the heavenly bodies remain at a constant distance from the earth: it is a weakness in the system that it has no way of explaining differences in the brightness of the planets at different times.

This, then, was the astronomical model taken over by Aristotle. He acknowledges his debt to the mathematicians, but there are numerous obscurities in his account which raise doubts about the depth of his understanding of contemporary astronomy.[10] What is clear is that he constructed a physical description of the heavens, in which the spheres were not geometrical postulates but material bodies, and the most important element in this body of theory is his examination of the causes of the motions of the spheres.

7 FROM ASTRONOMY TO PHYSICS AND THEOLOGY

The astronomical model, as we have seen, used the motion of the sphere of the fixed stars as the base on which the other motions were overlaid. For the construction of a physical theory, this created a difficulty concerning the motions of all the planetary bodies except the outermost one, since the sets of planetary spheres are implanted in each other. Jupiter's set, to take an example, is inside the set of Saturn's spheres. But in the astronomical model the motion of the innermost of Saturn's spheres – the sphere that carries Saturn on its equator – is obviously not identical with that of the sphere of fixed stars; its function is precisely to justify Saturn's deviation from that motion. To preserve the geometrician's scheme, however, Jupiter's outermost sphere must move with the motion of the fixed stars. Consequently the physical theory must return to this base, by interpolating a set of spheres whose motions *cancel out* the special motions of Saturn.

Let S^1, S^2, S^3, S^4 be the spheres that explain Saturn's motions; S^4 is the one that carries Saturn. Then Aristotle postulates, inside S^4, a sphere S^{-4}, which rotates on the same axis and at the same speed as S^4, but in the reverse direction. Its motion is thus identical with that of S^3. He postulates S^{-3}, and S^{-2}, in similar fashion. Now S^{-2} has the same motion as S^1 – i.e. the motion of the fixed stars. The first of Jupiter's spheres, J^1, has its poles fixed inside the sphere S^{-2}.

For some reason, a *complete* set of spheres, starting from the motion of the fixed stars, is postulated for each planetary body. The point is this. The outermost sphere belonging to Jupiter, J^1, moves with the motion of the fixed stars. But so does its outer neighbour, S^{-2}. So one of these is redundant. The same applies to all of the inner planetary bodies. It is not clear why Aristotle did not economize in this way.

In fact, Aristotle took over Callippus' modifications of the Eudoxan system, and held to the thesis of a complete and separate set of spheres for each planetary body. They can be listed as follows (positive followed by counteracting spheres):

Saturn	4	+	3
Jupiter	4	+	3
Mars	5	+	4
Mercury	5	+	4

Venus	5	+	4
Sun	5	+	4
Moon	5		

No counteracting spheres are required for the moon, since there are no heavenly bodies beneath it; so the total is 55. It seems that the outermost sphere of Saturn is identical with the sphere of the fixed stars, which is not counted separately.[11]

But before leaving the subject of the heavens, we must raise the question that from some points of view appears to be the most important of all: what is the *cause* of the motion of the spheres? Since Aristotle concludes that circular motion is natural to the element of which the heavenly spheres are made, it might seem that there is no further cause to be specified: it might be the case that it is just a fact of nature that this element moves in circles, unless something prevents it, and the position of the poles of each sphere and their relation to each other determines what particular circular orbit is traced out by each particular bit of the aetherial element. Since in *On the Heavens* he attacks Plato's theory that the heavens are moved by their soul, and is silent (in general) about the existence of an external mover, it is tempting to think that in the period when that work was put together Aristotle held a mechanical theory of the motions of the heavens.[12] The whole system of cosmic motions, both in the heavens and in the sublunary world, might then be held to work on the same mechanical principle – the natural self-motion of the five elements. This would fit well enough with one interpretation of Aristotle's well known definition of 'nature', in *Physics* 2.1, as an internal principle of motion and rest.

But it can hardly be so simple. Change in general, including loco-motion, is analysed by Aristotle as the actualization of a potency: he insists that there must be some kind of agent that is actual in the required sense, and something that is not yet but can become actual in this sense; and that these two must be distinct. They may be parts or aspects of the same substance, but they must be distinct from each other. The nearest to an example of a self-mover is an animal: what moves it is its soul, what is moved is its body. But he contrasts this example explicitly with the motions of the elements: the elements cannot be self-movers even in this sense, because if they were, they could (like animals) stop themselves as well as put themselves into motion.

Aristotle never makes it entirely clear what causes the natural fall of earth or the natural rise of fire; but in the last chapters of *Metaphysics* 12 (Lambda) he introduces the external mover of the heavenly spheres. God is their mover, himself unmoved whether by himself or any other being. This Unmoved Mover is pure actuality, with no potentiality for internal change. As such, he is the guarantor of the eternity of the motions of the heavens.

In the relation between mover and moved, the motion is often brought about in some way that necessitates a motion performed by the *mover*: for example an artist or craftsman produces something out of the available materials by *doing* something to them. The prime example of a motion that is *not* brought about in this way is one that is caused by the thought and desire of the moved object – that is to say, when the moved object conceives of the actuality represented by the mover as good and consequently desirable. This is, remarkably, the model chosen by Aristotle for the motions of the heavens.

The model entails a degree of animism in his cosmology: the heavenly spheres, if they are to be capable of thought and desire, must possess souls. Aristotle presents his theology in a notably impressionistic way. It seems (in *Metaphysics* 12.8) that each of the fifty-five spheres must have its own mover; yet we are not told how such beings can be individuated, and in some of the few paragraphs devoted to this all-important topic it appears that a single unmoved mover is envisaged. At least it is clear that if there is a plurality it is an organized plurality: Aristotle ends the book with a quotation from Homer: 'The rule of many is not good: let there be one ruler.'[13]

Aristotle's cosmic deities are remarkably non-providential: their function in his system is to sustain the motions of the cosmos eternally. They have no hand in the creation of the cosmos, since it had no creation but has existed in its present form from all eternity; and they have apparently no thought for the welfare of any particular species or for the whole, except in so far as the eternal survival of the whole system and of all its natural kinds is a matter of concern.

In the surviving works of Aristotle there is astonishingly little on this subject, which one might have expected to be crucial. In the theological chapters of *Metaphysics* 12 (Lambda), he speaks of God in the singular, but introduces plural gods as movers of the spheres without clarifying the change from singular to plural. He describes the activity of the 'first mover' in strikingly reverential words:

> On such a principle, then, depend the heavens and the world of nature. And its life is such as the best which we enjoy, and enjoy but for a short time. For it is ever in this state (which we cannot be) since its actuality is also pleasure. And thought in itself deals with that which is best in itself. . . . If, then, God is always in that good state in which we sometimes are, this compels our wonder; and if in a better, this compels it yet more. And God is in a better state. And life also belongs to God; for the actuality of thought is life, and God is that actuality.
>
> (Aristotle *Metaphysics* 12.7, 1072b14–29, tr. Ross)

But the content of God's thought is never described, and remains a matter of controversy.[14]

❧ 8 MATTER AND ITS QUALITIES IN THE ❧ SUBLUNARY WORLD

At the end of the fourth century, Democritus put forward the theory of atoms. All of the 'being' in the universe, in his view, took the form of unbreakably solid pieces of matter, invisibly small individually but capable of combining temporarily into compounds large enough to be perceived. The only other item in the universe, endowed with a kind of being but sometimes also contrasted with atoms and characterized as 'not-being', was void space – itself absolutely without any properties except spatial extension. All the objects in the familiar world perceived by us were composed of atoms with some quantity of void interspersed between them. The perceptible qualities of things were explained as the outcome of the number and shapes of the component atoms, the quantity of void between them, and their motions in the void.

Plato, in his cosmological dialogue *Timaeus*, rejected this simple 'bottom up' type of explanation, although he did not entirely abandon the concept of atoms. In his theory, the beings primarily responsible for the characteristics of the physical world are the immaterial Forms, accessible to the mind rather than directly to the senses. Physical objects derive their properties from the Forms that they 'partake in' or 'imitate'. The properties of perceptible bodies are, however, related to the nature of the particles which they contain. Plato describes the mathematical structure of particles of the four traditional elements, earth, water, air, and fire. The quality of heat, for example, is related to the sharply angled pyramidal shape of particles of fire. But Plato's particle theory is different from Democritus' atomism in that his particles are not described as having solidity or resistance. They may be regarded as a conceptual analysis of the qualities associated with them, rather than as results of a breakdown of a compound into material components.

Aristotle's theory was in more complete contrast with Democritus than Plato's, in that he abandoned corpuscles altogether in favour of a continuous theory of matter. He himself analyses the argument which, he says, induced Democritus to introduce 'indivisible magnitudes' into his theory. It was a response to the paradoxes of the Eleatic Zeno, and went like this, in brief (*De gen. et corr.* 1.2, 316a11 ff.). Suppose that there are *no* indivisible magnitudes: then every magnitude would be divisible ad infinitum. Suppose such a division ad infinitum were completed: then one must be left either (a) with a collection of undivided magnitudes (which contradicts the hypothesis that every magnitude is divisible), or (b) with a collection of parts with no magnitude (which could never be put together to make a magnitude), or (c) with nothing at all. Hence, Democritus concluded, there must be indivisible magnitudes. Aristotle's response was that every magnitude is indeed divisible every-where, but not everywhere *simultaneously*. Hence there are no indivisible magnitudes, but in dividing one never arrives at an infinite collection of simultaneous parts.

It would be a comparatively easy business to describe his theory if he had made it clear what exactly composes his continuum. Difficulties arise because he fails to make clear whether or not we are to consider the continuum as being composed of 'prime matter', without any qualities beyond those of three-dimensional spatial extension and resistance, or as being invariably endowed with further qualities.

There is no doubt that he adopted the four elements first clearly identified by Empedocles, and taken over by Plato: earth, water, air, and fire.[15] He rejected Plato's theory that the four differ from each other because of the mathematical shape of their particles: instead he allocated to each of them (in addition to natural motion, upwards or downwards) a pair of the primary qualities, hot, cold, dry, and wet. Thus earth is cold and dry, water cold and wet, air warm and wet, fire warm and dry. Unlike Empedocles, he held that that the elements change into each other by exchanging qualities. For example, evaporation is analysed as the replacement of water's coldness by warmth.

But water is not *simply* coldness and wetness: cold and wet are qualities that give form to a substratum: water is *something* that is cold and wet. The 'something' that underlies the qualities is barely described by Aristotle; hence there arises a controversy as to whether or not he had a conception of 'prime matter'. His theory of elementary change does not require a stage at which there exists prime matter without any qualities: what changes into air, to continue with the example of evaporation, is water, and it changes directly, with no intermediate stage. But each of the four elements has three-dimensional extension and resistance, and these properties remain in place (in some sense, if not exactly) when a given quantity of water changes into air. If that is enough to constitute a theory of prime matter, then it seems undeniable that Aristotle held such a theory. But his account of change requires that there never exists an instance of prime matter without qualities.

The four elements are given the familiar names of earth, water, air, and fire, but that is misleadingly simple. The element 'earth' gathers in everything that is solid, water everything that is fluid or pliable, air everything that is misty or gaseous. Fire is to some extent *sui generis*, and does not fit well into this scheme.

∞ 9 FOUR LEVELS OF MATERIAL BEING ∞

1 The four elements ('primary bodies')
2 Homoiomerous bodies
3 Anhomoiomerous parts
4 Organisms

The main point of this classification is to distinguish (2) from (3), and the distinction depends on whether the part (*meros*) has the same name as the whole. If we take a part of a substance such as blood or bone or skin, each of them has the same name as the whole: a bit of bone is bone, and so on. At the next level, the same is not true: a bit of a hand is not a hand (nor 'hand'), nor a bit of a face a face (or 'face'). 'Anhomoiomerous' means 'having parts that are dissimilar'. The anhomoiomerous parts are made of the homoiomerous tissues: a hand is made of skin, bone, muscle, etc.

This distinction serves only to distinguish level (3) from (4), not (1) from (2). Earth, water, air, and fire are homoiomerous.

⤛ 10 THE FORMATION OF COMPOUNDS ⤜

Out of the elements, the tissues: out of these, as matter, the whole of nature's works. But though they are all out of these said elements as *matter*, in respect of their *real being* they are [determined] by their definition.

This is always clearer in higher-level things, and in general in things that are for an end, like tools. It is clearer that a corpse is a man in name only; similarly, then, a dead man's hand, too, is a hand in name only . . . ; such things are less clear in the case of flesh and bone, still less in fire and water, because the final cause is least clear here, where matter predominates.

. . . Such parts, then [sc. the simpler elements of organic compounds], can come-to-be by heat and cold. . . . But the complex parts composed of these – for example head, hand, foot – no one would believe to be composed in this way. Though cold and heat and motion are causes of bronze and silver's coming-to-be, they are no longer the causes of a saw or a cup or a box.

(Aristotle *Meteorologica* 4.12, excerpted)

Aristotle's anti-reductionist stance, in strong opposition to Democritus, is clearly announced in this last chapter of book 4 of his *Meteorologica* (which I take to be a genuine book serving as a bridge between his physical and biological works).[16] He has given an account of the four simple bodies and their motions; he has shown how they combine to make the next layer of his hierarchy of materials – the 'tissues', or 'the homoiomerous bodies', to use his own technical term. But he wants to make it clear that this 'bottom-up' procedure is *not* the way to analyse the physical world. Material elements are the ingredients, but they do not make the natural compound. Empedocles and Democritus were wrong.

Much more important than the material cause is what he designates here as the *logos*, which I have translated 'definition' in the passage above. We shall examine this again in the next section: for the moment, two points must be made.

First, Aristotle's claim is that to know what a thing really is is not just to know what it is made of, by taking it to bits, so to speak, nor just to trace the motions that its ingredients performed in composing it, but rather to know something about it as a present whole. In the case of an artifact, we shall want to know what it is *for*, the final cause; in the case of a living thing, we shall want to know what it *does* so as to survive and reproduce. So we know about *this* object (for example a saw), not when we discover what are the shapes, numbers, and dispositions of its component atoms or other material ingredients (although we shall want to know *something* about its components), but rather when we see that it is to cut wood and understand how its components enable it to do that. We know about *this* object (for example a frog) when we see where and how it gets a living and understand how its parts enable it to live and to reproduce.

So much is an epistemological point: form, or definition (which puts form into words), takes priority over material ingredients for the purpose of knowledge. But this is true about knowledge just because the same priority operates in reality. Matter-in-motion, by itself, does not make a saw or a cup or a box, still less a head or a hand or a foot. The forms or kinds that exist in nature are the primary data. As causes of the production of individual members of species they take priority over the earth, water, air, and fire that are used in the production. It is form that dominates. *How* it dominates and operates as a cause is what we must examine.

Aristotle's theory of the roles of matter and form in the processes of nature bears a strong resemblance to Plato's distinction in the *Timaeus* between Necessity and Mind. It is true that Plato locates the operation of these two causes in the *creation* of the physical world by the Craftsman God, whereas Aristotle uses them to explain the continuous cycles of coming-to-be and passing-away. But the function of the two causes is very much the same in both theories. Plato's Craftsman copies the Forms in a material base; he makes the best possible copies, given the limitations imposed by the Necessity of the materials. In Aristotle's theory, it is the forms themselves, without the designing mind of a Craftsman God, that shape and guide the potentialities of the four simple bodies and the material compounds formed out of them. For Aristotle, the materials represent Necessity in two guises. Materials with certain definite qualities are *necessitated* by the nature of the form they are to take on – a saw-blade must necessarily be of metal, not wood, and a bone must be made of something rigid, not liquid. They are also *necessitating*, in that they necessarily bring with them the whole set of their own properties, whether or not these are all necessitated by the forms. Thus the saw's metal is necessarily liable to rust as well as being capable of being sharpened, the bone is necessarily fragile as well as rigid, if it is not to be too ponderous.[17]

Aristotle's point against the Atomists is not that simple kinds of matter have no necessitating or causative properties, but that these properties *alone* cannot bring about the complex forms observed in nature. What they *can* bring about is described in the fourth book of *Meteorologica*, where he distinguishes four layers of complexity of natural objects, as we have seen. The point Aristotle makes in the quotation at the beginning of this section is that the necessitating properties of matter become less and less dominant with each step up through the layers. They have the greatest effect in the formation of the homoiomerous tissues from the elements. The active powers of heat and cold in the simple bodies work on the passive qualities of moisture and dryness to produce compounds that differ from each other by being, in different degrees, solidified, meltable, softenable by heat, softenable by water, flexible, squeezable, ductile, malleable, fissile, cuttable, viscous, compressible, combustible, and capable of giving off vapours (this is Aristotle's list, in *Meteorologica* 4.8, 385a12–19). The nature of the homoiomerous bodies is determined by these properties, together with the degree of heaviness or lightness imported by the proportions of each of the simple bodies in their composition.

Given the heating action of the sun, then, and the seasonal changes in that action brought about by the sun's motion in the ecliptic circle, we may believe that the continuum of the four simple bodies must be so stirred up into qualitative interaction that many varieties of compound bodies may be formed withot the intervention of other causes. Even at this level, Aristotle's theory is not reductionist: he did not hold that all these different qualities were 'nothing but' different degrees of hot, cold, dry, and wet, nor that the homoiomerous bodies are 'nothing but' earth, water, air, and fire in different proportions. They are all to be thought of as real features of the natural world, generated by the interactions of the simple bodies but not reducible to them.

But even at this level, the generation of the complex out of the relatively simple is rarely caused solely by matter in motion. Homoiomerous tissues like oakwood, fishskin or cowhide are plainly enough *not* brought into being by the action of the sun and the natural properties of the four simple bodies, and nothing else. Aristotle says no more than that the causative action of form is *less* obvious at the lower stages, not that it is entirely absent.

❦ 11 THE FOUR CAUSES ❦

The four are listed in *Physics* 2.3:

> In one way, that out of which a thing comes to be and which persists, is called a cause, for example the bronze of a statue. . . .
>
> In another way, the form or the archetype, i.e. the definition of the essence and its genera, are called causes. . . .

Again, the primary source of the change or rest. . . .
Again, in the sense of end or that for the sake of which a thing is done. . . .

These are traditionally referred to as the material, formal, efficient, and final causes. 'The causes being four, it is the business of the student of nature to know about all of them, and if he refers his problems back to all of them, he will assign the "why?" in the way proper to his science' (*Physics* 2.7, 22–25). But there are reasons for being hesitant about the word 'cause' as a translation of Aristotle's *aition* or *aitia*. No single translation is adequate for all contexts – the bronze of which a statue is made, for instance, is not naturally called a 'cause' of the statue. The basic idea is to classify those items which are responsible for a thing's being what it is. Closest to the modern 'cause' is the third in Aristotle's list, the efficient cause – the sculptor, in the case of the statue. But the bronze of which it is made may well be cited as being responsible for some aspects of its nature; so also its form, and the end or purpose for which it was made.

In the last chapter of the *Meteorologica*, quoted at the beginning of the last section, Aristotle insists that it is inadequate to mention material constituents alone as responsible for the nature of the compound: in anything but the simplest objects in the world, form is of much greater importance. But form alone is still insufficient: it is necessary to specify whatever it is that is responsible for giving *this* form to *this* matter – the efficient cause. And in many cases, for a full explanation we need to know the goal or end served by the possessor of this form in this matter. This simple schema dominates Aristotle's studies of the natural world. It guides his inquiries, and gives shape to his presentation of the results.

12 ARISTOTLE'S ZOOLOGICAL WORKS

The major works are *Parts of Animals* (*PA*), *Generation of Animals* (*GA*), and *History of Animals*.

The first of these provides two introductions to zoological studies. *PA* 1.5 is a fluently written and rather elementary 'protreptic', urging students not to be contemptuous of biology as opposed to 'higher' studies such as metaphysics or astronomy, which deal with eternal rather than perishable things. In the realm of biology, we have the advantage of being closer to the subject matter, and are therefore better able to study it. Moreover, the philosophical mind will find great satisfaction in discovering and analysing the causes at work in plants and animals, where Nature offers much that is beautiful to the discriminating eye.

PA 1.1 is a discussion of causes, and above all a defence of the view that the final cause is most prominent in the works of nature. Lacking a theory of the evolution of species, Aristotle treats as the starting point for biology the form of the grown specimen – the adult horse or man, the full-grown oak tree. This is in opposition to those who started from the material elements – for example, Democritus. The first step is to understand the mode of life of the animal, and to observe what it needs for survival and for reproduction. These are the two essentials for understanding structure and behaviour. Each animal exists in a particular kind of environment, and the nature of the environment determines what will be good for the animal's survival and reproductive capacity. The student of nature, therefore, will observe the animal and its parts, and decide first what contribution each part makes to survival and reproductive capacity. This is the 'cause' *for the sake of which* the part exists and has the structure that it is observed to have. The student will understand the nature of the animal when these causes are understood.

Aristotle uses the word 'cause' (*aitia*) in its usual Greek sense, as that which is responsible for the phenomenon to be explained. But he does not mean to imply that the parts of animals are *caused to grow* (in our sense of 'caused') by capacities that lie in the future: the hooked beak of the (individual) hawk is not caused by its capacity, when grown, to tear up the flesh of its prey. The key to Aristotle's teleology, in the biological realm, is the identity of the form of the (male) parent and the offspring.[18] The parental hawk (to continue the example) survived to produce offspring just because its beak was of a kind well adapted to its mode of life; such a beak was an essential attribute of the form of the hawk; and this form is transmitted to the offspring. The final cause – that 'for the sake of which' the part of the creature exists – is thus subsumed into the efficient cause. The semen of the parent carries the form of the parent and transmits it, as efficient cause in the process of generation, to the offspring.

The mechanism by which this transmission of form is achieved is described in detail in *Generation of Animals*. Aristotle dismisses the theory that the semen is drawn from all the parts of the parent's body (pangenesis). That theory, which is set out in the surviving Hippocratic treatise *On Seed*, and was probably also defended by Democritus, was based on the resemblances of children to their parents. Aristotle argues that this proves too much or too little. Children resemble their parents in characteristics such as their manner of movement which is not determined by physical structure. Moreover children sometimes resemble grandparents or other family members, rather than parents. His own theory depends on his metaphysical distinction between form and matter. The matter of the embryo is provided by the mother, the form by the father.

The semen carries in it the 'movements' that will cause the parts of the embryo to grow in the proper order and form. These movements are not simply instructions, nor an abstract design or formula: they are derived from the soul of the adult parent, and they are embodied in a material substance carried in the semen, called *pneuma*. *Pneuma* is a concept that plays a large part in Greek physiology, from the earliest times, when it is equated more or less exactly with the breath of life. But Aristotle's use of the concept is ill defined. He speaks of the 'connate *pneuma*'; it is clearly necessary for life, and is especially associated with the faculties of soul such as sensation and movement. It carries also the idea of vital heat. But he does not give it the precise and detailed description that forms an important part of Stoic theory, and he does not explain its relation to the four material elements. There is a single mysterious hint (*GA* 2.3, 737a1, mentioned above, in section 5) that it is 'analogous to the element of the stars'.[19]

The *History of Animals*, in ten books, has sometimes been taken to attempt a classification of animals – not by the process of 'dichotomizing' (dividing genera progressively by two into narrower classes) practised by Plato but rejected by Aristotle – but by more complicated methods. Recent researches, however, have shown that that the motivation of these treatises is rather to examine the differentiae of animals (for example the shape and size of legs, the apparatus of the senses, the modes of protection) and to relate them to the needs of the animal to get food, to ward off predators, and to bring up the next generation.[20]

Aristotle uses the terms *genos* and *eidos*, which became the standard words for what later biologists denote by 'genus' and 'species'. But it is clear from examination of the texts that *genos* in Aristotle can denote classes of varying degrees of generality, and *eidos* is not always subordinate to *genos*. What Aristotle seeks to do is to identify the kinds of animals there are, as defined by their mode of life in their environment, and to present comparative studies of the structure and organization of their parts as they are adapted to their function. Hence the supreme importance of the final cause. The biologist above all seeks to explain the connection between each of the characteristic actions of each animal kind, and the structure of the parts of the body that enable the animal to perform these actions.

➳ 13 *PSYCHE* ➳

Psyche is usually translated by the English word 'soul', and it is convenient to use the word in spite of its misleading modern connotations.[21] Aristotle treats the *psyche* as the defining principle of life: the four material elements have no *psyche*, in spite of their natural tendency to seek for their natural place in the cosmos; compounds of the elements have no *psyche*, unless they possess at least the faculties of nutrition and reproduction. Aristotle constructs a *scala naturae* in which each higher step of the ladder is distinguished by the addition of further faculties of the soul. Plants and animals have the basic faculties of nutrition and reproduction; in addition to these, animals have sensation, although not all of them have all of the five senses; some animals, but not all of them, have also the capacity to move themselves; man has all of the animal faculties, with the addition of imagination (*phantasia*) and reason, which are also shared, in some small degree, by the higher animals.

There is thus an ascending order of plant and animal species to be found in the world. This is not, however, an order produced by evolutionary processes: on the contrary, all of the species now in existence have always existed, in Aristotle's view, and will continue to exist. We will discuss the relations between the species briefly in the next section.

It is, of course, a crucial ingredient of Aristotle's theory that the soul is not an entity separate from the body, nor indeed separable in any way except by abstraction in thought (there could be no transmigration of souls in his theory). The soul is 'the first actuality of a natural body that is possessed of organs' (*On the Soul* 2.1, 412b5). If a body is to have soul, it must have the organs that give it the potentiality of carrying out some of the functions of life. The soul is described as the *first* actuality because it is not necessary for the functions of the living body to be *in action* to qualify the body as 'ensouled'. The eyes of a corpse or a statue are not alive, but the eyes of a sleeper are alive although they are not seeing. The soul is a state of readiness, in bodily organs, to perform their function. It can thus be described as a second potentiality, as well as a first actuality.

The conception of an ascending order among living species, with the stages defined by the number and complexity of functions capable of being performed by the plant or animal, gives Aristotle the conceptual apparatus for working out a comprehensive classification of species. There is indeed some evidence that such a classification was a goal of his biological work, but it is not achieved in his surviving writings, where he is concerned above all, it appears, with understanding the differences between animals, and especially with putting the differences into relation with the organic parts.[22] It has been remarked, too, that many of the ingredients of a theory of evolution of species are foreshadowed in his theory, but he was firmly against such an idea, as we have observed.

This is not the place for a lengthy assessment of Aristotle's achievement in biology, but a few points may be mentioned. He was handicapped by his belief, inherited from some earlier physiologists (against the view of Plato), that the heart, rather than the brain, is the seat of the sensitive soul.[23] The nerves had not yet been identified as such, and the blood was taken to be the vehicle for the transmission of messages from sense organs to the centre and vice versa. Blood was thought to be, or to contain, food for the tissues of the body – the circulation of the blood was not, of course, discovered for many centuries after Aristotle. He took respiration to be a way of moderating the natural heat of the body of animals with blood in their system, although he had a use for the concept of *pneuma* or breath, which has been mentioned in section 5.

The *Generation of Animals* contains a detailed study of the reproduction of many species. Aristotle did not understand the contribution of the female of the species to the reproductive process: in his theory semen is the vehicle that conveys the formal structure of parent to offspring, while the female contributes only the material constituents of the embryo, and (in some species) a protective site for its development. But there are remarkable insights in his analysis of the function and structure of semen. It contains both the formal and the efficient cause of the offspring: it contains in potentiality the specific form and some, at least, of the individual characteristics that will be passed on from the parent, and it contains also the 'instructions' for the motions needed to embody these in the embryo. The transmission takes place not by some crude exchange of materials, but in the form of 'encoded' messages.

An odd feature of his 'embryology' is his continuing belief in the spontaneous generation of members of some species. Some creatures (*testacea*) originate from sea water; some plants (for example mistletoe) and animals (grubs) from putrefying matter. What is supplied from sources other than parents in these cases is *pneuma*, which is the material vehicle of life, and warmth. So much is perhaps not hard to understand: there is more difficulty in understanding how matter and warmth alone can supply the form, which in the case of sexual generation requires the subtle and complex contributions of the semen.[24]

❧ 14 THE UNITY OF THE COSMOS ❧

Plato's cosmos, as described in the *Timaeus*, was itself an organism – a *zôon* or animal; Aristotle never talks of the whole cosmos in such terms. He does, however, in various ways and from time to time indicate clearly enough that he regards the cosmos as being appropriately named: the word carries with it the idea of good order.

> We must consider also in which of two ways the nature of the whole contains the good or the highest good, whether as something separate and by itself, or as the order (*taxis*) of the parts. Probably in both ways, as an army does. For the good is found both in the order and in the leader, and more in the latter; for he does not depend on the order but it depends on him. And all things are ordered together somehow, but not all alike – fishes and fowls and plants – and they are not so disposed that nothing has to do with another, but they are connected. For all are organised together with regard to a single thing.
> (Aristotle *Metaphysics* 12.10, 1075a11–19, tr. Ross, slightly adapted)

In the context it would seem that Aristotle draws an analogy between the commander of an army and the supreme deity in command of the cosmos – perhaps the mover of the sphere of the fixed stars, or perhaps 'the divine' in a collective sense, meaning all of the movers of the spheres. The good that they achieve is the eternity of the cosmic order. That is to say, they ensure directly the eternal continuity of the motions of all the heavenly spheres, and hence the eternal interchange between contraries in the sublunary world, and the eternal continuance of all living species.

Aristotle repeats one brief sentence many times, in various contexts: 'nature does nothing without purpose' (*matên*, sometimes translated 'randomly' or 'in vain'). This is a notoriously puzzling claim: there seems to be no room in Aristotle's theory for a single personified 'Nature', acting purposively like a rational being. Each natural thing has its own nature, and some of the effects of the nature of a thing are purposive only in a very loose sense, if at all. The sentence seems to be a summing up of the manner of biological processes; it does not carry us far towards an understanding of the order of the cosmos as a whole.

There is a striking statement in the *Politics*:

> The viviparous species have sustenance for their offspring inside themselves for a certain period, the substance called milk. So that clearly we must suppose that nature also provides for them in a similar way when grown up, and that plants exist for the sake of animals and the other animals for the good of man, the domestic species both for his service and for his food, and if not all at all events most of the wild ones for the sake of his food and of his supplies of other kinds, in order that they may furnish him both with clothing and with other appliances. If therefore nature makes nothing without purpose or in vain, it follows that nature has made all the animals for the sake of men.
>
> (Aristotle *Politics* 1.3, 1256b13 ff.)

This is a claim that sounds more like Stoicism than Aristotelianism. In the zoological treatises, animals are described in a more autonomous fashion; it is not asserted that the function of any characteristic of oxen, for instance, is to supply beef or leather. Man is indeed the 'highest' of the animals, because man shares the divine capability of reason. But the function of the parts of animals is not, apparently, to provide for man, but to provide for the continued life of their own species.

What Aristotle has in mind is that we can observe a 'rightness' in the constituents of the cosmos and their modes of behaviour. It manifests itself in different ways. In the case of the elements, it consists in their natural motions – towards, away from, or around the centre. In the heavenly spheres, it consists in their positions and in the regularity of their motions. In the case of the sun, it shows itself in the daily and annual cycles of light and darkness, summer and winter, which have their effects on the mode of life and generation of biological species. The complement of these features of the cosmic spheres is that each species has its 'niche' in the world. The species did not in any sense *find* their niche, or grow to fill a previous vacancy: it just is

(Aristotle thought) an observable fact that the physical cosmos provides variously characterized environments, and the living species have just those features that enable them to take advantage of them.

Aristotle thus differs both from Democritus and from Plato. He differs from Plato's *Timaeus*, as we have observed, in denying that the cosmos is the work of a purposive Creator. But he differs even more from Democritus, in denying that the world comes about through accident or material 'necessity'. The cosmos just is as it is. It is like a well disciplined army, commanded by a good and effective General who keeps his troops up to the mark in performing their various traditional tasks.

 NOTES

1   See Barnes [1.28]; for more detailed discussion of *Posterior Analytics*, see chapter 2, below.
2   See section 12 for discussion of the translation of *aitia* as 'cause'.
3   On this subject, see especially Owen [1.72, §8].
4   This subject is continued in section 8.
5   One argument is derived from Plato's *Timaeus*, although it was in fact used neither by Plato nor by Aristotle, and those who use the argument do not, it seems, think of aether as the element of the heavens. The argument is that there are five regular solids, and so there should be a fifth element corresponding to the dodecahedron, which was assigned by Plato to the shape of 'the whole'. This argument is found in the pseudo-Platonic *Epinomis* (981b ff.) and apparently in Plato's sucessor Xenocrates (fr. 53 Heinze, from Simplicius).
6   See section 13.
7   Aristotle acknowledges his debt to these two in *Metaphysics* 12.8.
8   The third and fourth spheres enable the model to accommodate the retro-gradation of planets. But Aristotle is quite vague about the details of these motions, being content, apparently, to leave them to the mathematicians.
9   Later Greek astronomers put Venus and Mercury between the moon and the sun.
10 For comparison of Aristotle's description with astronomical theory, see [1.63] Neugebauer, *History* Part II, pp. 675–89, with diagrams in Part III, pp. 1357–8.
11 At 1074a12–14, Aristotle says that if the extra spheres added by Callippus to the sun and the moon are removed, the total should be 47. But something has gone wrong with the text or the calculation. If Aristotle states the condition correctly, the number should be 49.

Another interesting puzzle about the numbers may be mentioned at this stage; it was first raised, so far as I know, by Norwood Russell Hanson [1.87]. It turns on the question whether the axis on which each sphere turns should be regarded as an *axle*, with a certain thickness in diameter, or as a geometrical line. If it is an axle, and is fixed at its ends in the surface of its outer neighbour, then when its poles coincide with those of the outer neighbour it should rotate along with that neighbour. Thus we have a problem at the junction between two planetary sets. To take the example used above, S^{-2}, which has the rotation of the fixed stars, must impart its own rotation to the *axle* of J^1, and since J^1 rotates about its own axle with the motion of the fixed stars, the sphere J[1] will be rotating with *twice* that rotation, i.e. in 12 hours. The first sphere of Mars will rotate in 6 hours, the first of Venus in 3 hours, and so on.

The solution to this is simply to treat the axis of each sphere as a geometric construction and its poles as dimensionless points. This is consistent with the physical nature of the spheres themselves, and abolishes the consequence of a double rotation. The points of contact do not *rotate*, although of course they are carried around with the surface in which they are located whenever they do not coincide with the poles of the superior sphere.

12 For a clear discussion of the problems about motion in *On the Heavens*, see the introduction to [1.14] Guthrie.

13 *Iliad* 2.204; *Metaphysics* 12.10, 1076a5. The problems connected with the unmoved mover or movers of the spheres has of course been very much discussed. Some notable examples: [1.8] Ross, pp. 94–102; [1.14] Guthrie, introduction; [1.85] Merlan.

14 See recent discussions in [1.86] Norman, [1.83] DeFilippo, and [1.74] Waterlow.

15 See section 4, above.

16 See the discussion of this book in [1.62] Furley, chapter 12. Its authenticity has been, and still is, doubted by some scholars.

17 See [1.80] Sorabji, and [1.77] Cooper.

18 This is well explained in [1.81] Woodfield.

19 The fullest account of *pneuma* is found in *De motu animalium*. See [1.9] Nussbaum, especially pp. 143–64.

20 See especially [1.18] Balme, Introduction to books 7–10, p.17; [1.90] Pellegrin, and [1.64] Lloyd ch.1 and ch.12.

21 See also chapter 3, below.

22 See [1.64] Lloyd, ch.1 and ch.12.

23 See below, chapter 10, for Galen's refutation of Aristotle's view.

24 There is a considerable recent literature on Aristotle's theory of spontaneous generation. See, for example, [1.89] Balme, and [1.90] Lennox.

BIBLIOGRAPHY

ITEMS RELEVANT TO CHAPTERS 1–4

1.1 The edition of the Greek text of Aristotle, to which reference is standardly made by page, column and line numbers: *Aristotelis Opera*, ed. I. Bekker, 5 vols (Berlin, 1831–70).

1.2 *Index Aristotelicus* [Greek word index], ed. H. Bonitz (Berlin, 1870).

Complete English translation

1.3 *Aristotle: The Revised Oxford Translation*, ed. Jonathan Barnes (Bollingen series), (Princeton, NJ, Princeton University Press, 1984).

Greek texts with English commentary – some notable editions

1.4 *Prior and Posterior Analytics*, ed. W.D. Ross (Oxford, Clarendon Press, 1949).
1.5 *Physics*, ed. W.D. Ross (Oxford, Clarendon Press, 1936).
1.6 *Aristotle on Coming-to-be and Passing-away* (*De generatione et corruptione*), ed. H. Joachim (Oxford, Clarendon Press, 1922).
1.7 *De anima*, ed. R.D. Hicks (Cambridge, Cambridge University Press, 1907).
1.8 *Metaphysics*, ed. W.D. Ross (Oxford, Clarendon Press, 1924).
1.9 *De motu animalium*, ed. M. Nussbaum (Princeton, NJ, Princeton University Press, 1978).

Greek texts with English translation (Leob Classical Library, Harvard University Press)

1.10 *The Categories, On Interpretation* ed. H.P. Cooke; *Prior Analytics*, ed. H. Tredennick (1938).
1.11 *Posterior Analytics*, ed. H. Tredennick; *Topics*, ed. E.S. Forster (1938).
1.12 *On Sophistical Refutations, On Coming-to-be and Passing-away*, ed. E.S. Forster; *On the Cosmos*, ed. D.J. Furley (1955).
1.13 *Physics*, ed. P.H. Wickstead and F.M. Cornford (1929–34).
1.14 *On the Heavens*, ed. W.K.C. Guthrie (1953).
1.15 *Meteorologica*, ed. H.D.P. Lee (1952).
1.16 *On the Soul* and *Parva naturalia*, ed. W.S. Hett (1936).
1.17 *Generation of Animals*, ed. A.L. Peck (1943).
1.18 *Historia animalium* books 1–4 and 5–8, ed. A.L. Peck (1965 and 1970); books 7–10, ed. D.M. Balme (1991).
1.19 *Parts of Animals*, ed. A.L. Peck, with *Movement of Animals*, ed. E.S. Forster (1937).
1.20 *Minor Works*, ed. W.H. Hett (1936).
1.21 *Problems*, ed. W.H. Hett (1926).
1.22 *Metaphysics*, ed. H. Tredennick, with *Oeconomica* and *Magna Moralia*, ed. G.C. Armstrong (1993).
1.23 *Nicomachean Ethics*, ed. H. Rackham (1926).
1.24 *Athenian Constitution, Eudemian Ethics*, and *Virtues and Vices*, ed. H. Rackham (1935).
1.25 *Politics*, ed. H. Rackham (1932).
1.26 *Rhetoric*, ed. J.H. Freese (1926).

English translations of separate works, with commentary, in the Clarendon Aristotle series (Oxford University Press)

1.27 *Categories* and *De interpretatione*, by J.L. Ackrill (1963).
1.28 *Posterior Analytics*, by Jonathan Barnes (1975).
1.29 *Topics*, books 1 and 8, by R. Smith (1994).

1.30   *Physics*, books I and II, by W. Charlton (1970); books III and IV, by Edward Hussey (1983).
1.31   *De generatione et corruptione*, by C.J.F. Williams (1982).
1.32   *De anima*, books II and III, by D.W. Hamlyn (1968).
1.33   *De partibus animalium* I and *De generatione animalium* I, by D.M. Balme (1972).
1.34   *Metaphysics*, books Gamma, Delta, and Epsilon, by C. Kirwan (1971); books Zeta and Eta, by D. Bostock; books M and N, by J. Annas (1976).
1.35   *Eudemian Ethics*, books 1, 2, and 8, by M. Woods.
1.36   *Politics* 1 and 2, by T.J. Saunders (1995); 3 and 4, by R. Robinson (1962); 5 and 6, by D. Keyt (1999); 7 and 8, by R. Kraut (1997).

Bibliographies

Recent bibliographies in [1.39] *The Cambridge Companion to Aristotle* (1995); also Barnes, Schofield and Sorabji [1.53].

General Introductions to Aristotle

1.37   Ackrill, J.L., *Aristotle the Philosopher* (Oxford, Oxford University Press, 1981).
1.38   Barnes, J., *Aristotle* (Oxford, Oxford University Press, 1982).
1.39   Barnes, J., ed., *The Cambridge Companion to Aristotle* (Cambridge, Cambridge University Press, 1995) (contains an extensive bibliography).
1.40   W.K.C. Guthrie, *A History of Greek Philosophy*, vol. VI: *Aristotle: An Encounter* (Cambridge, Cambridge University Press, 1981).
1.41   W.D. Ross, *Aristotle* (London, Methuen, 1923).

Proceedings of the Symposium Aristotelicum

1.41a *Aristotle and Plato in the Mid-Fourth Century*, ed. I. Düring and G.E.L. Owen, Göteborg, 1960).
1.42   *Aristote et les problèmes de méthode*, ed. S. Mansion (Louvain, Publications Universitaires, 1961).
1.43   *Aristotle on Dialectic: The Topics*, ed. G.E.L. Owen (Oxford, Oxford University Press, 1968).
1.44   *Naturphilosophie bei Aristoteles und Theophrast*, ed. I. Düring (Heidelberg, Lothar Stiehm, 1969).
1.45   *Untersuchungen zur Eudemischen Ethik*, ed. P. Moraux and D. Harlfinger (Berlin, De Gruyter, 1971).
1.46   *Aristotle on the Mind and the Senses*, ed. G.E.R. Lloyd and G.E.L. Owen (Cambridge, Cambridge University Press, 1978).
1.47   *Etudes sur la Métaphysique d'Aristote*, ed. P. Aubenque (Paris, 1979).
1.48   *Aristotle on Science: the 'Posterior Analytics'*, ed. E. Berti (Padua, Antenore, 1981).

1.49 *Zweifelhaftes im Corpus Aristotelicum: Studien in einigen Dubia*, ed. Paul Moraux and Jurgen Wiesner (Berlin and New York: De Gruyter, 1983).

1.50 *Mathematics and Metaphysics in Aristotle*, ed. Andreas Graeser (Bern/ Stuttgart, Paul Haupt, 1987).

1.51 *Aristoteles' 'Politik'*, ed. Günther Patzig (Göttingen: Vandenhoecht and Ruprecht, 1990).

1.52 *Aristotle's Rhetoric*, ed. D.J. Furley and A. Nehamas (Princeton, NJ, Princeton University Press, 1994).

Other collections of essays by various authors

1.53 Barnes, Jonathan, Schofield, Malcolm, and Sorabji, Richard (eds), *Articles on Aristotle:* vol. 1 Science; vol. 2 Ethics and Politics; vol. 3 Metaphysics; vol. 4 Psychology and Aesthetics (London, Duckworth, 1975).

1.54 Seeck, Gustav Adolf (ed.), *Die Naturphilosophie des Aristoteles* (Darmstadt, Wissenschaftliche Buchgesellschaft, 1975).

1.55 Gotthelf, Allan (ed.), *Aristotle on Nature and Living Things: Philosophical and Historical Studies* (Bristol Classical Press, and Mathesis Publications, Pittsburgh, 1985.

1.56 Gotthelf, Allan, and Lennox, James G. (eds), *Philosophical Issues in Aristotle's Biology* (Cambridge, Cambridge University Press, 1987).

1.57 Matthen, Mohan (ed.), *Aristotle Today: Essays on Aristotle's Ideal of Science* (Edmonton, Alberta, Academic Printing and Publishing, 1987).

1.58 Devereux, Daniel, and Pellegrin, Pierre (eds), *Biologie, Logique et Métaphysique chez Aristote* (Paris, CNRS, 1990).

1.59 Judson, Lindsay (ed.), *Aristotle's Physics: A Collection of Essays* (Oxford, Clarendon Press, 1991).

❧ BIBLIOGRAPHY FOR CHAPTER 1 ❧

General works on Greek science and philosophy of nature

1.60 Sambursky, S., *The Physical World of the Greeks* (London, Routledge and Kegan Paul, 1956).

1.61 Dicks, D.R., *Early Greek Astronomy to Aristotle* (London, Thames and Hudson, 1970).

1.62 Furley, David, *Cosmic Problems* (Cambridge, Cambridge University Press, 1989).

1.63 Neugebauer, O., *A History of Ancient Mathematical Astronomy* (Berlin/Heidelberg/ NY, Springer Verlag 1975).

1.64 Lloyd, G.E.R., *Methods and Problems in Greek Science: Selected Papers* (Cambridge University Press, 1991).

1.65 Sorabji, Richard, *Time, Creation, and the Continuum: Theories in Antiquity and the Early Middle Ages* (London, Duckworth, 1983).

1.66 —— *Matter, Space, and Motion: Theories in Antiquity and their Sequel* (London, Duckworth, 1988).

General studies on Aristotle's philosophy of nature

1.67 *Aristotle Today: Essays on Aristotle's ideal of science*, ed. Mohan Matthen (Edmonton, Academic Printing and Publishing, 1989).

1.68 Barnes, Schofield and Sorabji [1.53], vol 1, Science.

1.69 Barnes [1.39] *The Cambridge Companion to Aristotle*. [With good bibliography.]

1.70 Graham, Daniel W., *Aristotle's Two Systems* (Oxford, Oxford University Press, 1987).

1.71 Mansion, Augustin, *Introduction à la physique aristotélicienne*, 2nd edn (Louvain, 1946).

1.72 Owen, G.E.L., *Collected Papers in Greek Philosophy*, ed. Martha Nussbaum (Ithaca, NY, Cornell University Press, 1986). Especially no. 8 'Aristotle: method, physics and cosmology' and no. 10 '*Tithenai ta phainomena*'.

1.73 Solmsen, Friedrich, *Aristotle's System of the Physical World* (Ithaca, NY, Cornell University Press, 1960).

1.74 Waterlow, S., *Nature, Change, and Agency in Aristotle's Physics* (Oxford, Clarendon Press, 1982).

Causation

1.75 Annas, J., 'Aristotle on inefficient causes', *Philosophical Quarterly* 32 (1982), 319.

1.76 Balme, D.M., 'Teleology and necessity', in Gotthelf and Lennox, [1.56], 275–86.

1.77 Cooper, John M., 'Hypothetical necessity and natural teleology', in Gotthelf and Lennox [1.56], 243–74.

1.78 Gotthelf, Allan, 'Aristotle's conception of final causality', in Gotthelf and Lennox [1.56], 204–42.

1.79 Lennox, James, 'Teleology, chance, and Aristotle's theory of spontaneous generation', *Journal of the History of Philosophy*, 20 (1982), 219–38.

1.80 Sorabji, Richard, *Necessity, Cause and Blame: Perspectives on Aristotle's Theory* (London, Duckworth; Ithaca, NY, Cornell University Press, 1980).

1.81 Woodfield, Andrew, *Teleology* (Cambridge, Cambridge University Press, 1976).

Motion and theology

1.82 Bogen, James, and McGuire, J.E., 'Aristotle's great clock: necessity, possibility and the motion of the cosmos in *De caelo* 1.12', *Philosophy Research Archives* 12 (1986–87), 387–448.

1.83 DeFilippo, Joseph, 'Aristotle's identification of the prime mover as god', *Classical Quarterly* 44 (1994), 393–409.

1.84 Kahn, C., 'The place of the prime mover in Aristotle's teleology', in Gotthelf [1.55].

1.85 Merlan, P., 'Aristotle's unmoved movers', *Traditio* 4 (1946), 1–30.
1.86 Norman, Richard, 'Aristotle's Philosopher-God', *Phronesis* 14 (1969), 63. Repr. in Barnes, Schofield and Sorabji [1.53], vol. 4, 183–205.
1.87 Hanson, N.R., 'On counting Aristotle's spheres', *Scientia* 98 (1963), 223–32.

Matter and elements

1.88 Moraux, Paul, 'Quinta essentia', in Pauly–Wissowa, *Realencyclopädie* 24, 1171–226.

Biology

1.89 Balme, D.M., 'Development of biology in Aristotle and Theophrastus: theory of spontaneous generation', *Phronesis* 7 (1962), 91–104.
1.90 Lennox, James 'Teleology, chance, and Aristotle's theory of spontaneous generation', *Journal of Hellenistic Studies* 20 (1982), 219–38.
1.91 Pellegrin, Pierre, *La Classification des animaux chez Aristote: Statut de la biologie et unité de l'Aristotélisme* (Paris, Les Belles Lettres, 1982).

CHAPTER 2

Aristotle's logic and metaphysics
Alan Code

❧❦❧

❧ OVERVIEW OF ARISTOTLE'S LOGIC ❧

The Aristotelian logical works are referred to collectively using the Greek term '*Organon*'. This is a reflection of the idea that logic is a tool or instrument of, though not necessarily a proper part of, philosophy. In the traditional ordering of these works the *Categories* comes first. It deals, among other things, with the simple terms (subjects and predicates) that when combined go together to form simple statements, and it characterizes primary substances as the ultimate subjects for predication. It also contains a treatment of ten categories, with particular emphasis on the four categories of substance, quantity, relation and quality. The *De Interpretatione*, which is placed second, discusses the statements that result from combining nouns and verbs, and includes a treatment of various modal relations between statements. The main topic of the two *Analytics* is demonstration (*epideixis*), the type of valid deductive argument, or syllogism, (*sullogismos*) involved in scientific knowledge (*epistêmê*). The *Prior Analytics*, which contains a formal theory of syllogistic reasoning, shows how statements combine to form arguments, and in the *Posterior Analytics* demonstrations are analyzed as explanatory syllogisms from first principles. This work combines the notion of syllogistic inference with an account of the nature of scientific first principles in its analysis of the structure of science. The *Topics* is chiefly concerned with dialectical debate, and the work *On Sophistical Refutations* contains a treatment of various kinds of fallacies in dialectical argument. At the conclusion of this work Aristotle indicates that unlike his other inquiries, such as his treatment of rhetoric, that build upon the results of his

40

predecessors, prior to his own efforts there simply was no general inquiry concerning syllogistic reasoning. The *Rhetoric*, not itself included in the *Organon*, is concerned with the use of rhetorical argumentation for the purpose of persuading an audience.

❧ PREDICATION, AND SUBSTANCE AS SUBJECT ❧

Predication

In the *Categories* (using terminology not employed for this purpose outside that work) predication is characterized in terms of the two relations 'said of a subject' and 'present in a subject'. The relata are 'things that are' (*onta*), and this type of predication may be dubbed 'ontological'. Although the verb translated 'to be predicated' (*katêgoreisthai*) is used extensively outside the *Categories*, the way in which the phrases 'said of' and 'present in' are used here is idiosyncratic to this work. Due to the way it is connected with the notion of definition, it is convenient to describe the relation 'being said of a subject' as *essential* predication. Essential predications say what a subject is intrinsically, or *per se*.[1] By way of contrast, the relation 'being present in a subject', which in the *Categories* covers all types of predication other than essential predication, is *accidental* predication.[2]

Although these two relations are taken as primitives in the *Categories*, remarks there provide a partial characterization.[3] The 'said of' relation is transitive, and as will be seen below, is connected with definition in a way that the 'present in' relation is not. Given that *man* is predicable of Socrates, anything predicable of man, for instance, is thereby predicable of Socrates. The definition of the species man applies to him as well. The class of things 'present in a subject' are described as being present not in the way that a part is present in a whole, and as incapable of existing separately from some subject that they are in. These two types of ontological predicability help account for linguistic predicability (the application of a linguistic predicate to a subject). A simple subject–predicate sentence is used to make a simple affirmative statement in which one item is predicated of another, usually distinct, item. The linguistic predicates 'man' and 'grammarian' are applicable to some subject just in case the species man and grammatical knowledge, respectively, are ontologically predicable of that subject.

The notion of predication is employed in *De Interpretatione* 7 to distinguish particulars from universals. A 'universal' (*katholou*) is an item of such a nature as to be predicable of a plurality of things; a 'particular' (*kath' hekaston*) is an item that cannot be predicated, either essentially or accidentally, of a plurality. Aristotle sometimes uses the term 'individual' (*atomon*) for items not essentially predicable of other things (thus leaving it open whether an individual is accidentally predicable of something distinct from itself).

The *Categories* distinguishes between the simple linguistic expressions (things spoken of without combination) of which statements are composed, and the entities those expressions signify. The name 'man', for instance, and the verb 'runs' are simple significant expressions that combine to form the declarative subject–predicate sentence 'Man runs'. Although when used without combination, neither of these words has a truth-value, they may be combined to form a statement that is either true or false. The word 'man' signifies man, the word 'runs' signifies the activity of running, and one uses the sentence 'Man runs' to truly affirm some predicable (namely, *running*) of some subject (namely, *man*). The word 'man', which may serve as either a subject or a predicate expression, signifies a substance,[4] for it signifies the species man, and that is a substance. There are also particular substances, like Socrates, which are the signification of names that function as grammatical subjects, but never as grammatical predicates. The particular itself is always an ontological subject, and never a predicable.

According to *Categories* 4 the ten kinds of things that are signified by simple expressions are: substances, quantities, qualities, relatives, places, times, positions, states, doings and undergoings. Although Aristotle does not himself explain the rationale for this list, it is a classification of the kinds of things that could be said of something in response to a question asked about it. When we say of some particular substance what it is, as when we say of Socrates that he is a man, the simple expression (here 'man') signifies a substance. However, in addition to predicates offered in response to the question (1) 'What is it?' when asked of a particular substance, there are other kinds of linguistic terms that are given in response to other kinds of questions. For instance, we may ask of something (2) 'How large is it?' and elicit a reply such as 'six feet'. In a like manner each of the other entries on this list classifies a kind of answer to some other kind of question: (3) 'What is it like?' (to which we might answer 'pale'); (4) 'What is it in relation to something?' (A double, a half); (5) 'Where is it?' (in the Lyceum); (6) 'When was it?' (yesterday, last year); (7) 'What position is it in?' (lying down, or sitting); (8) 'What state is it in?' (armed); (9) 'What is it doing?' (cutting); or (10) 'What is being done to it?' (being cut). Just as questions such as 'What is Socrates?' and 'What is Bucephalus?' collect predicate expressions such as 'man', 'horse' and 'animal' that signify substances, these other nine questions collect predicate expressions that signify other kinds of predicables.

The ten kinds of things signified by these kinds of expressions are standardly referred to as the Aristotelian categories. Aristotle frequently uses the Greek word '*katêgoria*' to mean 'predicate', or 'kind of predicate'. When the term is used in this sense, particular substances are not themselves in the 'category' of substance (since they are always subjects and never predicates). Elsewhere when Aristotle makes use of a classification of 'categories', this full list of ten does not appear.[5] For instance, *Metaphysics* Delta 7 correlates the various *per se* senses of 'to be' with an eight-fold categorial schema of the sort suggested by this list.

A subject's essential predicates are those that signify *what it is*. The subject is called what it is synonymously from such predicates. In the first chapter of the *Categories*, two things are *homonyms* just in case, although there is a term that applies to both, the definitions associated with the two applications are distinct; two things are *synonyms* just in case the same term applies to both, and the associated definition is the same as well. Some universal X is said of some subject Y if, and only if, both the name and the definition of X truly apply to Y. For this reason whenever a universal is said of a subject, the universal and its subject are 'synonyms'. The word 'man', for instance, is applicable to the particular man because the universal it signifies, the species man, is predicable of him. However, not only does the name of the species apply, its definition applies as well. The definition of man is an account saying what man is, and the definition that applies to Socrates is the definition of the species man. Assuming for illustrative purposes that the account that defines man is 'biped animal', it is true that whatever is a man must be a biped animal. The definition of the species man applies to particular men, and the species is predicated essentially of those particulars. The defining expression that signifies the essence of a particular just is the definition of its species.

In the *Organon* universals, not sensible particulars, are the objects of definition. The definition appropriate for a particular is the definition of the species to which it belongs. In order for a particular to be a logical subject, or subject of predication at all, it must be something essentially. The species to which a particular belongs, although not identical with the particular, is what the particular essentially is. It is the definable something the particular must be essentially if it is to be anything at all.

Not only substantial universals, but any object of definition whatsoever is a subject for essential predication. The color white, for instance, is a color, and hence color is predicable of white. Substances and non-substances alike may possess definitions, and hence be endowed with essential natures. In addition to the names of substantial universals, there are also names of the universals that are accidentally predicable of substances. Although, in some cases, the name of a non-substantial universal (the name 'white', for instance) applies to the substances to which the universal is present, in general not the name itself, but rather some linguistic predicate associated with the name, is applicable to all and only those things having the universal as an accidental property. Socrates is called 'brave', not 'bravery'. Despite this, the definition of any universal X that is accidentally predicable of a subject Y can never be truly applied to Y. Although the name 'white' applies to white particulars in virtue of the fact that they all have the color white, the definition of that color is not linguistically predicable of any of them. They are not called white in virtue of what they are.

If a non-substantial property is present in a subject, then (in general) its name does not apply to that subject, but there will be some associated expression that differs in ending, which is applicable to the subject. In such cases the subject is called what it is called *paronymously* from that property. Although the noun 'bravery' cannot be truly predicated of Socrates, the adjective 'brave' is applicable to Socrates because bravery is present to him. The brave thing is a paronym.

Substance as subject

Translators of Aristotle's Greek typically render the abstract substantive *'ousia'* as 'substance',[6] suggesting the idea that substances are the subjects of predication. In the *Categories* all beings except for primary substances are predicable (either essentially or accidentally) of primary substances. On the other hand, a primary substance is a primary substance because it is a subject (*hupukeimenon*) for the other things, but is not itself predicable of anything further. Each primary substance is an individual subject of predication that is not itself predicable of a substance, and as such is 'some this' (*tode ti*).

In this treatise all primary substances are particulars – the particular man, the particular horse, and so on. Aristotle here treats individual men, horses, and the like as primary substances. In the *Metaphysics* he also considers the claims of their matter and form to be substance, but in this work the individual is not subjected to the hylomorphic analysis found both in his natural science and the *Metaphysics*. There is no discussion in the *Organon* of matter, nor of the relations between the individual man, his body and his form (or soul).

In the *Categories* primary substances are particulars, and their natural kinds (i.e., their species and genera) are universals. These natural kinds are called 'secondary substances', and are the only substances other than the primary substances. The only universals in the *Categories* are (1) secondary substances, (2) their differentiae, and (3) the various quantities, qualities, and other non-substantial items that are had by the substances.[7] Some linguistic predicates, such as 'man', signify universals that are essentially predicable of all the substantial particulars of which they are predicable. These terms classify particulars according to their natural kinds.

In addition to its distinction between primary and secondary substance, with the attendant designation of the primary substances as the subjects for everything else, the *Categories* also lists a number of the distinctive characteristics (*idia*) of substances, quantities, relatives and qualities. For instance, substances do not have contraries, nor do they admit of degrees. Most importantly, anything that can persist through time as numerically one and the same while receiving contrary properties must be a primary substance. One and the same individual man can be pale at one time, dark at another; hot at one time, cold at another; bad at one time, good at another. In this way the ultimate subjects of predication are treated as the persisting subjects for accidental change.

THE STRUCTURE OF SCIENTIFIC KNOWLEDGE

Syllogistic

The theory of syllogistic reasoning in the *Prior Analytics* concerns the relation between the premises and the conclusion of a syllogism. The conclusion *follows of necessity from* the premises. In his account of this relation he appeals to characteristics of arguments that abstract from the content of the statements involved. He identifies a few obvious (perfect) cases of this relation, and then shows that all non-obvious (imperfect) cases can be reduced to the obvious.

The notion of syllogistic inference is utilized both in Aristotle's analysis of scientific reasoning and in his treatment of dialectical argument. A scientific demonstration is a syllogism that proves its conclusion by showing how it necessarily follows from its explanatory principles. Knowing scientifically requires this kind of argument from indemonstrable starting points. Reasoning from necessarily true explanatory principles to necessarily true scientific conclusions takes place in a variety of sciences that do not share a common genus or kind. This is why a general account of this relation must abstract from the particular content of the statements of any given science. In this sense his theory is sometimes described as 'formal'.

In a similar manner, the logical expertise exemplified by a dialectician in two person question–answer exchanges involves the production of valid inferences, and this ability is not confined to a single domain. In the first book of the *Topics* dialectical skill is characterized as the ability both to reason syllogistically from credible opinions (*endoxa*) to conclusions that necessarily follow from them, and to avoid being refuted by one's own concessions in argument. Dialectic is useful for intellectual training, for persuading a general audience and for philosophical knowledge. It enables one to develop and examine the arguments on both sides of philosophical puzzles (*aporiai*), thereby facilitating the discernment of truth. Furthermore, the dialectical scrutiny of credible opinions provides a path that leads to the first principles of the sciences. Unlike scientific arguments which argue from first principles and are concerned with items within a single subject genus, dialectical argument is possible concerning any subject matter whatsoever, and in this sense is topic neutral. Hence a general account of the way in which a dialectician shows that credible opinions and an interlocutor's concessions necessitate further conclusions requires abstraction from subject matter. In dialectical argument one asks questions, and produces syllogisms using the answers as premises. However, since such arguments do not reason from explanatory premises already known by the respondent, they do not result in knowledge. Although credible opinions, which can include commonly accepted views as well as the opinions of the wise, must not be obvious falsehoods, they may in fact be false, and certainly need not be explanatory first principles. Reasoning from them is in any case no guarantee that the conclusions reached are true, and even where the premises are true, they (typically) do not explain the truth of the conclusion.[8]

In the first chapter of the *Prior Analytics* Aristotle informally characterizes a syllogism as an account[9] in which certain things being posited, something other than what has been posited follows of necessity in virtue of the former's being the case. He further explains that 'in virtue of their being the case' means 'resulting through them', and that this involves not needing any term outside of those in the premises for the generation of the necessity. A syllogism is a case of a valid argument in which the conclusion follows of necessity from the premises, and does so in virtue of the way subject and predicate terms are combined. The heart of his syllogistic is a general characterization of those valid arguments that contain a pair of simple statements as premises, have a simple statement as conclusion, and involve just three terms: major, middle, minor. In aid of generality, actual Greek terms (like 'animal' or 'pale') are replaced by Greek letters (like 'A' and 'B') used as schematic letters. The forms of the four basic types of statements (the 'assertoric' propositional forms) are characterized in terms of their quantity and quality, and his three syllogistic 'figures' are characterized by reference to the order of the major, middle and minor terms of an argument.[10] In addition, Aristotle presents a number of rules of conversion. He identifies within the three 'figures' the syllogisms, or valid arguments, and believes that every scientific demonstration and every syllogism in the informal sense can be captured by a string of two premise syllogisms from these figures (and ultimately from the first figure).

Although the *Prior Analytics* does not explicitly refer to the *De Interpretatione*, its account of syllogistic inference builds upon ideas about statements that can be found in the latter. There both designating terms and verbs are said to have a signification on their own (though not a truth-value). They can, however, be combined to form simple sentences.[11] A statement (*apophansis*) is a sentence that is capable of either truth or falsehood. The *Organon* has no further discussion of sentences that lack a truth-value (such as prayers), and leaves them as a topic of discussion for rhetoric and poetics. Every simple statement is either an affirmation (*kataphasis*) or a denial (*apophasis*) An affirmation affirms some predicate of a subject, whereas a denial denies some predicate of a subject.

Both particulars and universals may serve as the subjects of a statement, but the predicate of a statement is always universal. Where both the subject and the predicate are universals, one may further specify whether the affirmation or denial is of the subject taken as a whole, or merely as a part. The statement that 'every animal is pale' affirms *pale* of its subject, *animal*, as a whole. Such a statement is called 'universal' in quantity. By way of contrast, 'some animal is pale' affirms *pale* of only a part of its subject. Such a statement is called 'particular' in quantity.[12] One may specify in terms of their quantity (universal or particular) and quality (affirmative or negative) the four so-called assertoric categorical propositional forms employed in Aristotle's syllogistic: universal affirmative, or A propositions (for example, every man is mortal); universal negative, or E propositions (for example, no man is mortal); particular affirmative, or I propositions (for example, some man is mortal); and particular negative, or O propositions (for example, some man is not mortal).[13] Aristotle tried to show that all valid arguments could be put into syllogisms constructed of premises and conclusions of these forms. However, his account does not give axioms or rules for the propositional connectives, or statements containing either nested quantification or relational predicates. This drastically limits its scope of application. An additional problem results from the fact that use of a categorical statement in a syllogism presupposes that its terms have instances. (For instance, if it is true that all men are mortal, it is also true that some men are mortal.)

There are logical relations that obtain between the different propositional forms. Consider four propositions, or statements, sharing the same subject and predicate but each exemplifying a different propositional form. The A and O propositions are *contradictories*,[14] as are the E and the I; the A and E are *contraries*;[15] I is the *subalternate* of A, and O the *subalternate* of E.[16] The *Prior Analytics* captures some further basic relations between the propositional forms by means of the following three conversion rules:

C1   if every S is P, some P is S
C2   if some S is P, some P is S
C3   if no S is P, no P is S

These are not themselves syllogisms, and function in effect as rules for valid arguments having a single assertoric premise and a single assertoric conclusion.

The syllogisms given formal treatment in this account consist of two premises and a conclusion, and each has both a *figure* and a *mood*. Statements are composed of terms, and the notion of *figure* is characterized by specifying the relationships between the terms occurring in the premises and the conclusions. The two *extreme terms* are the subject and the predicate of the conclusion, the *major term* being the predicate of the conclusion, the *minor term* being its subject. The *middle term* is the one that occurs in both premises, but not in the conclusion. The *major premise* is the premise containing the major term, and the *minor premise* is the premise containing the minor term. An argument is in the *first figure* if the major term is the predicate of the major premise, and the minor term is the subject of the minor premise. In such cases the middle term is the subject of the major premise, and the predicate of the minor premise. An argument is in the *second figure* when the middle term is the predicate of both premises, and in the *third figure* when the middle term is the subject of both premises.

The syllogisms, or valid arguments within the three figures may be specified in terms of their *mood*, where the mood of a syllogism can be represented as a trio of propositional forms: the form of the major premise, the minor premise and the conclusion (in that order). *Prior Analytics* A4–6 states all the valid and invalid moods of the three figures. The valid moods of the first figure are AAA, EAE, AII, EIO (plus the subaltern moods AAI, EAO).[17] Invalid moods are shown to be such by producing counterexamples – that is, instances of a figure and mood combination in which the premises can be true, and the conclusion false.

Having specified the syllogisms of the first three figures, Aristotle reduces the so-called 'imperfect' syllogisms of the second and third figure to the 'perfect' syllogisms of the first figure. The perfect syllogisms of the first figure are basic cases in which nothing other than the premises themselves are needed in order for it to be evident that the conclusion follows of necessity from the premises. Although in an imperfect syllogism the conclusion does necessarily follow, in order to make this evident one must do more than simply present the premises. The reduction shows that a valid argument that uses second or third figure resources to derive a conclusion can be replaced by valid reasoning that derives the same conclusion from the same premises relying upon only the obvious inferences of the first figure, together with the conversion rules.[18] In some cases a direct reduction utilizing conversion is possible, but where this is not possible (second figure AOO and third figure OAO), he resorts to *reductio ad absurdum*.[19] A *reductio* argument shows that the premises have a certain syllogistic consequence by producing a direct deduction of the contradictory of one premise from the other premise taken together with the contradictory of the conclusion.

Demonstration and first principles

For Aristotle the universe can be rendered intelligible, or understood, by humans. *Metaphysics* Epsilon 1 divides all knowledge into the theoretical, the practical and the productive. Whereas the goal of a productive science is always some product distinct from the exercise of the science itself (such as a shoe, a statue or health), and the goal of practical knowledge consists of the activities of life, theoretical knowledge is an understanding of the truth merely for its own sake. Theoretical knowledge itself is divided into the mathematical sciences, the natural or physical sciences and theology. The practitioner of a theoretical science knows, or understands, something by grasping its 'why' or 'cause'. Knowledge is attained when something is explained by means of starting points or principles (*archai*) that are even better known than what is explained.

The account in the *Posterior Analytics* of the structure of a demonstrative science is both patterned after and inspired by the way in which the Ancient Greek mathematical sciences, especially geometry, had developed in the direction of axiomatization. Ideally, the premises of a mathematical proof both *necessitate* the conclusion, and *explain* why it is true. It is with this ideal in mind that he says in *Posterior Analytics* A2 that we think that we have knowledge or understanding (in the unqualified sense) whenever we suppose both (1) that we know its 'cause' (the reason it is the case), and (2) that it could not possibly be otherwise. The word 'cause' is used here to translate the Greek term '*aitia*', but it should be stressed that the range of applicability of the Greek term overlaps with, but is not coextensive with that of our word 'cause'. Anything that can be explained has an *aitia*, regardless of whether it is the type of thing that we would ordinarily describe as 'caused'. For instance, the premises of a mathematical proof, although not causes, nonetheless explain the truth of the conclusion, and may reasonably be said to be responsible for it. The *aitia* of something is what is responsible for its being a certain way, and as such is an explanatory factor the grasp of which constitutes knowing why something is the case. What is known in the unqualified sense of that term must be a necessary truth.

Building on his key insight that knowledge requires both an understanding of 'causes' and the necessity of what is known, the treatise goes on to discuss the different kinds of first principles, and how they are related to theorems. The necessary truths that constitute the body of a demonstrative science are exhaustively partitioned into indemonstrable first principles, and their demonstrable consequences. The former are understood through themselves. Their consequences, the theorems, are known or understood only through their 'causes' and principles. Our knowledge of the latter is demonstrative in that such knowledge involves deducing them from first principles that explain why they are the case.

Posterior Analytics A2 states that the principles must be true, primary, immediate, better known than, prior to and explanatory of those things of which they are the principles. Since a first principle is known through itself, and not through other things, there is no explanation as to why the principle is true. It is not explained or 'caused' by anything, and hence it cannot be known by tracing it back to causes. A first principle is indemonstrable, for it is both primary and immediate. To be immediate, it must be primary in the sense that there is nothing prior to it in terms of which it is understood or known. If it is a statement (such as a definition) with both a subject and a predicate, there is no middle term that explains or mediates the connection between its subject and its predicate. A first principle cannot itself be explained by deducing it from prior principles or causes, and in this way is indemonstrable.[20] The other necessary truths of a science are explained or 'caused' by something other than themselves. They are known by tracing them back to principles, and 'causes' that are known through themselves. Such theorems are known only when one understands why they must be true. Theorems are known by deducing them from necessarily true first principles that are their 'causes', and the first principles must themselves be known independently of, and prior to demonstration. Demonstration itself is a scientific syllogism, a syllogism by virtue of which we know.

Aristotle thinks that all knowledge comes from pre-existing knowledge. In the case of knowledge of theorems, the pre-existing knowledge is the knowledge of the principles. However, since the first principles are better known than the conclusions of any demonstrative argument, although knowledge of them also comes from pre-existing knowledge, they must come to be known in some way other than demonstration. In connection with this topic Aristotle draws a distinction between what is known to us and what is known without qualification. What is known to us, prior to knowing first principles, is what we know through sense perception. This is not scientific knowledge, or knowledge without qualification. Our task is to move from what is known to us to knowledge of what is most knowable without qualification. These are the intelligible principles that will in turn explain and account for the original sensible phenomena from which we started. In the last chapter of the *Posterior Analytics*, B19, Aristotle explains that we come to know first principles through induction (*epagogê*), an argumentative procedure that proceeds to a generalization from some group of its instances. Aristotle is aware that such inferences are not deductively valid, and unfortunately does not develop a set of rules governing such inferences. Consequently, details of his views about this procedure cannot be described with confidence. What he does say indicates that induction is supposed to be the means by which an inquirer advances from what is initially knowable (to that individual) to what is knowable without qualification. In B19 it is said that *knowledge* of first principles is based on *experience*, that experience in turn is based on numerous *memories*, and finally that memories themselves result from numerous and repeated *perceptions*. All animals, ourselves included, have natural discriminative perceptual capacities. Perception provides the ultimate inductive basis for knowledge of first principles. The epistemic state the exercise of which constitutes knowledge of principles is called '*nous*', or intelligence. Very little is said about it here, and when it is discussed elsewhere, in *De Anima* Gamma 4 and 5, the text is highly controversial and notoriously difficult.

Each demonstrative science has both a kind term that demarcates its subject matter and a set of attributes that it studies. *Posterior Analytics* A7 and A10 show that a demonstrative science makes use of first principles in order to prove its conclusions about those objects that are encompassed by the general kind that it studies. Such demonstrated conclusions ascribe to these objects those properties that pertain to them *intrinsically*. A science studies items mentioned in the definitions of those things falling within the scope of its subject genus, as well as those definable things themselves, and their demonstrable attributes. These additional items are properties, or 'modifications' (*pathê*) either of the things within the scope of the genus, or of the genus itself. They are not included in the definitions of the subjects that possess them, and consequently demonstrations must be given to show that they belong to their subjects intrinsically. Geometry studies figures, and seeks causes and principles that govern each kind of figure *qua* that kind of figure. An example would be the proof of the theorem that the angles of a triangle equal two right angles. In general, the geometer appeals to first principles to explain what belongs to various kinds of figures insofar as, and because, they are figures.

Aristotle put forward his account of scientific knowledge in opposition to the Platonic conception of a general dialectical science of being. Whereas Platonic dialectic purported to yield scientific understanding of the principles of the departmental sciences, Aristotle's rival account was designed to uphold the independence or autonomy of the departmental sciences. The statements within such a science include propositional first principles as well as the theorems in which the 'modifications' of various types of figures are demonstrated.[21] Aristotle divided the first principles of a science into axioms and theses, and divided the latter into hypotheses and definitions. Whereas the definition of X is an account signifying what X is, a hypothesis is an existence postulate that states of what is defined *that* it is. The definitions and hypotheses of a science are employed only in that branch of knowledge, and being first principles are not demonstrated by some other science. A definition is immediate in the sense that the predicate of a definition signifies just what the subject is, and hence the connection between subject and predicate is not explicable by reference to a middle term.

By way of contrast with theses, the axioms are common to all sciences. Aristotle describes axioms as the principles from which reasoning arises, and as such they must be known in order to learn or scientifically understand anything at all. The two most important examples of axioms are the law of non-contradiction, and the law of the excluded middle (the principle that there cannot be an intermediate between contradictories). The axioms are common to all of the sciences, and knowledge of the axioms is common to all scientific understanders. This is relevant to Aristotle's conception of metaphysics as general ontology, a science which among other things investigates the axioms (for which see pp. 60–1).

A science does not study just any attribute that might happen to belong to its subject matter, for there is no science of the accidental. In order to determine which statements, terms and first principles are appropriate for a given science with a given subject matter, one must specify the *respect* in which the science in question studies the application of the various terms to the subject it studies. For instance, the biologist does not study all the properties of living things, but only those that apply to them in respect of being living beings. Biology studies both the definitions of each species of living things and the properties that belong to each species *per se*, or intrinsically.

A science studies what must belong to a subject in some respect, and in so doing investigates what belongs to it intrinsically, or *per se*.[22] *Posterior Analytics* A4 distinguishes the following three distinct ways in which something can belong to a subject *per se*. First, if something is in the account saying what some subject is (i.e., in the definition of the subject) it belongs to that thing *per se*. It is in this way that both biped and animal belong to the species man intrinsically$_1$. In a second way something belongs to a subject intrinsically if that item is such that the subject in question is in its definition. It is in this way that 'male' and 'female' hold good of animal intrinsically$_2$. Finally, in still another way, an item is said to belong to a subject in respect of itself if that item belongs to the subject because of, or on account of the subject. In this third way, 'being-receptive-of-grammar' belongs to man intrinsically$_3$; 'having-interior-angles-equal-to-two-right-angles' belongs to triangle intrinsically$_3$. What does not belong to a subject intrinsically$_1$ or intrinsically$_2$ is sometimes called by Aristotle 'accidental'. Consequently, items that intrinsically belong to something in this third way are sometimes called *per se*, or intrinsic accidents. He also distinguishes things that are beings intrinsically from things that are beings accidentally. Something is a being intrinsically, or *per se*, just in case it is not called what it is called through being something else that happens to be that. By way of contrast, a pale thing, or a cultured thing, is a being accidentally since it is called what it is called (namely 'pale' or 'cultured') through being something else, a man, that happens to be called 'pale' or 'cultured'.

The first sense of 'intrinsic', or *per se*, is the most basic of all, and because of its connection with definition can be used to characterize the notion of essence. The essence of each thing is what it is said to be intrinsically$_1$, and it is essentially predicable of that of which it is the essence. *Topics* A5 states that a definition (*horos* or *horismos*) is an account (*logos*) signifying the essence of that thing. (Rather than using a single word to mean essence here, he employs a phrase that corresponds to the English 'what it is (for it) to be' (*to ti ên einai*). The essence of something is the entity signified by the entire account saying what it is. Although he argues that the Platonic method of collection and division cannot demonstrate a definition, the influence of that method can be seen in Aristotle's own conception of definition as a complex expression that mentions both the *genus* to which the item belongs and the *differentiae* that distinguish it from other coordinate members of that genus.

A definition is an account signifying an essence. An account signifying what something is signifies its essence, and the definition of something is the account that says what it is.[23] If the definition of man is 'biped animal', then biped animal is the essence of man. Just as the word 'man' signifies the species man, the definition of man signifies the essence of man. To predicate an essence of that of which it is the essence one may linguistically predicate the appropriate associated defining expression, thereby saying what that thing is. A definable item is one and the same as the essence signified by its definition. Whenever some universal is defined, the subject of the definition is the same as the essence signified by the definiens. Thus if man is correctly defined as 'biped animal', then the species man and the essence signified by the phrase 'biped animal' are the same thing.

For this reason definitions are immediate principles. The statement of essence says what a thing is intrinsically$_1$, and is even better known than any theorem, but its truth is not demonstrated by any argumentative procedure. His account of the nature of a deductive science is built around this idea of indemonstrable statements of essence. Scientists know things by knowing their essences. The essences signified by real definitions function as middle terms in scientific demonstrations. They are the 'causes' that explain the intrinsic connection between subject and predicate in a scientific theorem.

PART 2: METAPHYSICS

OVERVIEW OF ARISTOTLE'S *METAPHYSICS*

There is disagreement as to how much of the collection of fourteen treatises called the *Metaphysics* was originally intended to be part of a single work, but it is generally agreed that their final organization is not due to Aristotle. By the first century BC an Aristotelian corpus was organized following the Stoic division of philosophy into logic, natural science and ethics. The topics investigated in the *Metaphysics* do not readily fall under these headings, and it is possible that the title was meant to indicate a supra-sensible subject matter, or perhaps the fact that it is to be studied after natural science. However, this label may mean no more than 'the things after physics', and hence indicate no more than a decision to place it in the corpus after the treatises on natural science. The title is not Aristotle's own, and he himself described the science it investigates using the labels 'wisdom', 'first philosophy' and 'the science of "that which is" *qua* "thing that is"'. Different books of the *Metaphysics* give different characterizations of this science, and the treatise as a whole does not contain a completed overall project.

Many scholars have thought that at least Books A-elatton, Delta and K were added later by editors. A-elatton, the brief second book, deals with philosophy as the knowledge of truth, as well as the connection between the finitude of causes and the possibility of knowledge. It has the appearance of an introduction, and according to one tradition consists of notes taken by

Pasicles, the nephew of Eudemus of Rhodes, on lectures delivered by Aristotle. Delta, which may have circulated independently in antiquity, is a lexicon of philosophical terms, many of which play a crucial role in the *Metaphysics*. It includes entries on 'principle', 'cause', 'substance', 'being', 'prior' and 'posterior'. However, it lacks entries on many key metaphysical terms (for example, 'essence', 'subject', 'matter', 'form', 'some this' and 'separate'). Book K contains alternative versions of parts of B, Gamma and Epsilon, as well as some excerpts from the *Physics* on such topics as luck, change, infinity and continuity.

Book A begins with the famous dictum that all humans by nature desire to know. After a description of a progression starting from 'perception', and going through 'memory', 'experience' and 'skill' to 'theoretical knowledge', it describes the goal of the investigation as wisdom (*sophia*), a kind of knowledge of the causes and principles of things. Such a science would involve a general account of the causes and principles of all things, and would involve an understanding of the highest good. In the course of arguing that it is pursued for its own sake, he explains that philosophy begins in wonder, and above all we engage in it when we are puzzled, and cannot explain why things are the way they are. Next, A3–9 presents a lengthy survey of the views of his predecessors on the causes of things. Having discussed, among others, Thales, Anaximenes, Anaxagoras, Empedocles, Democritus, Leucippus, Parmenides, the Pythagoreans and Plato, he concludes in A10 that nobody has employed a type of cause other than those he named in the second book of his *Physics*: the material, formal, final and efficient.

The organization of material in the treatise as a whole is in part a reflection of Aristotle's belief that investigation involves a methodology according to which one starts with what is familiar to us initially, and moves towards an understanding of first principles that are knowable by nature. He starts with a review of the previously held opinions. In a general way this is accomplished by the survey in Book A, but where relevant there are other references to what has been thought by others. Second, there should be a statement of the puzzles[24] that these views give rise to. Prior to arriving at explanatory starting points, an inquirer is in a state of ignorance and puzzlement–thought is tied up in knots. Concerning the nature, scope and subject matter of wisdom, the most general science of the causes, there are opposing views, each supported by considerations having at least some degree of credibility. Book B contains a collection of brief sketches of puzzles about the causes of things. Some are more thoroughly investigated and answered elsewhere in the *Metaphysics*. This list both initiates and structures metaphysical investigation, the goal of which is the understanding that results from the resolution of such puzzles. It includes both puzzles about the unity of what later turn out to be the various parts of metaphysics, as well as probing questions about the proper characterization of the highest explanatory entities. Insofar as these arguments arise from *endoxa*, this part of philosophical investigation involves an exercise of dialectical skill. The final stage consists of a presentation of solutions, ideally making use of starting points or principles that are both natural and explanatory. Although sometimes there are clear indications that a solution is being offered, often it is not easy to determine whether a passage is presenting his own view rather than developing a puzzle to be solved.

Book Gamma asserts the existence of a general science that studies 'that which is' *qua* 'thing which is'. By virtue of its generality it is contrasted with those sciences that study only some part of what there is. It also solves some of the puzzles of Book B by arguing, among other things, first that general ontology is also the science of substance, and subsequently that it studies those concepts, such as unity and plurality, that apply to things quite generally. General ontology also studies such basic logical principles as the law of non-contradiction and the law of excluded middle. In the course of pursuing the latter there is a lengthy examination and putative refutation of the Protagorean doctrine of truth.

Book Epsilon divides theoretical knowledge into mathematics, natural science and theology. Most parts of mathematics deal with things that are unchanging but do not exist separately; the physical sciences deal with realities that do exist separately (although their forms cannot exist except in matter), and are subject to change; finally, theology studies separate and unchanging substance. First philosophy will be theology if such substances exist (otherwise it will be natural science), and it is here claimed that first philosophy will also be the universal science that studies 'that which is' *qua* 'thing that is'. This book also reiterates a four-fold distinction found in Delta 7 according to which the word 'being' (*on*) can be used for (1) 'that which is' so and so *per accidens* (where the predicate does not belong intrinsically or *per se*[25] to its subject; for example, a human is cultured, but not in its own right), (2) 'that which is' so and so intrinsically or *per se* (where the predicate does belong *per se*, and typically the subject and predicate are in the same category of 'that which is'), (3) 'that which is' so and so either potentially or in actuality (i.e., the predicate belongs either actually or potentially to the subject) and (4) 'that which is' in the sense of that which is true. General ontology is not concerned with either the first or fourth. There simply is no science of the accidental (this happening neither always nor for the most part), and since truth depends upon the combination and separation of things in the mind, it is simply a modification of thought. Accordingly, the following three books begin with a discussion of 'that which is' in connection with categories, and later move to a discussion of the further division of 'that which is' into potential and actual.[26]

The so-called middle books, Zeta, Eta and Theta (as well as Lambda 1–5) are concerned with sensible substance, and draw on some of the basic principles employed in Aristotle's hylomorphic physics. Zeta presents a complex set of arguments that eventually leads to the view that the form of a sensible substance, rather than its matter or the sensible composite itself, is a primary substance. It is argued that definition and essence belong primarily to substances, and that no universals are substances. Additionally there are arguments against the existence of Platonic Forms, and against the claim that particulars are definable.

In addition to the concepts of matter and form, the middle books bring in from his natural science a distinction between actuality (or activity) and potentiality. Books Eta and Theta make use of these concepts in an attempt to clarify further the relationship between the matter and form of a sensible composite, and the sense in which the form is an activity or actuality. Eta 6 treats the form of a composite and its matter as one and the same thing in the sense that the form is in actuality what the matter is potentially. Thus material composites are unities in their own right, and not merely one *per accidens*. The matter is not itself another actual substantial individual, and is 'some this' only in potentiality, not in actuality. A living thing is ultimately composed of inanimate materials (ultimately, of earth, air, fire and water), but its proximate matter is its organic body, and this is not separate from the substance of which it is the matter.

Book Iota is close in topic to other concerns of general ontology as construed in Gamma 2. It discusses the various kinds of unity and plurality, and in connection with the latter distinguishes the four forms of opposition: contraries, contradictories, privations and relative terms.

The discussion in Lambda 1–5 of the principles and causes of sensible things partially overlaps with the middle books. Lambda 1 divides substances into sensible and non-sensible, and further divides the former into the perishable (sublunary substances) and the eternal (the heavenly bodies). Non-sensible substances are both eternal and immutable, and it is pointed out that some have divided this group into (Platonic) Forms and mathematical objects.

Next, Lambda 6–10 present some of Aristotle's own positive theological views about non-sensible substance, and present arguments for the existence of an eternally actual unmoved mover of the outermost sphere of the cosmos. This is the god of his metaphysical system, and is identified with thought thinking itself.

Books M and N are concerned with rival views concerning whether there are, besides the sensible substances, any eternal, immutable substances. They contain an exposition and criticism of Platonist accounts both of the existence and nature of Forms and of the objects of the mathematical sciences (for instance, numbers, lines and planes). There are arguments challenging the explanatory role that Pythagoreans on the one hand, and various Platonists on the other, envisaged for numbers, as well as arguments against the existence of the Forms. Against the Platonist view that mathematical objects are separate substances it is argued that the mathematician studies physical objects *qua* indivisible units, or *qua* lines, or *qua* planes, etc., and that such things as lines, numbers and planes do not have separate being. As for the Forms, alternative versions of the attacks on the existence and putative explanatory power of separate, Platonic Forms in chapters A6 and 9 are to be found in M4 and 5, together with some material not in the earlier book.[27]

METAPHYSICS AS GENERAL ONTOLOGY

The general science of causes is general ontology

Gamma 1 begins with the assertion that there is a science that studies 'that which is' *qua* 'thing which is' and what belongs to 'that which is' intrinsically, or *per se*.[28] By virtue of its generality this science is contrasted with the departmental sciences that cut off merely some part of 'that which is' and study the properties that are unique to that part. To study 'that which is' *qua* 'thing that is' is not to study some special object called 'that which is *qua* thing that is'. The '*qua*' locution is here used to indicate the respect in which this science studies its subject matter, and indicates that it deals with those ubiquitous truths that apply to each 'thing that is'. The metaphysician must *both* state the general (propositional) principles that apply to 'that which is' as such *and* treat of their properties or features. An example of a metaphysical principle that belongs to beings as such is the principle of non-contradiction (PNC). To study what belongs to 'that which is' *per se* also involves a study of the terms that apply to 'things that are' as such (for instance, 'same' and 'one'), and to investigate truths about them.

This concept of general ontology is further clarified by the way in which Aristotle proceeds to deal with issues raised by four puzzles stated in B1 about the nature of the metaphysical enterprise itself. These are four of the first five items on the list, and they concern the characterization of the universal science that deals in the most general way possible with the causes and starting points of all things. The second puzzle (995b6–10), for instance, assumes that this science will at the very least deal with the principles of substance, and inquires whether it will also deal with the common axioms – those principles 'from which everybody makes proofs'. Does it, for instance, study the PNC? Gamma 3 solves this puzzle by showing that the science of substance is the science that studies the common axioms. Gamma also provides answers to at least portions of the other puzzles, though without explicitly referring back to them. For instance, after Book B has queried whether the science of substance also studies the *per se* accidents of substances, it goes on to ask whether it will study in addition to these accidents such terms as 'same', 'other', 'similar', 'dissimilar', 'contrariety', 'prior' and 'posterior', and then concludes by asking whether it will also study even the *per se* accidents of these last mentioned items. This is to ask whether in addition to investigating the definitions of the *per se* accidents of substance, it will also study such issues as whether each contrary has a single contrary. Gamma 2 is in part devoted to answering these last two questions in the affirmative.

In some respects, general ontology exhibits the kind of structure that is analyzed in the *Posterior Analytics*. It involves both a certain subject matter, and a set of items, both propositions and terms, that belong to its subject matter in respect of itself. However, the various kinds of 'things that are' are not themselves species of a single genus, and 'that which is' is not a generic kind predicable in common of all the 'things that are'.[29] Substance, quality, quantity and so on are different categories of being, but these categories cannot be subsumed under a single genus. Nonetheless, there can be a single science of 'that which is'. Such a science studies what belongs to a 'thing that is' in respect of its being a 'thing that is' – the things that pertain to it simply insofar as and because it is one of the 'things that are'.

General ontology as the science of substance

Aristotle uses his term *'ousia'* ('substance') for the fundamental explanatory principles of his general ontology. Strictly speaking, each science is the science of that primary thing by reference to which the other items within the scope of that science are called what they are called.[30] This strategy, when applied to the expression 'thing that is' allows him to conclude that the science of general ontology is in fact the science of substance.

As the first sentence of Gamma 2 declares, 'that which is', although spoken of in a plurality of ways, is nonetheless always spoken of in relation to a single thing, i.e., some single nature, and that single starting point is *ousia*, or substance. Although there is no single condition in virtue of which all 'things that are' are properly called 'things that are', some things are so called in a primary way, others in a derivative way, and a single science studies them all. The subject matter of ontology is not in the ordinary sense a generic kind, but this does not distinguish it from *all* special sciences. For instance, there is a single departmental science that studies everything that is healthy, despite the fact that the different kinds of healthy things do not come together under a single generic kind. A single science taking for its subject healthy things is possible because everything that is healthy is so called with reference to a single item, namely health. A diet is healthy because it maintains health, medicine because it produces health, a complexion because it signifies health, and a body because it receives health. In general, every-thing that is healthy is so called because it stands in some relation to a single thing, health. The relation of course varies for the different kinds of healthy things, but that with reference to which they are called 'healthy' is the same in all cases.

It is in this way that there is a sort of subject for general ontology as well. The term 'thing that is' is not ambiguous in its application to substances, qualities, quantities, and so on, and yet it applies primarily to substances, and derivatively to all else. Substances are 'things that are' simply because they are substances. The applications of this label to things other than substances must be explained by relating them in appropriate ways to substances, the primary 'things that are'. Every non-substantial kind of 'thing that is' is a kind of 'thing that is' by virtue of bearing the right kind of relation to the primary kind, to substance. However, just as in the case of health, the relation varies from one kind of non-substantial 'thing that is' to another. There is no single explanation for the application of the term 'thing that is' to non-substances. Qualities, for example, are 'things that are' because for a quality to *be* just is for it to *qualify* a substance; quantities, of course, do not stand in this relation to substance, but rather are 'things that are' by virtue of being the magnitudes of substances.

How and why general ontology studies ubiquitous terms

In addition to its concern with principles that apply to all 'things that are' solely in virtue of being 'things that are', general ontology also deals with certain principles that do not apply to absolutely everything. Having asserted that there is a single, unified science that studies 'that which is' *qua* 'thing that is', and having explained that such a science studies the causes and principles of substance, the remainder of Gamma 2 shows that general ontology also studies the ubiquitous terms that apply to 'that which is' as such.

Gamma 2 argues that 'one', 'many', 'same', 'other', 'similar', 'dissimilar', 'equal', 'unequal', 'different' and 'contrary' are all examples of *per se* attributes of 'that which is'.[31] These are *per se* modifications, or *idia* of 'that which is' *qua* 'thing that is'. To study them, one both states their definitions and proves theorems about them. This is one respect in which general ontology conforms to the model for knowledge found in *Posterior Analytics*. For instance, one might define contraries as things differing maximally within the same kind, and then demonstrate a *per se* accident of contrariety by proving as a theorem that each contrary has exactly one contrary.

General ontology must study unity (the signification of the ubiquitous term 'one') for the following reason. There is a single science that investigates all of the types of 'things that are' *qua* 'things that are', as well as their various sub-types. Since each 'thing that is' is in its own right, or *per se*, one thing that is, and there are just as many types of the 'that which is' as there are of 'that which is one', general ontology must study unity and its varieties. The three types of unity are sameness, similarity and equality, and so general ontology treats of the definitions of each of these. Furthermore, there is always a single science for opposites, and since plurality is the opposite of unity, general ontology must also study plurality and its forms. The three types of plurality are otherness, dissimilarity and inequality, and so general ontology also studies these and their various sub-types. One type of otherness is difference, and contrariety is a type of difference. Contrariety, then, is one type of difference; difference is one type of otherness; otherness is one type of plurality; plurality is the opposite of unity; and finally, unity belongs *per se* to 'that which is'. Hence contrariety itself must be dealt with by the general ontology.

How general ontology studies basic logical principles

General ontology is not only the science that studies what it is for terms to be contradictories, but also studies truths about the subjects to which such terms can be applied. In this spirit Gamma 3 claims, alluding to one of the puzzles of Book B, that we must state whether the science of substance just described also investigates the things that are called axioms in the mathematical sciences. This question is answered in the affirmative because the science of substance is the general science of 'that which is' *qua* 'thing that is', and this studies what belongs *per se* to all 'things that are'. Each common axiom applies to all 'things that are' *qua* 'things that are', and does not have an application merely in one particular kind apart from the rest of what there is.

These common principles are indemonstrable, and metaphysical argument does not demonstrate their truth. However, this science can prove things *about* these axioms. Gamma 3, for instance, attempts to prove that the principle of non-contradiction (PNC) is the firmest of all principles. The PNC is the principle that it is impossible for the same thing (predicate) to belong and not belong to the same thing (subject) at the same time, in the same respect. This is equivalent to saying that it is impossible for both members of a contradiction to be true (at the same time, in the same respect, etc.).

According to the account given in *De Interpretatione* 6 a contradiction (*antiphasis*) is a pair of opposed (*antikeimena*) statements, one of which is an affirmation (*kataphasis*), the other of which is a denial (*apophasis*). The affirmation and the denial are statements about the same subject, but what is affirmed of the subject in the former is precisely what is denied of it in the other. In *Metaphysics* Iota 7 a 'contradiction' is characterized as an *antithesis* such that for anything whatsoever, one part or the other of the antithesis is present, there being nothing between the two members of the antithesis.[32] Iota 4 classifies contradiction as the primary type of opposition, the other three types being contrarieties, privations and relative terms (pairs such as master/slave).

Book B cites the PNC as an example of the common beliefs that all employ in proof, and Gamma argues that it is the firmest of all such principles in that one could never be in error with respect to it (since it is impossible to believe a contradiction). Being the firmest of all principles, it is the most knowable, and must be grasped and understood by anybody who is able to understand anything at all, and can never be employed merely as a hypothesis.

To show the impossibility of believing a contradiction he argues as follows. He starts by asserting that it is impossible for contraries to simultaneously belong to the same subject. This is a consequence of the PNC. The notion of contrariety involved is that mentioned above and characterized in Delta 10. Contraries are those things belonging to the same kind that differ as widely as possible within that kind. Assuming that beliefs are attributes of believers, we are told that a belief that contradicts another is the contrary of that belief. Consequently, it is impossible for a believer to believe both members of a contradiction at the same time; for were somebody to have both beliefs, that person would be in contrary states – but that is impossible.

Gamma 4 claims that it has been proven by means of the principle itself that the PNC is the firmest principle. It then goes on to state that although the PNC cannot be demonstrated, it can be given a demonstration elenctically. In *Prior Analytics* B20 an *elenchus*, or refutation, is a syllogism, the conclusion of which is the contradictory of some proposition maintained by the opponent, and the premises of which are conceded by the interlocutor. The premises need not be, and typically are not, prior to and explanatory of the conclusion, and hence typically an elenctic demonstration does not yield knowledge of its conclusion.

The elenctic demonstration outlined in Gamma 4 begins by having an opponent signify something both to himself and to another. The elenctic proof that follows is intended to refute an interlocutor who denies the PNC, and to do so by showing that certain commonly known things that the opponent believes actually entail the PNC (or at least particular instances of it). As such this argument is not a scientific demonstration, but rather an *elenchus*. The *elenchus* shows that the principle is already known by anybody who knows anything. However, being a first principle no premises could possibly show why it is true, and a valid deduction of the PNC is not a demonstration, for nothing is prior to and explanatory of the PNC.

METAPHYSICS AS THE THEORY OF SUBSTANCE

Sensible substance: being as a definable 'this something'

Although *Metaphysics* Zeta and Eta may originally have formed an independent treatise on substance, they nonetheless do carry out an important part of the task of general ontology. As Z1 explains, its main question, 'What is substance?' is in fact the fundamental ontological question 'What is "that which is"?', a question over which both Aristotle and his predecessors have repeatedly puzzled. Accordingly, the inquiry into substance is pursued within the context of his program for general ontology. The opening lines of Zeta begin this inquiry with the assertion that 'that which is' (*to on*) is spoken of in many ways, and then elaborate upon this claim by listing some of its significations in connection with the categories. On the one hand being, or 'that which is', signifies both 'what X is' (*ti esti*) and 'some this' (*tode ti*); additionally (now turning to other categories) it signifies either a quality ('what X is like') or quantity ('how much X' is), or each of the other things predicable in the way these latter things are. He takes it as clear that of the various significations of the phrase 'that which is', the primary signification is the 'what X is' which signifies a substance. That is, the most basic kind of being is the being expressed by a definition that answers the 'What is it?' question when asked of a substance. All other things are beings, or 'things that are', derivatively. Anything that is a 'thing that is', but not in the primary way, is properly called a 'thing that is' by virtue of standing in some appropriate relation of ontological dependence to something that is a 'thing that is' in the primary way. Some things are beings because they are qualities of substances; others because they are quantities of substances; and so on. As required by the account of 'being' (or 'that which is') given in Gamma 2, the term '*on*' applies primarily and without qualification to substances, and derivatively to all else. General ontology is indeed the science of substance.

Although Gamma proclaimed the ontological priority of substance, it did not explain what it is to be a substance. To advance the project of general ontology Zeta now initiates an investigation designed to arrive at an account of substance. For this general project to succeed, it must characterize substance in such a way that every type of 'thing that is' will be accounted for by reference to what substances are. In order for substances to play this role, their being (i.e., what they are) cannot in turn be explained by appeal to any causes or explanatory factors external to them. A substance cannot be a 'thing that is' by virtue of standing in some relation to something other than itself. Substances are 'things that are' simply because they are substances. Hence each substance is what it is intrinsically, or *per se*. A substance is *both* 'some this' and a 'what X is'. Being intrinsically a particular subject, it is 'some this'; being something essentially, it will also be a 'what X is'.[33]

Furthermore, Z1 states that substances are primary in all of the ways in which something can be primary. This is because: (1) only substances are separate, (2) the account of the being of each non-substantial item must contain an account of the being of some substantial item (from which that non-substantial item cannot be separated, and upon which its being depends), and (3) understanding, or knowledge, of each thing proceeds from an understanding of the substances signified by definitions. The subsequent investigation in the middle books aims at a general account of perceptible substance that meets these conditions on the primacy of substance. The last three conditions imposed upon the analysis of substance stem not from some particular theory of substance, but from the single idea that strictly speaking the subject matter of general ontology is substance.

Here, as elsewhere, investigation must begin with what is known, or familiar, to the inquirer. Since Aristotle takes it that there is widespread agreement that at least some perceptible bodies are substances, his inquiry into substance must begin with them. The eventual goal is to have moved from these to an understanding of what is most knowable by nature. Aristotle investigates perceptible substances in order to consider later such questions as whether there is, in addition to the matter of sensible substances, another kind of matter, and whether we need to inquire into some other kind of substance (for instance, numbers, or something of that sort). Z17 says that the new starting point that it offers might help us to get clear about that substance that exists separated from perceptible substance.

Accordingly, in Z2 he starts by listing various types of things that have been thought to be substances. The items thought to be the clearest examples of substance are bodies. This includes not only the four basic elements (earth, water, air and fire), but also living things, both plants and animals, as well as their parts, and anything that is either a part of or composed of bodies. The entry on substance in Delta 8 explains why bodies are called substances. It is because they are not predicable of a subject, but the other things are predicable of them. This is the condition uniquely satisfied by primary substances in *Categories* 5. What makes something a primary substance in the *Categories* is that it satisfies this very condition. Z2 neither endorses nor rejects this or any other view about what things are in fact substances, or what makes them so. Z16 subsequently reveals that the parts of animals are not actual substances, but rather things that exist in potentiality in that they fail to be separate, and that the four elements are not substances in that they are like heaps rather than unities. In general, most of the things thought to be clear examples of substance (including items treated in the *Categories* as primary substances), turn out to be potential beings, and not substances in actuality.

Next, after also touching on various Platonist views that treat (separate) Forms and/or mathematical objects as substances, Aristotle says that what is needed is a consideration of such questions as whether there are any substances besides the sensible ones, and what is the manner of being for both the sensible substances and for whatever non-sensible substances there may be. Later he will argue that there are no (separate) Forms,[34] and Books M and N defend his view that there are no non-sensible mathematicals that enjoy the status of separate substances. However, before answering the question 'What things are substances?', Z2 advises that we first sketch out an answer to the question 'What is substance?' This involves determining what explains what makes it the case that some substance is a substance. The explanatory entity E that explains why some substance X is a substance may be called 'the substance of X'. The task at hand is to say what it is for something to perform that explanatory role, and then to say in a general way which of X's causes is the entity E that performs it.

Z3 begins this search by listing as possible candidates for the substance of X four items that are familiar from Aristotelian logic:[35] its *essence*, a *universal* it instantiates, a *genus* to which it belongs or some *subject* associated with it. The first three correspond to the predicate position of a statement, and are items that a dialectician might invoke as an answer to the question 'What is X?' The fourth candidate for substance is a *subject* of which other items are predicable. The 'subject' is thought most of all to be substance, and Z3 explains that the 'subject' is that of which all other things are said, but is not itself said of anything further. Consequently, the substance of X would be something that is not said of a subject, but rather is that of which the other things are said.

This characterization of the substance of X as the subject for predication should be compared with the claim in *Categories* 5 that the primary substances are those things of which all else is predicable, they themselves being predicable of nothing further. Whatever its merits as a characterization of the class of substances, in Z3 it is found inadequate as a specification of the substance of some substantial being X. Within a hylomorphic context, the matter, the form and the composite may each be called a 'subject', and the logical subject condition for substance by itself does not provide an adequate account of what it is about a substance that makes it the case that it is a substance. Aristotle argues that on its own it leads to the materialist view that the substance of a material object (i.e., what it really is) is some matter that is the ultimate subject of all its predicates. By stripping off in thought all predicables, one arrives at an ultimate subject of predication that is nothing in its own right, and has whatever predicates it does only accidentally. However, such matter is neither separate nor 'some this',[36] and hence cannot be the substance for which we are searching. Although recent scholarship has raised serious problems for taking this to commit Aristotle to the existence of an indeterminate ultimate subject of predication, traditionally this chapter has been read as introducing Aristotle's own concept of prime matter. Prime matter has also been thought of both as a principle of individuation for numerically distinct material objects, and as the persisting substratum for the basic elemental transformations in his natural science.

The hylomorphic analysis of perceptible substance is invoked in Z3 without explanation as something already familiar. It is not entailed by the general characterization of the science of 'that which is' *qua* 'thing that is', nor is it involved in his logic. Rather it is taken over from Aristotle's natural science, and depends upon some of the basic constitutive principles of the science that treats of the general principles that govern natural bodies insofar as they are subject to change. Although the substances of the *Organon* are persisting subjects for non-substantial changes, in the logical works there is no treatment of the causes of change, and substances are not analyzed as compounds of matter and form. The technical concept of matter is never employed in the logical works, nor is the correlative notion of form. In these works the word '*eidos*' is used not for the hylomorphic conception of form, but rather for a secondary substance, the species (and sometimes for the Platonic Form). The notion of form introduced in Z3 must be understood within the context of this kind of hylomorphic analysis. It is the formal component of a particular hylomorphic compound.

He turns next to a discussion of another candidate for substance: the essence. In connection with his inquiry into substance, Z4, 5 and 6 deal with the logical concepts of definition and essence. In the logical works an essence is simply the ontological correlate of a definition (an answer to a 'What is X?' question). Z4 and Z5 argue that only substances have definitions in the primary sense, and consequently there are essences (in an unqualified sense) only for substances. Nonetheless, in a derivative way, items from other categories are also definable and endowed with essences. Z6 attempts to establish the principle that all things that are primary, and called what they are called intrinsically, are one and the same as their essence. This thesis expresses the view that the definiens and the definiendum must, in a correct definition of a substance, signify one and the same entity. A substantial form is identical with its essence. However, neither accidental unities (such as a pale man) nor hylomorphic composites are identical with an essence.

On Aristotle's view the requirement that a substance be 'what X is' leads to the view that a primary substance is identical with a definable form. This form is not the species, for later[37] the species is analyzed as a universal composite of matter and form, and as such is not a primary substance. There is currently considerable scholarly controversy as to whether Aristotle considered substantial forms to be particulars, universals or neither particulars nor universals. One reason for holding that they are universals is that substances are first in the order of definition and knowledge, and definition is thought to be of the universal.[38] A chief reason for taking them to be particulars is that a substance must be a separately existing 'this something', but universals are ontologically dependent upon particulars.[39]

This initial discussion of definition and essence is followed in Z7, 8 and 9 by a treatment of the material, formal and efficient causes of natural, artistic and spontaneous generation. These three chapters argue that all generated objects are composites of matter and form, and that the formal component of a substance is its essence. This 'physical' conception of an essence is different from but related to the 'logical' notion of an essence (i.e., the signification of the definition of a thing). Z10 and Z11 resume the inquiry into definition and essence within a hylomorphic context, and Z12 subsequently takes on the problem of the unity of definition.

Z3 listed the universal as a candidate for substance, and Z13, 14, 15 and 16 discuss various topics connected with the claim that universals are substances. The genus being one type of universal, these chapters also deal with its credentials for being substance. Since the objects of definition are thought to be universals, these issues naturally follow an exploration of definition and its objects. The claim of universals to be substances stems from the fact that to the Platonist they seem to satisfy best the requirement that a substance be 'what X is'. However, Z13 argues that since the substance of something is unique to that of which it is the substance, no universal is a substance. This would suggest that if the 'what X is' requirement is to be met at all, it is the essence that will meet it. However, in order to count as a substance, an essence would also have to be 'some this'. The essence, an item originally introduced as a predicable, should also satisfy the subject condition for substance. It is the essence that is identical with hylomorphic form that plays this role. If the 'what X is' requirement is to be met by one of the first three candidates listed in Z3, it is the essence that will meet it.

In order to count as a substance, an essence would have to be a particular, determinate subject, and not a universal. Aristotle thinks that the Platonic view that what is predicable in common of particulars is separate and a 'this something' leads to an infinite regress that he refers to as the 'third man'.[40] Although the reconstruction of this argument is difficult, it seems to have involved the idea that if the particulars have a Form in common, and this Form is a separately existing 'this something', then there must be an additional Form that both the particulars and the first Form have in common, and so on *ad infinitum*. According to Aristotle, however, the form of a perceptible substance does not exist separately, but always requires perceptible matter.

Although it is clear that Z13 presents arguments against the claim that universals are substances, these arguments are presented as part of an aporematic investigation, and as such are linked up with the results of earlier chapters in order to formulate a problem (*aporia*). The problem is that no substance is composed of universals or of actual substances, and so substances must be incomposite, and hence indefinable; yet it was argued in the earlier treatment of definition in Z4 and Z5 that strictly speaking only substances are definable. However, if substances are not definable, then nothing is.

This problem is not directly solved in Z13–16, but Z17 makes a fresh start in the attempt to answer the question 'What is substance?' From its new perspective, the primary cause of being for a material composite is the essence that is responsible for the fact that the matter constitutes that composite. The substance of X is neither one of the material elements of which X is composed nor an element present in its essence, and is itself both simple and definable. This cause is in turn identified with the form. The form of X is its substance, and is the primary cause of its being. A substantial form is separate in definition, and hence prior in both the order of definition and knowledge. Nonetheless, it cannot exist without matter, and in the case of perceptible things it is only the composite that is separate without qualification.

Sensible substance: actuality and potentiality

The substance of a living thing is its soul. It is because a soul is present to a body that the body constitutes a living, functioning organism. The body is the matter, and is the thing in potentiality, whereas the form is the activity or actuality that must be present if that body is to be actually alive. According to a hylomorphic theory of this sort, a person lives a human life in virtue of having the capacities assigned to the various parts of human soul, the principle of human life. Soul is that by virtue of which (in the primary sense) we live, think, perceive, etc. The form (or substance of) the species man is that form (i.e., human soul) that makes a human body alive in virtue of the fact that the body has it. The word 'man' is applicable to Socrates in virtue of his matter (his body) having a substantial form. The substantial form or essence is strictly speaking a 'this something', and Socrates is a 'this something' because of the form that his body has.

Book Theta initiates a more extended treatment of the distinction between 'that which is' in actuality, and 'that which is' potentially. To understand what an actuality (*energeia*) is, Aristotle begins by considering the kind of potentiality (*dunamis*) that is correlated with change, because this is the most basic and most familiar kind of potentiality. Change, unlike substantial form, is a kind of incomplete activity or actuality, but an understanding of the relation between change and the potential for change enables one to comprehend the way in which substantial form is an actuality (or activity). Theta 6 explains the concept of an *energeia* by means of a set of analogies. An actuality is something that stands to something else in the way that a change stands to its correlated potentiality. Both a substantial form and a change can be called 'actuality' (although the form is a more perfect actuality), for as a change stands to its potentiality, so the substance (i.e., the form) stands to its matter. Substantial form is an actuality that is the fulfillment of the potentiality the matter has for being 'this something'. As a goal and fulfillment, it is the primary cause of the composite's being what it is.

❧ METAPHYSICS AS THEOLOGY ❧

Aristotle has argued that in the sensible world there are substances, and what makes them such is their form. These forms are internal principles, or natures, and as such cannot exist without matter. The next major step in the general ontological program is to investigate supra-sensible reality. There is reason to think that there are non-perceptible substances that exist separately, and perhaps they are the things entirely knowable by nature. The last three books of the *Metaphysics* are concerned with the various non-sensible items that have been thought to be substances. Although a discussion of this sort is needed to complete the general inquiry into 'that which is', these books may not have been written as a part of the larger work. They are not explicitly coordinated with the treatment of sensible substance in the middle books, nor do they attempt to put their topics within the framework of the general ontology of Gamma.

Books M and N argue that (1) although mathematical objects exist, they are not substances, and (2) Platonic Forms do not even exist. Nonetheless, there are on his view supra-sensible beings of a different kind, and at least one of these is the unmoved mover, or god of his metaphysics. Lambda 6–10 contains an account of this unmoved mover. Although itself unchangeable, it is an eternal source of the motion of the outermost celestial sphere, and being the final cause of that motion, it moves as an object of love. God is incapable of being other than it is, and as such has no matter, but rather is a being the substance of which is actuality (*energeia*).[41] This actuality is activity of the best sort: intelligent activity (*nous*). Being eternally engaged in the best kind of thinking, god is a living being. God's intelligence is not a thinking of us or of the universe, but rather is a thinking of thinking or intelligence itself (1074b34). He argues both that this activity is the good, and that it is the source of the order and goodness of the universe.

Although perceptible substances are the substances that are initially most familiar to us, metaphysical inquiry is ultimately for the sake of coming to an understanding of this first principle. One moves towards an understanding of divine substance by starting with the causes of the things that are most familiar to us and proceeding towards an understanding of the highest causes. Lambda 4 states that the causes and principles of different things are in one sense different, but in another sense, speaking generally and by analogy, they are the same for all things (1070a31–33). The unmoved mover is a cause analogous to those causes and principles of perceptible substances studied by the special sciences. God is the final cause of motion in the outermost sphere, and this is analogous to the way in which the nature of an animal of some type is the final cause of the coming-to-be of animals of that type. The eternal, continuous activity that is god's nature is analogous to the actuality of a perceptible substance. To understand actuality, we start with an understanding of the manner in which a change is an actuality, and then move to an understanding of the substance of a perceptible body as an actuality. However, the highest cause is grasped when we attain an understanding of the best and most perfect actuality, and this is an understanding of god.

❧❧❧ NOTES ❧❧❧

1　See p. 52 for the use of this phrase.

2　Aristotle sometimes employs other conceptions of the accidental, including one according to which the accidental is the contingent.

3　See *Categories* 2, 3, 5.

4　(*ousia*): see p. 000.

5　With the possible exception of the ten-fold list of predicables in *Topics* A9. This list begins with 'what x is' (instead of 'substance'), suggesting a classification of predicates answering to the various kinds of questions that can be asked about any subject at all, substance or otherwise.

　　Another way of classifying predicates is represented by the four-fold distinction in *Topics* A5 between genus, definition, *proprium* and accident. This classification is useful for his analysis of a science in terms of a subject genus, definitions of the items investigated, and theorems relating *propria* to the defined kinds it studies. The accidental is that which falls outside the scope of a science. See 51–52 below.

6　The translation is not ideal since it, unlike the Greek, has no connection with the verb 'to be'.

7　There is at present still debate as to whether the non-substantial individuals of *Categories* 2 are particulars or universals.

8　*On Sophistical Refutations* 2 classifies arguments used in discussion into four classes: didactic, dialectical, peirastic and eristic. Didactic arguments use as premises truths from some science that are not yet the beliefs of the learner, and such arguments are in effect demonstrations. Dialectical arguments deduce the contradictory of an opponent's thesis from *endoxa* (which may or may not represent the opponent's own beliefs), and peirastic arguments constitute that subset of dialectical arguments in which the premises are both believed by the respondent and must be known by anybody purporting to have knowledge. Eristic arguments are not dialectical, and produce either real or apparent syllogisms not from *endoxa*, but from apparent *endoxa*.

9　*Logos*: this Greek term is used in this context to mean something like 'argument'. The term has many uses for Aristotle, including its application to definition (for which see p. 52 below).

10　Here only the theory of the assertoric syllogism (i.e. one composed of statements) is discussed. Since scientific knowledge of a theorem involves knowing that it is necessary, an analysis of demonstration would seem to require a modal syllogistic dealing with statements of necessity and possibility. *Prior Analytics* A8–22 attempts to develop a theory of syllogistic inferences that involve modal categorical statements. It is unsuccessful in that its treatment of modality is inconsistent, and apparently conflates sentential and adverbial readings of the modal operators.

11　Since a sentence is a linguistic item, the terms of which it is composed should also be linguistic. However, I will follow Aristotle's usage in sometimes calling the objects picked out by its linguistic terms the 'terms' of a statement. Thus Socrates and the species man are sometimes referred to as the 'terms' of the statement that Socrates is a man.

12 Using this terminology in translations is potentially confusing since in calling a proposition 'particular' one is not thereby saying that its subject is a particular. Although occasionally Aristotle will use singular premises in syllogistic inferences, the theory he develops in fact applies solely to arguments composed of statements of A, E, I or O form.

13 The technical vocabulary of the *Prior Analytics* typically reverses the order of subject and predicate, and picks out the four forms corresponding to these kinds of schemata, labeled respectively 'A', 'E', 'I', and 'O': P *belongs to every* S; P *belongs to no* S; P *belongs to some* S; P *does not belong to some* S. The letters 'A', 'E', 'I', and 'O' are mnemonic devices taken from the first two vowels in the Latin words 'affirmo' and 'nego'.

14 Both cannot be true together, and both cannot be false together. For the application of this concept to singular statements, see p. 60.

15 They cannot both be true, but both can be false.

16 A entails I, and E entails O.

17 Following Aristotle, the major premise is listed first. These argument forms have come to be called Barbara, Celarent, Darii, Ferio (Barbari and Celaront), respectively, the vowels indicating the propositional forms. The valid moods of the second figure are EAE, AEE, EIO and AOO, plus the subaltern moods EAO, AEO (Cesare, Camestres, Festino, Baroco, plus Cesaro and Camestrop). Those of the third figure are AAI, EAO, AII, IAI, OAO, EIO (Darapti, Felapton, Datisi, Disamis, Bocardo and Ferison). A fourth figure (in which the major term is the subject of major premise, and the minor term is the predicate of minor premise) exists. The fourth figure is not discussed as such by Aristotle, although the *Prior Analytics* shows awareness of its valid moods AAI, AEE, IAI, EAO, EIO. (There is a subaltern mood AEO as well.)

18 He also shows that Darii and Ferio can be derived using Celarent.

19 He also shows how a third figure OAO (as well as AAI and IAI) can be established by a method of *ekthesis*.

20 Furthermore, Aristotle argues that demonstration of principles cannot proceed in a circular fashion, nor can there be an infinite series of principles which would enable each principle to be demonstrated by a prior principle (see *Posterior Analytics* A3).

21 This topic is pursued further below on pp. 59–60.

22 *Kath' hauto*; also translated as 'in itself' or 'in its own right'.

23 These remarks apply only to so-called 'real' definitions. *Posterior Analytics* B10 distinguishes various ways in which the term 'definition' is used, including so-called 'nominal' definitions (accounts of what a term signifies) and 'real' definitions (accounts that make evident why something is). At least some of the former are of non-existent things, whereas the latter never are.

24 *Aporiai*. When applied to a journey, the word '*aporia*' indicates a condition of difficulty (being without a way of passage) that prevents further progress towards one's destination. B1 applies this term both to the condition of the intellect when faced with credible, but opposing arguments, and to the arguments themselves.

25 In either of the first two senses explicated in *Posterior Analytics* A4. See p. 25.

26 See Z1, 1028a11–13 and Theta 1, 1045b27–1046a2.

27 See also M9.

28 'That which is *qua* thing that is' translates '*to on hêi on*', an expression often rendered as 'being *qua* being'.

29 See *Posterior Analytics* B7, and *Metaphysics* B3.

30 Gamma 2, 1003b16–17.

31 Later the chapter adds without further argument: 'complete', 'prior', 'posterior', 'genus', 'species', 'whole' and 'part'.

32 It is an opposition to which the Law of Excluded Middle applies.

33 Despite the fact that the question 'What is it?' is answered by reference to a definable universal, it is nonetheless proper to apply the label 'what X is' to particulars as well. The phrase 'what X is' may be used as a place-holder for terms such as 'man' or 'horse.' For instance, 'what Socrates is' is a man. Since he is a man, it is correct to say that Socrates is 'what he is' (i.e., the definable species man).

34 In Z8,14 and 16; see also M4,5,9 and A6 and 9.

35 See pp. 41, 44, 50–53.

36 Z3, 1029a26–28.

37 Z10, 1035b27–31.

38 Z11, 1036a28–29 with B6, 1003a5–17.

39 Z13, 1039a1–2 with note 38.

40 Z13, 1038b35–1039a3; also see passages in note 34.

41 1071b20.

SELECT BIBLIOGRAPHY ON ARISTOTLE'S LOGIC AND METAPHYSICS

GENERAL

For Greek texts, English translations and commentaries, general bibliographies, general introductions to Aristotle and collections of essays, see [1.1] to [1.59].

Further texts and commentaries relevant to Aristotle's logic

2.1 Burnyeat, M. and others (eds), *Notes on Book Zeta of Aristotle's Metaphysics*, Study Aids Monograph No. 1 (Sub-faculty of Philosophy, Oxford University, 1979).

2.2 —— (eds), *Notes on Books Eta and Theta of Aristotle's Metaphysics*, Study Aids Monograph No. 4 (Sub-faculty of Philosophy, Oxford University, 1984).

2.3 Frede, M. and Patzig, G., *Aristoteles 'Metaphysik Z': Text, Übersetzung und Kommentar*, 2 vols (Munich, C.H. Beck, 1988). [Includes Aristotle's *Metaphysics* in Greek with a German translation.]

2.4 Montgomery, M., *Aristotle: Metaphysics Books VII–X, Zeta, Eta, Theta, Iota* (Hackett, 1985).

2.5 Smith, R., *Aristotle: Prior Analytics* (Indianapolis, Hackett, 1989).

Books containing introductions to Aristotle's logic

2.6   Bochenski, J.M., *Ancient Formal Logic* (Amsterdam, 1951).
2.7   Kneale, W.C. and Kneale, M., *The Development of Logic* (Oxford, 1962).

⚬ BOOKS AND ARTICLES ON LOGIC ⚬
AND METAPHYSICS

2.8   Ackrill, J.L., 'Aristotle's theory of definition: some questions on *Posterior Analytics* II.8–10', in Berti [1.48], 359–84.
2.9   Albritton, R., 'Forms of particular substances in Aristotle's *Metaphysics*', *Journal of Philosophy* 54 (1957) 699–708.
2.10 Aubenque, P., *Le Problème de l'être chez Aristote* (Paris, 1962).
2.11 Bambrough, R., ed., *New Essays on Plato and Aristotle* (London, 1965).
2.12 Barnes, J., 'Aristotle's theory of demonstration', in Barnes, Schofield and Sorabji [1.53], vol.1, 65–87. [Revised version of paper published in *Phronesis* 14 (1969) 123–52.]
2.13 —— 'Proof and the syllogism', in Berti [1.48] 17–59.
2.14 Bogen, J. and McGuire, J.E., eds, *How Things Are* (Dordrecht, 1985).
2.15 Bolton, R., 'Definition and scientific method in Aristotle's *Posterior Analytics* and *Generation of Animals*', in Gotthelf and Lennox [1.56], 120–66.
2.16 —— 'Essentialism and semantic theory in Aristotle: *Posterior Analytics* II, 7–10', *Philosophical Review* 85 (1976) 514–44.
2.17 Burnyeat, M., 'Aristotle on understanding knowledge', in Berti [1.48], 97–139.
2.18 Charles, D., 'Aristotle on meaning, natural kinds, and natural history', in Devereux and Pellegrin [1.58], 145–67.
2.19 Cherniss, H.F., *Aristotle's Criticism of Plato and the Academy*, vol. I (Baltimore, 1944).
2.20 Code, Alan, 'The aporematic approach to primary being in *Metaphysics* Z', in Pelletier, F.J. and King-Farlow, A., *New Essays on Aristotle, Canadian Journal of Philosophy*, supplement 10 (Edmonton, 1984), 1–20.
2.21 —— 'Aristotle's investigation of a basic logical principle', *Canadian Journal of Philosophy* 16 (Sept. 1986), 341–57.
2.22 —— 'Metaphysics and logic', in Matthen [1.57], 127–49.
2.23 —— 'No universal is a substance: an interpretation of *Metaphysics* Z13, 1038b8–15', *Paideia*, Special Aristotle Issue (Dec. 1978) 65–74.
2.24 —— 'On the origins of some Aristotelian theses about predication', in Bogen, J. and McGuire, J. eds, *Language and Reality in Greek Philosophy* (Athens, 1985), 101–31, 323–6.
2.25 Cohen, S. Marc, 'Essentialism in Aristotle', *Review of Metaphysics* 32 (1979) 387–405.
2.26 Corcoran J., ed., *Ancient Logic and its Modern Interpretations* (Dordrecht, 1974).
2.27 Dancy, R.M., *Sense and Contradiction* (Dordrecht, 1975).
2.28 Decarie, V., *L'Objet de la métaphysique selon Aristote* (Montreal, 1961).
2.29 Driscoll, J. A., '*Eide* in Aristotle's earlier and later theories of substance', in O'Meara, D.O., ed., *Studies in Aristotle* (Washington, 1981), 129–59.

2.30 Evans, J.D.G., *Aristotle's Concept of Dialectic* (Cambridge, 1977).

2.31 Ferejohn, M., *The Origins of Aristotelian Science* (New Haven, 1991).

2.32 Frede, M., 'Categories in Aristotle', in O'Meara, D.O., ed., *Studies in Aristotle* (Washington, 1981), 1–24; reprinted in Frede [2.34], 29–48.

2.33 —— 'The definition of sensible substances in *Metaphysics* Z', in Devereux and Pellegrin [1.58], 113–29.

2.34 —— *Essays in Ancient Philosophy* (Minnesota,1987).

2.35 —— 'Stoic vs. Aristotelian syllogistic', *Archiv für Geschichte der Philosophie* 56, 1–32; reprinted in Frede [2.34], 99–124.

2.36 —— 'Substance in Aristotle's *Metaphysics*', in Gotthelf [2.40], 17–26; reprinted in Frede [2.34], 72–80.

2.37 —— 'The unity of general and special metaphysics: Aristotle's conception of metaphysics', in Frede [2.34], 81–95.

2.38 Furth, M., *Substance, Form and Psyche: An Aristotelian metaphysics* (Cambridge, 1988).

2.39 Gill, M.L., *Aristotle on Substance: The paradox of unity* (Princeton, 1989).

2.40 Gotthelf, A., ed., *Aristotle on Nature and Living Things* (Bristol, 1985).

2.41 Graham, D.W., *Aristotle's Two Systems* [1.70].

2.42 Hartman, E., *Substance, Body, and Soul* (Princeton, 1977).

2.43 Hintikka, K.J.J., 'Aristotle and the ambiguity of ambiguity', *Inquiry* 2 (1959) 137–51; reprinted with revisions as Ch. 1 of Hintikka [2.45], 1–26.

2.44 —— 'On the ingredients of an Aristotelian science', *Nous* 6 (1972), 55–69.

2.45 —— *Time and Necessity: Studies in Aristotle's theory of modality* (Oxford, 1973).

2.46 Irwin, T.H., *Aristotle's First Principles* (Oxford, 1988).

2.47 —— 'Homonymy in Aristotle', *Review of Metaphysics* 34 (1981) 523–44.

2.48 —— 'Aristotle's concept of signification', in Schofield, M. and Nussbaum [2.96], 241–66.

2.49 Jaeger, W., *Aristoteles, Grundlegung einer Geschichte seiner Entwicklung* (Berlin, 1923); trans. by Richard Robinson, *Aristotle: Fundamentals of the History of his Development* (Oxford, 2nd edn 1948).

2.50 Kahn, C., 'The place of the prime mover in Aristotle's teleology', in Gotthelf [2.40], 183–205.

2.51 —— 'The role of *nous* in the cognition of first principles in *Posterior Analytics* II 19', in Berti [1.48], 385–414.

2.52 Kapp, E., 'Syllogistic', in [1.53], 35–49; originally published as 'Syllogistik' in Pauly–Wissowa, *Real-Encyclopädie der classischen Altertumswissenschaft*, vol. IVA, cols. 1046–1067 (1931).

2.53 Kosman, L. A., 'Substance, being and *energeia*', *Oxford Studies in Ancient Philosophy* 2, 1984, 121–49.

2.54 —— 'Understanding, explanation and insight in Aristotle's *Posterior Analytics*', in Lee et al. [2.58], 374–92.

2.55 Kung, J., 'Aristotle on thises, suches, and the third man argument', *Phronesis* 26 (1981) 207–47.

2.56 Lear, J., 'Active *Epistêmê*', Graeser [1.50], 149–74.

2.57 —— *Aristotle and Logical Theory* (Cambridge, 1980).

2.58 Lee, E.N., Mourelatos, A.P.D. and Rorty, R., eds, *Exegesis and Argument* (Assen, 1973).

2.59 Le Blond, J.M., 'Aristotle on definition', in ([1.53], vol. 3), 63–79; originally published as 'La Définition chez Aristote', *Gregorianum* 20 (1939) 351–80.

2.60 —— *Logique et méthode chez Aristote* (Paris, 1939; 2nd edn 1970).

2.61 Lesher, J.H., 'Aristotle on form, substance and universals: a dilemma', *Phronesis* 16 (1971) 169–78.

2.62 Lesher, J.H., 'The meaning of *nous* in the *Posterior Analytics*', *Phronesis* 18 (1973) 44–68.

2.63 Lewis, F., *Substance and Predication in Aristotle* (Cambridge, 1991).

2.64 Lezl, W., *Logic and Metaphysics in Aristotle* (Padua, 1970).

2.65 Loux, M. J., '*Ousia*: a prolegomenon to *Metaphysics* Z and H', *History of Philosophy Quarterly* 1 (1984) 241–66.

2.66 —— *Primary Ousia: An essay on Aristotle's Metaphysics Z and H* (Ithaca, NY, 1991).

2.67 Lukasiewicz, J., *Aristotle's Syllogistic from the Standpoint of Modern Formal Logic* (Oxford, 1951; 2nd edn 1957).

2.68 McCall, S., *Aristotle's Modal Syllogisms* (Amsterdam, 1963).

2.69 McKirahan, R.D., *Principles and Proofs: Aristotle's theory of demonstrative science* (Princeton, 1992).

2.70 McMullen, E., ed., *The Concept of Matter in Greek and Medieval Philosophy* (Notre Dame, 1963).

2.71 Mansion, S., *Le Jugement d'existence chez Aristote* (Louvain, 1946; 2nd edn 1976).

2.72 Matthen, M., see [1.57].

2.73 Merlan, P., see [1.85].

2.74 —— 'On the terms "metaphysics" and "being-*qua*-being"', *Monist* 52 (1968) 174–94.

2.75 Moravcsik, J.M.E., ed., *Aristotle: A collection of critical essays* (Garden City, NY, 1967).

2.76 Morrison, D.R., 'Separation in Aristotle's metaphysics', *Oxford Studies in Ancient Philosophy*, vol. 3, 1985, 125–57.

2.77 Mueller, I., 'Aristotle on geometrical objects', *Archiv für Geschichte der Philosophie* 52 (1970) 156–71; reprinted in [1.53] vol. 1, pp. 96–107.

2.78 O'Meara, D.J., ed., *Studies in Aristotle* (Washington, D.C., 1981).

2.79 Owen, G.E.L., 'Aristotle on the snares of ontology', in Bambrough [2.11], 69–95; reprinted in Owen [1.72], 259–78.

2.80 —— 'Logic and metaphysics in some earlier works of Aristotle', in Düring and Owen [1.41], 163–90; reprinted in Owen [1.72], 180–99; and in Barnes *et al.* [1.53], 13–32.

2.81 —— *Logic, Science and Dialectic: Collected papers in Greek philosophy*, see [1.72].

2.82 —— 'Particular and general', *Proceedings of the Aristotelian Society* 79 (1978–9), 1–21; reprinted in Owen [1.72], 279–94.

2.83 —— 'The Platonism of Aristotle', *Proceedings of the British Academy* 51 (1966), 125–50; reprinted in Owen [1.72] 200–20; and in [1.53] Barnes *et al.* vol.1, 14–34.

2.84 —— '*Tithenai ta Phainomena*', in Mansion [2.71], 83–103; reprinted in Moravcsik [2.75], 167–90; also in Barnes *et al.* [1.53] vol.1, 113–26; and in Owen [1.72], 239–51.

2.85 Owens, J., *The Doctrine of Being in the Aristotelian Metaphysics* (Toronto, 1951; 2nd edn 1963; 3rd edn 1978).

2.86 Patzig, G., *Aristotle's Theory of the Syllogism* (Dordrecht, 1968). [First published in German as *Die aristotelische Syllogistik* (Göttingen, 1959).]

2.87 —— 'Logical aspects of some arguments in Aristotle's *Metaphysics*', in Aubenque [1.47], 37–46.

2.88 —— 'Theologie und Ontologie in der *Metaphysik* des Aristoteles', *Kant-Studien* 52, 1960–61, 185–205; published in English as 'Theology and ontology in Aristotle's *Metaphysics*', in Barnes *et al.* [1.53] vol.3, 33–49.

2.89 Pelletier, F.J. and King-Farlow, J.A., eds, *New Essays on Aristotle, Canadian Journal of Philosophy* Sup. Vol. 10 (Edmonton, 1984).

2.90 Preuss A., and Anton, J.P., eds, *Aristotle's Ontology: Essays in ancient Greek philosophy* 5 (Albany, 1992).

2.91 Rijen, J. van, *Aspects of Aristotle's Logic of Modalities* (Dordrecht, 1989).

2.92 Rijk, L.M. de, *The Place of the Categories of Being in Aristotle's Philosophy* (Assen, 1952).

2.93 Rose, L.E., *Aristotle's Syllogistic* (Springfield, Ill.: Charles C. Thomas, 1968).

2.94 Scaltsas, T., *Substances and Universals in Aristotle's Metaphysics* (Ithaca, NY, 1994).

2.95 Scaltsas, T., Charles, D. and Gill, M.L., eds, *Unity, Identity and Explanation in Aristotle's Metaphysics* (Oxford, 1994).

2.96 Schofield, M. and Nussbaum, M., eds., *Language and Logos: Studies in ancient philosophy presented to G.E.L. Owen* (Cambridge, 1982).

2.97 Sellars, W., 'Aristotle's metaphysics: an interpretation', in *Philosophical Perspectives* (Springfield, Ill., 1967) 73–124.

2.98 —— 'Substance and form in Aristotle', *Journal of Philosophy* 54 (1957) 688–99.

2.99 Smiley, T., 'What is a syllogism?', *Journal of Philosophical Logic* 2 (1973) 136–54.

2.100 Solmsen, F., *Die Entwicklung der aristotelischen Logik und Rhetorik* (Berlin, 1929).

2.101 Waterlow, S., *Passage and Possibility* (Oxford, 1982).

2.102 Witt, C., *Substance and Essence in Aristotle: An interpretation of Metaphysics VII–IX* (Ithaca, NY, 1989).

2.103 Woods, M. J., 'Universals and particular forms in Aristotle's *Metaphysics*', *Oxford Studies in Ancient Philosophy*, Sup. Vol. (Oxford, 1991) 41–56.

CHAPTER 3

Aristotle: Aesthetics and philosophy of mind

David Gallop

❦

❧ AESTHETICS ❧

Aesthetics, as that field is now understood, does not form the subject-matter of any single Aristotelian work. No treatise is devoted to such topics as the essential nature of a work of art, the function of art in general, the differences between art and craft, or the concepts of meaning and truth in the arts. Nor does Aristotle anywhere examine, in a general way, the status of what would now be called 'aesthetic judgments', or seek a rational foundation on which they might be based. He hardly even possessed a vocabulary in which such questions could be raised.

His writings nevertheless contain some of the most suggestive and influential remarks concerning the arts that have ever been penned. These are to be found mainly in the *Poetics*,[1] a short treatise on poetic composition, from which only the first of two books has survived. That work has provided principles of criticism which have lasting interest and relevance, not only for drama and epic, but for literary genres unknown to Aristotle himself, and also, though to a lesser extent, for the non-literary arts.

The most convenient starting point for consideration of Aristotelian aesthetics is provided by Plato's treatment of the arts (cf. *Routledge History of Philosophy*, vol. I, ch. 12), and especially by his notorious banishment of poetry from the 'ideal state' depicted in his *Republic*. Plato's own poetic impulse had evidently been a source of severe internal conflict. Especially in *Republic* X, his attack had been so vehement, and framed in such personal terms (for example 595b–c, 607e–608b), as to suggest that in banishing poetry he was renouncing an ardent passion of his own. Poetry had been branded as the arch-enemy of philosophy, and Socrates made to speak of a 'long-standing quarrel' between them (607b). Yet Plato would spare poetry if he

76

could. For, in closing, he had made Socrates challenge lovers of poetry 'to speak on its behalf in prose', and to show 'that it is not only pleasant but beneficial' (607d–e).

The *Poetics* is, in effect, a response to that challenge. It is true that Plato is nowhere named in the treatise, and that Aristotle does not expressly claim to be answering him. Nevertheless, in the dry phrases of the *Poetics* and in its major contentions we can hear the elements of just such a prose defence of poetry as Plato had invited.

The Poetics *and 'poetry'*

The treatise begins with a survey of poetry in relation to other art forms, a classification of its principal genres (chapters 1–3), and a short history of their development (chapters 4–5). The bulk of the extant work is devoted to a discussion of tragedy (chapters 6–22), followed by a shorter treatment of epic (chapters 23–4), solutions to some problems in literary criticism (chapter 25), and a comparative evaluation of tragedy and epic (chapter 26). The lost portion of the work probably included a discussion of comedy (promised at 49b21–2).

The project of the *Poetics* is announced in its opening sentence. Aristotle there proposes to consider 'the poetic craft itself and its species, the power (*dunamis*) that each species possesses, and how plots should be put together if the composition is going to prove successful' (47a1–3).

It is significant that plot-construction is introduced at the outset. For this at once reveals how Aristotle conceived of the subject. That subject was not 'poetry' as we now use the term. The noun *poiêsis* was formed on the verb *poiein*, which meant, quite generally, 'to make'. Although the noun can bear the wider sense of 'making', it was often used specifically for composition in verse, a curious narrowing of usage noticed in Plato's *Symposium* (205c–d). In the same context Plato had assimilated poetic composition to various other forms of creative activity, regarded as so many different expressions of love. But he had not challenged the limitation of literary *poiêsis* to metrical verse.

Aristotle does challenge this. On the first page of the *Poetics* he mentions the pre-Socratic cosmologist Empedocles. Although that thinker had composed his account of the world in Homeric hexameters, he deserves to be called a natural scientist rather than a poet (47b18–20). Later (51b2–4) Aristotle observes that if the works of the historian Herodotus were put into verse, they would still be 'history of a sort'. On the other hand, the mimes of Sophron and Xenarchus and Socratic dialogues, dramatic sketches and conversations in prose, are mentioned (47b10–11) as if they shared something in common with 'poetic' art.

Metre, therefore, is neither a sufficient nor a necessary condition for the craft examined in the *Poetics*. If it is taken for a defining property of 'poetic' utterance, it will follow that 'poetry' and its cognates are mistranslations of key terms in the treatise. Even the broader English use of 'poetic' to mark certain features of diction or style misses what Aristotle treats as central. The *Poetics* deals mainly with only two genres, epic and tragedy, both of which happen to use metre and poetic language. But those features are, for Aristotle, incidental to their status as *poiêsis*. What made Homer or Sophocles masters of that craft was their skill in putting together a story.

This brings us to the nub of Aristotle's response to Plato. Plato's attack was misguided, in Aristotle's view, because it had misrepresented the nature and the impact of fiction. Aristotle's project was not, then, to give an account of all that we should call 'poetry', but to examine the foundation of the two fictional genres most highly developed in his time. In doing so, he not only 'answered' Plato, but became an effective mediator in the 'long-standing quarrel between poetry and philosophy'. For through his examination of poetic fiction, he showed how an art form, far from being an enemy of philosophy or the sciences, might be seen as their ally. To have shown that was no small contribution towards a philosophy of art.

Aristotelian mimêsis

In *Republic* II–III and X Plato had used the concept of *mimêsis* to denigrate artists and especially poets. The concept is no less central to Aristotle's aesthetics than it had been to Plato's. But Aristotle uses it to restore the poets to a place of honour. How does he achieve this?

The *Poetics* begins by classifying the major poetic genres along with music, dance and the visual arts, as so many different forms of *mimêsis* (47a13–18). These are differentiated according to the media they use (chapter 1), the objects they represent (chapter 2), and their mode of representation (chapter 3). The last of these differentiae turns upon the distinction between poetic narrative and dramatic enactment.

Unfortunately, however, the *Poetics* contains no explicit definition of *mimêsis* itself. In the broadest terms, we can understand it as 'making or doing something which resembles something else' (Lucas [3.6], 259). But that formula is too vague to be useful, and it harbours a tiresome obscurity which bedevils Greek discussions of the whole subject. *Mimêsis* can mean – as its English derivatives 'mime' and 'mimicry' suggest – enactment or impersonation. It was upon that sense of *mimêsis* that Plato had partly relied when he chastised the poets in *Republic* III (especially 394d–398b) for their use of dramatic enactment: poetry is 'mimetic' by virtue of mimicking the words or actions of characters whose roles are enacted.

But *mimêsis* can also mean producing a likeness or representation of some original subject, as painters depict pieces of furniture such as beds and tables, or human figures such as carpenters and cobblers. In the broader polemic of *Republic* X Plato had condemned poetry as 'mimetic', not for its mimicry, but on the wider ground that it represented particular objects, people, scenes or events in the sensible world. This charge had included epic poetry no less than drama. Indeed, by calling Homer 'the original teacher and leader of all those fine tragedians' (595c), Plato had deliberately blurred the distinction which he had himself drawn earlier between narrative and enacted modes of poetic fiction (393a–b, cf. 394b–c).

Which of the two kinds of *mimêsis* has Aristotle in mind in the *Poetics*? With respect to poetry, at least, the answer is not always clear. In his sketch of the early history of poetry (chapter 4) Aristotle traces it to two 'causes', both natural (48b5). The first of these is the natural human tendency to 'imitate' (*mimeisthai*), evidenced by the earliest learning of children. Does *mimeisthai* here mean mimicry or representation? The human species is differentiated from others by virtue of being 'thoroughly mimetic' (*mimêtikôtaton*, 48b7). But does this mean that human beings alone tend to mimic and thereby learn from the behaviour of others, for example in learning to talk? Or does it mean that they alone are given to making likenesses of things, such as pictures or sculptures? The latter characteristic does in fact differentiate them more markedly than the former, since mimicry also occurs in non-human species (cf. *Historia Animalium* 536b9–21, 597b22–9). Elsewhere (*Politics* 1338a40–b2, cf. a17–19) Aristotle urges that children be taught to draw, not for its practical utility but because it makes them observers of physical beauty. When he speaks in the *Poetics* of 'the earliest lessons' of children (48b7–8), he is probably thinking of their drawing, painting or modelling before they learn to read or write.

It is clearer that he has representational *mimêsis* in mind when he turns to the second 'cause' for the development of poetry. For this is the human tendency to take pleasure in representational objects (*mimêmata*), which are exemplified by visual likenesses (48b9–12). Aristotle observes that we delight in viewing precisely detailed likenesses of things, even if their originals are inherently painful. The pleasure is attributed to 'learning' and 'inferring': 'it comes about that in viewing they learn and infer what each thing is, for example that this [person] is that one' (48b16–17). Here the composition of poetic fiction is treated as analogous to drawing or sculpting. We enlarge our understanding of the world both by making representations ourselves and by viewing those made by others. Thus Aristotle accounts for both the impulse to compose fiction and the widespread enjoyment of it. Both are traced to our natural desire to learn.

It is often objected that he here places undue emphasis upon mere recognition as a factor in the appreciation of a work of art. Neither artistic merit nor aesthetic pleasure depends upon a work's recognizable fidelity to a real original. The original may be quite unknown to us, or dead or non-existent, yet the work may still give pleasure, indeed greater pleasure than many a good likeness of a familiar subject.

In reply it is sometimes suggested that what is at issue is the recognition of the likeness as typifying a *class* of subjects, and as highlighting what is characteristic of that class. Such an interpretation, if it could be squared with the text, would fit neatly with Aristotle's later contention (51b6–11) that fiction deals with 'universals' rather than particulars. The representational work, though it depicts an individual, is of interest as exhibiting features of a type: this is the way that such-and-such people will generally appear or behave. Aristotle's pronouns are, however, demonstrative, not sortal. So unless we emend them, he is plainly speaking of inferring the identity of an individual: 'this person (in the portrait) is that person (whom we already know)'. But then what does mere identification of a familiar individual have to do with pleasurable learning from a work of art?

Some light is thrown upon Aristotle's meaning by a closely parallel text from the *Rhetoric*:

> Again, since learning and wondering are pleasant, it follows that such things as acts of representation must be pleasant – for instance painting, sculpture, poetic composition – and every product of skilful representation: this latter, even if the object represented is not itself pleasant: for one does not delight in that, but there is an inference that this is that, with the result that one learns something.
>
> (1371b4–10, trans. after revised Oxford translation)

This passage anticipates the *Poetics* in stressing 'inference' and 'learning' from a representation, even of objects that are inherently painful. Its point is not, however, limited to the subjects of human likenesses, since the pronouns in the inference schema ('this is that') are neuter. Moreover, the pleasure taken in learning is derived from 'wonder'. The work prompts its viewers to ask questions of it, and presumably contains features from which answers may be inferred. Thus it both arouses and gratifies human curiosity. The pleasure lies in identifying something that is not expressly named or asserted, but is merely shown. Something is suggested by the representational object, which its viewers can learn only by figuring it out for themselves. In short, a representational work of art demands *interpretation*.

This point is crucial for grasping what is distinctive in the Aristotelian conception of *mimêsis*. When Aristotle insists upon the mimetic status of poetic fictions, he is, in effect, distinguishing their contents from the declarative assertions of history, philosophy or natural science (cf. Halliwell [3.17], 72–3, 172). By means of that distinction, he effectively undermines Plato's objection that poetic fiction is inimical to truth. A *mimêsis* lays no claim to assert truth, because it makes no explicit assertion at all. Whatever truth it contains is merely implicit, and its viewers are left to seek out and identify that truth for themselves.

This notion of *mimêsis*, though visible throughout the *Poetics*, is especially prominent in Aristotle's remarks about organic structure in tragic plot (chapters 7–8); in his distinction between poetic fiction and history (chapter 9); and in his concept of *mimêsis* in epic poetry (chapters 23–4). We shall consider these topics in turn.

Organic structure

Organic concepts and illustrations occur frequently in the *Poetics*.[2] They stem, in part, from Aristotle's conception of a poetic fiction as a *mimêsis* of its subject. He thinks of the subject as a living creature, whose likeness the poet aims to capture, as painters aim to capture the likeness of human or animal models. Greek used the same noun (*zôion*) for 'picture' as for 'animal', and the Greek word for 'drawing' or 'painting' (*zôgraphia*) embodied a connection between those arts and the living subjects they depicted. Accordingly, a representational work must, so far as its medium allows, be so structured as to exhibit the features of the creature which it represents.

Plato in the *Phaedrus* (264b–d, cf. 268c–d, 269c) had already observed that in any composition, an organic principle should govern the ordering of the materials. Aristotle uses organic models extensively, especially in *Poetics* chapters 6–8, to enunciate several broad aesthetic principles, whose influence upon artistic composition and criticism has extended far beyond tragedy.

After giving a formal definition of tragedy (49b22–8), he deduces from its essential nature what he calls its six 'qualitative parts': plot, character, thought, diction, choral ode and spectacle. As noticed above, the 'part' to which he attaches prime importance is plot (*muthos*), He calls the plot of a tragedy its 'first principle and, so to speak, its soul' (50a38–9). The metaphor is derived from his psychology (see pp. 90–104 below). The 'soul' (*psuchê*) of an animal is the 'form' of its living body, i.e. the set of powers possessed by the adult member of its species, which determine its physical make-up and direct every stage in its growth. Likewise the plot of a tragedy determines everything that happens in it, shaping the entire action from beginning to end.

The primacy of plot is indicated also by a visual analogy. It is compared with an outline sketch of some definite object, in contrast with colours laid on at random (50b1–4). Here the 'action' represented by the play is conceived as an organism, whose structure the plot must reveal, just as a black-and-white figure reveals that of an animal.

The same idea underlies Aristotle's directions for plot-structure (chapters 7–8). The action must be 'complete' or 'whole'. 'Whole' is explicated in terms of the plot's containing 'a beginning, a middle and an end' (50b26–7). Aristotle thinks of its successive phases as analogous to an animal's head, trunk and tail. Just as the parts of the animal's body are connected, so the plot should represent a *nexus* of events, so arranged that each renders necessary, or at least probable, the one that follows it. Only in this way can a fictional *mimêsis* exhibit the sorts of causal connection that hold in the real world. Aristotle distinguishes causal order from mere temporal succession (52a18–21), and sharply criticizes dramatists whose plots are 'episodic' (51b33–5). For a disjointed plot, lacking causal connection between its incidents, cannot suggest those general truths about human character and conduct which it is the business of fiction to display.

Equally far-reaching are Aristotle's remarks regarding the proper length for a tragic plot and the criteria for beauty (50b34–51a6). Here the appreciation of a play is expressly compared with the study of an animal. A due proportion or balance between the parts and the whole is of prime importance in the appreciation of beauty, whether in natural objects or in artistic representations of them. The work must therefore be large enough for its parts to be separately discernible, yet not so large that the observer loses all sense of its unity or wholeness. A conspectus of the parts in relation to each other and to the whole is needed for the appreciation of a representational work, just as it is for the observation of an animal. In both cases we need to be able to grasp the contribution made by each element to a well co-ordinated, functioning whole.

Aristotle also emphasizes unity in plot. Here too his remarks have a wider aesthetic relevance, although the requirement of unity in drama has sometimes been extended in ways which lack any basis in his text. Nowhere does the *Poetics* insist upon 'unity of place' or 'unity of time'. All that it demands is 'unity of action'. Aristotle observes that this is not secured merely by stringing together unrelated episodes in the life of a single individual (51a16–22). Just as, in the composition of an animal, nature makes nothing without a purpose, so each element in a well-structured plot should be placed where it is for a reason. Everything that happens should have a discernible bearing upon what happens elsewhere in the play. A grasp of those relationships must be possible through a conspectus of the entire work. For only through a survey of the entire action can the viewer draw inferences regarding the import of the play. Because a structured and unified plot displays necessary or probable connections in the real world, the foregoing remarks lead Aristotle directly into his celebrated contrast between 'poetry' and history.

Poetic fiction and history

Whereas the historian's task is to record events which *have* occurred, the poet's is to speak of 'the kinds of events which *could* occur and are possible by the standards of probability or necessity' (51a36–8, trans. Halliwell). Here Aristotle implicitly rejects Plato's characterization of the poet as a mere 'imitator' of sensible particulars. For poetic fiction has a generalizing purpose. It aims to show the *sort* of thing that happens, by using plot-structures in which the behaviour of certain *sorts* of agent is displayed (51b6–11). Aristotle has here pinpointed the essential difference between history and fiction. The first duty of historians is not to exhibit general truths, but to record particular events, as they have grounds for believing them to have occurred. Authors of fiction, by contrast, can tailor the events of their stories to exhibit whatever general truths they wish to suggest. This distinction between poetic and historical aims is clearer in comedy than in tragedy, Aristotle remarks (51b11–15), because comedy made more frequent use of invented plots.

Thus, 'poetry is more philosophical and more serious than history, since poetry speaks more of universals, history of particulars' (51b5–7). Poetic fiction aims to show truths that have a larger significance than particular historical facts, because they emulate the generalizations of scientific theory. Yet we must firmly grasp that a poetic *mimêsis* does not directly assert, but merely suggests, those truths about character and conduct whose workings it displays. Its audience must infer truths to which its action points, but which it does not expressly affirm.

The contrast between fiction and history, Aristotle further argues (51b29–32), need not prevent poets from basing their works upon fact, since real events may be as well suited as fictional ones to show the sort of thing that is likely to happen. 'Historical fiction' is not, indeed, a contradiction in terms. If Aristotle took the figures and events of traditional legend to have been real, then most of the tragic repertoire performed in his time would have been, for him, what Shakespeare's so-called 'histories' are for us. A sufficiently powerful fiction may sometimes acquire the status of fact. Shakespeare's Henry V and Richard III became, respectively, the warrior-hero and the arch-villain of English school history books. Nevertheless, to regard the content of such plays as being straightforwardly 'affirmed' by the dramatist is, from Aristotle's perspective, to misapprehend their purpose altogether.

Mimêsis in epic poetry

So far we have interpreted Aristotle on the assumption that poetic *mimêsis* generally means 'representation' rather than mimicry. But a vexing passage in his discussion of epic places this once more in doubt.

> Among Homer's many other laudable attributes is his grasp – unique among epic poets – of his status as a poet. For the poet should speak as little as possible in his own person, since it is not by virtue of that that he is a *mimêtês*.
>
> (60a5–8, trans. after Halliwell)

It is usually supposed that Aristotle here refers to the distinction that Plato had drawn in *Republic* III between narrative and *oratio recta*. For Plato had there used the expression 'speaking in his own person' (393a6, cf. 394c2–3) to contrast Homer's narrative sections with the frequent passages in which his characters speak directly. If that is what Aristotle means, then he has switched, without warning, to the sense of *mimêsis* in which it means 'mimicry', and he is suggesting that only in passages of *oratio recta* is the epic poet a genuine *mimêtês*. Yet that interpretation creates the utmost difficulty. It restricts *mimêsis* more narrowly than Aristotle's usage in the treatise would generally suggest. It is flatly inconsistent with his own earlier distinction between narrative and enactive modes of *mimêsis* (48a19–29). And it is equally inconsistent with his repeated labelling of epic poetry as 'narrative *mimêsis*' (59a17, 59b33, 59b36–7).

Aristotle does not explain the phrase 'speaking in his own person', and we need not take him to mean exactly what Plato had meant. He goes on to castigate other epic poets as 'constantly competing in their own persons' and as 'representing few things on few occasions' (60a8–9). Here, as elsewhere (51a6–11, 51b35–52a1, 53b7–11, 62a5–11), he has his eye on the way in which artistic aims can be perverted by the pressures of performance. He means that inferior poets used a thin plot as a platform from which to harangue the audience in their own voice, instead of allowing a richly elaborated story to makes its own impact, as Homer did. Such an interpretation fits with what we have earlier said of *mimêsis*. For poets practise it not by virtue of what they directly assert, but by virtue of what they leave their audiences to infer.

The present text need not, therefore, be taken to restrict *mimêsis* to sections of direct enactment or *oratio recta*. Nevertheless, we can observe a special connection between those sections and what is distinctive about Aristotle's conception of *mimêsis*. Enacted drama and *oratio recta* in epic afford the clearest cases of mimetic utterance, because it is there that the authors' detachment from the content of their works is most obvious. They need not be identified with their characters' words, nor taken to endorse anything they say. Thus enacted drama and *oratio recta* exemplify authorial detachment in its purest form. They provide a standard of disengaged utterance to which all works of art should aspire. We have here, in embryo, a conception of representation in which literary artists are completely detached from all utterances in their works. The work speaks entirely for itself, with no direct statement or comment from its author (cf. Halliwell [3.17], 173–4). On such a view, to condemn artists, as Plato did, for failing to attain truth, is to misrepresent the very nature of their enterprise.

Mimetic pleasure

We can now return to our earlier difficulty regarding the pleasure taken in representational objects. Aristotle had said (48b17–19) that if we should not have seen the original of such an object before, it will not give pleasure *as* a representation, but only through such features as its workmanship or colour. We need to ask what analogue exists in tragedy or epic to satisfy this requirement. For, clearly, it is Aristotle's view that we do enjoy those genres as representations, and not merely for their workmanship or colour. Yet in what sense must we have 'previously seen' what they represent? In order to enjoy, say, *Oedipus Rex* as a representation, what must the audience have 'seen before'?

Not, of course, the legendary Oedipus himself, whom no audience in historic times could be supposed to have seen. Nor could Aristotle have made it a requirement of enjoying Sophocles' play that one must have prior knowledge of the Oedipus story. For although most tragedies in his day used traditional stories for their plots, he expressly notes that they could give pleasure to everyone, even though the stories were 'familiar only to few' (51b25–6). He also notes that newly invented plots, whose stories were known to no one, could still give pleasure (51b21–3). Obviously, neither the characters nor the story of a wholly invented plot could be regarded as needing to be 'seen before' as a condition for enjoyment of the work.

Yet one phrase of Aristotle's suggests a sense in which the pleasure given by tragedy or epic requires prior acquaintance with its subject-matter, even when its characters are unknown or wholly invented. He calls tragedy a representation 'not of human beings but of actions and of life' (50a16–18, cf. 50b24–5, 52a1–2). The individual human beings may be quite unknown to us, and so may their particular stories. But what *is* already known to us is 'life', connected here as in the *Nicomachean Ethics* (1098a18–20, 1100a4–9) with human actions or fortunes over a period of time or an entire career. Sophocles' tragedy represents 'the changes and chances of this mortal life', no less familiar to ancient audiences than to modern ones. Life's dynamics, its changes from prosperity to adversity, its complex interplay of character with circumstance, its ambiguities and uncertainties, its moral dilemmas and mental conflicts, its ironies and contradictions, its surprises and coincidences, are already familiar to us, and their highlighting in fictional representation is a source of pleasure. We enjoy the tragedy of Oedipus because we can recognize in his story misconceptions, misfortunes, failings and follies, and a grim inevitability, that are typical of human life. Our pity and fear are evoked through our recognition of human frailty embodied in the story. Human vulnerability, and therefore our own, are powerfully brought home to us. The enjoyment with which we respond to all this is what Aristotle calls the pleasure that is 'proper' to tragedy (53b10–11, cf. 53a35–6, 59a21, 62b13–14).

This pleasure is neither limited to nor dependent upon theatrical enactment. It can be gained no less from reading or hearing a fictional narrative than from seeing a play performed (50b18–20, 53b3–7, 62a12, a17–18). Literary and theatrical values need not coincide, and they may, for Aristotle, even conflict (51a6–11). The pleasure 'proper' to tragedy does not require live performance because it depends crucially upon inferences from the content and structure of the plot. Even when a tragedy is performed, the pleasure proper to it cannot be fully experienced while the performance is still in progress, but can be gained only through a retrospect upon the completed action (cf. 53a30–9). That is why Aristotle can treat metrical language, choral odes, and visual elements as mere adornments of tragedy, as 'seasonings' (49b25–9, 50b16) rather the main dish. The pleasure that they give is not integral to tragedy's distinctive function as a *mimêsis* of action.

What he says of 'spectacle' is especially revealing. He rates it as the element 'least integral to the poetic art' (50b17), as 'belonging more to the sphere of the property man than of the poet' (50b20). He dismisses as 'quite outside the sphere of tragedy' (53b10) those poets who relied on lavish staging to achieve sensational effects. For the pleasure proper to tragedy is not morbid. It depends not upon the horror that can be produced by terrifying stage-effects, nor upon the thrill caused by pain or cruelty, but upon the compassion we feel for fictional characters who are caught up in the events of a pitiful tale. We respond to an emotional content inherent in the play (53b13–14) rather than to the gimmickry of production.

Tragic katharsis

The emotional content of tragedy brings us, finally, to the much vexed question of tragic *katharsis*. Aristotle's formal definition of tragedy runs as follows:

> Tragedy is a representation of an action which is serious, complete, and of a certain magnitude – in language which is garnished in various forms in its different parts – in the mode of dramatic enactment, not narrative – and by means of pity and fear effecting the *katharsis* of such emotions.
>
> (49b24–8, trans. after Halliwell)

The concluding clause has generally been held to contain an 'answer' to Plato's condemnation of poetry for its harmful effect upon control of the emotions. But what was that answer? What did Aristotle mean by the tantalizing term *katharsis*?

We must first notice, and put aside, the modern use of 'catharsis' to mean the release of pent-up emotion. That is psychiatric jargon, which derives from an influential way of reading the present text, as a glance at the

Concise Oxford Dictionary (s.v. 'catharsis') will confirm. If we insist upon reading that use back into Aristotle, we risk prejudging his meaning, even when we retain his own word.

Basically, *katharsis* meant 'cleansing', frequently, though not solely, through medical purging or religious purification. Neither of those metaphors, however, enables a satisfactory account to be given of *katharsis* in the context of tragedy.

First 'purgation'. A purging of pity and fear has sometimes been taken to mean their complete elimination from our emotional system. Against that, it has been rightly objected that, according to Aristotle's own ethical teaching, the proper feeling of those and other emotions plays an indispensable part in human well-being. It has seemed inconceivable that he should defend tragedy on the ground that it eliminates the emotions altogether.

On the other hand, if 'purging' the emotions simply means venting them in the theatre, for example by having a good cry, the *katharsis* clause seems a cumbersome way of expressing that idea. For it seems, absurdly, to represent pity and fear as a means to their own discharge. Collingwood ([3.36], 51) glosses *katharsis* as an 'emotional defecation', which 'leaves the audience's mind, after the tragedy is over, not loaded with pity and fear but lightened of them'. Against this, one must protest that to interpret *katharsis* as 'emotional defecation' saddles Aristotle with a view of the emotions which he simply did not hold. Moreover, merely to reiterate the fact, well known to Plato himself and heavily underscored by him, that audiences gain a pleasurable sense of relief by discharging feelings of pity and fear, would do nothing to counter his argument that such discharges are psychologically harmful.

'Purification' of the emotions is equally problematic. In the *Nicomachean Ethics* (1105b19–25) Aristotle distinguishes between occurrent states of emotional arousal (*pathê*) and our natural capacities (*dunameis*) for feeling such states. Clearly, the former could not be purified, for to speak of 'purifying' a twinge of pity or a fit of terror is nonsense. 'Purifying' might possibly be a metaphor for improving our capacity to feel pity or fear, if tragedy could somehow cause us to feel them more appropriately than certain people do. Yet, although Aristotle has sometimes been credited with a therapeutic theory of that sort (cf. House [3.38], 108–11), it has never been made clear just how tragedy produces such an effect, or indeed why that should be necessary for an audience of ordinary sensibility and sound mind. One might even wonder whether tragedy could affect an audience at all unless its emotional apparatus were already more or less in order. Anyone who does not feel special revulsion, for example, at child-murder, matricide or incest, will hardly be moved, let alone improved, by watching *Medea*, *Electra* or *Oedipus Rex*.

Some scholars have therefore tried another tack. *Katharsis* is not the only word whose meaning is in doubt. The phrase usually rendered 'of such emotions' (*toioutôn pathêmatôn*) could also be translated 'of such afflictions'. The clause would then mean, 'accomplishing by means of pity and fear the *katharsis* of pitiful and fearful afflictions'. That would make good sense, if *katharsis* could be taken to mean, as several scholars have recently urged (for example Golden [3.50], 145–7; Nussbaum [3.39], 388–91, 502–3, nn.17–18), 'clarification'. On that construal, Aristotle would be saying that tragedy, through pity and fear represented in the play, achieves a clarification of just such afflictions in real life. Tragedy enlightens its audience by deepening their understanding of just such sorrows as are typified by the play. For it traces those sorrows to various kinds of psychological conflict which are 'clarified' by its action.

Such an interpretation is attractive. Linguistically, it fits perfectly. It allows us to connect *katharsis* with Aristotle's remarks about 'learning' from mimetic works, and about the generalizing power of fiction. It also makes a claim about tragedy that can be amply supported from the experience of actual plays.

It founders, however, upon two reefs. First, it tends to beg the question against Plato's attack. Tragedy's power to move us is a familiar and incontestable fact. To defend it as serving a purely intellectual purpose, on the basis of a formal definition, is simply to ignore that impact which it is known to have, and for which Plato had condemned it.

Secondly, an intellectualist interpretation disregards a passage in the *Politics*, which – baffling though it is – cannot lightly be set aside. Aristotle there speaks (1341b32–42a16) of a *katharsis* induced in certain mentally disordered people by exposure to 'kathartic melodies' (*ta melê ta kathartika*). He mentions a pleasurable 'lightening' effect produced by orgiastic music, alleviating their frenzied state. In a medical context (*Problemata* 955a25–6) the term 'lightening' (*kouphizesthai*) is used of the relief felt after coitus by people who suffer from excessive sexual desire. If the *katharsis* of the *Politics* has any bearing upon that of the *Poetics*, to which it expressly refers (1341b39–40), it seems unlikely that the latter should be understood as a purely cognitive experience. Tragic *katharsis* is unlikely, then, to mean 'clarification', but probably included a component of 'lightening' or relief. But if so, what was that component, and how was Plato 'answered' by making reference to it?

The *katharsis* clause can be interpreted as a pointed and effective response to Plato if we notice (following Sparshott [3.54], 22–3) that it contains a Platonic allusion which Aristotle's audience would readily have picked up, and which would account for the sudden introduction of the term *katharsis* without explanation. In the *Phaedo* Socrates had exalted the true philosopher as one whose soul is cleansed by achieving freedom from bodily appetites and passions. He speaks (69b–c) of the philosopher's virtues as 'a kind of *katharsis* from all such things [sc. pleasures, fears and all else of that sort]' (69c1) and of wisdom herself as 'a kind of purifying rite' (*katharmos tis*). Plato here describes neither a purging nor a purifying *of* the emotions, but a liberation of the soul *from* them (reading the Greek genitive as 'separative'), in which the philosopher achieves the serenity, and especially the immunity from fear of death, so conspicuously shown by Socrates himself. It is not the emotions which are purified or purged, but *the soul* which is cleansed from servitude to them through release from its bondage to the body. In Aristotle's reference to the '*katharsis* from such emotions', which echoes Plato's wording at 69c1 almost exactly, we can still catch an allusion to that very *katharsis* which Plato had extolled. Paradoxically, it is by means of the emotions aroused in tragedy that that state of tranquillity is achieved. Pity and fear, enacted by the performers and aroused in the audience, so far from causing surrender to such feelings, are the very means by which we may be delivered from their power. The emotional harrowing of tragedy enables us to accept our own frailties as the common lot of mankind, and thereby raises us above a self-absorbed pity, fear or grief.

Tragedy has this mysterious, uplifting power. Through compassion and admiration for its victims, we are somehow elevated above our own selfish turmoil. This response is evoked especially when we behold exemplary magnanimity or dignity in face of undeserved suffering. George Orwell once remarked that '[a] tragic situation exists precisely when virtue does *not* triumph but when it is still felt that man is nobler than the forces which destroy him' (*Collected Essays*, vol. 4, 338). That sentiment is profoundly Aristotelian (cf. 53a4–17), and it could be illustrated by any number of tragedies, ancient or modern. An immortal illustration, however, lay at Aristotle's elbow, as it still lies at ours. In the *Phaedo* Socrates had shown miraculous nobility in face of monstrous injustice and a universal human terror. Though not a tragedy by all of Aristotle's formal criteria, its impact exemplifies the very *katharsis* which it stresses itself, and it has made just such an impact upon its readers across the centuries.

Aristotle responds to Plato, then, by claiming for tragedy precisely that effect which Plato had extolled and achieved in the most moving of his own dialogues. Poetic fiction, rightly understood, can provide just that benefit which Plato had claimed for philosophy. Thus, as Aristotle says, 'poetry is both more philosophical and more serious than history' (51b5–6): 'more philosophical', because it implicitly suggests 'universals' which are the domain of philosophy; and 'more serious', not because it is more edifying than history, or shows virtue as any more triumphant, but because it celebrates the power of the human spirit to rise above injustice, misfortune, suffering and death.

On that interpretation, it is mistaken to ask whether *katharsis* is intellectual *or* emotional, cognitive *or* affective. For the response just outlined evidently has both intellectual and affective elements. Feeling and thought are interactive. The more thoroughly we understand a tragedy, the more deeply it will engage our emotions. Conversely, the more deeply we are moved by a play, the more we shall be disposed to seek meaning in it. Emotional impact and the quest for understanding are mutually reinforcing. Precisely in that sense *katharsis* is achieved 'through pity and fear'. Those feelings are not a means to their own discharge or improvement. Rather, their arousal through a poetic *mimêsis* is a means to spiritual peace.

On the view defended above, *katharsis* is the attainment of a calm or tranquil frame of mind, an outlook that is 'philosophical' in a popular sense of the word also traceable, ultimately, to the *Phaedo*. It is paradoxical (and Aristotle's wording in the *katharsis* clause reflects this), that emotional arousal should be a means to emotional serenity. But the paradox needs no sophisticated medical theory of 'homoeopathic cures' to ground it. It is simply common experience, not only of tragedy but of other high art forms, that they can move us profoundly, yet thereby leave us more at peace with ourselves and with the world we inhabit. That experience lies at the core of Aristotle's aesthetic; and his single reference to it deserves attention, not as mere *ad hominem* polemic in an ephemeral debate with Plato, but because it points towards a wider account of art which holds perennial truth.

❧ PHILOSOPHY OF MIND ❧

Aristotle's chief contributions to the philosophy of mind are to be found in *De Anima* (*DA*), a general preface to his lectures on zoology, and in a collection of essays now known as the *Parva Naturalia* (*PN*). Also relevant are a short work on animal movement, *De Motu Animalium*, and the zoological treatises, *De Partibus Animalium* and *De Generatione Animalium*. The account that follows will be based mainly upon *De Anima* and the *Parva Naturalia*.[3]

De Anima has come down to us in three books. The first contains a survey of problems about the 'soul' and a critique of previous theorists. The second begins with Aristotle's own general account of the soul. Its remainder, together with the whole of the third book, deal with the various powers possessed by living things. The order of discussion corresponds, albeit very roughly (cf. Hutchinson [3.62]), with the hierarchy of powers in plants, animals and human beings, ascending from the powers of nutrition and reproduction shared by all organisms to those possessed only by animals (perception and imagination), and then to the power of intellect, which is possessed (within the natural order) by mankind alone. Animal desire and locomotion are also discussed.

The essays of the *Parva Naturalia* form a series of appendices to *De Anima* covering a variety of special subjects in psycho-biology. Those of greatest interest for present-day philosophy of mind are the first five in the series, which deal with sense-perception, memory, sleep, dreams, and divination through sleep.

The expression 'philosophy of mind' does not, however, map neatly on to either *De Anima* or the *Parva Naturalia*. On the one hand, they include empirical psychology and physiology as well as philosophy. On the other hand, many questions now central to the philosophy of mind find no place in them at all. If we ask of them, for example, how mental events are related to physical ones, or how we can know the existence and contents of minds other than our own, we shall ask in vain. Such questions are, in effect, by-passed in Aristotle's approach to the whole subject.

The difficulty in aligning *De Anima* with 'philosophy of mind' is connected with the problem of translating its title term, *psuchê*. 'Soul', though it will generally be used below, has religious associations which are alien to Aristotle's scientific interests. Although he sharply criticizes earlier scientists, he shares their concern to explain the powers of growth and self-movement which distinguish living from non-living things, and the perceptual, emotional and cognitive powers which distinguish animals from plants. At the outset (*DA* 402a7–8) he characterizes *psuchê* as 'the principle of animal life'. He expressly warns against limiting the inquiry to human beings (*DA* 402b3–9), and subsequently attributes *psuchê* to all living things. Since we do not credit plants, or even animals, with souls, there are many places where 'soul' as a translation of *psuchê* will sound unnatural.

Traditionally, the *psuchê* had been thought of as a shadowy simulacrum of the living body, which can survive its death, and persist in a disembodied state in Hades. It foreshadowed the concept of a ghost, an entity whose *post mortem* existence is of its very essence (as remains true of 'soul' in English). Aristotle, in effect, undermined this tradition by linking the concept of *psuchê* with that of organic life, and by considering, more closely than his predecessors had done, the implications of that linkage. Thus, he transformed what had been a partly religious concept into a wholly scientific one. Against that background, the question whether the *psuchê*, or any aspects of it, can exist separately from the body naturally played a larger part in his debate with earlier thinkers than it has played in more recent philosophy of mind.

Equally dubious, as a translation of *psuchê*, is the English 'mind'. In its ordinary use, as roughly equivalent to the human intellect, it is too narrow for the range of powers associated by Aristotle with *psuchê*, since it does not include nutrition, growth or reproduction, and is not generally attributed to animals. As for its extended use by philosophers since Descartes, to mean the subject of conscious awareness or thought, although Aristotle may be said to have possessed the idea of such a subject, he explicitly resists its identification with the *psuchê*. In a famous passage, to which we shall return, he observes:

> to say that it is the *psuchê* that is angry is as if one were to say that it is the *psuchê* that weaves or builds. It is surely better not to say that the

psuchê pities or learns or thinks, but rather that the *human being* does this *with* the *psuchê*.

(*DA* 408b11–15)

One further aspect of *psuchê* needs to be dissociated from *De Anima* and the *Parva Naturalia*. Aristotle is unconcerned in these treatises with the 'true self', that precious element in human beings whose well-being had been a matter of paramount concern for Socrates and Plato. Even in his ethical writings, talk of *psuchê* is different in tone from Plato's. Although he defines human well-being in terms of 'activity of *psuchê*' (*Nicomachean Ethics* 1098a16), he tends not to speak of 'souls' (*psuchai*) as entities either possessed by or identified with individual human subjects. In his mature psychology the individual soul as a subject of moral attributes, or as a moral agent, receives no attention.

This important difference stems largely from Aristotle's rejection of Platonic dualism, the notion that the soul is an independent substance, lodged within the body during life, yet capable of separate existence. Although Aristotle had embraced that idea in his youth, the treatises of his maturity present a strikingly different picture. That picture is drawn, in broadest outline, in the first three chapters of *De Anima* II, to which we may now turn.

Soul and body

Aristotle's central thesis is that the soul of a living thing is related to its body as 'form' (*morphê*) is related to matter (*hulê*). The soul is the structure whereby bodily matter is so ordered as to form a living animal or plant. Soul and body are not two separate entities, somehow temporarily conjoined. Rather, they are, like form and matter in general, complementary aspects of a single entity, the whole complex living creature. This thesis is sometimes called 'hylemorphism'.

The 'form' of a living thing is attained when the potential of its constituent matter becomes actualized in a full-grown member of its species. In attaining that form, a creature develops certain powers, whose exercise is necessary for its preservation and well-being, and for the perpetuation of its species. Most of these powers are exercised by means of 'organs', parts of the body conceived as tools fashioned for specific tasks. Indeed, the very word *organon* means a tool or implement. Tools and bodily organs both provide Aristotle with models to illustrate his account of the soul.

An axe is not just wood and iron, but wood and iron so structured as to be an implement for chopping. Its chopping purpose dictates both its form and its matter, and is essential for grasping its essential nature, 'what it is to be an axe' (*DA* 412b10–15). Aristotle distinguishes, moreover, between its 'first actuality', attained when the wood and iron have been fashioned into an implement with power to chop, and its 'second actuality', attained when it is being used for chopping. The axe's essential nature is given by the 'first' actuality rather than the 'second'. For it does not cease to be an axe when the woodsman lays it aside, but only when it becomes so blunted or otherwise damaged that its chopping power has been lost.

Similarly, an eye is not just a lump of translucent jelly, but gelatinous material so structured and situated within the body that its owner possesses the power of sight. Should that power be destroyed, the jelly will remain an 'eye' in name only (*DA* 412b18–22). The connection between the eye and sight is not, indeed, a merely contingent one. We cannot see with anything except our eyes, nor can we use our eyes for any purpose except seeing. It is sight which defines the eye; and it does so in terms of the 'first' actuality rather than the 'second'. For the organ does not cease to be an eye at times when its owner is not seeing anything, for example while asleep or in the dark. What is necessary for its being an eye is simply that under appropriate conditions its owner be capable of seeing with it.

We can now understand the phrases in which Aristotle formally defines the soul. He calls it 'the first actuality of a natural body which potentially has life' (*DA* 412a27–8), and immediately explicates this as 'the first actuality of a natural body possessing organs' (*DA* 412b5–6). As sight stands to the eye-jelly, so does the complete set of powers possessed by an organism stand to its body as a whole. To ascribe soul to it, then, amounts to saying that it is a body *in working order*. To credit X with soul, it is not necessary that X should now be absorbing food, reproducing itself, walking, seeing, imagining, remembering, feeling angry, thinking or talking. It is only necessary that it should possess the capacity for whichever of those activities are characteristic of its species.

From this account it follows at once that soul can no more exist separately from body than an axe's chopping power or an eye's power of sight can exist when the axe or the eye has been destroyed. It is a gross conceptual error to regard an animal's soul as some sort of receptor or motor within its body, whether a material one, as certain pre-Socratic thinkers had supposed, or an immaterial one, as Plato's Socrates had affirmed in the *Phaedo*. It is, in terms made famous by Gilbert Ryle, a 'category mistake' to view the soul as a substance in its own right, rather than a set of powers which living things possess. For any given animal or plant species, its 'soul' cannot be understood without reference to the bodily apparatus needed to exercise the powers in question: 'it is not a body, but is something relative to a body. That is why it is *in* a body, and in a body of some definite kind' (*DA* 414a20–2, trans. after revised Oxford translation).

This idea is anticipated in a sharp criticism of theories of trans-migration. Such theories, Aristotle drily observes, are akin to saying that the art of carpentry could enter into flutes: 'just as a skill must use its own tools, so a soul has to use its own body' (*DA* 407b25–6). Carpentry uses, amongst other tools, saws. To cut timber, a saw must have teeth. Since a flute lacks teeth, its use for sawing is not even imaginable. It is therefore absurd to suggest that carpentry could be practised with tools designed to serve the ends of a quite different skill. If an animal's soul is a certain set of capacities, then it can only belong to a body equipped to exercise those capacities. Just as the idea of a flute's being used for carpentry is (not just false but) absurd, so it is absurd to suppose, with Plato's Socrates, that the body of a donkey might house the soul of a human being, or that the soul of a bee might enter a human body (*Phaedo* 82a–b). For the body of a donkey does not equip it to weave a cloak or build a house; no more does a human body enable its owner to pollinate flowers or to produce honey.

As we saw earlier, Aristotle prefers to say that 'the human being does things with the soul', instead of ascribing those activities to the soul itself (*DA* 408b13–15). He compares saying that the soul is angry with saying that the soul weaves or builds. Here too he is combating the idea of the soul as a separable inner agent which can have experiences or perform actions independently of the body. Since bodily movements play an essential part in weaving or building, the absurdity of attributing those tasks to the soul alone is clear. Similarly, Aristotle argues, to attribute anger, pity or other mental phenomena to the soul alone is to disregard the bodily apparatus through which the relevant capacities must be displayed. To say that a person does things 'with the soul' is to say that certain capacities are exercised through the appropriate physical apparatus.

In a similar vein, Aristotle distinguishes a physiologist's account of anger, 'a boiling of the blood and hot stuff around the heart', from a philosopher's definition of it, 'a desire for retaliation' (*DA* 403a29–b1). The latter account gives the 'form' of anger, the former provides the 'matter' in which it has to be realized. Aristotle also suggests that the true student of nature will combine both sorts of account. The physiology of the emotions plays an essential part in a full understanding of them. Anger is not a pure state of feeling, but is inseparable from the bodily responses in which it is vented. Yet it cannot be simply equated with those responses. The bodily arousal typical of a given emotion may be present when there is little or no occasion for that emotion to be felt (cf. *DA* 403a19–24). To identify an emotional state specifically as one of anger, we do not take a man's pulse or measure his blood-pressure. Rather, we interpret his bodily reactions and behaviour as part of a pattern, a wider context within which anger is typically provoked and displayed, and in the light of which it has to be understood.

Modern philosophy has pressed further the question of how mental events or states are related to bodily reactions or behaviour. It is assumed that there are radically distinct sorts of item: private experiences on the one hand and observable processes on the other. But from Aristotle's perspective that distinction is entirely problematic. Anger, understood as the urge to retaliate, can occur only in animals that respond to attack or injury with certain bodily reactions or overt behaviour. If we insist upon asking how their urge to retaliate is related to their physical response, Aristotle would reply that 'one need not inquire whether the soul and the body are one, any more than whether the wax and its shape are one' (*DA* 412b6–7). Just as the wax and the impress made in it by a seal are inseparable aspects of a single waxen object, so a certain bodily response and the urge to strike back are inseparable aspects of the single phenomenon that we call anger. A purely chemical or neurological description of anger, however minute its detail, if it makes no reference to the kinds of stimulus that typically provoke anger, the goals sought by an angry animal, and the role of anger in an animal's preservation and well-being, will miss what is of primary significance in the whole phenomenon.

Basic to Aristotle's account of the soul, then, are the tasks that a creature can perform with its body. To speak of its soul is to refer, compendiously, to the set of powers possessed by creatures of its type. In the higher animals, and especially in mankind, these powers are both numerous and complex, and a full account of them will vary widely from one species to another. This theory, as Aristotle observes (*DA* 414b20–8), is too general to provide information for any specific form of life. In his zoological writings, however, it is applied fruitfully to a huge variety of animal species. It is there shown in marvellous detail why different species develop the organs they have, and how those organs are fitted for the tasks they must perform if they are to contribute to the survival and well-being of the whole animal. In *De Anima*, by contrast, we find only a broad survey of the various powers possessed at each level of life. These must now be considered in turn.

Nutrition and reproduction

The powers of growth, nourishment and reproduction are attributed by Aristotle to the 'nutritive' soul. Because they are shared by all living things, 'living' is defined with reference to them alone (*DA* 415a23–5). So long as they remain operative, an animal or human being may be said to 'live', even should its higher faculties be impaired. Aristotle calls the intake of food and reproduction the 'most natural of functions for living things' (*DA* 415a26–7). For it is through them that living things achieve the only sort of permanence available to them. Although they must perish individually, they are enabled, through the generation of offspring like themselves, to perpetuate their species. Thus 'they share in the eternal and the divine in the only way that they can' (*DA* 415a29–b1). This recalls the teaching of Diotima in Plato's *Symposium* (207a–208b): the reproductive urge in all animals is an aspiration to immortality, in which mortal creatures unconsciously emulate the divine.

The capacities of the 'nutritive' soul will strike most philosophers of mind as falling outside their province. Since growth, nourishment and reproduction are not 'mental' processes, they seem to raise no 'mind–body problem'. No philosopher now asks, for example, how mind and body are related in the digestion of food, since we normally remain unconscious of that purely 'physical' process. Only with *in*digestion can the philosopher of mind get a foothold, by asking how dyspepsia is related to the sensation of heartburn. But nothing could illustrate better the shift that has occurred in the locus of philosophical concern. Ever since Descartes, the central issues for the philosophy of mind have arisen only with respect to sentient creatures. Because growth and nutrition can occur in non-sentient substances, those processes fail to qualify, as it were, for 'mental' status.

Aristotle's map, however, is differently drawn. The question of how *psuchê* is related to the body arises for any sort of living thing, whether sentient or not. For plants as for animals, we may distinguish form from matter, actuality from potentiality. Plants may be seen as conforming, no less than animals, to Aristotle's definition of the soul as 'the first actuality of a natural body possessing organs'. Their parts can be viewed as rudimentary organs with specific jobs to perform: 'for example the leaf serves to shelter the pod, and the pod to shelter the fruit; the roots are analogous to the mouth, since both take in food' (*DA* 412b1–4). In the case of plants, we cannot, of course, ask how sensations, feelings or thoughts are related to their physical make-up. But we may well ask how their capacities for nourishment and reproduction are related to their material constituents. And we may take a set of chemical processes in a plant (for example the absorption of heat and moisture through its roots) to constitute the material basis for realization of its form. It is only when those processes are explained as the intake of nourishment and a means to growth, that we have understood their significance in the plant's life.

Perception

Animals are distinguished from plants by their powers of perception. These powers enable them to move about, seek food, adapt to their environment and defend themselves, and thus to survive and flourish (cf. *DA* 434a30–b8; *PN* 436b8–437a3). The minimal power, found even in the simplest animals, is the sense of touch. But most species possess a more complex apparatus, in which several different sensory powers are somehow combined in a single, unified system. How are these powers related to one another and to the bodily organs through which they are exercised? And how, in detail, does Aristotle understand what happens in perception?

In this connection, he repeatedly uses phrases which need a word of explanation. He will speak of certain items as 'inseparable, yet separate in account', or as being 'the same yet different in their being'. By this he means that a single thing can answer to two or more different descriptions. A lump of sugar, for example, is both white and sweet. 'The white thing' is identical with, or inseparable from, 'the sweet thing'. Yet its 'being white' is different from its 'being sweet': we would give distinct accounts of what it is to be white and what it is to be sweet. The two descriptions have, as we should say, different senses but the same reference. The relation of the morning star to the evening star is a familiar modern example.

This point plays an important part in Aristotle's view of the relation of the senses to one another and to an animal's other powers. He will often say of two or more powers that they are 'the same, yet differ in their being' (for example *DA* 413b29–32, 424a26, 427a2–3, 432a31–b4, 432a31–b3, 433b21–5; *PN* 449a14–20, 459a15–17). For he wishes to insist both upon their inseparability, as belonging to a single, unified system, and upon the need for distinct accounts of their respective operations. He regards the sense-organs as different parts of a single, connected apparatus centred in the heart. Perception can occur only when the impulses initiated by an external object's impact upon the organs have travelled to the central sensorium. This centre, and the apparatus which it controls, will be differently described for each of the various functions it enables its owner to perform.[4]

In his essay on sleep (*PN* 455a20–2), Aristotle writes: 'For there exists a single sense-faculty, and the master sense-organ is single, though its being differs for the perception of each kind of thing, for example of sound or colour.' Similarly, in his treatise on sense-perception (*PN* 449a16–20) he argues that there must be a single sense-faculty, yet each of the modes in which it operates (visual, auditory, etc.) is different. A single apparatus is capable of receiving data from a variety of external stimuli through several different types of receptor. Hence different accounts of what it is (the 'being' of this apparatus) will be required for each mode of its operation.

Why must there be a single central sensorium upon which all the sense-organs converge? Because, Aristotle argues, it is one and the same subject that sees, hears, imagines, desires, thinks, moves and acts. All of these powers alike can be exercised by a single animal when it is awake, and all alike are cut off when it is asleep. Our ascription of perception, desire and movement to a single creature requires that it be possessed of a single central apparatus, where all input from the sense-organs is registered, and from which all its responses originate.

We might think of the central sensorium as analogous to a multi-purpose tool, a single thing, yet also as many different things (for example knife, corkscrew, screwdriver) as the functions which it enables its owner to perform. A full understanding of 'what it is', of its 'being', calls for a differentiated account of its role in each of those tasks. But it remains a single 'master' organ, whose functioning is essential for every part of the creature's sensory apparatus, and much else within it, to work. Aristotle calls it the 'primary sense-organ'. Although he himself identified it with the heart, in modern physiology it finds a close analogue in the brain.

Since the sensory apparatus is centred at the heart, it is understandable that Aristotle should sometimes speak as if the soul were in the heart. Thus, he can speak of conscious awareness (for example being angry or frightened) as due to movements or changes within the heart (*DA* 408b5–11). But such language should not be taken to mean that consciousness resides in some spatial region of the heart. The power of sight is 'in' the eye, but unlike the eye it has no spatial extension (*DA* 424a24–8). It is not 'in' the eye in the sense in which the pupil is in it. Similarly, to assign the soul to the heart is not to locate consciousness there, but is simply to say that an animal's perceptual (and other) powers can function only if certain physical processes occur in the central organ.

Aristotle's hypothesis of a single centre controlling all sensory (and other) functions of higher animals is intelligible in broad outline. But much detail in his account of perception remains obscure. We have spoken of input from the sense-organs as 'registered' in the central sensorium, and of the animal's 'responses'. What exactly is the nature of this 'registering' or of these 'responses'? Aristotle's answer is elusive and controversial. He says that the power of perception is 'the capacity to receive the sensible forms without the matter' (424a17–19, 425b23–4). But how is that to be understood? Perception obviously differs from nutrition in that the matter of perceived objects is not absorbed into the percipient's body. A piece of bread must be ingested if it is to nourish, but not if it is merely seen, touched, smelt or tasted. But in what sense can an object's 'sensible form' be received without its matter? Is it meant that when we see a red flag, for example, the eye-jelly takes on its properties, literally reflecting the flag's redness? Or does 'receiving the form' refer to a change in the percipient's consciousness, the visual awareness of red? Or does it refer to both of these, regarded as two different aspects of a single event?

Aristotle compares what happens in perception with the impress received by wax from a bronze or golden seal: the shape of the seal is reproduced in the wax, whereas the bronze or gold is not (424a19–21). When someone sees a red flag, its matter is not absorbed into the percipient's body, yet its redness is somehow transmitted to the observer. Aristotle supposes that a continuous series of impulses is relayed from the flag to the eyes, and thence to the heart. These impulses must preserve (in some fashion which is not made clear) the structure of the flag's sensible properties, yet without importing into the percipient any of the matter of the flag itself. This account has been well compared with the modern idea of signals emitted from physical objects, and relaying their sensible properties in coded 'messages' via the sense-organs and nervous system to the observer's brain (Ackrill [3.29], 67). Aristotle probably does not mean that the eye-jelly is literally reddened. For he says only that the seeing organ is coloured 'after a fashion'

(*DA* 425b22–3). It could, however, receive a structure which represents the flag's red colour, without itself turning red. Such a structure would suffice to explain, as Aristotle says, why, for example, after-images can persist in the sense-organs when the external stimuli have gone (*DA* 425b24–5; cf. *PN* 459b5–18).

Aristotle's use of the waxen imprint as a model for what occurs in perception recalls his caution, quoted earlier, that 'we need no more inquire whether the soul and the body are one than whether the wax and its shape are one' (*DA* 412b6–7). Perceiving should not be described either in purely physiological terms or in purely psychological ones; and a description of the latter type, which gives the 'form', is not reducible to one which gives the 'matter'. If that interpretation is correct, it will follow that for perception, as for the analogous case of anger, both sorts of story need to be told for a complete account. And, as in the case of anger, it needs to be shown how perceptual powers are conducive to the subject's preservation and overall well-being. Beyond this, as we have seen, Aristotle recognizes no 'mind–body' problems of the kind that have dominated modern philosophy of mind.

Imagination and related powers

Aristotle next turns to imagination (*phantasia*), a power of great importance in human beings and in the higher animals. His main account of it is given in *De Anima* III. 3, but it also plays a major role in the essays on memory, sleep and dreams in the *Parva Naturalia*, and on desire and movement in *De Motu Animalium*.

Aristotle relates imagination to the power of perception in the terms he had used to express the relationship of the different senses to one other and to the primary sense-faculty: they are 'the same yet differ in their being' (*PN* 459a14–16). That is, they share a common physical basis in the sensorium centred at the heart. But since that apparatus works differently in its different roles, a separate account is needed for its 'imagining' operations.

The story of those operations forms a sequel to Aristotle's story about ordinary perception, later crystallized in Thomas Hobbes's phrase 'decaying sense'. Movements produced by external objects in an animal's sense-organs will often persist as traces in the organs when the original stimuli are no longer present. These movements are carried from the sense-organs, through the veins, to the heart, where (by a process which remains obscure) they are stored, and may later be reactivated. They are then experienced as mental images, memories or dreams. Imagination thus enables waking animals to visualize or recall objects in their absence, and to be attracted or repelled by them, according as they are envisaged as pleasant or painful. It also collaborates with desire and (in human beings) with thought, to produce movement. An animal's desire for pleasure and its aversion to pain impels it to pursue objects envisaged as pleasant or beneficial, and to shun those envisaged as painful or harmful.

So far the role of imagination is limited to the storage of sense-impressions and their retrieval as mental images. But Aristotle's account has a further dimension, which reflects the kinship of the word *phantasia* with 'appearing'. Modern descendants from the same word-group include 'fancy', 'fantasy' and 'phantom'. The word-group covers many kinds of phenomena, including not only 'appearances' in ordinary perception but also what 'appears' pleasant or good, and is 'fancied' as an object of desire. It also covers deceptive appearances (for example optical and other sensory illusions), after-images, dreams, delusions, apparitions and hallucinations.

No single English word is wide enough to cover all these 'appearances'. 'Imagination' is an acceptable translation of *phantasia* where mental imagery is involved. But in several cases mentioned by Aristotle as instances of *phantasia*, images find no place: the sun 'appears' only one foot across (*DA* 428b3–4; *PN* 458b28–9, 460b18–20); a single stick held between crossed fingers 'appears' as if it were two (*PN* 460b20–2); to a person gripped by strong emotion, a stranger 'appears' as a loved one or an enemy (*PN* 460b3–11); to feverish patients, cracks in their bedroom walls 'appear' as animals (*PN* 460b11–16); land 'appears' to be moving to those who are sailing past it (*PN* 460b26–7); the likeness of a man or a centaur may be seen in shifting cloud-formations (*PN* 461b19–21). In such cases *phantasia* signifies the way an experience registers with, or is interpreted by, the subject. At its broadest, it is the capacity whereby things presented to an observer, in any mode of experience, appear to that subject in the way that they do. It determines what content the objects have for the observer, what they are seen *as*. We may conveniently label it 'interpretive *phantasia*'.

Phantasia in this broad sense has received much attention in recent philosophy of mind, and Aristotle shows a powerful insight in calling attention to it. Yet it remains unclear whether he holds any unifying theory linking it with the capacity for forming mental images, or indeed what such a theory would look like. For the latter capacity can be exercised, on Aristotle's own showing, only in the absence of the original objects whose sensory traces produce images. By contrast, interpretive *phantasia* must be exercised concurrently with the experience itself: a stick is felt as two only while it is being touched with crossed fingers. On the face of it, image-formation and interpretive *phantasia* seem quite different. The hypothesis of 'decaying sense' has no apparent relevance to the latter, and it is not obvious how both can be explained as operations of a single power.

Aristotle rightly distinguishes between imagination and belief or judgment (*doxa*). The exercise of interpretive *phantasia* is compatible with widely differing beliefs as to whether things really are the way they appear. A paranoid man may be firmly convinced that a stranger is his enemy, whereas someone who assimilates a cloud to a centaur does not believe for a moment that it is one. Patients may or may not think that the cracks in their walls are animals, depending on the severity of their illness. When we say of an object seen indistinctly, that 'it appears to be a man', we register uncertainty as to whether or not it really is one (*DA* 428a13–15). Judgment, then, may either endorse or oppose the deliverances of imagination, or it may remain non-committal.

More dubious are two further distinctions between imagination and judgment (*DA* 427b16–24). First, we can imagine things at will, whereas we cannot judge them to be the case at will. Secondly, 'when we judge something terrible or fearful, we straightway feel accordingly', whereas with imagination we are in the same state as people viewing terrible things in a picture. The first of these points is plausible only with respect to voluntary image-formation; with respect to interpretive *phantasia* it seems far more debatable. The second distinction seems clearly untenable, at least with respect to some workings of the imagination: bad dreams or memories may be as terrifying as things judged terrible in reality. In comparing the imagining of terrible things with viewing them in a picture, Aristotle does not say, and is unlikely to mean, that we feel no emotion at all (cf. Belfiore [3.35], 243–5). For it would then be hard to explain the power of mimetic objects to stir our emotions, so clearly recognized in the *Poetics*. But the present text does suggest a distinction, perhaps implicit also at *Poetics* 53b12, between the full-scale pity or terror aroused by events judged to be real, and the 'distanced' feeling of those emotions in response to a representational work of art.

Aesthetic experience, however, receives virtually no attention in either *De Anima* or the *Parva Naturalia*. Their focus is upon the role of imagination in animal desire and goal-directed movement. Aristotle's interest, as usual, lies in the faculty's contribution to animal survival and well-being. This circumscribes his treatment rather narrowly. For the imagination, as we think of it, is not merely the capacity for forming images or interpreting experience. It includes creative or inventive powers, especially those displayed in mimetic works of art. Poetic fictions are pre-eminent among its products. Aristotle may, indeed, have recognized a connection between *phantasia* and artistic ability. He identifies aptitude for poetic metaphor with an inborn flair for 'seeing resemblances' (*Poetics* 1459a6–8), a gift which has obvious connections with interpretive *phantasia*. Yet he nowhere explores the role of that power in artistic creation as a subject in its own right.

Intellect

No aspect of Aristotle's thought is more controversial than his treatment of the intellect (*nous*). Nor is anything in his writings more puzzling or harder to reconcile with his wider philosophical outlook.

In general, as we have seen, he treats mental faculties as inseparable from their physical basis. In line with this, we should expect the intellect to be realized in an appropriate kind of matter, and therefore to exist only within a living human body. Aristotle sometimes entertains this view, especially when making thought dependent upon imagination. Thus he writes: 'But if this too [sc. thinking] is a form of imagination or does not exist apart from imagination, it would not be possible even for this to exist without the body' (*DA* 403a8–10). Since the soul is later declared never to think without imagery (*DA* 431a14–17), and since both practical and theoretical thinking are said to require imagery (*DA* 431b7–10, 432a8–14), we might infer that the intellect can exist only within a living human being. For thought requires imagination, imagination in turn requires perception, and both the latter powers are inseparable from a properly functioning body.

Yet Aristotle remains unwilling to draw that inference. His remarks about intellect are tentative in tone and cryptic in content, but they consistently postulate a special status for it, exempting it from material embodiment, hence from perishing: 'the intellect seems to be engendered in us as some sort of independent substance and not to be destroyed' (*DA* 408b18–19); unlike our capacity for memory or love, which ceases with bodily decay, 'the intellect is probably something more divine, and is unaffected' (*DA* 408b29); 'it seems to be a distinct kind of soul, and it alone admits of being separated, as the immortal is separable from the perishable' (*DA* 413b25–7); and, by contrast with powers requiring bodily activity (such as walking, nutrition, perception), 'it remains that only intellect enters from outside and only intellect is divine. For its activity is not bodily activity' (*De Generatione Animalium* 736b27–9; cf. *DA* 413a7, 429a22–7). Alone among our mental faculties, then, the intellect is no mere aspect of a form–matter composite, but is pure form without matter. Since it needs no material embodiment, it can exist separately from the body, and is therefore capable of surviving death. It has an equally privileged status in Aristotle's ethics, where its exercise in philosophical study (*theôria*) affords the highest happiness and the only immortality possible for mankind (*Nicomachean Ethics* 1177a11–18, 1177b26–1178a3).

Two factors, in particular, mark the intellect as exceptional. First, it requires no bodily organ for its exercise. In thinking we can apprehend all manner of objects, far and near, material and immaterial, sensible and abstract. Objects of thought, unlike those of perception, require no bodily apparatus to be apprehended. They are grasped directly, yet without physical contact. Moreover, thought, unlike perception or emotion, is attended by no bodily changes or processes of which we are conscious while we think.

Secondly, thinking is not restricted to human subjects, but is also, in Aristotle's larger scheme of things, a function of immaterial beings, including God, whose sole mode of activity it is. Human thinking is conceived, analogously, as the operation of a divine element within us, a substance in its own right, whereby we can imitate, albeit imperfectly and intermittently, the continuous and eternal thinking of God.

In an enigmatic chapter of *De Anima* (III.5) Aristotle distinguishes 'active' or 'productive' intellect from 'passive' intellect, and says of the former that 'in its separate state it alone is just that which it is, and it is this alone which is immortal and eternal' (430a22–3). The point of this distinction remains obscure, and it may not embody any doctrine that was ever clearly formulated by Aristotle himself. Possibly, he would have distinguished two levels of intellectual activity: (1) a mundane level at which thought requires images, is dependent upon the body, and must therefore perish with it; and (2) a loftier level at which neither images nor their bodily correlates are required, because the objects of thought are purely abstract or formal in nature. If the second level were the domain of the 'active' intellect, its capacity for separate existence might be defended (not very cogently), on the ground that imageless thought needs no physical embodiment. Aristotle's remarks suggest, however, that the active intellect is somehow operative in *all* human thinking, enabling even the passive intellect to function in its own domain. Without a divine operator at work in us, we could not think at all. Whether the operator is merely god-*like* or whether, as one tradition of commentary has maintained, it is to be identified with God himself, has been the subject of an age-old and still inconclusive debate (cf. Rist [3.33], 177–82).

That debate belongs more to the history of Aristotle's metaphysics and theology than to his philosophy of mind. One may in fact doubt whether he would ever have arrived at a doctrine of separable intellect had he been concerned with human psychology alone (cf. Wilkes [3.47], 116). The doctrine is so strongly redolent of Platonic dualism that many would happily write it off as an outmoded relic from an early stage of Aristotle's development. In view of its persistence throughout *De Anima*, and its appearance in the biological and ethical treatises, it cannot be so easily dismissed. Yet it remains in tension with the generally monistic tenor of Aristotle's psychology. He may well have been aware of the tension himself. For on this topic, above all, he gives the impression of wrestling with problems rather than presenting cut-and-dried solutions: 'concerning the intellect and the power of thinking, nothing is clear as yet' (DA 413b24–5). After more than two millennia, those words remain as true as ever.

In conclusion, we may recall Aristotle's characterization of the plot of tragedy as its 'soul' (*Poetics* 50a38–9). The full significance of that remark should now be apparent. We have seen that the soul of a living thing is the structure which enables a plant or an animal to exercise the powers characteristic of its species. Similarly, the plot of a tragedy is the structured nexus of events which enables the power characteristic of that genre to be exercised. Just as without soul there can be no living thing, so without plot there can be no tragedy. The declared aim of the *Poetics* is to examine the 'power' (*dunamis*) which each species of poetry possesses (47a8–9). A tragedy or an epic is designed to make a certain impact. Its 'soul' is the structure whereby it can move and enlighten its viewers concerning the vicissitudes of human life. A poetic fiction, like other mimetic objects, complements scientific inquiry into human powers, by displaying them at work and by engaging them in the service of self-understanding.

According to Aristotle's ethical teaching, human well-being lies in excellent 'activity of soul', i.e. in the best use of those capacities for rational thought and action by which mankind is differentiated. We have seen how those capacities are exercised with pleasure in the experience of poetic fiction, and of other mimetic objects. As representations of human behaviour, those objects depict, and give play to, the very powers which define their makers and their viewers. Through their distinctive appeal to the mind and the senses, they satisfy needs rooted in our nature. Hence the two themes of this chapter are, at bottom, interconnected. Aristotle's aesthetics complement, as they are also conditioned by, his philosophy of mind. His work in both fields reflects the naturalism which is the dominant strain in his thought, and the scientific outlook which is its hallmark.

NOTES

1 All references to the *Poetics* are to R. Kassel's text [3.5], with the initial '14' omitted from Bekker page-numbers. References to other Aristotelian treatises are to the relevant Oxford Classical Texts. Translations are my own unless otherwise noted.
2 For a fuller study of them, see Gallop [3.49]. With permission, some material from that study has been used below.
3 References to *De Anima* and the *Parva Naturalia* are to W.D. Ross's texts [3.12] and [3.14], with titles abbreviated to *DA* and *PN*. Translations are my own except where noted.
4 See Gallop [3.8], pp. 124–6. I draw upon this study occasionally below.

SELECT BIBLIOGRAPHY

ORIGINAL LANGUAGE TEXTS AND EDITIONS

Aesthetics

3.1 S.H. Butcher, *Aristotle's Theory of Poetry and Fine Art*, 4th edn, New York 1911; repr. New York 1951.
3.2 I. Bywater, *Aristotle on the Art of Poetry*, Oxford, Oxford University Press, 1909.

3.3 E.M. Cope, *The Rhetoric of Aristotle*, 3 vols, rev. J.E. Sandys, Cambridge, 1877.

3.4 G.F. Else, *Aristotle's Poetics: The argument*, Cambridge, Mass., Harvard University Press, 1957.

3.5 R. Kassel, ed., *Aristotelis De Arte Poetica Liber*, Oxford, Clarendon Press, 1965.

3.6 D.W. Lucas, ed., *Aristotle: 'Poetics'*, Greek text, with intro., notes and appendices, Oxford, Clarendon Press, 1968.

3.7 W.D. Ross, ed., *Aristotelis 'Ars Rhetorica'*, Oxford, Clarendon Press, 1959.

Philosophy of mind

3.8 D. Gallop, ed., *Aristotle on Sleep and Dreams*, with trans., intro., notes and glossary, Warminster, Aris and Phillips, 1996.

3.9 W.S. Hett, trans., *Aristotle's 'De Anima' and 'Parva Naturalia'*, Loeb Classical Library, London and Cambridge, Mass., Harvard University Press, 1936.

3.10 R.D. Hicks, ed., *Aristotle: 'De Anima'*, with trans., intro. and comm., Cambridge, Cambridge University Press, 1907.

3.11 M. Nussbaum, ed., *Aristotle, De Motu Animalium*, with trans., intro., comm. and exegetic essays, Princeton, Princeton University Press, 1978.

3.12 W.D. Ross, ed., *Aristotelis 'De Anima'*, Oxford, Clarendon Press, 1959.

3.13 —— ed., *De Anima*, with intro. and comm., Oxford, Clarendon Press, 1961.

3.14 —— ed., *Parva Naturalia*, with intro. and comm., Oxford, Clarendon Press, 1955.

3.15 P. Siwek, ed., *Parva Naturalia*, with Latin trans. and comm., Rome, 1963.

❧ ENGLISH TRANSLATIONS AND EDITIONS ❧

Complete works

3.16 J. Barnes, ed., *The Complete Works of Aristotle. The Revised Oxford Translation*, 2 vols, Princeton, Princeton University Press, 1984.

Separate works

Aesthetics

3.17 S. Halliwell, ed., *The Poetics of Aristotle*, trans. with intro. and comm., Chapel Hill, University of North Carolina Press, 1987.

3.18 M.E. Hubbard, trans., *Poetics*, in D.A. Russell and M. Winterbottom (eds), *Ancient Literary Criticism*, Oxford, Oxford University Press, 1972.

3.19 J. Hutton, ed., *Aristotle's 'Poetics'*, with trans., intro. and notes, New York, W.W. Norton and Co., 1982.

3.20 R. Janko, ed., *Aristotle: 'Poetics'*, with trans., intro. and notes, Indianapolis, Hackett, 1987.

3.21 G.A. Kennedy, *Aristotle on the Art of Rhetoric: A theory of civic discourse*, trans. with intro., notes and appendices, Oxford, Oxford University Press, 1991.

Philosophy of mind

3.22 K. Foster and S. Humphries, trans., *Aristotle's 'De Anima' in the Version of William of Moerbeke and the Commentary of St. Thomas Aquinas*, New Haven and London, Yale University Press, 1951.

3.23 D.W. Hamlyn, ed., *Aristotle's 'De Anima', Books II and III (with parts of Book I)*, with trans., intro. and notes, Oxford, Clarendon Press, 1968.

3.24 H. Lawson-Tancred, ed., *Aristotle: 'De Anima'*, with trans., intro. and notes, Harmondsworth, Penguin, 1986.

3.25 R. Sorabji, ed., *Aristotle on Memory*, trans. with intro. and notes, London, Duckworth, 1972.

ANTHOLOGIES AND BIBLIOGRAPHIES

3.26 J. Barnes *et al.*, eds, *Articles on Aristotle*, vol. iv, Psychology and Aesthetics, London, Duckworth, 1979. [Bibliography, pp. 187–90.]

3.27 A.O. Rorty, ed., *Essays on Aristotle's 'Poetics'*, Princeton, Princeton University Press, 1992. [Bibliography, pp. 425–35.]

3.28 M.C. Nussbaum and A.O. Rorty, eds, *Essays on Aristotle's 'Philosophy of Mind'*, Oxford, Clarendon Press, 1992. [Bibliography, pp. 401–19.]

See also chs 6 and 9 of [1.39] J. Barnes, ed., *The Cambridge Companion to Aristotle* (1995) with bibliographies at pp. 337–45 and 379–84. Comprehensive Bibliographies are given also in works by E. Belfiore and S. Halliwell listed below ([3.35], 365–80 and [3.37], 357–64).

GENERAL STUDIES OF ARISTOTLE'S THOUGHT

3.29 J.L. Ackrill, *Aristotle the Philosopher*, Oxford, Oxford University Press, 1981. [Esp. ch. 5.]

3.30 D.J. Allan, *The Philosophy of Aristotle*, Oxford, Oxford University Press, 1949; 2nd edn 1970. [Esp. ch. 6.]

3.31 J. Barnes, *Aristotle*, Oxford, Oxford University Press, 1982. [Esp. chs 15 and 19.]

3.32 G.E.R. Lloyd, *Aristotle: The growth and structure of his thought*, Cambridge, Cambridge University Press, 1968. [Esp. chs 9 and 12.]

3.33 J.M. Rist, *The Mind of Aristotle: A study in philosophical growth*, Toronto, University of Toronto Press, 1990. [Esp. ch. 9.]

3.34 W.D. Ross, *Aristotle*, London, Methuen, 1923. [Esp. chs 5 and 9.]

❧ OTHER BOOKS ❧

Aesthetics

3.35   E. Belfiore, *Tragic Pleasures: Aristotle on plot and emotion*, Princeton, Princeton University Press, 1992.

3.36   R.G. Collingwood, *The Philosophy of Art*, Oxford, Oxford University Press, 1938. [Esp. ch. 3.]

3.37   S. Halliwell, *Aristotle's 'Poetics'*, Chapel Hill, University of North Carolina Press, 1986.

3.38   H. House, *Aristotle's 'Poetics': A course of eight lectures*, revised with preface by C. Hardie, London, Hart-Davis, 1956.

3.39   M. Nussbaum, *The Fragility of Goodness: Luck and ethics in Greek tragedy and philosophy*, Cambridge, Cambridge University Press, 1986. [Esp. pp. 378–91.]

3.40   E. Schaper, *A Prelude to Aesthetics*, London, Allen and Unwin, 1968. [Esp. ch. 3.]

Philosophy of mind

3.41   J.I. Beare, *Greek Theories of Elementary Cognition*, Oxford, Oxford University Press, 1906.

3.42   W.W. Fortenbaugh, *Aristotle on Emotion*, London, Duckworth, 1975.

3.43   W.F.R. Hardie, *Aristotle's Ethical Theory*, Oxford, Oxford University Press, 2nd edn 1980, chs 5 and 16.

3.44   G.E.R. Lloyd and G.E.L. Owen (eds), *Aristotle on Mind and the Senses*, Cambridge, Cambridge University Press, 1978.

3.45   D. Modrak, *Aristotle: The power of perception*, Chicago, 1987.

3.46   F. Nuyens, *L'Évolution de la psychologie d'Aristote*, Louvain, 1948 (originally published in Flemish, 1939).

3.47   K.V. Wilkes, *Physicalism*, Atlantic Highlands, N.J., Humanities Press, 1978. [Esp. ch. 7.]

❧ ARTICLES AND CHAPTERS ❧

Aesthetics

3.48   J. Bernays, 'Aristotle on the effect of tragedy', English trans. J. and J. Barnes from *Zwei Abhandlungen über die aristotelische Theorie des Drama* (Berlin, 1880; first published Breslau, 1857), in [3.26], 154–65.

3.49   D. Gallop, 'Animals in the *Poetics*', *Oxford Studies in Ancient Philosophy* 8, ed. J. Annas (1990), 145–71.

3.50   L. Golden, '*Mimêsis* and *Katharsis*', *Classical Philology*, lxiv 3 (1969), 145–53.

3.51   S. Halliwell, 'Pleasure, Understanding and Emotion in Aristotle's *Poetics*', in [3.27], 241–60.

3.52 R. Janko, 'From Catharsis to the Aristotelian Mean', in [3.27], 341–58.
3.53 J. Lear, 'Katharsis', *Phronesis* xxxiii 3 (1988), 297–326, repr. in [3.27], 315–40.
3.54 F.E. Sparshott, 'The Riddle of *Katharsis*', in *Centre and Labyrinth: Essays in honour of Northrop Frye*, ed. E. Cook *et al.* (Toronto, University of Toronto Press, 1983), 14–37.
3.55 S. White, 'Aristotle's favourite tragedies', in [3.27], 221–40.

Philosophy of mind

3.56 J.L. Ackrill, 'Aristotle's definitions of *Psuchê*', *Proceedings of the Aristotelian Society* 73 (1972–73), 119–33, repr. in [3.26], 65–75.
3.57 J. Barnes, 'Aristotle's concept of mind', *Proceedings of the Aristotelian Society* 72 (1971–72), 101–14, repr. in [3.26], 32–41.
3.58 I. Block, 'The order of Aristotle's psychological writings', *American Journal of Philology* 82 (1961), 50–77.
3.59 M.F. Burnyeat, 'Is an Aristotelian philosophy of mind still credible? (a draft)', in [3.28], 15–26.
3.60 D. Gallop, 'Aristotle on sleep, dreams, and final causes', *Proceedings of the Boston Area Colloquium in Ancient Philosophy*, vol. iv (1988), eds J.J. Cleary and D.C. Shartin (Lanham 1989), 257–90.
3.61 W.F.R. Hardie, 'Aristotle's treatment of the relation between soul and body', *Philosophical Quarterly* 14 (1964), 53–72.
3.62 D.S. Hutchinson, 'Restoring the order of Aristotle's *De Anima*', *Classical Quarterly* 37 (ii) (1987), 373–81.
3.63 C.H. Kahn, 'Sensation and consciousness in Aristotle's psychology', *Archiv für Geschichte der Philosophie* 48 (1966), 43–81, repr. in [3.26], 1–31.
3.64 M.C. Nussbaum and H. Putnam, 'Changing Aristotle's mind', in [3.28], 27–56.
3.65 M. Schofield, 'Aristotle on the imagination', in [3.44], 99–129, repr. in [3.26], 103–32.
3.66 R.K. Sorabji, 'Body and soul in Aristotle', *Philosophy* 49 (1974), 63–89, repr. in [3.26], 42–64.

CHAPTER 4

Aristotle: Ethics and politics

❦

⟡ ETHICS ⟡

Roger Crisp

❧ BACKGROUND AND METHOD ❧

Aristotle wrote no books on ethics. Rather, he gave lectures, the notes for which subsequently were turned by others into two books, the *Nicomachean Ethics* (*NE*) and the *Eudemian Ethics* (*EE*). There is much dispute over the relative dating and merit of these works, but the traditional view is that the *Nicomachean Ethics* represents Aristotle's philosophical views on ethics in their more developed form, perhaps at around 330 BC, the *Eudemian Ethics* probably having been composed earlier for a more popular audience (though see Kenny [4.12]). There is a third ethical work sometimes attributed to Aristotle, the *Magna Moralia*, but this is probably post-Aristotelian.

NE contains ten 'books', while *EE* contains eight. Oddly, they have books in common: books 4–6 of *EE* are the same as books 5–7 of *NE*. Scholarly disagreement has focused particularly on which work these books properly belong to. Controversy continues, but the more widely held view, based on study of Aristotle's discussion of pleasure in the common books, is that they belong to the *EE*.

It is *NE* which has traditionally been studied, along with the common books, so it is on that work that we shall concentrate. But *EE* should not be ignored by serious readers of Aristotle. Its differences from *NE* are subtle and interesting, and even if *EE* is earlier, it illuminates how Aristotle's ethical thought developed. Whatever the relation between the works, it cannot be denied that *NE* is one of the most important works in ethics ever composed, both from the historical point of view and that of contemporary moral philosophy.

Aristotle lectured in a room containing a three-legged table, wooden sofas, a whiteboard, and a bronze statue and globe. On the walls were, among other things, lists of virtues and vices, and depictions of Socrates. His audience would have consisted primarily of young men, of more than humble origin, who might hope to make their way in a career that was at least partly political. As Aristotle spoke from his notes, it is almost certain that he would have expanded upon or clarified certain points, perhaps in response to questions from his audience. The style in which we have *NE* has had the result that much Aristotelian scholarship has been, and continues to be, pure interpretation of what he says. But in the last few decades in particular, his views have been seen as the foundation for a modern ethics, based on virtue.

Aristotle's audience would have been able to make a difference to fourth-century Athens, and *NE* is explicitly practical in intent. This is most certainly not an anthropological work, attempting dispassionate study of the common morality of the day. Aristotle, like Socrates and Plato before him, believed that certain aspects of that common morality were deeply mistaken. He wished to persuade his readers of this, intellectually and practically: 'Our present study is not, like the others, for intellectual purposes. For we are inquiring into what virtue is not so that we may know, but to become good men, since otherwise it would be pointless' (1103b26–9).

What, for Aristotle, is ethics? A modern work on ethics will concern duties, obligations, responsibilities, rights. Those notions do have analogues in Aristotle's ethical treatises, but he is primarily concerned with the question of the good life for human beings. The central ethical question for Greek philosophers was not, 'What morally ought I to do or not to do?', but, 'What is *eudaimonia*?' *Eudaimonia* is usually translated as 'happiness', and we shall conform to that usage (see Kraut [4.22]). But some prefer to use notions such as 'well-being' or 'flourishing', in order to remove any implication that *eudaimonia* is a matter of contentment or short-term pleasure. It should not be forgotten, either, that *daimon* is Greek for 'luck', and that *eu* means 'well'. In *NE* 1.9, indeed, Aristotle discusses the question of whether happiness is merely a matter of good fortune.

Greek culture was a culture of excellence, in the sense that young men were widely encouraged to compete with one another in many areas of life, including, of course, athletic, intellectual and aesthetic activity. (The Greek word for excellence, *aretê*, has its root in *anêr*, 'man', as opposed to 'woman'.) One of the central questions asked by Socrates, who provided the inspiration for Plato and hence the whole of Western philosophy, was, 'What is *aretê*?' *Aretê* has traditionally been translated 'virtue', and we shall again conform to tradition. But it should be remembered that, according to ancient Greek usage, a horse that ran fast or a knife that cut well could be said to have an *aretê*, as could a person who told good jokes, as we shall see below.

110

Greek philosophers, then, were concerned to map the relations of happiness and virtue. Most of what we know of Socrates is through the depiction of him in Plato's dialogues, but from these it appears that Socrates held that virtue is knowledge. This has the implication, as radical then as now, that the person who performs a vicious action does so out of ignorance. Socrates held also that knowledge, virtue and happiness were very closely related, and, indeed, put his view dramatically into practice. Given the chance to escape the death penalty imposed upon him by the city of Athens, he chose to remain, believing virtue to be 'the most precious possession a man can have' (Plato, *Crito*, 53c7).

Plato continued the Socratic tradition, identifying *dikaiosunê* (usually translated 'justice', though the term covers morality more broadly) with an ordering of the parts of the soul in which reason governs desire and the emotions. For both Socrates and Plato, then, virtue was an extremely important component in human happiness, just how important being a central issue in modern discussions. Aristotle is most plausibly seen as working within the same tradition, asking the same sorts of questions and employing the same sorts of concepts, though his account is of course informed by the philosophical apparatus he developed in other areas of his own thought. Two things set him apart from Socrates and Plato. First, and here again we meet Aristotle's emphasis on practicality, virtue itself is of no value; what matters is actually performing virtuous actions. Secondly, for Aristotle virtuous activity is the only component of happiness. Again, this has some very radical philosophical implications.

The methods of the three philosophers were, however, quite different. Socrates proceeded by asking questions of those around him, and then subjecting the answers he received to searching scrutiny. Plato wrote his philosophy down, in the form of dialogues between Socrates and others. But in his later work, the dialogue form is merely a way to express his own radical metaphysical and moral views. Aristotle was quite reflective about method in ethics, and *NE* 1145b2–7 is one of his clearest statements. Here he says that, when considering an ethical issue, one should first set out (*tithenai*) the *phainomena* (which here means the views long accepted by most people, and the views of philosophers), then formulate the *aporiai* or puzzles that emerge, and finally do one's best to resolve these puzzles in the light of the original *phainomena*.

The way Aristotle goes on to treat the problem of *akrasia* just after this statement is a good example of this method at work. (For our purposes, we can translate *akrasia* as 'weakness of will', though we should not forget that there is some dispute about whether the Greeks had a concept of the will.) On the one hand, nearly everyone accepts that reason can come into conflict with desire, and lose. I know that this large cream cake will make me feel sick, but my desire for it is such that I cannot resist. On the other hand, because virtue is knowledge, Socrates refused to allow that people knowingly took what they knew to be the worse course of action. Aristotle seeks to resolve the puzzle by suggesting that people do indeed do what they know to be worse, but that they 'know' only in an attenuated sense. When I say, 'I know this cake is going to make me sick', I am merely spouting the words, like a drunk or an actor on stage, without a full grip on their content.

Aristotle faces the problem all philosophers face, that he can set out the views of others and the philosophical problems that arise only from his own perspective. It can be questioned whether he really keeps to his methodological principles, and, if so, whether he is not heading in the direction of conservatism. There is no doubt that the *tithenai* method is often quite far from his mind, when he is engaging in straightforward philosophical argument, based either on premises from elsewhere in his philosophy or on what is generally believed. But even here, as we shall see in the case of his discussion of happiness, he is keen to show that his view chimes with the views of the many and the wise. That is something Socrates and Plato in their ethics never tried to do. They have more in common with those moral philosophers known as 'intuitionists', who suggest that there are certain fundamental truths about ethics which many people cannot see. Aristotle's moral epistemology has some similarity to the forms of 'coherentism' which dominate contemporary philosophy, such as the 'reflective equilibrium' of John Rawls, which attempts to bring philosophical principles into harmony with our reactions to particular cases (see Rawls [4.52]). But, as already suggested, some of Aristotle's views in ethics, and indeed in politics (see below), were far from conservative.

Aristotle's audience, as we saw, would have consisted primarily of well-off young men. They also had to be well brought-up. There is no point, Aristotle suggests, in those who are too young to understand ethics coming to lectures on the subject. In that respect, ethics is unlike mathematics, where prodigies are possible. The reason is that ethical understanding comes not only through philosophy, but first through ethical activity itself. We learn by doing. So to benefit from Aristotle's lectures – to become better – you will need what he calls *to hoti*, 'the that', a basic grasp of the notions of virtue, happiness, and all that they entail. After reflection, aided by the lectures, will come *to dihoti*, 'the because', an understanding of the principles that lie behind ethics (*NE* 1095b6–7).

Because of the importance of practical experience, ethics is unlike mathematics in its capacity for precision (and the same goes for politics: see pp. 127, 133). This is something that Aristotle stresses several times early in *NE* (1.3; 1098a20–b8). A mathematics lecture can tell you exactly how to carry out a particular differential calculus, but an ethics lecture can give you only rough guidance on how to act in a particular case. The circumstances of human life are indefinitely complex and unpredictable, to the point that often experience is the only guide. As we shall see below, cultivating the intellectual virtue of *phronêsis* ('practical wisdom') will consist partly in developing a sensitivity to the salient features of particular cases that does not consist in mechanically subsuming the case under an explicit rule one has learned.

This aspect of Aristotle's understanding of ethics also explains something that some of his readers find peculiar. The core of *NE*, rather than offering us sets of principles or rules, consists in a set of portraits of the virtuous man. The point of these portraits, however, is to enable us to 'latch on' to the nature of the virtue in question, and what it requires, so as better to be able to develop and to practise that virtue ourselves.

❧ HAPPINESS ❧

Aristotle is keen to point out to the potential politicians in his audience that ethics is a preliminary to politics (*NE* 1.2). He places the fields of human understanding in a hierarchy, those above in the hierarchy governing those below. At the top is politics, which governs the other disciplines in that it legislates when they are to be studied. Now the point of studying ethics is to understand the nature of individual human happiness; this is the 'end' of studying ethics. Politics will include that end, in the sense that it will decide how the human good is to be pursued within a city, and how the good of one person is to be balanced against that of another.

Just as now, there was no shortage of views in fourth-century Athens concerning the human good. Aristotle splits the most common of these views into three (*NE* 1.5). First, he suggests, most people identify happiness with pleasure (this is the view known as hedonism). Aristotle dismisses the life of pleasure as the life of an animal, leaving it to later philosophers such as Epicurus and John Stuart Mill to draw attention to conceptions of happiness that stressed the non-bodily pleasures. Politicians are more sophisticated, he claims, seeing happiness as consisting in honour, the second view. This, however, is to be rejected because it depends on the opinions of others. We tend to believe that the basis of happiness is not as fragile as this. And, anyway, people pursue honour only to assure themselves of their own goodness, so that virtue is prior to honour. But virtue cannot be happiness either, since one could be in a coma or suffering the worst evils and be virtuous, and no one would count a person in such a position as happy. The third type of life Aristotle mentions is the contemplative life, and this receives substantial discussion at the end of *NE* (10.7–8).

We can already see how Aristotle allows commonly accepted views about happiness – such as that the person in a coma cannot be happy – to shape the argument alongside his own philosophical arguments – such as that virtue is prior to honour. The two methodologies come together shortly afterwards in his putting certain conceptual constraints on the notion of happiness, which are intended to be uncontroversial (1097a15–1097b21). Again, the notion of a hierarchy of goods or ends is central. Some goods or ends are clearly subordinate, or less 'final' (*teleios*), than others. When I go to town to buy a flute, my goal – the flute – is merely subordinate to some other goal, such as enjoying music. The highest good, Aristotle suggests, is thought to be unconditionally final, in the sense that it is never sought for anything else, while other things are sought for it. Happiness is unconditionally final, since we choose it for itself and not for other things, while we choose other things – flutes, honour, pleasure, the lot – for the sake of being happy.

The notion of 'self-sufficiency' (*autarkeia*) was important in the philosophical world at the time *NE* was composed, and Aristotle points out how reflection upon this notion shows us something about the nature of happiness: 'We take a self-sufficient thing to be what, on its own, makes life worthy of choice and lacking in nothing; and this is what we think happiness does' (1097b14–16). Again, then, happiness is final. Nor should happiness be counted as one good among others, since then it would not be self-sufficient or the most worthy of choice of all goods. For it would always be improvable.

Quite what Aristotle means here has been subject to a great deal of philosophical discussion (see, for example, Ackrill [4.18]; Crisp [4.20]; Keyt [4.24]; Kenny [4.23]; Kraut [4.22]). On one view, ascribing to Aristotle what is called the dominant view of happiness, he is arguing that happiness must be the most worthy of choice of all goods, and so superior to other goods. As we shall see below, there are strong reasons for identifying such a good with 'contemplation' (*theôria*). On another view, Aristotle holds an inclusive view of happiness, believing it to be the most final good in the sense that it includes all others. Flutes, honour, pleasure, and so on, are all, in some sense, parts of happiness.

The inclusive view, on the face of it, seems to fit better with Aristotle's stress on a hierarchy of ends the higher items of which 'include' (*periechoi*, *NE* 1094b6) those below. His famous 'function' argument, which we shall discuss below, does throw up a serious problem for the inclusivist interpretation, but we should first attempt to be clearer about just what notion of inclusion is in play.

Help is at hand in the form of Aristotle's discussion of Eudoxus at *NE* 1172b23–34. Eudoxus had argued that pleasure was the good (that is, the highest good), since pleasure, when added to any other good, makes it more worthy of choice, and the good is increased by the addition of itself. This is a poor argument, of course, but what matters here is Aristotle's comment upon it. He says that all Eudoxus proves is that pleasure is one of the goods, and goes on to note that Plato uses the same sort of argument to show that pleasure is not the good. The pleasant life, Plato argued, is more worthy of choice when combined with wisdom, so it is not the good. For the good is such that nothing can be added to it to make it more choiceworthy.

Aristotle does not mean in his claims about finality either that a happy life has to contain all the goods or that a happy life cannot be improved upon.

The discussion of Eudoxus and Plato shows that he is primarily thinking of conceptions of happiness when he speaks of inclusion. A conception of happiness – that is, a list of the things that happiness consists in – must be complete. If I can add some good (such as wisdom) to a proposed list, then that list is, to that extent, faulty. So the correct conception of happiness must include all the goods there are. As we shall now see, this poses a serious problem of interpretation of Aristotle's own view.

Having set out the conceptual requirements on any conception of happiness, Aristotle suggests that we may be able to identify exactly what happiness consists in if we can discover the *ergon*, or 'function', of a human being (*NE* 1097b24–1098a20). Again, though there are problems with it, 'function' is the traditional translation here, so we shall continue to use it. The *ergon* of X is X's characteristic activity, the sort of thing engaging in which makes X what it is. Thus, the *ergon* of a knife is to cut. That is also its function, of course, but the notion of function introduces the notion of some external purpose which is not present in the Greek.

What, then, is the function, the characteristic activity, of a human being? It cannot be nutrition or growth, since these are common to humans and plants. Nor can it be sense-perception, since that is common to humans and other animals. All that is left is rationality or reason. Now the function of a lyre-player is to play the lyre, and the function of a good lyre-player to play the lyre well. So if we assume that the human function is that activity of the soul that expresses reason, then the good man's function is to do this well. Doing anything well is doing it while expressing a virtue, so the human good turns out to be that activity of the soul that expresses virtue.

Happiness, then, is virtuous action. This explains why Aristotle spends most of *NE*, a work concerning happiness, offering accounts of the nature of virtuous action. Before going on to consider the conclusion of the function argument in the light of the conceptual requirements that precede it, let us first consider the function argument itself. Aristotle's argument here is a form of perfectionism, that is, a view which holds that the human good consists in the perfection of human nature. An old objection to his argument is its proceeding by elimination. Why should the human function not include, say, sense-perception? And how can excelling in rational activity be characteristic of human beings when the gods engage in just such activity?

This objection, however, fails to take into account an obvious assumption lying behind the function argument, namely that plants and animals are not the sort of beings to which we ascribe happiness. So, given that humans are happy, it makes sense to seek the characteristic that distinguishes humans from plants and animals. True, this characteristic may be, indeed is, shared with the gods, but that does not matter for the purposes of the argument here.

Another objection is more serious. Aristotle, it is said, forgets the distinction between 'the good man' and 'the good for man' (Glassen [4.21]).

I may well accept that the good or paradigm example of a human being is one whose life exemplifies the virtues. But it does not follow that such a life is the best life for the person who lives it. For it could be that by going against one's nature one can obtain a life that is better for oneself.

Finally, there is a general concern about perfectionist arguments as a whole, that they come too late. Most perfectionists imply that they are carrying out an independent inquiry into human nature, and then allowing their conception of the human good to be shaped in the light of their understanding of human nature. But all too often it can be suggested that the perfectionist is allowing his already-formed views of what happiness consists in to guide his conception of human nature itself. So the notion of human nature is left as a wheel spinning idly. In our conclusion below, we shall discuss the important role the notion of human nature plays in Aristotle's politics, and raise a similar concern.

There are, then, problems with the function argument. But the function argument is not Aristotle's only way of arguing for his conception of happiness as virtuous activity. As we suggested, the portraits he paints of the attractions of the virtuous life, and the bad features of the vicious life, particularly in the middle books of *NE*, can be seen as speaking in favour of the virtuous life.

Two further problems concerning Aristotle's conception of happiness remain. The first concerns the relation between the conceptual requirement of inclusiveness and the idea that happiness consists in virtuous activity. Recall how the argument of Plato referred to in the Eudoxus discussion worked. If I suggest that happiness consists in pleasure, my claim can be refuted by showing that a life that contains wisdom as well as pleasure is better than a life which contains (the same amount of) pleasure. My list is incomplete, and I must add wisdom to it. The conclusion of the function argument leaves Aristotle with one item on his list: virtuous activity. Why should we not criticize him in the same way, by insisting that he add other goods, such as pleasure, wisdom or friendship, to his list?

Arisotle's response here would be that virtuous activity itself includes these goods (*NE* 1.8). The virtuous man will find true pleasure in virtuous actions, the exercise of virtue essentially involves wisdom, and friendship is one of the virtues. Aristotle even has a response to those who suggest that happiness requires 'external goods', such as money. For virtuous action will itself require such goods. You cannot, for example, be generous unless you have something to be generous with.

Aristotle's view of happiness, however, does have a very radical implication, so radical that it throws some doubt on the plausibility of the view. According to Aristotle's account of happiness, there is nothing good in the life of the vicious person, since happiness consists in virtuous activity. This is a brave and interesting claim, and solidly within the Socratic–Platonic tradition, but it is too strong. Aristotle's response to the objection just discussed above fails properly to individuate goods. For him to demonstrate that pleasure need not be added to the list, he has to show not only that virtuous activity involves pleasure, but that there is no pleasure independent of virtuous activity. This, however, would seem very hard to support. Can the vicious man not enjoy a good meal as much as the virtuous man? Some pleasures, and some other goods, are independent of virtuous activity, and will provide some rationale for the vicious life. Aristotle would then have to retreat to the less exciting, but more plausible, view that virtuous action offers the best prospects of happiness. This, however, would be enough for his view to be of practical import for his audience.

The other problem of interpretation concerns the relation between the virtues 'of character' – courage, generosity, and so on – and the activity of contemplation. Aristotle begins *NE* 10.7 as follows: 'If happiness is activity expressing virtue, it is reasonable that it express the highest. This will be the virtue of the best thing.' He goes on to suggest that the 'best thing' is understanding (*nous*), the activity expressing which is contemplation (*theôria*), and to defend the claim at length that contemplation is 'final' (*teleios*) happiness.

There are many interpretations available of these claims of Aristotle, from the idea that he is straightforwardly inconsistent in his views concerning happiness to the notion that these chapters are an 'end-of-term joke', at the expense of Plato (Ackrill [4.18]; Moline [4.26]). One of the most common views has been that contemplation is indeed what Aristotle has meant all along by virtuous activity: the function argument does, after all, conclude that, if there are more virtues than one, happiness will be that which expresses the best and 'most final' (*NE* 1098a17–18).

Aristotle throws dust in our eyes by attempting in *NE* to answer several questions at once. One is the question of what goes on the list of goods that constitute happiness, and his answer there is virtuous activity. Such activity can involve either contemplation or the virtues of character, and happiness can be found in either (1178a9). Another question, however, is, given this conception of happiness, which activity is the most conducive to happiness. And here his answer is, in the ordinary way of things, contemplation.

It may have been that some in Aristotle's audience were disappointed by the conclusion of *NE*. For Aristotle gives no explicit guidance on which kind of life to go for, that of the philosopher or of the politician. But he would have argued that which life is likely to be the happiest for any one individual depends on the particular circumstances of the case. His general advice is that contemplation is peculiarly valuable, so if one is capable of it in any reasonable degree, the life of the philosopher is probably the one to aim for. But if one is not a talented thinker but an excellent politician, one should probably choose the life of action. And there is nothing to prevent one, in the manner perhaps of Plato's 'philosopher kings', attempting to combine both activities within the same life.

To sum up our discussion so far. Aristotle's enquiry is essentially a political one, concerning the running of a city. Political arrangements will be concerned with the promotion of human happiness, and this turns out to be virtuous activity. So from happiness, we are, like Aristotle, led into discussing virtue. And virtue, Aristotle points out (*NE* 1102a7–13), is again anyway a central topic of politics, since the 'true politician' spends more time on attempting to instantiate virtue in his citizenry than on anything else.

❧ VIRTUE ❧

Happiness is virtuous activity, and virtuous activity is activity of the soul. So it is important, Aristotle says, for the politician to have some understanding of the soul itself (*NE* 1.13). The soul can be divided into rational and nonrational parts. The rational part, with which, for example, we contemplate, is correlated with the 'intellectual virtues', the most important of which in connection with ethics is *phronesis*, or 'practical wisdom'. The nonrational part can be subdivided, one of its subdivisions being concerned with nutrition and growth. The other part, however, has more in common with reason. We know that it exists, as Plato pointed out in the *Republic*, because there is something in us that struggles with reason in certain circumstances, such as when we are weak-willed. This part is also capable of obeying reason, as in the case of the continent man. Its virtues, the 'virtues of character', are courage, generosity, temperance, and so on. *NE* is concerned primarily with the virtues of character, though, as we shall see below, intellectual virtues have an important role to play in full virtue.

Virtue of thought comes mostly from teaching, and there are some cases in which it is acquired very early. Think, for example, of a mathematical prodigy. But the virtues of character arise through habit (*ethos*) (*NE* 2.1). Teaching, of course, is important in steering people into the correct habits, but there is nothing in acquiring virtue analogous to the 'flash of inspiration' one finds in learning mathematics. Becoming virtuous is more like learning a skill, such as building. One learns to build a wall by doing it, and if one does it well, one will become a good builder. So performing just actions or courageous actions will result in one's becoming just or courageous. Since the habits we get into are very much a result of the guidance we receive, it is essential for the moral educator – a parent at the individual level, a politician at the social level – to understand the role of habit.

Someone might here raise a puzzle (*NE* 2.4). Surely, a person who is building is already a builder, and similarly someone who is performing just or generous actions is already virtuous? Aristotle points out that someone learning to build may just be following instructions, and notes that, for an agent to be virtuous, he must not only perform virtuous actions, but perform them in the right way: knowing what he is doing, choosing them for their own sake, and doing them out of a well-grounded disposition.

The second of these three conditions provides a possible link between Aristotle's ethics and the later ethics of Immanuel Kant (1724–1804). According to Kant, moral worth attaches to an action only in so far as it is motivated by respect for the moral law. This has seemed objectionable to some philosophers, who believe, for example, that an action motivated by a loving concern for another person is morally praiseworthy. Here we find Aristotle telling us that a virtuous action is chosen for its own sake, not, for example, so that another person can be helped. Elsewhere he says that the virtuous man chooses virtuous actions for the sake of *to kalon*, 'the fine' or 'the noble' (*NE* 1115b12–13), and it is plausible to see this as, for him, equivalent to choosing them for their own sake. Again, however, there is no reference to concern for others: the focus is on oneself and on the quality of one's actions.

Virtues, then, are dispositions (*hexeis*), engendered in us through practice. Aristotle characterizes the nature of virtue using his famous 'doctrine of the mean' (*NE* 2.6). The idea of the mean had developed in Greek medicine, the basic thought being that the different bodily elements should be neither excessive nor deficient, but in harmony. Aristotle was probably influenced also by Plato's conception in the *Republic* of the harmony of the elements in the best soul. Virtue of character aims at the mean in the following way:

> We can, for example, be afraid or be confident, or desire, or feel anger or pity, or in general feel pleasure and pain both too much and too little, and in both ways not well; but at the right times, about the right things, towards the right people, for the right end, and in the right way, is what is intermediate and best, and this is proper to virtue. Likewise, there is an excess, a deficiency and a mean in the case of actions as well.
>
> (*NE* 1106b18–24)

It is important to be clear that Aristotle is not advocating here a doctrine of moderation. In the case of anger, for example, one should be moderate only if moderate anger is required in the circumstances. In some cases, such as a mild slight, mere crossness will be called for, in others, absolute fury. It all depends on the case.

In the case of anger, then, the person with the virtue of even temper will feel angry at the right times, about the right things, in the right degree and so on. Imagine that something happens to me at three o'clock, the reasonable and virtuous response to which is anger. How is this 'in a mean'? For Aristotle cannot intend us to think that it is in a mean between getting angry at two o'clock and getting angry at four o'clock!

In the case of anger, you can err in two ways regarding when you get angry. You can get angry when you should not, or you can fail to get angry when you should. Both will be vicious, and if you have a disposition to either, you have a vice. The same goes for the other conditions: you can get angry with the wrong people, or fail to get angry with the right people, get angry for the wrong reasons, or fail to get angry for the right reasons, and so on. So, as Aristotle says, there is only one way to get it right, but many ways to go wrong (*NE* 1106b28–35).

The passage quoted above primarily concerns feelings, and some authors have written as if there is a feeling underlying each of Aristotle's virtues of character. But this is not so, for example, in the case of a central virtue, generosity (*NE* 4.1). In fact, more to the fore in Aristotle's discussions of the individual virtues are the actions that exemplify them. And our account above shows how to understand the notion of an action's being in a mean. Generosity is concerned with the giving away of money. The generous man is the one who gives it away, for example, at the right times, whereas the prodigal man will give it away at the wrong times, and the ungenerous man will fail to give it away when he should.

It is sometimes suggested that there is something almost tautologous about the doctrine of the mean: you should do what is right, and what is right is what is not wrong (see Barnes [4.15]). But in fact the doctrine of the mean represents an important ethical discovery by Aristotle. He divides human life into certain central 'spheres', concerning the control of money, social life, sexual desire, common emotions such as anger or fear, and so on, and notices that there is a right way to act or to feel in each of these spheres, depending on the circumstances. And unlike an ethics of constraint (a list of 'don'ts'), Aristotle sees that ethics requires positive action or feeling, not mere avoidance. Each sphere is, as it were, neutrally characterized: if I know that you have given away money, I cannot yet tell whether that is vicious. The virtuous man is the one who acts and feels well, and the vicious are those who perform the same actions and feel the same feelings at the wrong time or in the wrong way, or fail to do so when they should.

What, then, are the virtues of character, according to Aristotle, and what are their spheres? Consider the following table:

Virtue	Sphere	Discussion in NE
Courage	Fear and confidence	3.6–9
Temperance	Bodily pleasure and pain	3.10–12
Generosity	Giving and taking money	4.1
Magnificence	Giving and taking money on a large scale	4.2
Magnanimity	Honour on a large scale	4.3
(Nameless)	Honour on a small scale	4.4

Even temper	Anger	4.5
Friendliness	Social relations	4.6
Truthfulness	Honesty about oneself	4.7
Wit	Conversation	4.8

Aristotle also briefly discusses shame, which he says is not really a virtue, and righteous indignation (*NE* 1108a30–b6; 4.9). He devotes the whole of book 5 to justice, and his notorious attempts to force this virtue into his framework fail (1133b29–1134a13). The reason for this should be clear from our discussion above: in the case of justice there is no neutrally characterizable action or feeling which the virtuous man can do or feel at the right time. Books 8 and 9 of *NE* concern another virtue, *philia*, usually translated as 'friendship', though it is in fact wider than this.

Justice, then, is a problem with the doctrine, and there are more technical difficulties with particular virtues such as courage. But the doctrine of the mean on the whole provides Aristotle with a sound framework in which to discuss and systematize the virtues and vices. The list is interesting, in that it contains nothing corresponding to what we might call benevolence or kindness, a general concern for others at large. Some have said that this demonstrates the size of the cultural gap between pre- and post-Judaeo-Christian societies. But one might suggest that the core of the virtue of benevolence is located elsewhere by Aristotle, primarily in the virtue of friendship. The Aristotelian virtuous man may perhaps be excessively concerned with 'the fine', but this does not make him heartless. It has to be admitted that the notion of general benevolent concern for humanity at large does not play any significant role in Aristotle's ethics. But it must also be admitted that general benevolent concern, as opposed to concern for those with whom the agent has some personal connection, plays a smaller part in modern ethical life than many of us like to admit.

What is the relation of the intellectual virtues to the mean and to the virtues of character in general? Aristotle begins his discussion of the intellectual virtues in such a way that it sounds as if he is agreeing with those who find the doctrine of the mean to be empty (*NE* 6.1). Telling someone that the right action is in a mean between two extremes, he says, is rather like telling an ill person to take the drug the doctor would prescribe. But we should remember here Aristotle's insistence that the listener to his lectures should have a basic grasp of the elements of ethics. Someone who has that can then use it as a starting-point for reflection on the nature of the virtues, and consequent character change. I might, for example, reflect upon the large number of times I have been angry with students over the last few weeks, and follow Aristotle's advice to steer myself in the opposite direction in future.

But really getting it right on every occasion, Aristotle says, will require that one's feelings and actions are in accordance with 'correct reason' (*orthos logos*). This is not a matter of habituation, but something more intellectual, and will require the possession of the intellectual virtue of practical wisdom.

Practical wisdom is broad, and includes an ability not only to find the right means to certain ends, but the ability to deliberate properly about which ends are worthy of pursuit (*NE* 6.8–9; 6.12). The person with practical wisdom, then, will have the correct understanding of happiness, and the role of virtue in constituting happiness, and be able to apply his understanding in everyday life.

But practical wisdom is not like, say, mathematical ability, which can be acquired early and operates according to the application of certain explicit rules. Practical wisdom, like the virtues of character, develops with experience, and has as much to do with seeing the salient features of certain situations, and acting and responding appropriately in the light of them, as with any ability for explicit deliberation. Some have seen Aristotle's discussion of practical wisdom as disappointing, perhaps because they hope for some explicit and detailed ethical rules by which to live. Aristotle does offer some pretty specific rules – such as that you should ransom your father from pirates rather than repay a debt to someone (*NE* 1164b33–1165a2) – and the general rules 'be virtuous' and 'aim at the mean' are of course always in the background. But Aristotle is insistent, and surely correct, that one cannot learn virtue solely from philosophical books or lectures.

Practical wisdom, since it involves seeing in the right way, is a necessary condition for possessing any virtue. And if in any particular case you have the general capacity to see what is right and do it, you will have it in all cases. So, though Aristotle is prepared to distinguish one virtue from another, he is not ready to allow that one can possess one virtue and lack another (*NE* 6.13). One cannot, for example, be generous and cowardly. One important reason for Aristotle's holding this view is his thought that virtue requires getting it right. For vices can distort the deliverances of any disposition, however close it may be to being a full-blooded virtue. In a situation where generosity required conquering fear, the person might not do the generous thing, and that would mean that he lacked the virtue. Good intentions are not enough.

❧ ARISTOTLE AND CONTEMPORARY ❧ ETHICS

Aristotle's ethics were immensely influential. They were the focus of Hellenistic ethics, and were also extremely important in the Christian tradition, most strikingly in the work of Thomas Aquinas (*c.*1225–1274). Of course, it was not only the Aristotelian ethics which were significant during this period, but the whole Aristotelian world view. With the scientific revolution of the seventeenth century, however, Aristotelian science began to decline in importance, and the ethics met with the same fate. In the place of

Aristotelian ethics developed modern systems of ethics, many of them employing notions alien to Aristotelian thought. The two main developments were Kantian ethics, according to which morality is a universal law of reason and individual rights are sovereign, and utilitarian ethics, according to which one should act so as to produce the greatest amount of happiness.

In science, the move away from Aristotle was not complete. In his famous work on the circulation of the blood, for example, William Harvey refers to Aristotle more than to any other thinker. And the same is true in ethics: the Kantian emphasis on reason in ethics cannot help but remind us of the function argument (see p. 115) and practical wisdom, while utilitarian concern for happiness has its roots in Greek eudaimonism. But over the second half of the twentieth century, there has been a self-conscious attempt by certain philosophers to return to a more explicitly Aristotelian ethics. This movement began in 1958, with the publication of Elizabeth Anscombe's article 'Modern Moral Philosophy' [4.46]. Anscombe, following Schopenhauer, argued that modern ethics revolved around notions of legalistic obligation which made little sense in the absence of a divine lawgiver. She suggested that philosophers desist from moral philosophy, and turn to psychology. 'Eventually', she claimed, 'it might be possible to advance to considering the concept "virtue"; with which, I suppose, we should be beginning some sort of a study of ethics' (Anscombe [4.46] 15).

This was the beginning of what has come to be known as 'neo-Aristotelian virtue ethics'. The 'neo-' here is, however, rather important. For certainly these writers have not sought to revive Aristotelian ethics. Indeed it might be argued that the differences between their views and those of Aristotle are such that the link between them is only as strong as the link between Aristotle and Kant or Aristotle and the utilitarians.

Virtue ethicists, like Aristotle, begin with the notion of *eudaimonia*, or human flourishing, considering the agent and his life as a whole, rather than concentrating on individual and isolated right and wrong actions. But this is not a difference in substance between them and the Kantians and utilitarians, for these latter theorists can also offer an account of the good life and moral character. It is just that often they have not bothered.

No modern writer has adopted the strong Aristotelian view that happiness consists only in virtuous activity. Indeed many modern virtue ethicists, such as Philippa Foot [4.48] or Alasdair MacIntyre [4.50], are sceptical about objective accounts of the human good. Even those who are less sceptical, such as Rosalind Hursthouse [4.49], tend to see the virtues as instrumental to human flourishing, understood independently from the virtues themselves, thus taking the 'best bet' strategy we mentioned above.

Another important difference between Aristotle's eudaimonism and that of most modern writers is his apparent acceptance of egoism, the view that reasons justifying action must ultimately rest on the agent's own self-interest. There is nothing in the Aristotelian corpus to suggest other than that

Aristotle's aim was to offer to his listeners an account of the best life for a human being in order that they might pursue it for themselves. The idea of reasonable self-sacrifice for others is quite absent, since there is no gap between self-interest and the virtues (*NE* 9.8).

Perhaps the most direct Aristotelian influence can be seen in the writings of John McDowell [4.51], David Wiggins [4.54], and others who stress the notion of a sensitivity to the morally salient features of situations as constituting the heart of virtue and morality itself. But even here the importance of 'mother wit' in Kant, or the role of perception in the de-ontological intuitionism of W.D. Ross (1877–1971), himself a great Aristotelian scholar, should not be forgotten. The utilitarian tradition, it is true, has tended to place more emphasis on calculation than moral perception, but again this is a matter of contingency. Utilitarians need some account of practical wisdom or moral judgement as much as any other moral theorist.

The above discussion is intended to suggest that the distinctions drawn between different schools in modern ethics are not as precise or useful as many believe them to be. Ultimately, the real difference between one moral philosopher and another lies in how they tell us to live, and the reasons they give for living in that way. No one now speaks ordinarily of *megalopsuchia* (usually translated as 'magnanimity', but not meaning what is now meant by that term), which for Aristotle was the crown of the virtues (*NE* 4.3). The magnanimous man thinks himself worthy of great things, and has one concern above all others: honour. He stirs himself only when some great achievement is at stake. There is indeed much to be learned from Aristotle's account of the virtues, but his moral ideal is a long way from 'neo-Aristotelian' modern writers, particularly those who emphasize the virtue of care for the vulnerable.

Most importantly, perhaps, we should remember the political context in which Aristotle was writing (see below). His virtues are intended for fourth-century Athenian noblemen, inhabiting a city-state with a population of tens of thousands rather than of millions. This is not to say that Aristotle is any kind of relativist, grounding his account of virtues in whatever social context they were to appear in. Rather, he believed that the Greek polis was, universally, the best form of human society, and that the virtues that it made possible were largely the reason for this. For this reason, it is dangerous to draw conclusions about what Aristotle would have thought about how individuals should live in modern societies entirely different in their details and general nature from the Greek polis. Perhaps the correct way to approach Aristotelian ethics is not to claim him as an ally in or authority for one's own views about modernity. Rather, he should be read carefully and sensitively, with an understanding of historical, social and political context, as one of the best sources of insight into the human ethical condition available to us.

THE *POLITICS*

Trevor J. Saunders

INTRODUCTION

It is a fair test of a political philosopher to ask him to describe what in his view is the best form of communal human life. Aristotle would give you this reply: 'It is to live as a citizen in that special kind of aristocracy which I describe in my *Politics*, in what you moderns call "books" 7 and 8. You and your fellow-aristocrats would not be numerous: you would be able to address them all in a single gathering. The territory of your state would be correspondingly modest. Your citizenship would be granted you on the strength of your high moral and political virtue, which you would have acquired as a result of systematic exposure to a carefully contrived programme of private and state education. The other members of your household would be your wife, children, servants, and slaves. Your resources, ample but not great, would come from your land; but you would not need to bother your head much about that, as your slaves would do the work. Trade and handicrafts would be confined to free men who are not citizens; for such people, though necessary to the state, would not be *parts* of it. You would spend much of your time on leisure activities – not just play, but rather the serious intellectual and cultural pursuits of what you would now call a gentleman. Why do I think this the ideal life? Pray read the rest of my *Politics*.'[1]

Taking the Master's advice calls for effort. Though of the highest importance and influence, the *Politics*, unlike the *Nicomachean Ethics*, is a rather ragged work. Aristotle employs his usual elegantly plain style, which can at times be spare to the point of sketchiness and even obscurity. But that is not the real bother. Though substantial stretches of the text are structured and beautifully written wholes, there are frequent puzzles in the detail: unclear references back and forth, enquiries left incomplete, and sudden changes of subject-matter and standpoint. To reconstruct Aristotle's full thought on a given subject, it is usually necessary to thumb through the entire work and collect the relevant passages – which are not always consistent with each other. The abundant references given below are designed to speed the reader's thumb. (Unless otherwise stated, all references are to the *Politics*.)

On the global scale too, the structure and sequence of the eight books seem strange, and have prompted many commentators into reordering them in accordance with *a priori* views about the natural disposition of their contents, or with theories about Aristotle's philosophical development. The debate was substantially enriched by Jaeger in 1923 ([4.84] 259–92), who argued powerfully for an Aristotle gradually freeing himself from Platonic political assumptions and methods, an emancipation traceable in various strata of the text. But this controversy, though inky, has proved inconclusive, and 'genetic' analyses are not now in vogue. It is perfectly reasonable to do what most interpreters now do in practice, that is take the *Politics* as it comes, and to assume that however Aristotle composed the parts, he intended to present the ensemble as we have it, failing only to tighten the nuts and bolts.[2]

Nevertheless, a brief survey of three of the more conspicuous difficulties of structure will serve to provide some idea of the contents of the work as it has come down to us. (1) Book 2, on certain theoretical utopias (notably Plato's *Republic* and *Laws*), and on three historical states (including Sparta) in fine repute, looks as if it may have been written first, as the standard Aristotelian review, at the start of a work, of his predecessors' contributions to the subject in hand. Why then does book 1, a strongly sociological analysis of the state and its parts, and philosophically the richest book of all, precede it? Does it contain theoretical groundwork of which Aristotle realized the need only when composing the rest of the *Politics*? (2) Why is the closing sentence of 3, a book devoted to questions of political power in the various constitutions, similar to the opening one of 7, on the ideal state? Both speak of the need to examine the 'best' constitution. But books 4–6 are full of historical analysis, and advice on the reform of existing and *imperfect* states. So have they been inserted between 3 and 7 by some clumsy editor? Even if they have been, the implications for our understanding of the *Politics* as a whole are mysterious. (3) Why does book 8, the last, break off in mid-discussion? It is unlikely that Aristotle simply became bored with political theory, since on his own showing knowledge about the working of the state, *politikê epistêmê*, is the supreme, all-embracing knowledge, that is of how to achieve the highest human good (*NE* 1.2, *Politics* 1.1 ad init.). Perhaps he died pen in hand. If that is so, it suggests that books 7 and 8 are not his early thoughts, inspired by Plato-style idealism, but the genuine conclusion and practical aspiration of the entire work.

Perhaps the best advice to give a reader of the *Politics*, particularly a new reader, is to be aware of such specialized academic problems, for they can affect interpretation, but not to become obsessed by them. For in spite of variations in detail, Aristotle's political philosophy is clearly a fundamentally consistent whole, underpinned by firm and constant philosophical foundations.

～ NATURE ～

In 1.2, utilizing a long-established optimistic and progressivist tradition in Greek historical anthropology, Aristotle tells the following story. Civilization has advanced sequentially, through three 'associations', *koinôniai*:

1 household (*oikos*), formed of the two primitive 'associations' of man–woman, master–slave;
2 village (*kômê*), formed of several households;
3 state (*polis*), formed of several villages.

The naturalness of each association is stressed heavily. Man–woman: they have a natural urge to breed; master–slave: natural ruler and natural ruled; household: formed by nature for everyday purposes; village: 'by nature to an especial degree, as a colony of a household – children and grandchildren'; state: it exists by nature, for all men have a natural impulse towards such an association.

Each stage incorporates its predecessors, and brings an increase in material resources, presumably because of increasing specialization of function and opportunities for exchange of goods and services. In part, material comfort and security are what all these associations are for. But at stage 2 Aristotle's ulterior preoccupation begins to emerge: the village is formed for 'other than daily purposes'; and at stage 3 the state, which is a 'complete' association and totally self-sufficient, 'came into being for the sake of life, *zên*, but exists for the sake of the good life, *eu zên*'. By 'self-sufficiency' Aristotle means here not merely an assured supply of all necessary material goods from domestic or foreign sources, but the opportunities afforded by the complex demands of life in a polis for the full exercise of a man's natural potentialities for rational conduct in conformity with the moral virtues (on these, see pp. 118–22 above). Such conduct both leads to, and is, human 'happiness', *eudaimonia*; it is the 'good' life for which the state exists (cf. 7.1, 13, *NE* 1097b1 ff.). Hence, in Aristotle's celebrated formulation, man is a *phusei politikon zôion*, 'an animal (fit) by nature for (life in) a polis' (cf. 1278b15 ff.). For this animal is unique in possessing reason and speech, and a capacity for shared moral values (1253a7–18). Hence again, a man who does not live and act in a state is a man indeed, but no more a full man, i.e. a fully functional man, than a hand made of stone is a functional hand. He is functionally stunted, and the measure of happiness he attains is limited.

This latter point is worth developing. To Aristotle, it is no more a matter for surprise or indignation that one man should by nature be better equipped than another for acquiring virtue and thereby achieving happiness than that he should be by nature stronger physically, with a greater potential for (say) weight-lifting. 'Happiness' is on a sliding scale: one can have more or less of it (1328a37–40, 1331b39–1332a7). Hence he has an immediate answer to the objection that vast numbers of people ('barbarians', i.e. non-Greeks) live and apparently flourish in societies other than Greek *poleis*. That they are happy up to a point, he would concede; that they are fully so, he would deny. In a Greek polis, did they but know it, they would be happier (cf. 7.7). Happiness is not, or not only, a subjective feeling of satisfaction in achievement (see p. 110): it is an objective and definable state of affairs, of human flourishing, that is to say rational activity in accordance with the virtues; for this is man's natural function (see p. 115).

Further objections spring up, as many as the heads of the Hydra. Several, centring on the notion of 'function' in human behaviour, have been explored already (pp. 115–16). In addition: (1) Even in terms of Aristotle's own natural philosophy, in which the paradigm of the 'natural' is biological growth (see *Physics* 2.1), the state is hardly natural. It is much more like an artefact, full as it is of elaborate constitutional and social contrivances that certainly do not develop naturally, as an embryo develops naturally into an adult member of its species, of its own accord, given all facilitating conditions (see Keyt [4.86]. (2) But even if we grant that the development from primitive pairings through household and village to state may properly be conceived on a biological model, in virtue of natural urges to develop such associations, difficult questions confront us: for example, can the same analysis be applied to a process involving many individuals in many changing relationships as is applied to a single individual's physical growth into an adult? (3) More generally, how far ought we to privilege certain human characteristics, or certain patterns of human social behaviour, on the strength of either parallels to them or differences from them in the characteristics or behaviour of animals?[3]

Perhaps the best we can do for Aristotle is to extend the notion of 'natural' to embrace anything which is the product of man's natural faculties, conspicuously reason, and which conduces to his happiness; and indeed Aristotle himself at times speaks in this way (for example 1279a8–13, 1287b36–41; on his 'political naturalism', see Miller ([4.91], 27–66). But as we shall see, he is prepared to be very specific indeed about 'anything'; for human institutions are, he believes, capable of normative assessment. Some things conduce to happiness, some do not. Human skill should follow and supplement nature (cf. 1337a1–3). Consequently, relativism in social and political values and institutions is to be firmly rejected. No doubt all sorts of theoretical and practical controversies are possible; but in the end they are capable of definitive solution by reference to the fulfilment of men's natural capacities, to the *sort of being* a man naturally and peculiarly is.

Aristotle's natural teleology has three important consequences for political theory and practice. (1) A man in a state of nature is not someone living in simple primitive 'happiness' in a nudist camp; nor is he Hobbes' natural man, naked and shivering in the wind before achieving such protection and comfort as society affords him. Rather, to be in a natural condition is to be a functionally fulfilled member of a polis: one goes not back to nature, but forward to it. (2) Though the state is indeed a device to ensure peace and protection, its role is not simply to hold the ring in a minimalist or merely contractualist manner, between socially or commercially contesting individuals or groups (3.9). It should take comprehensive care of every department of life, economic, social, political, military, private, public, secular, religious; in particular, it should take extreme pains to ensure the proper moral formation of its members (8.1). (3) Despite that, the state is not a super-entity, with interests and purposes independent of, or superior to, those members' happiness; for happiness is ultimate: men can have no higher aim (see p. 114); and that aim is the 'common task', *koinon ergon*, of the association, *koinônia*, which is the state. The polis is therefore essentially a communal and co-operative enterprise, depending heavily on reciprocal services and mutual benefits. These benefits are to be won not by men conditioned or brainwashed into being social and political robots, but by men with discretion founded on *phronêsis*, practical wisdom (on which see pp. 121–2).

Hence, although Aristotle has much to say about the ways in which one section of a polis may pursue its own interests at the expense of other parts, or of the whole, he never confronts directly the issue so vital to us in this century, of 'totalitarianism', the subjugation of the interests of the individual and of subordinate organizations to the interests of the state itself, as a super-entity. The point of the thesis at 1253a18 ff., which sounds so alarming, that the state is 'prior by nature' to household and individual, is that while the state can flourish without any particular individual, no individual can attain 'happiness' without *it*, i.e. when he is not fully functional as one of its citizens. Aristotle drives no wedge between the interest of the individual and those of the state: to him, a totalitarian polis would not be a polis at all.[4]

AIMS AND METHODS

How then does Aristotle tackle the political theory and practice of his day? Four strands in his text are readily discernible:

1 Theoretical fixed points: a technique of analysis based on a cluster of such concepts as nature, function, virtue, and happiness, deployed teleologically.
2 Practical fixed points: the institutions of the 'best' state, in which the concepts of 1 are instantiated in as feasible a form as possible (1328b35–9).

But the best state does not exist (though it could). So the great bulk of Aristotle's discussion is taken up with:

3 Description and analysis of the (mistaken) theoretical underpinning and actual practices of less-than-ideal constitutions or states existing or merely proposed, with comment which at times becomes exceedingly censorious. Aristotle is nevertheless prepared to judge a state or constitution in the light of its success or failure in achieving its 'hypothesis', i.e. its own political aims and standards, as in book 2 *passim*; for such standards can have some limited merit. In general, he has considerable respect for *endoxa*, common reputable opinions (cf. pp. 111–12, and his handling of the controversies about slaves and about justice in constitutions, pp. 137 and 131–2).

4 Implicit in (3), recommendations for correcting existing theory, and for improving existing practice in order to make it approximate more closely to the ideal; for the 'statesman' (citizen active in state affairs, see p. 132 and n. 11 below) has a 'duty of care' even to inferior constitutions (4.1).[5]

These four strands mesh in complex ways; and the abundant historical detail which Aristotle cites (sometimes with impressive induction) as evidence for his arguments lends his text both colour and authenticity.[6] In short, he is at once philosopher, don, critic, data-processor, and political reformer.

APPLICATIONS

Admittedly, Aristotle as a political reformer is not a familiar figure. There is a common idea that it was Plato who was the reformer *par excellence* (consider only the Philosopher-Kings of his *Republic*), whereas Aristotle stuck more closely to the realities of Greek life – so closely, in fact, as make his political philosophy a mere rationalization of the status quo. This is a half-truth at best. Aristotle's conceptual apparatus, in which nature is central, is capable of yielding the most radical political ideals, very much askew to the standard assumptions of his day. I take four examples.

1 Constitutions and citizenship

Aristotle defines a 'constitution', *politeia*, in terms of a power-structure which embodies and promotes the state's social aims and moral values. It is 'an ordering (*taxis*) which states have concerning their offices (*archai*) – the manner in which they have been distributed, what the sovereign (*kurion*) element of the constitution is, and the purpose (*telos*) of each association (*koinônia*, i.e. state)' (1289a15–18, cf. 1.1, 1295a34–b1). His typology of constitutions contains therefore both a formal element and a moral element:

the identity, number, and economic status of the sovereign rulers, and the character of their rule. It is also interlarded with lengthy analyses of the social, economic, and psychological factors which make for the preservation and destruction of the various constitutions. The texts are lavish but scattered, mainly in 3.6–18 and books 4–6. For a new reader, 3.6–8 and 4.2 form the best introduction, followed by the 'chief texts' listed below.

Straight or correct constitutions, operating in the common[7] interest:

Kingship, *basileia*: a species of 'rule by one' *monarchia*. Aristotle considers this to be ideally the best constitution, provided that a monarch of supreme virtue and political wisdom is available; but he never is. Chief texts: 3.13–18; 5.10, 11.

Aristocracy, *aristokratia*: 'power of the best', *aristoi*. Rule by few, typically of noble breed, wealthy, cultured, and virtuous. Chief texts: 3.18; 1289a30–3; 4.7–8; 5.7.

Polity, *politeia* (awkwardly: this is also the general word for 'constitution'): rule by many, specified variously. For there appear to be three forms: (i) rule by heavy-arms bearers; (ii) a 'mixed' system, judiciously combining elements of oligarchy and democracy; (iii) rule by a large middle class, i.e. persons who are neither rich nor poor, and who have only moderate appetites for wealth and power; this composition of a state is 'by nature' (1295b27–8).[8] Chief texts: 1265b26–9; 3.7; 4.7–9, 11, 13; 1307a5–33.

Bent or deviated constitutions, operating in the interests of the rulers only:

Tyranny, *turannis*: a species of 'rule by one' *monarchia*. Chief texts: 4.10; 5.11, 12.

Oligarchy, *oligarchia*: 'rule by few'; *oligoi*, typically wealthy. Chief texts: 4.4, 6; 5, 1, 6, 9, 12; 6.6, 7.

Democracy, *dêmokratia*: 'power of the people', *dêmos*. Rule by many, typically poor. Chief texts: 1284a17 ff.; 4.4, 6, 9, 12; 5.1, 5; 1310a22 ff.; 6.2, 4. On restricted democracies, see 1274a11 ff., 1281b21 ff., 1297b1 ff.

This schema, which has antecedents in Plato and elsewhere, is fundamental to the entire *Politics*; and it is subject to numerous and at times bewildering refinements and elaborations, which reflect the extraordinary variety of Greek political practice. But Aristotle gives us more than static description of complex constitutional facts: he provides a dynamic, psychological analysis of how they come about. The root cause, he claims, is varying perceptions of 'the equal' (*to ison*), and 'the just' (*to dikaion* 5.1 ff.). Democrats argue that since they are equal in one respect, free birth, they ought in justice to be equal in all, i.e. political power; oligarchs believe that since they are unequal, i.e. superior, in one thing, wealth, they ought in justice to be unequal in all, i.e. they ought to have greater political power. When political facts collide too sharply with these political beliefs, civil strife, *stasis*, can break out; hence the frequent modifications to, and indeed complete changes of, constitutions. Aristotle, by contrast, thinks that the sole proper claim to political power is political virtue, that is the practical ability to further the purposes for which the polis naturally exists (3.9, 12, 13); and in this endeavour political power ought to be distributed differentially to different degrees of political virtue, more to more, less to less,[9] though both wealth and numbers have some contribution to make (3.11; 1283a16–22, b27–34, 1293b34 ff., 1309a4–7). By ensuring that constitutions are not extreme, and by cultivating the political beliefs and habits of the population in the spirit of the existing constitution, a measure of stability can be won (1260b8 ff., 1310a12 ff.). Finally, the rule of impartial law is essential to the very existence of a constitution (1291b39–1292a38).

Aristotle's functional analysis of entitlements to rule dovetails with his functional definition of a citizen (3.1–2): 'he who shares in deliberative and judicial office'.[10] That is, a citizen, *politês*, is one who is active in 'running the affairs of the polis', *politeuomenos*, in accordance with its constitution, *politeia*, as a 'statesman', *politikos*.[11]

From all this it follows, in Aristotle's view:

i that across the entire range of constitutions, the number of citizens strictly conceived varies sharply: few or very few in oligarchies and aristocracies, many or very many in democracies;[12]

ii that in all oligarchies and in some democracies (those with some property-qualification for citizenship) there will be variable numbers of native free adult males who are not citizens in the full sense, but only equivocally (like women and children, cf. 1278a4–5); slaves and foreigners, of course, qualify in no sense;

iii that in deviated constitutions, although the citizen-body, *politeuma*, operates in its own interests, it may, and prudentially should, pay some attention to the interests of others. The few rich, if sovereign, should not 'grind the faces of the poor', and the numerous poor, if sovereign, ought not to 'soak the rich' beyond endurance; for either excess may lead to *stasis* (1295b13 ff.; 4.12; 1308a3 ff., 1309a14–32, b14–1310a12; also 5.11, on tyrannies);

iv that there is a distinction to be made between the good citizen and the good man. The former is befitted by his personal sympathies, virtues, and attainments to be a citizen under a particular imperfect constitution; the latter is befitted by his to be a citizen under the 'best' constitution (cf. 8.1). The virtue of the former is pluriform, for there are many imperfect constitutions; the virtue of the latter is not only perfect but single, for there is in principle only one best constitution (3.4; 1310a12 ff., cf. *NE* 1135a3–5);

v   that both good citizens and good men exercise their virtue, i.e. that of practical wisdom, *phronêsis*, most fully when ruling; but since they are all equal, and since obviously not all may rule simultaneously, they must take it in turns to rule and be ruled, in some principled manner laid down in the constitution (1279a8 ff., 1332b12 ff.). Their virtue is therefore twofold: to know how to rule and be ruled well; indeed, by engaging in the latter they learn to do the former (1277a25 ff.).[13]

Given, then, that the ideal single ruler does not exist and is never likely to, and that the natural capacity of men for developing virtue and thereby achieving 'happiness' varies widely, it is scarcely surprising that Aristotle, in seeking the 'best' state, should look to some form of aristocracy. For only in an aristocracy are good man and good citizen one and the same person, because the criterion for office-holding is not only wealth but virtue (3.18; 4.7, 8). Aristotle's fundamental intentions are plain: what he wants to see above all in his citizens is education and virtue; for these are at once the conditions of 'happiness' (7.1, esp. 1323b21 ff.; 8.1), and the criteria for the holding of office (cf. 1326b15, 'merit'); and in an aristocracy, by definition, the best (*aristoi*) men exercise power.[14]

Nevertheless, Aristotle never calls his 'best' state an aristocracy, perhaps because as aristocracies go it is highly unusual.[15]

i   The members of an aristocracy, i.e. its citizens, are typically wealthy. But the members of Aristotle's aristocracy do not value wealth: they are to possess only moderate resources, which are all that is necessary for life; what matters to them is the 'goods of/concerning the soul' (7.1, cf. 1. 8–10).

ii   The members of an aristocracy are normally few, in relation to the total free adult male population of the state (aristocracy is a kind of oligarchy, 1290a16–17). Yet it is possible, though Aristotle gives no figures, that the restricted level of private resources in his own aristocracy would permit it to be more widely diffused: a few dozen or even a few hundred members look rather too few for his purposes.[16] But it is clear that he would not wish to see any approximation to Plato's diffused aristocracy (Magnesia) in his *Laws*, where the adult male citizens number 5040; such a total, he believes, is outrageously large (1265a10 ff., cf. 7.4). (In many other respects, however, there are marked similarities between Magnesia and Aristotle's best state (Barker [4.71] 380–2).)

iii According to Aristotle's typology of constitutions, aristocracy is the rule of a few virtuous persons over many non-virtuous, but in the common interest. In his own best state the position seems to be subtly different: the aristocrats' interests *are* the common interests – simply because there are no other citizens: the aristocrats *are* the state.[17] That is, there is no body of persons other than themselves with a claim on their strictly *poli*tical attention. At any rate, Aristotle is quite explicit, indeed emphatic, that all other adult males – agricultural workers (who are preferably to be slaves, 1330a25 ff., cf. 1255b30–40), artisans, and traders (and of course their dependants) – are not 'parts' of the state:[18] they are merely its essential conditions. How far this would matter in practice is hard to judge: Aristotle's aristocrats presumably cannot ignore such people, and have to make some arrangements for their activities and welfare (for example 1331b1–4); and a poor person is not necessarily worse off materially just because he lacks the formal but ambiguous status of 'citizen' without the citizen rights of office-holding, etc., except perhaps that Aristotle's aristocrats can afford to be generous to him less well than historical aristocrats. But there can be no doubt that Aristotle has sharpened the political distinction between citizens and others.

iv The cultural and artistic activities Aristotle recommends as pursuits for his citizen aristocrats (book 8) look very different from the huntin'-shootin'-fishin' engaged in by historical landed aristocrats.

v Aristotle allocates the civic functions of his best state by age-groups: as a young man, one's function is to be a soldier, not to hold political office; later, at some unspecified mature age, one exchanges being ruled (exclusively) for the alternation of being ruled and ruling, and deliberates and judges; in old age one assumes a priesthood (7.9; 1332b25–7). This three-fold division is more systematic than common historical practice; for to deprive arms-bearers of office is remarkable, and Aristotle is at pains to justify it (1329a2 ff., 1332b32 ff.); see further Mulgan ([4.74], 95–6).

Aristotle's best state is therefore both like and unlike historical states. It is something of a hot-house plant, nurtured in the rich soil of natural teleology; for all the above conditions are justified, immediately or implicitly, by an appeal to nature.

i In one way or another, nature provides for most of our needs, in sufficient but not excessive quantities; agriculture is an especially natural source of supply (1.8). To seek to acquire endless wealth is a misuse of our faculties, and so unnatural (1258a8–10).

ii A small aristocracy is justified on a variety of pragmatic grounds, but notably the danger of a large population making the natural aims of the state hard to achieve because of its sheer size and complexity (7.4–5).

iii Many free men perform only the lowly tasks of manual work, crafts, and trade, which preclude them from virtuous activity and therefore happiness (1323b21–2), and approximate them to slaves (1260a36 ff., 1278a9–11, 20–1, 1328a37–9); and indeed some men are slaves by nature (1.6).

iv   Cultural pursuits promote virtue (1341b11), which is necessary to happiness, our natural aim.

v   This sequence follows the dictates of nature: the human body and soul just naturally develop like that – bodily strength when one is young, wisdom when older (cf. 1336b40–1337a3; *NE* 1094b27 ff.).

2 Trade

One prominent category among the non-citizens of the best state is traders. They are recognized as essential to its economic self-sufficiency, but their activities are kept at arm's length in an area separate from the leisured pursuits of the citizens (1321b12 ff; 7.6, 12). Yet there is a paradox here; for in 1.9–10 (taken with *NE* 5.5) Aristotle pronounces trade to be unnatural.[19] How then can it be both unnatural and essential?

Briefly, Aristotle believes that trade tends to undermine civic order. The key terms in his analysis are acquisition, exchange, proportionality, equality and justice. The natural forms of *acquisition* are (a) from nature (farming, etc.), (b) by exchange, which beneficially irons out unevennesses in supply: I breed many pigs, you make many shoes; let us therefore *exchange* pigs for shoes in a certain *proportion* (6 pairs of shoes for 1 pig, *vel sim.*); or (c) let me purchase shoes from you using money which I have received in the past from someone else for my pigs, and which I have found it useful to keep, as a mere substitute for goods, until I need your shoes. The proportion in which the pigs and shoes are exchanged between us leaves us equal: each of us is in the same economic position after the transaction as before (each of us 'has his own', 1132b11–20), and neither can feel aggrieved. So far, so natural: exchange facilitates the economic life of the polis; 'by proportionate reciprocity the state endures'.[20]

Trade befouls the purity of this model, and not only or primarily because traders are commonly small-minded persons obsessed with maximizing their monetary profit, since they assume (Aristotle claims) that just as the aim of the art of medicine is unlimited health, the aim of the art of acquisition is unlimited wealth; whereas in truth wealth is not an end but a means to life, and life does not require a vast amount of it (1257b25 ff.). His real point is sharper, and is apparently contained in the cryptic statement that the skill of acquisition from trade 'is justly censured, since it is not in accordance with nature, but is *from each other*' (1258b1–2). That is, presumably, the trader's profit is to the disadvantage of the buyer, who pays more that the 'proportionate' value;[21] he comes off worse, and resents it as an injustice; and injustice in general is, according to Aristotle, precisely the deprivation of that which would enable a person to live a virtuous life, in accordance with his natural potentialities; for such a life demands a certain level of material goods.[22] This resentment of injustice can be corrosive of the social and political structure; for it does not make for harmony, *homonoia*, and friendship, *philia* (*NE* 9.6).[23] Usury, Aristotle claims, attracts even greater odium than trade; of all modes of acquisition, it is the most contrary to nature: it is 'money born of money'. Trade at least achieves that for which money was invented: the exchange of real goods.

If this reconstruction of Aristotle's admittedly problematical texts is correct, his assessment of trade, like his economic theory as a whole, is driven philosophically, by reference to first principles, the natural purposes of the polis; and it draws support from (what he takes to be) common perceptions about equality and justice. Nevertheless, pioneering and radical though he may be in point of theory, he nowhere recommends radicalism in practice; for clearly the suppression of trade would bring any existing state to a stop, and the remedy for the ills generated by traders would be worse than the disease. In his 'best' state, trade simply slots into place as the imperfect activity of imperfect persons, who are not fully capable of *eudaimonia*, but who are essential to the state even if not 'parts' of it.

How the estates of the aristocrats are to be insulated from trade Aristotle does not say. Presumably their managers would traffic with traders (1255b30–7, 1331a30–b13), and they themselves would not feel resentment concerning profit; they are after all not in a relationship of 'political justice' with persons who are not parts of the polis (cf. *NE* 1134a25 ff.)

3 Slaves[24]

From a modern point of view, perhaps the most surprising thing Aristotle says about slavery is that it is a benefit to the slave, *doulos*. This is because his relationship with his master is symbiotic (cf. 1252a24–34). The master has powers of reason, the slave has them only minimally: 'he participates in reason so far as to apprehend it but not so far as to possess it'; he wholly lacks deliberative capacity (and therefore *eudaimonia*, 1280a32; *NE* 1177a8–9). Presumably this means he can understand the orders he receives, but could not have worked out independently in advance what he should do. His function is manual work, and the performance of essential routine tasks is his benefit to his master, who possesses him as a 'living tool' (*NE* 1161b4), and who benefits him in turn by controlling his life by reason. In a similarly minimal way the slave possesses enough virtue[25] to carry out orders in a willing spirit. Nevertheless, the master who can afford it has little to do with his slaves, and employs an overseer of their work; but he himself should be responsible for inculcating their virtue.

Aristotle's statements about slavery are not always consistent, partly because the several different models (for example master is to slave as soul is to body, or whole to part) by which he attempts to express the essence of slavery and the master–slave relationship seem to have conflicting implications (cf. Smith ([4.95]). More crucially, the relationship of mutual benefit sketched above is undercut elsewhere (1333a3–5; *NE* 1160b30) by a grimly instrumental one, in which apparently the only benefit is to the master; 1278b32–7 tries to marry the two positions. On the other hand, Aristotle frankly admits that the slave's ability (presumably thanks to his minimum rationality and virtue) 'to participate in law and contract' creates the possibility of friendship between him and his master (1255b12–14; *NE* 1161b4–6); but even here there is a heavy qualification, that the friendship is 'not with slave *qua* slave, but *qua* man'.

Aristotle never questions the justice of the institution itself; but in one complex chapter (1.6), in which he arbitrates in a contemporary controversy about it, he subjects it to sharp restriction. Some people, he reports, assert that slavery is just, on the grounds that what is captured in war belongs to the conqueror; others attack it as unjust, since it is imposed by force. Aristotle thinks both sides are right, and both wrong. Only *natural* slaves – i.e. persons whose natural mental and physical capacities befit them to be slaves – should be *actual* slaves; for that is expedient and just. Hence the defenders of slavery are correct up to a point: natural slaves may be forcibly enslaved (cf. 1255b37–39, 1256b23). Conversely, the attackers are also right in part: those who are not slaves by nature ought not to be enslaved. Aristotle in effect admits that some men are slaves who ought not to be, and vice versa. In his own best state, presumably, only natural slaves will be actual slaves (1324b36–41); but how this is to be contrived he does not say. He apparently assumes that natural slaves will breed natural slaves. Nor does he face the obvious possibility that a naturally 'free' man, *eleutheros*, may become slavish by habituation.

The point is this. By a clear application of natural teleology Aristotle arrived at a view of slavery which, if anyone had ever tried to put it into effect, would have caused uproar; for at least some slaves – those with high natural potential – would have had to be freed, and some free men – those of low natural talent – would have had to be enslaved. Aristotle lacks such practical reforming zeal; but his ideas are dynamite to the basis of contemporary practice.[26]

4 Women

Aristotle's view of women is in one fundamental and obvious respect the same as his view of slaves; for both are ruled by their natural superiors in point of reason and virtue (1252a31–4, 1254b12–15). Like a slave, a woman needs specific virtues in a form which equips her to fulfil her function (1259b40–1260a24). But the slave needs 'little' virtue, whereas the woman (i.e. the free woman, typically the wife of the free male) needs more: she has to be 'good' (*spoudaia*, 'sound', 1260b14–19). Unlike the slave, she possesses deliberative capacity – but it is 'without authority' (1260a13). The precise nature of the deficiency is unclear; but presumably the man possesses deliberative capacity in some stronger or more synoptic form, which entitles him to overrule her choices (cf. Fortenbaugh [4.80]).

There is nothing here to disturb the view of women commonly held by the Athenian male, unless he makes the mistake of treating his wife like a slave (see 1252b4–7). Perhaps more radical in its implications is the remark in 1.12 that a man rules over his wife *politikôs*, 'in the manner of a statesman', 'as one statesman rules another'. Yet it is important not to over-estimate the significance of this. 'Political' rule is over free and equal persons by turns (see pp. 133–4); but, as Aristotle hastens to explain, a woman is not the equal of a man: she is inferior, and therefore never rules, either in state or in household (except presumably over children and slaves). By *politikôs* Aristotle probably means not merely that a man rules his wife with a concern for her welfare, but accepts that in so doing he is one rational agent dealing with another, who needs persuasion, not orders. This is a considerable corrective to any view of women as essentially emotional and witless things (there is plenty of such prejudice on display in Greek literature). At any rate, Aristotle sees an important continuity between a man's treatment of his fellow-citizens in the public arena and his treatment of his wife in the private.

❧ CONCLUSION ❧

Natural teleology, then, makes Aristotle a far more potent challenger to contemporary ethical values and political practices than he may appear to a reader who merely notices that often enough the teleology endorses them. But even then, it is not intrinsic to natural teleology that it should confer approval on the status quo unquestioningly. For instance, so far from challenging the institutions of the private household and of private property, he vigorously condemns Plato's proposal to abolish them for his Philosopher-Guardians of the *Republic* (*Politics* 2.1–5). He subjects both to critical examination, and pronounces both conducive to happiness.[27]

But Aristotle faces three linked problems: (1) He assumes that, in some sense pertinent to the achievement of happiness in activity, the nature of each individual man is the same, variations being deficiencies in the ideal. He cannot accept that someone with (say) a natural bent towards manual work has a nature as effective for achieving happiness as the nature of someone with a natural bent towards politics or philosophy. (2) Even if we grant his assumption, however, deciding precisely what human characteristics or activities are natural can seem arbitrary; and some of his attempts to distinguish them are to say the least more plausible than others (cf. p. 116). (3) Why has nature a special status? Can we not seek to rise above it? Why do we assume that nature is best for us? If we need not assume that, then as Keyt

([4.70], 147) has neatly put it, 'The bedrock upon which Aristotle's theory comes to rest is also the rock on which it founders.' Nevertheless, nature as a standard of conduct has a seductive allure: it seems to be sure and fixed, and to offer an unchallengeable alternative to ethical and political relativism, liberalism, and individualism, and in fact to any creed that in principle not merely tolerates but encourages a plurality of values and practices in an 'open' society.

It is for this reason that some modern communitarians, for example MacIntyre [4.89], have looked to Aristotle for inspiration and support (cf. p. 123). Now communitarians are a rather various school, but their core belief is that it is essential to the mental health of the individual and to the cohesion of society that the latter should espouse some single moral, social and political tenet, or coherent set of tenets, with a range of reciprocal rights and duties derivable therefrom. For a single tenet (or set) can be shared across a whole society; conflicting tenets cannot (cf. 1253a15–18). For these purposes Aristotle's natural teleology is ready-made. For one has only to assume a single human nature, and lay out a set of social and political structures and relationships based (allegedly) on what man essentially is. But obviously that singleness does not have to be either 'natural' or specifically Aristotelian.

 NOTES

1 Good discussions of Aristotle's 'best' state are Mulgan [4.74] 78–101, and Huxley [4.82].
2 For accessible overviews of the problems of structure see Keyt and Miller [4.70] and Rowe [4.93].
3 On the biological dimension in Aristotle's political thought, see Mulgan [4.92], Kullmann [4.87]; on Aristotle and Darwinian biology, Arnhart [4.75].
4 Some crucial texts: 1280b29 ff., 1323b21 ff., 1325a7–10, b23–32, 1332a3–7; 8.1. The whole issue, too large for consideration here, is debated by Barnes and Sorabji [4.77], and by Miller ([4.91] 191–251). For related questions of political rights and duties in Aristotle, see in general Everson [4.79], Miller [4.91]; on the resolution of conflict, Yack [4.96].
5 1289a1–7. One has to say 'implicit' recommendations, because although the purpose of political knowledge is action (*NE* 1094b27 ff.), Aristotle does not on the whole give direct advice to statesmen 'in the field' on how to set about tactically the amelioration of an imperfect state or constitution. He sets targets, or approximations to them (cf. pp. 112–13), and shows that policy or practice or situation *a* will achieve them, and *b* will not; and he then assumes that statesmen, after reading the *Politics*, will choose *a* not *b*. But the 'true' statesman needs more than empirical rules of thumb: he needs to grasp the first principles of 'political knowledge', notably of how politics embraces ethics (*NE* 1.1–2; 1102a5 ff., 10.9; cf. pp. 113, 118).
6 For most of his historical evidence he presumably relied on the research reports,

compiled in the Lyceum, of the constitutions of Greek states (see *NE* 1181b17). There were 158 'Constitutions', but only one survives, and only in part: *The Constitution of the Athenians.*

7 For an analysis of Aristotle's application of this slippery adjective, see Miller ([4.91] 191–213).

8 The tangled (and controversial) relationships between these three are investigated by Robinson ([4.66b] 99–103), Mulgan ([4.74] 76–7), and Johnson ([4.85] 143–54)

9 That is, by 'geometrical' equality (equality for equals, inequality for unequals, cf. 1325b7–10), not 'arithmetical' equality (for example one man one vote): see Harvey [4.81].

10 'Executive' office seems assumed. Aristotle discusses various difficulties in the definitions, which may be passed over here. 'Judging' refers to courts, with or without popular juries; what we would now call 'civil' and 'criminal' cases often had political importance.

11 'Statesman' is obviously a bad translation, but it is sanctioned by usage. 'Politician' is misleading, since it suggests professionalism.

12 Strictly, a tyrant or king would be the sole citizen; persons delegated to particular duties of ruling would not have authority in their own right.

13 There are some problems here, for example (a) What is one to do with one's *phronêsis* when being ruled? (b) Is the reciprocity of ruling and being ruled consistent with Aristotle's preference for an ideal monarchy? (c) What is the relationship between the 'contemplative' life and the 'active' life of a *politikos*? See 7.2–3 and pp. 117–18 above.

14 1279a35–7, where the alternative etymology, 'because [it looks to] the best for the state', seems improbable.

15 Indeed, Johnson ([4.85] 155–69) argues that the 'best state' is in fact the 'middle' constitution of 4.11. Cf. Huxley [4.81], Kraut [4.66d] 52.

16 At any rate, to judge from 1295a25 ff., 1324a23–5, *NE* 1099b18–20. Aristotle is also aware of the practical dangers of a 'shortage of men': 1278a26–34, 1299a31–b13, 1326b2–3; cf. 1297b26; but contrast *NE* 1171a6–8. (Greek *poleis* were in size much more like our towns or even villages than like our cities; Athens, which had *c.*30,000 adult male citizens in the fourth century, was 'off the scale'.)

17 1332a34–5: 'for us/for our purposes' (i.e. the best state) 'all the citizens share in the constitution.' But artisans etc. do not so share; therefore they are not citizens, even in a technical attenuated sense – or so it seems.

18 7.9. It is this point that formally exempts Aristotle's constitution from the charge of being itself a 'deviated' constitution, as pursuing its members' interests only; for there are no other interests embraced by the state for it to pursue.

19 I assume what I argue in Saunders ([4.66a] 88–90), that these three chapters essentially cohere, though they are different in immediate preoccupation. The following two paragraphs are a bald summary of my extended discussion there. For a complete analysis of Aristotle's economics see Meikle [4.90].

20 Aristotle assumes, and in *NE* 5.5 tries to identify, a fixed basis of commensurability; but he fails. As a sighting shot, he suggests 'need'.

21 Hence, in modern terms, while Aristotle recognizes in a commodity both use-value and exchange-value, and possibly labour-value (1258b25), he fails to acknowledge the value of distribution as a legitimate charge on the buyer.

22 *NE* 1099a31 ff., 1129b17–19; on justice, see Miller [4.91], esp. chs 3 and 4.
23 On 'political' friendship, i.e. as between one *politês* or *politikos* and another, co-operating in the purposes of the polis, see Cooper and Annas [4.78].
24 Except where otherwise indicated, this section is based on material in 1.3–7 and 13.
25 That is, the virtue of being ruled, not of ruling; master and slave possess different virtues, which are not on the same scale; see Saunders ([4.66a] 98–100).
26 Schofield ([4.94] 11) puts the same point more gently, in an excellent discussion of the relationship between Aristotle's 'ideology' (in a 'broadly Marxist' sense of the word) of slavery and his philosophical analysis of it.
27 Private property he defends by an intriguing combination of economic, social, and psychological reasons: Irwin ([4.83] 200–25), Miller ([4.91] 321–5), Saunders ([4.66a] 118–20). But he imposes certain conditions, notably a considerable degree of common use: 1263a21 ff., 1329b39–1330a2.

❦❦❦ BIBLIOGRAPHY ❦❦❦

❦ ETHICS ❦

Original language editions

4.1 Bywater, J. (ed.), *Ethica Nicomachea*, Oxford, Clarendon, 1894.
4.2 Walzer, R.R. and Mingay, J.M., *Ethica Eudemia*, Oxford, Clarendon, 1991.

Commentaries

4.3 Burnet, J., *The Ethics of Aristotle*, London, Methuen, 1900.
4.4 Grant, A., *The Ethics of Aristotle*, 2 vols, London, Longmans, 1885.
4.5 Woods, M., *Aristotle's Eudemian Ethics*, Books 1, 2 and 8 (see [1.35]).

English translations

4.6 *Eudemian Ethics*, trans. Solomon, in [1.3].
4.7 *Nicomachean Ethics*, trans. Irwin, T., Indianapolis, Hackett, 1985.

General works

4.8 Barnes, J., Schofield, M. and Sorabji, R. (eds), *Articles on Aristotle*, vol. 2 (see [1.53]).
4.9 Broadie, S., *Ethics With Aristotle*, New York and Oxford, Oxford University Press, 1991.
4.10 Hardie, W.F.R., *Aristotle's Ethical Theory*, 2nd edn, Oxford, Clarendon, 1980.

4.11 Irwin, T., *Aristotle's First Principles*, Oxford, Clarendon, 1988.

4.12 Kenny, A., *The Aristotelian Ethics: A Study of the Relationship between the Eudemian and Nicomachean Ethics of Aristotle*, Oxford, Clarendon Press, 1978.

4.13 Rorty, A. (ed.), *Essays on Aristotle's Ethics*, Berkeley and Los Angeles, 1980.

4.14 Urmson, J.O., *Aristotle's Ethics*, Oxford, Blackwell, 1988.

Method

4.15 Barnes, J., 'Aristotle's Method of Ethics', *Revue Internationale de Philosophie* 34 1981, 490–511.

4.16 Owen, G.E.L., 'Tithenai ta Phainomena', in S. Mansion (ed.) [1.42], and Barnes, J., Schofield, M., Sorabji, R. (eds), [1.53] vol. 1, 113–26.

4.17 Roche, T.D., 'On the Alleged Metaphysical Foundation of Aristotle's Ethics', *Ancient Philosophy* 8 1988, 51–62.

Happiness

4.18 Ackrill, J.L., 'Aristotle on Eudaimonia', *Proceedings of the British Academy* 60, 1974; repr. in Rorty [4.13] 15–33.

4.19 Cooper, J., *Reason and Human Good in Aristotle*, Cambridge, Mass., Harvard University Press, 1975.

4.20 Crisp, R., 'Aristotle's Inclusivism', *Oxford Studies in Ancient Philosophy* 10, 1994, 111–36.

4.21 Glassen, P., 'A Fallacy in Aristotle's Argument about the Good', *Philosophical Quarterly* 7, 1957, 319–22.

4.22 Kraut, R., *Aristotle on the Human Good*, Princeton, Princeton University Press, 1989.

4.23 Kenny, A., *Aristotle on the Perfect Life*, Oxford, Clarendon, 1992.

4.24 Keyt, D., 'Intellectualism in Aristotle', *Paideia* Special Issue 1978; repr. in Anton, J.P. and Preus, A. (eds), *Essays in Ancient Greek Philosophy*, Albany, NY, State University of New York Press, 1983, 364–87.

4.25 McDowell, J., 'The Role of Eudaimonia in Aristotle's Ethics', *Proceedings of the African Classical Association* 15, 1980; repr. in Rorty [4.13], 359–76.

4.26 Moline, J., 'Contemplation and the Human Good', *Nous* 17, 1983, 37–53.

Virtue and the doctrine of the mean

4.27 Barnes, J., 'Introduction', in *Aristotle, Nicomachean Ethics*, trans. Thomson, J.A.K., Harmondsworth, Penguin, 1976, 9–43.

4.28 Hursthouse, R., 'A False Doctrine of the Mean', *Proceedings of the Aristotelian Society* 81, 1980–81, 57–72.

4.29 Hutchinson, D.S., *The Virtues of Aristotle*, London, Routledge and Kegan Paul, 1986.

4.30 Joseph, H.W.B., 'Aristotle's Definition of Moral Virtue and Plato's Account of Justice in the Soul', *Philosophy* 9, 1934; repr. in his *Essays on Ancient Philosophy*, Oxford, Clarendon, 1935, 156–77.

4.31 Losin, P., 'Aristotle's Doctrine of the Mean', *History of Philosophy Quarterly* 4, 1987, 329–41.

4.32 Nussbaum, M.C., 'Non-relative Virtues: An Aristotelian Approach', in French, P.A., Uehling, T.E. and Wettstein, H.K. (eds), *Midwest Studies in Philosophy 13: Ethical Theory: Character and Virtue*, University of Notre Dame Press, 32–53.

4.33 Pears, D., 'Courage as a Mean', in Rorty [4.13] 171–87.

4.34 Sherman, N., *The Fabric of Character*, Oxford, Clarendon, 1989.

4.35 Williams, B., 'Acting as the Virtuous Person Acts', in R. Heinaman (ed.), *Aristotle and Moral Realism*, London, UCL Press, 1995, 13–23.

Other central topics in NE

4.36 Burnyeat, M., 'Aristotle on Learning to be Good', in Rorty [4.13], 69–92.

4.38 Cooper, J., 'Friendship and the Good', *Philosophical Review* 86, 1977; repr. as 'Aristotle on Friendship' in Rorty [4.13], 301–340.

4.39 Furley, D., 'Aristotle on the Voluntary', in Barnes, Schofield and Sorabji (eds) [1.53], 47–60.

4.40 Gosling, J. and Taylor, C.C.W., *The Greeks on Pleasure*, Oxford, Clarendon, 1982.

4.41 Owen, G.E.L., 'Aristotelian Pleasures', *Proceedings of the Aristotelian Society* 72 (1971–2); repr. in Barnes, Schofield and Sorabji (eds.) [1.53], 92–103.

4.42 Price, A., *Love and Friendship in Plato and Aristotle*, Oxford, Clarendon, 1989.

4.43 Sorabji, R., *Necessity, Cause and Blame*, London, Duckworth, 1980.

4.44 Wiggins, D., 'Weakness of Will, Commensurability, and the Objects of Deliberation and Desire', in his *Needs, Values, Truth*, 2nd edn, Oxford, Blackwell, 1991, 239–67.

4.45 Williams, B., 'Justice as a Virtue', in Rorty [4.13], 189–99.

Aristotle and modern ethics

4.46 Anscombe, G.E.M., 'Modern Moral Philosophy', *Philosophy* 33, 1958, 1–19.

4.47 Cottingham, J., 'Partiality and the Virtues', in Crisp, R. (ed.), *How Should One Live?*, Oxford, Clarendon, 1996, 57–76.

4.48 Foot, P., *Virtues and Vices*, Oxford, Blackwell, 1978.

4.49 Hursthouse, R., *Beginning Lives*, Oxford, Blackwell, 1987.

4.50 MacIntyre, A., *After Virtue*, London, Duckworth, 1981.

4.51 McDowell, J., 'Virtue and Reason', *Monist* 62, 1979, 331–50.

4.52 Rawls, J., *A Theory of Justice*, Cambridge, Mass., Harvard University Press, 1971.

4.53 Wallace, J., *Virtues and Vices*, Ithaca, NY, Cornell University Press, 1978.

4.54 Wiggins, D., 'Deliberation and Practical Reason', in his *Needs, Values, Truth*, 2nd edn, Oxford, Blackwell, 1991, 215–37.

4.55 Williams, B., *Ethics and the Limits of Philosophy*, London, Fontana, 1985.

 POLITICS

Greek text

4.60 Ross, W.D., *Aristotelis Politica*, Oxford, Clarendon Press, 1957.

Translations

4.61 Saunders, T.J., *Aristotle, The Politics* (trans. T.A. Sinclair, rev. T.J.S.), Harmondsworth, Penguin Classics, 1981.
4.62 Stalley, R.F., *Aristotle, The Politics* (trans. E. Barker, rev. R.F.S.), Oxford, World's Classics, 1995.
4.63 Reeve, C.D.C., *Aristotle, Politics*, Indianopolis/Cambridge, Hackett Publishing Company, 1998.

Commentary with Greek text

4.64 Newman, W.L., *The Politics of Aristotle*, 4 vols, Oxford, Clarendon Press, 1887–1902.

Commentary with German translation

4.65 Schütrumpf, E., *Aristoteles: Politik*, vol. 1 (containing book 1), Berlin, Akademie Verlag, 1991; vol. 2 (containing books 2 and 3), Darmstadt, Wissenschaftliche Buchgesellschaft, 1991; vol. 3 (containing books 4–6) with H.-J. Gehrke, Berlin, Academie Verlag, 1996.

Commentaries with English translation

4.66a Saunders, T.J., *Aristotle, Politics*, Books 1 and 2, Oxford, Clarendon Aristotle Series, 1995 [1.36].
4.66b Robinson, R., *Aristotle, Politics*, Books 3 and 4, Oxford, Clarendon Aristotle Series, 1962 (repr. with supplementary essay by D. Keyt, 1995) [1.36].
4.66c Keyt, D., *Aristotle, Politics*, Books 5 and 6, Oxford, Clarendon Aristotle Series, 1999 [1.36].
4.66d Kraut, R., *Aristotle, Politics*, Books 7 and 8, Oxford, Clarendon Aristotle Series, 1997 [1.36].

Bibliographies

In Saunders [4.61] and [4.66a], Stalley [4.62], Reeve [4.63], Schütrumpf [4.65], Robinson [4.66b], Keyt [466c], Kraut [466d], and in Barnes [1.38], Keyt and Miller [4.70], and Miller [4.91] below. Comprehensive critical bibliography:

4.67 Touloumakos, J., 'Aristoteles' "Politik", 1925–1985', *Lustrum* 32 (1990), 177–282, 35 (1993), 181–289; in progress.

Collections of essays

4.68 Barnes, J., see [1.53] vol. 2.
4.69 Patzig, G. (ed.) see, [1.51].
4.70 Keyt, D. and Miller, F.D., *A Companion to Aristotle's 'Politics'*, Oxford and Cambridge, Mass., Blackwell, 1991.

Influence of the Politics

4.71 Barker, E., *The Political Thought of Plato and Aristotle*, London, Methuen, 1906, 497–522.
4.72 Dunbabin, J., 'The reception and interpretation of Aristotle's *Politics*', in Kretzmann, N. *et al.* (eds), *The Cambridge History of Later Medieval Philosophy*, Cambridge, Cambridge University Press, 1982, 723–37.
4.73 Langholm, O., *The Aristotelian Analysis of Usury*, Bergen, Universitets- forlaget, 1984.

General account

4.74 Mulgan, R.G., *Aristotle's Political Theory*, Oxford, Clarendon Press, 1977.

Books and articles

4.75 Arnhart, L., 'The Darwinian biology of Aristotle's political animals', *American Journal of Political Science* 38 (1994), 464–85.
4.76 Barker, E., *Greek Political Theory: Plato and his Predecessors*, 4th edn, London, Methuen, 1951.
4.77 Barnes, J., 'Aristotle and political liberty', in Patzig [1.51], 249–63, with comments by R. Sorabji: 'State power: Aristotle and fourth century philosophy', 264–76.
4.78 Cooper, J.M., 'Political animals and civic friendship', in Patzig [1.51], 220–41, with comments by J. Annas, 242–8.
4.79 Everson, S., 'Aristotle on the foundations of the state', *Political Studies* 36 (1988), 89–101.
4.80 Fortenbaugh, W.W., 'Aristotle on slaves and women', in Barnes, Schofield and Sorabji [1.53] vol. 2, 135–9.
4.81 Harvey, F.D., 'Two kinds of equality', *Classica et Mediaevalia* 26 (1965), 101–46; 27 (1965), 99–100.
4.82 Huxley, G., 'On Aristotle's best state', in Cartledge, P. and Harvey, F.D. (eds), *Crux: Essays presented to G.E.M. de Ste. Croix on his 75th birthday*, Exeter, Imprint Academic, 1985, 139–49.

4.83 Irwin, T.H., 'Aristotle's defence of private property', in Keyt and Miller [4.70] 200–25. Original version in *Social Philosophy and Policy*, 4 (1987), 37–54.

4.84 Jaeger, W., *Aristotle: Fundamentals of the History of his Development*, 2nd edn, Oxford, Oxford University Press, 1948.

4.85 Johnson, C., *Aristotle's Theory of the State*, London, Macmillan, 1990.

4.86 Keyt, D., 'Three basic theorems in Aristotle's *Politics*', in Keyt and Miller [4.70] 118–41. Original version in *Phronesis* 32 (1987), 54–79.

4.87 Kullmann, W., 'Man as a political animal in Aristotle', in Keyt and Miller [4.70] 94–117.

4.88a Lloyd, G.E.R., 'The idea of nature in the *Politics*', in his *Aristotelian Explorations*, Cambridge, Cambridge University Press, 1996, 184–204. Original version (in French) in Aubenque, P. and Tordessillas, A. (eds), *Aristote, Politique*, Paris, Presses Universitaires de France, 1993, 135–59.

4.88b Lord, C., *Education and Culture in the Political Thought of Aristotle*, Ithaca, NY, Cornell University Press, 1982.

4.89 MacIntyre, A., *After Virtue*, London, Duckworth, 1981.

4.90 Meikle, S., *Aristotle's Economic Thought*, Oxford, Clarendon Press, 1995.

4.91 Miller, F.D., *Nature, Justice, and Rights in Aristotle's 'Politics'*, Oxford, Clarendon Press, 1995.

4.92 Mulgan, R.G., 'Aristotle's doctrine that man is a political animal', *Hermes* 102 (1974), 438–45.

4.93 Rowe, C.J., 'Aims and methods in Aristotle's *Politics*', in Keyt and Miller [4.70] 57–74. Original version in *Classical Quarterly* 27 (1977), 159–72.

4.94 Schofield, M., 'Ideology and philosophy in Aristotle's theory of slavery', in Patzig [1.51] 1–27 (with comments by C.H. Kahn, 28–31).

4.95 Smith, N.D., 'Aristotle's theory of natural slavery', in Keyt and Miller [4.70] 142–55. Originally in *Phoenix* 37 (1983), 109–22.

4.96 Yack, B., *The Problems of a Political Animal: Community, Justice and Conflict in Aristotelian Political Thought*, Berkeley, University of California Press, 1993.

CHAPTER 5

The Peripatetic school[1]
Robert W. Sharples

❡

The history of Peripatetic philosophy after Aristotle falls into two phases, divided by the renewal of interest in the works we now possess after their publication by Andronicus in the first century BC.

Initially, Aristotle's own associates in the Lyceum and their successors carried on the work of the school. When Aristotle left Athens for Euboea at the news of the death of Alexander the Great in 323 BC, the headship of the school passed to Theophrastus of Eresus, who had collaborated with Aristotle at least since the latter's stay in Assos in Asia Minor in 347–345 BC. When Theophrastus died in 288/7 or 287/6 BC, he was succeeded by Strato of Lampsacus, who remained head of the school until his own death eighteen years later. The school was initially a centre of Macedonian influence in Athens, as it had been in Aristotle's own lifetime; Demetrius of Phalerum, a member of the school, was regent in Athens for Cassander from 318 to 307, and it was probably he who gave Theophrastus, though a resident alien, the right of owning property. The philosophical schools were expelled from Athens for a year after Demetrius' fall, and this may well have been motivated by hostility to the Peripatetics in particular.

The early activity of the school was characterised, as it had already been in Aristotle's lifetime, by the collection and interpretation of information in every field, and by the raising and the attempted resolution of theoretical difficulties. Examples of two very different themes in the collection of information are provided by the best known of the surviving works of Theophrastus. The *Characters* is a series of sketches of more or less imperfect personality types; it has been variously interpreted as material for a study of comedy, for the presentation of character in rhetoric, or for the study of character which the ancients called 'ethics' but we might rather classify as

147

psychology. Theophrastus' botanical writings, the *Researches on Plants* (*Historia plantarum*) and *Explanations of Plants* (*De causis plantarum*) are the earliest systematic botanical texts to survive. The contrast between the *Researches* and *Explanations*, between the collection of data and the more theoretical work, reflects Aristotle's own practice in his zoological writings; but we should beware of assuming that the collection of material, and particularly its arrangement, is not already guided by theoretical considerations. The botanical subject-matter indeed requires conscious consideration, or tacit re-adjustment, of the Aristotelian theoretical framework; what is unnatural may become natural with time (*Explanations of Plants* 4.11.7), and the way in which art helps nature in the cultivation of plants, both art and nature setting out to achieve what is best, prompts consideration of whether the true end of a tree's growth is to produce fertile seed or edible fruit – edible by humans, that is (cf. especially *Explanations of Plants* 1.16). Theophrastus is prepared, in discussing wild and cultivated species, to speak about natural kinds in a flexible way, describing reversion from cultivated to wild varieties as changes of kind (*genos*).[2] But – whatever view one takes of Aristotle's own position on the fixedness of natural kinds in zoology[3] – Theophrastus does not explicitly present his approach to natural history as different from that of Aristotle.

The Lyceum was also active in collecting the views of earlier scholars: Eudemus compiled a history of mathematics, Menon of medicine, and Theophrastus the opinions of earlier philosophers about the natural world and about sense-perception. Among other historical activities were the work of Theophrastus' contemporaries Aristoxenus (on music) and Dicaearchus (on cultural history and biographies of philosophers and poets). Theophrastus' fellow-townsman Phainias wrote on botany (fragments 36–49 Wehrli) and on political history. Theophrastus' concern with earlier writers was not, however, purely historical; like Aristotle himself, he discussed their views as a basis for establishing his own[4] – though he does seem to have gone into more detail than Aristotle, and some interest in historical detail for its own sake cannot be excluded.

There are similarities between the activity of the Lyceum in this period and those of the scholars and scientists of Ptolemaic Alexandria. The two traditions indeed overlapped; Hermippus, described as a 'Peripatetic' biographer (of a somewhat sensationalist kind) was a follower of the Alexandrian scholar Callimachus, and other historians too are described as Peripatetics. The contributions of the two centres differed in different fields. In zoology the Peripatetics wrote as natural scientists, the Alexandrian scholars as literary scholars and encyclopaedists, at one remove from their scientific subject-matter and concerned especially with the explaining of classical literary texts. In human anatomy and physiology, on the other hand, the Alexandrians, aided by their practice of dissection, were in the forefront.[5]

It has often been held that Theophrastus, and to an even greater extent Strato, changed the emphasis of Peripatetic philosophy, with a progressive movement towards on empiricism and materialism. There is *some* truth in this picture; the pseudo-Aristotelian *Problems*, and other works wrongly attributed to Aristotle such as the *Mechanics* and *On Things Heard* (*De audibilibus*) which show this tendency, derive from this period of the school, and a notable example of empirical observation is Strato's proof that falling bodies accelerate, from the fact that water which falls as a continuous stream breaks into separate droplets further down (fragment 73 in [5.57]). But the contrast with Aristotle himself can be overstated. For our knowledge of much of Theophrastus' activity and all of Strato's we are dependent on fragmentary reports by later writers. Writers like Plutarch, a Platonist, and Cicero, emphasising the differences between philosophers of the same school in the interests of neo-Academic sceptical debate, may not be the best guides to whether or not Strato is a good Aristotelian.[6] Plutarch indeed explicitly presents Strato as denying the involvement of purpose in the natural world, but this may be tendentious; for Aristotle also, in *Physics* 2, nature is not a *conscious* force.

To show that there is a basis in *some* passages of Aristotle for a position adopted by Theophrastus or Strato does not indeed establish that it is not in some sense un-Aristotelian; divergence can take the form of selective emphasis and omission as well as of straight contradiction. But such divergence may be unconscious and unintentional; and since selective emphasis of particular aspects of Aristotle's thought is not confined to Theophrastus and Strato, or even to Plutarch and Cicero, but is found among modern interpreters as well, we need to be aware of the standpoint from which a judgement of what is or is not Aristotelian is being made. Those who regard metaphysics as the central philosophical issue and theology, in the sense of the study of incorporeal principles, as central to metaphysics may well regard not only Theophrastus and Strato but later ancient Peripatetics too as neglecting or rejecting what *they* regard as Aristotle's chief contributions. In a recent masterly short account of Aristotle, Jonathan Barnes devoted just two pages ([5.164] 63–5) out of eighty-eight to Aristotle's theology and the theory of the Unmoved Mover. This might have surprised St Thomas Aquinas and some other leading interpreters of Aristotle, ancient, medieval and modern; but Theophrastus and Strato might have found Barnes' Aristotle more familiar than Aquinas'.

One of the Theophrastean works to survive is his so-called *Metaphysics* (the original title is unknown). This has often been described as 'a fragment'; it seems in fact to be complete, but it raises questions rather than answering them. In questioning two central Aristotelian doctrines, the explanation of natural phenomena in terms of purpose and the theory of the Unmoved Mover, it can readily be seen as indicating Theophrastus' rejection of central Aristotelian doctrines – especially when Theophrastus can be seen as paving the way for Strato. However, Most in [5.50] has shown that some (but only some) of the examples of purpose in nature apparently rejected by Theophrastus are ones equally rejected by Aristotle himself, and has suggested that Theophrastus' discussion is aimed not against Aristotelian teleology but against a more thorough-going Platonist version. And Theophrastus' treatise does have a positive message, which is that the universe is an organised system in which the same degree of purposefulness and goodness should not be expected at every level (2 6a2, 5 8a3, 7 8a27; cf. Laks in [5.50] 237 ff.) – a theme we shall find recurring in later Peripatetics too. Theophrastus also emphasises the need for limits to enquiry (*Metaphysics* 8 9b21 and fragments 158–9 FHS and G).

That Theophrastus did reject Aristotle's Unmoved Mover seems probable enough; but Aristotle did not accept the theory of the Unmoved Mover throughout his career, and in any case raising objections is a thoroughly Aristotelian way of proceeding. Critics have been too ready to forget the problematic and exploratory nature of much of Aristotle's own surviving works, and too ready to interpret his successors as abandoning what they themselves regard as crucial features of Aristotelianism rather than as continuing Aristotle's enquiries (or sharing in them, for there is no reason to suppose that Theophrastus' *Metaphysics* was not written in Aristotle's lifetime).[7]

Even where Aristotle's own position can be easily determined those of his successors are not always clear. Steinmetz in [5.41] claims, as will be discussed in detail later, that Theophrastus modified the Aristotelian system of four sublunary elements. Theophrastus certainly begins his surviving treatise *On Fire* by raising general questions about the Aristotelian theory, but, characteristically, then turns aside from the general questions to investigate particular phenomena – concerning which some of his remarks do seem to reveal un-Aristotelian assumptions. At this point we may, like Steinmetz, suppose that Theophrastus did indeed develop a distinctive theory of his own, and look for other reports of Theophrastus' views that seem to confirm this; or we may, with Gottschalk ([5.65] 80–1; [5.42] 24–6), suppose that Theophrastus couples a general adherence to an Aristotelian framework with a flexibility and readiness to speculate in particular details. Gottschalk stresses, indeed, that Theophrastus paved the way for Strato to adopt a more revolutionary approach to physics.

After Strato the Lyceum rapidly fell into decline. Strato's successor Lyco (head of the school for forty-four years from 270/69 or 269/8 BC) was notable for his oratory, social standing and love of luxury rather than for science or philosophy; his successor Ariston of Ceos was noted chiefly for his biographical studies. It is probably to Ariston that we owe the preservation of the wills of Aristotle and Theophrastus, and perhaps the list of Aristotelian titles in Diogenes Laertius. In the second century Critolaus, who accompanied the Academic Carneades and the Stoic Diogenes of

Babylon in their visit to Rome in 155 BC, was philosophically active, chiefly in defending Aristotelian positions (the eternity of the world, the fifth heavenly element, and the inclusion of bodily and external goods as well as virtue as a constituent of happiness) against the Stoics; but he seems to have been the exception rather than the rule.

Those for whom the most important aspects of Aristotelianism are those which they see Aristotle's immediate successors as questioning, rejecting or neglecting have tended to see the decline of the Peripatetic school as a natural consequence of the change of emphasis. Others, themselves favouring an empiricist approach to the natural world, have seen Theophrastus and Strato as advancing scientific enquiry where Aristotle's attitudes hindered it;[8] this equally seems to overstate the contrast between Aristotle and his successors.

The real reasons for the decline of the Lyceum may be harder to recapture. Certainly the special sciences in the Hellenistic period developed an impetus of their own in institutions other than the Lyceum – notably medicine in Ptolemaic Alexandria; but that does not explain why zoology and botany, the sciences Aristotle and Theophrastus had made their own, declined in the Lyceum without developing elsewhere. Where philosophy in a narrower sense is concerned, the answer may be easier. Aristotle's thought is guided by certain structures and assumptions, but within that framework it is characteristically questioning, open-ended and provisional. And Aristotle explicitly stressed, against Plato, the relative independence of the different branches of philosophical enquiry. For those who were attracted by comprehensive and dogmatic philosophical systems the Lyceum had nothing to offer that could compare with Epicureanism or the Stoa;[9] while for those who rejected dogmatism the Aristotelian approach must have seemed a poor second-best to the aggressive scepticism introduced to the Academy by Arcesilaus in the middle of the third century BC. Strato's successors emphasised those aspects of the school's activity, present indeed from the outset, that related to the general literary and rhetorical culture of the period, and this too may have lessened the distinctive appeal of the school. There is nothing un-Aristotelian in attention to the views and concerns of people in general, as a glance at the *Nicomachean Ethics* will show; but for Aristotle himself it was only the foundation on which he built.

To speak of how Aristotle's 'unpublished' writings might have seemed to Hellenistic readers assumes, indeed, that those who might have wanted to read them could have done so. The decline of the Lyceum is linked by Strabo and Plutarch with a story that Aristotle's and Theophrastus' writings, left by Theophrastus not to Strato but to Neleus of Scepsis in the Troad, passed from Neleus to his descendants. They, having no interest in philosophy, hid the books in a cellar to prevent their seizure by the kings of Pergamum, who wanted to create a library to rival the one in Alexandria. Thus, according to the story, the 'unpublished' works of Aristotle – those which we now have, the originally 'published' works having been lost later in antiquity – were inaccessible until rediscovered in the first century BC, and the Peripatetics were unable 'to do philosophy in a systematic way' without them. The manuscripts were eventually recovered by the bibliophile Apellicon, who took them to Athens and published them, but inaccurately; they were then seized by the Roman general Sulla when he sacked the city in 86 BC, and taken to Rome, where they were copied by the grammarian Tyrannio. From his copies a new collection, which is the basis of the arrangement of Aristotle's writings that exists today, was produced by Andronicus of Rhodes; this also included some works of Theophrastus.[10]

It is true, as we shall shortly see, that the revival of Aristotelianism dates from Andronicus, and that it is different in character from what had preceded it; where the earlier Peripatetics had sought to continue Aristotle's work, later writers are essentially looking back to it and commenting upon it. It is significant that Strabo supposes that one *could not be* a Peripatetic philosopher without access to texts of Aristotle himself; concentration on the study of canonical texts was a general characteristic of the period.[11]

What is much less certain is that Aristotle's works were indeed inaccessible in the intervening period. It is unlikely that even 'unpublished' works existed in only one copy; we know that different, and differing, copies of Aristotle's *Physics* existed in the lifetime of Theophrastus, for Eudemus (fragment 6 Wehrli) wrote to him about a variant reading, and Strato left to Lyco 'all the books, apart from those I have written myself' (Diogenes Laertius 5.62).[12] The possibility remains that, if Aristotle's works were little read in the Hellenistic period, this was not because they were unavailable but because – however strange this may seem to modern interpreters for whom Aristotle is a central figure in the whole history of philosophy – they were not considered of great interest.

Aristotelian doctrines were indeed still referred to; but characteristic of the Hellenistic period is, not the study of Aristotle's own works, but the compilation and use of summaries of the sort that underlie Cicero's knowledge of Aristotle and the account in Areius Didymus (below). Examples of this type of writing include the 'Aristotelian Divisions' preserved in Diogenes Laertius' life of Plato and in a manuscript in Venice[13] and the source of the account of Aristotelian philosophy in book 5 of Diogenes Laertius' *Lives of the Philosophers*.[14]

The revival of Aristotelian studies which began with Andronicus' collection (on which see Gottschalk [5.77] 1089–97) was different in kind from what had gone before, for the status of Aristotle's text had changed. Aristotle's immediate successors had indeed taken his works as a starting point; Eudemus' *Physics* essentially followed Aristotle's while clarifying certain issues (Wehrli [5.57] vol. 8: 87), and Boethius presents Theophrastus (fragment 72A FHS and G) as filling in the points that Aristotle had not fully covered. But for the early Peripatetics it was a matter of continuing

Aristotle's work, not of regarding him as the canonical authority to be interpreted.

The writing of summaries of Aristotelian doctrines did not cease; but use was now made – to differing extents – of the treatises edited by Andronicus.[15] Nicolaus of Damascus, a courtier of Herod the Great, compiled, in addition to historical and ethnographical writings, a summary of Aristotle's philosophy which collected together material on similar topics from different Aristotelian texts. This survives in a Syriac summary and in other fragments. A treatise by Nicolaus on plants, possibly part of the compendium, was translated from Syriac into Arabic in the ninth century AD, thence into Latin in the second half of the twelfth century, and thence back into Greek. In the process it became mis-attributed to Aristotle himself, and it is this re-translation that appears as *On Plants* in modern editions of Aristotle, though the falsity of the attribution was already realised in the Renaissance.[16]

Areius Didymus, a Stoic and 'court-philosopher' to the emperor Augustus, wrote summaries of the teachings of the various schools. Of his treatment of the Peripatetics we possess the section on ethics, quoted at length by Stobaeus, and fragments of the section on physics; the doctrines they present are Aristotelian in content, and Areius sometimes used the texts made available by Andronicus, but the terminology and emphasis reflect Hellenistic preoccupations and Areius' concern to stress the similarities between Peripatetic and Stoic ethics.[17]

Other scholars, however, concentrated on the writing of commentaries on the newly popular Aristotelian texts. The earliest of these are now lost except for scattered quotations, having been replaced by later, often Neoplatonic works. Andronicus and his pupil Boethus[18] commented on the *Categories* and on other works; so too did Alexander of Aegae, teacher of the emperor Nero. The earliest surviving complete commentary is that of Aspasius (first half of the second century AD) on the *Nicomachean Ethics*; Adrastus of Aphrodisias' explanations of the literary and historical references in the *Ethics* were incorporated into the later anonymous commentary on books 2–5.[19] But the earliest author from whom a considerable number of commentaries survives is Alexander of Aphrodisias, described as 'the commentator' by his successors; though even of his works only a part survives. Interest in Aristotle's 'published' works declined as that in the 'unpublished' works in Andronicus' collection developed; for Cicero, who either did not know of or was not interested in the texts edited by Andronicus, Aristotle still meant the Aristotle of the 'published' works, but he is perhaps the last major writer for whom this is true.

The Lyceum may have ceased to exist as an institution at the time of Sulla's sack of Athens.[20] But Athens continued to be a centre for philosophers of all schools. In AD 176 Marcus Aurelius established posts there for teachers of the four principal philosophies (Platonic, Aristotelian, Stoic and

Epicurean), and it may be to an appointment at Athens that Alexander refers in the dedication of his treatise *On Fate*, written between AD 198 and 209. Alexander of Aphrodisias would not in any case have been the first holder of the Athenian post; that may have been his older namesake, Alexander of Damascus. The institution of the imperial appointments only confirmed a situation that already existed; philosophers of the different schools were teaching in Athens – and engaging in lively polemic against each other – throughout the second century AD.

Alexander's commentaries do not yet show the adaptation to a context of formal teaching apparent in the later, Neoplatonic commentaries. They are discursive and open-ended, presenting alternative interpretations without always indicating a preference between them.[21] They seem to reflect the results of teaching and discussion rather than an actual record of the process. We also possess some collections of short discussions attributed to Alexander; there were once more that are now lost. Some of these take the form of problems in Aristotelian doctrine, or in the interpretation of particular texts, followed by solutions; others are expositions of particular passages, or summaries of texts or doctrines. Whether they are by Alexander himself has to be considered text by text. Since many of them are connected with themes dealt with in Alexander's commentaries or in monographs by him, it is natural to assume that they at least originate from his school. But it has recently been suggested that some of them may be considerably later in date, though still concerned essentially with Aristotelian issues.[22] And this highlights a problem: that of the second disappearance of Aristotelianism, or rather its absorption into Neoplatonism.

We know the names of Alexander's teachers, and can identify some of their doctrines and his reaction against them. But we do not know the names of any of his pupils; and with one exception all ancient commentators on Aristotle after Alexander whose writings are known to us are Neoplatonists. There had long been a tendency on the part of Platonists to incorporate Aristotelian ideas into their expositions of Plato; some, notably the second-century AD Platonist Atticus, rebelled against this, but they were in the minority. Plotinus himself had the works of Aristotle and the commentaries of Alexander, among others, read in his school (Porphyry, *Life of Plotinus* 14). Subsequently, with the formalisation of the Neoplatonic philosophical curriculum, selected works of Aristotle were studied as a preliminary to the reading of Plato. The emphasis was on the logical and physical treatises and the work *On the Soul*; that explains why Aspasius' commentary on the *Ethics* survived – there was no incentive to replace it – and why we have to wait until the twelfth century AD for commentaries on the *Parva Naturalia*, the zoological works, and the *Rhetoric*.[23]

The exception to the general dominance of Platonists after Alexander is Themistius, who in the fourth century AD combined epideictic rhetoric with the production of explanatory paraphrases of Aristotle's works. But

Themistius' Aristotelianism has no clear heritage; we cannot trace either its immediate antecedents or his successors. There are occasional references to other individuals as 'Peripatetics', such as the bishop Anatolius of Alexandria in the third century AD; and as late as AD 500 Dorus from Arabia is described as having spent more of his life in the study of Aristotle than he should have, before being introduced to the higher study of Plato by Isidorus.[24] But none of this amounts to the continued existence of a distinctive Aristotelian tradition.

The second decline of Aristotelianism is a topic we will return to. First, however, it will be convenient to consider developments in each branch of Aristotelian philosophy in turn throughout the period of the five centuries separating Aristotle from Alexander.

∾ LOGIC ∾

Theophrastus and Eudemus continued and developed the study of formal logic which Aristotle had instituted in the *Prior Analytics*. There are two areas in which they made a particular contribution. The first is in modal logic, the logic of necessity and possibility. Aristotle had utilised a notion of possibility according to which 'possible' excludes not only what is impossible but also what is necessary; while this is intuitive (it is not natural to say 'it is *possible* that 2+2=4', for example), it removes the expected parallelism between statements of possibility and statements of fact. For with this type of possibility 'it is possible that all B are A' implies 'it is possible that no B are A', and 'it is possible that no B are A' does not imply 'it is possible that no A are B' (for it may be that all B have the possibility of either being A or not being A, but that there are some other A that cannot be B at all). Second, while it may seem natural to suppose that a conclusion cannot be stronger than the weakest of the premises from which it follows – the 'weakest-link-in-the-chain' principle, or, as medieval logicians put it, *sequitur conclusio partem deteriorem*, 'the conclusion follows the weaker part' – Aristotle argued that it made a difference which premiss was concerned. For him 'necessarily all B are A' and 'all C are B' yield 'necessarily all C are A', while 'all B are A' and 'necessarily all C are B' yield only 'all C are A' and not 'necessarily all C are A'.

On both these issues Theophrastus and Eudemus, who are regularly cited together in our sources, adopted the opposite view; in both cases the effect is to make modal logic simpler and tidier. Statements of possibility now behave like statements of fact, and the modality of the conclusion in all syllogisms is determined by a simple rule. If Aristotle was influenced in taking the view he did by extra-logical considerations (for example, that being as a matter of fact a member of a group implies possessing necessarily the properties that all members of the group possess necessarily), the changes made by Theophrastus and Eudemus may indicate a move from logic conceived in terms of its applications in the real world to logic as a purely formal system. It is, however, one thing to assert this with hindsight, quite another to claim that Theophrastus and Eudemus would have seen the change in these terms.

Theophrastus also developed the study of argument forms mentioned by Aristotle but not fully discussed by him. It seems highly probable that these included the forms of argument with conditional, conjunctive and disjunctive premisses which were to form the basis alike of Stoic logic and of modern propositional logic. But it also seems likely that Theophrastus saw these simply as one among several types of secondary argument form, the categorical syllogism remaining primary, and that he did not anticipate Chrysippus' development of propositional logic as a comprehensive system.[25]

The eventual decline of the Stoic school, and the adoption of Aristotelian texts into the Neoplatonic curriculum, ensured the victory of Peripatetic logic over Stoic logic as the subject of formal study. But the contribution of Aristotelian writers after Theophrastus and Eudemus to the development of logic was not great. The innovations came from writers outside the school, such as Galen (even though it is not true, as once thought, that Galen discovered the fourth figure of the 'Aristotelian' syllogism[26].) Alexander wrote extensive commentaries on Aristotle's logical works (only those on *Prior Analytics* 1 and on the *Topics* now surviving) and a separate monograph, now lost, on *Syllogisms with Mixed Premisses* (that is, premisses of differing modalities).

PHYSICS AND METAPHYSICS; FATE AND PROVIDENCE

Aristotle defined time as the numbered aspect of motion (*Physics* 4.11 219b5), indicated most clearly by the movement of the heavenly sphere, though not to be identified with this (*Physics* 4.14 223b23). Theophrastus and Eudemus followed Aristotle's view, but Strato rejected it on the grounds that motion and time are continuous whereas number is discrete[27] and defined time as quantity or measure both in motion and in rest, thus giving it an existence independently of motion (fragments 75–9 Wehrli). He was followed in this by Boethus.[28] Alexander explicitly rejected such a theory, and identified time as the number of the motion of the outermost heavenly sphere more definitely than Aristotle himself had done. Where Aristotle had suggested that there could be no time without soul, as without soul there could be no numbering (*Physics* 4.14 223a21 ff.), Alexander argued that time is in its own nature a unity and is divided by the present moment only in our thought. This suggests that time itself can exist without any actual *numbering*; and

Alexander appears to identify time in this sense with the continuous *numerable* movement of the outermost heavenly sphere. Characteristically, Alexander's approach combines a claim to be stating and defending the 'Aristotelian' position with a new development and emphasis of his own.[29]

Theophrastus assembled a series of difficulties for Aristotle's definition of place as the innermost unmoved limit of what surrounds a thing (Aristotle *Physics* 4.4 212a20; Theophrastus fragment 146 FHS and G.) We do not know whether these difficulties led Theophrastus actually to reject the Aristotelian conception of place. The Neoplatonist commentator Simplicius, after outlining the view of place held by his predecessor Damascius, mentions in passing that Theophrastus seems to have anticipated this, interpreting place as the proper position of a part in a complex whole.[30] Strato (fragment 55 Wehrli, cf. fragments 59–60 Wehrli) certainly rejected Aristotle's view of place, and defined it instead as the interval or extension delimited by the outermost surface of what is contained or the innermost surface of what contains it – which amounts to saying that the place of a thing is, not as for Aristotle what contains it, but the space that it occupies.[31]

For Aristotle sublunary things are composed of the four elements, earth, air, fire and water (which can be and are transmuted into each other), while the heavenly spheres are composed of ether, the fifth element, which has the capacity for movement but for no other kind of change; fire and air naturally move upwards, towards the heavens, and earth and water downwards. Steinmetz [5.41] argued that Theophrastus both rejected the fifth element and argued that fire requires a substrate in a way that the other elements do not. It is true that in the opening section of *On Fire* Theophrastus draws attention to the fact that terrestrial fire needs a constant supply of fuel, which might be thought to conflict with its status as a primary element; and he also speculates over whether the sun, if not actually fire, may not be at least hot.[32]

Such thoughts might lead to a world-picture radically different from Aristotle's – if indeed Aristotle's own views were consistent throughout.[33] It is not, however, clear how far Theophrastus pursued the implications. For the introductory discussion of *On Fire* ends inconclusively, and Theophrastus turns to more specific questions, not before pointing out that the need for replenishment applies not just to fire but to all the sublunary elements (*On Fire* 8). As for the fifth element, Philoponus suggests that Theophrastus (fragment 161A FHS and G) retained it, and the evidence to the contrary is at best dubious.[34] Strato (fragment 84 Wehrli) certainly rejected the fifth element and held that the heavens are composed of fire. He also held that all the elements naturally move to the centre of the universe (fragments 50–2 Wehrli).[35] The fifth element was later rejected also by Xenarchus, a Peripatetic of the time of Augustus.[36]

Steinmetz also suggested that Theophrastus emphasised the role of heat, especially that of the sun, in causing physical change, and that he modified the Aristotelian explanation of meteorological phenomena by dry and moist exhalations from the earth and the water on it, reducing the dry one to mere reflection of the heat of the sun. But both Theophrastus' *Meteorology* and his treatise *On Fire* suggest less divergence from Aristotle's views than Steinmetz supposed.[37] And, once again, there is the question of Aristotle's own consistency; for Longrigg ([5.67] 216–21), who argues that Theophrastus treated fire as active and the other three elements as passive, finds that both this and Theophrastus' distinction between the generative heat of the sun and terrestrial fire develop themes already present in Aristotle's physiological and biological writings, as opposed to his general physical theory. The Stoics rejected a fifth element and gave a major role to fire, and later, with Chrysippus, *pneuma*, as embodiments of the active principle in the universe; but the presence of similar tendencies in Aristotle's own successors does not mean that their enterprise of continuing and developing Aristotle's thought should be seen only as a transition paving the way for Stoicism.

Although Theophrastus denied the existence of the Unmoved Mover, he continued to hold, like Aristotle,[38] that the heavens are ensouled (fragments 159, 252 FHS and G). That the heavens are ensouled was later the belief of Alexander of Aphrodisias, and of his teacher Herminus (Simplicius, *On the Heaven* 380.3 ff.).[39]

Aristotle maintained the infinite divisibility of matter and the absence of any void. Scholars have drawn particular attention to contexts where Theophrastus, in the explanation of physical processes, makes use of the notion of passages or pores (notably *On Fire* 42). There is no inconsistency between this and Aristotelian physical theory, unless we are to suppose that the pores contain vacuum; they may well be thought of rather as containing matter more tenuous than what surrounds them. Strato was certainly prepared to allow the existence of 'microvoids' within material bodies (fragment 65a Wehrli).[40] Theophrastus *did* it seems employ the principle of 'nature abhorring a vacuum' in the explanation of winds,[41] but this and the idea of microvoids are not equivalent, as Furley [5.68] 156 ff. points out. Both ideas influenced the Alexandrian physician Erasistratus, who had been a fellow-pupil of Theophrastus with Strato, in his explanations of physiological processes; and the influence of Strato's theory has also been seen in the technological writer Hero of Alexandria.[42] But all this is still far removed from the Atomist conception of discrete particles of matter moving within an otherwise empty space. A tendency to materialistic explanations can be seen in Theophrastus' introduction of material effluences into the explanation of odour, which Aristotle had interpreted rather as the propagation of a change in the intervening medium. Even light was explained by some Peripatetics in material terms.[43]

On issues of physical theory such as these the Peripatetics of the Roman Empire, concerned as they were to explain the Aristotelian texts, returned to more orthodox Aristotelian positions. (Alexander of Aphrodisias had a particular interest in the theory of vision, inherited from his teacher Sosigenes.) But on other aspects of the organisation of the natural world later Peripatetics found themselves constrained to develop 'Aristotelian' positions on issues to which Aristotle himself had devoted little or no direct attention. The Stoics, in particular, had made fate and divine providence central topics of philosophical debate. Aristotle himself had little to say about the former, and his account in *Metaphysics* Λ of the Unmoved Mover as engaged in self-contemplation, causing movement as an object of desire without itself being affected, seems to rule out divine providence altogether.

The nature of divine involvement with the universe forms the climax of the treatise *On the World* (*De mundo*), attributed to Aristotle (and so contained in our standard editions) but probably in fact a composition of the Roman period.[44] In this treatise God is likened to the Persian King, ruling by delegated authority; divine influence is present in the world, but God himself is remote in a way that is appropriate to his dignity. Aristotle himself in *Metaphysics* Λ 10, arguing that goodness is to be located both in the Unmoved Mover and in the orderliness of the world dependent on it, but more in the former than in the latter, had employed the images of a military commander and the head of a household; these were to play an important part in subsequent discussion, as we shall see. Other interpreters, however, took a harsher line, and the standard view attributed to Aristotle in both pagan and Christian sources – among them Areius Didymus and Diogenes Laertius – is that the heavens are the objects of divine providence while the sublunary region is not. This view may derive originally from Critolaus (fragment 15 Wehrli).[45] The Platonist Atticus (fragment 3 des Places) in the second century AD attacked Aristotle vehemently for holding such a view (and also for denying the immortality of the soul, of which more later); Aristotle's views, he argued, are really no different from those of Epicurus, but at least Epicurus had the courage of his convictions and denied providence altogether, whereas Aristotle allows its existence but only in a context where it cannot directly benefit us.

It was apparently in reply to Atticus that Alexander of Aphrodisias developed an alternative 'Aristotelian' theory of providence, preserved partly in his treatise *On Providence* which survives in two Arabic versions, and partly in various short texts attributed to him. Providence is located in the heavens, he argues, in the sense that it is exercised from the heavens over the sublunary region, which, being subject to coming-to-be and passing-away, is the only part of the universe that actually needs providential care. However, providence extends to the sublunary only in preserving the eternity of natural kinds; there is no involvement of providence in the lives of individuals. Alexander can thus account for the occurrence of misfortunes in the lives of individuals, and also avoid an involvement of the divine in things that would be beneath its dignity – something for which he repeatedly criticises the Stoics.[46]

Alexander's theory of providence is a re-working of authentically Aristotelian materials in a new guise. That the movements of the heavens, and especially the seasonal movements of the sun, preserve the continuity of sublunary coming-to-be and hence of natural kinds is argued by Aristotle himself in the penultimate chapter of his *On Coming-to-be and Passing-away*, and the eternity of natural kinds had been used as an argument for that of the world by Critolaus (fragment 13 Wehrli).[47]

Similarly where fate is concerned Alexander's position is an adaptation of Aristotelian themes. For Aristotle what is natural applies for the most part but not always; and Alexander, in his treatise *On Fate*, states that an individual's fate is their nature or, quoting Heraclitus, their character, which for the most part determines what happens to them, but not always. Alexander may not have been the first to put forward this view; certainly one of the texts attributed to him endeavours to read such a notion of fate back into Aristotle's own two uses of the adjective 'fated', into Theophrastus and into an otherwise unknown Polyzelus.[48]

What Alexander's view of fate emphatically rules out is the Stoic concept of fate as inexorably determining everything. The unity of the universe, he argues, is preserved not by the chain of causes and effects, but by the regular movement of the heavens; as in a household, so in the universe minor variations in matters of detail do not affect the orderliness of the whole (Alexander, *On Fate* ch. 25). The similarity to Alexander's theory of providence is apparent; so too is the place in Peripatetic thought of the conception of the universe as a hierarchy in which the same degree of order, goodness and perfection is not to be expected at every level. It is tempting to see the remoteness of God in the *De mundo*, and Alexander's attacks on the Stoics for involving God in every detail of the management of the world, as reflecting the increased remoteness of earthly rulers when the Greek city state was replaced first by the Hellenistic monarchies and then by the Roman Empire; but the fact that the hierarchical picture is already implicit in Aristotle *Metaphysics* Λ 10 itself may argue for caution here.

Theophrastus and Strato devoted little attention to problems of general metaphysics such as the nature of universals; indeed, Strato's materialism is reflected in his emphasising the effect of one element in overcoming another rather than the division into matter and form (Gottschalk [5.58] 150, cf. Brink [5.1] 948). With the revival of Aristotelianism and the placing of the *Categories* at the beginning of the whole sequence of Aristotle's works the status of universals became a central issue. Once again, the thinker on whose views we are most fully informed is Alexander, though his views were anticipated by Boethus,[49] and some of the evidence comes from short texts which may not all be by Alexander himself. Definitions, it is argued, are of specific or generic forms; these do not include any of the peculiarities of individuals due to their matter, such as Socrates' snub nose, and yet are not in themselves *universal*; the nature of human being would be the same even if only one human being existed. Socrates exists because 'human being' exists, and not the other way round; yet 'human being' would not exist if no individual human being at all existed. The implication seems to be that each human being has the same nature or form, the form of the species human being, but that my form and yours are the same only in kind (or 'form'; the Greek is the same), not numerically; or, putting it another way, to speak of 'the same form' does not mean that there is a single numerically individual form that you and I share.[50]

Alexander's position has been criticised both in ancient and in modern times for being nominalist and hence un-Aristotelian. Some of those criticisms are, however, from a Platonist standpoint.[51] For Aristotle as well as for Alexander universals have their existence as *post rem* mental constructs;[52] but it is important that those mental constructs are not arbitrary but reflect the fundamental reality of the specific forms. The latter are the product of the abstracting power of intellect (Alexander, *On Soul* 90.2–11), but that does not mean that it is up to us which features we abstract. On the contrary, the important thing about every human being is that he or she is a *human being*, the various accidents due to matter being secondary to this. This explains why texts attributed to Alexander can say that the universal is prior to any *particular* individual;[53] and, while it may be questionable whether we should use ideas from one area of Alexander's philosophising to settle an issue in another, the emphasis in his theory of providence on the preservation of the species agrees with an emphasis on the reality of specific form. Lennox [5.175] indeed sees eternity in species through reproduction as the context for understanding what is meant by 'being one in form'.

Alexander has also been regarded as un-Aristotelian in diminishing the role of form in comparison with that of matter. But this is chiefly in the context of his doctrine of soul, to which we should now turn.

SOUL

Aristotle defined the soul as the form of the living creature. It is thus neither a separable immaterial entity (as Plato had supposed), nor a distinct material ingredient in the whole creature (as Epicurus for example was to argue). But neither is it, for Aristotle, simply a product of the arrangement of the bodily parts, reducible to the latter; body is to be explained in terms of soul, and in general compounds of matter and form are to be explained in terms of the latter. A human body has a certain structure in order to enable the human being to function in the way that human beings do.

However, that body is to be explained in terms of soul and not vice versa need not mean that a certain arrangement of bodily parts is not a necessary condition for the existence of a certain type of soul. In the case of perceptive soul the bodily organ that relates to a particular soul-faculty is evident; the eye in the case of sight, the ear in that of hearing. It is less obvious how we are to relate the soul to the body in general – both in terms of how soul and body interact, and in terms of whether some part of the body plays a particularly vital role. Aristotle had seen 'connate spirit' (*pneuma*) as the physical means by which soul operated, and the heart as the particularly vital organ, the first to develop in the embryo. He had also asserted that intellect, alone of the soul-faculties, was not correlated with any particular organ, and had spoken, in the notorious chapter 3.5 of *On Soul*, of a distinction in intellect between 'that which makes everything' and 'that which becomes everything', apparently presenting the former, active intellect as imperishable in a way in which the latter, passive intellect was not. The history of subsequent Peripatetic psychology is largely that of attempts to clarify these issues, attempts that were affected to varying extents by contemporary attitudes and the positions of other philosophical schools. It will be convenient first to discuss the nature of the soul as a whole and its relation to the body, and then to consider the question of intellect separately.

Among Aristotle's immediate pupils, Dicaearchus is said (fragments 11–12 Wehrli) to have regarded the soul as a 'harmony' or mixture of the four elements in the body, a view which some reports present as equivalent to denying the existence of the soul at all (fragments 7–8 Wehrli). Annas [5.160] 31 sees Dicaearchus' theory of the soul as eliminativist, with the *caveat* that our sources may be tendentious). Aristoxenus, too, is said (fragments 119–20 Wehrli) to have regarded the soul as a harmony or attunement of the body, simply. It is possible that both writers were prompted by Plato's attack on the Pythagorean theory of soul as a harmony in the *Phaedo* (86ad, 92a–94e) and that their interest was chiefly in attacking Plato's position. We do not know whether they actually presented their interpretations as 'Aristotelian'. Strato certainly brought some highly pertinent criticisms (fragments 122–7 Wehrli, cf. Gottschalk [5.58] 164 ff.) against Plato's arguments for immortality in the *Phaedo*, and was followed in this by Boethus.[55] Even less interest in Aristotle's theory is shown by Heraclides of Pontus (a pupil both of Aristotle and of Plato's successor Speusippus; he is a follower of the Academy rather than a Peripatetic, though sometimes treated as such), and by Clearchus, another writer on the fringes of the Peripatetic school; both were interested in 'out-of-the-body' experiences.[56]

Strato emphasised the role of *pneuma*, 'breath' or 'spirit', in the functioning of the soul. Aristotle and Theophrastus had used *pneuma* to explain bodily processes,[57] and for Strato (fragments 119–20 Wehrli) soul-activities were explained by *pneuma* extending throughout the body from the 'ruling part', which he located not in the chest (as both Epicurus and the Stoics did) but in the head, or more precisely in the space between the eyebrows. The term for 'ruling part' in our sources (*hêgemonikon*) is Stoic, but even if Strato did not use this actual word the idea is implied. Tertullian illustrates Strato's theory with the analogy of air in the various passages of a musical pipe (Strato, fragment 108 Wehrli); the Stoics were to use that of the tentacles of an octopus (*SVF* 2.836). Strato was influenced here by developments in contemporary medicine and anatomy; Erasistratus investigated the function of the nerves by dissection and argued that they contained 'psychic' *pneuma* extending from the brain. All sensation, Strato held, was felt in the ruling part of the soul, rather than in the bodily extremities (fragments 110–11 Wehrli); all sensation involved thought (fragment 112 Wehrli), and there is no thought not derived from sensation (fragment 74 Wehrli). Some have drawn a contrast between Strato's views on thought itself and those of Aristotle, emphasising Strato's empiricism; but the contrast sometimes depends on attributing to Aristotle himself a belief in intuition as a mode of cognition distinct from the senses, and this is at least questionable.[58]

Lyco's successor Ariston of Ceos may have stressed the distinction between rational and irrational soul, against the Stoics,[59] but perhaps in an ethical rather than a psychological context. Critolaus described the soul as made of ether, the fifth element (fragments 17–18 Wehrli; Annas [5.160] 33). It has been suggested that soul itself and ether were more closely linked in Aristotle's 'published' works than in those that survive; but this is questionable.[60] Cicero says that Aristotle identified the soul with ether, but this may reflect a misunderstanding, aided by the familiarity of materialistic theories of soul in other schools, of a reference in Aristotle's early *Eudemus* to soul as a fifth *incorporeal* nature besides the four material elements recognised at that stage.[61]

Andronicus defined the soul as the power arising from the mixture of the bodily elements,[62] and was followed in this by Alexander (*On Soul* 24.21–3). Alexander has been criticised for interpreting Aristotle in a materialist way, treating soul as form, indeed, but making form secondary to matter.[63] His treatment of soul as the culmination of an analysis which starts from the simple physical elements and builds up through successively more complex structures does suggest that he sees form in general and soul in particular as the product of material arrangement. However, it is not un-Aristotelian to say that a certain bodily arrangement is a *necessary condition* for the existence of soul.[64] Indeed, Alexander may have intended to defend an authentically Aristotelian position against more materialist interpretations. His view does indeed exclude any personal immortality; but so does Aristotle's own, with the *possible* exception of his cryptic remarks about the Active Intellect (see p. 165).

Andronicus probably, and Alexander certainly (*On Soul* 22.7 ff.), compared soul as a principle of movement with the nature of the simple bodies, for example the weight of earth. It was by appeal to this conception of nature (itself Aristotelian enough; Aristotle, *Physics* 2.1 192b21) that Alexander explained the application to the simple bodies of Aristotle's claim that everything that moves is moved by something (Aristotle, *Physics* 8.4 254b24), defending it in a treatise surviving only in Arabic.[65]

❧ INTELLECT ❧

Discussion of Aristotle's theory of intellect begins already with Theophrastus, who suggests that the reason that we are not always thinking is because of the mixture of the active intellect with potential intellect and body (Theophrastus fragments 320–1 FHS and G). A further problem was how intellect, which can have no nature of its own if it is to be able to receive all intelligible forms, can ever begin to perform the task of abstraction by which it separates forms from their matter (cf. Theophrastus fragments 307, 309, 316–17 FHS and G). Alexander *On Soul* 84.24–7 later expresses the point by saying that our intellect, at birth, is not so much like a blank wax tablet as like the blankness of the wax tablet; and Xenarchus suggested, whether seriously or as a *reductio ad absurdum*, that potential intellect was to be identified with prime matter. It was natural to see Aristotle's remarks in *On Soul* 3.5 about an active intellect which 'makes all things', contrasted with the passive intellect 'which becomes all things', as indicating some solution to this problem.

In the treatise *On the Generation of Animals*, moreover, Aristotle refers, in passing and with no very clear explanation, to intellect, alone of our soul-faculties, as entering into the father's seed, 'from outside' (Aristotle *Generation of Animals* 2.3 736b27) At some point this was linked with the Active Intellect of *On Soul*. One of the minor works attributed to Alexander, *On Intellect*, records – only to criticise in its turn – an answer to the objection that such an intellect could not 'come from outside' since, being immaterial, it could not change place at all. The objection and reply follow on a previous section introduced as 'from Aristoteles'; this is probably to be taken as a reference to its content being an interpretation of Aristotle's own doctrines, and in any case the identity of the person whose views are reported in this section, and of the originator of the following reply to the objection concerning change of place, are uncertain – the text may be disjointed.[66]

The section introduced as 'from Aristoteles' explains the role of the Active Intellect. It is not an element in the soul of each individual separately; rather, it is identified with the supreme intelligible, the Unmoved Mover, and acts upon our intellects to develop their potentiality through our thinking of it. The objection concerning movement is then answered by the argument that the Active Intellect is present everywhere throughout the world, but can only produce intelligence in those parts of matter that are suitable – i.e. human beings (and any superior intelligences there may be). To this the author of *On Intellect* himself replies with objections similar to those which Alexander elsewhere brings against Stoic pantheism, complaining that involvement of the divine in the sublunary world is inconsistent with the divine dignity. Gottschalk [5.77] 1160–2 stresses, however, that the rejected account differs from Stoicism in not regarding its omnipresent intellect as *material*.

The author of *On Intellect* shares the view that the Active Intellect acts upon our intellects; it does so by our becoming aware of it so that it becomes, as it were, a paradigm of the intelligible for us. The difficulty with this view is that it suggests that God is the first thing we think of, whereas it would be more plausible for awareness of him to be the culmination of our understanding. And in Alexander's own, certainly authentic *On Soul* we find two other explanations of the role of the Active Intellect; being the supreme intelligible itself, it must be the cause of other things being intelligible, and it is also the cause of things being intelligible because, as Unmoved Mover, it is the cause of their having being in the first place (Alexander, *On Soul* 88.24–89.8 and 89.9–19 respectively).[67] Neither explanation, however, indicates *how* the Active Intellect causes us to have intelligence; they simply provide ingenious grounds for asserting *that* it does so. Such concentration on solving the immediate problem is typical of Alexander. An explanation would indeed be available if we were to suppose that the divine intellect already contained within itself the thoughts that we can come to apprehend; but that is essentially the position of Plotinus, and while he may be indebted in various respects to Alexander's account of intellect, there is no indication that Alexander himself took this particular step.

It has been debated whether Alexander's *On Soul* is an attempt to improve on *On Intellect*, or the reverse. Both accounts alike, by identifying the Active Intellect with God rather than with a part of the individual's soul, deny personal immortality. Since thought, for Alexander as for Aristotle, is identical in form with its objects, and the Unmoved Mover is pure form without matter, our minds in a sense become the Unmoved Mover while they think of it, and can thus achieve a sort of temporary immortality; but that is all (*On Soul* 90.11–91.6).[68] Whether this claim is to be seen in mystical terms, or whether it is simply the by-product of Alexander's undoubted ingenuity in attempting to clarify Aristotelian doctrine, is debatable. It is also questionable as exegesis of Aristotle; Aquinas was later to argue, against Alexander and Averroes, that Aristotle *had* intended the Active Intellect to be a personal element in each individual's soul and had thus intended a personal immortality.

❧ ETHICS, POLITICS, RHETORIC ❧

Throughout our period Peripatetic ethics are characterised by a contrast with the paradoxical extremes of Stoicism. Cicero repeatedly portrays

Theophrastus as weakening virtue by recognising external goods, subject to fortune, as necessary for happiness (Theophrastus fragments 493, 497–9 FHS and G; so too Ariston of Ceos, cf. Wehrli [5.60] 580). Theophrastus' position is not that far removed from some aspects of Aristotle's; the latter had after all said that to call someone being tortured happy is absurd (*Nicomachean Ethics* 7.13 1153b19; cf. Cicero *Tusculan Disputations* 5.24, and Fortenbaugh [5.30] 218–23). Lyco is attacked by Cicero (*Tusculan Disputations* 3.77 = Lyco fragment 19 Wehrli; cf. 3.76) for seeking to reduce distress by arguing that it is caused by disadvantages of fortune and of the body, not by evil in the soul.

The claim that happiness involves all three classes of goods, of the soul, of the body, and external, is attributed to Critolaus (fragments 19–20 Wehrli), though he also argued that if those of the soul were placed on one side of a balance and bodily and external goods on the other, the former would far outweigh the latter (fragments 21–2 Wehrli). Areius Didymus (cited by Stobaeus *Ecl.* 2.7.3b p. 46.10–17 Wachsmuth), however, seeking to reconcile Peripatetic and Stoic ethics, explicitly rejects Critolaus' view, which he interprets as making all three types of goods *parts* of human excellence; this is also the view attributed to Aristotle by Diogenes Laertius (5.30; Moraux [5.87] 276). For Areius bodily and external goods are rather *used by* virtuous activity; a similar view is later held by Aspasius (*On the Nicomachean Ethics* 24.3 ff.[69] Areius holds that there is no happiness without external goods as well as virtue; however, while lack of external goods does not necessarily lead to actual unhappiness, lack of virtue always does.[70]

Opposition to extreme Stoic ethical views played a part in the renewed interest in Aristotelianism on a popular level in the Imperial period. It is particularly notable in the treatment of *pathos* or 'emotion', which Aristotle had regarded as fundamental to ethics. The Stoics confined the term to emotional reactions that went beyond right reason, and therefore regarded *pathê* as such as uniformly bad (though also recognising a class of 'good feelings', *eupatheiai*, such as 'watchfulness' by contrast with fear; Critolaus rejected this distinction, fragment 24 Wehrli, cf. Wehrli [5.57] vol. 10 p. 69 and [5.60] 588). The Peripatetics characteristically recommended not the absence of passions, *apatheia*, but *metriopatheia*, moderation in the passions; as Aristotle himself had taught, failure to show anger when anger is due is a shortcoming (*Nicomachean Ethics* 2.7 1108a8; cf. Diogenes Laertius 5.31; Philodemus, *On Anger* XXXI.31–9 Wilke; Cicero, *Tusculan Disputations* 4.43–4; Aspasius *On the Nicomachean Ethics* 44.12–19; Moraux [5.75] 282 n. 197, [5.87] 278).

According to Areius Didymus (Stobaeus *Ecl.* 2.7.1, 38.18–24 Wachsmuth), Aristotle regarded *pathos* not as an excessive movement of the soul but as an irrational movement *liable* to excess. Andronicus and Boethus too defined it as a movement of an irrational part of the soul (Aspasius, *On the Nicomachean Ethics* 44.20 ff.); but Andronicus shared with the Stoics the view that all *pathos* involves a supposition that something is good or bad, and Boethus held that it was a movement possessing a certain magnitude. Aspasius rejected both these points, distancing the Peripatetic position further from the Stoic one (Aspasius, *On the Nicomachean Ethics* 42.13 ff.).

Aspasius' role in the development of Aristotelian ethics as a subject of study has been a topic of recent debate. His commentary on the *Nicomachean Ethics* includes the 'common books' which are transmitted both as part of the *Nicomachean Ethics* and of the *Eudemian* (*Nicomachean Ethics* 5–7 = *Eudemian* 4–6). It is from the time of Aspasius that the *Nicomachean Ethics* rather than the *Eudemian* is the work regularly studied and cited (as in the *Ethical Problems* attributed to Alexander, for example). Perhaps it was Aspasius who was responsible for the placing of the 'common books' in their Nicomachean context, but this seems more questionable.[71]

The Stoics based their ethics on the 'appropriation' (*oikeiôsis*) or recognition by living creatures of their own selves. The most fundamental impulse was that to self-preservation, which developed in two ways in human beings as they grew older, firstly by the person coming to recognise virtue and reason as true self-interest, and secondly by the recognition of other people as akin to oneself. Attempts have been made to trace the origin of this Stoic doctrine to the post-Aristotelian Peripatos.[72] It was indeed attributed to Aristotle by Areius Didymus (ap. Stobaeus, *Ecl.* 2.17.3, 116.21–128.9 Wachsmuth),[73] Boethus and Xenarchus (Alexander of Aphrodisias, *Supplement to the book On the Soul* (*De anima libri mantissa*) 151.3–13), but this may simply reflect Stoic influence and, in the case of Areius at least, a desire to assimilate Stoic and Aristotelian thought to one another.[74] Theophrastus spoke of 'affinity' (*oikeiotês*) between all human beings and animals (fragment 531 FHS and G; cf. fragment 584A FHS and G), but this is hardly the same as the process of 'appropriation' described by the Stoics. Some have argued that the account of moral development in terms of 'appropriation' at Cicero, *On Ends* 5.24–70 derives from Theophrastus, even though the book as a whole represents the views of the syncretising Antiochus of Ascalon,[75] but this is at best open to debate.

Dicaearchus in his *Tripoliticus* (fragments 70–1 Wehrli) set out the doctrine of the mixed constitution, a combination of monarchy, aristocracy and democracy superior to each of these. The concept was already present, applied to Sparta, in Plato (*Laws* 4.712d) and Aristotle (*Politics* 2.6 1265b33);[76] it was later to be applied to Rome by Polybius (6.11.11) and Cicero (*Republic* 1.69–70, 2.65) and appears in Areius Didymus (ap. Stobaeus *Ecl.* 2.7.26, p.151.1 Wachsmuth). Cicero presents Dicaearchus and Theophrastus as advocates of the active and contemplative lives respectively, continuing a debate already present in Aristotle *Nicomachean Ethics* 10.7–8 (Dicaearchus fragment 25 Wehrli, Theophrastus fragment 481 FHS and G).

Theophrastus developed Aristotle's study of rhetoric, elaborating from Aristotelian materials a doctrine of the four virtues of style (correctness, clarity, appropriateness, and ornament) which became standard for later writers, and dealing with rhetorical delivery, a subject Aristotle had neglected. Theophrastus' *Characters* may well relate to the rhetorical portrayal of character as much as to comic drama or the study of ethics; these purposes are not indeed mutually exclusive. Subsequently, however, the study of rhetoric became a subject in its own right and grew apart from Peripatetic philosophy.[77]

CONCLUSION

The history of Aristotelianism as a separate tradition in the ancient world comes to an end with Alexander and Themistius. Part of the reason for Alexander's having no distinguished followers in his own school is undoubtedly the decline in interest in formal higher education in the third century by contrast with the second. But that does not on its own explain why Aristotelianism declined where Platonism did not. Once again, as in the third century BC, the lack of a distinctive doctrinal appeal may have played a part; where Platonism had a radical and distinctive message, Aristotelianism appealed to scholars and, on a different level, to common sense. The difference was that, where Aristotelianism in the Hellenistic period lacked a distinctive identity except in so far as the pursuit of enquiry itself provided one, the revived Aristotelianism of the Empire was limited in its scope by being too closely tied to the exposition of the Aristotelian texts. More might indeed have been made of those texts and their implications; but if Alexander had developed his ideas concerning intellect further, he would, as already indicated, have been adopting a position not unlike that of the Neoplatonists themselves.

Merlan ([5.2] 122–3 n.4) and Movia ([5.128] 63–81) both assess Alexander in terms of a tension between naturalism and mysticism. Merlan goes further, suggesting that the whole history of the Peripatetic tradition in antiquity can be seen in terms of an uneasy oscillation between a materialism insufficiently distinct from Stoicism, on the one hand, and a belief in immaterial principles insufficiently distinct from Platonism, on the other; the school declined because it lacked a distinctive enough position of its own (Merlan [5.2] 122. Merlan's perspective is indeed explicitly Platonist; but it was after all Platonism that eventually prevailed).

In another sense, however, the decline of Aristotelianism was only apparent. The continued study of Aristotle's writings was a fundamental part of the Neoplatonist curriculum, and Greek philosophy passed to the Islamic world in a form which combined Platonic and Aristotelian elements. It was the latter which, in a new guise indeed, became central to the philosophies of Avicenna, Averroes, Aquinas and many others. But to tell that story now would take more space than we have already used.

∾ NOTES ∾

1 It will be immediately apparent how much the following account owes to the writings of others, and in particular to those of Paul Moraux and of Hans Gottschalk. Important too is the survey of Peripatetic writers from Theophrastus to Nicolaus of Damascus in Wehrli [5.60]. I am particularly grateful to Fred Schroeder for his permission to refer to work in progress at the time of writing. Numbered references in [brackets] are to the bibliography; for fragments of Peripatetic writers, Wehrli = [5.60] and FHS and G = [5.25].

2 Theophrastus, *Explanations of Plants* 1.9.1, 1.16.12, 1.18.2. Cf. Einarson and Link [5.6] vol. 1, xvii–xviii. I am grateful to Geoffrey Lloyd for emphasising the importance of this to me.

3 Cf. Pellegrin [5.184]; Lennox [5.176].

4 See Steinmetz [5.41] 334–51; Gottschalk [5.42] 20; Mansfeld [5.153], [5.179] and [5.180] especially 67–70.

5 See Annas [5.160] 26–8.

6 Plutarch, *Against Colotes* 14 1114F = Strato fragment 35 Wehrli; Cicero, *On the Nature of the Gods* 1.35 = Strato fragment 33 Wehrli; cf. *Academica Posteriora* 1.121 = Strato fragment 32 Wehrli. Repici [5.62] 117–56; on the other side, van Raalte [5.51] 203.

7 Cf. Devereux [5.49], especially at 182. Balme [5.53] similarly argues that Theophrastus' views on spontaneous animal generation antedate Aristotle's own latest views.

8 So, recently, Isnardi-Parente [5.173] 125–8 and Marenghi [5.69] 9–11, 33–6.

9 This is not to deny that both these schools showed philosophical acumen and subtlety; the loss of interest in Aristotle was not a loss of interest in philosophical argument as such.

10 Strabo 13.1.54; cf. Plutarch *Life of Sulla* 26.1–3 and, for Andronicus, also Porphyry, *Life of Plotinus* 24. I use 'published' and 'unpublished' as equivalents for the traditional 'exoteric' and 'esoteric' respectively; the latter, in particular, could have misleading connotations. That Andronicus produced a definitive *edition* in the sense of a standard text, as opposed to a standard arrangement of works, has been called into question by Barnes in [5.79] and in his contribution to [5.98]. Against Düring's claim that Andronicus produced his collection in Rome cf. Gottschalk [5.77] 1093.

11 Gottschalk [5.77] 1088, 1098 n.96, and 1173. Cf., for the second century AD in particular, Ebbesen [5.165] vol. 1, 54–6.

12 Moraux [5.87] 248–9. Cf. also Athenaeus 1.4 3ab with Gottschalk [5.77] 1084–6, who suggests that the books inherited by Neleus may never have left Athens and (speculatively) that Apellicon may have stolen the books and made up the whole story to conceal the fact.

13 Ed. H. Mutschmann, Leipzig: Teubner, 1906. Translation and commentary in Rossitto [5.90].

14 On which see Moraux [5.87], emphasising Diogenes' use of a Hellenistic source which, he suggests, impressed him because of its antiquity.

15 Cf. also Gottschalk [5.77] 1129–31, on the classifications in the pseudo-Aristotelian treatise *On Virtues and Vices* and the adaptation of this, combined

with Stoic material, in the work *On Passions* falsely attributed to Andronicus himself.

16 On Nicolaus see Moraux [5.74] 445–514; Gottschalk [5.77] 1122–5. On the treatise *On Plants* in particular Moraux [5.74] 487–9, with bibliography, and Drossaart-Lulofs and Poortman [5.86]. For the reception of the work in the Renaissance, cf. Schmitt [5.185] 299–300, 307–8.

17 On Areius see Moraux [5.74] 259–444; Fortenbaugh [5.82]; Gottschalk [5.77] 1125–9; Hahm [5.83]. For the historical evidence for his personal relationship with Augustus see Hahm [5.83] 3035–8. The identity of the author of our texts with the friend of Augustus has recently been called into question by Göransson [5.167].

18 On Boethus see Moraux [5.74] 143–79.

19 In [5.94]; cf. Gottschalk [5.77] 1155, against Kenny [5.95] 37 n.3, who attributed the *whole* commentary to Adrastus. On Adrastus generally cf. Moraux [5.75] 294–322.

20 So Lynch [5.3] 161–2, 200–7. Gottschalk [5.77] 1093–4, however, argues that the school continued to exist in some sense at least for the rest of the first century BC, and that Andronicus was its head.

21 Gottschalk [5.77] 1159–60 notes the same tendency in Alexander's teacher Sosigenes, and suggests it may have been a didactic technique. Cf. Moraux [5.137] 169 n. 1; Sharples [5.131] 97.

22 Schroeder [5.117]. Cf. also, on *Quaestio* 1.11, Sharples [5.119] 50 n. 126.

23 There is a convenient list of the published commentaries in Sorabji [5.78] 27–30.

24 Damascius ap. Suda s.v. Doros (no. 1476, vol. 2 p. 137.3–15 Adler). Dorus is also mentioned in Damascius' *Life of Isidorus*, 131. Cf. Brink [5.1] 947.

25 So Barnes [5.40]; cf. Ebert [5.166] 15–19, arguing against Barnes that there is no evidence for Theophrastus using variables to represent propositions rather than terms, as the Stoics did. On Theophrastus' logic in general cf. Kneale and Kneale [5.174] 100–12.

26 Cf. Kneale and Kneale [5.174] 183–4; Gottschalk [5.77] 1171.

27 Simplicius *On the Physics* 788.34 ff. = Theophrastus fragment 151B FHS and G = Eudemus fragment 91 Wehrli = Strato fragment 75 Wehrli.

28 Simplicius *On the Categories* 434.2 ff., cf. Gottschalk [5.77] 1108.

29 Cf. Sharples [5.139] and Gottschalk [5.77] 1168.

30 Theophrastus fragment 149 FHS and G. Cf. Sorabji [5.44] and [5.186] 158, 202–15; Algra [5.45]; [5.25] commentary volume 3.1, 54–60.

31 Cf. Gottschalk [5.58] 169; Sorabji [5.186] 158.

32 Cf. on this [5.25] commentary volume 3.1, 89–90, 115–16; Battegazzore [5.43].

33 Cf., on the question of the fifth element, Furley [5.68] 193–5.

34 On Theophrastus fragment 232 FHS and G – a report of Xenophanes' views, not of Theophrastus' own as Steinmetz and others have supposed – see most recently Runia [5.47].

35 Furley [5.68] 159. Theophrastus at *On Winds* 22 already seems to imply that *air* naturally moves downwards, Longrigg [5.67] 221.

36 Gottschalk [5.77] 1119. On Xenarchus see Moraux [5.74] 197–214.

37 As Gottschalk ([5.42] 24) has pointed out.

38 Cf. Guthrie [5.170] xxix–xxxvi.

39 Zeller regarded this as un-Aristotelian in Herminus and Alexander, and

Gottschalk ([5.77] 1159) describes it as startling; but if it is so it is as a return to Aristotelian orthodoxy.

40 Gatzemeier [5.66] 94–7 argued that no more than a theory of potential void was to be attributed to Strato; but cf. Furley [5.68] 151–3, Algra [5.159] 58–69, and, against Gottschalk's attribution of a belief in actual void to Theophrastus, Furley [5.68] 141–3.

41 Steinmetz [5.41] 30; and see now Daiber [5.14] 279, 283 and Kidd [5.46] 303, against Gottschalk [5.42] 24 and [5.58] 159 ff., who regarded the relevant section of Theophrastus' *Meteorology* (13.13–17 and 13.50, pp. 28–9 in Daiber [5.14]) as contaminated by Strato's views.

42 Cf. Furley [5.68] loc. cit., and references there.

43 Cf. Gottschalk [5.58] 155, [5.65] 76.

44 Cf. Moraux [5.75] 1–82, Gottschalk [5.77] 1132–9. Reale [5.89] claimed that the *De mundo* is a genuine early work of Aristotle himself, but this has not found general acceptance.

45 Cf. Moraux [5.87] 282 and Gottschalk [5.77] 1126 and n. 237; Mueller [5.182] 155 n. 42 is, however, more doubtful.

46 See further Sharples [5.127] 1216–18, and references there.

47 Moraux [5.141] 199–202, before the Arabic text of *On Providence* was known, criticised Alexander's theory of providence for being 'mechanistic'; in fact the Arabic text makes it clear that Alexander does want to assert that the divine is aware of its beneficial effects on the sublunary, though how he reconciled this with *Metaphysics* Λ we do not know.

48 Cf. Donini [5.129] 159–61 and [5.151] 182; Sharples [5.127] 1218–19 and references there.

49 Cf. Lloyd [5.144] 52, Gottschalk [5.77] 1109.

50 The first way of putting it suggests a doctrine of individual forms (not, of course, in the sense that each person's form will include individual *peculiarities*); the second, that a form is the sort of thing to which questions of numerical identity or difference do not apply. Cf. Lloyd [5.144] 49 ff., especially 54, and Lennox [5.175] 77–8. (But Lennox goes further, arguing that we should not speak of 'the same *form*', or of your form and mine being the same in *form*, at all; it is *compounds* of form and matter that are or are not the same as each other. Ibid. 88–9.) The question whether or not *Aristotle* believed in 'individual forms', and if so in what sense, has been a major topic of contemporary debate; cf., recently, Halper [5.171] 227–55.

51 Simplicius, *On the Categories* 82.22; Dexippus, *On the Categories* 45.12. Cf. Sharples [5.127] 1199, and references there.

52 Lloyd [5.144] 2 ff., 49 ff., though noting expressions in Alexander which could encourage what he calls 'back door Platonism'.

53 Cf. Sharples [5.127] 1201 against Lloyd [5.144] 51, but also [5.122] 50 n.126.

54 So Annas [5.160] 30–1. See also Gottschalk [5.168].

55 Gottschalk [5.77] 1117–19.

56 Cf. Annas [5.160] 30–2. The testimonia to both writers are included in Wehrli [5.57]. Cf. also Gottschalk [5.61] 98–108.

57 Cf. Solmsen [5.70] 560–3, 567–8, arguing that in Aristotle the theory is in the early stages of its development and that there is no indication of channels through which *pneuma* passes in the body; with a rather different emphasis,

linking *pneuma* with the blood in the blood-vessels, Peck [5.183] 593. Cf. also Verbeke [5.188] 198, Annas [5.160] 18–19, and Longrigg [5.178] 173–4. There is, however, no hint in either Aristotle or Theophrastus of the distinctive position of Praxagoras and Erasistratus (below) that the arteries normally contain *only* air, the veins blood.

58 Cf. Barnes [5.163] 256–7. On Strato's psychology cf. further Gottschalk [5.58] 164 and Annas [5.160] 28–9. At 33 Annas describes him as the only member of the Hellenistic Lyceum with interesting views on the soul.

59 This depends on whether a report at Porphyry ap. Stobaeus *Ecl.* 1.49.24 p. 347.21 Wachsmuth is to be assigned to him, as it is by Movia [5.181] 150–5, Ioppolo [5.182] 272–8 and Annas [5.160] 33, but not by Wehrli [5.57] vol. 6, or to the Stoic Ariston of Chios (= *SVF* 1.377).

60 Cf. Gottschalk [5.61] 106–7.

61 So Easterling [5.64]; see also Moraux [5.63] 1206, 1229–30, and Theophrastus fragment 269 FHS and G.

62 Galen, *Quod animi mores* 44.18 Müller. Cf. Moraux [5.74] 132–4, Gottschalk [5.77] 1113. Galen himself argues for it being the mixture, simply.

63 Moraux [5.141] 29–62, comparing Alexander here with Strato; Robinson [5.145], especially 214–18. See Sharples [5.127] 1203 and references there; also my reply to Robinson at *Classical Review* 43 (1993) 87–8.

64 Gottschalk [5.77] 1114, while stressing the similarity of Alexander's position to that of Dicaearchus and Aristoxenus, notes the affinity of Dicaearchus' view with Aristotle's *own* position – though his source for this is the Platonist Atticus, whose intentions are hostile.

65 See Pines [5.136], and for a full translation of the text Rescher and Marmura [5.138]. Alexander's view is seen by Pines as an ancestor of the impetus theory used by Philoponus to explain the forced motion of projectiles and passed on to medieval science; where projectiles are concerned Alexander himself holds the orthodox Aristotelian view that their movement is caused by the transmission of movement through the air behind them.

66 Moraux [5.99] interpreted the remark as a reference to Alexander's teacher Aristoteles of Mytilene, arguing that the doctrines in *On Intellect* are *not* in fact contained in the works of Aristotle (the Stagirite). That does not mean that the ingenious might not have found them there; that the reference is after all to the Stagirite has been re-asserted against Moraux by Thillet [5.123] xv–xix and Schroeder and Todd [5.116] 22–31. Accattino and Donini in [5.115] xxvii n. 77 side with Moraux. I am grateful in particular to Jan Opsomer for illuminating discussion of this passage, to be developed more fully elsewhere. The identification of the person referred to does not affect the fact that an identification of the Active Intellect and the 'intellect from outside' was asserted by someone early enough to be criticised, and defended, before the work *On Intellect* attributed to Alexander criticised the defence in its turn. However, Schroeder [5.117] has raised doubts not only about the attribution of *On Intellect* to Alexander (which has long been debated; cf. Sharples [5.127] 1211–14) but also about its date (see above, n. 22).

67 On the first argument cf. Lloyd [5.177] 150, defending it against Moraux [5.141] 90–2 who criticises it as based on Platonist rather than Aristotelian suppositions. The second argument will apply more easily to things subject to coming-to-be

and passing-away than to those that are eternal. Cf. Sharples [5.127] 1206–8 and nn.

68 In the sixteenth century Nicoletto Vernia argued that Alexander did believe in personal immortality, but this is a misinterpretation; cf. Mahoney [5.142].

69 Cf. Moraux [5.87] 276; Gottschalk [5.77] 1127; Hahm [5.83] 2981, 3010.

70 For an assessment of Areius' position as an interpretation of Aristotle, and a favourable comparison in this regard with Antiochus of Ascalon, see Annas [5.161] 415–25.

71 Cf. Kenny [5.95] and Gottschalk [5.77] 1101, 1158.

72 Cf. Brink [5.55], Gottschalk [5.77] 1117, 1127–8, and the references they provide.

73 Cf. Görgemanns in [5.82] and Hahm [5.83] 2991, 2998–3000.

74 Cf. Hahm [5.83] 3001–11, and, for a comparison between Areius' account of *oikeiôsis* and Aristotle's theory of friendship, Annas [5.161] 279–87.

75 Cf. Gigon [5.56]; Magnaldi [5.84].

76 Also of Athens under Solon, Aristotle, *Politics* 2.12 1273b38.

77 This process is traced in Fortenbaugh and Mirhady [5.71].

BIBLIOGRAPHY

This bibliography combines (i) an attempt to survey the most important literature in the field and (ii) references to all works that there has been occasion to cite in the course of the discussion.

GENERAL SURVEYS

[5.1]   C.O. Brink, 'Peripatos', in Pauly–Wissowa, *Realencyclopädie der Altertumswissenchaft*, suppl. 7 (1940) 899–949.

[5.2]   P. Merlan, 'The Peripatos', in A.H. Armstrong, ed., *The Cambridge History of Later Greek and Early Medieval Philosophy*, Cambridge, Cambridge University Press, 1967, 107–23.

[5.3]   J.P. Lynch, *Aristotle's School*, Berkeley, University of California Press, 1972.

THEOPHRASTUS: TEXTS AND TRANSLATIONS; SURVIVING WORKS

Researches on Plants (Historia plantarum)

[5.4]   A. Hort, *Theophrastus: Enquiry into Plants*, London/Cambridge, Mass., Heinemann/Harvard University Press (Loeb Classical Library), 1916–26. Greek text, annotated English translation. Also includes *On Odours* and the spurious *On Weather-Signs*.

[5.5]   S. Amigues, *Théophraste: Recherches sur les plantes*, Paris, Budé, 4 volumes, 1988–, in progress). (Greek text, French translation, commentary.)

Explanations of Plants (De causis plantarum)

[5.6]   B. Einarson and G.K.K. Link, *Theophrastus: De causis plantarum*, Cambridge, Mass., Harvard University Press (Loeb Classical Library), vol. 1 1976, vols. 2 and 3 1990. (Greek text, annotated English translation.)

On the Senses

[5.7]   in H. Diels, *Doxographi Graeci*, Berlin, Reimer, 1879, 497–527. (Greek text.)

[5.8]   G.M. Stratton, *Theophrastus and the Greek Physiological Psychology before Aristotle*, London/New York, Allen and Unwin/Macmillan, 1917. (Greek text, English translation, commentary.)

On Stones

[5.9]   E.R. Caley and J.C. Richards, *Theophrastus On Stones*, Columbus, Ohio University, 1956. (Greek text, English translation, commentary.)

[5.10]   D.E. Eichholz, *Theophrastus: De lapidibus*, Oxford, Clarendon Press, 1965. (Greek text, English translation, commentary.)

On Fire

[5.11]   V. Coutant, *Theophrastus: De Igne*, Assen, Vangorcum, 1971. (Greek text, translation, commentary.)

On Odours

See [5.4] above; also

[5.12]   U. Eigler and G. Wöhrle, eds, *Theophrastus: De odoribus*, Leipzig and Stuttgart, Teubner, 1993. (Greek text, German translation, commentary.)

On Winds

[5.13]   V. Coutant and V. Eichenlaub, *Theophrastus: De ventis*, Notre Dame, University of Notre Dame Press, 1975. (Greek text, English translation, commentary.)

Meteorology (preserved only in Syriac and Arabic)

[5.14]   H. Daiber, 'The *Meteorology* of Theophrastus in Syriac and Arabic translation', in [5.37] 166–293. (Arabic and Syriac texts, English translation, commentary.)

Metaphysics

[5.15]   W.D. Ross and F.H. Fobes, *Theophrastus: Metaphysics*, Oxford, Oxford University Press, 1929. (Greek text, English translation, commentary.)

[5.16]   M. van Raalte, *Theophrastus: Metaphysics*, Leiden, Brill, 1993. (Greek text, English translation, commentary.)

[5.17]   A. Laks and G. Most. Paris, Budé, 1993. (Greek text, annotated French translation.)

On Fish

[5.18]   R.W. Sharples, 'Theophrastus: *On Fish*', in [5.37] 347–85. (Greek text, English translation, commentary.)

Characters

[5.19]   R.G. Ussher, *The Characters of Theophrastus*, London, Macmillan, 1960. (Greek text, commentary.)

[5.20]   P. Steinmetz, *Theophrast: Charaktere*, Munich, Max Hueber, 1960–2. (Greek text, commentary.)

[5.21]   J. Rusten, *Theophrastus, Characters*, Cambridge, Mass., Harvard University Press (Loeb Classical Library; with Herodas and Cercidas), 1992. (Greek text, English translation.)

Minor works

For other surviving minor works (*On Sweats*, *On Giddiness*, *On (Types of) Fatigue*)

[5.22]   a new edition to be published by Brill is in preparation by W.W. Fortenbaugh, R.W. Sharples and M. Sollenberger, but meanwhile reference must still be made to

[5.23]   F. Wimmer, *Theophrasti Eresii opera*, vol. 3, Leipzig, Teubner, 1854–62, or to

[5.24]   —— *Theophrasti Eresii opera*, Paris, Didot, 1866, reprinted 1964.

∾ THEOPHRASTUS: COLLECTIONS OF ∾
FRAGMENTS AND TESTIMONIA

In general

[5.25]   W.W. Fortenbaugh, P.M. Huby, R.W. Sharples (Greek and Latin) and D. Gutas (Arabic), eds, *Theophrastus of Eresus*, Leiden, Brill, 1992. (Greek/Latin/Arabic text and English translation; commentary vol. 3.1,

R.W. Sharples, *Sources on Physics*, with contributions on the Arabic material by Dimitri Gutas, 1998; vol. 5, R.W. Sharples, *Sources on Biology*, 1995; others forthcoming.)

Fragments on particular topics

Logic

[5.26]   A. Graeser, *Die logischen Fragmente des Theophrast*, Berlin, De Gruyter, 1973. (Greek text, commentary.)

[5.27]   L. Repici, *La logica di Teofrasto*, Bologna, Il Mulino, 1977. (Greek text, Italian translation, commentary.)

Physical doxography

[5.28]   Diels ([5.7]) 473–95. (Greek texts.)

Intellect

[5.29]   E. Barbotin, *La Théorie aristotélicienne de l'intellect d'après Théophraste*, Louvain, Publications Universitaires, 1954. (Greek text, French translation, commentary.)

Ethics

[5.30]   W.W. Fortenbaugh, *Quellen zur Ethik Theophrasts*, Amsterdam, Grüner, 1984. (Greek text, commentary.)

Piety

[5.31]   W. Pötscher, *Theophrastos* Peri Eusebeias, Leiden, Brill, 1964. (Greek text, German translation, commentary.)

Laws

[5.32]   A. Szegedy-Maszak, *The* Nomoi *of Theophrastus*, New York, Arno, 1981. (Greek text, commentary.)

❧ THEOPHRASTUS: STUDIES ❧

General

Fundamental are:

[5.33]   O. Regenbogen, 'Theophrastos', in Pauly–Wissowa, *Realencyclopädie der Altertumswissenchaft*, suppl. 7 (1940) 1354–562.

[5.34]   F. Wehrli in [5.187] 474–522.

Numerous papers on various aspects of Theophrastus' work in:

[5.35]   W.W. Fortenbaugh, P.M. Huby and A.A. Long, eds, *Theophrastus of Eresus: On his Life and Work* (Rutgers University Studies in Classical Humanities, 2), New Brunswick, Transaction, 1985.

[5.36]   W.W. Fortenbaugh and R.W. Sharples, eds, *Theophrastean Studies* (Rutgers University Studies in Classical Humanities, 3), New Brunswick, Transaction, 1988.

[5.37]   W.W. Fortenbaugh and D. Gutas, eds, *Theophrastus: His Physical, Doxographical, and Scientific Writings* (Rutgers University Studies in Classical Humanities, 5), New Brunswick, Transaction, 1992.

[5.38]   Jan van Ophuisjen and Marlein van Raalte, eds, *Theophrastus: Reappraising the Sources* (Rutgers University Studies in Classical Humanities, 8), New Brunswick, Transaction, 1998.

Logic

[5.39]   I.M. Bochénski, *La Logique de Théophraste*, Fribourg en Suisse, Librairie de l'Université, 1947.

[5.40]   J. Barnes, 'Theophrastus and hypothetical syllogistic', in [5.189] 557–76, and in [5.35] 125–41.

Physics

[5.41]   P. Steinmetz, *Die Physik des Theophrast* (Palingenesia, 1), Bad Homburg, Max Gehlen, 1964.

[5.42]   H.B. Gottschalk, Review of [5.41], in *Gnomon* 39 (1967) 17–26.

[5.43]   A.M. Battegazzore, 'Spigolature filologiche e note esegetiche al *De igne* Teofrasteo', *Sandalion* 10–11 (1987–8) 49–66.

[5.44]   R. Sorabji, 'Theophrastus on Place', in [5.36] 139–66.

[5.45]   K. Algra, 'Place in Context', in [5.37] 141–65.

[5.46]   I.G. Kidd, 'Theophrastus' *Meteorology*, Aristotle and Posidonius', in [5.37] 294–306.

[5.47]   D.T. Runia, 'Xenophanes or Theophrastus', in [5.37] 112–40.

Doxography

[5.48]   J.B. McDiarmid, 'Theophrastus on the Presocratic Causes', *Harvard Studies in Classical Philology* 61 (1953) 85–156.

Metaphysics

[5.49]   D.T. Devereux, 'The relation between Theophrastus' *Metaphysics* and Aristotle's *Metaphysics Lambda*', in [5.36] 167–88.

[5.50]   A. Laks, G.W. Most and E. Rudolph, 'Four notes on Theophrastus' *Metaphysics*', in [5.36] 224–56.

[5.51]   M. van Raalte, 'The idea of the cosmos as an organic whole in Theophrastus' *Metaphysics*', in [5.36] 189–215.

Biology

[5.52]   G. Senn, *Die Pflanzenkunde des Theophrast von Eresos*, ed. O. Gigon, Basel, Universität, 1956.
[5.53]   D.M. Balme, 'Development of biology in Aristotle and Theophrastus: theory of spontaneous generation', *Phronesis* 7 (1962) 91–104.
[5.54]   G. Wöhrle, *Theophrasts Methode in seinen botanischen Schriften*, Amsterdam, Grüner, 1985.

Ethics

[5.55]   C.O. Brink, '*Oikeiôsis* and *Oikeiotês*; Theophrastus and Zeno on Nature in moral theory', *Phronesis* 1 (1956) 123–45.
[5.56]   O. Gigon, 'The Peripatos in Cicero's *De finibus*', in [5.36] 259–71.

❦ OTHER PERIPATETICS OF THE HELLENISTIC PERIOD ❦

Texts

The fragments of these writers are collected by
[5.57]   Wehrli, F., *Die Schule des Aristoteles*, Basel, Schwabe, 2nd edn, 1967–78. (Greek texts, German commentary.)

supplemented, for Strato, by

[5.58]   H.B. Gottschalk, 'Strato of Lampsacus: some texts', *Proceedings of the Leeds Philosophical and Literary Society, Literary and Historical Section*, 11.6 (1965) 95–182.
[5.59]   A series of texts, English translations and discussions will appear in *Rutgers Studies in Classical Humanities*; the first on Dicaearchus and Demetrius of Phalerum (*Rutgers Studies* 9 and 10, ed. W.W. Fortenbaugh *et al.*), the next on Eudemus.

Studies: general

A survey of the whole period in
[5.60]   F. Wehrli, 'Der Peripatos bis zum Beginn der römischen Kaiserzeit', in [5.187] 459–599.

On specific writers:

[5.61]   H.B. Gottschalk, *Heraclides of Pontus*, Oxford, Clarendon Press, 1980.
[5.62]   L. Repici, *La natura e l'anima: saggi su Stratone di Lampsaco*, Torino, Tirrenia, 1988.

Studies: particular topics

Physics

[5.63] P. Moraux, 'Quinta essentia', in Pauly–Wissowa, *Realencyclopädie der Altertumswissenchaft*, 24.1 (1963) 1171–263.

[5.64] H.J. Easterling, 'Quinta natura', *Museum Helveticum* 21 (1964) 73–85.

[5.65] H.B. Gottschalk, 'The *De coloribus* and its author', *Hermes* 92 (1964) 59–85.

[5.66] M. Gatzemeier, *Die Naturphilosophie des Straton von Lampsakos*, Meisenheim am Glan, Anton Hain, 1970.

[5.67] J. Longrigg, 'Elementary physics in the Lyceum and Stoa', *Isis* 66 (1975) 211–29.

[5.68] D.J. Furley, *Cosmic Problems*, Cambridge, Cambridge University Press, 1989.

[5.69] G. Marenghi, *[Aristotele]: Profumi e miasmi*, Naples, Arte Tipografica, 1991.

Biology

[5.70] F. Solmsen, 'Greek philosophy and the discovery of the nerves', *Museum Helveticum* 18 (1961) 169–97, reprinted in id., *Kleine Schriften* vol. 1, Hildesheim, Olms, 1968, 536–82.

Rhetoric

[5.71] W.W. Fortenbaugh and D.C. Mirhady, eds, *Peripatetic Rhetoric after Aristotle* (Rutgers University Studies in Classical Humanities, 6), New Brunswick, Transaction, 1994.

Aristotelian bibliography and the transmission and editing of his works

[5.72] P. Moraux, *Les Listes anciennes des ouvrages d'Aristote*, Louvain, Éditions universitaires, 1951.

[5.73] I. Düring, *Aristotle in the Ancient Biographical Tradition*, Göteborg/ Stockholm, Almqvist and Wiksell, 1957.

∼ PERIPATETICS OF THE ROMAN PERIOD ∼

General

There is a very full survey in

[5.74] P. Moraux *Der Aristotelismus bei den Griechen*, vol. 1, Berlin, De Gruyter, 1973.

[5.75] —— vol. 2, 1984.

[5.76] —— vol. 3, ed. J. Wiesner, forthcoming.

A shorter survey in

[5.77] H.B. Gottschalk, 'Aristotelian Philosophy in the Roman world', in H. Temporini and W. Haase, eds, *Aufstieg und Niedergang der römischen Welt*, vol. II.36.2, Berlin, De Gruyter, 1987, 1079–174.

See also

[5.78] R. Sorabji, ed., *Aristotle Transformed: The Ancient Commentators and their Influence*, London, Duckworth, 1990.

Andronicus

[5.79] J. Barnes, 'Roman Aristotle', in J. Barnes and M. Griffin, eds, *Philosophia Togata II*, Oxford, Clarendon Press, 1997, 1–69.

Arius Didymus

[5.80] Fragments of the physical epitome in [5.7] 447–72.
[5.81] Text of the ethical epitome in Stobaeus, *Ecl.* 2.7 (vol. 2 pp. 37–152 in C. Wachsmuth, ed., *Ioannis Stobaei Anthologii duo libri priores*, Berlin, Weidemann, 1884).

Studies

[5.82] W.W. Fortenbaugh, ed., *On Stoic and Peripatetic Ethics: The Work of Arius Didymus* (Rutgers Studies in Classical Humanities, 1), New Brunswick, Transaction, 1983.
[5.83] D.E. Hahm, 'The ethical doxography of Arius Didymus', in H. Temporini and W. Haase, eds, *Aufstieg und Niedergang der römischen Welt*, vol. II.36.4, Berlin, De Gruyter, 1990, 2935–3055.
[5.84] G. Magnaldi, *L'oikeiôsis peripatetica in Ario Didimo e nel 'De finibus' di Cicerone*, Florence, Le Lettere, 1991.

Nicolaus of Damascus

Texts in
[5.85] H.J. Drossaart Lulofs, *Nicolaus of Damascus on the Philosophy of Aristotle*, Leiden, Brill, 1965. (Syriac text, English translation and commentary of fragments of books 1–5 of Nicolaus' compendium.)
[5.86] H.J. Drossaart Lulofs and E.J. Poortman, *Nicolaus of Damascus 'De plantis'; Five translations*, Amsterdam, North-Holland Publishing, 1989 (Verhandelingen der Koninklijke Nederlandse Akademie van Wetenschappen, Afd. Letterkunde, Nieuwe Reeks, Deel 139).

Other eclectic writings

For Diogenes Laertius' account of Aristotle's views see

[5.87]   P. Moraux, 'Diogène Laërce et le *Peripatos*', *Elenchos* 7 (1986) 247–94.

[5.88]   [Aristotle] *De mundo* appears in editions of the collected works of Aristotle; cf. especially E.S. Forster and D.J. Furley, *Aristotle: On Sophistical Refutations*, etc., London/Cambridge, Mass., Heinemann/Harvard University Press (Loeb Classical Library), 1955, and bibliography there.

Reale's view that the work is a genuine early one of Aristotle is argued in

[5.89]   G. Reale (1974) *Aristotele: Trattato sul cosmo*, Naples, Loffredo, 1974; revised edn, Giovanni Reale and Abraham P. Bos, eds, *Il trattato* Sul cosmo per Alessandro *attributo a Aristotele*, Milan, Vita e Pensiero, 1995.

On the 'Aristotelian' *Divisions* see

[5.90]   C. Rossitto, ed., *Aristotele ed altri: Divisioni*, Padua, Antenore, 1984.

[5.91]   [Andronicus] *On the Passions* is edited by A. Glibert-Thirry, *Pseudo-Andronicus de Rhodes, Peri pathôn*, Leiden, Brill, 1977 (Corpus Latinum Commentariorum in Aristotelem Graecorum, suppl. 2).

Adrastus and Aspasius

[5.92]   Aspasius' commentary on the *Nicomachean Ethics* is edited by G. Heylbut in *Commentaria in Aristotelem Graeca* vol. 19.1, Berlin, Reimer, 1889.

[5.93]   Annotated English translation of Aspasius by H.P. Mercken, forthcoming: London, Duckworth.

[5.94]   The anonymous scholia on *Nicomachean Ethics* 2–5 incorporating material from Adrastus are edited by G. Heylbut in *Commentaria in Aristotelem Graeca* vol. 20, Berlin, Reimer, 1892.

See also

[5.95]   A. Kenny, *The Aristotelian Ethics*, Oxford, Clarendon Press, 1978.

[5.96]   F. Becchi, 'Aspasio e i peripatetici posteriori: la formula definitoria della passione', *Prometheus* 9 (1983) 83–104.

[5.97]   —— 'Aspasio, commentatore di Aristotele', in H. Temporini and W. Haase (eds), *Aufstieg und Niedergang der römischen Welt* vol. II.36.7, Berlin, De Gruyter, 1994, 5365–96.

[5.98]   A. Alberti and R.W. Sharples, eds, *Aspasius: The Earliest Extant Commentary on Aristotle's Ethics*, Berlin: De Gruyter, 1999.

On Aristoteles, argued by Moraux to be the teacher of Alexander of Aphrodisias, see

[5.99]   P. Moraux, 'Aristoteles, der Lehrer Alexanders von Aphrodisias', *Archiv für Geschichte der Philosophie* 49 (1967) 169–82.

❧ ALEXANDER OF APHRODISIAS ❧

Texts and translations

[5.100] Greek texts in *Commentaria in Aristotelem Graeca* vols 1–3, Berlin, Reimer, 1883–1901 (commentaries; various editors) and in

[5.101] I. Bruns, ed., *Supplementum Aristotelicum* 2.1–2, Berlin, Reimer, 1887–1892 (other works). For spurious works see the bibliography in [5.127].

Editions of texts surviving in Arabic, many with translations, are listed in [5.127] and in

[5.102] R. Goulet and M. Aouad, 'Alexandre d'Aphrodise', in R. Goulet, ed., *Dictionnaire des philosophes antiques* vol. 1, Paris, Éditions du CNRS, 1989, 125–39,

to be modified in the light of

[5.103] A. Hasnawi, 'Alexandre d'Aphrodise vs Jean Philopon: notes sur quelques traités d'Alexandre 'perdus' en grec, conservés en arabe', *Arabic Sciences and Philosophy* 4 (1994) 53–109.

[5.104] F.W. Zimmermann, 'Proclus Arabus rides again', *Arabic Sciences and Philosophy* 4 (1994) 9–51.

Editions, translations and commentaries of particular works

Commentaries on Aristotle

[5.105] J. Barnes, S. Bobzien, K. Flannery and K. Ierodiakonou, *Alexander of Aphrodisias On Aristotle Prior Analytics 1.1–7*, London, Duckworth, 1991. (Annotated English translation.)

[5.106] W.E. Dooley, *Alexander of Aphrodisias: On Aristotle Metaphysics 1*, London, Duckworth, 1989. (Annotated English translation.)

[5.107] W.E. Dooley and A. Madigan, *Alexander of Aphrodisias: On Aristotle Metaphysics 2 and 3*, London, Duckworth, 1992. (Annotated English translation.)

[5.108] A. Madigan, *Alexander of Aphrodisias, On Aristotle Metaphysics 4*, London: Duckworth, 1993. (Annotated English translation.)

[5.109] W. Dooley, *Alexander of Aphrodisias: On Aristotle Metaphysics 5*, London, Duckworth, 1993. (Annotated English translation.)

[5.110] G. Fine, *On Ideas: Aristotle's Criticism of Plato's Theory of Forms*, Oxford, Clarendon Press, 1993. (Discusses material from Alexander's commentary on Aristotle, *Metaphysics* A.)

[5.111] E. Lewis, *Alexander of Aphrodisias: On Aristotle Meteorology 4*, London: Duckworth, 1996. (Annotated English translation.)

[5.112] M. Rashed, 'Alexandre d'Aphrodise et la 'Magna Quaestio': Rôle et indépendance des scholies dans la tradition byzantine du corpus aristotélicien', *Les Études Classiques* 63 (1995) 295–351. (On fragments of Alexander's *Physics* commentary.)

[5.113] M. Rashed, 'A "new" text of Alexander on the soul's motion', in R. Sorabji, ed., *Aristotle and After*, University of London, School of Advanced Studies, 1997 (*Bulletin of the Institute of Classical Studies*, suppl. vol. 68), 181–95.

On the Soul

[5.114] A.P. Fotinis, *The 'De Anima' of Alexander of Aphrodisias*, Washington, University Press of America, 1979. (English translation and commentary; also includes *On Intellect*.)

[5.115] P. Accattino and P.L. Donini, *Alessandro di Afrodisia: L'anima*, Rome and Bari, Laterza, 1996. (Italian translation and commentary.)

On Intellect

[5.116] F.M. Schroeder and R.B. Todd, *Two Aristotelian Greek Commentators on the Intellect: The De Intellectu attributed to Alexander of Aphrodisias and Themistius' Paraphrase of Aristotle De Anima 3.4–8*, Toronto, Pontifical Institute of Medieval Studies, 1990. (Medieval Sources in Translation, 33.)

On the dating see

[5.117] Frederic M. Schroeder, 'The Provenance of the *De Intellectu* attributed to Alexander of Aphrodisias', *Documenti e studi sulla tradizione filosofica medievale* 6.1 (1995).

On Providence

[5.118] S. Fazzo and M. Zonta, *Alessandro d'Afrodisia*, Sulla Provvidenza, Milan, Rizzoli, 1998.

Quaestiones *and* Ethical Problems

[5.119] R.W. Sharples, *Alexander of Aphrodisias: Quaestiones 1.1–2.15*, London, Duckworth, 1992. (Annotated English translation.)

[5.120] —— *Alexander of Aphrodisias: Quaestiones 2.16–3.15*, London, Duckworth, 1994. (Annotated English translation.)

[5.121] —— *Alexander of Aphrodisias: Ethical Problems*, London, Duckworth, 1990. (Annotated English translation.)

On Fate

[5.122] R.W. Sharples, *Alexander of Aphrodisias: On Fate*, London, Duckworth, 1983. (Greek text, English translation, commentary.)

[5.123] P. Thillet, *Alexandre d'Aphrodise: Traité du Destin*, Paris, Budé, 1984. (Greek text, annotated French translation.)

[5.124] A. Magris, *Alessandro di Afrodisia, Sul Destino* (collana 'I rari'), Firenze, Ponte alle Grazie S.p.A., 1996. (Italian translation, commentary.)

[5.125] C. Natali, *Alessandro di Afrodisia: Il Destino*, Milan, Rusconi, 1996. (Italian translation, commentary.)

On Mixture

[5.126] R.B. Todd, *Alexander of Aphrodisias on Stoic Physics*, Leiden, Brill, 1976. (Greek text, English translation, commentary.)

Studies: general

A general survey, with full bibliography, in

[5.127] R.W. Sharples, 'Alexander of Aphrodisias: Scholasticism and Innovation', in H. Temporini and W. Haase, eds, *Aufstieg und Niedergang der römischen Welt*, vol. II.36.2, Berlin, De Gruyter, 1987, 1176–243.

A much fuller survey in [5.76].

[5.128] G. Movia, *Alessandro di Afrodisia tra naturalismo e misticismo*, Padua, Antenore, 1970.

[5.129] P.L. Donini, *Tre studi sull' aristotelismo nel II secolo d.C.*, Turin, Paravia, 1974.

[5.130] —— *Le scuole, l'anima, l'impero*, Turin, Rosenberg and Sellier, 1982.

[5.131] R.W. Sharples, 'The School of Alexander', in [5.78] 83–111.

[5.132] G. Abbamonte, 'Metodi Esegetici nel commento *in Aristotelis Topica* di Alessandro di Afrodisia', *Seconda Miscellanea Filologica, Università degli Studi di Salerno, Quaderni del dipartimento di scienze dell'antichità 17*, Naples, Arte Tipografica, 1995, 249–66.

[5.133] P.L. Donini, 'Alessandro di Afrodisia e i metodi dell' esegesi filosofica', in *Esegesi, parafrasi e compilazione in età tardoantica: Atti del Terzo Congresso dell' Associazione di studi tardoantichi*, a cura di C. Moreschini, Naples, 1995, 107–29.

[5.134] R.W. Sharples, 'Alexander and pseudo-Alexanders of Aphrodisias, *scripta minima. Questions* and *problems, makeweights* and prospects', in W. Kullmann, J. Althoff and M. Asper, eds., *Gattungen wissenschaftlicher Literatur in der Antike* (ScriptOralia Bd. 95 = Altertumswissenschaftliche Reihe Bd. 22), Tübingen: Günter Narr Verlag, 1998, 383–403.

Studies on particular topics

Logic

[5.135] K.L. Flannery, SJ., *Ways into the Logic of Alexander of Aphrodisias* (Philosophia Antiqua, 62), Leiden, Brill, 1995.

Physics

[5.136] S. Pines, 'Omne quod movetur necesse est ab aliquo moveri: a refutation of Galen by Alexander of Aphrodisias and the theory of motion', *Isis* 52 (1961) 21–54. Reprinted in id., *Studies in Arabic Versions of Greek Texts and in Medieval Science*, Jerusalem and Leiden, Magnes Press/Brill, 1986, 218–51.

[5.137] P. Moraux, 'Alexander von Aphrodisias *Quaest.* 2.3', *Hermes* 95 (1967) 159–69.

[5.138] N. Rescher and M. Marmura, *Alexander of Aphrodisias: The Refutation of Galen's Treatise on the Theory of Motion*, Islamabad, Islamic Research Institute, 1969.

[5.139] R.W. Sharples, 'Alexander of Aphrodisias, *On Time*,' *Phronesis* 27 (1982) 58–81.

[5.140] S. Fazzo and H. Wiesner, 'Alexander of Aphrodisias in the Kindî-circle and in al-Kindî's cosmology', *Arabic Sciences and Philosophy* 3 (1993) 119–53.

Psychology and metaphysics

[5.141] P. Moraux, *Alexandre d'Aphrodise: Exégète de la noétique d'Aristote*, Liège/Paris, Faculté des Lettres/E. Droz, 1942.

[5.142] E.P. Mahoney, 'Nicoletto Vernia and Agostino Nifo on Alexander of Aphrodisias: an unnoticed dispute', *Rivista critica di storia della filosofia* 23 (1968) 268–96.

[5.143] P.L. Donini, 'L'anima e gli elementi nel *De Anima* di Alessandro di Afrodisia', *Atti dell' Accademia delle Scienze di Torino*, classe di scienze morali, storiche e filologiche, 105 (1971) 61–107.

[5.144] A.C. Lloyd, *Form and Universal in Aristotle* (*ARCA, Classical and Medieval Texts, Papers and Monographs*, 4), Liverpool, Francis Cairns, 1981.

[5.145] H. Robinson, 'Form and the immateriality of the intellect from Aristotle to Aquinas', in H. Blumenthal and H. Robinson, eds., *Aristotle and the Later Tradition* (*Oxford Studies in Ancient Philosophy*, supplementary volume), Oxford, Clarendon Press, 1991, 207–26.

[5.146] D.K.W. Modrak, 'Alexander on *phantasia*: a hopeless muddle or a better account?', *Southern Journal of Philosophy* 31 (1993), supplement, 173–97.

[5.147] J. Ellis, 'Alexander's Defense of Aristotle's Categories', *Phronesis* 39 (1994) 69–89.

[5.148] A. Madigan, 'Alexander on Species and Genera', in Lawrence P. Schrenk, ed., *Aristotle in Late Antiquity*, Washington, DC, The Catholic University of America Press, 1994, 74–91.

[5.149] R.W. Sharples, 'On Body, Soul and Generation in Alexander of Aphrodisias', *Apeiron* 27 (1994) 163–70.

[5.150] P. Accattino, 'Generazione dell'anima in Alessandro di Afrodisia, De anima 2.10–11.13', *Phronesis* 40 (1995) 182–201.

Fate

[5.151] P.L. Donini, 'Stoici e megarici nel de fato di Alessandro di Afrodisia', in G. Giannantoni, ed., *Scuole socratiche minori e filosofia ellenistica*, Bologna, Il Mulino, 1977, 174–94.

[5.152] D. Frede, 'The dramatisation of determinism: Alexander of Aphrodisias' *De fato*', *Phronesis* 27 (1982) 276–98.

[5.153] J. Mansfeld, 'Diaphonia in the argument of Alexander *De fato* chs 1–2', *Phronesis* 33 (1988) 181–207.

[5.154] P.L. Donini, 'Il *De fato* di Alessandro: questioni di coerenza', in H. Temporini and W. Haase, eds, *Aufstieg und Niedergang der römischen Welt*, vol. II.36.2, Berlin, De Gruyter, 1987, 1244–59.

[5.155] R. Gaskin, 'Alexander's sea battle: a discussion of Alexander of Aphrodisias *De fato* 10', *Phronesis* 38 (1993) 75–94.

[5.156] —— *The Sea Battle and the Master Argument: Aristotle and Diodorus Cronus on the Metaphysics of the Future*, Berlin, De Gruyter, 1995.

[5.157] P.L. Donini, 'Doti naturali, abitudini e carattere nel *De fato* di Alessandro', in K.A. Algra, P.W. van der Horst, D.T. Runia, eds, *Polyhistor: Studies in the History and Historiography of Ancient Philosophy Presented to Jaap Mansfeld on his Sixtieth Birthday*, Leiden, Brill, 1996, 284–99.

[5.158] S. Bobzien, 'The inadvertent conception and late birth of the free-will problem', *Phronesis* 43 (1998) 133–75.

❧ OTHER WORKS CITED ❧ (MISCELLANEOUS)

[5.159] K. Algra, *Concepts of Space in Greek Thought*, Leiden, Brill, 1995. (Philosophia Antiqua, 65.)

[5.160] J.E. Annas, *Hellenistic Philosophy of Mind*, Berkeley, University of California Press, 1992.

[5.161] —— *The Morality of Happiness*, New York, Oxford University Press, 1993.

[5.162] H. von Arnim, *Stoicorum Veterum Fragmenta*, Leipzig, Teubner, 1903–24 (= *SVF*).

[5.163] J. Barnes, *Aristotle's Posterior Analytics*, Oxford, Clarendon Press, 1975.

[5.164] —— *Aristotle*, Oxford, Oxford University Press, 1982.

[5.165] S. Ebbesen, *Commentators and Commentaries on Aristotle's 'Sophistici Elenchi'* (Corpus Latinum Commentariorum in Aristotelem Graecorum, 7), Leiden, Brill, 1981.

[5.166] T. Ebert, *Dialektiker und frühe Stoiker bei Sextus Empiricus*, Göttingen, Vandenhoeck and Ruprecht, 1991.

[5.167] T. Göransson, *Albinus, Alcinous, Arius Didymus* (Studia Graeca et Latina Gothoburgensia, 61), Göteborg, Acta Universitatis Gothoburgensis, 1995.

[5.168] H.B. Gottschalk, 'Soul as harmonia', *Phronesis* 16 (1971) 179–98.

[5.169] A. Gotthelf, ed., *Aristotle on Nature and Living Things: Philosophical and Historical Studies Presented to David M. Balme*, Pittsburgh, Mathesis, 1985.

[5.170] W.K.C. Guthrie, *Aristotle: On the Heavens*, London/Cambridge, Mass., Heinemann/Harvard University Press (Loeb Classical Library), 1939.

[5.171] E.C. Halper, *One and Many in Aristotle's 'Metaphysics': The Central Books*, Columbus, Ohio State University Press, 1989.

[5.172] A.M. Ioppolo, *Aristone di Chio*, Naples, Bibliopolis, 1980.

[5.173] M. Isnardi Parente, *Filosofia e scienza nel pensiero ellenistico*, Naples, Morano, 1991.

[5.174] W. Neale and M. Kneale, *The Development of Logic*, Oxford, Clarendon Press, 1963.

[5.175] J.G. Lennox, 'Are Aristotelian species eternal', in [5.169] 67–94.

[5.176] —— 'Kinds, forms of kinds, and the more and less in Aristotle's biology', in A. Gotthelf and J.G. Lennox, eds., *Philosophical Issues in Aristotle's Biology*, Cambridge, Cambridge University Press, 1987, 339–59.

[5.177] A.C. Lloyd, 'The principle that the cause is greater than its effect', *Phronesis* 21 (1976) 146–56.

[5.178] J. Longrigg, *Greek Rational Medicine: Philosophy and Medicine from Alcmaeon to the Alexandrians*, London, Routledge, 1993.

[5.179] J. Mansfeld, 'Aristotle, Plato, and the Preplatonic doxography and chronography', in G. Cambiano, ed., *Storiografia e dossografia nella filosofia antica*, Turin, Tirrenia, 1986, 1–59.

[5.180] J. Mansfeld, '*Physikai doxai* and *Problemata physika* from Aristotle to Aëtius (and beyond)', in [5.37] 63–111.

[5.181] G. Movia, *Anima e intelletto*, Padua, Antenore, 1968.

[5.182] I. Mueller, 'Hippolytus, Aristotle, Basilides', in Lawrence P. Schrenk, ed., *Aristotle in Late Antiquity*, Washington, DC, The Catholic University of America Press, 1994, 143–57.

[5.183] A. Peck, *Aristotle: Generation of Animals*, London/Cambridge, Mass., Heinemann/Harvard University Press (Loeb Classical Library), 1942.

[5.184] P. Pellegrin, 'Aristotle: a zoology without species', in [5.169] 95–115.

[5.185] C.B. Schmitt, 'Aristotelian textual studies at Padua: the case of Francesco Cavalli', in A. Poppi, ed., *Scienza e filosofia all' università di Padova nel quattrocento*, Padua, Edizioni LINT, 1983, 287–314.

[5.186] R. Sorabji, *Matter, Space and Motion*, London, Duckworth, 1988.

[5.187] F. Ueberweg, ed. H. Flashar, *Grundriss der Geschichte der Philosophie, Die Philosophie der Antike*, 3, Basel, Schwabe, 1983.

[5.188] G. Verbeke, 'Doctrine du pneuma et entéléchisme chez Aristote', in G.E.R. Lloyd and G.E.L. Owen, eds, *Aristotle on Mind and the Senses*, Cambridge, Cambridge University Press, 1978, 191–214.

[5.189] J. Wiesner, ed., *Aristoteles, Werk und Wirkung: Paul Moraux gewidmet*, vol. 1, Berlin, De Gruyter, 1985.

[5.190] —— vol. 2, 1987.

[5.191] E. Zeller, *Die Philosophie der Griechen* 3.2⁴, Leipzig, Reisland, 1903.

CHAPTER 6

Epicureanism

Stephen Everson

It is tempting to portray Epicureanism as the most straightforward, perhaps even simplistic, of the major dogmatic philosophical schools of the Hellenistic age. Starting from an atomic physics, according to which 'the totality of things is bodies and void' (*Hdt* 39 (LS 5A)),[1] Epicurus proposes a resolutely empiricist epistemology, secured on the claim that every appearance (and not merely every perception) is true, maintains a materialist psychology and espouses hedonism in ethics. Indeed, it is perhaps not too far-fetched to see in Epicurus' work an attempt to return to the natural philosophy of the pre-Socratics, and especially that of his atomist predecessor Democritus. However, even if there is some truth in this, the natural philosophy we find in him is much more sophisticated than any produced before the work of Plato and Aristotle. Epicurus certainly eschews dialectic and rejects the central role given to definition in the acquisition of *epistêmê*, understanding, but he nevertheless builds on the sophisticated empiricism we find in Aristotle. Again, whilst he returns to an earlier tradition of natural philosophy in denying the place accorded to teleological explanation by Plato and Aristotle, unlike his predecessors he is duly aware of the need to meet the challenge posed by those who deny that natural change and the development of natural substances can be properly explained without the use of such explanation. Moreover, whilst Epicurus is at pains to reject natural teleology, he seems not to renounce formal as well as final causes: we find no attack on Aristotle's contention that one must distinguish a substance from its material constitution. Most importantly, perhaps, Epicurus is concerned to provide the kind of systematic ethical theory which was simply unknown before the *Republic* and the ethical writings of Aristotle.

The temptation to render Epicurus more simple than he actually is is perhaps made more intense by the fact that his philosophical ambitions are congenial to a scientifically minded contemporary taste. Not least, of course,

Epicurus seeks to explain all natural phenomena as the result of the motion of atoms through space. Furthermore, his system is a firmly naturalistic one. What he attempts is precisely to explain the behaviour of material substances (including those material substances which are human beings) in a way which is consistent with his atomistic materialism. Abstract objects, such as Platonic Forms or the objects of Aristotelian *nous* play no role in his system. His theories are moreover radically constrained by the available perceptual evidence and he does not seek to crown his enquiry by the acquisition of the sort of necessary universal knowledge required by Plato and Aristotle. In contrast to Plato, who mistrusted the evidence of the senses, and Aristotle, who, whilst renouncing this Platonic mistrust nevertheless denied the ability of the senses to provide genuine knowledge, Epicurus places perception (together with the related capacity for *prolêpsis*) right at the centre of his scientific method and is very cautious about forming beliefs that go beyond what is given in perception. In his espousal of materialism and empiricism, Epicurus seems a very modern ancient philosopher, someone who rejects precisely those parts of Platonism and Aristotelianism which can make them appear alien to the contemporary reader. Materialism and empiricism can take many forms, however, and, as we shall see, we must be careful not to assimilate Epicurus too quickly to their popular contemporary versions.

LIFE AND WORKS OF EPICURUS

Although an Athenian citizen, Epicurus was born on the island of Samos in 341 BC, where his father had gone from Athens as a settler ten years before. It is possible that he was first introduced to philosophical enquiry by Pamphilus, a Platonist who also lived on the island, and possible too that, when still young, he came under the influence of Nausiphanes, a follower of Democritus. Certainly he acquired a knowledge of early atomism from Nausiphanes, although this may have been after he visited Athens. When Epicurus was 18, he went to Athens to do his military service, and it is reported that he went to the Academy to hear Xenocrates lecture. After his two-year stint in the army, Epicurus joined his father in Colophon, where the latter had gone after the Athenian settlers had been ordered out of Samos by Perdiccas. Little detail is known of the next fifteen years of his life. He probably worked as a school teacher in Colophon, before moving to Mytilene in 311 to teach philosophy. A lost polemical work, *Against the Philosophers at Mytilene*, suggests that he did not fit in to the philosophical scene there very happily, and he seems to have left quite soon for Lampsacus, forming there a philosophical circle around himself. In 307 he returned to Athens, and, in order to set up a philosophical school, he bought a house which came to be known as the 'Garden'. Epicurus lived there until his death in 271 BC. Although there is strong secondary evidence that Epicurus was a keen and vitriolic literary polemicist, there is also compelling evidence that he was a highly good-natured man in person, and inspired great loyalty amongst his students.

He wrote a great deal. Forty-one works are cited in Diogenes Laertius' biography of him (in book X of his *Lives of the Philosophers*), but this list is of Epicurus' 'best works': according to Diogenes, his complete works ran to around three hundred rolls, so that he surpassed all previous writers in the number of his books (X.26). Unfortunately, very little of this has come down to us. Diogenes reproduces three philosophical letters written to Epicurus' followers: the *Letter to Herodotus* (*Hdt.*), in which he provides an epitome of his natural science; the *Letter to Pythocles* (*Pyth.*), an outline of his theories about celestial phenomena; and the *Letter to Menoeceus* (*Men.*), which gives the basics of his ethics. Diogenes also cites forty 'Principal Beliefs' (*Kuriai Doxai, KD*), and a further collection of maxims survives in a manuscript in the Vatican (*Vaticanae sententiae, VS*). In addition, some of the papyri found at Herculaneum have contained fragments of perhaps his principal work, the *De Natura*, which, according to Diogenes, ran to thirty-seven books.

In addition to these few works which have survived, we have various other sources for Epicurean doctrine. Most important is the *De Rerum Natura* of the first-century BC Roman poet Lucretius, in which he sets out Epicurean teaching in helpful detail. The papyri discovered at Herculaneum have also contained works by Philodemus, another Epicurean of the first-century BC. More bizarrely, many fragments have been found in central Turkey of a wall erected by one Diogenes of Oenoanda to set out the principles of Epicureanism. In addition to these Epicurean sources, there is quite a lot of evidence for Epicurean philosophy in the work of Cicero and Plutarch, two opponents of Epicureanism. Given the state of our evidence, we do not have much reason to find developments either in Epicurus' own work, or even in that of his followers. Thus, later writers are generally taken to provide pretty straightforward evidence for Epicurean claims and arguments. I shall follow that practice here, but it is worth noting at least the possibility that later Epicureans may manifest doctrinal shifts from Epicurus' own claims.

One reason perhaps why Epicurus' philosophical system has seemed more simple than those of Plato and Aristotle and of his Hellenistic opponents is that the most accessible of his own writings to have survived are the letters, which are precisely intended to present introductory outlines of his views and arguments. It is clear from the works which survive on papyrus, both those of Epicurus himself and of Philodemus, that there was a proper place for detailed and technical argumentation within Epicureanism, but this has so far played a minor role in forming our general sense of the nature of Epicurus' work, not least perhaps because deciphering the remains of the papyri is a tremendously difficult and uncertain process.

❦ PERCEPTION AND COGNITION ❦

Throughout his work, Epicurus shows himself to be epistemically cautious. He is keenly aware of the danger of holding false beliefs and is duly anxious to provide a method which, if followed, will allow one to believe only truths. Central to this method is a reliance on perception – which, together with *'prolêpseis'* and the 'primary affections' of pleasure and pain, provide the 'criteria of truth' (DL X.31).

Epicurus provides an reasonably elaborate account of what happens in perception, according to which we perceive when we are struck by the films of atoms (*eidôla*) which are constantly emitted from the solid bodies around us. These preserve the shape of the objects from which they emanate (*Hdt.* 46 (LS 15A1)) and it is by coming into contact with these *eidôla* that we see and think of shapes (*Hdt.* 49 (LS 15A6)), since these delineations penetrate us 'from objects, sharing their colour and shape, of a size to fit into our vision or thought, and travelling at high speed, with the result that their unity and continuity then results in the impression' (*Hdt.* 49–50 (LS 15A8)). Hearing, too, involves the reception of atoms: it 'results from a sort of wind travelling from the object which speaks, rings, bangs or produces an auditory perception in whatever way it may be' (*Hdt.* 52 (LS 15A14)). Smell, too, 'just like hearing, would never cause any affection if there were not certain particles travelling away from an object and with the right dimensions to stimulate this sense, some kinds being disharmonious and unwelcome, others harmonious and welcome' (*Hdt.* 53 (LS 15A18)).

Thus, we are able to perceive because we are receptive to the various kinds of atoms emitted by the solid objects around us. Indeed, perception just is the conscious reception of these atoms, its content entirely determined by their nature and properties: 'all perception, says Epicurus, is irrational and does not accommodate memory. For neither is it moved by itself, nor when moved by something else is it able to add or subtract anything' (DL X.31 (LS 16B1–2)). The content of a perception is thus not to be explained by reference to anything other than what produces that perception, although the objects of perception are distinct from the direct causes of the perception. In *Hdt.* 46, we are told that the *eidôla* have the same shape as the solid objects from which they emanate, but are much finer than the things which are apparent – what are apparent in perception, then, are not the *eidôla* themselves but the solid objects (cf. Lucretius IV.256 ff.). (It is for this reason, of course, that Epicurus has to argue for his account of how we perceive: if we perceived the *eidôla* which cause the perceptions, then the truth of that account would be given in perception and not stand in need of argument.)

Since the *eidôla* in fact preserve the relevant properties of the objects from which they are emitted, the perceptual affection reports correctly the nature of the solid object:

And whatever impression we get by focusing our thought or senses, whether of shape or of properties, that is the shape of the solid body, produced through the *eidôlon*'s concentrated succession or after-effect. But falsehood and error are always located in the belief which we add.

(Hdt. 50 (LS 15A9–10))

It is the passivity of perception – its inability to add or to subtract anything from the stimulus – which secures its utter epistemic reliability, and it is not until the mind begins to work with the perceptual reports that the possibility of error arises. Whilst the content of perception is entirely determined by the nature of the stimulus which produces it (and so by how things are), the content of belief is not so constrained and our beliefs can thus mis-report how things are.

The claim that all perceptions are true is, of course, an extremely strong one. The occurrence of perceptual conflict was, after all, something which had been the subject of epistemological scrutiny since Protagoras' move to global subjectivism in order, if we are to believe Plato's *Theaetetus*, to preserve the reliability of perception despite the occurrence of prima-facie conflicting appearances. Thus, if, for instance, the same wind seems cold to one person and warm to another, the mistake, according to Protagoras, would be to think of these perceptions as both seeking to represent the same state of affairs – in this case, the temperature of the wind – when, of course, they could not both be true. Rather, each correctly reports a distinct state of affairs; the wind's temperature relative to the individual perceiver. The wind is in fact warm for the one perceiver and cold for the other. Perceptions report truly how things are for the perceiver (and, importantly, not merely how they seem to the perceiver).

Protagoras' wholesale subjectivism – the account is intended to apply not just to temperatures and colours but to all properties universally – was an extreme, and not obviously coherent, reaction to the possibility of perceptual conflict, and it did not find favour with either Plato or Aristotle, who had to find other ways to deal with the problem. Plato did so by denying that perceptions can be true or false at all: he treats them as mere sensations which provide the materials for beliefs. Aristotle, who did allow perceptions themselves to have propositional content, and so to be capable of being true and false, avoided the difficulties of perceptual conflict by denying that all perceptions are true: thus, in a case of perceptual conflict, at least one of the conflicting perceptions will be false and will be the result of a defect on the part of the perceiver.

Against this background, Epicurus' re-affirmation of the truth of all perceptions, without a move to any kind of subjectivism, can be seen to be very bold indeed – so bold, indeed, as to seem like hopeless epistemic optimism. Moreover, the argument which Diogenes Laertius cites as supporting this claim seems to be clearly insufficient to do this:

All perception, he says, is irrational and does not accommodate memory. For neither is it moved by itself, nor when moved by something else is it able to add or subtract anything. Nor does there exist anything which can refute perceptions: neither can like sense refute like, because of their equal validity; nor unlike since they are not discriminatory of the same things; nor can reason, since all reason depends on the senses; nor can one individual perception, since they all command our attention.

(DL X.31–2 (LS 16B1–7))

Thus, there is nothing which can convict any particular perception of error, since in any case where some state seems to cast doubt on the truth of a perception, that state can itself have no greater epistemic security than the perception which it calls into question. Even if this were right, however, it would not give Epicurus the conclusion he needs, since it would be consistent with this that there are indeed false perceptions, even though we can never have sufficient reason to believe of any particular perception that it is false.[2] Since there is nothing here to block the possibility of conflicting perception, the most sensible response when that possibility is realised would seem to be that of the sceptic; suspension of judgement. Indeed, in a case of two conflicting perceptions of the same sense, it would seem to be impossible to assent to both, since this would be to believe a contradiction.

We are given a different argument by Sextus:

For just as the primary affections, that is pleasure and pain, come about from certain agents and in accordance with those agents – pleasure from pleasant things and pain from painful things, and it is impossible for what is productive of pleasure not to be pleasant and what is productive of pain not to be painful but that which produces pleasure must necessarily be naturally pleasant and that which produces pain naturally painful – so also with perceptions which are affections of ours, that which produces each of them is always perceived entirely and, as perceived, cannot bring about the perception unless it is in truth such as it appears.

(*Math.* VII.203)

Here it is the passivity of the senses which secures their veridicality: they are such as to present the cause of the perception just as it is. This provides a much better route to Epicurus' conclusion – and, indeed, it accords with the very start of Diogenes' report of what Epicurus has to say about perception (and also with the remark at Cicero *De Finibus* I.64 that one will not be able to defend the judgement of the senses without knowing the nature of things). It also provides a rather different kind of epistemological strategy from what we would have if we took the burden of the argument for the claim that all perceptions are true to be carried by the argument for the irrefutability of perceptions. The latter might look very much like an a priori epistemological argument, but the argument from the passivity of the senses is part of a theory about the way in which we are related perceptually to the world – and not itself given in experience. Given this, it is better to take the irrefutability argument as a subsidiary argument, an attempt to show that the universal conclusion – that all perceptions are true – is consistent with the available perceptual evidence, and thus does itself not fall foul of Epicurus' scientific methodology. *Eidôla* are theoretical entities which we have reason to believe in because they explain things which are apparent. It is not part of the content of perception that we perceive because we are struck by atoms from the solid objects around us.

His argument for the role of *eidôla* in perception, then, is an instance of his general method for establishing the truth of claims which are not directly supported by the evidence of perception itself. Unfortunately, our evidence for the details of this method is sketchy. In his brief report, Diogenes simply uses Epicurus' technical terms without explicating their meaning: a belief will be true if it is 'attested or uncontested' and false if it is 'unattested or contested' (DL X.34 (LS 18B)). There is a much fuller account in Sextus, although doubt has been cast on its reliability. According to this, attestation is 'apprehension through what is evident of the fact that the object of belief is such as it was believed to be', and non-contestation 'is the following from that which is evident of the non-evident thing posited and believed'. Contestation, alternatively, conflicts with non-contestation, being 'the elimination of that which is evident by the positing of the non-evident thing', whilst non-attestation 'is opposed to attestation, being confrontation through what is evident of the fact that the object of belief is not such as it was believed to be'. Sextus concludes his report: 'Hence attestation and non-contestation are the criterion of something's being true, while non-attestation and contestation are the criterion of its being false. And the evident is the foundation and basis of everything' (*Math*. VII.211–6 (LS 18A)). One obvious question here is why Epicurus needed two modes of assessment for beliefs rather than just one. The answer to this would seem to be that different types of belief will be assessed in different ways. Thus, if a non-perceptual belief (i.e. one which does not derive directly from perception) is nevertheless about something which can be perceived, then it should be assessed for whether it is attested or non-attested by perception. Sextus' example of this is that of seeing someone from a distance: if I believe that the far-off figure is Plato, then that belief, which is not currently given by the perception itself, can be attested or non-attested by a later perception when the person is closer. In contrast, there are theoretical beliefs which can never be directly verified by reference to perception – such as Epicurus' beliefs about *eidôla* – and it is these which are contested or non-contested by the perceptual evidence.

Now, whilst it is reasonably straightforward to understand what it is for a belief to be either attested or contested by perceptual experience, matters are more difficult when it comes to construing the other two epistemic relations, those of non-attestation and non-contestation. The trouble is that whilst the words themselves, and perhaps also Epicurus' own practice, suggest that nothing more or less than simple consistency with the perceptual evidence is sufficient for it to be either non-contested or non-attested (depending on what type of belief it is), Sextus' account clearly places much stricter constraints on what the relations between beliefs and perceptions can be if the former are to be non-contested or non-attested by the latter. Furthermore, there would seem to be very good reason for this more restrictive view, since to accept a theoretical belief just on the grounds that it is consistent with the evidence seems extraordinarily lax, and to reject (rather than merely to hold in doubt) a perceptual belief just on the grounds that it is not attested by perception seems extraordinarily strict. What we should rather expect are three categories in each case: beliefs which our perceptions provide reason to accept, beliefs which they provide reason to reject, and those for which there is not perceptual evidence either way. Diogenes indeed does report a category of beliefs as those which 'await' – 'for example waiting and getting near the tower and learning how it appears from near by' – (DL X.34 (LS 18B)), and this suggests that Epicurus did allow that there could be beliefs which were neither contested nor un-contested, nor attested nor un-attested.

There is much room for interpretative manoeuvre on this point, but no space to effect that manoeuvring here. What can be said is that consistency with the perceptual evidence must certainly be a minimal condition for a theoretical belief to stand as non-contested – and a condition Epicurus is indeed concerned to show is satisfied when arguing for such beliefs – but that it may be that more is required than this. Indeed, the more minimal the constraints on what it is for a belief to be non-contested, the less important will be that notion for Epicurean science. Thus, whilst Epicurus introduces the *eidôla* at *Hdt.* 46 (LS 15A1), merely by saying that it is not impossible that there are such delineations of atoms, he continues by claiming that *eidôla* provide the most effective way of producing perception (*Hdt.* 49 (LS 15A6–8)). The theory is thus secured by something stronger than mere consistency with the perceptual evidence – what recommends it is not just that it provides a possible explanation of the evidence, but that it provides the best explanation of it. Again, at *Hdt.* 55–6, when he argues that we should not think that there are atoms of all sizes, he supports this by saying that 'the existence of every size is not useful with respect to the differences of qualities', where this seems to mean that we do not need to posit all sizes of atoms in order to explain the various qualities of visible bodies. If the only constraint imposed on theoretical claims was that they should not conflict with the perceptual evidence, however, then there would be no good reason to restrict the range of properties one attributed to the atoms. In the light of this, and of both Sextus' report and the presence of the category of 'that which awaits' in Diogenes Laertius, there is some reason to think that non-contestation of a theoretical belief requires that it should be needed for an adequate explanation of the perceptual evidence. Even if we resist this, however, we can accept that in practice the Epicurean justification of theoretical beliefs did not stop at showing the mere consistency of those beliefs with the evidence of perception, and that if this is indeed all that is required to demonstrate that they are non-contested, then Epicurus seems to have required more for theoretical justification than non-contestation.

In any case, the irrefutability argument in Diogenes can now be seen not to be a piece of a priori epistemological reasoning, but rather an attempt to show that the theoretical claim that all perceptions are true meets the minimal condition for acceptability – that it does not conflict with the perceptual evidence. The best explanatory account of perception gives us reason to think that our perceptions are always true and this claim is consistent with our perceptual experience itself, despite the fact that one might think that there are perceptual conflicts.

I have so far been contrasting beliefs with perceptual evidence, but this is slightly misleading, since Epicurus' criteria of truth are not limited to perception itself. The proper contrast is, as we have seen, between belief and what is evident, and things can be evident to us not merely through perception, but also through *prolêpsis* (plural: *prolêpseis*). If we are to understand Epicurus' epistemology – and hence his natural science – we need to have some sense of the cognitive role played by *prolêpsis*. Perception is an entirely passive process, and the nature of the perceptual affection is determined entirely by the nature of the stimulus which produces it. In bringing *prolêpseis* into his account of cognition, Epicurus is able to extend the range of information the subject is able to receive. According to Diogenes' brief exposition of *prolêpsis* (DL X.33), it is, for instance, in virtue of having the *prolêpsis* of man or horse that one can think and talk about men or horses and such *prolêpseis* are both self-evident and acquired through perception. Thus, what *prolêpseis* someone has depends upon his previous perceptual experience, and so these will differ between subjects. Thus, someone can talk and think about, say, cows and horses because he has *prolêpseis* of cows and horses – and he will have these if he has had sufficient previous perceptual experience of cows and horses.

This is not, however, to say that he has had previous perceptions whose content is about the condition of cows and horses. Thus, the *eidôla* flowing from a horse will preserve the shape and colour of the horse, and so, in receiving them, one will have the perception that an object of a certain shape has a certain colour. This is guaranteed by the mechanism of the reception of the *eidôla*, but is not yet sufficient for the subject to have an experience with the content that that horse is that colour. In order to have an experience with that content, the subject must have some concept of a horse and it is here that *prolêpseis* come into play. In acquiring a *prolêpsis* of something, the subject acquires a recognitional ability for things of that kind. This requires repeated perceptual exposure to such things, after which one will be able to recognise newly perceived examples as similar to the ones he has already seen. This does not require any articulated theorising about what it is to be that kind of thing: it is important for Epicurus' cognitive theory that *prolêpseis* operate prior to the level of belief, since this is what secures their ability to stand as criteria of truth for beliefs. People will differ in what *prolêpseis* they possess – in virtue of differing in their perceptual histories – but the acquisition of a *prolêpsis* is just as non-rational as having a perception. If someone has sufficiently many perceptions caused by horse-*eidôla*, he will come to have the *prolêpsis* of a horse and so will be able to distinguish horses from other types of thing both when he perceives them directly and when he thinks about them.

ATOMS AND VOID

Our direct experience is of solid objects in the world around us. In virtue of perception proper we can know that these objects have certain properties – such as size, shape and colour – and in virtue of *prolêpsis* we can come to recognise what sorts of objects they are (although this will always be in terms of properties which are perceptually apparent). Theory is required, however, if we are to come to know how these solid objects are materially constituted and how this explains their behaviour. In this section, I shall provide a brief outline of Epicurus' theory of matter, generally citing his claims and argu-ments rather than discussing them. This is not because those arguments are uninteresting – indeed Epicurus' arguments for the nature of the atoms are some of his more sophisticated – but because to discuss them seriously would require more in the way of historical context (in particular, Aristotle's arguments for the continuous nature of matter and against the existence of void) than is possible here. As it is, this section should be seen just as an exposition of Epicurus' basic physical theory.

Epicurus begins the exposition of his physical theory in the *Letter to Herodotus* by affirming the temporal infinity of the basic constituents of the universe. 'Nothing', he claims, 'comes into being out of what is not – for in that case everything would come into being out of everything with no need for seeds' (*Hdt.* 38 (LS 4A1)). Epicurus thus secures his claim on something we observe, which is that when things are generated, they are generated from the relevant kind of seed (cf. Lucretius I.169–73 (LS 4B4–5)). Thus, in order to grow an oak tree, we need to start with an acorn – for it is only an acorn which has the potential to generate an oak tree. If things could be generated *ex nihilo*, however, then there would be no necessary determinate conditions for their generation, and so no need for seeds. (Of course, it might be objected that Epicurus moves too quickly here from the generation of things with which we are acquainted to the claim that nothing can be generated *ex nihilo*. After all, we have no perceptual evidence that atoms do not come into existence spontaneously, merely that composite bodies do not, and this might be a respect in which the non-evident is dissimilar from the evident.) In any case, Epicurus holds to the analogy between the observed and the unobserved in this respect, and takes the universal need for composite things to be generated from bodies which possess the potential to generate those things to confirm the general thesis that nothing can be generated *ex nihilo*. He also maintains that nothing can pass away into nothing: if it could, then everything would already have perished. Given these two claims – that things cannot be created from nothing and they cannot perish into nothing, we can accept that the basic constituents of the universe persist for ever, since they will not have come into existence and cannot go out of existence.

Epicurus' next move is to establish the nature of those basic constituents:

> Moreover, the totality of things is bodies and void. That bodies exist is universally witnessed by perception itself, in accordance with which it is necessary to judge by reason that which is non-evident, as I said before; and if place, which we call 'void', 'room', and 'intangible substance' did not exist, bodies would not have anywhere to be or to move through in the way they are observed to move. Beyond these nothing can even be thought of, either by imagination or by analogy with what is imagined as completely substantial things and not as the things we call accidents and properties of these.
>
> (*Hdt.* 39–40 (LS 5A))

According to Epicurus, there are two basic kinds of substance (existing thing): bodies and void. Now, this is not yet a statement of atomism, since Epicurus tells us that the fact that bodies exist is given in perception, and we do not perceive atoms. Thus, the bodies which we know through perception to exist are the solid bodies which, he will argue, are composed of atoms. For Epicurus' present purpose, however, this is quite sufficient, since we do perceive that there are solid bodies and this is enough to show that there are bodies which are extended and tangible. In itself, however, this does not show that void exists – what does show *that* is not that we perceive material objects, but that we see that they move. What is distinctive of void is that it is not solid: it offers no resistance. If all space were occupied by things which were solid, then solid objects would not be able to occupy a different space from the one they occupy at any time, and so could not move. Since we know from perception that bodies do move, we can infer that there is space which offers no resistance to the impact of bodies, and thus that void exists.

Having established the existence of both bodies and void, Epicurus moves to discuss the nature of bodies. All bodies are either compounds or the basic constituents of compounds, and the latter are incapable of either alteration or dissolution: 'the primary entities, then, must be atomic kinds of bodies' (*Hdt.* 40–1 (LS 8A)). Epicurus' atoms are uncuttable: it is physically impossible to split them. This is because, unlike those bodies which have atoms as constituents, they contain no void, and it is the presence of void in a body which renders it vulnerable to alteration (cp. Lucretius I.528–39 (LS 8 B2)). In expounding the existence of bodies which could not be divided, Epicurus was returning to the physical theory of Democritus and Leucippus in opposition to Aristotle, who had argued that matter must be continuous, that is, infinitely divisible. Epicurean atomism was more radical than that of his predecessors, however, since not only did he maintain that there are bodies which are physically indivisible, but he argued that there are minima which, whilst extended, have no parts at all – that is, they cannot be divided even conceptually. Each atom is perpetually in motion and if it were able to travel through the void without interference from other atoms, it would be carried downwards by its weight, and all atoms would travel at the same speed.[3] However, the trajectory of atoms, although not their velocity, can be affected by collisions with other atoms, so that one can have, for instance a system of atoms constituting some solid object. Although each atom will indeed be constantly moving, the trajectories of the constituent atoms will be such that the object which is constituted by them remains stationary.

The basics of Epicurus' atomic theory, then, are that matter is not continuous, but atomic, and that the physical atoms – the bodies which cannot be further divided physically – are constituted by minimal parts which are not even conceptually divisible. Every body – that is, every entity which is extended and solid – is either an atom or constituted by atoms. There are infinitely many atoms, and an infinite space for them to occupy and move about in. Each atom, because of its weight, has a natural tendency to move downwards (at a speed 'as quick as thought'), but the locomotive history of many atoms is limited by the fact that they collide with other atoms. A collection of atoms can constitute a stable solid object when the atoms mutually deflect each other's motion so as to maintain each other in a pattern. Even then, the atoms will not be at rest but will oscillate at their natural speed.

❧ SOUL, BODY AND PROPERTIES ❧

Atoms and void are the primary entities of Epicurean physics, and bodies and void are the only things which exist '*per se*'. Although Epicurus does not want to deny, for instance, that there are properties, he takes these to be parasitic on the existence of *per se* existents. Indeed, he is careful on this point:

> Now as for the shapes, colours, sizes, weights, and other things
> predicated of body as permanent attributes – belonging either to all
> bodies or those which are visible, and knowable in themselves through

perception – we must not hold that they are *per se* substances: that is inconceivable. Nor, at all, that they are non-existent. Nor that they are some distinct incorporeal things accruing to the body. Nor that they are parts of it; but that the whole body cannot have its own permanent nature consisting entirely of the sum total of them, in an amalgamation like that when a larger aggregate is composed directly of particles, either primary ones or magnitudes smaller than such-and-such a whole, but that it is only in the way I am describing that it has its own permanent nature consisting of the sum total of them. And these things have their own individual ways of being focused on and distinguished, yet with the whole complex accompanying them and at no point separated from them, but with the body receiving its predication according to the complex conception.

(Hdt. 68–9 (LS 7B1–2))

There are some properties which all bodies must have (shape, size, weight) and some which all visible bodies must have (colour). These are 'permanent' attributes of bodies: as Lucretius reports, they are those properties which 'can at no point be separated and removed without fatal destruction resulting – as weight is to stones, heat to fire, liquidity to water, tangibility to all bodies, and intangibility to void' (I.451–4 (LS 7A3)). Such properties are thus not merely permanent, but necessary. This necessity is not merely physical, but conceptual: one cannot conceive of the body without that property. They are not, however, *per se* substances like bodies themselves – they exist only as the properties of bodies, and so their existence is in that way derivative. In addition to these permanent properties, bodies can also have accidental properties: 'by contrast slavery, poverty, wealth, freedom, war, peace, and all other things whose arrival and departure a thing's nature survives intact, these it is our practice to call, quite properly, accidents' (I.455–8 (LS 7A4)).

Epicurus' distinction here between visible and invisible bodies makes it clear that he does not think that atoms possess all the properties possessed by complex bodies. The only properties which atoms possess are those of shape, weight, size and the necessary concomitants of shape (*Hdt.* 54 (LS 12D1)), and so one cannot in general explain the fact that a complex body has some property by appealing to the possession of that very property by its constituent atoms. This is again made clear by Lucretius, who says that 'you should not suppose those white objects which you see before your eyes as white to consist of white primary particles or those which are black to be the product of black seeds' (II.731–33 (LS 12E1)). This, he points out, actually allows for a more satisfying explanation of the behaviour of coloured objects:

> Besides, if primary particles are colourless, and possess a variety of shapes from which they generate every kind of thing and thus make colours vary – since it makes a great difference with what things and

in what sort of position the individual seeds are combined and what motions they impart to each other and receive from each other – it at once becomes very easy to explain why things which a little earlier were black in colour can suddenly take on the whiteness of marble, as the sea when its surface has been churned up by great winds, is turned into waves whose whiteness is like that of gleaming marble. All you need to say is that what we regularly see as black comes to appear gleaming white as soon as its matter is mixed up, as soon as the ordering of its primary particles is changed, as soon as some particles are added and some subtracted. But if the sea's surface consisted of blue seeds, there is no way in which they could turn white. For things that are blue could never change to the colour of marble, no matter how you were to jumble them up.

(Lucretius *De rerum natura* II.499–514 (LS 12A3))

Given that Lucretius allows here that atomic change to a complex body can involve not merely the re-arrangement of atoms but also their loss and addition, the argument here doesn't quite work – since one could accept that individual atoms cannot change, but maintain that when the sea changes colour it is indeed because there are blue atoms on the surface which are displaced by white atoms. Nevertheless, the passage is important because it suggests strongly that Epicurus accepts that the properties of a complex substance (a substance which has atoms as constituents) are determined by the properties – including the arrangement and motion – of its constituent atoms. For Lucretius infers the claim that the different atomic shapes and arrangements make the colours of a substance change from the general claim that the primary particles 'possess a variety of shapes from which they generate every kind of thing'. That Lucretius feels entitled to infer from this that they are responsible for colours, and changes in colour, shows that what are 'generated' by the atoms are not just objects, but their properties as well – that is, that there is a particular arrangement of atoms of particular shapes that will determine not just that there is a certain kind of complex substance, but that that substance has the properties it does.

The Epicurean treatment of the relation between macroscopic and microscopic properties can perhaps be best illustrated by considering his account of the *psuchê* – the 'soul' – as this represents his most sustained attempt to explain the nature and behaviour of complex substances by reference to the nature and arrangement of their constituent atoms. For Epicurus, an animal body, like all solid objects, is a compound of atoms, and the *psuchê* is itself a material part of a living body: it is a 'fine-structured body' diffused throughout the whole (*Hdt.* 63 (LS 14A1)). Thus, the *psuchê* is itself a body – that is, it is an individuated entity with its own distinctive atomic constitution. According to a report in Aetius, Epicurus took the material constitution of the *psuchê* to be specific to it: 'it is a blend (*krama*) consisting of four things, of which one kind is fire-like, one air-like, one wind-like, while the fourth is something which lacks a name' (Aetius 4.3.11 (LS 14C)). Although it is thus possible to specify the atomic constituents of the matter of the *psuchê*, what is important for the explanation of psychic functioning is that they form a 'blend'. This is emphasised by Lucretius:

> The primary particles of the elements so interpenetrate each other in their motions that no one element can be distinguished and no capacity spatially separated, but they exist as multiple powers of a single body. . . . Heat, air and the unseen force of wind when mixed form a single nature, along with that mobile power which transmits the beginning of motion from itself to them, the origin of sense-bearing motions through the flesh.
>
> (III.262–5; 269–72 (LS 14D1))

Because the elemental atoms are blended, they constitute a body which has particular powers lacked by things which are not so constituted – when contained within a larger body, it is, for instance, capable of sensation and thought.

This last qualification is important for Epicurus, who enthusiastically denies that the *psuchê* can survive the death of the body, and emphasises the mutual dependency of psuche and the body which contains it. So, whilst it is indeed the *psuchê* which is responsible for perception, it is only able to produce that capacity in virtue of being contained within the body. Once the body disintegrates, the atoms of the *psuchê* are dispersed and so it loses its own capacities (*Hdt.* 63–4 (LS 14A3)). Neither the *psuchê* nor the body can survive the demise of the other, and it is the combination of body and *psuchê* which constitutes the living animal, not the *psuchê* by itself: 'since conjunction is necessary to their existence, so also theirs must be a joint nature' (Lucretius, III.347–8). Thus, it is not just the *psuchê*, but the whole body, which enjoys perception, which is, as Lucretius says, an affection which is common to the mind and the body (III.335–6).

From the mere fact that Epicurus takes the *psuchê* to be itself a material body, one can tell very little about what relation he postulates between the psychological properties of the living animal and the movement of the atoms which constitute the *psuchê*. However, this becomes clearer if one reflects on his arguments for this materialist thesis.[4] The psuche must be material since, if it were not material it would be void, and 'void can neither act nor be acted upon, but merely provides bodies with motion through itself' (*Hdt.* 67 (LS 14A7)). Since it is evident that the *psuchê* does act on things and is, in turn, acted on, the idea that it is incorporeal is incoherent. That is, it is evident that there are psychological causes and effects, and if this is so, then what is changed and produces change must be something material, since immaterial things cannot be the agents or patients of change. The claim that only material things can bring about or undergo change will be well-motivated if it is assumed that all changes are either themselves atomic events, or are determined by those.

That Epicurus accepts that psychological events require the occurrence of atomic events is clear from his arguments for the nature of the *psuchê*'s atomic constitution. So, according to Lucretius, the mind is 'exceedingly delicate and is constituted by exceedingly minute particles' (III.179–80):

> Nothing is seen to be done so swiftly as the mind determines it to be done and initiates; therefore the mind rouses itself more quickly than any of the things whose nature is seen plain before our eyes. But that which is so readily moved must consist of seeds exceedingly rounded and exceedingly minute, that they may be moved when touched by a small moving power.
>
> (III. 182–8)

In accordance with Epicurean scientific method, Lucretius starts off from something evident – that the mind produces its effects more rapidly than anything else does – and infers from this that the atoms of the *psuchê* are smaller and rounder than any other atoms. For this inference to work, however, psychological changes must require atomic changes, otherwise there would be no necessity that the atoms should be able to move as rapidly as the mind works. Again, when Lucretius comes to explain the occurrence of emotions, he does so by reference to the atoms which constitute the mind. When one is angry this is because of the heat in the *psuchê* and when one is frightened, this is the result of its coldness, 'the companion of fear, which excites fright in the limbs and rouses the frame' (III. 288–93). Here there is a material explanation for the effects of the emotion. When one is afraid and one's limbs shake, this can be explained by reference to the cold, the 'companion' of fear. For the emotion to have the effects it does – and that psychological states have causes and effects is the datum from which Epicurean theorising about the *psuchê* begins – there must be atomic events which determine those effects.

In trying to understand Epicurus' natural science, it is tempting to think that he must be a reductionist just because he espouses atomism – which can strike the contemporary reader as somehow an intrinsically 'scientific' theory of matter. This temptation should be resisted, however. There is no sign that Epicurus attempted to identify, say, the mental properties or events of people with their atomic properties or events. The cold is, after all, only the companion of fear and not the emotion itself. In this respect, Epicurus is perhaps more Aristotelian than he is sometimes given credit for being – for Aristotle too accepted a genuine role for material explanation within his natural science and psychology. Aristotle distinguished efficient causation from material causation: changes involving material substances are to be explained both by reference to the capacities of the agent and patient of the change and to the underlying material events on which the changes supervene. That Epicurus maintains an atomic theory of matter rather than one according to which matter is continuous, and that he renounces a teleological explanation of natural phenomena, puts no pressure on him to give up the distinction between efficient and material causes – and there is good reason to think that he does not give it up (even if he does not continue with the terminology). For if it is the properties of the *psuchê* which have causes and effects, and if Epicurus does not identify those properties with the arrangements of atoms which generate those properties but still thinks that the operations of the *psuchê* can be explained by reference to the arrangements of its constituent atoms, then, like Aristotle, he must distinguish antecedent causes from material causes and allow both a role in the determination of changes.

✷ ACTION AND RESPONSIBILITY ✷

Lucretius gives the following account of the causation of action:

> Now I shall tell you . . . how it comes about that we can take steps forward when we want to, how we have the power to move our limbs, and what it is that habitually thrusts forward this great bulk that is our body. First, let me say, images (*simulacra*) of walking impinge on our mind and strike it, as I explained earlier.[5] It is after this that volition occurs. For no one ever embarks upon any action before the mind first previews what it wishes to do, and for whatever it is that it previews there exists an image of that thing. So when the mind stirs itself to want to go forwards, it immediately strikes all the power of the spirit distributed all over the body throughout all the limbs and frame: it is easily done because the spirit is firmly interlinked with it. Then the spirit in turn strikes the body, and thus gradually the whole bulk is pushed forward and moved.

(IV. 877–91)

Here we have, as we should now expect, an account of what happens when we act which makes use of a mixture of both psychological and material causation. In order to walk, for instance, the person needs to form the intention to walk, and so needs to think about walking. For this to happen, he must have an image, or images, of walking and these come in the form of *eidôla* from outside.[6] These images have both a psychological and a material aspect: they are constituted by atoms whose impact on the mind will have mechanical effects, but they are pictorial in that they present an image to the mind. As the mind decides to walk, it transmits an impulse to the spirit which in its turn strikes the relevant parts of the body so that they move. We thus have a story which can be told at two levels. Mechanically, the atoms of the image strike those of the mind which impact those of the spirit which impact those of the body, whilst, psychologically, the mind responds to the image of walking by deciding to walk, thus causing the person to walk. The person walks because he decides to (and, in order to decide to, he must think about walking). This causal explanation is taken to be consistent with the determination of these psychological events by the material events which underlie them.

Allowing that psychological events are determined by the movements of the atoms which constitute the person's *psuchê* and body, however, was taken by some to raise the threat of a determinism inconsistent with moral responsibility. Epicurus deals with this threat in the remnants of Book 25 of his *De Natura*. There he distinguishes between a person's atomic constitution and what he calls 'developments' – and it is in virtue of the latter that we are responsible for actions (XXXIV.21–2 Ar2 (LS 20B)). The passage is notoriously obscure, but it is most happily read as providing a response to someone who seeks to excuse bad behaviour as the result of material causation, that is, as brought about by the motions of one's constituent atoms. Epicurus is thus not concerned with the sort of determinist argument against moral responsibility which has become more familiar – that if our actions are caused by our mental states, which are themselves caused, then we are cannot be held responsible for how we act. Epicurus, like Aristotle, does not think that the fact that our actions are the effects of our practical deliberations provides any reason at all to deny that we are responsible for them. His response to his opponent here is to point out that our actions are not, or not only, determined by the motions of our constituent atoms, but by the 'developments', which, presumably, are our psychological states. The determinist's mistake is to seek to explain our actions only by reference to their material causes, and so to leave out of account the psychological states which are the antecedent causes of our actions.

Some have seen in this an Epicurean rejection of physicalism – a denial that our psychological states are in fact determined by the motions of our constituent atoms.[7] This is not required by the text, however, and would, as we have seen, go against the position we find implied elsewhere. Moreover, when Epicurus does move to deny determinism as such, he does so by positing indeterminacy at the atomic level. So, Cicero reports that, in order to avoid 'the necessity of fate', Epicurus posits an atomic swerve, fearing that 'if the atom's motion was always the result of natural and necessary weight, we would have no freedom, since the mind would be moved in whatever way it was compelled by the motion of atoms' (*De Fato* 22–3 (LS 20 E2–3)). Thus Epicurus, it seems, modified his atomic theory so that not only could atomic motion result from the atom's own weight, and from the impacts of other atoms, but it could also occur spontaneously as a minimal deviation from its existing trajectory – a swerve. This was introduced in order to preserve the ascription of moral responsibility. Epicurus seems to have accepted that if all atomic events were determined by previous atomic events, and if psychological events were determined by atomic events, then we could not properly ascribe responsibility to people for their actions. In order to preserve the *prolêpsis* that we are so responsible, he modifies the atomic theory so as to introduce indeterminacy at certain points, so that the chains of causation do not stretch back infinitely. That he was driven to this, however, confirms rather than casts doubt on the thesis that atomic events determine psychological events, since, if this were not so, there would be no need to deny that all atomic events are determined.

It is difficult to regard Epicurus' doctrine of the swerve as a great success. For, even if it does introduce indeterminacy into his system, it would not seem to do so in the right way. For, whilst it will serve to deny that there are infinite chains of atomic causes, it does nothing in itself to make these relevant to the determination of mental events and of actions, and it is difficult to see how Epicurus thought the mere denial of infinite causal chains of atomic events could make a relevant and constant difference to the determination of actions.[8] It is hard here not to support Carneades' judgement, reported by Cicero, that in fact Epicurus did not need his swerve, but, having accepted that 'a certain voluntary motion of the mind was possible', this in itself provided what was needed against those who would deny that we are responsible for our actions: 'a defence of that doctrine was preferable to introducing the swerve, especially as they could not discover its cause' (Cicero, *De Fato*, 23 (LS 20E4)).

PLEASURE AND THE GOOD LIFE

Epicurus thus sees no conflict between the thought that we are material substances whose behaviour can be explained by reference to the movements of our constituent atoms, and the fact that we are capable of intentional action and practical deliberation. Such deliberation, according to Epicurus, is always conducted by reference to pleasure: 'we recognise pleasure as the good which is primary and congenital; from it we begin every choice and avoidance, and we come back to it, using the affection as the yardstick for judging every good thing' (*Men.* 129). Whenever we act, we do so to gain some pleasure, and our actions will be successful in so far as they achieve this. Pleasure and pain, the 'primary affections'; are, we remember, Epicurus' third criterion of truth, along with perceptions and *prolêpseis* – they have the same kind of epistemic reliability as these other states.[9] If something seems pleasurable to someone, then it is pleasant, and if it seems painful, it is indeed painful.

That pleasant things are to be pursued and painful things avoided is evident to anything which is capable of experiencing pleasure and pain: 'as soon as it is born, every animal seeks after pleasure and rejoices in it as the greatest good, while it rejects pain as the greatest bad and, as far as possible, avoids it; and it does this when it is not yet corrupted, on the innocent and sound judgement of nature itself' (Cicero *De Finibus* 1.30 (LS 21A2)). This 'cradle argument' should not be taken simply to express an unhappy prejudice in favour of untrained, infantile or animal tastes: the point is that the badness of pain, and the goodness of pleasure, are evident simply in their perception. The judgement is 'nature's' because it is delivered by the causal interaction with the world around us: it is not something whose truth needs to be established by theorising. '[Epicurus] thinks these matters are sensed just like the heat of fire, the whiteness of snow and the sweetness of honey, none of which needs confirmation by elaborate arguments' (I.29).

This provides the foundation for Epicurus' account of the good life, which he identifies with a life of pleasure (properly conceived). He maintains, that is, not just that pleasure is a good but that it is the highest good, the final end of action. This is stated clearly by Torquatus, the spokesman for the Epicurean school in Cicero's *De Finibus*:

> We are investigating what is the final and ultimate good, which as all philosophers agree must be of such and such a kind that it is the end to which everything is the means, but is not in itself the means to anything. Epicurus situates this in pleasure, which he wants to be the greatest good, with pain the greatest bad.
>
> (I.29 (LS 21A1))

The terms here are Aristotelian, and it was indeed Aristotle's discussion of happiness (*eudaimonia*) which set the terms for Hellenistic ethical discussions. According to Aristotle, happiness is formally the final end of action: it is something which cannot be chosen for the sake of anything else, whereas other things are chosen for its sake. Thus, 'we call that which is never desirable for the sake of something else more final than the things which are desirable both in themselves and for the sake of that other thing, and therefore we call final without qualification that which is always desirable in itself and never for the sake of something else' (*Ethica Nicomachea* I.7, 1097a31–5). That happiness is final without qualification is a formal condition on any substantive account of happiness, and Aristotle's own substantive account satisfies this by distinguishing between those things which are desirable both for themselves and for the sake of happiness – such as virtue, intellectual activity and pleasure – and happiness, which is only valuable for itself. One achieves happiness precisely by engaging in those activities and having those things which are intrinsically valuable and are thus the components of happiness.

The difference between the Aristotelian and Epicurean conceptions of happiness will immediately be apparent. Aristotle, like Epicurus, takes pleasure to be something intrinsically valuable (although he would not accept the claim that our perceptions of what is pleasant are incorrigible), but whilst he places pleasure as a constituent of happiness, along with other goods, Epicurus moves actually to identify it with happiness. A further formal condition which Aristotle set down for any account of happiness was that a happy life should be 'self-sufficient' – that is, it must be such that it lacks nothing of value (otherwise there would a better good which would consist of happiness together with whatever it lacks, and this further good would then be more final than happiness itself). The danger for Epicurus' identification of happiness with pleasure is that it will fail to meet this condition, because it will leave out of account those things other than pleasure which are intrinsically valuable, thus allowing a life which included these as well to be better than a life of pleasure. To make good his identification of the final end with pleasure, Epicurus will need to show either that other things are not in fact intrinsic goods or that, even if some are, we can, and perhaps always do, also desire these things for the sake of pleasure.

There is no reason in principle why Epicurus' conception of happiness should be radically less complex than that offered by Aristotle. Whether it is will depend, in part, on how he understands the relation between pleasure and what affords it. So, if he were to think of pleasure as a feeling or sensation which is produced in one by doing things, then his account of happiness would certainly be more simple than Aristotle's: a happy life would just be one in which the subject enjoyed a great deal of that feeling, and enjoying that feeling would be the only thing worth pursuing. Other things will only be instrumentally valuable – valuable just in so far as they give rise to this feeling. If, alternatively, he were to identify pleasure with pleasurable activity, or make the degree and quality of the pleasure dependent on the type of activity which produces it, then his idea of what happiness would be like need not be substantially different from Aristotle's. The happy life could just be one which involved the enjoyment of valuable activities, where the activities are pleasurable precisely because they are themselves valuable. This would allow Epicurus, for instance, to treat virtuous activity as Aristotle does – something which is desirable in itself and, for that reason, something which can be chosen for the sake of happiness.

These different conceptions of pleasure will result in accounts of happiness which differ in another respect as well. Treating pleasure as a feeling leads naturally to a subjective account of happiness, for if one takes pleasure to be a feeling which can be produced indifferently by various things, then those activities will be pleasurable for someone just if they happen to produce that feeling in him, and there is no reason to require that the same activities will be pleasant for everyone. Although it will be the case that for everyone to lead a happy life is to enjoy (a great deal of) the feeling, how one acts to achieve that can differ between people. If, alternatively, one takes pleasure to be dependent on the value of the activities and experiences which give rise to it, then one might be able to specify those activities and experiences which will be part of a happy for life for anyone.

When we turn to consider what Epicurus has to say about pleasures, it would seem that he is no subjectivist:

> So when we say that pleasure is the end, we do not mean the pleasures of the dissipated and those that consist in having a good time, as some out of ignorance and disagreement or refusal to understand suppose we do, but freedom from pain in the body and from disturbance in the soul. For what produces the pleasant life is not continuous drinking and parties or pederasty or womanising or the enjoyment of fish and the other dishes of an expensive table, but sober reasoning which tracks down the causes of every choice and avoidance, and which banishes the beliefs that beset souls with the greatest confusion.
>
> (*Men.* 131–2 (LS 21A5))

Someone whose life was focused on what are sometimes called the pleasures 'of the flesh' would not, according to Epicurus, achieve happiness through these. His conceptions of happiness and of pleasure, then, are not sympathetic to the idea that it does not matter how one lives if one is to be happy, so long as what one does produces pleasure.

This is not because he thinks, as some have, that such pleasures are not genuine pleasures or denies that they are good. Rather, as this passage suggests, they turn out to be the wrong kind of pleasure to be identified with the final end. They are, that is, kinetic pleasures, whereas the states he identifies with being happy, *aponia* and *ataraxia*, freedom from bodily and mental pains, are what he calls *katastematic*, or static, pleasures. In the *De Finibus* the distinction is illustrated by the difference between the pleasure one gets from quenching thirst and the pleasure of having had one's thirst quenched (II.9). The first is an active pleasure – a pleasure of doing something or, perhaps, having something happen to one – whilst the second is static and results from the absence of pain or distress. It is not clear from our sources whether Epicurus thinks that whenever we have satisfied a desire there is a corresponding static pleasure; this would perhaps be a somewhat odd thing to think (how long would such a pleasure last?). Instead of taking the pleasure to be that, for instance, of having quenched one's thirst (a different static pleasure from that of, say, having satisfied one's hunger), one could rather take it to be the condition one is in when one has no unsatisfied desires and is not in pain or distress. If one were thirsty, then one would need to drink to achieve this, and if one were hungry, one would need to eat. The static pleasure which would result in the two cases would be the same (and its achievement would be contingent on the absence of other causes of bodily distress).

The importance of the distinguishing between kinetic and *katastematic* pleasure is that it makes more plausible the identification of happiness, objectively conceived, with pleasure. According to Torquatus in the *De Finibus*, the greatest pleasure we experience is not any kind of gratification, but what is perceived once all pain has been removed: 'For when we are freed from pain, we rejoice in the actual freedom and absence of all distress' (*De Finibus* I.37). Pleasure is the necessary consequence of the removal of pain, since there are no states which are neither painful nor pleasurable. This thesis is central to Epicurus' hedonism. Whenever one is not suffering from pain or distress, one will be in a state of pleasure, and, further, this condition is not one which can be made more pleasurable: 'Epicurus, moreover, supposes that complete absence of pain marks the limit of the greatest pleasure, so that thereafter pleasure can be varied and differentiated but not increased and expanded' (*De Finibus* 1.38).[10] Thus, the combination of *aponia*, the absence of bodily pain, and *ataraxia*, the absence of mental distress, places one in a condition which one cannot rationally wish to improve. Once one has achieved these, life cannot get any better.

At first sight this looks very odd. Epicurus accepts that every pleasure is something good (*Men.* 129), and this must include kinetic as well as static pleasures, but seems to deny that one's life can be made better by pursuing more kinetic pleasures. Whilst pleasure is a good, it is not the case that more pleasures are better. That one should find this paradoxical is a sign, for Epicurus, that one has misunderstood the nature of pleasure, and so will not be able to organise one's life to achieve what he takes everyone to aim at, i.e. the most pleasant life. For to pursue different kinetic pleasures as a means to achieving a more pleasurable life assumes that one can be in a state which is intermediate between pleasure and pain – and this, of course, is just what Epicurus denies. As long as one is not in pain or distress, then one is in a state of pleasure, and since there are not degrees – but merely varieties of – pleasure, one's state cannot be improved by adding particular kinetic pleasures.

Aponia and *ataraxia* thus together constitute happiness, which is the final end of action – that for which everything else is desired. Now, one could grant happiness this status without having to claim that whenever one acts one does so in order to achieve it. The claim could merely be that whilst all others goods can intelligibly be chosen for the sake of happiness, it cannot be chosen for the sake of anything else. Epicurus, however, seems to maintain the stronger thesis. Having identified happiness with *aponia* and *ataraxia*, he claims that achieving these is the goal of every action: 'this is what we aim at in all our actions – to be free from pain and anxiety' (*Men.* 127 (LS 21B1)). Again, this seems an absurdly strong thesis to hold. At least generally, one's desires are for more specific things, such as eating or sleeping or listening to music or playing soccer – and even if one were to accept that in pursuing such things one was thereby aiming at achieving a good life, it is vastly implausible that their role in achieving this higher end is because they free one from pain. Epicurus, however, does not need to maintain that we always do, in fact, act in order to achieve *aponia* or *ataraxia*: his claim need be only that when we act, we always do so in order to get some pleasure or other. However, once we understand the nature of the static pleasures, we will see that these can, and should, provide the goal for our practical reasoning. Thus, he is clear that whilst all pleasures are good, not all are choiceworthy, so that whilst one always has some reason to choose something which will afford pleasure, there can be stronger reason not to choose it. 'No pleasure is something bad *per se*: but what produces some pleasures produces stresses many times greater than the pleasures' (*KD* 8 (LS 21D1)). Thus, the rational agent will resist some pleasures because satisfying the desire for them will lead to greater overall distress than leaving it unsatisfied. If such calculations are to be properly made, the choice must be referred to the goal of achieving *aponia* and *ataraxia*.

To help with the successful pursuit of that goal, Epicurus classifies desires into three classes: 'Some desires are natural and necessary, some natural but not necessary, whilst others are neither natural nor necessary but arise from empty belief' (*KD* 29). This is explicated by a *scholion* which has survived in our manuscripts of Diogenes Laertius' text, which reports that the first class of desires are for things which bring relief from pain, the second for things which will vary pleasure rather than remove pain, and the third are for such things as crowns and the erection of statues (DL X.149 (LS 21I)). In the *Letter to Menoeceus*, Epicurus himself expands on what it is for a desire to be necessary: 'of the necessary, some are necessary for happiness, others for the body's freedom from stress, and others for life itself' (*Men.* 127 (LS 21B1). This classification of desires is not immediately obvious – in particular, it is not obvious how a desire can be natural without being necessary. If what it is for a desire to be natural is for it to be such that, given our nature, we cannot avoid having it, then how could such a desire not be necessary? Taking our cue from Epicurus' own explication of necessary desires, we should think of necessary desires here as desires whose satisfaction is necessary for happiness, *aponia* or survival. These desires will not be as specific as, for instance, is the desire for some expensive food. What is necessary for survival is just the desire to eat. Nevertheless, the desire to eat an expensive food is clearly not unrelated to that necessary desire but is rather a specific instance or version of it.[11] Epicurus can thus intelligibly take it to inherit its naturalness from the more general desire, although its satisfaction is not necessary for the person's survival. Indeed it is not important for its being non-necessary that it should be a desire for some expensive food: all particular types of food are such that a desire for them is not necessary. This is why Epicurus recommends that we stick to the more general desires, since the more general the desire, the less likely it is to go unsatisfied.[12] (Of course, desires for expensive things are, in the normal course of things, more likely to go unsatisfied than desires for things which are cheap and readily available.)

All desires are either natural or empty, and empty desires according to *KD* 29 are empty because they are based on 'empty' belief. We know from

Epicurus' methodological discussions that empty beliefs are false beliefs which are not secured by reference to the criteria of truth. Thus, to reject a perception will be to confound perceptions with 'empty belief' and so actually to lose the criterion of perception altogether (*KD* 24 (LS 17B1)), and if one does not grasp the relevant *prolêpsis*, the words one uses will also be 'empty' (*Hdt.* 37 (LS 17C1)). Emptiness in one's beliefs and language is the consequence of not securing them on the criteria of truth. As empty words are words which do not succeed in picking anything out, and empty beliefs are those which do not correspond to how things are, so empty desires will be those which are not for things which are genuinely pleasant. Thus, Epicurus can allow that people can have desires which arise from bad evaluative theories of the world – so that, for instance, they are persuaded, in whatever way, that crowns and public renown are pleasurable things to have – and they will not in fact gain pleasure from the satisfaction of these desires. Thus, although Epicurus accepts the primary affections of pleasure and pain as criteria of truth, this does not force him to accept that anything anyone believes to be pleasant is so, since such beliefs can be, and no doubt often are, unsecured by the appearances.[13]

❧ THE GOOD LIFE AND OTHERS ❧

For Epicurus, then, as for Aristotle, happiness is the central notion for practical reasoning. One worry for a theory of this kind is that it can seem to provide a necessarily selfish account of practical reasoning, since it looks as if all actions are ultimately to be judged by reference to whether they contribute to the agent's own well-being. Aristotle escapes this – as do the Stoics after him, who identify happiness with virtue – because he takes the constituents of happiness to be desirable in themselves: they are constituents of happiness just because their value is autonomous. Thus in order for virtuous activity to contribute to the agent's happiness, it must be chosen for its own sake, and not merely as something instrumental to his happiness. The virtuous person will indeed take pleasure in acting virtuously, but this pleasure comes from his awareness that he is acting well, that he is doing what he has reason to do anyway, and does not motivate his action. It is less clear that Epicurus, in identifying happiness with pleasure, even the static pleasures of *ataraxia* and *aponia*, can similarly escape the charge that he renders all practical reasoning ultimately selfish, concerned only with the good of the agent himself.

The difference in principle between the two accounts can perhaps be helpfully illustrated by a non-ethical component of Aristotelian happiness: intellectual activity. Aristotle takes such activity to be the highest activity of which we are capable, and so the most valuable. Because of this, gaining a scientific understanding of the world is the most pleasurable activity and a component of the good life. For Epicurus, in contrast, understanding the world is not something autonomously valuable: if we were not alarmed by celestial phenomena and the prospect of death, there would be no need to study natural science (*KD* 11). Such study is necessary, since 'one would not be able to banish fear about the most important things, if one did not know the nature of the whole universe' (*KD* 12). People have a fear of the divine and of death, and they need to come to understand the nature of the gods and of the *psuchê* to see that neither of these fears is justified. If the gods exist at all, they lead a completely happy life, unconcerned with human lives and so of no threat to human happiness. Similarly, once one recognises that the *psuchê* perishes at the death of the person, one will see that one cannot be harmed after death and so death is 'nothing to us'.[14] However, if we were not inclined to take cosmic events as signs of divine wrath or to think of death as a grave harm, we should have no need to understand the nature of the universe. The study of natural science is useful just because it dispels mental distress and so helps to achieve *ataraxia*. Its value is merely instrumental to the achievement of pleasure and thus happiness.

Of course, this difference between Aristotle and Epicurus might have arisen just because Epicurus took a more philistine attitude to intellectual activity than did Aristotle, but it certainly exemplifies a general concern with his account of happiness. So, he says that 'if you fail to refer each of your actions on every occasion to nature's end, and stop short at something else in choosing or avoiding, your actions will not be consequential on your theories' (*KD* 25 (LS 21E)). From this it looks very much as if Epicurus sets up as the over-arching principle of practical reasoning that whenever one acts one should do so in order to achieve pleasure for oneself. This was indeed the view of practical deliberation we find attributed to the Cyrenaics, who denied that happiness was the final end of action and who thought that one should act towards other people just so as to gain the most pleasure and least pain for oneself.[15] Epicurus, however, was no Cyrenaic and precisely seems to have wanted to allow that one can rationally be concerned with the good of others. The difficulty is seeing how this might be so, given his hedonism.

Thus, Epicurus placed great store in the importance of friendship, saying that even though it will at least initially be motivated by utility, it is nevertheless something intrinsically valuable (*Vatican Sayings* 23). However, if one's relationships with other people are motivated and controlled by a concern for one's own pleasure, then whatever relationships they are, they won't be much like friendships. It is clear from a passage in *De Finibus* I that the Epicureans were themselves worried by this, since Torquatus there reports different Epicurean accounts of the relationship between pleasure and friendship (without, unfortunately, ascribing any to Epicurus himself). Some, it seems, bit the bullet and allowed that 'the pleasures which belong to friends are not as desirable *per se* as those we desire as our own' (*De Finibus* I.66 (LS 22OI)). Even according to these Epicureans, however, we come to care about our friends as much as we do for ourselves, even though our concern is mediated by our own pleasures:

> Without friendship we are quite unable to secure a joy in life which is steady and lasting, nor can we preserve friendship itself unless we love friends as much as ourselves. Therefore friendship involves both this latter and the link with pleasure. For we rejoice in our friends' joy as much as in our own and are equally pained by their distress. The wise man, therefore, will have just the same feelings towards his friend that he has for himself, and he will work as much for his friend's pleasure as he would for his own.
>
> (*De Finibus* I.66–7 (LS 22 O))

This, however, seems to restate and preserve the problem rather than to resolve it, maintaining both that one has to care about one's friend for his own sake and that one's own pleasures are more desirable *per se* than those of one's friend.

Of course, the fact that one treats something as having value in itself does not commit one to thinking that it has as much value as other things one values: one could accept that one's friend's pleasure is *per se* desirable whilst denying that it is as *per se* desirable as one's own pleasure. However, this would not provide a satisfactory reconciliation. One would hardly think someone a proper friend if he were willing to promote one's interests just so long as they never conflicted with his own. In fact two different strategies are suggested in the text for reconciling hedonism and the demands of friendship. The first is to maintain both that a friendship is something which is in one's own overall interests, but also that it cannot be conducted unless one does take one's friend's interests to have equal value to one's own. Thus, as a matter of practical rationality, one would decide, in respect of one's friend, to put into abeyance the general principle of referring every action to the criterion of one's own pleasure, allowing the friend's interests equal weight with one's own. The second way would be to appeal to the psychological fact that one comes to be co-affected with the friend: one comes to rejoice in one's friend's joy as much as in one's own and to be equally pained by his distress. Once this has happened, one can in fact appeal to the principle of pursuing one's own pleasure in order to act in the interests of one's friend, since, for instance, knowing that he is hungry or thirsty will disturb one's own pleasure as much as if one were hungry or thirsty oneself.

Whilst this is consistent with maintaining that one's own pleasure is more desirable *per se* than that of other people, one can see why other Epicureans might have felt it unstable. These Epicureans, according to Torquatus, 'though intelligent enough, are a little more timid in facing the criticisms from you Academics: they are afraid that if we regard friendship as desirable just for own pleasure, it will seem to be completely crippled' (*De Finibus* I.69 (LS 22 O)). It would be at least slightly odd to maintain that one does have as much reason to promote one's friend's interests as one's own, but only because one will be pained as much as he will if one does not. Thus, the second Epicurean response is to allow that whilst one does first make contact with people and form relationships with them for the sake of one's own pleasure, once 'advancing familiarity has produced intimacy, affection blossoms to such an extent that friends come to be loved just for their own sake even if no advantage arises from the friendship' (*De Finibus* I.69 (LS 22 O)). This is a more interesting, if perhaps less subtle, position than the first, and accords with what Epicurus himself seems to have said in *VS* 23. It is more interesting, because it seems to allow the extension of the goodness of pleasure from oneself to other people. That is, in coming to love the friend for himself, his interests in themselves will provide one with reasons for action. One can still refer one's actions to the criterion of whether they produce pleasure, but the range of relevant pleasures will have been extended to include those of one's friend. It is not, of course, that one will not take pleasure in his well-being, but, in contrast to the first view, this is no longer the motivation for particular acts of friendship.

There is nothing in Epicurus' account of pleasure to provide an obstacle to such an extension: certainly we need first to experience our own pleasure in order to understand its nature, but, having grasped that, we can then understand what it is for someone else to gain pleasure and recognise this as a good. We do not, however, find in Epicurus any wholesale move in this direction as we do, say, in Mill: there is no attempt to argue that having come to recognise the goodness of pleasure, we should recognise that it is equally good whoever's pleasure it is. Our ability to love the friend for himself comes about because we are close to him, and there is no argument to the effect that we should seek to extend this sort of concern beyond our friends.

If Epicurus allowed this move to secure his account of friendship, it was not available to him when he came to place the virtues within the good life. This is a particular difficulty in the case of justice, since this requires that one take into account the interests of other people even when one has no affection for them. However, just as Epicurus was concerned to reconcile his official hedonism with the practices of friendship, so he assiduously maintained that it was compatible with virtue. Indeed, he maintained that the happy life was not possible unless the agent was virtuous. So, prudence 'teaches' that one cannot live pleasurably without living prudently, honourably and justly, and if one lives prudently, honourably and justly, one must live happily: 'for the virtues are naturally linked with living pleasurably, and living pleasurably is inseparable from them' (*Men.* 132 (LS 21B6)). One's first reaction to this, however, is that it is just too blithe: one wants to know how it is that prudence – practical rationality – teaches this, and Epicurus does not go on to provide an argument here. As we have seen, Aristotle could allow that acting virtuously can contribute to one's happiness just because such activity is intrinsically valuable. The virtuous agent will indeed take pleasure in acting virtuously. This is where Epicurus' identification of happiness with the static pleasures causes difficulty – for the pleasure of acting well, even if he recognised it, would be a kinetic pleasure, and thus not something which could be a component of happiness. Although he avoids the dangers of subjective hedonism by identifying happiness with *aponia* and *ataraxia*, the effect of this identification is to make difficult any attempt to bring acting in other people's interests within the sphere of the agent's own happiness (except in the case of friendship).

So, although the Epicurean wise man will, we are told, act in accordance with virtue, this has to be just because he is himself better off by doing so, and not because he recognises any reason to do so which is independent of his own well-being. In *De Finibus* I (42–54), Torquatus is duly at pains to show that the Epicurean will act virtuously. So, we are told that vices such as rashness, lust, cowardice and injustice trouble the mind by their very presence (50). Moreover, if one acts unjustly, one can never know that this will not be discovered, and so one will be troubled by the possibility of punishment. As Torquatus points out, reasonably enough, someone who has attenuated his desires in line with the Epicurean injunction to follow only those which are natural and necessary will in fact have little reason to act unjustly (52–3). Nevertheless, properly speaking, justice is not to be chosen for itself, but because it provides pleasure (53). It does so because if one treats other people properly, one will gain their affection, which is pleasant in itself, and one's life will be made more secure. Thus, although Epicurus recognises that there are requirements of justice – requirements which he seems to have taken to be generated by social contracts – he does not allow that these do not provide reasons for action because justice is in itself a good thing (or injustice a bad thing, *KD* 34 (LS 22A4)) but rather because acting unjustly will produce more distress than acting justly: 'The just life is most free from disturbance, but the unjust life is full of the greatest disturbance' (*KD* 17 (LS 22B3)).

Epicurus' theory of the good life is thus a strange mixture of the revisionary and the conservative. It is perhaps in its account of pleasure that it is most revisionary: the states of *aponia* and *ataraxia*, the static pleasures, look very unlike the sort of things which had ben taken to be pleasures. Having set these up as the pleasures which are constitutive of happiness, however, Epicurus is then able to provide hedonistic arguments for restricting the rational agent's pursuit of kinetic pleasures: once one has achieved them, one's well-being cannot be increased through the addition of more of the latter. This prevents the Epicurean from espousing a view according to which one will be happier the greater number of pleasures one can experience. Given this, it is indeed plausible enough to think that the Epicurean wise man will in fact lead a life which does not violate the norms of virtue (although it will no doubt be easy enough to imagine situations where he might). However, Epicurus does not manage to show that his account of the good can accommodate the idea that the virtues present reasons for action which are autonomous: when the Epicurean acts virtuously this is because he regards this as the most effective means of achieving *ataraxia*. In the case of friendship, Epicurus is able to allow genuinely altruistic action because of the fact that one can come to care as much about the friend's well-being as one does about one's own. In the case of justice, however, his motivational concerns are not ultimately displaced from his own well-being.

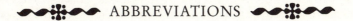

ABBREVIATIONS

Sources frequently quoted are abbreviated as follows:
DL Diogenes Laertius, *Lives of the Philosophers*. X = book 10
Hdt. Epicurus, *Letter to Herodotus*
KD Epicurus, *Kyriai Doxai* (*Key Doctrines*)
Math. Sextus Empiricus, *Adversus mathematicos*
Men. Epicurus, *Letter to Menoeceus*
Pyth. Epicurus, *Letter to Pythocles*
VS Vaticanae sententiae (words of Epicurus found only in a Vatican MS)

NOTES

1 Where possible – and, fortunately, this is frequently – I cite the translation given by Long and Sedley [6.3] in their *The Hellenistic Philosophers*, although I have very occasionally adapted their translations. Thus 'LS 5A' refers to passage A in section 5 of that work. I have done this not merely out of laziness, but because it seems to me helpful if the texts one cites, even in translation, have an existence which is independent of their employment in a particular context, so that the reader can more readily check up on how properly they are employed. Of course, one still needs to remember that these are translations of the real thing and not the thing itself.

2 In fact the argument as it stands is not a good one, even for the weaker conclusion, since it might well be that a series of perceptions can cumulatively provide compelling evidence against a single deviant perception, particularly if one has a theory of how that perception was produced. The argument would seem to miss the point, for instance, of Aristotelian warnings against accepting the perceptions of sick people rather than providing a rebuttal of such a strategy.

3 For the claim that all would travel downwards see Lucretius I.984–991 (LS 10B4), and for the claim that all atoms travel at the same speed, see *Hdt*. 61 (LS 11 E1).

4 Perhaps it is helpful here just to clarify a distinction between what I shall call 'materialism' and what I shall call 'physicalism'. I take a materialist thesis to concern substances: materialism about a certain kind of substance requires that one accept that substances of that kind have a material constitution. Physicalism, in contrast, is concerned with the relation between events (and perhaps states of

affairs), and will give some sort of priority to physical events. Although Epicurus is straightforwardly a materialist about the *psuchê*, it is not yet obvious whether he thinks that, for instance, psychological events are determined by physical (in context, atomic) events.

5 Lucretius *De rerum natura* IV.722 ff.

6 It is not just perception which requires the impact of external *eidôla*, but all appearances and thoughts.

7 This is argued by David Sedley in his 'Epicurean anti-reductionism', in J. Barnes and M. Mignucci (eds) [6.8].

8 Long and Sedley argue that volition itself can cause an atomic swerve, but there is no direct evidence for this, and if it were correct then all Epicurus' opponents on this matter would be guilty of *ignoratio elenchi*.

9 See Sextus *Math*. VII.203, cited above p. 193.

10 Cf. *KD* 3: 'The removal of all pain is the limit of the magnitude of pleasures. Wherever pleasure is present, as long as it is there, pain or distress or their combination is absent.'

11 This elucidation here is the same as that offered by Julia Annas [6.18], Chapter 11.

12 See *Men*. 130–2(LS 21B4–6).

13 Even non-necessary natural desires can arise from empty beliefs (when, however strongly felt, their frustration would not lead to pain – *KD* 30 (LS 21E3)): presumably the thought is that one might form a strong desire, say, to listen to minimalist music because it was fashionable, so that this desire, although a specific version of a natural and necessary desire, would not give rise to pleasure when satisfied.

14 'Accustom yourself to the belief that death is nothing to us. For all good and evil lie in perception, whereas death is the absence of perception. Hence a correct understanding that death is nothing to us makes the mortality of life enjoyable, not by adding infinite time, but by ridding us of the desire for immortality. For there is nothing fearful in living for one who genuinely grasps there is nothing fearful in not living' (*Men*. 124 (LS 24A1)).

15 Pleasures for the Cyrenaics were firmly of the kinetic kind – they had no truck with taking such things as *aponia* and *ataraxia* to be genuine pleasures.

BIBLIOGRAPHY

ITEMS RELEVANT TO CHAPTERS 6–8

Texts and translations

6.1 Diogenes Laertius, *Lives of Eminent Philosophers*, edited and trans. by R.D. Hicks, Cambridge, Mass., Harvard University Press, 1925, reprinted with new introductory material 1972; especially book 4 (Sceptics), book 7 (Stoics), book 10 (Epicurus).

6.2 Sextus Empiricus, *Outlines of Pyrrhonism* and *Adversus Mathematicos* (= *Against the Logicians, Against the Physicists, Against the Ethicists, Against the Professors*), trans. by R.G. Bury, Loeb Classical Library, Harvard University Press, 1933–49 (repr. 1976–87).

6.3 Long, A.A. and Sedley, D.N., *The Hellenistic Philosophers*, 2 vols, Cambridge University Press, 1987. Selected texts, with English translation, commentary, and bibliography.

6.4 *Hellenistic Philosophy: Introductory Readings* trans. by Inwood, B. and Gerson, L.R., Indianapolis, Hackett, 1988.

Proceedings of the Symposium Hellenisticum

6.5 Schofield, M., Burnyeat, M., Barnes, J., eds, *Doubt and Dogmatism: Studies in Hellenistic Epistemology*, Oxford, 1980.

6.6 Barnes, J., Brunschwig, J., Burnyeat, M., eds, *Science and Speculation: Studies in Hellenistic Theory and Practice*, Cambridge/Paris, 1982.

6.7 Schofield, M. and Striker, G., eds, *The Norms of Nature: Studies in Hellenistic Ethics*, Cambridge/Paris, 1986.

6.8 Barnes, J., and Mignucci, M., eds, *Matter and Metaphysics*, Naples, Bibliopolis, 1988.

6.9 Brunschwig, J. and Nussbaum, M., eds, *Passions and Perceptions: Studies in Hellenistic Philosophy of Mind*, Cambridge, 1993.

6.10 Laks, A. and Schofield, M., *Justice and Generosity: Studies in Hellenistic Social and Political Philosophy*, Cambridge, 1995.

Other collections of essays

6.11 Brunschwig, J., *Papers in Hellenistic Philosophy*, Cambridge, 1994.

6.12 Flashar, H., Gigon, O. and Kidd, I.G., *Aspects de la philosophie Hellénistique*, Geneva, Fondation Hardt, 1986.

6.13 Dillon, J.M. and Long, A.A., *The Question of 'Eclecticism': Studies in Later Greek Philosophy*, University of California, 1988.

6.14 Griffin, M. and Barnes, J., eds, *Philosophia Togata: Essays on Philosophy and Roman Society*, Oxford, 1989. Vol. 2, 1997.

6.15 Striker, G., *Essays on Hellenistic Epistemology and Ethics*, Cambridge, 1996.

Books on Hellenistic philosophy

6.16 Algra, K. and others, eds, *The Cambridge History of Hellenistic Philosophy*, Cambridge, Cambridge University Press, 1998.

6.17 Annas, J., *Hellenistic Philosophy of Mind*, Berkeley and Los Angeles, University of California Press, 1992.

6.18 Annas, J., *The Morality of Happiness*, New York, Oxford University Press, 1993.

6.19 Flashar, H., ed., *Die Philosophie der Antike*, Band 4: *Die Hellenistische Philosophie*, Basel, 1994 (with detailed bibliographies).

6.20 Hicks, R.D., *Stoic and Epicurean*, London, 1910.

6.21 Long, A.A., *Hellenistic Philosophy*, 2nd edn, London/Berkeley/Los Angeles, University of Calilfornia Press, 1986.

6.22 Nussbaum, M.C., *The Therapy of Desire: Theory and Practice in Hellenistic Ethics*, Princeton, Princeton University Press, 1994.

6.23 Sharples, R.W., *Stoics, Epicureans and Sceptics: An Introduction to Hellenistic Philosophy*, London and New York, Routledge, 1994.

6.24 Zeller, E., *Stoics, Epicureans and Sceptics*, London, 1880 (translation, by O. Reichel, of Zeller's *Die Philosophie der Griechen in ihre historischen Entwicklung*, vol. 3.1, 1852, rev. E. Wellmann, 1923).

❧ EPICUREAN BIBLIOGRAPHY ❧

Texts

6.25 Arrighetti, G., *Epicuro: Opere*, Torino, Einaudi, 1st edn, 1960; 2nd edn revised, 1973. Complete, with Italian translation.

6.26 Bailey, Cyril, *Epicurus: The Extant Remains*, Oxford, Clarendon Press, 1926. Main texts, with English translation.

6.27 Bailey, Cyril, *Lucretius: De Rerum Natura*, Oxford, Clarendon Press, 1947. Latin text with English translation and commentary.

6.28 Smith, Martin Ferguson, ed., *Diogenes of Oenoanda. The Epicurean Inscription*, Naples, Bibliopolis, 1993. Text with English traslation and commentary.

Bibliography

Full and recent bibliography in [6.16] *Cambridge History of Hellenistic Philosophy*. See also Flashar [6.19].

General studies

6.29 Bailey, Cyril, *The Greek Atomists and Epicurus*, Oxford, Clarendon Press, 1928.

6.30 Boyancé, P., *Lucrèce et l'Épicurisme*, Paris, 1963.

6.31 Rist, J.M., *Epicurus: An Introduction*, Cambridge, 1972.

Collected papers

See above, [6.5–6.15].

Special topics

6.32 Asmis, E., *Epicurus' Scientific Method*, Ithaca, NY, Cornell University Press, 1984.

6.33 Clay, D., *Lucretius and Epicurus*, Ithaca, NY and London, Cornell University Press, 1983.

6.34 Englert, W.G., *Epicurus on the Swerve and Voluntary Action*, Atlanta, 1987.

6.35 Everson, S., 'Epicurus on mind and language', in *Companions to Ancient Thought 3: Language*, ed. S. Everson, Cambridge, 1994.

6.36 Festugière, A.J., *Epicurus and his Gods*, Oxford, Blackwell, 1955.

6.37 Furley, D.J., *Two Studies in the Greek Atomists*: (1) Minimal Parts; (2) The Swerve, Princeton, Princeton University Press, 1967.

6.38 Furley, D.J., 'Democritus and Epicurus on Sensible Qualities', in Brunschwig and Nussbaum [6.9], 72–94.

6.39 Furley, D.J., 'Nothing to us?' (on death), in Schofield and Striker [6.7], 75–92.

6.40 Mitsis, P., *Epicurus' Ethical Theory: The Pleasures of Invulnerability*, Ithaca, NY and London, Cornell University Press, 1988.

6.41 Nussbaum, M.C., 'Therapeutic arguments: Epicurus and Aristotle', in Schofield and Striker [6.7], 31–74.

6.42 Sedley, D., 'Two conceptions of vacuum', *Phronesis* 27 (1982), 175–93.

6.43 Sedley, D., 'Epicurus' refutation of determinism', *Syzetesis* (Fest. Gigante), Naples, Bibliopolis, 1983, 11–51.

6.44 Sedley, D., 'Epicurean anti-reductionism', in Barnes and Mignucci [6.8], 295–328.

6.45 Striker, Gisela, 'Epicurus on the truth of sense impressions', *Archiv für Geschichte der Philosophie* 59 (1977), 125–42.

6.46 Taylor, C.C.W., 'All perceptions are true', in Schofield *et al.* [6.5], 105–24.

CHAPTER 7

Stoicism[1]

Brad Inwood

❦

~ 1 FROM SOCRATES TO ZENO ~

More than eighty years passed between the death of Socrates in 399 BC and
the arrival in Athens of Zeno in 312. Athenian society had undergone
enormous upheavals, both political and social. The Greek world had been
reshaped by the rise of Macedonian military and political power and by
Alexander the Great's conquests in the East, which opened up new regions
for commercial and political expansion. This was also one of the most
creative periods of philosophical development in the history of the ancient
world. It encompassed the careers of Plato and Aristotle; the schools which
carried on their legacy developed and matured. There was continued
Pythagorean activity. Mathematics and geometry flourished. Other philosophical movements arose in surprising numbers; some of these, like
Epicurus' Garden and the Stoa itself, were to thrive and become a permanent
part of the philosophical landscape, though many were ephemeral.

Zeno, the founder of Stoicism, came to Athens from Citium on Cyprus
when he was in his early twenties (DL 7.28); according to one source (DL
7.31), his appetite for philosophy had already been stimulated by reading
'Socratic books' brought back by his father, a merchant, from his voyages.[2]
Zeno himself is said to have come to Athens on a commercial voyage, but it
is hard not to suspect that the real attraction was philosophy. And when he
arrived the philosophical scene was rich and varied. Plato, of course, had been
dead for a generation. The fourth head of his school, Polemo, had just taken
over; Platonic dialogues were standard reading. Aristotle had fled Athens and
died in Euboea ten years before. His associate Theophrastus was still at the
head of the school founded to continue Aristotle's programme of work.
Philosophers from nearby Megara were also active on the Athenian scene;
one of them, Stilpo, was a sophisticated practitioner of dialectic and also had

strong interests in ethics and metaphysics. Other dialecticians contributed to a heady atmosphere of argument and logical challenge: perhaps the most famous was Diodorus Cronus. A particularly striking feature of Athenian intellectual life at the time was the emergence of the 'Cynics'. These were a loose group of philosophers who claimed Socratic inspiration for their distinctive interest in ethics, in the cultivation of the excellences of character as the key to human fulfilment. They combined radical social criticism with an ascetic devotion to natural simplicity and frank speech; equally Socratic was their dedication to the rational articulation of their social ideals. For the Cynics, ethical and social norms were only as good as the justification that could be given for them. They claimed to stand for 'nature', as opposed to baseless social convention; they aimed to undermine, by their speech and their example, what they regarded as the empty and hypocritical conventions of Greek city life.

This double concentration, on reason and on nature, must have appealed to Zeno. After arriving in Athens he drifted by a book shop, where book two of Xenophon's *Socratic Reminiscences* was being read aloud;[3] Zeno enthusiastically asked where he could find men like the ones described there (DL 7.2–3). A Cynic philosopher, Crates of Thebes, was passing by, and the bookseller said 'follow him'. Zeno did, and spent many years in his company. Crates, of course, had been a follower of Diogenes of Sinope. Diogenes, in turn, was supposedly an associate of Antisthenes, a close follower of Socrates, a contemporary and rival of Plato, and (according to tradition) the founder of Cynicism.

The dual influence of Socrates and Cynicism shaped the central concerns of the Stoic school from its foundations. Zeno's predilection for ethical and political philosophy no doubt had its roots in his years with Crates. But Zeno was a restless philosopher, and sought out other teachers too. The Megarian Stilpo left his mark on many aspects of Zeno's philosophy. Diodorus Cronus led him in the direction of serious work in logic, which remained a central interest of the school for centuries. There was even a longish period of study in the Academy. Polemo's special expertise in ethics can only have confirmed the Socratic interests which had brought Zeno to philosophy in the first place. The impact of the Academic division of philosophy into logic, ethics, and physics was fundamental for the development of Stoicism; but the strong systematizing tendencies of the school may also owe something to the influence of Aristotle's followers, who laboured away in the Lyceum of Theophrastus. Zeno never joined that rather specialized group of scientists and philosophers, but he can hardly have ignored the influence of a lecturer like Theophrastus, who was apparently able to draw a crowd of two thousand for his public lectures.[4]

Zeno obviously took advantage of the wealth of philosophical opportunity available to him in Athens, and when he began to give his own public lectures in the famous Painted Stoa his system showed the influence of this breadth of education and interest. This breadth is sometimes disparaged as evidence of a merely synthetic philosophy, but a mere synthesis would never have had the impact of the school which Zeno founded, a school which lasted for half a millennium and which for much of that time was the leading philosophical movement of the day. It is more plausible to think of his lectures, and the system which developed out of them, as being the result of a rich tradition of theory and argumentation, focused by the critical intelligence of Zeno and his successors.

2 NATURE AND PHILOSOPHY

'Nature' as a philosophical concept had a long history in Greek culture. The emergence of philosophy itself is closely connected with the demarcation of what is 'natural' – what happens apart from the intervention of anthropomorphic beings – as a subject of investigation. The understanding of nature as what functions without anthropomorphic intervention came into renewed prominence in the sophistic movement of the fifth century, with the contrast between nature and 'convention' (*nomos*); here the foil for nature is human society, its values, and its institutions.

In such contrasts nature usually has a positive value. To say something is natural is to claim that it is reliable in a way that nothing can be which is dependent on changeable personal decisions or social norms. Speaking in broad terms, nature is viewed with approval because it is in principle stable and consistently explicable, and these are traits regularly favoured by philosophers, ancient and modern. Hence in the fourth century BC philosophers frequently claimed as natural those features of their systems which they regarded as fundamental. For Plato the Forms and certain facts about moral and political reality are 'natural'; Aristotle finds that goal-directedness is a basic feature of the natural world ('Nature does nothing in vain'); Epicurus calls the basic entities of his physical system, atoms and void, 'natures' and grounds his hedonism on the belief that all animals naturally desire and pursue pleasure. The Cynics urged that we should follow nature, properly understood, and not mere convention; hence the famous slogan of Diogenes 'deface the currency' (*nomisma*), which plays on the etymological linkage between *nomos* and *nomisma*.

Stoicism, though, is the ancient school most solidly associated with the concept of nature. In their ethics the Stoics claimed that the key to human fulfilment lay in living a life according to nature; they devoted a great deal of intellectual energy to physics, the study of the natural world; they argued that a godlike rationality was the central feature of human nature and even identified nature with god. Nature was formally defined as 'a craftsman-like fire, proceeding methodically to creation (*genesis*)' (DL 7.156): the rational plan controlling the organization and development of the world and materially immanent in it. Zeno's decision to build his new system around the concept of nature was triggered by the influence of Cynicism, but the rich conception of nature which he built into so many parts of his philosophy brings together the entire tradition.

A striking feature of Stoicism was its insistence on the unity and co-ordination of all the traditional aspects of philosophical activity. From the beginnings until the time of Plato philosophical enquiry ranged widely over many kinds of subject matter: the physical world, the nature of human perception and understanding, the organization of society, the nature of a good life, etc. Even in Plato there is no neat division between ethics and metaphysics, between epistemology and logic. But in the late fourth century philosophers became more self-conscious about the relationships between the various subjects philosophy dealt with. Epicurus grouped what we might call epistemology, logic, and scientific method under the heading 'canonic'; and two of Plato's followers, Xenocrates and Aristotle, developed their own views on the branches of philosophical enquiry. Aristotle's division is complex and based on the belief that different subject matters had their own independent first principles of explanation. But Aristotle matters less than the Platonist Xenocrates, who first divided philosophy formally into three parts: logic, physics, and ethics. Zeno seems to have adopted this division from his teacher Polemo and it became the standard for the school. With the exception of Aristo of Chios, who rejected everything but ethics (and was later regarded as unorthodox), all Stoics accepted this division, calling the branches variously 'topics', 'species', or 'kinds' (DL 7.39). Cleanthes subdivided further into six parts: logic into dialectic and rhetoric, ethics into ethics proper and politics, physics into physics proper and theology (DL 7.41).

Philosophy as a whole was variously described as 'the pursuit of wisdom', as 'the pursuit of correctness of reason', and as 'the knowledge of things human and divine and their causes'. But the formal division of philosophy does raise questions about the relationship between the parts and their appropriate pedagogical order. Here there was a natural and healthy difference of opinion within the school. The disagreement was expressed through a variety of similes describing the relationship of the parts to each other (DL 7.40). Some compared philosophy to an animal: logic was the bones and sinews, ethics the flesh, and physics the soul. Or it was like an egg: logic is the shell, the white is ethics, and the yolk is physics. Alternatively, logic is the wall around an orchard, with physics being the land and trees and ethics the fruit.[5] Various pedagogical orderings were proposed, though all Stoics seem to have agreed that since the separation of parts was not absolute the teaching would also have to be mixed to some extent. Plutarch (*Stoic Self-contradictions* 1035ab) preserves the view of Chrysippus, the third head of the school (after Cleanthes), whose views are often treated as the standard version of early Stoicism; he preferred the order logic, ethics, physics, ending with theology.

In practice it was impossible for the school to maintain a clean separation between the parts of philosophy, however those parts were conceived: those Stoics who championed the inseparability of one part from another, both in substance and in teaching, were proven right.

3 LOGIC AND *LOGOS*

Logic must be understood in two distinct senses. As the Stoics themselves used the word, it designates that part of philosophy which deals with *logos*, reason or articulate speech, in any of its various aspects. The narrower sense of 'logic' is more familiar to modern readers: a systematic and formal study of propositions, arguments, their relationships to each other and their validity. The Stoics are of enormous importance for the history of logic in this narrower sense, but it is important to bear in mind that this was only one part, perhaps in their eyes not the central one, of the study of *logos*.[6]

In the broad sense, logic is divided into two branches of knowledge.[7] Rhetoric is the study of relatively long, continuous speeches and dialectic is the study of discussions conducted by means of short questions and answers. Each aims at speaking well in its own domain. But what are those domains? Traditionally, rhetoric aimed at persuasion as such, rather than at knowledge. This goal could be held in contempt, as it was by Plato in the *Gorgias*, or taken at face value, as it was by most rhetorical theorists, or rehabilitated philosophically, as it was by Aristotle. This traditional understanding of the goal could not have been irrelevant to the Stoics, since they also followed the tradition in their division of rhetoric into forensic, deliberative, and encomiastic (panegyric) or epideictic, and in their breakdown of the parts of the standard forensic speech (DL 7.42–3). Yet they could not accept that rhetoric, as a kind of knowledge and so as a part of the life of the virtuous wise man, aimed at no more than persuasion, disregarding the truth and the purpose of the speech. 'Speaking well' also meant speaking truly and virtuously.

Rhetoric was taught by the Stoics, but in such a way that it challenged rather than accommodated the more conventional understanding of rhetoric and its function.[8] Its aim seems to have been the same as that of dialectic: the attainment of truth through ordered discourse and argument. The difference between rhetoric and dialectic, then, came down to a matter of form: rhetoric is broader and more extensive in its presentation of argument; dialectic denser and more compact. Zeno tried to illustrate this difference with a comparison. Dialectic is a like a tightly closed fist and rhetoric like the same hand opened out with fingers extended. Same hand, different configuration. We don't know how far Zeno wanted this comparison to be pushed, but one might note that a fist typically has a great deal more power and impact than an open palm. Dialectic could punch; rhetoric merely slapped.

This conception of rhetoric drained much of the strength from traditional rhetorical practice. Lawyers and politicians do not limit themselves to giving sound arguments for what they believe to be true conclusions. But Stoic rhetoric hobbled speakers in yet another way. The style used by the Stoic orator was to be plain, simple, direct, and unemotional. No wonder that Cicero dismissed the rhetorical theory of Cleanthes and Chrysippus as fit only for someone who wants to learn the arts of silence (*De Finibus* 4.7).

Dialectic is by far the more important part of logic. In contrast to rhetoric, it deals with discourse in question and answer format, in the tradition represented by Plato's Socratic dialogues and Aristotle's *Topics*. The root meaning of the term 'dialectic' in Greek is 'conversation', and the context of live philosophical encounter was never far from centre stage. It was a crucial part of philosophical activity in the early years of the school's history. Arcesilaus, head of the Academy and chief Platonist of his day, only philosophized orally. Carneades, some decades later, did the same. The Megarian style of argumentation also reflects oral debate.

But the characterization of dialectic as knowledge of what is true, what is false, and what is neither true nor false points to a much broader and more ambitious study of human discourse and its relation to what is real. The standard breakdown of dialectic into its component topics confirms this (DL 7.43–4). Dialectic, we are told, covers the content of human discourse, i.e., what is signified by our utterances, as well as the utterances themselves. 'What is signified' covers both the representational contents of sense perception (presentations, *phantasiai*) and the propositions and predicates which depend on them. Thus most of what we would consider epistemology could be treated as a part of dialectic by the Stoics. But since the ontological status of things like propositions is evidently problematic (not least for a school which held a form of materialism) this area of dialectic also touches on metaphysics and philosophy of mind.[9]

'Utterance' itself is also understood quite broadly. It includes (among other things) what we would call purely linguistic and grammatical phenomena: a physical account of utterance as sound appropriately set in motion by the speech organs; a discussion of the letters of the alphabet and the phonemes native to the Greek language; regional dialects; the canons and criteria used to settle questions of proper usage and good style; and the linguistic phenomena distinctive of poetry. The analysis of the parts of speech is also part of the study of utterance.

It is curious that the parts of speech (name, common noun, verb, conjunction, article)[10] are treated under the heading of 'utterance' as linguistic and grammatical matters, while apparently similar matters (the categorization of sentences into types such as propositions, questions, oaths, imperatives, the difference between active and passive propositions, and so forth) should be treated under the heading of 'things signified'. The reasons

227

for this are not particularly clear in our sources,[11] but for present purposes two points are most important. First, as professional philosophers the Stoics influenced and were influenced by professional grammarians, providing a philosophical rationale (however unclear it might be to us now) for their analysis which competed with the more straightforwardly descriptive principles developed by grammarians. Second, the Stoic analysis of grammar is the culmination of the philosophical contribution to grammar which began with the Sophists in the fifth century BC and continued in the work of Plato, Aristotle and their followers. After the creative interaction of grammar and philosophical analysis of language in the Hellenistic period,[12] Greek grammar more or less went its own way, marked for ever by the contribution of Stoicism.

Let us now turn to the narrower and more familiar sense of logic, the study of forms of inference, arguments, and validity. One view about the role of logic in the Stoics' system suggests that logic has a defensive function – it is like the wall around a garden or the shell around an egg (DL 7.40); Posidonius compared logic to the bones and sinews of an animal, which suggests a more integral role for logic, giving shape and definition as well as strength to the flesh and soul (physics and ethics).[13] That dialectic is a virtue, though, seems to be the view of all orthodox Stoics (Aristo of Chios apparently disagreed – DL 7.160–161). It was valued for its contribution to the living of a stable and orderly life as well as for its help in establishing the truth; most Stoics would have thought these two functions to be intimately connected. Here is one account of the contribution made by dialectic and its parts:

> They say that the study of syllogisms is extremely useful; for it indicates what is demonstrative, and this makes a big contribution towards correcting one's opinions; and orderliness and good memory indicate attentive comprehension. . . . Dialectic itself is necessary and is a virtue which contains other virtues as species. Freedom from hasty judgement is knowledge of when one ought to assent and when not. And level-headedness is a strong-minded rationality with respect to what is likely, so that one does not give in to it. And irrefutability is strength in argument, so that one is not swept away by it to an opposite opinion. And intellectual seriousness is a disposition which refers presentations to right reason. Knowledge itself, they say, is either a secure grasp or a disposition in the reception of presentations not reversible by argument. And the wise man will not be free of error in argument without the study of dialectic. For truth and falsity are distinguished by it and persuasive and ambiguous statements are properly discerned by it. And without it methodical question and answer are impossible.

Hasty judgement in assertions has an impact on events, so that those who are not well exercised in handling presentations turn to unruliness and aimlessness. And there is no other way for the wise man to show himself to be sharp, quick-witted and, in general, clever in arguments. For the same man will be able to converse properly and reason things out and also take a position on issues put to him and respond to questions – these are the characteristics of a man experienced in dialectic.

(DL 7.45–48)

As Ian Mueller puts it, logic had 'both an epistemological and a moral significance for the Stoics'.[14] It helps a person to see what is the case, reason effectively about practical affairs, stand his or her ground amid confusion, differentiate the certain from the probable, and so forth. Moreover, it protects him or her from being misled by captious argumentation and fallacies, such as the *sôritês*. Beyond that, the study of argument and inference had become an independently interesting and important part of philosophy. The formal study of logic began with Aristotle and was further stimulated by the deliberately provocative use of paradoxes and puzzles by the Megarians; and the Stoics (especially Chrysippus), unlike the Epicureans, sought to develop logic as a discipline.

Aristotle's syllogistic deals primarily with the relations between terms (usually symbolized by letters of the alphabet) which are connected into statements and arguments by means of quantifiers ('all', 'none' or 'some') and predicating expressions ('is' and 'is not'). The fundamental and simplest syllogistic form is:

All B is A
All C is B
∴ all C is A.

This form of inference and a few others are self-evidently valid ('perfect'), and Aristotle's formal logic is largely taken up with study of these inference forms, their relations to each other, and their relation to other valid inference forms. Aristotle held that the validity of any valid inference form could in some way be derived from the perfect syllogisms. These, consequently, are basic to his system.

Unlike Aristotle, the Stoics took propositions (symbolized by ordinal numbers) to be the basic units of analysis in logic. They worked with a small set of operators which they used to link propositions: 'if', 'and', 'not', and exclusive 'or'. They recognized five basic inference forms, or indemonstrable arguments, and seem to have held that any valid argument form could be derived from these indemonstrables by purely logical means. This gave the Stoics a sound procedure for assessing and explaining validity. The five indemonstrables are as follows:

I
If the first, the second.
But the first.
∴ the second.

II
If the first, the second.
But not the second.
∴ not the first.

III
Not both the first and the second.
But the first.
∴ not the second.

IV
Either the first or the second.
But the first.
∴ not the second.

V
Either the first or the second.
But not the second.
∴ the first.

It is not clear how much effort Stoic logicians put into the attempt to show
formally that any valid inference form could be reduced to these forms. But
it is known that they had at least four 'rules' or logical principles which they
used in the analysis of arguments and argument forms. One example of this
sort of analysis is preserved for us by Simplicius in his commentary on
Aristotle's *De Caelo* (236.33). The third 'rule' is this: if from two propositions
(a, b) a third (c) follows, and from this conclusion (c) and a further proposition (d) another conclusion (e) follows, then the final conclusion (e) follows
from (a), (b), and (d). The example given by Simplicius is from physics.

    (a) Every body which is in a place is perceptible.
    (b) No perceptible body is infinite.
    (c) No body which is in a place is infinite.
    (d) What is outside the heavens is in place.
    (e) There is no infinite body outside the heavens.

There is also a Stoic criterion for validity (Sextus Empiricus, *Outlines
of Pyrrhonism* 2.137): an argument is valid if a conditional which has
the premises of the argument as antecedent and the conclusion of the argument as consequent is itself sound. Suppose the argument to be tested for
validity is:

> If it is day it is light
> But it is day
> ∴ it is light.

This will be valid if the following conditional is sound:

> If (it is day) and (if it is day it is light)
> then it is light.

In such a simple case the criterion will not tell us anything that our logical intuitions do not already recognize. But for more complex or less clear argument forms such a test could be quite useful.

The logical relations used by the Stoics deserve a brief comment. As noted, the 'or' they employed is exclusive; by contrast modern formal logic generally uses an inclusive 'or'. 'And' is straightforward, while the main point of interest about 'not' is the care which the Stoics took to be clear about the scope of the negation. Sometimes 'not' negates a term in a proposition, and sometimes it negates an entire proposition. In Stoic logic, which works with propositions rather than terms, 'not' can be used deliberately to negate whole propositions and normal Greek word order is violated to make this clear. It is as though we were to re-express 'Socrates has not conversed with Aristotle' as 'Not: Socrates has conversed with Aristotle' or 'It is not the case that Socrates has conversed with Aristotle'. The rephrasing sounds awkward, but can be very useful in clarifying the meaning of a sentence and therefore avoiding fallacies which turn on ambiguity. The use of logical analysis to diagnose and avoid fallacies and sophisms was an important function of dialectic for the Stoics, and we have abundant evidence of their ongoing interest in the sort of logical puzzles prized by the Megarians (for example DL 7.25). One such is known as the Nobody argument. In one version it goes like this (DL 7.82, cf. 7.187):

> If someone is here, he is not in Rhodes.
> But someone is here.
> ∴ there is not someone in Rhodes.

The conclusion, that there is no one in Rhodes, is evidently false. Care about the handling of negation and about the use of the indefinite pronoun (which is used equivocally in this sophism) dissolves the paradox.

The conditional ('if' ... 'then') is a crucial logical relation. From a logical point of view, 'if' can mean a number of different things. We know of several ancient interpretations of 'if' (Sextus *Outlines of Pyrrhonism* 2.110–12): One of these, attributed to Philo the Megarian, is equivalent to the material conditional and has a strictly truth-functional meaning: a conditional is sound if it does not have a true antecedent and a false consequent. Diodorus Cronus held that a sound conditional was one of which it neither was nor is possible that it should have a true antecedent and a false consequent. Knowing of these interpretations, the Stoics adopted a third instead: a conditional is sound when the opposite of the consequent conflicts with the antecedent. The Stoic interpretation certainly renders at least part of their logic non-truth-functional, and so from a modern formal viewpoint less powerful. But the applicability of the conditional to inferences about facts and relations in the world is enhanced by their interpretation. When we find an intelligible connection in nature, the Stoic conditional will express it adequately. 'If you release a stone in mid air it falls' is true, and expresses something important about a world which has an intelligible causal structure; it is properly expressed in a Stoic conditional because there is a clear conflict between the release of the stone and having it not fall. Compare a Philonian conditional: 'if it is day, I am conversing'. This must be regarded as sound whenever it is day and I am conversing. But such a conditional tells us nothing of interest about facts and relations in the world. The Stoics used their logic not just to solve paradoxes, but as a tool for physics.[15] It is worth noting that when discussing astrological predictions Chrysippus was careful *not* to express the (allegedly) regular connections between astral and terrestrial events by means of the conditional (Cicero *De Fato* 12–15). It may be that it is not the case both that Fabius was born at the rising of the dog-star and that Fabius will not die at sea. But Chrysippus would not express this as 'if Fabius is born at the rising of the dog-star he will not die at sea' precisely because he was not convinced that there was a necessary causal linkage between being born at that time of year and dying on dry land; such a view would conflict with his attempt to develop a non-necessitarian determinism (see p. 239). Chrysippus preferred the negated conjunction; Philo, whose conditional was truth-functional, would have seen no difference between the two ways of expressing the matter.[16]

We thus come back to the question of the use of logic within Stoicism. It prepares the philosopher for paradoxes and helps him to solve them; this is vital, since the persistence of paradoxes threatens the belief that the world is a well-ordered and rational whole. Stoic logic is also designed to be of use in discovering and expressing causal relations. The use of dialectic to explore all the arguments for and against a given position,[17] which was cautiously approved by Chrysippus, is essential to the establishment of a true and stable understanding of the world.

Aristotle handled the basic question of how humans come to know the world around us in a number of different works. The *Posterior Analytics* has an important chapter (2.19) on the perceptual foundations of our knowledge of the world; the *Metaphysics* opens (1.1) with reflections on a similar theme; the theory of human perception which attempts in part to explain how this works is found in a treatise on natural philosophy, *On the Soul*. Similarly, the Stoics handled epistemological issues throughout their philosophy; the theory of how our sensory apparatus works is part of physics, but dialectic includes their account of the representational content of sense perception.

If dialectic is to be used to discover the truth about an explicable and rationally ordered world, then clearly we humans must have access to reliable basic information about that world. Sense perception is the source of information, and in Stoicism we can see the nascent empiricism of Aristotle's theory developed more fully.[18] The Stoics held that our senses, when in good condition and used under normal circumstances, tell us the truth about the world. The truths of sense perception form the basis of our knowledge of the world. If one could show in some way that sense perception cannot be relied on to tell us the truth about the world, then the entire edifice of our knowledge about the external world collapses. The building is only as solid as its foundations.

Sceptics, in particular Academics like Arcesilaus and Carneades, aimed to undermine the claims of Stoicism in exactly this way. The target of their epistemological critique was the key theoretical item in Stoic epistemology, the presentation (*phantasia*). A presentation is an 'impression'[19] in the physical stuff of the soul, a physical alteration caused by changes in the matter of the external world. Such an impression also carries information; it reveals both itself and the external event or thing which causes it (*SVF* 2.54). The informational content of the presentation is conveyed, in rational animals, as non-corporeal 'meanings' or *lekta*. Just how this was accomplished is one of the more puzzling features of Stoic philosophy of mind. But the account preserved in Diogenes Laertius makes the basic point clear: 'the presentation is first, and then the intellect, which is verbally expressive, puts into rational discourse what it experiences because of the presentation' (DL 7.49. Cf. DL 7.63, Sextus M 8.70). The intelligible content of our perceptions is then either accepted by the perceiver or not. The assent given to the content of the presentation may be conscious or unconscious, and belief ensues when our mind accepts the presentation as representing the world. Hence the Stoics can readily account for the common experience of seeing but not believing.

This alteration and its informational content can be stored as a memory; it also contributes to the process of shaping of our basic conceptions and beliefs about the world. Hence our concepts and untutored beliefs are only as secure as our presentations. When sceptics attacked the reliability of presentations as sources of information about the world, the Stoics had to respond. The debate which ensued is too complex for summary here,[20] but one or two general remarks should be made. First, the clear isolation of assent from other aspects of the process of perception and belief obviates some sceptical moves; the Stoics do not claim that humans are passive prisoners of their perceptual experience. It is up to us to judge among our presentations. So if (to use the hackneyed example which originates in this debate) the straight oar looks bent under water, we can deny assent to the perception;

and we will do so since it conflicts with the information received from other perceptions or because we understand the refraction of light in different media.

But this ability to choose which presentations to accept requires us to have some criterion to apply in doing so. Here the Stoics' response to sceptical challenge is less successful. They claim that the criterion is a special kind of presentation, which they designated with a rather rebarbative label: cataleptic. A cataleptic presentation is stipulated to be one which exactly represents a part of the external world just as it is and has in addition a distinctive feature which indicates that it could not have been caused by any other source. It is allegedly self-validating. If, the Stoics say, we base our knowledge of the external world on such presentations, we will not err. The difficulty with this claim, however, is that a determined sceptical attack can easily reveal it as being either circular or arbitrary. In the end, the prolonged and complex debate between sceptics and Stoics about the criterion for reliability in sense perception reached no satisfactory resolution. The Stoic position ended where it began, with a commonsensical confidence in the veridical nature of sense perception, and the sceptical attack revealed that it is impossible to provide a foundational justification of what is itself meant to be a foundation for human understanding.

❧ 4 PHYSICS AND COSMOLOGY ❧

'Let us begin from Zeus.' With these words the Stoic astronomical poet Aratus opened his *Phaenomena*, one of the most influential didactic poems in antiquity. As a Stoic, Aratus celebrates the omnipresent beneficence of Zeus and emphasizes that we humans are 'of his race'. In Aratus' view, the well-organized character of the natural world and the fine articulation of the heavenly constellations are the work of Zeus, father of gods and men; the entire cosmos was organized as a sign for humans of how best to live.

Zeus was, of course, central in Greek religious thinking, and in particular for Hesiod, whose poetry had a profound impact on the early Stoics, not just on Cleanthes, the second head of the school (who was even moved to imitate him by writing his own epic verse in honour of Zeus.[21]) But the broader tradition of Greek philosophical cosmology also influenced the Stoics. Perhaps foremost they looked to Plato's *Timaeus*, with its creator god and its thorough-going teleological account of the physical world. But the Presocratics were also important, none more than Heraclitus (at least as he was understood in the period after Aristotle), who emphasized the central role of fire in the physical explanation of the world and also looked to Zeus as an organizing symbol for his thought about the relation of man to the cosmos. The influence of Empedocles is also detectable. The selection of the four basic forms of matter recognized by the Stoics (earth, air, fire, water) might also be the result of Platonic or Aristotelian influence, and the idea of a cosmic cycle might also be influenced by Pythagoreanism or the myth of Plato's *Statesman*. But Empedocles was also an important forerunner.

As Epicureanism represented the current version of atomistic thinking about the nature of the universe, so Stoicism represented, in the Hellenistic period, the most widespread and up-to-date version of the traditional non-atomistic cosmology. The cosmos, as the Stoics saw it, is finite and spherical, with the earth at the centre. The four basic types of matter (earth, water, air, and fire)[22] are arranged in roughly concentric spheres around the centre of the cosmos, which coincides with the centre of the earth. For the Stoics, as also for Plato and Aristotle, the four basic types of matter are not unchangeable. Empedocles had worked with the assumption that they are elemental and not derivable from each other or from any simpler physical reality. Stoicism offered a theory about the nature and derivation of the four basic types of matter which resembles Aristotle's theory more closely than it does Plato's.

Another point of difference from earlier cosmologies lies in the Stoic view about what is outside the cosmos. For Aristotle the answer was simple. Nothing is outside the cosmos just because the cosmos is the sum total of all physical reality. This view flew in the face of atomistic claims that our cosmos (like all the others) is surrounded by an infinite void. The Stoics accepted some of their arguments that there must be infinite void outside the cosmos. But it is open to question whether they interpreted 'infinite' in the same sense as the atomists did. Not having an infinity of material stuff or an infinity of worlds to find a place for, they did not need actual infinity of the sort that Aristotle argued against in his *Physics*. Perhaps, then, they understood 'infinite' in the older sense found in Anaximander: the void outside the cosmos was indefinitely large.

Another reason for the Stoics to accept extra-cosmic void lies in their commitment to the theory that the cosmos has a beginning and an end in time. Like Epicurus and many Presocratics (but emphatically unlike Aristotle), the Stoics believed that the cosmos was created by the cosmogonic activity of Zeus and would one day end by being reabsorbed into the cosmic fire out of which it was born. And when it did end in the grand conflagration destined for it, it would expand in volume (as does anything when it is heated or burned). Evidently, the Stoics reasoned, if the cosmos will one day expand then there must be empty space for it to expand into. That, they held, was the extra-cosmic void.

The life of each cosmos begins with the death in conflagration of its predecessor. In the form of fire, the entire raw material of the universe is in its most divine state and is identified with Zeus, the craftsman-god. The first cosmogonic act of Zeus/fire is the generation of the four elements:

In the beginning, then, he was by himself and turned all substance into water via air; and just as the seed is contained in the seminal fluid, so this, being the spermatic principle of the cosmos, remains like this in the fluid and makes the matter easy for itself to work with in the generation of subsequent things. Then it produces first the four elements: fire, water, air, earth.

(DL 7.136)

Starting out as fire, Zeus produces four elements, one of which is fire. These four are then the stuff of which the world as we know it is generated. What is striking here is the dual role of fire, both as the fundamental cosmic principle which alone survives the cycle of destruction and re-creation, and as a created element. This double role for fire is reflected in the immanence of divine powers in the world. For the intelligent guiding power represented by Zeus/fire is omnipresent and ever-present in the world. As Zeno said, the entire cosmos and the heaven are the substance of god.[23] Hence Stoicism has often been seen as a forerunner of various later forms of pantheistic thinking.

It is, in fact, crucial to Stoicism that the creative and shaping force active in the world should be immanent. For this power is a causal power, and the Stoics took as the foundation of the physical theory a carefully considered corporealism which rested on the argument (derived ultimately from Plato's *Sophist*)[24] that the only realities are things which can act and be acted upon, and that these are bodies. So for the Stoics, anything which is going to have causal efficacy must be a body.[25] If god is going to control and govern events in the world, then he must be a body in the world. The presence and force of the divine in the physical world become manifest in several ways.

We see it first in their account of the basic formation of the elements. The Stoics distinguished between elements (earth, air, fire, water) and principles. The principles are the 'active' and the 'passive'. These principles are eternal and interact to create the elements, which perish at each conflagration. Moreover, the principles are formless, whereas elements take on definite characteristics. Most importantly, the principles are corporeal. Consequently the elements and the cosmos made up of them are a blend of the active and passive principles. When, therefore, they go on to identify the active principle with god and the passive principle with matter, they lay the foundations for a simple but elegant corporealism built on the foundations of Platonic and Aristotelian thought about the physical world. The power of god is everywhere in the active and explicable causal structures we see in the world at every level of analysis. In so far as any material object has shape and definite characteristics it has in it something comprehensible and therefore divine.

Stoic corporealism attempts to answer some of the problems left unresolved by the Stoics' predecessors. The explanatory gap between the intelligible and the physical was a crux for Plato, and in some sense he had to relegate physical objects to a lesser ontological status. Their relationship to the intelligible realities which alone could actually explain things was always doubtful. Aristotle's mature hylomorphism bridged this gap to some extent, by recognizing that the individual object was an inextricable composite of form and matter, neither of which could exist separately from the other. Yet even in Aristotle problems remained, both in the area of psychophysical causation and in theology. For Aristotle's god, the teleological cause of the order in the natural world, is remote from that world and of a different order of being. In the ancient world as in the modern, there has always been dissatisfaction with the notion that god only moves the world by being loved, that the first cause itself *does* nothing. For many, and certainly for the Stoics, that is not an adequate account of causation.[26] The suggestion that god could be identified with the active cause structuring each object and rendering it formally complete and intelligible, though it leaves problems about the relation between this principle, fire and *pneuma* (for which see below), brings divine teleology and causal explanation together in a novel and relatively satisfying way.

At some point, probably with Chrysippus, the Stoic attempt to grapple with these problems was reconfigured so that less emphasis fell on the element fire and more on a physical stuff best thought of as being composed of fire and air.[27] *Pneuma* became, in mature Stoicism, the principal locus of divine immanence in the natural world. It was used to account for a wide range of phenomena, from the cohesion of the cosmos itself (always a problem for the Stoics, who did not rest content with Aristotle's explanation in terms of natural motion) to the nature of the human soul.[28] In all of its manifestations the most useful characteristic of this kind of matter was its elasticity and tensile strength. *Pneuma*, then, was alleged to be omnipresent, and its tensional or vibratory motion gave objects of any magnitude their internal cohesion and basic physical properties.[29] The fact, then, that it penetrated the whole cosmos explains its cohesion. That it penetrates, for example, stones explains their solidity and density. Its presence in iron explains its hardness. Its presence in silver explains its shiny colour. It is but a slight extension of this idea to use the notion of *pneuma* as an organizing principle for the cosmos as such, using variations in its tensility to explain the basic categories of beings in the world. It is a quirk of our sources that Philo of Alexandria preserves some of the clearest descriptions of this hierarchical description of the natural world (see *SVF* 2.458), but the authenticity of the basic idea is confirmed by more conventional sources, such as Diogenes Laertius.[30]

Pneuma is present in stones and other inert objects in the form of a basic disposition (*hexis*); at the next highest level of organization it is found in plants as nature (*phusis*). In animals *pneuma* appears as soul (*psychê*), and in rational animals it appears as reason (*logos*). As *hexis* it holds an object together and gives it unity and its basic physical characteristics. This is a function of *pneuma* which is also found in plants, though in them *pneuma* also creates powers of growth, nutrition, and reproduction. Clearly the lower functions are subsumed in the higher, and this is continued all the way up this *scala naturae*. Because the higher powers subsumed the lower ones, all entities remained satisfactorily unified in Stoic physics.

Interesting results begin to appear at the highest level of description, the cosmos itself. For since *pneuma* is the organizing power of Zeus in the world, it is not out of place to describe the world as a single entity unified by the same *pneuma* which explains the objects which form parts of the whole. If there is one *pneuma*, then the world is one object. Evidently it is alive – at least as much as plants are. So it is proper to describe the world as being or having a nature. Indeed, Stoics often identified the world and god with nature.[31] But it also lives as animals do. For how else could it produce and contain animals? So it has a soul and is a living animal – just as Plato held when he described a world soul in his *Timaeus*. But it is also rational, being governed by and identical with Zeus, evidently run according to a well-organized and providential plan, a plan of the sort so admired by Aratus. But if that is so, then the world is a rational animal, and an immortal one as well. Indeed, it is a god, the very Zeus whom Aratus hymned in his *Phaenomena*.

But if on this cosmic level of description the world is a single thing, then everything else, no matter how unified it might be on its own, is but a part of the whole. And yet human beings have the same rationality as Zeus. Are we not, then, as Seneca said with typical terseness (*Letters on Ethics* 92.30), his allies as well as his parts? It follows, at least for a Stoic, that in looking at the place of human beings in the world as described by Stoic physics one must always use bifocal spectacles, considering human beings under both descriptions, both as separate entities and as parts of a larger and more fully rational whole.

The cosmos which is organized by Zeus runs on strictly causal principles. That is only natural, since the basic manifestation of Zeus' power in the world is through the causal power operating in every thing. To be caused by an organized and structured power like Zeus is to be explicable; the Stoic cosmos, then, is in principle fully determined. There is, in the Stoic view, a cause for every event in the history of the cosmos, without exception. Any other state of affairs would jeopardize its rational comprehensibility. At least from the time of Chrysippus, and possibly from the foundation of the school,[32] Stoics held that fate consisted in the causal determination of each and every event in the history of the cosmos. Nothing corporeal could escape the nexus of cause and effect, and nothing incorporeal can have effects or be caused.

Stoic determinism is grounded in their logic as well as their physics. Diodorus Cronus had forced the issue with his Master Argument.[33] Chrysippus, whose strong support of the principle of bivalence even for future-tense propositions[34] already committed him to a form of determinism which we would regard as merely logical, evidently had to find a compromise between fate and moral responsibility as we normally understand it. The solution he came to is a compromise, perhaps one that neither determinists nor libertarians would welcome.[35] Human actions, for which we are normally held to be responsible, are explained in terms of their causes, which are twofold. There is an external stimulus to act (a presentation) and an internal state of character or moral temperament. Actions occur when the conjunction of these two factors causes an assent, which is in turn the cause of the action. Thus no human action is uncaused and determinism is preserved; but the causal chain necessarily runs through the character of and events in the soul of the agent, so that there is a reasonable basis for holding the agent responsible for his or her actions. Chrysippus attempted to argue that this kind of causation did not *necessitate* human action (Cicero *De Fato* 41–3), and in so doing made use of a complex theory of different kinds of causes; but in the end the important point is that human action is fully determined by the nexus of cause and effect and that nevertheless it is perfectly reasonable to hold agents responsible for their behaviour. The Stoics aimed to avoid the kind of fresh starts and breaks in causal sequence associated with Epicurean and Aristotelian theory, and to defend the meaningfulness of our habits of praise and blame. To judge the success or failure of this endeavour requires of the modern reader a clear sense of his or her own philosophical position.

5 ETHICS AND THE FRUITS OF PHILOSOPHY

Logic is the wall around the garden; physics is the soil and the trees; ethics is the fruit growing on those trees. Ethics is the part of philosophy which justifies its claim to be an *ars vivendi*, a craft concerned with how to live. In ancient thought, a craft is characterized by at least three features: it will be based on a body of knowledge; it will consist in a stable disposition of the craftsman; and it will have a function and goal. Ethics is based fundamentally on a knowledge of the nature of the cosmos and man's place in it and, more particularly, of the value of things. The disposition of the agent is his or her character, ideally virtue. And the goal of the art of living is 'happiness', *eudaimonia*.[36]

Most ancient ethical theories work from the assumption, best articulated by Aristotle (*Nicomachean Ethics* 1095a14–20; note the striking anticipation by Plato, *Symposium* 205a), that everyone agrees that *eudaimonia* is the goal of life, the major dispute being about what happiness consists in. Some might say that it consists in a life of physical pleasures, others in a life of political power or social prominence; others might think that complete happiness lies in a life characterized by an abundance of intellectual endeavour and achievement, or in a life of selfless devotion to the welfare of others. In each case, the conception of happiness adopted would affect one's whole life, serving as a reference point for actions and decisions.

Zeno's characterization of this goal of life was simple. 'Zeno first, in his book *On the nature of man*, said that the goal was to live in agreement with nature, which is to live according to virtue' (DL 7.87). Another source gives us a more nuanced picture of development and clarification in the school:

> Zeno defined the goal thus: to live in agreement, i.e., to live according to one harmonious *logos*, since those who live inconsistently are unhappy. His followers refined the definition and proposed the following: to live in accordance with nature, supposing that Zeno's formulation was a deficient predicate.[37]
>
> (Stobaeus *Eclogae* 2.75.11–2.76.3)

Our source goes on to credit Cleanthes with the refinement and to report at length on the different formulations of the goal given by later Stoics from Chrysippus ('to live in accordance with experience of what happens by nature') to Antipater. The significance of the differing formulations lies partially in Stoics' attempts to defend their view against Academic criticism. The main point throughout the school's development is clear, though. The goal, the basic reference point for human life, is nature.[38] And nature clearly guides us to virtue as the exclusive[39] source of the happiness which constitutes the fulfilment of human life.

Nature guides human beings to virtue by processes immanent in us; as Cleanthes said, every human has a natural inclination to virtue (Stobaeus *Eclogae* 2.65.8), and the very conception of good is in some way natural to us (DL 7.53). As soon as we are born (and the Stoics held that we are born in an uncorrupted state) it becomes apparent that we (like all other animals) are committed to the preservation and enhancement of our own selves. This basic commitment is a feature of nature as such, and it is even shared with plants (whose distinctive level of organization is, as we have seen, described as 'nature'). A summary account attempts to show how this fundamental attachment to oneself and one's own nature is related to the claim that virtue is natural to us.

> They say that an animal's first impulse is to preserve itself, because nature made it committed to itself from the beginning, as Chrysippus says in book one of *On Goals*, stating that for every animal its first commitment is to its own constitution and the reflective awareness of this. For it is not reasonable that nature would make an animal alienated from itself, nor having made the animal, to make it neither committed to nor alienated from itself. Therefore, the remaining possibility is to say that having constituted the animal she made it committed to itself. For in this way it repels injurious influences and

pursues that which is proper to it. The Stoics claim that what some people say is false, viz. that the first impulse of animals is to pleasure.[40] For they say that pleasure is, if anything, a by-product which supervenes when nature itself, on its own, seeks out and acquires what is suitable to the animal's constitution. It is like the condition of thriving animals and plants in top condition. And nature, they say, did not operate differently in the cases of plants and of animals; for it directs the life of plants too, though without impulse and sense-perception, and even in us some processes are plant-like. When, in the case of animals, impulse is added (which they use in the pursuit of things to which they have an affinity), then for them what is natural is governed by what is according to impulse. When reason has been given to rational animals as a more perfect governor, then for them the life according to reason properly becomes what is natural for them. For reason supervenes on impulse as a craftsman.

(DL 7.85–6)

The Stoic commitment to nature emerges here very clearly. It is not just human nature, for (like the Cynics and Epicureans) the Stoics use animals to illustrate the patterns of desire and satisfaction which define the inevitable and undeniable foundation of human excellence and happiness, and in doing so they reveal both the universal immanence and the overall teleology which are key features of their physics. A greater challenge for the Stoics, though, lies in explaining how human beings progress from their initial and apparently animal-like state of concern with self-preservation to a mature and rationally articulated commitment to a rational life as such. To judge from a later Stoic account, in *Letter* 121 of Seneca, the answer must be that as humans mature our constitution develops, so that our commitment to our constitution develops along with it. When our nature becomes fully rational at the age of fourteen, our commitment develops into a desire to preserve and enhance that rationality. Hence the Socratic commitment (see Plato *Crito* 46b, 48c and *Gorgias passim*) to do whatever is dictated by the best argument is grounded by the Stoics in a well-developed theory of human character development. To consider the extreme case: should it turn out that the argument dictates that our own life be sacrificed in the name of rationality, then the commitment to our rational nature will override our commitment to self-preservation. Hence Socrates calmly allowed himself to be executed and the Stoics consistently maintained that a well-thought-out suicide was a reasonable option in extreme circumstances.

It follows for the Stoics that one of the principal jobs of ethics, as a branch of philosophy, is the working out of what reason dictates. The principal reference point for doing so was the Socratic tradition in ethics, especially the version of it that we know through Plato's 'Socratic' dialogues. Perhaps the first Socratic passage to reflect on is *Meno* 77–8, which appears to establish that the good (in the sense of what one believes to be beneficial to oneself) motivates every agent. 'Benefit' becomes crucial in establishing the difference between what is good, what is bad, and what is indifferent (i.e., neither good nor bad), both for Socrates (*Meno* 87–9, *Gorgias* 467–8, *Euthydemus* 278–82, cf. Xenophon *Memorabilia* 4.6.8) and for the Stoics (DL 7.102–3). The apparent good (as Aristotle termed it) always motivates a rational agent, but obviously if one is wrong about what is beneficial then one will also act incorrectly. On Socratic and Stoic principles, a genuine good is what invariably gives the agent true and lasting benefit. However, few of the goods as conventionally understood provide this: wealth, social standing, even bodily health can all lead to unpleasant results in some circumstances. This was common ground among the Stoics, as even the debate between Aristo of Chios and more conventional Stoics shows (M 11.64–7).[41] In fact, it is argued, there really is nothing except virtue (and, of course, things which participate in virtue) which can be relied on to produce real benefit in every circumstance. Other things are all indifferent to the achievement of happiness, the goal of life.

But such things are not for that reason absolutely indifferent, as are things like the exact number of hairs on one's head. For some things obviously make a positive contribution to the kind of life for which we humans have been designed by nature, while others actively hinder such a life. The former, then, are termed 'preferred' and the latter 'dispreferred' (a typical instance of Stoic neologism): health and prosperity and reputation are preferred because they make a real contribution to a normal human life, while disease and poverty and social disapproval are the opposite (see DL 7.103–5). Nevertheless, the Socratic argument which lies at the heart of Stoic ethics urged that such things, considered on their own, could not make a person happy, that all that mattered is how one uses them. Even disease and death can be handled by a virtuous person in such a way that good will come of it. The key, of course, is virtue. With it, happiness is assured, and without it one is bound to fall short.

The Stoics also followed Socrates in accepting some version of the Socratic thesis of the unity of the virtues, best known from the *Protagoras*. Yet they also adopted the Platonic schematization of the virtues into a canonical set of four distinct virtues (prudence or practical intelligence, courage, justice, temperance or self-control (DL 7.92)), with the others organized as subtypes of these. There was debate within the school over the relationship between these individual virtues and their foundation (which is a form of practical and critical intelligence, properly oriented towards the fulfilment of human nature as part of a larger and rational cosmos). Aristo is identified with the view that there really is in the human soul only one condition which constitutes virtue, though it is called by different names as it is applied in different circumstances and in the face of different challenges and various human weaknesses. When applied to threatening situations, it is courage, but if we are tempted by pleasures, we call it self-control, and so forth. Chrysippus, on the other hand, held that each virtue represented a genuinely distinct feature of the state of our souls, but that these distinct virtues are inseparable in fact so that the presence in the soul of one entails the presence of all. As far as we can tell, Zeno's view seems to have been somewhere between these two extremes. But all Stoics seem at least to have held that the virtues are inseparable and that they are based on *knowledge* of what is good, what is bad, and what is indifferent, a knowledge which is a fully habituated state of the agent's soul.

Virtue, then, depends in large measure on knowing the value of things. The awareness that things like health are preferable but not good (in the relevant technical sense – for Chrysippus sensibly allowed the normal and looser meaning of 'good' as well) will affect the way an agent acts (see Plutarch *Stoic Self-contradictions* 1035cd and 1048a) For the Stoics (again, starting with Zeno) distinguished clearly between actions which are appropriate and reasonable for humans to do and those which are also virtuous. Appropriate actions (*kathêkonta*) are defined as those which 'when done admit of a reasonable justification' (LS 59B) (and the reasonableness can be relativized to the nature of the agent). Thus animals, too, can carry out appropriate 'actions'. In contrast, actions which are appropriate and in addition flow from the virtuous disposition of an agent are described as 'right actions' (*katorthômata*). The distinction between appropriate and right actions is crucial for an understanding of how Stoic theories about the value of things and the goal of life were meant to be put into practice.

Appropriate actions are described at two levels of generality. Sometimes our sources describe general types of action as being appropriate for humans, such as taking care of one's health, earning a living, attending to one's family, engaging in political activity; the opposites of such actions are stigmatized as inappropriate; other types of action are classed as neither appropriate nor inappropriate, such as holding a pen or picking up a stick. Yet in concrete circumstances any of these actions can in fact become the appropriate thing to do. Stoic interest naturally centred on actions which in general are inappropriate or irrational (such as maiming oneself) but on some occasion, as a result of peculiar circumstances, turn out to be the reasonable thing to do; they are labelled 'appropriate in the circumstances'. The justification which lies behind the general prescriptions for appropriate actions is often easy to intuit; what is less clear from our sources (except late ones, like Cicero's *De Officiis* and Seneca's *De Beneficiis*) is the kind of moral reasoning which the Stoics recommended as a way of determining the best and most justifiable action in a given circumstance. Yet it is clear that the Stoics did regard this as a matter of reasoning, for one standard characterization of appropriate actions is 'what reason constrains us to do' (DL 7.108) – interestingly, this is exactly the phrase used by Plato's Socrates to describe his own commitment to reasoning out the best thing to do in a given circumstance.

Reasoning about what to do and what not to do is extraordinarily difficult for humans, in view of our relative ignorance and fallibility, especially about the future. (Overcoming this, to the best of our abilities, is one of the main applications of logic and physics.) Another later Stoic, Epictetus (who worked in the late first century AD), preserves Chrysippus' reflections on the problem:

> as long as it is unclear to me what comes next, I always cling to what is naturally more suited for getting what accords with nature; for god himself made me prone to choose things. But if I really did know that it is now fated for me to be sick, then I would even pursue that.
>
> (Epictetus *Discourses* 2.6.9–10)

Even illness, then, and death can be the objects of rational choice, *if* one has a clear enough view about the plan worked out for oneself by the providential order of the world; but normally one does not, so that normal prudence guides the vast majority of our actions. Only when it is clear that fate is drawing us on to some definite outcome do we abandon that endeavour and follow fate, knowing of course that it is all for the best in the larger cosmic pattern.

But appropriate actions are only the foundation of morality. No action, however reasonable and well justified, is *right* unless it is done from a virtuous disposition. This, of course, is the principal difference between appropriate and right actions, and in considering right actions it is crucial to recall that they are defined as a subset of appropriate actions: they are 'perfect' or 'complete' appropriate actions. Even the genuinely virtuous person, who is wise and perhaps as rare as the mythical phoenix, needs to figure out the appropriate thing to do, and there is no reason to believe that this process is any different for the person of virtue than it is for the ordinary person making moral progress.[42] It is difficult to determine in detail how the possession of virtue changes each action. Our sources seem to emphasize the completeness of a right action (it covers all the 'aspects') and the firmness of the moral disposition which produces the action (Ecl. 5.906.18–5.907.5 = LS 59 I). The nature of the motivation (knowing that what is done is done for its own sake) may also have been important. The crucial points, though, are that only a completely virtuous person can perform a right action, and that only the wise man has virtue. The rest of mankind are, strictly speaking, fools and full of vice.

Much of Stoic ethical writing, then, focused on fools – Panaetius, in the second century BC, made a point of emphasizing this aspect of Stoic ethics (see Seneca *Letter* 116.5), but he was certainly not alone in this. In all periods of the school's long history Stoics wrote about appropriate actions at least as much as they did about virtue and the sage. Their appeal lay not just in the clear and uncompromising conception of virtue and right action; it lay also in the emphasis they placed on moral progress and the writings they devoted to promoting it. Perhaps the most important aspect of their campaign to promote virtue is their focus on the passions. For here, though it is clear that their theory of the passions (such as pleasure, pain, fear, and desire) was based on their rigorous conception of the good and virtue, the recommendations they made for fighting against such passions were calculated to work even for those who had not and would not attain wisdom and complete virtue.

The Stoics' theory of passions is based on their analysis of the human soul; the key position is one on which they disagreed with both Plato and Aristotle, though they no doubt thought they were in the spirit of Socratic intellectualism: they rejected any fundamental difference between cognitive and affective parts or functions of the soul, maintaining that every function of the soul has both a cognitive and an affective aspect and that the cognitive aspect is the causally important one. Within this framework, they defined a passion as an irrational and excessive movement in the soul.[43] It is treated as a cognitively determined event in the soul – either identical with or the inescapable result of an assent to a seriously incorrect proposition about the value of things. It is when one judges that (for example) the death of one's sister is bad (and not just dispreferred) or that wealth is good (and not just preferred) that one falls into the kind of overreaction which constitutes a passion – in these cases grief and desire. Ideally all such mistakes would be avoided; that would lead to freedom from passion or *apatheia* – a mental condition far from that connoted by our word 'apathy'.

The Stoic view seems to be that confusion about the kind of value things have lies at the heart of our tendency to unhealthy emotional reactions. These reactions are wrong not because they engender subjectively unpleasant feelings (in fact, some of them are quite enjoyable – pleasure is an irrational 'uplift' in the soul), but because they invariably produce inconsistency and vacillation, cloud our judgement, over-commit us to certain short-term courses of action and feeling, and block our normal rational concern with longer-term planning. Passions are also wrong because they routinely put us into conflict with the naturally and providentially ordained course of events – this is one of the senses of irrationality captured in the definition – and deprive us of the adaptability which any rational agent must have to survive and prosper in a determined but unpredictable world.

The ideal state of mind, then, is not the absolutely unfeeling condition suggested by our term 'stoical', but an affective life characterized by stable and healthy emotional reactions to events. But how does one get to this condition? What is the cure for passions? Obviously, to get straight about values, to learn the difference between what is really good or bad and what is merely preferred or dispreferred. For Stoics, who did not think that there was a distinct emotive part of the soul, this ought, in principle, to be the proper cure, and this was apparently promoted by Cleanthes as the only cure for such mental confusion. But although this accords well with the school's intellectualist philosophy of mind, its impracticality will be immediately obvious to anyone actually counselling a friend in the grip of a strong passion. The practicality of the school's approach to ethics is confirmed by Chrysippus' improvement on this (Cicero *Tusculan Disputations* 3.76): he thought that the starting point would have to be to convince the patient (for the Stoics made extensive use of the medical metaphor in discussing passions) that it was not reasonable or right to overreact to one's feelings, and to leave until later the fundamental issue of the nature of good, bad, and indifferent.

6 CONCLUSION

The guiding ideas of Stoicism throughout its history are nature and reason. Though much changed in the school over its history (Stoicism avoided the static character of Epicureanism as well as the extraordinary variability seen in the Platonic tradition), the centrality of these notions never varied. Nature, whether on a large or a small scale, is rational and reasonable, and so at heart is every human being. Hence, they thought, we fit into nature not as merely physical objects, but as rational animals. Perhaps they saw themselves as having found the ideal middle ground between two tempting positions: the notion that man's rationality puts him fundamentally at odds with the physical world; and the idea, represented by other materialists in the ancient world, that we are our physical selves and nothing more. The bold claim made by the Stoics was that the natural and the rational are in the final analysis identical, and that human beings can only find themselves by looking to nature, to the orderly, purposive, and explicable whole of which they are privileged parts.

7 DEVELOPMENT IN THE SCHOOL

In this discussion I have treated Stoicism as a single whole, with considerable emphasis on the early stages which determined its basic character. There were, of course, significant developments over its nearly 500-year history. But I believe, although this is a controversial claim, that the differences and developments which one can detect and document are on matters of detail. Here and there we find doubts about the literal truth of the idea of conflagration or cosmic recurrence, strong Platonic sympathies in psychology, or Aristotelian leanings in natural philosophy (these last two items associated with Posidonius, perhaps the most innovative of later Stoics). Certainly each Stoic writer was a unique individual, so that there are real differences of outlook among a 'professional' philosopher like Chrysippus, a court adviser like Seneca, an ex-slave like Epictetus, and a Roman emperor like Marcus Aurelius Antoninus. But because the central ideas of the school were shared by all (and because Stoicism never asked that its adherents follow blindly a canonical version of its tenets), an account of the divergences and developments in the school's history would require a degree of detail incompatible with the limits of a chapter like this one. On these matters, as on many others, the interested reader will have to find his or her own way with the assistance of some supplementary reading (listed in the bibliography).

 ABBREVIATIONS

Sources frequently quoted are abbreviated as follows:
DL Diogenes Laertius, *Lives of the Philosophers* [7.6]
Ecl. John Stobaeus, *Eclogae* [7.7]
FDS Hulser, K., *Die Fragmente zur Dialektik der Stoiker* [7.1]
LS Long, A.A. and Sedley, D.N., *The Hellenistic Philosophers* [6.3]
SVF Arnim, H. von, *Stoicorum veterum fragmenta* [7.2]

NOTES

1 I would like to thank the Social Sciences and Humanities Research Council of Canada for a subvention which contributed to the writing of this chapter.
2 Themistius (*FDS* 101) points to the *Apology of Socrates* (presumably Plato's) as influential; but we have no idea what evidence he relied on.
3 It would be interesting to know which part of book 2 was supposed to have had this effect on young Zeno. Perhaps it was the allegory of Heracles and virtue in 2.1.21 ff.
4 There is considerable controversy about how much influence Aristotelian ideas had on Zeno and other early Stoics. If – and this is to my mind an open question – we can believe the stories about the disappearance of Aristotle's library when Theophrastus died, then any influence of the Peripatos on Stoicism was most likely to have occurred in the 25 years during which Zeno was at Athens and Theophrastus led the Peripatos. While Theophrastus lived, the library was surely available to those who were interested; and if Zeno never formally studied with him, his younger contemporary, the Academic Arcesilaus, certainly did, and his critical attacks certainly shaped Stoic thinking on a number of issues. I suspect, however, that Aristotelian books and ideas were pretty generally available to serious philosophers in Athens throughout the Hellenistic period, and that their influence was a significant factor in the development of Stoic thinking. See, however, F.H. Sandbach [7.20].
5 The comparison of philosophy to a 'city, beautifully fortified and administered according to reason' does not tell us much about the partitioning of philosophy.
6 There is an excellent discussion of Stoic dialectic by A.A. Long, 'Dialectic and the Stoic sage' in Rist [7.17].
7 Or rather, at least two. Some Stoics also included as distinct branches of logic the study of definitions and a form of epistemology. See DL 7.41.
8 The best general discussion of Stoic rhetoric and its relation to dialectic is by

Catherine Atherton, 'Hand over fist: the failure of Stoic rhetoric', *Classical Quarterly* 38 (1988), 392–427.

9 It is hard to be sure how much of this material would be treated under dialectic and how much under physics. But it is clear that dialectic was meant to include at least partial coverage of these themes.

10 Our traditional grammatical categories for the parts of speech are obviously related to these, but there are differences. Note, for example, the absence of 'adverb' in this classification. The Stoics built on earlier and cruder analyses; professional grammarians, in Greek and Latin (and then in vernacular languages during the Renaissance and after) expanded and refined the theory. One feature of interest is the Stoic distinction between name and common noun: in DL 7.58 the difference is expressed in metaphysical rather than grammatical terms (names indicate individual quality and common nouns indicate common quality), despite the fact that the parts of speech are discussed under the heading of 'utterance'.

11 The best discussion of these issues is by Michael Frede, 'The principles of Stoic grammar' in Rist [7.17].

12 One other feature of this creative period is the debate over 'analogy' and 'anomaly' in the analysis of the workings of language. This is too large a topic to develop here, but it clearly turned in part on the Stoics' views about etymology and word derivation. Here again one might best treat this as a moment in the history of linguistics, but for the Stoics the questions were essentially philosophical ones: nothing which dealt with *logos* and its relation to reality could be treated as anything but philosophical.

13 DL 7.40, Sextus M 7.19. Sextus gives a reason for this order further on in the passage. In M 7.23 he notes that physics comes last because it is more 'divine' and intellectually demanding. In DL the Posidonian view is not attributed to him by name, and reverses the positions of physics and ethics, making physics the analogue of the soul. This is either a confusion in DL or further evidence of the variety of positions taken on this question.

14 In Rist [7.17]. This is a splendid overview of Stoic logic, from the perspective of formal logic. See also Mates [7.16].

15 Their views on determinism are worked out in part through reaction to Diodorus Cronus' so-called Master Argument, which is closely linked to his own understanding of the conditional.

16 One might also note the use of the negated conjunction in formulating *sôritês* arguments (DL 7.82).

17 See Plutarch *Stoic Self-contradictions* chs 8–9, DL 7.182–4.

18 Epicureanism also moved sharply in the direction of well formulated empiricism at about the same time. The philosophical climate obviously inclined in this direction, and this was not just a result of Aristotle's influence. But it is precisely in epistemology and philosophical psychology that our sources present Stoic ideas in a form most closely related to Aristotle's.

19 Either literally an impression or figuratively. Chrysippus held that by impression Zeno meant 'alteration'; see DL 7.50; M 7.227–31, 7.372–73. This improved the theory and protected it from some criticisms. But the main thrust of Academic attack is not diverted by this clarification.

20 Basic evidence and clear philosophical discussion can be found in LS [7.3] 39–41.

21 The *Hymn to Zeus* is extant (see LS [7.3] 541), and there are short quotations from other poems.

22 The Stoics distinguished two types of fire: terrestrial fire, which was destructive, and 'craftsmanlike fire' which played a creative role in cosmogony. The latter was identified with the fire of the heavenly bodies and the animal heat which sustains life. They did not, therefore, follow Aristotle in postulating a fifth kind of element for the heavenly bodies. Another difference between Aristotle and the Stoics is that Aristotle described his elements in terms of *two* of the basic qualities (hot, cold, wet, dry) and an underlying substrate while the Stoics only posited *one* basic quality for each element.

23 DL 7.148. This is the orthodox view; note that Boethus, a later Stoic, wanted to restrict god's substance to the sphere of the fixed stars.

24 See Long and Sedley [7.3], commentary on §45. For discussion of the nature and philosophical motivation of Stoic corporealism, see LS §§27–30, and J. Brunschwig in [7.10] 19–127.

25 The exceptions to this corporealism are few: void, place, time, and *lekta*. Souls, however, are bodily (though made of a very different stuff from the body). Certain problems are created by this doctrine for Stoic philosophy of mind, since intelligible contents (for example *lekta*) are incorporeal; yet to hold that the content of our thoughts has no causal influence on the actions of our bodies is most strange. The Stoics had no trouble with the notion that souls influenced bodies; but how, one must ask them, can thought contents be related to the physical events in our souls? Limitations of space preclude a discussion of the important Stoic analyses of time and of spatial concepts.

26 It is in the Hellenistic period, and in particular in Stoicism, that the notion of cause began to narrow towards the idea of active causation which we most often use. See M. Frede, 'The Original Notion of Cause' in [7.22], 217–49.

27 Air and fire are described as the sustaining elements, being the locus of the cold and the hot; *pneuma* is made up of them.

28 It has been suspected that the Stoic emphasis on *pneuma* had its roots in Aristotle's later work on animal psychology. The *De motu animalium* gives *pneuma* a prominent role in bridging the gap between soul and body in explanations of animal action. It also had a special role in explanations of reproduction. The Stoics also share with Aristotle (against Plato) the view that the central and cognitive functions of the soul are carried out in the heart. But it is worth noting that *pneuma* was generally important in Hellenistic biology, and that the Stoic development of a corporeal account of the perceptual and motor systems, based on *pneuma* and with the heart at the centre of activity, parallels the empirical results generated by contemporary medical scientists in Alexandria, at least some of whom practised dissection. The medical discovery of the arterial system seems to have been particularly important for supporters of the heart-centred model of soul.

29 One interesting problem which bulks surprisingly large in our sources for Stoicism arises from this theory. If *pneuma* is a physical stuff and what it organizes is a physical stuff, then how are we to describe the mixture of them? The Stoics described the mixture as 'complete' (*di' holou*) and they compared it to the mixture between fire and iron in a piece of red-hot iron.

30 More evidence is gathered and discussed in chapter 2 of my *Ethics and Human Action in Early Stoicism* [7.14].

31 The standard Stoic definition of nature was: 'a craftsmanlike fire proceeding methodically to generation' (DL 7.156).

32 Long and Sedley ([7.3] 1, 392) argue that neither Zeno nor Cleanthes adopted the all-inclusive causal understanding of fate which Chrysippus embraced and hence that they did not share his need to reconcile fate with moral responsibility.

33 He seems to have argued that the following three propositions are incompatible: (1) everything past and true is necessary; (2) something impossible does not follow from something possible; (3) there is something possible which neither is nor will be true. Diodorus himself rejected (3) and so supported his own definition of the possible as 'what either is or will be true'; Cleanthes rejected (1); Chrysippus, somewhat implausibly, denied (2). See Long and Sedley [7.3] §38.

34 Contrary to the view taken by Aristotle, *De Interpretatione* 19.

35 The literature on this problem is enormous. See, for example, Charlotte Stough, 'Stoic determinism and moral responsibility', ch. 9 in Rist [7.18]; A.A. Long, 'Freedom and determinism in the Stoic theory of human action', ch. 8 in his *Problems in Stoicism*; and various chapters of Richard Sorabji's *Necessity, Cause, and Blame* [1.80]. In the ancient world, the Aristotelian commentator Alexander of Aphrodisias gives the most effective and sustained argument against the Stoic view in his *De Fato*.

36 'Happiness' is a notoriously unsatisfactory translation for the Greek term, but I will retain the traditional term for the sake of simplicity and familiarity. It should be understood throughout as a term of art.

37 This phrase is a technical term in the analysis of *lekta*, indicating that the verbal expression was elliptical and needed to be completed by a noun in an oblique case, viz. 'with nature'.

38 As to the sense of nature being invoked, Chrysippus held that the 'nature, in consistency with which we must live [is] . . . both the common and, specifically, the human nature. Cleanthes includes only the common nature, with which one must be consistent, and not the individual' (DL 7.89). Why Cleanthes took this view is not clear. But since humans are parts of universal nature, the difference between the two heads of the school was probably only one of emphasis.

39 Notoriously, the Stoics held that virtue is not just necessary but also sufficient for happiness. Peripatetics argued against this position, as did the Academic Antiochus of Ascalon. But it remained official school doctrine until the end.

40 This is a criticism of the Epicurean argument in favour of hedonism. For discussion of these arguments, see J. Brunschwig, 'The cradle argument in Epicureanism and Stoicism', ch. 5 in [6.7].

41 Aristo argued that there could be no meaningful distinction among things, except that between virtue and vice. Mainstream Stoics disagreed. The debate is an important one, but here I limit myself to a presentation of the mainstream Stoic doctrine.

42 See G.B. Kerferd, 'What does the wise man know?', in Rist [7.18].

43 Much of this discussion is based on ch. 5 of my *Ethics and Human Action in Early Stoicism* [7.14].

BIBLIOGRAPHY

MAJOR COLLECTIONS OF SOURCE MATERIAL

7.1 Hülser, K., *Die Fragmente zur Dialektik der Stoiker*, Stuttgart, Frommann-Holzboog, 1987.

7.2 Arnim, H. von, *Stoicorum veterum fragmenta*, Stuttgart, Teubner, 1905.

7.3 [= 6.3] Long, A.A. and Sedley, D.N., *The Hellenistic Philosophers*, Cambridge, Cambridge University Press, 1987. The philosophical commentary is indispensable.

7.4 [= 6.4] Inwood, B. and Gerson, L.P., *Hellenistic Philosophy*, Indianapolis, Hackett, 2nd edn, 1997, contains primary sources in literal translation, quoted in this chapter with the publisher's permission.

7.5 Giannantoni, G., *Socraticorum reliquiae*, Naples, Bibliopolis, 1983, contains evidence for fourth-century minor Socratics.

SOURCE MATERIAL IN ANCIENT AUTHORS

7.6 [= 6.1] Diogenes Laertius, *Lives of the Philosophers*, ed. R.D. Hicks, revised, Cambridge, Mass., Harvard University Press, 1972.

7.7 John Stobaeus, *Eclogae*, ed. Wachsmuth and Hense, Berlin, Weidmann, 1884.

7.8 *Panaetii Rhodii Fragmenta*, ed M. van Straaten, 3rd edn, Leiden, Brill, 1962.

7.9 Posidonius, *Fragments*, ed. L. Edelstein and I.G. Kidd, with translation and commentary, Cambridge, Cambridge University Press, 1988.

[For Cicero, Seneca, Epictetus, Plutarch, Sextus Empiricus, and Marcus Aurelius, see Loeb Classical Library or other editions.]

SECONDARY READING

[The following works are fundamental and readily accessible. A more detailed advanced bibliography can be found in vol. 2 of LS.]

7.10 [= 6.8] Barnes, J. and Mignucci, M., eds, *Matter and Metaphysics*, Naples, Bibliopolis, 1988.

7.11 Epp, R., ed., *Recovering the Stoics = Southern Journal of Philosophy* 23 Suppl. 1985.

7.12 [= 6.12] Flashar, H., Gigon, O., and Kidd, I.G., *Aspects de la philosophie Hellénistique*, Geneva, Fondation Hardt, 1986.

7.13 Hahm, D., *The Origins of Stoic Cosmology*, Columbus, Ohio State University Press, 1977.

7.14 Inwood, B., *Ethics and Human Action in Early Stoicism*, Oxford, Oxford University Press, 1985.

7.15 [= 6.21] Long, A.A., *Hellenistic Philosophy*, 2nd edn, London/Berkeley/Los Angeles, University of California Press, 1986.

7.16 Mates, B., *Stoic Logic*, 2nd edn, Berkeley and Los Angeles, University of California Press, 1961.

7.17 Rist, J.M., ed., *The Stoics*, London/Berkeley/Los Angeles, University of California Press, 1978.

7.18 Rist, J.M., *Stoic Philosophy*, Cambridge, Cambridge University Press, 1969.

7.19 Sandbach, F.H., *The Stoics*, London, Chatto and Windus, 1975.

7.20 Sandbach, F.H., *Aristotle and the Stoics*, Cambridge Philological Society Suppl. Vol. 10, 1985.

7.21 [= 6.7] Schofield, M. and Striker, G., eds, *The Norms of Nature*, Cambridge, Cambridge University Press, 1986.

7.22 [= 6.5] Schofield, M., Burnyeat, M., and Barnes, J., eds, *Doubt and Dogmatism*, Oxford, Oxford University Press, 1980.

7.23 [= 6.23] Sharples, R.W., *Stoics, Epicureans and Sceptics: an Introduction to Hellenistic Philosophy*, London and New York, Routledge, 1996.

CHAPTER 8

The sceptics
Michael Frede

❀❖❀

❧ INTRODUCTION ❧

When we speak of 'scepticism' and of 'sceptics', we primarily think of a philosophical position according to which nothing is known for certain, or even nothing can be known for certain. There are certain ways in which we go about things when we try to find out the truth about something or other. But these ways at best are such that, in following them, we come to believe something which actually is true, but they are never such that what we come to believe, given the way we came to believe it, is guaranteed to be true. Hence, we never know for certain whether what we come to believe to be true actually is true. We perhaps hope that it is, or even are confident that it is, but it might be not.

This, though, is not what those ancients who called themselves 'sceptics' (*skeptikoi*) for the most part meant by 'scepticism'. To the contrary, the very term 'sceptic', at least sometimes, was meant to suggest, among other things, that a sceptic is not going to claim that nothing can be known. '*Skepsis*' is a word which in Greek ordinarily was used to refer to one's looking at or considering or reflecting on something. But it also came to be used to refer to one's inquiry into a matter, and thus became, along with '*zêtêsis*', a term to refer to any kind of inquiry, but in particular the kind of methodical inquiry philosophers and scientists are engaged in. And it surely is no accident that ancient sceptics not only were called, or called themselves, 'sceptics', but also 'zetetics' (DL IX, 69; *Pyrrh*. I, 7). Given the formation of the words, a sceptic or zetetic should be a person who is prone or inclined to inquire into things, or shows particular ability or persistence in doing so. So a sceptic should be somebody who is not going to content himself with any conclusion, until the inquiry has run its full course and all possibilities have been explored. As Sextus Empiricus, himself a sceptic, tells us at the end of the second century AD in his introduction to scepticism, the *Outlines of*

Pyrrhonism, we talk of 'scepticism', because sceptics inquire (*Pyrrh*. I, 7). We would like to know why the sceptics think of themselves as inquisitive in a way which singles them out. Sextus begins his account of scepticism (*Pyrrh*. I, 1–4) explaining precisely this. He says that of those inquiring into something, there are (1) those who at some point think they have found the answer; there are (2) those who give up the inquiry, claiming that the question or problem cannot be resolved; but there are (3) also those who think that the question so far has not been resolved, and thus go on inquiring. The suggestion is that both the first and the second group, each in their own way, give up on the inquiry, before it has come to an end. The first group of inquirers are so eager to have an answer to the question that they jump to a conclusion, though it is not warranted by the inquiry so far. The second group of inquirers similarly terminate the inquiry, before it has come to an end, with a rash verdict, namely the verdict that the matter cannot be resolved, though not everything that could perhaps be said about the matter has been taken into consideration. It is only the third group of inquirers who insist, like the second group, that the matter has not yet been resolved, but also insist that not all possibilities to resolve it have yet been explored and that hence any final verdict is out of place.

Many interpreters do not take this self-characterization of the sceptic seriously; they might even regard it as disingenuous. For, according to these interpreters, the sceptic surely must believe, whatever he says, that no question can be resolved, that the truth cannot be known; and hence it is disingenuous of the sceptic to claim that he continues to look for an answer to the questions which have arisen or arise. But this criticism seems to be guided by an unjustified preconception of what a sceptic is; it fails to take into account the fact that the sceptic is quite right in insisting that, though at any point in our inquiry we may be able to say that the question has not been resolved, there seems to be no point in our inquiry at which we can say that it cannot be resolved, given that we have not considered everything which could be brought to bear on the issue. So the sceptic perhaps thinks that no question has been resolved so far. And he may have little expectation that any questions will be resolved. But it is a big step to go beyond this to claim that no question can be resolved. And, as we will see, there is a further consideration which will possibly discourage a sceptic from taking this step.

In any case, Sextus identifies the three kinds of inquirers as (1) the dogmatics, properly so called, those who believe that they have found the answers to at least some questions, for instance the Peripatetics, or Epicureans, or Stoics; (2) the Academics, who believe that the questions one inquires into cannot be resolved, that the truth cannot be grasped or known (they are dogmatic in a wider sense in that they at least claim that nothing can be known for certain); (3) the Pyrrhoneans, who will claim no such thing, but will go on with the inquiry. So at least Pyrrhonean sceptics reject any suggestion that they claim that nothing can be known for certain.

But we also have to take into account that Pyrrhoneans in general, and hence also Sextus, have some difficulty in justifying their own existence by claiming that their position is radically different from that of the Academics. As we will see, Pyrrhonean scepticism, the kind of scepticism Sextus Empiricus is an exponent of, arose as a reaction against the particular form Academic scepticism had taken in the first century BC. At that time Academics claimed that nothing can be known for certain, as we can see from Cicero's *Academica*. And it was in part for this reason, as we can see from Photius' report (*Bibliotheca* c. 212, 169b 38 ff.), that Aenesidemus, the founder of Pyrrhonean scepticism, rejected the Academic scepticism of his time. But we can also see that this had not always been the position of Academic sceptics, and that Sextus himself is aware of this (cf., for example, *Pyrrh*. I, 226; 232). So, both Pyrrhoneans and Academics down to a certain time refused to claim that nothing can be known for certain.

It is also easy to see why they would refuse to make such a claim. If the way we come to believe something is questionable in that there is no guarantee that, given the way we have come to have this belief, the belief is true, because at any point on the way we may have taken the wrong turn, then our having taken this way not only does not guarantee that our belief is true and hence allows us to claim that we know, it does not even provide any justification for just having the belief. In any case, the argument of the Pyrrhoneans and the early Academics, like Arcesilaus, is that for any reason you offer in support of your belief to justify it, there is a reason to the contrary to undermine your justification, and thus your belief is unjustified, even if it should happen to be true. Thus Pyrrhoneans and early Academics not only do not claim that nothing can be known, they do not make any claims whatsoever. They do not make any claims whatsoever because they think that the questions that these claims purport to answer have not been settled, and that, short of settling them, one has no justification for any claim as to how they should be answered. Hence sceptics in antiquity also are called 'aporetics' (DL IX, 69; cf. *Pyrrh*. I.7) and 'ephectics' (ibid.). However far we have got in an inquiry, as long as the question is not settled, they are at a loss as to how to answer the question. And hence they suspend judgement, refrain from taking a position on the matter. Now, there is also a question as to whether anything can be known for certain or not. Hence it would be curious, if sceptics who refused not only to assume that any question was definitively settled, but even to assume that one could take any position on a question which was not settled, of all questions would make an exception for this question, and claim that nothing can be known for certain. They not only do not believe that they know that nothing could be known for certain, they do not even take any kind of a position on this question, so as to claim that nothing can be known. This, then, is the standard understanding of scepticism in antiquity.

Nevertheless, it is easy to see, at least in broad outline, how the term 'scepticism' came to be understood in the way it standardly is understood nowadays. There were, towards the end of the history of Academic scepticism, sceptics who did claim that nothing can be known for certain, and who, quite generally, were ready to espouse beliefs or opinions, provided it be understood that they did not know for certain that these beliefs are true. It was these Academics who prompted Aenesidemus to restore scepticism in the form of Pyrrhonean scepticism. But this late form of Academic scepticism which is attacked by Aenesidemus is represented in Cicero's *Academica*. In fact, it is the form of Academic scepticism espoused by Cicero himself. It also is the form of scepticism attacked by Augustine in his 'Contra Academicos'. And given the enormous authority and influence both Cicero and Augustine had, it is not surprising that it was this position which came to be associated with the term 'scepticism'; and this all the more so, as the rivalling view that a sceptic should not even have any belief as to the answer to the questions which arise, plausibly seemed so untenable, given the needs of ordinary life.

Hence, to study ancient scepticism in its own historical setting, we will have to consider Academic scepticism and Pyrrhonean scepticism, even if most of these sceptics in their scepticism were not even prepared to commit themselves to the claim that nothing can be known. But, we first of all will have to have at least a brief look also at some earlier philosophers, especially given that the Academics themselves appealed to them as their precursors. And we will also, before we can turn to Academic scepticism, have to look at a philosopher in the generation before Arcesilaus who was some sort of sceptic, namely Pyrrho. We will have to do this not just because Pyrrho is a figure of considerable interest in his own right in the history of scepticism understood in a broader sense. His position also is relevant, because, though Arcesilaus himself did not appeal to Pyrrho as a precursor, already some of Arcesilaus' contemporaries believed they could claim or suggest that there are important similarities between Pyrrho's and Arcesilaus' position (DL IV, 33). Moreover, when Aenesidemus in the first century BC tried to revive a more radical scepticism, he at least claimed to be articulating a position which went back to Pyrrho. Hence scholars for a long time were quite prepared to believe that Pyrrho had been at least a proto-Pyrrhonist. And, to the extent that one was prepared to believe this, it also was difficult to resist the temptation to believe that the striking similarities between Pyrrhonean scepticism and Arcesilaus' position, which Sextus Empiricus himself acknowledges (*Pyrrh*. I, 232), were in part due to Pyrrho's influence on Arcesilaus.

 ARCESILAUS' PRECURSORS

Arcesilaus obviously felt that he somehow had to explain why it should be thought to be appropriate that he, given his radical scepticism, should be the scholarch of Plato's Academy, the guardian of the venerable tradition going back to Plato and beyond to Socrates. It is reasonably clear that Arcesilaus did make an effort to explain in which way his work was in the best tradition of the Academy. We will discuss this, when we come to deal with Arcesilaus in detail. But it also seems that even without the efforts of Arcesilaus himself, at least later Academics tried to explain that Arcesilaus' scepticism could rely on a tradition of sceptical thought going back to philosophers from Xenophanes to Metrodorus of Chius (cf. Cicero, *Ac. Post.* I, 44; *Ac. Pr.* II, 13 ff.; 72 ff.). And, indeed, we find enough evidence for some form of scepticism or other in the modern sense of the term among these earlier philosophers, that Sextus Empiricus, possibly partly in light of such Academic claims, thinks it necessary to argue, for instance, that Democriteanism should not be confused with scepticism (*Pyrrh.* I, 213 ff.). Such appeals to Presocratic predecessors, of course, are easier to understand if they come from later Academics who did believe that nothing can be known for certain, rather than from Arcesilaus, who would have had to argue that these philosophers had taken a first step in the direction of scepticism, but had failed to take the further step or further steps, just as he is supposed to have claimed to have gone a step beyond Socrates in not even allowing himself to say that he knows that he knows nothing (*Ac. Post.* I, 45).

It is easy to see why sooner or later doubts would arise about the possibility of knowledge, if not of any knowledge whatsoever, then at least of any knowledge which went beyond the trivial and which for that very reason one might aspire to, a deeper knowledge and understanding of why the world works the way it does. I do not have the space to consider how these doubts actually arose, for instance with Xenophanes (cf. DK B18; B34) or Alcmaeon (cf. DK B1). Such doubts were unavoidable, once Parmenides had claimed that reality is not at all as it appears to us in perception and as, on the basis of this, we think about it. For, according to Parmenides, thought shows that there is no motion, no change, no coming-into-being, no plurality, no diversity. So the senses are utterly unreliable, and hence also all belief based on observation. But, one had to ask, why should we believe that reason can be relied upon? The problem became acute with Democritus. Democritus thought (cf. Aristotle, *De generatione et corruptione* 325a 23 ff.) that in order to explain why, if reality is so different from what it appears to be, it nevertheless appears in the way it does, one at least has to assume that there is motion. So he assumed that in reality there are just atoms moving in a void, and that everything else, including colours and tastes, are just a matter of belief and convention (DK B9). But in saying this Democritus makes reason rely on the senses, to then in turn reject their judgement. For the only reason we have for saying that in reality there are many atoms moving, is that we perceive a changing manifold. So Democritus (DK B125) lets the senses complain, 'you wretched mind, you first take the evidence we offer and then overthrow us. But our overthrow is your downfall.' For, if we cannot trust the senses beyond their suggestion that we are dealing with a changing manifold, atoms moving in a void, we will never know in any particular case what we are dealing with, except atoms in the void (DK B6, 7, 8, 9, 10). And even this is questionable, as it relies on our perception of a changing manifold.

It is clear that Democritus must have used language like 'a thing is no more sweet than it is bitter' (cf. DK B156). Given what we have said, this should mean that in reality it is neither. And this is how Sextus Empiricus interprets this sort of language in Democritus (*Pyrrh.* I, 213). But there was another interpretation, the one Sextus Empiricus rules out. Already Democritus is claiming that, if different beings have conflicting perceptions or beliefs concerning something, one should say that the thing is no more this than that, because either it is neither, or it is utterly unclear which of the two it is. This will become important when we turn to Pyrrho.

Obviously under the influence of Democritus, a generation or two later, Metrodorus of Chius will conclude 'None of us knows anything, not even this whether we know or do not know' (*PE* XIV, 19, 9, DK B 1). Obviously, the addition 'not even this...' already involves a minimal refinement which presupposes some reflection on the bland claim 'none of us knows anything', for instance the kind of reflection we find in *Lucretius* IV, 469 ff. that somebody who believes that nothing is known also must think that this itself is not, or even cannot be, known. More intriguingly, Cicero (*Ac. Pr.* 73), like Eusebius, refers to the beginning of a book by Metrodorus, but then does not quote the remark quoted by Eusebius, but rather what looks like a further comment on the bland statement that we do not know anything. Unfortunately the translation of this comment is controversial, too. But it seems to run like this: I deny, he says, that we know whether we know anything or know nothing; we do not even know what it is not to know or to know; nor do we know whether there is anything or rather nothing. This would suggest that Metrodorus was aware of the possibility that the answer to the question whether anything is known also might depend on what we take knowledge to be. And, most tantalizingly, there might be the thought that there is no reality for us to know, against which the beliefs we have, following appearances in the conventional way, could be measured. If this is what Metrodorus was thinking about, we already have a rather developed state of the question whether anything can be known for certain.

With Metrodorus we also are within a generation or so of Pyrrho. Eusebius, having quoted Metrodorus as saying that we know nothing, not even this, whether we know or not, goes on to say that Metrodorus had prepared the way for Pyrrho (*PE* XIV, 19, 9). And there is no doubt that Pyrrho belongs to the group of philosophers influenced by Democritus that includes, for instance, Anaxarchus of Abdera, of whom Pyrrho is said to have been a student (DL IX, 61) and an associate (for example DL IX, 63).

PYRRHO

Pyrrho lived roughly from 365 to 275 BC. His main philosophical concern was ethical. He seems to have argued that everything was utterly indifferent, neither good nor bad, neither just nor unjust, and to have tried to live a life which dispenses with such value-judgements, but hence also is not burdened by the anxieties such beliefs cause us. His attempt to live such a life gave rise to a number of anecdotes, but the doctrine concerning the absolute indifference of things fell into oblivion, or was just remembered as a curious possible doctrine. In any case, Cicero in the *De finibus* repeatedly (for example V, 23), but also in the *Tusculans* (V, 85), speaks of it as a doctrine which had long been abandoned. It seems to be a fair judgement that Pyrrho would have disappeared almost without a trace from the history of philosophy if there had not been something more to his position, namely a side to it which made him appear to later Pyrrhoneans as their precursor. It is telling that the first thing Diogenes Laertius has to say, when he turns to Pyrrho's philosophy, is that Pyrrho was the first to introduce the idea of the *akatalêpsia* of things, of their unknowability, and of the suspension of judgement. So, supposedly, Pyrrho did not just say that nothing can be known, he also took the further step, crucial for the standard understanding of scepticism in antiquity, that the appropriate moral to draw from this is not just that our beliefs are mere opinions, but that one should suspend judgement altogether and have no beliefs.

But we have to proceed with utmost caution. Pyrrho himself did not leave any philosophical writings. There are anecdotes about him, some of them early, for instance those which were drawn from Antigonus of Carystus' biography of him (cf., for example, DL IX, 62). There are some important doxographical notices about him, some of which, certainly the most important one, goes back to Timon, a student of Pyrrho's, whose testimony, though, has to be treated with caution, as it is only too obvious that he tries to present Pyrrho as a philosophical hero by far superior to, for instance, Pyrrho's and his own Athenian contemporaries, including Arcesilaus.

Let us consider the first story, told by Diogenes Laertius (IX, 62) to show how consistently Pyrrho followed his doctrine in his life, a story drawn from Antigonus and taken by scholars to be particularly revealing: Pyrrho did not avoid anything or beware of it, faced everything: wagons, if it so happened, or precipices, or dogs, or whatever else of this kind. He entrusted nothing to his perceptions and was only saved because his acquaintances were following him around. Now the story could be interpreted in the following way: it is not that Pyrrho did not realize and believe that a wagon was coming his way or that a few steps separated him from a precipice. But he thought that everything was entirely indifferent and that hence it did not matter a bit, one way or another, whether he would be run over or not, or fall down the precipice or not. Moreover, by hard practice, he had learnt to take an attitude towards things which corresponded to what they are like, namely an attitude of indifference. It is not just that he thought they were indifferent, that they did not matter, he also had brought it about that, because they did not matter, they did not matter to him. And this he did not find easy, as another anecdote shows (DL IX, 66). He was reproached for being scared of a dog. He answered that it was difficult to shed humanity – indeed a fight and struggle – but that one could try to become indifferent, first by practising, but then, if needed, by thinking about things. Apparently many thought that Pyrrho had attained a remarkable and admirable degree of indifference and imperturbability. But all this has nothing to do with scepticism. To the contrary, it would seem that Pyrrho tries to be indifferent, because he believes things to be utterly indifferent. Nevertheless, the interpretation which is put in Diogenes Laertius on the story about precipices is that Pyrrho did not entrust anything to the senses. That is to say, he withheld belief as to what he saw, even if it was a wagon coming his way, or a precipice in front of him. The story is interpreted as if the other story about the dog who scared him had the moral that it is so difficult to learn not to believe that a dog is pursuing and attacking one, when in fact the moral clearly seems to be that it is so difficult to learn, in theory and in practice, that it does not matter whether a dog is attacking one. But where does the sceptical interpretation come from, and is there any justification for it?

Let us next look at what Diogenes Laertius IX, 61 refers to as evidence to explain in which way Pyrrho was the first to introduce suspension of judgement, before, in IX, 62, he proceeds to tell the story about wagons and precipices as evidence that Pyrrho followed this theory in real life. Diogenes refers to an otherwise unknown Asconius of Abdera as his source. The explanation is that according to Pyrrho things in truth, in the nature of things, in reality, are neither good nor bad, and that human beings only act the way they do out of convention and habit, whereas things are no more this than that. It should be immediately clear that Pyrrho is not saying that we do not know whether something is good or not, or bad or not, and hence should suspend judgement. For he clearly is saying that in reality they are neither good nor bad, and that it is just in people's belief that they are just or unjust. This does not seem to have anything to do with scepticism. There is no suspension of judgement even just concerning values, it seems, except in the sense that Pyrrho will refuse to believe that things are good or bad. So why does Diogenes Laertius, or his source, adduce this as evidence for Pyrrho's scepticism?

This time, though, there is one element in the account which might provide a clue: Pyrrho's supposed claim that each thing is no more this than that, that is, presumably, no more good than bad, no more just than unjust, and so forth. To begin with, the parallelism to Democritus is striking. Democritus, too, had said, for instance with reference to sensible qualities, that things are not red or green, that they are red or green just in conventional belief, that they are no more red than green. And there was an interpretation of the 'no more this than that' phrase, rejected by Sextus, which would have turned Democritus into a sceptic. So perhaps Pyrrho could be interpreted as saying, or even meaning to say, that depending on how you look at them, things appear to be good or bad, but either they are completely indifferent or there at least is no way to tell whether they are good rather than bad, or bad rather than good.

But the obvious parallel to Democritus might also invite the thought that Pyrrho assumes that things are completely indifferent in every respect, not just as far as their evaluation is concerned, but also as far as their phenomenal characteristics are concerned, and that he was just particularly interested to make this point concerning the good and the bad, the beautiful and the ugly, and such characteristics, though he took the point to hold also for phenomenal characteristics. But in this case, again, we do not get suspension of judgement in the appropriate sense. It is not true that we suspend judgement as to whether what we see is a wagon about to run us over or not. For, on this view, we believe that there is no such thing as a wagon about to run us over. To believe otherwise would already be to believe that things are not indifferent. So, again, we would need a different interpretation of the 'no more this than that' phrase. But, on the face of it, the evidence Diogenes Laertius provides rather seems to suggest that Pyrrho did not understand indifference in this general way, but as being limited to evaluative predicates; and it also rather suggests that Pyrrho, if he used the 'no more this' phrase, did not understand it in the sense that things might be indifferent, insofar as we cannot tell whether they are good or bad; for he seems to have thought that they actually were neither good not bad, and, for this reason, to have assumed that, if we think that they are good or bad, this must have its source, rather than in the things, in our conventional way of thinking about them.

With this we can turn to our most important testimony concerning Pyrrho's thought. It is preserved in Eusebius' *Praeparatio evangelica*, XIV, 18, 2–4, which is mainly drawn from Timon.

According to Timon, if one wants to attain *eudaimonia*, one has to focus on these things: (1) what are things like in their own nature; (2) which attitude we should have with regard to them; (3) what is going to happen to one if one has this attitude. Timon then goes on to give us Pyrrho's answers to these questions. This at least suggests that these questions, their sequence, and their purported point reflect Pyrrho's thought. And, given what we have said so far, the thought behind them would seem pretty clear: if you want to have a good life, first of all you have to be clear about the fact that it is not things in themselves which are good or bad. Hence, secondly, you should not have an attitude towards them as if they were good or bad. Thirdly, if you manage to have the right attitude towards them, you will be rid of all your anxieties and be happy. These questions in their sequence in any case do not suggest any scepticism. To the contrary, they suggest that you can find out what things really are like, as opposed to what people say they are like. They suggest that it only seems reasonable to take an attitude towards things which is based on what things really are like, rather than on what they are customarily believed to be like. And they suggest that one can reasonably expect a tangible benefit from taking such a reasonable attitude.

Now the answers Pyrrho actually gives to the first two questions, according to Timon, are these: (1) things in themselves are indifferent and cannot be judged (*anepikrita*); (2) hence our perceptions and our beliefs concerning them are not true or false; hence one should put no trust in them, but remain without belief and unmoved, and think in each case that the thing is no more this way than not this way, or that it both is and is not this way, or that it neither is, nor is not this way; (3) Timon says that the answer (presumably Pyrrho's answer is meant here) is that the result will be first speechlessness, and then imperturbability.

Now, this report deviates from our expectations in various ways. And it does so systematically in the sense that most of the deviations correspond to the second understanding of the ambiguous 'no more this than that' phrase. 'Indifference' now does not mean 'neither this nor that', but rather 'neither this nor that, or at least we cannot tell which one'. Hence the inference now is not that perceptions and beliefs cannot be trusted, because they are false, but because we cannot say either that they are true or that they are false. Nor will we just say in each case that the thing is no more this than that, meaning that it is neither, but something a great deal more complicated. Indeed, this is Timon's understanding of the phrase 'no more', which in his *Pytho* he claimed to indicate that one did not determine anything to be the case, but withheld assent (DL IX, 76). The other major deviation is that Timon understands the indifference not to be restricted to evaluative predicates.

Given the complexity of the evidence, it may turn out to be impossible to reconstruct a reliable view of Pyrrho's, as opposed to Timon's, position. In fact, it seems to me that the way forward is, to begin with, to leave aside Pyrrho and reconstruct Timon's position in its own right, in order then to see what Pyrrho's position may have been. It is clear enough, at least in outline, what Timon's position was. He did think that things were indifferent in the sense that they were neither this nor that, or, if they were, we could not tell whether they were this or that, and that hence all we could do is to follow appearances, not worrying whether things actually are this or that.

ACADEMIC SCEPTICISM

ARCESILAUS

Arcesilaus of Pitane (316/15 BC–241/40 BC) became head of the Academy around 273, to govern it for more than 30 years. He is the founder of Academic scepticism. Under his scholarchate the Academy turned sceptic in the ancient sense of the word. Though initially there was some resistance to the new direction the school took with him, this direction was consolidated, it seems, under his successor Lacydes. There is no reason to insist that Arcesilaus was in no way influenced by Pyrrho. Arcesilaus must have been familiar with Pyrrho's thought through Timon. He was well read. He went out of his way, it seems, to refer to sceptical elements in the thought of earlier philosophers, and so would have had no difficulty acknowledging Pyrrho's scepticism. But there is, at the same time, plenty of reason to insist that one has to be able to understand Academic scepticism as a development within the Academy. Arcesilaus would not have managed to become, or to retain his position as, scholarch, if he had not been able to present himself with some plausibility as continuing the tradition of Socrates and Plato. It was his opponents who had an interest in presenting him as constituting a break in the tradition of the school, as somebody who relied on a tradition alien to the spirit of the Academy, for instance on Pyrrho.

It is rather difficult to reconstruct Arcesilaus' thought with the kind of detail that his position would, no doubt, deserve. Nevertheless, there does seem to be enough evidence to reconstruct Arcesilaus' position in rough outline. It seems, for instance, that we can rely on the evidence that suggests that Arcesilaus appealed to Socrates, and to a lesser extent to Plato, for his scepticism, but also on the evidence according to which Arcesilaus' position was formed in part in opposition to the Stoic Zeno's epistemology. In order to understand this, it may help to briefly consider the historical position Arcesilaus found himself in.

As is well known, Socrates had assumed that whether we attain the good life depends on whether we attain wisdom, the knowledge of what is good and what is bad and related matters. Also, notoriously, Socrates did not believe that he himself had attained this wisdom. Indeed, he thought that if he had any claim to any kind of wisdom, it lay in precisely this, that he did not pretend to have a knowledge he did not have, a pretence which obviously would stand in the way of making any effort to attain real wisdom. Hence Socrates in his search for the truth questioned others to see whether they knew more than he did, and to free them, if necessary, from the false conceit of knowledge. There was a method, later known as the Socratic *elenchus*, which admirably suited this purpose. It involved a questioner and a respondent. The questioner would elicit a thesis from the respondent. He would then ask a series of yes-or-no questions of the respondent, in answer to which the respondent would commit himself to a position on these questions. But the questioner would ask these questions in such a way that the answers to them, if possible, would form the premises of an argument the conclusion of which would contradict the original thesis. The respondent, having given the answers he did, could not honestly fail to respond to the appropriate final question but by answering it in contradiction to his original thesis. The way Socrates is presented in Plato, Socrates was a formidable dialectician who always managed to reduce his respondents to contradiction, thus showing that they were ignorant on the matter in question. For somebody who knows will not contradict himself on a question within the area of his expertise.

It is important to draw attention to several features of this practice. The 'refuted' interlocutor not only has been shown not to know the truth, he also has been put into a situation in which he no longer feels in a position to answer the original question at all. He is, as it is called, in an 'aporia'. He will have had some reason for the thesis, and he has now been revealed to also have reason for asserting the contradictory. And torn between these two opposing reasons, he no longer rationally can assert either the thesis or its contradictory, let alone claim that he does so as a matter of knowledge. And, if this is at least part of the point of the practice, it should be clear that the argument advanced against the thesis cannot be understood as a proof that the thesis is false. Otherwise there would be no aporia.

As to the questioner, we should note that he can engage in this questioning without knowing the truth concerning the thesis or the questions he asks. He can do this without even having a mere belief as to the truth concerning his questions. He certainly does not commit himself to a view in questioning the respondent. The answers are all the respondent's, and so is the argument. It is the respondent who assumes that he is faced with an argument which forces him to contradict himself. Now, if the questioner does think, as Socrates did, that he does not know the answers to the questions he asks, he also should think that he himself would not be able to withstand questioning, if properly questioned, without being made to contradict himself. And thus he would think himself to be in a genuine aporia as to what to answer to the questions he asks. It is not only that he thinks that he does not know, he also thinks it unwise even to just make a claim on the matter, which upon questioning would turn out to be indefensible and futile.

Now philosophers after Plato (who in writing dialogues constantly reminds us of Socrates and his practice, but also himself manages to avoid committing himself to any position, since it is others who in the fiction of a dialogue commit themselves to the positions which get discussed in the dialogue) unlike Plato increasingly forget Socrates' caution. They begin to produce ever more, and ever more extravagant and speculative, theories, built on mere belief and producing nothing but more mere opinions. Both

Epicureanism and Stoicism are in part reactions to this situation which these philosophers try to remedy by developing an epistemology which is supposed to show how we can overcome mere opinion and attain true knowledge and wisdom. In fact, for the Stoics Socrates, in his single-minded quest for practical wisdom and his refusal to content himself with mere opinion, is a paradigm of a philosopher. But, they think, Socrates was mistaken in thinking that his kind of elenctic questioning or, more generally, his kind of dialectical argument, however much one excelled in it, would ever lead to knowledge. Argument based on mere belief will just lead to more mere belief. What we need to realize is that, in addition to mere belief and knowledge, there is cognition. Cognition, unlike mere belief, which at best just happens to be true, is bound to be true, given the way it has come about. It still falls short of knowledge in that, unlike knowledge, it can be destroyed by rational means, for instance by dialectical questioning. One can have clearly realized something to be the case, only later to be talked out of it on the basis of false assumptions incompatible with it, which one also holds. That cognition is different from mere opinion we can see from perception. If one clearly perceives something to be the case, one's belief that it is the case surely is not just a matter of mere opinion. More specifically the Stoics suggested that nature in its providence provides us with the ability to form impressions of things, the so-called cognitive impressions, for instance perceptual impressions, which, given the way they come about, cannot fail to be true. If we, then, accept these impressions, we will have cognition, rather than mere belief, and in cognition, unlike mere belief, we will have a solid basis for knowledge.

This, then, is the situation Arcesilaus found himself in. We readily understand why Arcesilaus was as scandalized by the endless production of more empty philosophical opinion as the Stoics and the Epicureans were. But we also understand why Arcesilaus might have decided to curb, or put an end to, empty philosophical speculation by reverting to the Socratic *elenchus* to test the philosophical theses proposed, or rather by applying to philosophical theses a scrutiny which in substance amounts to the same as a Socratic *elenchus*, though in outward form it differs from Socrates' questioning. Arcesilaus did not go to the market to question his fellow citizens, but rather asked students in his school to propose a philosophical thesis which he then would argue against. Or he would take a thesis which had its adherents, and then himself would produce the arguments for and against. And, in arguing against it, he might not entirely rely on premisses endorsed by the advocates of the thesis in question, but also on premisses they at least could not just dismiss, especially since Arcesilaus also was prepared to provide arguments for those premisses which his opponents might not want to endorse.

This procedure, though in format it somewhat differs from Socrates' questioning, still has the same crucial features of the *elenchus*. Arcesilaus can reduce the adherents of a thesis to complete *aporia*, without having to claim any knowledge for himself, indeed without even committing himself to a position on the matters raised. In fact, we should expect Arcesilaus, too, to claim to be at a complete loss himself, and not to make any claims, knowing well that his claim would not be able to resist similar questioning, either. Thus it is easy to understand, against the background of Socrates' elenctic practice, a continued tradition of various forms of dialectical argument in the Academy, and Arcesilaus' concern over his philosophical colleagues' disregard for Socrates' strictures against mere opinion, how Arcesilaus might decide to avail himself in a Socratic spirit of a variety of forms of dialectic to stem the tide of speculative dogmatism. We thus would understand why Arcesilaus would be a sceptic concerning philosophical theses or beliefs, that is to say, why he would not only refrain from claiming any knowledge on philosophical matters, but even refuse to take any stand on the matters at issue. He could see himself as somebody who is at loss for an answer in these matters. It is tempting to think that the term 'aporetic', as an alternative name for a sceptic (*Pyrrh.* I, 7; I, 221), has its origins in this Academic context.

There is one respect, though, in which Arcesilaus does not just resume what he takes to be the tradition of Socrates and Plato, abandoned by Speusippus, Xenocrates, and their followers down to Zeno and the Stoics. It is not just their questionable speculations which seem to make Socratic questioning more indicated than ever. There is a deeper problem, made obvious by the attempts of the Epicureans and the Stoics to show what Socrates and his interlocutors would have had to do to gain the wisdom Socrates was after. The question was whether there was not another diagnosis for Socrates' failure to attain the wisdom he thought we ideally should have, or we would have to have, to guarantee us a good life. Perhaps it turns out that this wisdom is a matter of realizing that one has not attained it, that one may not attain it, but that it is worth while to make every effort to attain it, even if one does not attain it. For obviously Socrates down to the end of his life did not regret his rather single-minded effort to attain something which, by his own admission, he had not attained (cf. Aenesidemus' remark in Photius, *Bibliotheca* c. 212, 169b 27–9, for a parallel).

Tradition, though, presents Arcesilaus not just as a sceptic in a much stronger sense. It presents him as an unqualified sceptic, as a sceptic on any question, matter or issue, however trivial it may be. He is supposed to have counselled complete suspension of judgement or belief. There is nothing in the evidence concerning Socrates which suggests such a radical scepticism. It is true that Socrates must have said something to the effect that his own claim to wisdom, if any, would just be this: that he was aware of the fact that he did not know anything. But nobody would naturally infer from this that he claimed not to know anything about anything. One takes him naturally to refer to his scepticism concerning the issues discussed by philosophers of nature, but primarily to his ignorance concerning the questions he is presented as discussing in Plato's early dialogues, ethical questions. Socrates also is often presented as not letting on what he himself believed, but, however we interpret this, we do not think that it means that Socrates had no beliefs as to, for instance, the gate of the city one would enter if one came from Larissa. Arcesilaus' position, it seems, is much more radical; it is a position of complete suspension of belief. To understand how this comes about, or at least how the appearance of it comes about, one has to take into account that the dialectical situation has radically changed. Socrates had to discuss such questions as whether and how virtue can be acquired. Arcesilaus also had to discuss such questions as to whether and how real knowledge can be acquired, in particular the knowledge which Socrates was after and which constitutes wisdom and virtue. Arcesilaus had to discuss the epistemological theses of the Epicureans, but in particular those of the Stoics which were meant to show that and how we could break out of the circle of mere opinion, attain knowledge, and in particular the knowledge which Socrates was after. These theses crucially involved the assumption that perceptions constitute the secure basis on which all knowledge rests. A dialectical response to these theses could not but involve arguments to the effect that knowledge is not attainable, or that even if we perceive something, there is no reason to suppose that the belief which we have on the basis of our perception is more than mere opinion, but cognitive, a solid basis of knowledge. And such a dialectical response cannot but also call all our beliefs into question, to the extent that they are based on perception and the experience which it gives rise to.

Now, obviously Arcesilaus did also attack these epistemological theses. In fact, what is very conspicuous and striking about the evidence concerning Arcesilaus we have, is precisely this that, though Arcesilaus in his teaching addressed whatever philosophical theses his audience was ready to propose, his own thinking seems to have been very much focused on Zeno's attempts to show how knowledge and thus ultimately wisdom were possible. A crucial part of Zeno's theory was this: to believe something is to give assent to an impression which represents something as being a certain way; some impressions deserve assent, and some do not; an impression deserves assent if it has its origin in something which is the case and represents matters precisely as they are the case. So your impression that this book is green deserves assent, if your impression has its origin in a fact and if it precisely and accurately represents this fact. Tradition has it that Zeno, pressed by Arcesilaus, went one step further. He stipulated that impressions, in order to deserve our assent, had to represent things in such a clear and distinct way that they could not possibly be false. That is to say, if the book is red, but you have the impression that it is green, then your impression lacks the kind of clarity and distinctness which it would have, if the book were green and you saw it under normal conditions. Such an impression Zeno calls cognitive, because assent to it constitutes a cognition, and not just a mere opinion. And cognitions are the basis of all our knowledge.

The debates between Stoics and Academics from Arcesilaus' time onwards were focused on the question whether there are such cognitions and cognitive impressions. Academics found a plethora of arguments to question the existence of such impressions which by their very character are guaranteed to be true. For instance, they referred to vivid hallucinations, which seem, at least to those affected, to have the same character as impressions we have under normal conditions; also to the possibility that God or gods might induce an impression in you which in no way differs from the kind of impression you would have if you saw something under ideal conditions, but which nevertheless was false (Cicero, *Ac. Pr.* 49–50). It is difficult to determine which of these arguments go back to Arcesilaus.

But it is reasonable to assume that at least this much of the argument goes back to Arcesilaus. Suppose there are two men, twins, who look exactly alike. They also are dressed exactly alike. The visual conditions are ideal. You have the impression, looking at one of them, that Castor has a white dress on. This impression has its origin in a fact, rather than just being the product of an abnormal state of your mind, and it represents the fact with as much faithfulness as you could possibly desire. But what you see, under ideal conditions, actually is Pollux with a white dress on, who looks exactly like Castor with a white dress on. The Stoic response is that there are no two things which are not distinct, and that distinct things do not exactly look alike. Arcesilaus' answer is to question whether there are no two things which are exactly alike, and the Stoics have no way to definitely settle this question in their favour. We should note in passing that this indicates that Academic arguments do not have to rely exclusively on premises accepted by the opponent. In order for the argument to count as dialectical, it suffices, if a premiss cannot just be dismissed by the opponent. In any case, it seems in response to arguments like the one concerning the twins that Zeno stipulates that an impression, in order to be cognitive, has to be clear and distinct in such a way that it could not possibly be false. Hence, given that Castor and Pollux are distinct, the impression that Castor has a white dress on, if it is clear and distinct, cannot have its origin in the fact that Pollux is standing in front of one with a white dress on. For the impression, to be clear and distinct, will have to represent Castor as having a look which Pollux, being distinct, can never have.

Once this further stipulation is made, though, Arcesilaus argues that there is no impression, under however ideal circumstances it may have been obtained, such that one could not find an impression exactly like it which was false. And so he produced examples of impressions which we clearly would not trust to be true, because they are formed under abnormal conditions, but which arguably are exactly alike the impressions we form under ideal conditions. Hence, the Stoics had to argue that no impressions formed under abnormal conditions can have the character of clarity and distinctness which impressions obtained under normal conditions have, without, though, being able to settle this question. And, as this question was not settled, Arcesilaus felt free to assume that there are no cognitive impressions, that is to say impressions which could not possibly be false, given their character as impressions.

Now, presupposing these arguments, Arcesilaus could argue in the following manner. A wise man will not give assent to impressions which do not deserve assent, that is to say a wise man will not hold mere opinions. But there are no impressions which deserve our assent because they are cognitive. Hence a wise man will not give assent to any impression. For to do so would be to hold a mere opinion.

So Arcesilaus does argue that it is wise not to give assent to any impression, and, by implication, that it is wise not to have any beliefs whatsoever. This argument is the major source for the assumption that Arcesilaus advocated total suspension of judgement. But this argument does not constitute any evidence for this assumption. It is just another dialectical argument. That it contains a premiss not shared by the Stoics does not mean that it is not dialectical. In fact, it rests on a number of assumptions, for instance the assumption that there are no cognitive impressions that one could wisely assent to, which themselves are the conclusions of dialectical arguments which rest on assumptions of which it is difficult to see why Arcesilaus should commit himself to them, or even could himself commit to them, if he wanted to argue non-dialectically that one should always suspend judgement. It rests on the Stoic notion of cognitive impressions and the Stoic assumption that only cognitive impressions deserve assent. This particular argument, then, is just another dialectical argument to whose conclusion Arcesilaus is in no way committed. Its point is to put the Stoics into the awkward position to have to acknowledge that it is not clear, as they assume it is, that wisdom presupposes the existence of cognitions and cognitive impressions, as without them we would never attain knowledge. If the Stoics are so determined to defend the existence of cognitive impressions as they conceive of them, it is because they think that there is no other way in which we will be able to escape mere opinion and attain knowledge and wisdom. But the argument presents us with an alternative: we can avoid mere opinion by suspension of judgement, and perhaps this is what wisdom consists in, at least the wisdom attainable by us.

There is, apart from this argument that a wise man will suspend judgement, another major reason which might make one think that Arcesilaus actually advocates universal suspense of judgement. Obviously Arcesilaus' opponents challenged Arcesilaus' conclusion, claiming that life without belief is impossible. We should note that this claim can be understood in two ways. It might be the claim that a genuinely human life, a good life, is not possible without some assumptions about the nature of the world and about what is good and what is bad. This is what both Epicureans and Stoics claimed. This is what seems to have motivated late Academic sceptics to allow for beliefs. And this prompted yet later ancient philosophers to espouse views about the world and what is good, even if the epistemic status of these views seemed dubious even to them. But it also might be the more radical claim that life is impossible, if you do not allow yourself even such trivial beliefs as the belief that a wagon is coming your way, rather than just such beliefs as 'losing one's life is a bad thing'. But let us assume that the claim was the more radical claim. Now it is clear that Arcesilaus did accept the challenge by arguing that the sceptic in practice would follow what is reasonable (*eulogon*), without thereby giving assent to anything, making any judgement as to what is true or false (*Math.* VII, 158). It is tempting to infer from this that Arcesilaus, as he accepted the challenge, must have thought that he actually was committed to the view that one should never give assent to anything. But, though it is tempting to think this, to think so is to overlook the fact that Arcesilaus may not have felt committed to the thesis that one always should withhold assent (which, in any case, would have involved some kind of contradiction), but may have felt that the dialectic of this argument forced him to defend the possibility of a life without assent. For the argument to the effect that a wise man will always suspend judgement will not constitute a threat to the Stoic position, if its conclusion is not dialectically sustainable. The assumption of a life without assent is no threat to the assumption that there must be cognitive impressions, if there is to be wisdom, if it cannot be dialectically defended. The conclusion that it is wise always to withhold assent contradicts the Stoic thesis that it is wise sometimes to give assent, namely when one has a cognitive impression. This contradiction is no threat to the Stoic thesis, if the contradictory just can be dismissed. Arcesilaus' answer as to how one might wisely live without assent is no more than a dialectical move to ensure that the argument to the effect that it is wise to always suspend judgement retain its dialectical force.

Such an interpretation of Arcesilaus' arguments as being dialectical seems to me to be the best explanation of the evidence. To adopt such an interpretation is by no means to adopt the view that all Arcesilaus was concerned with was to expose the questionability of each and any philosophical thesis. Socrates clearly was concerned with the beliefs which guide us in what we think and what we do in daily life. The Stoics had a similar concern. The point of Stoic doctrine was to convince one, for instance, that only wisdom and virtue are a good, and that hence in real life one should not get excited, or anxious, over the mere thought that one had a lot of money in the bank. We should assume that Arcesilaus had a similar concern. And part of this concern must have been that what we think and what we do in everyday life is questionable to the extent that it is guided by beliefs which philosophically are questionable, like the beliefs which the Stoics want us to guide our lives by, for instance the belief that only wisdom and virtue are a good, or that we should only believe something if we have a corresponding clear and distinct impression, because only this will guarantee cognition. A prerequisite for our being able to see how questionable these beliefs are, is that we are disabused of the idea that we, or some authorities, know them to be true. To disabuse us of this idea, and at the same time to show how questionable these beliefs are, dialectical arguments are the ideal means.

❧ CARNEADES ❧

There is no clear evidence of any significant philosophical development in the Academy in the period between Arcesilaus and Carneades. The situation is dramatically different once we come to Carneades. According to Apollodorus (DL IV, 65) he was born in 214/13 BC; according to another tradition (*Ac. Pr.* 16) some five years earlier. He died in 129/28 BC. He succeeded Hegesinus as scholarch (DL IV, 60), certainly before 155 BC, when he was a member of an Athenian embassy to Rome whose other members, the Peripatetic Critolaus and the Stoic Diogenes, were scholarchs. That Carneades' scholarchate marked a new period in the history of the school is reflected, for instance, by the fact that, according to Sextus Empiricus (*Pyrrh.* I, 220), a third and New Academy (as opposed to the Old Academy of Plato and the Middle Academy of Arcesilaus) begins with Carneades. There is a good deal of evidence concerning Carneades' philosophical activity, and the evidence is a good deal better than the evidence we have for Arcesilaus. Though Carneades, like Arcesilaus, did not leave any writings, he had in Clitomachus an able successor who was a voluminous writer and who tried to defend Carneades' position, as he understood it, though there was a dispute about the correct interpretation of Carneades' position among Carneades' students. Moreover, Cicero, himself an Academic sceptic and our main source for Academic scepticism mainly through his *Academica*, was near enough in time to Carneades to know people who had listened to, or even had been students of, Carneades, for instance his Academic teacher Philo. Thus, whereas Arcesilaus already by the time of Cicero had become a shadowy figure of the distant past, interpreted and reinterpreted on the basis of very little hard evidence to suit the interests of his Academic successors and their opponents, the evidence we have concerning Carneades is much more direct, more detailed, and more vivid.

There are certain obvious differences between Arcesilaus and Carneades. Whereas Arcesilaus seems to have focused very much on Stoicism, and hence on Stoic epistemology, Carneades cast his net wider. Carneades also discussed ethical questions in a way which has left a mark in our evidence. And it seems, to judge from his discussion of the end of life, that he made an effort not just to attack particular actual theses on a given topic, but to think of them systematically as different possible theses to hold on a particular question, which would open up the way for a discussion of new possible theses which had not yet been espoused.

Another striking difference between Arcesilaus and Carneades is this. In the evidence concerning Arcesilaus we repeatedly find the claim that Arcesilaus thought not only that one could argue for and against any thesis, but that the arguments would balance each other out, would be of equal force (*isostheneia*), and hence would lead to suspension of judgement. There are obvious difficulties about this thought, if we want to avoid construing it as a dogmatic claim. Perhaps it is no more than the thought that if we look at dialectical arguments, for instance Socrates' arguments, it seems that for any thesis an equally plausible case always can be made on the other side of the question. Now, conspicuously, in the evidence concerning Carneades such a reference to the equal force of arguments on both sides is missing. There still is the assumption that there are arguments on both sides, but there is not the additional suggestion that they will balance each other out. This might reflect an attempt to avoid what might seem like a dogmatic claim. But it also might reflect the thought that, however much we argue on both sides of a question, there still is the possibility that, in the end, we find one view a lot more plausible than the other. And one reason for this might be that we have a view or a belief quite independently of any arguments we have to justify this view or belief. If I see a green book and believe that the book is green, it is not on the basis of an argument with the conclusion that this book is green that I have this belief. If challenged to produce an argument, I could try to do so. But there will be an argument to the contrary. And this might convince me that my argument is not conclusive, in fact that I have no justification for my belief. But it might still seem to me – I might still have the impression – that the book is green. I might still think that it is plausible that the book is green. And this might be so, not because I am stubborn and not open to reasoning. For I have understood and granted that my argument is not conclusive. But neither is the argument on the other side, and I did not have the belief on the basis of an argument in the first place. There are at least three different kinds of cases we need to distinguish here. There are beliefs which are induced by nothing but an argument. We would not have these beliefs, unless we had arguments to support them. Correspondingly, such beliefs will disappear, once we see, in the light of arguments to the contrary, that we have no justification for our belief. But there also are beliefs which we hold, not, or not just, on the basis of arguments, but, for instance, by appeal to authority, for instance the authority of scientists. Now, one might also successfully question whether one was rationally entitled to these beliefs. But then there are beliefs which one not only does not have for a reason, but of which it seems unreasonable to demand that one should only have them, if one has an argument to support them, though it may not be unreasonable to demand, given the appropriate circumstances, a justification for the belief. A case in question is the belief that the book in front of me is green. That I will not be able to come up with a conclusive argument to prove that the book is green, does not necessarily mean that it is just a reflection on my rationality, if I continue to have the impression or even the belief that the book is green. Whatsoever the arguments on either side, it still seems to me to be highly plausible that the book is green, especially if the arguments on the other side do not appeal to any features of the particular situation to cast doubt on my belief.

There are two kinds of evidence to suggest that in the case of Carneades such considerations may not be irrelevant. First, Cicero (*Ac. Pr.* 67) reports that Carneades advanced an argument which is an exact counterpart to the argument of Arcesilaus, which we discussed above, that the wise man will never give assent. Carneades' argument, however, in addition to the first premiss, that if the wise man ever gives assent, he will have mere opinions, took as a second premiss the denial of Arcesilaus' conclusion, to infer the denial of Arcesilaus' second premiss, and thus to conclude that even the wise man sometimes will have opinions. This again can be interpreted as a merely dialectical argument. Even if the first premiss will not be accepted by the Stoics, they cannot just dismiss it, because they can only reject it by relying on the questionable assumption that there are clear and distinct impressions. Without this assumption, on their own view, they would have to grant that even the wise man will sometimes have mere opinions. But, if cognitive impressions were just introduced to avoid this conclusion, not much progress seems to have been made. In fact, Arcesilaus' and Carneades' argument as a pair seem to confront the Stoic with the choice to assume either that the wise man will never give assent to anything or that he will sometimes hold mere opinions, unless they can produce reason to believe that there are cognitive impressions which substantially goes beyond the claim that otherwise we will never get beyond mere opinions.

But some Academics obviously interpreted Carneades' argument, as we can see from the passage in Cicero, not as a merely dialectical argument, but as expressing Carneades' view, just as they took the conclusion of Arcesilaus' argument to express Arcesilaus' view. As a result we would have a very substantial disagreement between Arcesilaus and Carneades. And the kinds of considerations adduced earlier would explain why one at least interpreted Carneades in this way. There are impressions and beliefs such that the bearing arguments can have on these impressions and beliefs is intrinsically limited, even if there is some bearing, as in the case of the belief that this book is green.

Secondly, there is all the evidence according to which Carneades distinguished different kinds of impressions. To begin with, just as Arcesilaus had said, in order to evade the argument that life without belief is impossible, that the sceptic will follow what seems reasonable (*eulogon*), without giving assent to an impression, so Carneades said that the sceptic will follow what seems plausible (*pithanon*), without giving assent. The term '*pithanon*' was rendered by Cicero as '*probabile*'. It is crucial that this term not be misunderstood. Cicero translates the term in this way, because Cicero himself believes that, if impressions have a certain kind of plausibility, are well considered, one can approve of them even as a sceptic, in a sense assent to them, as long as one keeps in mind that it is not certain whether they are true. And the reason why Cicero thinks this, is that he also thinks that impressions we have on the basis of due consideration of the matter are more probable in the sense of being more likely to be true. But, unless we take Carneades' argument that the wise man will sometimes have mere opinions to express his own view, we should assume that by 'plausible' Carneades does not mean 'something which is likely to be true'. For Carneades, plausibility to whatever degree is one matter; truth and probability are another matter. And for Carneades, evidence, similarly, is one thing; truth another (cf. *Ac. Pr.* 34). However evident it might seem to you that this book is green, this does not mean that it is true that it is green. For something to be plausible, or even evident, it suffices that something strikes you as being this way, however much you think about it and take the arguments to the contrary into account.

In fact, Carneades talks about the various ways in which we can test our impressions (*Ac. Pr.* 33; 36; *Math.* VII, 175–89; *Pyrrh.* I. 227–9). There is some confusion in our sources concerning these tests. But it seems to me that Carneades' idea is simply this. In the case of perceptual impressions, for instance, the Stoics themselves seem to take the view that an impression is guaranteed to be true, if it has come about in the right way, namely under normal conditions. So, one thing you can do to test an impression, is to check the conditions under which it arose or arises. Obviously, this is not in the spirit of the Stoic theory. For, according to Stoic theory, cognitive, that is to say clear and distinct, impressions are criterial, and hence, to rely on further evidence to establish their cognitivity, would be to give up on their status as criteria. Nevertheless, we can check impressions in this way, as the Stoics themselves assume we do. If the object is too far away, we move closer to establish normal conditions. But we can also test impressions for coherence with other impressions of the same object which we already have or might obtain. For any given impression to be tested we can use both tests. Obviously it does not matter in which order we do so. What does matter is that the further impressions we have, or obtain, on either test to use them as evidence, can themselves be subjected to both tests, which involves the use of further evidence which again can be evaluated critically. It is clear that this procedure, for however long we follow it, will never guarantee that the impression to be tested at the outset is true, because for this the evidence against which we test it would have to be guaranteed to be true. So this test will not allow us to establish an impression as cognitive, unless we already assume that we can decide that certain impressions are cognitive without some such test. But how then do we know that they are cognitive? If the answer is that they are clear and distinct or evident, we will again argue that evidence is no guarantee for truth.

There is another way, though, to understand Carneades' remarks about differences between impressions according to whether they pass certain tests. They can be understood as part of Carneades' answer to the question as to what one does in life, if one universally suspends judgement. The answer may be that one does what everybody else does. One follows one's impressions, and depending on how important and how urgent the matter is, one will test one's impressions to the extent that this seems possible and worth while, so as to content oneself in the end, for the purposes at hand, with an impression of which one knows, though, that it is not guaranteed to be true, since one always could continue the test. Such a response again could be understood dialectically. But it also could be interpreted as an observation by Carneades as to what people, including sceptics, actually do, it being understood that this in no way conflicts with their scepticism. The fact that an impression passes such a test up to some level does not mean that it is true, and need not be taken to mean that it is true by somebody who relies on such an impression for practical purposes.

So there are at least two aspects of Carneades' arguments which might make one wonder whether Carneades did not allow for the possibility that, even as a sceptic, one might have an impression which one accepts concerning the matters one perceives, or even concerning the matters which are the subject of philosophical debate. Whether this, then, should be called a 'belief' or not, in part is a matter of terminology, ancient and modern, in part a matter of how we should conceive of beliefs.

One thing, though, is rather clear. Carneades cannot unequivocally have said that a sceptic may have beliefs concerning matters at issue in philosophy. For otherwise his own students would not have disagreed as to whether this had been his view. And, if Carneades himself had such beliefs, he clearly managed remarkably well never to unequivocally commit himself to such a belief. For Clitomachus, his long-time follower, could claim that he was never able to find out what Cameades' view was.

❧ CLITOMACHUS AND PHILO ❧

Whatever Carneades' own view on the matter of beliefs may have been, it became a subject of controversy among Carneades' students: not only what Carneades had thought on the matter, but also what one as a sceptic should think about it. Metrodorus, later followed by Philo of Larissa, took the position that the sceptic can have beliefs, even concerning philosophical matters, as long as one is clear that there is nothing to guarantee the truth of these beliefs. This was to become the dominant position in the Academy under Philo. But it was Clitomachus who succeeded Carneades as scholarch, and Clitomachus took a very different view.

Clitomachus is the first sceptic we know of to distinguish two senses of 'withholding assent', and hence, by implication, two senses of 'assent' (*Ac. Pr.* 104). In the first sense of 'withholding assent' one will never in any way assent to anything. In the second sense one will withhold assent, if one refuses to answer questions in such a way as to approve or disapprove of anything, to say or deny anything. The way this is put is somewhat confusing and has raised doubts as to the text. But the explication which follows seems to make it clear enough what is meant. 'Assent' can be either understood in the sense of 'unqualified assent', or it can be understood in the sense of the assent involved when one accepts a perceptual impression or in a discussion answers questions with 'yes' or 'no', depending on whether one finds something plausible or not. Hence, if it is said that the wise man will withhold assent, this can be understood in two quite different ways. It can be understood in the sense that the wise man will never give his unqualified assent to anything. But it also can be understood as meaning that the wise man will never give his assent in the sense involved in accepting a perceptual impression or in answering questions. And Clitomachus seems to claim that the way one should understand the remark that the wise man always withholds assent is in the former sense, rather than in the latter. So, according to Clitomachus, there must be a qualified sense of assent, in which even a sceptic will give assent, both in everyday life, when, for instance, it comes to things one perceives, but also in discussions.

Such a distinction of two kinds of assent, and, correspondingly, of two kinds of senses of 'withholding assent' or 'suspending judgement', seems crucial to the further history of scepticism in antiquity. The distinction was drawn in different ways, but it seems subsequently to have been drawn by everybody, by Academics and then by Pyrrhonean sceptics. It allowed them all to continue to insist that a sceptic does universally suspend assent or judgement, namely unqualified assent, while at the same time allowing for assent in some qualified sense. This is the position of the pre-Roman Philonean Academics in Cicero, *Ac. Pr.* 148. It is the position of Aenesidemus, when he says in his *Pyrrhonean Discourses* that Pyrrho does not determine anything dogmatically, because of the arguments on both sides (DL IX, 106). The claim is not that Pyrrho does not determine anything unqualifiedly, that is to say that Pyrrho does not say anything, one way or the other, in whatever way or sense of 'determining' you wish. The claim rather is that Pyrrho does not say anything, one way or the other, dogmatically. For, as Aenesidemus continues, Pyrrho will follow the phenomena, that is to say accept and rely on what he cannot help but think about things, given how they appear to him. This seems to correspond to the distinction drawn by Sextus Empiricus, *Pyrrh.* I, 13, between two senses of 'dogma', of which only one is rejected. In fact, Sextus, too, explicitly says here, and will repeat in I, 15, that the sceptic will assent in certain cases in a certain way, namely when he is affected by the appearance of things in such a way that he cannot help but think about them in a certain way.

Now, to see more clearly what Clitomachus may have in mind, we should first see in which way he could intend to draw the distinction so as to yield a position which differs from that of Metrodorus and Philo, with whom, as we know, he disagreed. Perhaps we have to begin with the fact that on the Stoic view we just have assent to impressions. There may be a distinction between the sense in which children, or even animals, might be said to assent to impressions, and the sense in which mature, rational human beings assent to impressions. So there is a Stoic distinction in place, which a sceptic could make use of. But, as to mature human beings, in Stoicism there is just one kind of assent, namely an assent to a rational impression which constitutes a belief, more precisely, depending on the impression, a cognition or a mere opinion. In every case, in the case of mature human beings, assenting to an impression involves taking it to be true. Let us call such an assent to an impression which involves taking the impression to be true an unqualified assent. When a sceptic says that he withholds assent he means to say that he withholds unqualified assent, that is, he does not take an impression to be true. Now, Philoneans seem to think that we are able to refine our impressions in such a way that they are true, or if not true, pretty much like the truth or likely to be true, though we cannot tell in any case whether they are true. So, they might give qualified assent in the sense that they accept an impression, not in the sense that they take it to be true, but in the more complex sense that they take it to be, if not true, pretty close to the truth, or at least likely to be true. And one would understand why they thought that such an assent still would constitute a belief or an opinion. For they might agree that, if we have an opinion, this does not mean that we believe that what we, for the purpose at hand, take to be the case, actually is true, let alone that we are certain that it is true. There is a certain tension here, but this may be largely due to our use of the word 'belief', as opposed to the Greek word 'doxa'. But we certainly understand what it means to take something to be the case for the purposes at hand, or to go on the assumption that something is the case, without committing oneself unqualifiedly to the view that it actually is the case.

Now Clitomachus, to have a different view of the matter, just has to hold on to Carneades' understanding of the plausible, or at least his interpretation of Carneades' understanding. An impression may be plausible or even evident, but, however plausible it is, this does not mean that it is true, or even that it is pretty much like the truth or likely to be true. So one can take an impression to be highly plausible, but this, quite straightforwardly, does not mean that one gives assent to it in the unqualified sense in which this involves taking it to be true. And, if one is a Clitomachean, rather than a Philonean, one does not even take it to be likely to be true. So, what then is the qualified sense in which one as a Clitomachean might give assent to an impression? Here we should also take into account that it is characteristic of the Metrodorean and Philonean position that even a wise person may have opinions, whereas Clitomachus denies this. So the kind of assent Clitomachus allows for should be such that giving assent does not amount to having an opinion. This we can achieve, if we distinguish between a view and an opinion. Having a view is just having an impression one contents oneself with, perhaps after having considered the matter carefully, if it needs careful consideration. So this is the view one has, but however carefully one has considered the matter one does not even have the slightest inclination to think that it is true. Nevertheless, this is one's view. Having a view, even having a carefully considered view, does not involve believing that it is true, nor even that it is likely to be true, or pretty much like the truth. Pyrrhoneans later, in their attempt to create a distance between themselves and the Academics, will interpret Carneades and Clitomachus along Philonean lines. Just as a Philonean might be strongly inclined to think that something is true, as long as he does not unqualifiedly take it to be true (*Ac. Pr.* 148), so Pyrrhoneans will suggest that the followers of Carneades and Clitomachus, unlike Arcesilaus, follow the plausible with a strong inclination to take it to be true (*Pyrrh.* I, 230). But, though this is true of Philo and the Philoneans, it is not true of Carneades and Clitomachus. If, then, we assume that Clitomachus relied on such an austere notion of a view, such that having a view did not even entail believing it to be probably true, or being inclined to believe it to be true, we also understand why Clitomachus would have thought that a view, construed thus austerely, did not amount to a belief or an opinion. And so he could continue to say that the sceptic will have no beliefs or opinions, though he will have views, that is to say accept or give assent to impressions in this qualified sense.

Now the views a Clitomachean sceptic may have, according to Cicero, *Ac. Pr.* 104, explicitly were said to be of two kinds: they are the kinds of views one relies on in everyday life, like, for instance, perceptual views concerning the colour of things. But they are also views concerning the matters under discussion, for instance philosophical views. No matter how much one argues about the existence of motion or places, one might in the end still have the impression that things move and that they move to some place. This does not mean that one believes that there is motion or that there are places, but it does mean that, if one is asked what one thinks, one would say that one thinks that things move to some place.

Now Clitomachus also seems to claim, though, that he is interpreting Carneades. In any case, in the debate about Carneades' position, referred to in Cicero, *Ac. Pr.* 78 (cf. 108), Clitomachus claims that Carneades just agreed dialectically that the wise man sometimes will have opinions. But how will this be compatible with Clitomachus' claim that he never found out what Carneades' view was? Even, if we distinguish between a view and an opinion, there still will be the problem why Carneades avoided revealing his view, if, according to Clitomachus, there is nothing wrong for a sceptic not only to have a view, but also to say what it is. Perhaps Carneades in fact did not think that there was anything intrinsically wrong with saying what one's view is, but still systematically refrained from doing it, since he thought that it would be of no help to anybody to tell them his view, indeed it might be of some harm, because it might be thought that there was something authoritative about his views.

Against this background we can be brief about Philo of Larissa who succeeded Clitomachus as scholarch around 110 BC, and presided over what looks like the collapse of the Academy as an institution in the wake of Sulla's capture of Athens in 87 BC in the course of the Mithridatic War; Philo actually had already taken refuge in Rome where he continued to teach for almost another decade.

To understand the conflicting notices about Philo we have first of all to keep firmly in mind that Philo at least twice changed position in a radical way. He started out as a follower of Clitomachus and Carneades. He then adopted the kind of position for which he was best known, which he taught as scholarch in Athens, and to which he also converted Cicero. But finally, in his Roman days, he again switched position quite radically, to the surprise and, it seems, dismay of some of his earlier followers. For what he taught now, it seems, was no longer that the truth about things ultimately is beyond our firm grasp, that nothing can be known for certain. He now taught that things naturally can be known, that it is just that we do not have a criterion of truth of the kind the Stoics were claiming we had, which would allow us in any individual case to be certain that we actually did have knowledge of this particuiar matter. So there are lots of things we know, for instance the colours of things, but also many other things. For we are by nature constructed in such a way as to generally get things right, for instance in perception. It is just that we can never be sure in a particular case whether we got it right (*Pyrrh*. I, 235; *Ac. Pr.* 18). This view still can be called 'sceptical', in that it still involves the assumption that one should never give unqualified assent, since one never knows in a particular case whether what one assents to is true.

What infuriated some (cf. *Ac. Pr.* 11–12) was that each time Philo changed his position he rewrote the history of the Academy so as to make it appear that his new position had been the true position of the school all along. The first change was accompanied by a reinterpretation of Carneades, and perhaps also of Arcesilaus. The second change again was presented as in line with the teaching of the Academy from its very beginnings. Philo apparently argued that the position that nothing can be known, which by now had become identified with the Academic position, due to Metrodorus and his own teaching, was a position Arcesilaus had developed only relative to the Stoic doctrine of cognitive impressions and the conception of knowledge which goes with it (*Ac. Pr.* 18; *Pyrrh*. I, 235). So, it is relative to a conception like the Stoics have that nothing can be known. But Arcesilaus had never meant to argue that nothing can be known in any sense, Philo now claimed.

Philo's final turn seems not to have gained him any new followers who could have carried on the traditions of the sceptical Academy. His most important student, Antiochus, had decided already, in reaction to Philo's dogmatic and probabilistic scepticism, to declare the history of the Academy from Arcesilaus onwards an aberration, and to return to the doctrine of the Old Academy, which he set out to distil out of Plato, Aristotle, and the Stoics. There was some attempt to revive the Philoneanism of the pre-Roman period (*Ac. Pr.* 11), but there was no philosopher of sufficient stature to carry on this tradition. Academic scepticism of one form or another continued to have its adherents, for instance figures as diverse as Plutarch and Favorinus of Arelate. But it had ceased to exist as a school.

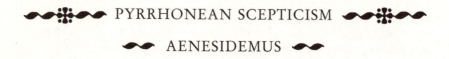

PYRRHONEAN SCEPTICISM

AENESIDEMUS

It is generally agreed nowadays that Pyrrhonean scepticism, whatever its precise relations to Pyrrho may be, owes the particular form in which we know it, primarily through the works of Sextus Empiricus, to Aenesidemus. It also seems that Aenesidemus must have written in the first century BC; recent scholarly opinion has moved away from a date late in the century, primarily to accommodate Cicero's silence on Pyrrhonism, to a date early in the century which, among other things, would best fit Aenesidemus' remarks on his Academic contemporaries.

What motivated Aenesidemus in his work is clear enough. Aenesidemus objected to the turn the sceptical Academy had taken under Philo. In his view, Academics had become virtually indistinguishable from Stoics, holding philosophical views, in fact more or less the same views, for instance in ethics, except that the Academics, equally dogmatically, claimed that, of course, nothing can be known. Photius, who reports this (*Bibliotheca* c. 212, 169b40 ff.), also talks as if Aenesidemus had been, or even had presented himself, as originally an Academic (169b33).

Aenesidemus wrote a good deal, for instance an *On Inquiry* (DL IX, 106), or an *Outline of Pyrrhonism* (DL IX, 78), but a major work of his was the *Pyrrhonean Discourses*, in 8 books (DL IX, 106), and we are fortunate in that for this work we at least have the short abstract made of it by Photius in his *Bibliotheca* (c. 212). The first book constituted some kind of introduction, presumably rather like the first book of Sextus Empiricus' *Outlines of Pyrrhonism*; it dealt at length with the difference between Academic scepticism and Pyrrhonism, but also gave a brief outline of the Pyrrhonist position as a whole. Books II to V dealt with questions of cognition and questions of nature, while the remaining three books were devoted to ethics. Obviously in the last book Aenesidemus argues against the claim that there is such a thing as the end of life, but in particular also against the claim that *eudaimonia* constituted the end (Photius, *Bibliotheca* c. 212, 170b31 ff.). Nevertheless in the introductory book, he holds out as a promise for those who follow the Pyrrhonean way that it will lead to *eudaimonia* (ibid. 169b27).

Scepticism in the ordinary, modern sense had been supported from the fifth century BC onwards by a number of observations which turned into commonplaces, for instance the observation that different people perceive the same things in different ways. Aenesidemus, it seems, collected them under ten headings as ten tropes, or modes of argument, one might avail oneself of in trying to question any given claim in order to achieve suspension of judgement. Obviously Pyrrhoneans set great stock on these tropes. Their discussion takes up paragraphs 36–163 of the first book of Sextus' *Outlines of Pyrrhonism*.

Pyrrhonism after Aenesidemus enjoyed a long history, though there is no indication that it ever gained a large following. DL IX, 116 provides us with a list of Pyrrhoneans which takes us to the beginning of the third century AD with Saturninus, another Empiricist doctor. But, though the school has a history of almost three centuries, we get no sense of a philosophical development. There are a good number of Pyrrhoneans we can identify and attach this or that fact or view to, but this never adds up to a distinctive philosophical profile. Obviously the doctrine of tropes was developed. The list of ten tropes was rearranged. A clever scheme of five tropes was introduced by Agrippa (DL IX, 88–9; *Pyrrh*. I, 164–77) whom we, though, cannot further identify. As Barnes has shown, they were almost certainly based in part on a reflection on Aristotle's remarks at the beginning of the *Posterior Analytics* about the need for first principles which do not require any proof, if there is to be demonstrative knowledge. For three of the five modes are the modes of infinite regress, of circularity, and of hypothesis, to which are added the modes of disagreement and of relativity. The modes apparently are meant to form a system such that in any discussion of any question they will jointly guarantee that one is able to neutralize any dogmatic claim.

∾ SEXTUS EMPIRICUS ∾

If we are quite well informed about Pyrrhonism, it is because two writings by its last major exponent in antiquity, Sextus Empiricus, have come down to us: the *Outlines of Pyrrhonism* in three books, and the *Adversus Mathematicos* in eleven books. The former consists of two parts: a general exposition of

Pyrrhonean scepticism in book I, and arguments against dogmatic positions in logic, physics and ethics in the last two books. The *Adversus Mathematicos* is entirely adversarial. The first six books criticize the doctrines within the liberal arts, apart from dialectic, the last five books criticize the philosophical doctrines in dialectic or logic, physics and ethics. Sextus Empiricus seems to have written before AD 200.

In Sextus Empiricus there is at least superficially a clear demarcation between dialectical arguments and remarks, on the one hand, and remarks *in propria persona*, as it were, on the other. There is an attempt on a large scale to systematically neutralize all major dogmatic theses in philosophy by dialectical arguments to the contrary. And there is at least some attempt to do the same for the liberal arts. These arguments often are layered in the sense that they not only question the thesis, but also the crucial notion involved in the thesis, arguing that it is ill-formed or at least controversial, such that it is not even clear what the dogmatic wants one to assent to. But it is clear that according to Sextus as a Pyrrhonean one not only suspends judgement concerning theses in philosophy or in the arts, but concerning any claim whatsoever, even concerning things which manifestly appear to be the case, the phenomena (*Pyrrh.* I, 8). Since there are conflicting phenomena or arguments advanced against particular claims of whatever kind, obviously these arguments are not to be understood as proving the claims to be false, but as showing them to be questionable. They are dialectical.

Now, as to the remarks make by the sceptic *in propria persona*, for instance the remarks made by Sextus Empiricus in *Pyrrh.*, book I, they are not to be understood straightforwardly, either, that is to say as claims to the truth. Sextus, right from the outset, in *Pyrrh.* I, 4, puts a rider on whatever he is going to say: he is just reporting his impressions, how things strike him at the moment, in the way an Empiricist doctor reports on his medical cases (*historia*). Sextus, towards the end of *Pyrrh.* I, in 187–209 (cf. DL IX, 74–7), has a long section on how particular sceptical phrases have to be understood, namely non-dogmatically, as not involving any claim to the truth.

But within these remarks thus qualified by a general caveat, Sextus also tries to explain how this scepticism of unlimited scope still leaves room for the sceptics' having certain impressions or views, rather than others, for instance the impressions or views Sextus reports them as having in book I of *Pyrrh.* And they obviously are not restricted to reports of perceptual impressions or views, but include thoughts and reflections, for instance as to what philosophers are trying to do, what they have done, and whether they have succeeded in what they have been trying to do. After all, as Sextus points out, we are beings who not just naturally perceive, but also think about things (*Pyrrh.* I, 24). And perceiving or thinking about things, there are certain impressions which one seems to be stuck with. However much you think about motion, in the end it still leaves you with the impression that things move. And Sextus is even willing to say that the sceptic gives his assent to such impressions, as he cannot help but have them (*Pyrrh*. I, 13; 19). He does not seem to be particularly concerned whether we call this an 'impression' or a 'belief' (*Pyrrh*. I, 13), as long as it is understood that there is nothing dogmatic about it, that such an acceptance of, or assent to, an impression does not in the least involve the assumption that it is true. Such impressions, which a sceptic cannot help but have, will offer him enough guidance to pursue his life.

The suggestion had been, in particular the Stoic suggestion had been, that a rational, a meaningful, a good life is impossible unless one has the right view about the world and about what is good and what is bad. This is why philosophers had tried to acquire wisdom. In the light of this assumption a sceptical life seems to be bound to be a failure, since it is not guided by such views. In fact, scepticism has the inherent tendency to eliminate such views, as one can help having them. So where does this leave the sceptic?

Sextus suggests that it turns out that it is the sceptic who will achieve, precisely because of his scepticism, what dogmatic philosophers had set out to achieve, namely peace of mind to the extent that this is a matter of our views or beliefs, and a minimum of suffering to the extent that this is unavoidable (*Pyrrh*. I, 25 ff.): in short happiness to the extent that this is attainable. The reason is this: the sceptic discovers that one can well live without having settled all the questions the dogmatic philosophers thought one had to have settled to have a good life. And the sceptic also discovers that being unencumbered by all these beliefs one actually can do without, one is no longer worried about things in the way one used to worry about them, when one had these beliefs. One may still worry about an illness, but one does not have the additional anxiety generated by the assumption that illness is an evil, or by assumptions as to what one might have to face, if one is going to die from this illness.

It would be a mistake, though, to think that a good life thus conceived of, namely a life unencumbered by self-imposed worries and concerns generated by dogmatic beliefs, was the end or ultimate aim of the sceptic in the sense in which philosophers talk about the end of life. It is not that the sceptic becomes a sceptic to attain this sort of life. It is that, having become a sceptic, he finds himself with this sort of life as a benefit, as it were. Nor is it the case that the sceptic all of a sudden turns into a dogmatic philosopher and claims that this is the good life, that this is the end which we should all aim at in all that we are doing. He is just making an observation, namely the observation that a sceptical life, far from being a disaster, in fact turns out to be the sort of life dogmatic philosophers in fact may have been looking for.

This life, the way Sextus imagines it, is not at all like the life of Pyrrho as suggested by the anecdotes about Pyrrho. It, at least on the face of it, is a rather conventional life (*Pyrrh*. I, 23-4). We follow the impressions we cannot help but have, given the way we perceive and think about things, we eat when we are hungry, we accept the traditional customs even in religious matters, and we exercise whatever art or craft we have learned. All this is possible, without being dogmatic about anything.

Needless to say, this attitude, however attractive it may seem to us, by the end of the second century AD increasingly seemed utterly unattractive, as people more and more obsessively were looking for the knowledge, or at least a set of beliefs, which would save the soul and which would provide some understanding of, and comfort in, a world in which one increasingly felt helplessly exposed to dark and obscure forces, which at any point might cruelly interfere with one's life, however piously one had followed the traditional customs of one's community. In any case, after the beginning of the third century AD we no longer hear of any Pyrrhoneans. There lingered on still, at least in the West under the influence of Cicero, a kind of enlightened scepticism, which is represented by Caecilius in Minucius Felix's *Octavianus*, and which at one point attracted Augustine. But, with the conversion to Christianity, the days of even such vestiges of scepticism were counted, too.

ABBREVIATIONS

The following abbreviations are used in this chapter.
Ac. Post. Cicero, *Academica Posteriora*
Ac. Pr. Cicero, *Academica Priora*
DK Diels, H. and Kranz, W., *Fragmente der Vorsokratiker*, 6th edn, Berlin, Weidmann, 1951
DL Diogenes Laertius, *Lives of the Philosophers* [6, 1]
Math. Sextus Empiricus, *Adversus Mathematicos* (*Against the Professors*)
PE Eusebius, *Praeparatio evangelica*
Pyrrh. Sextus Empiricus, *Pyrrhôneiai hypotupôseis* (*Outlines of Pyrrhonism*)

BIBLIOGRAPHY

TEXTS AND TRANSLATIONS

See [6.1] Diogenes Laertius; [6.2] Sextus Empiricus; [6.3] Long and Sedley.
8.1   Annas, J. and Barnes, J., *Sextus Empiricus: Outlines of Scepticism*, Cambridge, 1994.

COLLECTIONS OF PAPERS

See [6.5] Schofield, Burnyeat and Barnes, *Doubt and Dogmatism*; [6.7] Schofield and Striker, *The Norms of Nature*; [6.11] Brunschwig, *Papers in Hellenistic Philosophy*; [6.15] Striker, *Essays on Hellenistic Philosophy and Ethics*.

8.2   Burnyeat, M., *The Skeptical Tradition*, Berkeley, 1983.
8.3   Canto-Sperber, M., *Philosophie grecque*, Paris, 1997.
8.4   Frede, M., *Essays in Ancient Philosophy*, Minneapolis/Oxford, 1987.
8.5   Rorty, R., Schneewind, J., and Skinner, Q., *Philosophy in History*, Cambridge, 1984.
8.6   Voelke, A.J., *Le Scepticisme antique*, Cahiers de la Revue de Théologie et de Philosophie, 13, Geneva, 1990.

❧❧ BOOKS AND ARTICLES ❧❧

8.7   Allen, J. 'The skepticism of Sextus Empiricus', *Aufstieg und Niedergang der römischen Welt*, II 36 4, Berlin, 1990, 2582–607.
8.8   Annas, J., 'Doing without objective values', in [6.7] Schofield and Striker.
8.9   Annas, J. and Barnes, J., *The Modes of Scepticism*, Cambridge, 1985.
8.10   Barnes, J., 'The beliefs of a Pyrrhonist', *Proceedings of the Cambridge Philological Society* 28, 1982, 1–29.
8.11   Barney, R., 'Appearances and impressions', *Phronesis* 37, 1992, 283–313.
8.12   Bett, R., 'Carneades' *pithanon*', *Oxford Studies in Ancient Philosophy* 7, 1989, 59–94.
8.13   Brochard, V., *Les Sceptiques Grecs*, Paris, 2nd edn 1932.
8.14   Brunschwig, J., 'La Formule *hoson epi tôi logôi* chez Sextus Empiricus', in [8.6] Voelke, 1990, English trans. in [6.11] Brunschwig.
8.15   Brunschwig, J., 'Pyrrhon' and 'Le Scepticisme et ses variétés', in [8.3] Canto-Sperber.
8.16   Burnyeat, M., 'Can the Sceptic live his Scepticism?', in [6.5] Schofield, repr. in [8.2] Burnyeat.
8.17   Burnyeat, M., 'Tranquillity without a stop: Timon fr. 68', *Classical Quarterly* 30, 1980, 86–93.
8.18   Burnyeat, M., 'The sceptic in his time and place', in [8.5] Rorty.
8.19   Couissin, V., 'L'Origine et l'évolution de l' *epochê*,' *Revue des Études grecques* 42, 1929, 373–97, English trans. in [8.2] Burnyeat.
8.20   Frede, M., 'The Sceptic's beliefs', in [8.4] Frede.
8.21   —— 'The Sceptic's two kinds of assent and the question of the possibility of knowledge', in [8.5] Rorty.
8.22   —— 'Stoics and Skeptics on clear and distinct impressions', in [8.2] Burnyeat, repr. in [8.4] Frede.
8.23   —— 'A medieval source of modern scepticism', in R. Claussen and Daube-Schackart, eds, *Gedankenzeichen*, Düsseldorf, 1989, 65–70.
8.24   Giannantoni, G., ed., *Lo scetticismo antico*, Naples, 1981.
8.25   Glidden D., 'Skeptic semiotics', *Phronesis* 28, 1983, 213–55.
8.26   Glucker, J., *Antiochus and the Late Academy*, Göttingen, 1978.
8.27   Goedeckermeyer, A., *Die Geschichte des griechischen Skeptizismus*, Leipzig, 1905.
8.28   Hankinson, R.J., *The Sceptics*, London, 1995.
8.29   Ioppolo, A.M., 'The Academic position of Favorinus of Arelate', *Phronesis* 38, 1993, 183–213.

8.30 Long, A.A., 'Sextus Empiricus on the criterion of truth', *Bulletin of the Institute of Classical Studies* 25, 1978, 25–49.

8.31 Natorp, P., *Forschungen zur Geschichte des Erkenntnisproblems in Altertum*, Berlin, 1884.

8.32 Sedley, D., 'The motivation of Greek Skepticism', in [8.2] Burnyeat, 9–29.

8.33 Stough, C., *Greek Skepticism*, Berkeley, 1969.

8.34 ——'Sextus Empiricus on non-assertion', *Phronesis* 29, 1984, 137–64.

8.35 Striker G., 'Sceptical Strategies,' in Schofield [6.4] 54–83.

8.36 —— 'Über den Unterschied zwischen den Pyrrhoneern und den Akademikern', *Phronesis* 26, 1981, 153–69.

8.37 —— 'The ten tropes of Aenesidemus', in [8.2] Burnyeat, 95–115.

8.38 —— 'The problem of criterion', in S. Everson (ed.), *Epistemology*, Cambridge, 1990.

8.39 Stopper M.R., 'Schizzi pirroniani', *Phronesis* 28, 1983, 265–97.

8.40 Tarrant H., 'Scepticism or Platonism?', Cambridge, 1986.

CHAPTER 9

The exact sciences in Hellenistic times:

Texts and issues[1]

Alan C. Bowen

Modern scholars often rely on the history of Greco-Latin science[2] as a backdrop and support for interpreting past philosophical thought. Their warrant is the practice established long ago by Greek and Latin philosophers, of treating science as paradigmatic in their explanations of what knowledge is, what its objects are, how knowledge is obtained, and how it is expressed or communicated. Unfortunately, when they turn to the history of ancient science, these same scholars usually remain too much under the spell of the ancient philosophers. Granted, it is true that Greco-Latin science often served as a model and touchstone for philosophy and that, on occasion, this philosophy may have inspired science. But the marked tendency to follow Greek and Latin writers in viewing ancient science through the complex, distorting lens of ancient philosophy has hindered recognition that the various sciences of antiquity sometimes differ significantly from one another as well as from philosophy in their intellectual, literary, and social contexts. Moreover, it has encouraged scholars to ignore or even disparage clear indications that some of these sciences were deeply indebted in the course of their history to work outside the Greco-Latin tradition, in Akkadian, for example. And, what is worse, out of ignorance and neglect of the various contexts of ancient science, modern scholars have misrepresented the past fundamentally in numerous ways by resorting to alien predilections and concerns when trying to explain the origins, character, and development of Greek and Latin science.[3] In sum, the amorphous system of learned belief expressed now in handbooks on ancient science and currently underlying the modern interpretation of ancient philosophy, for instance, is largely inadequate and erroneous.

287

This failure of previous scholarship challenges historians of ancient science today to re-think the entire project from its beginning. In effect, it compels one to start afresh by imagining oneself the first modern scholar confronted with all the extant literary documents (papyri, inscriptions, manuscripts) and material artifacts (instruments) that come to us from the ancient Mediterranean and Near Eastern worlds. Such a prospect is admittedly daunting and brings to mind a variant of Meno's question (cf. Plato, *Meno* 80d–e): how can you seek to understand ancient science if you do not already know what it is, and how will you know that you have understood it? There are, of course, several well known ways to answer this in the abstract. But the real task is to work out a credible solution in the particular, that is, in the process of analyzing historical data. And, as I have found in studying ancient astronomy and harmonic science, this process involves a vital, corrective interplay between historical analysis and reflection on how this analysis proceeds. In fact, the process is, I think, heuristic in the sense that medicine was said to be heuristic on the grounds that the goal of the physician's craft, health, is articulated and known only through treating specific patients.

Given that the standard accounts of Greco-Latin science are at best controversial and should be abandoned in most part, and since the development of alternative accounts is still in its earliest stages, I must decline in what follows to attempt a survey. Instead, I propose to confine my remarks to a few sample texts in Greek written in the interval between the death of Alexander the Great in 323 BC and the beginning of the third century AD. There is no great significance to this period so far as the exact sciences themselves are concerned: it simply covers the range in time of the documents I have chosen to discuss. And I select these texts because they provide the earliest direct evidence of certain features of ancient science that will, I trust, be of interest to historians of science and philosophy.

In describing a text as direct evidence for some claim or other, I mean that the text itself is a sufficient basis for verifying the claim. Such direct evidence stands in sharp contrast to indirect evidence in the form of citations (that is, quotations, translations, paraphrases, and reports). For, one cannot verify a claim on the strength of indirect evidence alone; what one needs in addition is independent argument for maintaining that the citation is accurate and reliable. Since there are no general rules validating the accuracy or reliability of indirect evidence, such argument must be made case by case and is, in my experience, both difficult and rarely successful.

Restricting attention primarily to direct evidence may seem unduly cautious at first. But it is, I submit, the only policy that makes sense at the outset of any radically critical, historical investigation of the sort now called for. In any case, this policy does offer substantial advantages. To begin with, confirmation by recourse to direct evidence introduces an order of certainty that cannot be attained on the basis of indirect evidence or citations. The reason is that much of our indirect evidence concerns documents no longer available for inspection; thus, the most one may hope for in justifying reliance on this evidence is an argument for the probability of its accuracy. Such arguments, however, usually fail because they involve reading the historian's own expectations into the past, expectations often concerning empirical matters about which there may be considerable uncertainty and reasonable doubt. Next, if one is strict about how evidence is used and does not introduce indirect evidence except when it is demonstrably credible – and even then one should decline to build on it, since probabilities diminish when multiplied – the preference for direct evidence will counteract a major failing in traditional histories, the valorization of certain texts and authors at the expense of others. Finally, in dating the occurrences of concepts, theories, and the like, the historian may rely on direct evidence to identify the *latest* (that is, most recent) date possible for their introduction. This will seem a small gain, particularly to those who think it the proper business of historians to conjecture *earliest* possible dates. But such a program of conjecture is an enterprise to which there is no end except by convention. Moreover, by discouraging full appreciation of the documents we actually have, this fascination with the earliest dates assignable for the occurrences of concepts and theories in Greco-Latin science underlies in part the scholarly neglect of the Akkadian and Egyptian scientific traditions which, in various forms and sometimes through intermediaries, interacted with the Greek and Latin traditions.

The preceding will have to suffice as an *apologia* for my deciding to present the history of the exact sciences in Hellenistic times by way of narrowly defined case-studies. Though such an approach is not without precedent (cf., for example, Aaboe 1964), it is admittedly a departure from the great number of general surveys and narrative accounts currently available.[4] The texts I have selected are: Archimedes, *De lineis spiralibus* dem. 1; Geminus, *Introductio astronomiae* ch. 18; and Ptolemy, *Harmonica* i 1–2. These texts have no explicit connection. Nevertheless, they raise fundamental issues in the history of ancient science that are well worth pursuing (in studies that are, of course, suitably cognizant of historiographic matters). Indeed, there are running through these texts thematic concerns about the conception and mathematical analysis of (loco)motion, the nature of scientific communication, and the role in such communication of observation and mathematical theory.

MOTION IN MATHEMATICS: ARCHIMEDES

In his *De lineis spiralibus*, Archimedes (died 212 BC) analyzes fundamental properties of a curve of his own invention, now called the spiral of Archimedes. In the letter prefacing this treatise, the statement of the conditions under which this curve is produced comes first in a list of propositions about the spiral that are proven in the treatise proper (cf. Heiberg 1910–23, ii 14–23). Later, immediately after the corollary to dem. 11, this same statement reappears virtually unchanged as the first of a sequence of definitions. According to the latter formulation,

> if a straight line is drawn in a plane and if, after being turned round as many times as one pleases at a constant speed while one of its extremities is fixed, it is restored again to the position from which it started, and if, at the same time as the line is turned about, a point moves at a constant speed along the straight line beginning at the fixed extremity, the point will describe a spiral in the plane.
>
> (Heiberg 1910–23, ii 44.17–23; cf. 8.18–23)

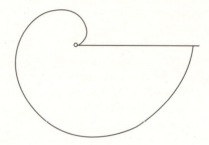

Figure 9.1 Archimedes' spiral (one revolution)

The first eleven demonstrations of the *De lineis spiralibus* establish what is necessary for the subsequent theorems on the spiral itself. The first two of these auxiliary demonstrations are devoted to properties of the motion of points on straight lines at constant speeds. In dem. 1 (Heiberg 1910–23, ii 12.13–14.20), Archimedes proposes to show that

> if a point moving at a constant speed travels along a line and two segments are taken in the line, the segments will have the same ratio to one another as the time-intervals in which the point traversed the segments.

The argument opens by specifying the task as follows (see Figure 9.2):

> let a point move along a line AB at a constant speed, and let two segments, CD and DE, be taken in the line. Let the time-intervals in which the point traverses CD and DE be FG and GH respectively. It is required to prove that the segment CD will have the same ratio to the segment DE as the time-interval FG will have to the time-interval GH.

Next, Archimedes makes some assignments:

let AD, DB be any multiples of CD, DE respectively, so that
AD > DB;   (1)

let LG be the same multiple of FG as AD is of CD, and   (2)

(let) GK be the same multiple of GH as BD is of DE.   (3)

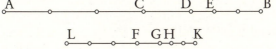

Figure 9.2 Archimedes, *De lineis spiralibus* dem. 1

The assignment in (1) is based on a lemma that Archimedes has stated in his covering letter to the treatise:

if there are unequal lines or areas, the excess by which the greater exceeds the less can, when added to itself, exceed any assigned [magnitude] belonging [in kind] to those which are compared with one another.   (4)

     (Heiberg 1910–23, ii 12.7–11: cf. *De sphaera et cylindro* post. 5;
     Quadratura parabolae praef.)

That is, in modern terms,

if a and b are magnitudes and $a < b$, there is a whole number n such that $n \cdot (b - a) > c$, where c is any magnitude of the same kind as a and b.[5]

The reasoning behind the assignment in (1) seems to be as follows. Any magnitude such as a line or area is divisible into a whole number of smaller magnitudes of the same sort. Thus, given any point D in AB and any whole numbers p and q, it is always possible to specify CD and DE such that

$$AD = p \cdot CD \text{ and } DB = q \cdot DE. \quad (5)$$

(This holds true, of course, regardless of whether AD and DB are commensurable or incommensurable, or whether AD > DB or AD = DB or AD < DB.) Now, since CB > DB and given the lemma in (4), there is, then, a whole number n such that

$$n \cdot (CB - DB) > DB \quad \text{that is, } n \cdot CD > DB. \quad (6)$$

But, either $n \cdot CD \leq AD$ or $n \cdot CD > AD$,
that is, in light of (5), either $n \leq p$ or $n > p$.
Thus, from (6) it follows that if $n \leq p$, then AD > DB,   (7a)
which is the case Archimedes considers,
       and that if $n > p$, then AD < DB,   (7b)
if one assumes also that n is the least number to satisfy (6).

After stipulating (1), (2), and (3), Archimedes draws attention to the fact that the point moves at a constant speed along AB. Obviously, he says, this point will then traverse each of the segments of AD that is equal to CD in the same time that it takes to traverse CD. Thus, given (2), he infers that LG is the time-interval in which the point traverses AD; and, similarly, given (3), that GK is the time-interval in which the point traverses DB. Accordingly, he maintains, since AD is greater than DB, the point will take more time to traverse AD than DB; that is,

$$\text{since AD} > \text{DB, therefore LG} > \text{GK.} \qquad (8)$$

Likewise, he says by way of generalization, if one takes any multiple of FG and any multiple of GH so that one of the resultant time-intervals exceeds the other, it will be proven that the line-segment corresponding to the greater time-interval will be greater, because these line-segments are to be produced by taking the corresponding multiples of CD and DE. In other words,

$$\text{if } r \cdot \text{FG} > s \cdot \text{GH, then } r \cdot \text{CD} > s \cdot \text{DE} \qquad (9a)$$

or

$$\text{if } r \cdot \text{FG} < s \cdot \text{GH, then } r \cdot \text{CD} < s \cdot \text{DE.} \qquad (9b)$$

where r and s are whole numbers.

Finally, Archimedes concludes that

$$\text{CD has the same ratio to DE that FG has to GH.} \qquad (10)$$

This conclusion that CD:DE :: FG:GH rests on an unstated condition for asserting that magnitudes are in the same ratio, a condition of the sort given by Euclid in *Elementa* v. def. 5:

> magnitudes are said to be in the same ratio, the first to the second and the third to the fourth, when, if any equimultiples whatever be taken of the first and third, and any equimultiples of the second and fourth, the former multiples alike exceed, are alike equal to, or alike fall short of, the latter equimultiples respectively taken in corresponding order.
>
> (Heath 1956, ii 114: cf. 120–6)

Thus, (10) specifically requires (9a) and (9b) as well as that

$$\text{if } r \cdot \text{FG} = s \cdot \text{GH, then } r \cdot \text{CD} = s \cdot \text{DE} \qquad (9c)$$

all which follow readily from the basic fact that the motion is constant.

A striking feature of the *De lineis spiralibus* is that Archimedes nowhere gives an explicit mathematical or quantitative definition of constant speed. The locutions he uses to express this concept suggest that he is starting instead from the qualitative notion that a body moves at the same or constant speed (*isotacheôs*) if it changes place at the same speed as itself (Heiberg

1910–23, ii 12.13–14: cf. 8.21, 44.21–2), that is, if it is unchanging in its swiftness or speed (*tachos*). This point will, of course, be lost if one insists on modern convention and supposes that, for Archimedes too, the speed of a body is the quotient of the distance it travels divided by the time taken to travel that distance. But this is not, in fact, how Archimedes *presents* speed: for instance, he characterizes sameness of speed not as an equality of quotients obtained when distances are divided by time-intervals, but by identifying the ratio of line-segment to line-segment and the corresponding ratio of time-interval to time-interval. This may, admittedly, be an artifact of the 'rules' of mathematical exposition during his time, in particular, of the formal condition that ratios be defined only between magnitudes of the same kind (cf. Euclid, *Elementa* v defs. 3–4); and so it may not be a sure guide to the way Archimedes actually conceived speed. (In the next section, I consider a text from the first century AD in which quotients of unlike quantities are in fact computed, though it is still not said that these quantities stand in a ratio to one another.) Accordingly, let us leave open the question of how Archimedes thinks of speed or swiftness and concentrate instead on how he expresses it. And, on this count, I find in dem. 1 and the rest of the *De lineis spiralibus* that he talks of speed as a quality of bodies that is quantifiable only in relation to other instances of this quality; and, moreover, that constancy of speed is to be understood as the sameness of this quality over time in a given body.

The next question, however, is whether such talk is supplanted by a quantitative definition in dem. 1. That is, does Archimedes, as some suppose, *posit* that traversing line-segments in equal times is just what motion at a constant speed is; or does he *infer* that a point will traverse equal line-segments in equal times from the fact that it moves with a constant speed (cf. Dijksterhuis 1987, 140–1)? The critical passage

> now, since it is posited that the point moves at a constant speed along the line AB, it is clear that it travels CD in the same amount of time as it also traverses each of the segments equal to CD.
>
> (Heiberg 1910–23, ii 12.30–14.4)

is, regrettably, not decisive. Nevertheless, there is, I think, compelling reason to maintain that Archimedes does not in fact identify motion at a constant speed with traversing equal segments of a straight line in equal times. For, as he is well aware, in the course of each revolution, though the generating point of the spiral always describes equal angles in equal times about the spiral's origin, that is, about the fixed extremity of the generating line, and though it always traverses equal segments of the generating line in the same equal times as well, this same point traces out arcs of the spiral itself that are not equal to another (cf., for example, dem. 12). In other words, the very construction of the Archimedean spiral entails that the generating line (and, hence, any point on it) will by virtue of its constant revolution define equal angles in equal times about the fixed extremity; and that the generating point will by virtue of its constant motion on the generating line traverse equal segments of this line in equal times. Yet, the combined motion of the generating point and line has the result as well that this point will not describe equal arcs of the spiral in equal times. Thus, from the vantage point of Archimedes' *De lineis spiralibus*, the qualitative idea of motion at a constant speed has to be more fundamental than the quantitative ideas of traversing equal segments of a straight line or equal angles of a circle in equal times. In fact, since these are the relevant ways of quantifying the motion of the generating point, and since they are not equivalent here, it would be a serious blunder to open a treatise on spirals with a demonstration presupposing that motion at a constant speed is to be *defined* simply as traversing equal segments of a straight line in equal times.

Let us now consider briefly the preface to Autolycus' *De sphaera quae movetur*. Autolycus begins by declaring that

> a point is said to move smoothly (*homalôs*) when it traverses equal or similar magnitudes in equal time-intervals. If a point moving smoothly along some line[6] traverses two segments, the ratio of the time-intervals in which the point traverses the corresponding segments and the ratio of the segments will be the same.

> (Mogenet 1950, 195.3–8)

The first sentence gives clear indication that smooth motion has been defined mathematically in terms of line-segments and time-intervals, albeit not as a quotient. In short, though this treatise and the *De lineis spiralibus* agree that motion can be characterized quantitatively, Autolycus' treatise alone stipulates that smooth motion is just traversing equal line-segments in equal times. Indeed, that Autolycus calls the point's motion smooth (*homalês*) rather than constant (*isotachês*) may signify that this definition was seen to obviate any need to present such motion in terms of a point's moving at the same speed as itself. Yet, while Autolycus explicitly defines (or reports a definition of) smooth motion, he simply states the theorem about the proportionality of time-intervals and line-segments. That is, he does not offer a proof covering the case of straight lines (such as Archimedes does in *De lineis spiralibus* dem. 1) or the case of circular arcs on a sphere, the latter of which is crucial for his treatise.

Two points emerge from this. First is that our understanding of the history of the exact sciences can only advance if proper attention is given to the language in which it is expressed. For example, any interpretation that renders both Archimedes' 'at a constant speed' and Autolycus' 'smoothly' by 'uniformly' will obliterate the complexity in the conceptual and linguistic apparatus that underlies the difference in their terminology. Indeed, to see that the very idea of 'uniform' motion is itself problematic in ancient texts, the reader should consult Aristotle, *Physics* 228b1–30. Second is that, so far as I can tell given the documentary evidence available, Archimedes was first to appreciate the complexity of the 'equal segments of a straight line in equal times', the 'equal arcs in equal times' and the 'equal angles in equal times' formulae in curvilinear motion and to ground them all in the qualitative idea that a body moving at a constant speed changes place at the same speed as itself.

Was Autolycus, then, the first to realize that, in the special case of a point's circular motion at a constant speed, the first formula was irrelevant, that the latter two formulae were equivalent, and that such motion (here called smooth) could be defined in terms of either? This question is difficult to answer. Perhaps he was, but the same ideas figure in the *Phaenomena* attributed to Euclid. Now, this treatise itself can be dated only to the period from the third to the first centuries BC.[7] Thus, to affirm priority for Autolycus in the mathematical definition of constant circular motion would require knowing his dates relative to Euclid's[8] and whether Euclid actually wrote the *Phaenomena*,[9] since the case for assigning Autolycus to the period from 360 to 290 BC (Aujac 1979, 8–10; cf., for example, Mogenet 1950, 5–7, 8–9) is nugatory.[10]

Apart from these concerns about the history of the idea of constant motion, it is important to realize that Archimedes' very inclusion of motion of any sort in the definition of his spiral is also remarkable. In the works of Euclid, for example, motion is limited to the construction of figures defined statically (cf. for example, *Elementa* i defs. 15–22, dem. 46) and to serving as a hidden assumption in proofs of such relations among figures as congruence (cf. Euclid, *Elementa* i not. com. 4, with Heath 1956, i 224–31).

Now, a common way of interpreting this contrast is to suppose that Euclid belongs to a stage in the history of Greek mathematics earlier than Archimedes. The case offered thus far for this view, however, is unavailing, resting as it does on no more than an ancient inference concerning an anecdote told also of Menaechmus, a mathematician of the fourth century BC, and Alexander the Great, as well as on two suspect citations in Archimedes' *De sphaera et cylindro* (see Bowen and Goldstein 1991, 246 n30). But, if Euclid's work is not demonstrably earlier than Archimedes', should one continue to view it as earlier in substance or form? This too is a difficult question, in part because it requires what has yet to be undertaken in any serious way, a critical study of the ancient *testimonia* about Euclid and the early history of Greek mathematics. In such a study of Proclus' reports, for example, the alternatives against which the claims are judged will have to be founded on more than the simple-minded dichotomy that Proclus is either lying or telling the truth. Indeed, it will have to be rooted in a full examination of Proclus' historiography, an examination informed by awareness of the numerous ways in which the ancients use history to make their cases and persuade their contemporaries. And should it turn out that Euclid's work draws on and even recasts earlier mathematical theory, it will still be valuable to discover its intellectual and cultural context, as this context was defined in the third century when Archimedes was active. This will, of course, require paying attention to philosophical, technical, and social issues bearing on the understanding and treatment of motion that have too long been ignored in the scholarly haste to locate Euclid in relation to Aristotle and the Academy.

THE ARITHMETICAL ANALYSIS OF LUNAR MOTION: GEMINUS

The *Introductio astronomiae* by Geminus dates from the century or so prior to Ptolemy (*c*.100–*c*.170 AD; cf. Toomer 1978, 186–7).[11] It is, accordingly, one of a number of valuable witnesses to the character of the astronomical theory which Ptolemy inherited and transformed. Of particular interest is Geminus' account of lunar motion in chapter 18. For it is here that Geminus not only shows some awareness of Babylonian astronomy, he undertakes to state its *rationale*. Granted, his account is historically incorrect, as we now know (cf. Neugebauer 1975, 586–7). But to focus on this is to miss the fundamental point that this chapter is the earliest Greco-Latin text available today that tries to explain the structure and derivation of a common Babylonian arithmetical scheme for determining the daily progress of a planet, the Moon.[12] So, let us turn to his account and examine it in detail.

Chapter 18 (18.1–19) begins by introducing the *exeligmos*, which Geminus describes as the least period containing a whole number of days, months, and lunar returns.[13] By 'month' Geminus understands a synodic month, that is, the period from one coincidence of the Sun and Moon at the same degree of longitude on the ecliptic (conjunction) to the next, or from one full Moon to the next. As for 'lunar return', Geminus explains that the Moon is observed traversing the ecliptic unsmoothly (*anômalôs*) in the sense that the arcs of the ecliptic which it travels increase day by day from a minimum to a maximum and then decrease from this maximum to the minimum. Thus, a lunar return – nowadays called an anomalistic month – is the period from one least daily lunar motion or displacement (*kinêsis*) to the next.

After claiming that, according to observation,

$$\text{one synodic month is nearly } 29 \ \overline{2} \ \overline{33} \ (= 29;31,49,5) \text{ days,} \tag{1}$$

and

$$\text{one anomalistic month is nearly } 27 \ \overline{2} \ \overline{18} \ (= 27;33,20) \text{ days,}^{14} \tag{2}$$

Geminus remarks that the problem was to find the least period containing a whole number of days, months, and lunar returns, that is, to discover the *exeligmos*. This period, he says (*Introductio astronomiae* 18.3; cf. 18.6), has been observed to comprise

669 (synodic) months, or   (3)
19,756 days,

in which there are

717 lunar returns (anomalistic months), or
723 zodiacal revolutions plus 32° by the Moon.

According to Geminus, since these phenomena, 'which have been investigated from ancient times' are known, it remains to determine what he calls the Moon's daily unsmoothness (*anômalia*) in longitude. Specifically, he continues, this means finding out what is its minimum, its mean (*mesê*) and its maximum daily displacement, as well as the daily increment by which this displacement changes, taking into account the additional observational datum that

$$11° < m < 12° \text{ and } 15° < M < 16° \qquad (4)$$

where m is the minimum daily displacement and M the maximum daily displacement. From (3), Geminus reckons that the Moon's

$$\text{(periodic) mean daily displacement} = \frac{723 \cdot 360° + 32°}{19756} = 13;10,35°, \qquad (5)$$

a value which he suggests the Chaldaeans discovered in this way, and that

$$1 \text{ anomalistic month} = \frac{19756}{717} = 27;33,20 \text{ days.} \qquad (6)$$

My insertion of 'periodic' in parentheses in (5) is for the reader's benefit, because throughout this chapter Geminus writes of two different and independent sorts of mean motion or mean daily displacement without making any terminological distinction. Thus far, he has computed the Moon's mean motion by taking the *periodic* relation stated in (3), converting the number of sidereal cycles to degrees, and dividing the resultant number of degrees by the number of days.

As for the computation in (5) itself, it actually yields 13;10,34,51,55...° as the value for the periodic mean daily displacement of the Moon; but Geminus' 13;10,35 may be excused as a rounding (cf. Aujac 1975, 95 n1). More puzzling, however, is the computation of the length of the anomalistic month in (6), since

$$\frac{19756}{717} = 27;33,13,18, 19...\text{days,} \qquad (6a)$$

which differs somewhat from Geminus' 27;33,20 days. (The difference amounts to 1;20 days in one *exeligmos*.)

One possibility is that Geminus has wrongly taken it for granted that his computation of the length of the anomalistic month in (6) yields the value stated in (2), namely, $27\ \overline{2}\ \overline{18}$ (27;33,20). Another possibility is that Geminus is here 'telescoping two different (Babylonian) methods into one' (Neugebauer 1969, 185: cf. 162). For, if one follows Neugebauer (1975, 586) and focuses only on the parameters of Geminus' account, it seems that Geminus is drawing on two different Babylonian text-traditions, namely, on texts from Uruk presenting a scheme in which the lunar displacement is $13;10,35^{o/d}$ and the length of the anomalistic month is $27;33,20^d$, and on Babylonian Saros-texts, the Saros being a cycle in which the length of the anomalistic month is 27;33,13,18, 19... days. A third possibility, and perhaps the most charitable, is that Geminus actually understands the number of anomalistic months in the *exeligmos* to be derived from the length of the anomalistic month by computing

$$\frac{19756}{27;33,20} = 716;57,5... \approx 717 \text{ anomalistic months.} \tag{6b}$$

Next, Geminus divides the anomalistic month of 27;33,20 days into four equal subintervals such that

$$I(m, \mu) = I(\mu, M) = I(M, \mu) = I(\mu, m) = 6;53,20 \text{ days,} \tag{7}$$

where, for example, $I(m, \mu)$ is the interval from the day of minimum lunar displacement to the day of (arithmetic) mean lunar displacement (μ). Then, he argues, since the Moon's

$$(\text{arithmetic}) \text{ mean daily displacement} = \mu = \frac{M + m}{2} = 13;10,35° \tag{8}$$

(cf. (5)), it follows that $M + m = 26;21,10^{o/d}$. $\quad$ (9)

This argument introduces a second type of mean motion. For here, Geminus presents μ as what I propose to call an *arithmetic* mean daily displacement, that is, the simple average of two extreme values for daily lunar displacement in longitude.

Now, according to Geminus, the sum of the maximum and minimum daily displacements is known from observation to be only 26°; the fractional part, 0;21,10°, apparently escapes observation by instruments. This means, he says, that one has to assign 0;21,10° to M and m in a way that meets three conditions (see (4), (9)):

$$M + m = 26;21,10^{o/d}, m \not> 12^{o/d}, \text{ and } M \not> 16^{o/d}.[15] \tag{10}$$

To do this, Geminus first reiterates that in each of the four subintervals of the anomalistic month (see (7)), the daily difference (d) – which is either incremental or decremental – is the same; this means, he remarks, that one has to find d such that

$$d \cdot 6;53,20 = k$$
$$11° < (\mu - k) < 12° \quad 15° < (\mu + k) < 16°, \text{ and} \tag{11}$$
$$((\mu - k) - 11°) + ((\mu + k) - 15°) = 0;21,10°$$

(see (9)), where k is the Moon's total displacement in longitude in 1/4 anomalistic month.

The value for the daily difference, he flatly declares in conclusion, is $0;18°$. For,

if $\qquad d = 0;18^{o/d}$ and $\mu = 13;10,35^{o/d},$ (12)

then $\qquad k = 0;18° \cdot 6;53,20^d = 2;4°$

and $\qquad M = \mu + k = 13;10,35 + 2;4 = 15;14,35^{o/d}$

$\qquad\qquad m = \mu - k = 13;10,35 - 2;4 = 11;6,35^{o/d}.$

This declaration of the scheme's basic parameters is, however, a *non sequitur*. Geminus does not supply enough information to deduce the value for the daily difference in the Moon's longitudinal motion. In fact, what he gives suffices only to specify a range of values for d. To see this, consider the values for d when $m\ (= \mu - k)$ and $M\ (= \mu + k)$ take on the extreme values of the range of possible values indicated in (11). Suppose, for instance, that

$$m = \mu - k = 11^{o/d}.$$

From (8) and (11) it would follow that

$$d = \frac{13;10,35-11}{6;53,20} = 0;18,57\ldots^{o/d}.$$

Similarly, if

$$m = \mu - k = 12^{o/d},$$

then

$$d = \frac{13;10,35-12}{6;53,20} = 0;10,14\ldots^{o/d}.$$

Accordingly, given (4),

$$0;10,14,\ldots^{o/d} < d < 0;18,57\ldots^{o/d}. \qquad (13)$$

Likewise, if $\quad M = \mu + k = 15^{o/d}$

it would follow from (8) and (11) that

$$d = \frac{15-13;10,35}{6;53,20} = 0;15,52\ldots^{o/d};$$

and, if $\qquad M = \mu + k = 16^{o/d},$

that $\qquad d = \dfrac{16-13;10,35}{6;53,20} = 0;24,35\ldots^{o/d}$

Again, given (4),

$$0;15,52 \ldots^{o/d} < d < 0;24,35 \ldots^{o/d}. \tag{14}$$

Therefore, from (13) and (14), it follows that

$$0;15,52 \ldots^{o/d} < d < 0;18,57 \ldots^{o}/d. \tag{15}$$

Obviously, one could select a value for d by rounding the lower bound in (15) upwards to $0;16^{o/d}$ or by truncating the upper bound to $0;18^{o/d}$ (cf. Neugebauer 1975, 587). It is, of course, not possible to decide in light of the text alone whether Geminus' claim that d is $0;18^{o/d}$ was reached by truncation. Indeed, one should not discount the possibility that the value Geminus assigns d was given at the outset or entailed in the information he had.

Chapter 18 is the earliest text extant in Greek or Latin to present an account of an arithmetical scheme of a type now associated with the Babylonians. Since Geminus mentions the Chaldaeans, and since he ascribes this account to no one else, it would seem that he is in fact reconstructing what he takes to be the theory underlying information that ultimately came to him from Mesopotamia. So one may reasonably ask, what did he actually have? Presumably, he had access either to tabular data itself, to a set of procedures for entering the data, or to an account of how this data was organized data. Unfortunately, there is no way to determine which was the case.

Still, it is true that in chapter 18 Geminus describes the arithmetical principles and parameters underlying tables for daily lunar motion, of a sort we now have from Uruk (Neugebauer 1969, 161–2; 1975, 480–1). In modern terms, these ephemerides are said to be structured according to a linear zigzag function (see Figure 9.3) in which

$$
\begin{aligned}
M &= 15;14,35° & \mu &= 13;10,35° \\
m &= 11;6,35° & \text{amplitude } (\Delta) &= (M - m) = 4;8° \\
d &= 0;18°
\end{aligned}
\tag{16}
$$

and, thus,

$$\text{period } (P) = \frac{2D}{d} = 27;33,20 \text{ days (cf. (12); Neugebauer 1975, 374–5).} \tag{17}$$

At the same time, Geminus' account of the *exeligmos* derives from a Babylonian eclipse-cycle now called the Saros (cf. Neugebauer 1969, 141–2). According to the Saros-cycle,[16] in a period of 223 synodic months, as the New or Full Moon returns 242 times to the same position relative to the same node, the Moon completes 239 cycles of its unsmooth motion in longitude, and travels through the zodiac 241 times and 10;30° (see Britton and Walker 1996, 52–4). In other words,

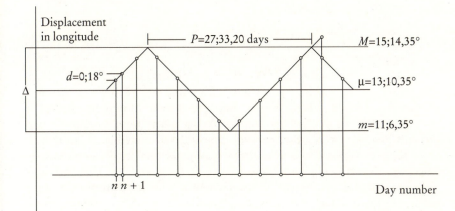

Figure 9.3 A linear zigzag function for lunar motion in longitude

223 synodic months = 239 anomalistic months = 242 draconitic months[17]

$$= 241 \text{ zodiacal revolutions by the Moon and } 10;30°[18]$$

$$= 6585;20 \text{ days.}$$

This cycle was certainly known in some form to Greco-Latin writers in Geminus' time. Pliny (*Historia naturalis* ii 56), for example, affirms that eclipses recur in cycles of 223 months.[19] The *Introductio astronomiae*, however, would seem to be the oldest surviving Greek or Latin text to introduce the *exeligmos*, an eclipse-cycle three times as long as the Saros-cycle, albeit without giving any indication of its purpose or its essential structure.[20] Geminus does not, for instance, connect the *exeligmos* with eclipses explicitly, and he does not mention the critical correlation of 669 (= 3 · 223) synodic months with 726 (= 3 · 242) draconitic months. Indeed, for a full statement of the *exeligmos* by a Greco-Latin writer, one must turn to Ptolemy, *Almagest* iv 2.[21]

Geminus is silent about the relation between his *exeligmos* and the Babylonian Saros. Now, it is possible that this is due to his ignorance of the fact that Saros is an eclipse-cycle and that the *exeligmos* is a longer version of the Saros. Yet, at the same time, it is also possible that he has suppressed this information in order to present the *exeligmos* as just another calendrical cycle of the sort he describes in *Introductio astronomiae* ch. 8. So, his silence permits no conclusions about the condition and form of the data that he reconstructs in chapter 18. Still, it is clear that, at the very least, he had Babylonian values for the Moon's mean daily displacement in longitude (13;35,10°), the daily difference in the Moon's displacement in longitude (0;18°), and the mean anomalistic month (27;33,20ᵈ), as well as the equation,

19756^{d} = 669 (synodic) months

= 717 anomalistic months

= 723 revolutions by the Moon + 32°.

Though Geminus is right that the Babylonians had long ago identified the *exeligmos*, his claim about how they did it is unwarranted and implausible. Indeed, when one considers Babylonian lunar ephemerides of the sort that lie behind his account (cf. Neugebauer 1955, nos 190–6), it is difficult not to conclude that he was either unfamiliar with them or that he failed to realize that their schematic character makes it virtually impossible to determine their observational basis.

Nevertheless, on its own terms, Geminus' account in chapter 18 of the *exeligmos* and of lunar motion in longitude is noteworthy, in the first place, because he seeks to derive the scheme by which the data in these ephemerides are organized from a few parameters. Granted, this derivation does not come with an epoch or starting-point for the anomalistic month: Geminus neither gives such a date nor indicates how to determine one. Thus, he does not recognize, or allow for, any interest there might be in actually determining the Moon's position in longitude at a given time. Next, Geminus' account is also notable because he identifies fundamental parameters as observational data. Admittedly, this is scarcely credible even on Geminus' own terms, if, as he reports (*Introductio astronomiae* 18.14), the best observation can do (with the aid of instruments) is to determine the sum of M and m to the nearest degree, a remark which is at odds with his claim that the values for the synodic and anomalistic months reported in (1) and (2) have been observed. And, as I have said, so far as history is concerned, though there is certainly some observational basis to the Babylonian Saros-texts and to the lunar tables from Uruk, there is no warrant for supposing that it consisted in observing the fundamental parameters of the arithmetical schemes structuring these tables. Still, Geminus' assumption that these basic parameters were observed is important as an indication of how he understands astronomy and its use of mathematics. For Geminus, apparently, his arithmetical scheme actually describes the Moon's unsmooth motion in longitude, and the accuracy of this description is guaranteed by the fact that it derives from arithmetical manipulation of observed parameters. Regrettably, he leaves unanswered pertinent questions about what counts as an observation, how observations are made, and so on.

Moreover, within the context of the *Introductio astronomiae*, Geminus' arithmetical account of lunar motion in longitude is also remarkable for two reasons. First is that it contrasts sharply with the rest of the treatise. Only in chapter 18 (and chapter 8, which concerns calendrical cycles) does Geminus introduce quantitative argument. Elsewhere, his remarks are qualitative and geometrical. Thus, in his account of the Sun's unsmooth motion in longitude (*Introductio astronomiae* 1.18–41), for example, though he supposes that it is only apparent because the Sun moves at a constant speed on a circle eccentric to the Earth, Geminus does not use his values for the lengths of the seasons (cf. 1.13–17) to specify the eccentricity of this circle and so on (cf. Neugebauer 1975, 581–4).

Second, and more striking, is that Geminus' account of lunar motion in chapter 18 is at odds with principles laid down earlier in the treatise. For, as he writes:

> It is posited for astronomy as a whole that the Sun, Moon, and five planets move at a constant speed [*isotachôs*], in a circle, and in a direction opposite to [the daily rotation of] the cosmos. For the Pythagoreans, who first came to investigations of this sort, posited that the motions of the Sun, Moon, and five planets were circular and smooth [*homalas*]. Regarding things that are divine and eternal they did not admit disorder of the sort that sometimes [these things] move more quickly, sometimes more slowly, and sometimes they stand still (which they call stations in the case of the five planets). One would not even admit this sort of unsmoothness [*anômalian*] of motion regarding a man who is ordered and fixed in his movements. For the needs of life are often causes of slowness and speed for men; but as for the imperishable nature of the celestial bodies, it is impossible that any cause of speed and slowness be introduced.
> For which reason they have proposed [the question] thus: How can one explain the phenomena by means of circular, smooth motions?
> Accordingly, we will give an explanation concerning the other celestial bodies elsewhere; but just now we will show concerning the Sun why, though it moves at a constant speed, it traverses equal arcs in unequal times.
>
> (*Introductio astronomiae* 1.19–22)

This means that the arithmetical scheme presented in chapter 18 does not describe the Moon's real motion in longitude; at best, it can represent the Moon's apparent motion – assuming, for the moment, with Geminus that the daily variations in the Moon's longitudinal displacement are indeed observable. But, if so, Geminus has yet to supply the account of the Moon's real motion in longitude that he has promised. Such an explanation would, of course, have to overcome a serious problem; namely, that there is no way, using resources presented in the treatise thus far, to construct a coherent argument that begins with the qualitative geometry of the Moon's real motions and concludes with the arithmetical detail of his scheme for the Moon's apparent motion. In short, by introducing the sort of arithmetical detail that he does in his account of the Moon's 'observed' variable motion in longitude, Geminus undermines his ostensible project of explaining this motion in terms of the smooth circular motion(s) that it supposedly makes in reality. In effect, chapter 18 exposes a problem at the heart of Greco-Latin astronomy of the time that becomes evident once it attempts to incorporate in its explanatory structure arithmetical procedures and results from Babylonian astronomy.

Geminus' mean daily displacement can only be an *apparent* lunar motion in longitude and not one the Moon *really* makes, if the mean in question is arithmetic. If the mean is periodic, however, the Moon's mean daily displacement can become a basis for specifying its true or real motion. But it would take Ptolemy to straighten out Geminus' conflated notion of mean motion and its relation to real and apparent planetary motion. Indeed, part of Ptolemy's genius lay in seeing that texts such as Geminus' *Introductio astronomiae* were typical of what was wrong with the astronomy of his time; that, in assimilating Babylonian astronomy, earlier and contemporary Greco-Latin writers betrayed a confused, inconsistent, and insufficiently sophisticated grasp of the proper role of arithmetic, geometry, and observation in astronomical argument (see Bowen 1994).

HEARING AND REASON IN HARMONIC SCIENCE: PTOLEMY[22]

In the opening chapter to his great astronomical work, the *Almagest*, Ptolemy presents himself as a philosopher. What this actually means to Ptolemy is a question that involves understanding not only his literary and scientific context but also how he appropriates and transforms this context in his own highly technical work.[23] Granted, there are scattered throughout Ptolemy's treatises tantalizing passages in which he talks of method and indicates a conceptual framework in which the sciences discussed somehow fit. There is even a treatise, the *De iudicandi facultate*, in which Ptolemy sets out an epistemology that is intended to explain and justify what one finds in his scientific works (cf. Long 1988, 193–6, 202–4). But research on these issues is still at a primitive stage primarily because scholars have yet to interpret this treatise and the related passages found in Ptolemy's other works in the light of the technical, scientific matters which give them their real meaning.[24] Yet the promise of such research is great, since Ptolemy is a pivotal figure in the history of western science.

Accordingly, in this final section, I will make a preliminary assault on the question of Ptolemy's philosophical views by examining the first two chapters of the first book of his *Harmonica* (Düring 1930, 3.1–6.13) with occasional reference to the *De iudicandi facultate*.[25] In these chapters, Ptolemy focuses on the question of criteria in the domain of music and on the related matter of the goal of the harmonic theorist, though he does mention astronomy and astronomers as well.

By Ptolemy's time, argument about the criteria of truth was prominent in intellectual circles: in fact, by then, the problem was to explain the contributions of reason and the senses to knowledge of external objects, and to determine what infallible means there are for distinguishing particular truths about these objects from falsehoods (cf. Long 1988, 180, 192). But Ptolemy recasts the problem. To begin, he decides to ignore the technical vocabulary current among philosophers of his time in favor of a simpler vocabulary that suffices to aid non-experts and to clarify reflection on the realities signified (cf. *De iudicandi facultate* 4.2–6.3). Accordingly, he proposes to use 'criterion' (*kritêrion*) to designate (a) the object about which one makes judgments, (b) the means through which and the means by which judgments about such objects are made, (c) the agent of judgment, (d) the goal of the judgments made, as well as the more usual sense, (e) the standard(s) by which the truth of judgments is assessed (cf. Blumenthal 1989, 257–8). Thus, given that in his view truth is a criterion *qua* goal of judgment (cf. *De iudicandi facultate* 2.1–2), Ptolemy represents the general problem as one of discovering the criterion of what there is (cf. 1.1). In the context of harmonic science (*harmonikê*), this becomes the problem of determining the criteria of what there is in the domain of music, that is, the criteria of *harmonia*, where *harmonia* is ultimately tunefulness or the way pitches should or do fit together properly.

Chapter 1 of the first book of the *Harmonica* opens with the assertion that

> Harmonic science is a capacity for apprehending intervals of high and low pitch in sounds,[26] while sound is a condition of air that is struck – the primary and most general feature of what is heard – and hearing and reason are criteria of tunefulness [*harmonia*] though not in the same way.
>
> (Düring 1930, 3.1–4)

I take this to mean that harmonic science is a branch of knowledge by which one is able to account systematically for intervals among pitches and to determine their *harmonia*. Obtaining and exercising this knowledge, however, is to draw on two faculties, hearing and reason, that serve as criteria in different ways:[27] as Ptolemy says, 'hearing is [a criterion] in relation to matter and experience (*pathos*); but reason [is a criterion] in relation to form and cause'.[28] To explain why hearing and reason are united in this way in developing or using harmonic science, Ptolemy first points out that

> even in general that which can discover what is similar [*to suneggus*] and admit precise detail [*to akribes*] from elsewhere is characteristic of the senses; while that which can admit from elsewhere what is similar and discover precise detail is characteristic of reason.
>
> (Düring 1930, 3.5–8)

That is, he continues,

> since matter is defined and delimited only by form whereas
> experiences [are defined and delimited] by the causes of motions, and
> since [matter and experience] are proper to sense-perception but [form
> and cause] are proper to reason, it follows fittingly that our sensory
> apprehensions are defined and delimited by our rational
> apprehensions, in that, at least in the case of things known through
> sense-perception,[29] the sensory apprehensions first submit their rather
> crudely [holoscheresteron] grasped distinctions to the rational
> apprehensions and are guided by them to distinctions that are
> precisely detailed and coherent.

(Düring 1930, 3.8–14)

The key to understanding Ptolemy's account thus far of the roles of
reason and the sense of hearing in harmonic science is the distinction between
to suneggus and *to akribes*. One possibility is that Ptolemy is concerned with
truth, that he means to affirm the approximate character of perception and
the accuracy of reason. Thus, as Barker translates the critical lines:

> ... it is in general characteristic of the senses to discover what is
> approximate and to adopt from elsewhere what is accurate, and of
> reason to adopt from elsewhere what is approximate, and to discover
> what is accurate.

(Barker 1991, 276)

The problem here, in the first place, is that Ptolemy does not actually say
that the senses characteristically discover *to suneggus* and so forth. What he
maintains instead is that some thing, which is capable of discovering *to
suneggus* and admitting *to akribes* from elsewhere, is characteristic of the
senses. Likewise for reason, he does not say that it characteristically discovers
to akribes and so forth, but that some thing, which is capable of discovering
to akribes and admitting *to suneggus* from elsewhere, is characteristic of it.
Now these items are, I submit, the *perceptum* and thought, respectively.
Second, it is important to realize that Ptolemy is not here directly concerned
with truth but with how information is transformed into knowledge. In
short, as his talk of matter and form suggests, the contrast he has in mind is
one between sensory information before and after it has been articulated
as knowledge, and not one between the approximate and the accurate.

Thus, I take Ptolemy's point to be that the scientific analysis of pitch
requires hearing to discern similarity and difference among pitches and
intervals, and reason to articulate this similarity or difference by quantifying
it numerically according to a theoretical system. This process of informing or
articulating and thereby appropriating what hearing discerns into a system
of knowledge involves introducing precision or numerical detail. Thus,
for Ptolemy, what hearing grasps is rather crude (*holoscheresteron*), either

306

because it is not numerically quantified at all or because it is quantified in a way not involving theory (as when someone hears an interval and simply says that it is a fifth, for instance). Thus, what is *holoscheresteron* is rather crude because it lacks the sort of precise detail it must have to be scientific knowledge, which does not mean of itself that it cannot be exact or accurate.[30]

Reason and the senses are criteria of science in the ways they are because, as Ptolemy says,

> it happens that reason is simple, unmixed, and, thus, complete in itself, fixed, and always the same in relation to the same things; but that sense-perception is always involved with matter which is confused and in flux. Consequently, because of matter's instability, neither the sense-perception of all people nor even that of the same people is ever observed to be the same in relation to objects similarly disposed, but needs the further instruction of reason as a kind of cane.
>
> (During 1930, 3.14–20; cf. *De iudicandi facultate* 8.3–5, 9.6).

In other words, assuming the principle that cognitive faculties are like their objects, reason alone is fit for articulating consistently what is grasped by the senses: the senses themselves cannot do this.

In saying this, Ptolemy has raised the related issues of disagreement among listeners and error. If hearing does not on every occasion discern the same distinction in what is heard though the circumstances are such that it should, it is important to discover whether reason may ever rely on hearing and in what way, if one is to account fully for the roles of reason and hearing in harmonic science. The question is, then: does hearing ever discern similarities and differences among pitches correctly and, if so, whose hearing is it?

Ptolemy answers by pointing out first that hearing may be brought to recognize its errors by reason.[31] So, under some circumstances at least, it is possible for hearing to discern things accurately. Then, Ptolemy affirms the stronger thesis that sometimes what hearing presents to reason does not need any correction at all. Let us consider these claims in turn.

Ptolemy maintains that reason can bring hearing to a knowledge of errors in its apprehensions, by way of an analogy:

> So, just as the circle drawn by the eye alone often seems to be accurate until the circle made by reason brings [the eye] to the recognition of one that is in reality accurate [*akribôs echein*], thus when some definite interval between sounds is taken by hearing alone, it will initially seem sometimes neither to fall short nor to exceed what is appropriate, but is often exposed as not being so when the interval selected according to proper ratio is compared, since hearing recognizes by the juxtaposition the more accurate [one] as something genuine, as it were, beside that counterfeit.
>
> (Düring 1930, 3.20–4.7)

Evidently, hearing is corrigible if reason, on the strength of theory, produces in sound what is correct (i.e., an interval defined by the proper ratio) so that hearing may apprehend it and thereby come to discern error.[32] Obviously, reason will be obliged to be equip itself with an instrument that it can employ in a way consistent with theory in order to produce the correct sounds – a point Ptolemy makes explicit later. In any case, Ptolemy clearly holds that both reason and hearing can detect errors in the apprehensions of hearing. But, though this entails that the apprehensions of hearing are sometimes accurate, it does not yet follow that reason may rely on hearing for information about differences among sounds.

The analogy illustrating how reason can bring the eye and hearing to discern error when none was recognized previously also suggests that the senses are better as judges than as producers of *percepta*. But to establish that hearing may apprehend distinctions correctly unaided by reason, Ptolemy must evaluate the capacity of the senses to make distinctions on their own.

He begins by affirming that it is in general easier to judge something than it is to do it. His elaboration of this premiss makes it clear that hearing will have better results in recognizing that an interval or melody is out of tune than when it guides the production of the interval or melody by means of some instrument such as the voice or *aulos*. Indeed, he explains,

> this sort of deficiency of our sense-perceptions does not miss the truth by much in the case of [our] recognizing whether there is a simple difference between them [*sc.* our sense-perceptions] nor, again, in the case of [our] observing the excesses of things that differ, at least when [the excesses] are taken in greater parts of the things to which they belong.[33]

(Düring 1930, 4.10–13)

The locution here may strike the modern reader as odd. The deficiency in question is, I think, the deficiency of the senses in apprehending what is in reality accurate, which he has just described. Now, as I understand it, the claim that this deficiency 'does not miss the truth by much' is a figure of speech: Ptolemy actually means that, when the senses discern a mere difference or report the amount of this difference (providing that the amount is suitably large), they do not under these circumstances miss the truth at all.[34] In other words, I maintain that, for Ptolemy, the apprehensions of hearing are in fact correct and accurate, when hearing attends to the mere occurrence of an interval between sounds or when it reports the amount of this interval (if the amount is large enough).

It is important that the amounts of the differences between the sounds be large in comparison to the sounds, that is, for example, that the difference between two intervals be large in comparison to the two intervals. As Ptolemy says of the senses in general, if the amounts of the differences they apprehend are a relatively small part of the things exhibiting them, the senses may not discern any difference at all; yet, when such apprehensions are iterated, the error or difference accumulates and eventually becomes perceptible.

The upshot is that Ptolemy assigns the senses a well-circumscribed reliability: sensory apprehensions of sameness and difference are for the most part deemed unreliable. Only in apprehending the fact of difference or the amount of this difference (when the amount is suitably large) do the senses such as hearing provide a reliable and fitting empirical basis for science (cf. *De iudicandi facultate* 12.4).[35]

The question of whose hearing it is still remains, and Ptolemy approaches it by considering the class of those instances when hearing by nature goes astray. After all, what hearing apprehends or reports can become scientific only when integrated by reason in an explanatory system;[36] and this means that reason will often have to deal with error in what hearing reports. As he says,

> just as for the eyes there is a need for some rational criterion through
> appropriate instruments – for example, for the ruler in relation to
> straightness and for the pair of compasses in relation to the circle and
> the measurements of parts – in the same way as well there must be for
> the ears, which are with the eyes especially servants of the theoretical
> or reason bearing part of the soul, some procedure [*ephodos*] from
> reason for things which [the ears] do not by nature judge accurately, a
> procedure against which they will not testify but will agree that it is
> correct.
>
> (Düring 1930, 5.3–10)

Ptolemy begins chapter 2 by identifying the instrument for correcting aural apprehensions as the harmonic canon or ruler (*kanôn*), adding that the name is taken from common usage and from its straightening (*kanonizein*) things in the senses that fall short regarding truth (cf. Düring 1930, 5.11–13). But what is this rational criterion of harmonic science, the third criterion that Ptolemy has designated as such thus far in the opening chapters of the *Harmonica*?

According to Ptolemy,

> it should be the goal of the harmonic theorist to preserve in every way
> the rational hypotheses [*hupotheseis*][37] of the canon as never
> conflicting in any way with the senses in the judgment of most people,
> just as it should be the goal of the astronomer to preserve the
> hypotheses of the celestial motions as in agreement with their
> observed periods, hypotheses that while they have themselves been
> taken from obvious and rather crude [*holoscheresteron*] phenomena,
> find things in detail accurately through reason so far as it is possible.
> For in all things it is characteristic of the theorist or scientist to display
> the works of nature as crafted with a certain reason and fixed cause,
> and [to display] nothing as produced [by nature] without a purpose or

by chance especially in its so very beautiful constructions, which sorts of things the [constructions] of the more rational senses, seeing and hearing, are.[38]

(Düring 1930, 5.13–24)

This third criterion, to which reason may appeal in distinguishing truth from falsehood in musical sound and on which it may rely, turns out, in fact, to be the consensus of the majority about what is heard when the canon is properly set up according to theory and actually struck.[39] For this criterion entails that, on such occasions, the standard of accuracy in determining not only the fact of differences among sounds but also, under certain circumstances, how great these differences are, is what most people hear. In sum, the hearing that stands as the reliable counterpart of, and standard for, reason in harmonic science is that of the majority.[40]

In the remainder of chapter 2, Ptolemy explains how rival schools fail to pursue this basic goal of the harmonic theorist (cf. Bowen and Bowen 1997, 111–12). But rather than pursue this, by way of conclusion I will now briefly address the question 'What does the harmonic theorist actually know?'

In the first place, the harmonic theorist understands *harmonia*, that is, the organization of differences in pitch. To say more than this, however, it is necessary to discover just what it is that the majority reports about such differences. In particular, one should at least ask whether the consensus of the majority concerns a subjective experience or the objects underlying this experience. Now, Ptolemy's answer to this question comes in the next chapters (*Harmonica* i 3–4), which discuss (a) the causes of high and low pitch in sound (*psophos*), and (b) musical notes (*phthoggoi*) and their differences. But this very distinction between sounds and musical notes suggests another feature of *harmonia* that one must not neglect, namely, that *harmonia* is fundamentally an aesthetic phenomenon, that the differences in pitch have an intrinsically aesthetic character. That is, implicit in Ptolemy's account of the third criterion is the view that *harmonia* is ultimately defined by the musical sensibilities or tastes of a community – no matter whether one assumes (as I do) that the phrase *kata tên tôn pleistôn hupolêpsin* means 'in the opinion of most people' or that it means 'in the opinion of most experts':[41] in either case, the harmonic theorist is to appeal to, and to rely on, a shared sense of differences in pitch and their melodic propriety.

It would seem, then, that in answer to the question 'What does the harmonic theorist know?', one might point out that harmonic science articulates systematically by means of number a communal sense of musical propriety. But, if so, does this science change over time? There is, after all, a tension in Ptolemy's account between reason and what most people hear, and I suspect that it is essential to his understanding of harmonic science itself: such tension is certainly built into his third criterion to the extent that agreement or consent is an issue.

One way to cast the problem is to ask, does hearing ever correct or bear witness against theory? Obviously, it must as the theoretical account of the music characteristic of a culture becomes more scientific and accurate, a possibility implicit in Ptolemy's criticism of contemporary and earlier theorists at the close of chapter 2, for instance, and elsewhere. But does theory ever have to adapt to changes in what most people hear when the canon is set up according to theory and struck? This is a question to bring to a careful reading of the *Harmonica*. For if Ptolemy denies that musical sensibility changes over time, harmonic science has a perfection it can reach in articulating the sense of musical propriety shared by most people. But, if he allows that it does change, then harmonic science must too and so it cannot have a final form. In this case, then, what most people hear when the canon is set up according to theory and then struck will serve not only to confirm theory and to correct practice, it will on occasion serve also to confirm practice and to correct theory.[42] And if observation may take on such a role in harmonic science, may it do the same in astronomy?[43]

CONCLUSION

It is perhaps appropriate to finish with a question, since a series of case-studies will hardly generate global results. To philosophers it is often given that one may grasp the universal in the particular; but rarely is this granted to historians of ancient science. Thus, for now, I content myself with the more mundane hope that the preceding studies of particulars in detail will at least raise questions leading to other particulars in a fruitful way.

NOTES

1 I take the exact sciences to include arithmetic, geometry and all those sciences involving arithmetic and geometry in a significant way (for example, astronomy, astrology, harmonics, mechanics, and optics). Isolating these sciences as a class is not a uniform characteristic of Greco-Latin thought. Still, it is a useful starting-point, particularly if one considers the various exact sciences throughout their histories and inquires of each whether it was in fact (always) viewed as scientific by the ancients, and to what extent the role of mathematics affected this decision.

2 When writing of Greek and Latin science, philosophy, and so on, I refer only to the respective languages in which the relevant texts are written.

3 See, for example, the critical studies by von Staden (1992) and Pingree (1992).

4 Of these, Lloyd 1984 is a useful and instructive contribution.

5 Following Dijksterhuis 1987, 147–9. According to Dijksterhuis, though this lemma bears an obvious formal resemblance to Euclid, *Elementa* v def. 4 (which posits that, if a and b are magnitudes and $a < b$, there is a whole number n such that $n \cdot a > b$), it is essential to Archimedes' indirect calculations of magnitudes

by means of infinite processes (cf. Dijksterhuis 1987, 130–3), because, in so far as it entails that the difference between two magnitudes is a magnitude of the same kind, it excludes the possibility of infinitesimals such as one would admit if the difference between two lines, say, were a point.

6 In the present context, the lines will be circular arcs on a sphere. Such arcs may be equal or similar: they are similar if they lie on parallel circles and are cut off by the same great circles (cf. Aujac 1979, 41 nn2–3).

7 The use of the names of the zodiacal constellations to designate the twelve equal arcs of the ecliptic in the *Phaenomena* would seem to place it after the fourth century and perhaps in the third (cf. Bowen and Goldstein 1991, 246–8). But note, however, that according to Berggren and Thomas (1992: cf. Berggren 1991), the aim of this treatise is to account qualitatively for the annual variations in the length of daytime, a concern characteristic of the second and first centuries BC. (Hypsicles' *Anaphoricus*, a treatise presenting a Babylonian arithmetical scheme for determining the length of daytime throughout the year, is commonly thought to belong to the second century BC.)

8 It is difficult to determine the relative dates of Autolycus and Euclid. The argument from evidence internal to their treatises (cf. Heath 1921, i 348–53) that Autolycus is prior to Euclid is, as Neugebauer (1975, 750) points out, 'singularly naive': there is no reason to dismiss the possibility that Autolycus and Euclid were contemporary.

9 See Bowen and Goldstein 1991, 246 n30.

10 See Bowen and Goldstein 1991, 246 n29.

11 Geminus' dates are uncertain. Scholars have traditionally supposed that he was active in the first century BC; but Neugebauer (1975, 579–81) has argued for a date in the first half of the first century AD.

12 So far as I am aware, P. Hibeh 27 (third century BC) is the earliest Greek text which organizes information according to a (modified) Babylonian scheme of the sort which Geminus attempts to explain: cf. *MUL.APIN* 1.3.49–50, 2.2.43–2.3.15; Bowen 1993, 140–1.

13 There are periods shorter than the one Geminus actually identifies as the *exeligmos*: see pp. 300–1 below, on the Saros.

14 Geminus represents numbers in two ways, either as whole numbers plus a sequence of unit-fractions (in decreasing order of size) or as sexagesimals. I will follow convention by writing unit-fractions by means of numerals with bars over them: thus, $\bar{n}$ stands for $1/n$ and $\bar{3}$ for $2/3$ (cf. Neugebauer 1934, 111). Moreover, I shall use the semicolon to separate sexagesimal units and the sixtieths, and commas to separate sexagesimal places to the right of the semicolon. See *Introductio astronomiae* 18.8, for an explanation – Manitius views this as a marginal gloss that has been moved into the text – of Geminus' nomenclature for sexagesimal fractions of a degree: first sixtieths are units of $\overline{60}$; second sixtieths, units of $\overline{60} \cdot \overline{60}$; and so on.

15 Since (4) rules out $m = 12^{o/d}$ and $M = 16^{o/d}$, it follows that $m < 12^{o/d}$ and $M < 16^{o/d}$.

16 For texts and analysis, see Aaboe, Britton, *et al.* 1991.

17 The draconitic month is the period of the Moon's return to the same node or point where its orbit crosses the plane of the ecliptic in the same direction. Determining the length of the draconitic month is useful in understanding eclipses, since they occur only when the Moon is at or near the nodes.

18 That is, 241 returns to the same star or sidereal months plus 10;30°. The Sun completes 18 zodiacal revolutions (sidereal years) and 10;30° in the same period.

19 Not all the manuscripts of Pliny, *Historia naturalis* ii 56 have 223 as the number of synodic months: cf. Mayhoff 1906, 144; Neugebauer 1969, 142.

20 In Geminus' version of the *exeligmos* – as in Ptolemy's (*Almagest* iv 2) – the Moon makes 723 zodiacal revolutions and then travels 32° farther, whereas, if one triples the Babylonian Saros-cycle, the Moon circles the zodiac 723 times but then travels only 31;30° farther.

21 Ptolemy's accounts of the shorter cycle (the Babylonian Saros) and of the *exeligmos* are consistent: he posits that in one Saros the Moon makes 241 zodiacal revolutions and 10;40°, and that the Sun makes 18 such revolutions and 10;40°.

22 I take the opportunity in what follows to revise and develop the analysis given in Bowen and Bowen 1997, 104–12.

23 See Grasshoff 1990, 198–216 and Taub 1993 for two recent attempts to discover Ptolemy's philosophical views.

24 See Bowen 1994 on Taub 1993: cf. Lloyd 1994.

25 Barker's translation (1989, 276–9) of *Harmonica* i 1–2 is helpful, albeit misleading in critical matters of philosophical and technical detail.

26 Cf. Gersh 1992, 149. See Bowen and Bowen 1997, 137 n22 for criticism of Solomon's analysis (1990, 71–2) of Ptolemy's definition of harmonic science.

27 Hearing and reason are both instrumental, though the mode of their instrumentality differs, as Ptolemy's use of different instrumental constructions at *De iudicandi facultate* 1.5, 2.2–4 indicates: hearing, like any other sense, is 'the means through which' one makes judgments and reason is 'the means by which' one does this. Note that one of the basic meanings of '*kritêrion*' is 'instrument': cf. *De iudicandi facultate* 2.3; Friedlein 1867, 352.5–6.

28 In this analogy, matter is, I presume, to be taken in relation to form and *pathos* in relation to explanation. Barker renders *pathos* by 'modification'; but it makes little sense to compare hearing to a modification (that is, to a change or enmattered form) in the present context. So, I propose instead to render *pathos* by 'experience': cf. Ptolemy, *De iudicandi facultate* 8.3, 10.1–3; Barker 1989, 280 n20.

29 Cf. Düring 1930 3.13: Barker (1989, 276) has 'at least in the case of things that can be detected through sensation'. See Ptolemy, *De iudicandi facultate* 10.5 which allows that there are things known by reason without the aid of the senses.

30 This is consistent with Ptolemy's usage in the *Almagest* (cf., for example, Heiberg 1898–1907, i 203.12–22, 270.1–9; ii 3.1–5, 18.1–5, 209.5–7). In most cases, the astronomical observations criticized by Ptolemy involve measurement; so number is already present in what the eyes report to reason: the problem is that the means by which these measurements were made is not known. One should compare Geminus' use of *akribes* and *holoscheresteron* at, for instance, Manitius 1898, 100.16–20, 114.13–18, 116.20–3, 118.10–12, and 206.17–21.

31 At this point, when Ptolemy turns to the problem of error, the meaning of *akribes* changes from 'detailed' to 'accurate' or 'true'.

32 The force of this analogy is not, as Barker (1989, 277 n9) supposes, that hearing alone can detect its unreliability (cf. *De iudicandi facultate* 8.3–5, 10.1–3). Reason, for example, may well avail itself of visual information to determine (again on the basis of theory) that the sound produced is incorrect. In *De iudicandi facultate*

10.4–5, Ptolemy writes that on certain occasions reason may choose to correct sense-perception through the means of sense-perceptions. Thus, if a sense is affected in a way inappropriate to the object sensed, reason may determine the error either through similar, unaffected or uncorrupted sense-perceptions when the cause of error involves the sense-perceptions, or through dissimilar sense-perceptions of the same object when the cause does not involve them but something external.

33 On Solomon's version (1990, 73–4) of these lines, see Bowen and Bowen 1997, 140 n33 and Barker 1989, 277.

34 Barker (1991, 118) does not recognize a rhetorical figure here, though the fact that hearing does sometimes disclose the truth is assumed in the next lines, when Ptolemy considers how imperceptible error in sense-perception may accumulate and eventually become perceptible. Cf., for example, Düring 1930, 23.19–24.8.

35 Long's claim (1988, 193) that, for Ptolemy, 'sense-perception is limited to the immediate experiences it undergoes and it cannot pass judgment on any external objects as such', though it neglects *kai epi poson apallagentôn* at *De iudicandi facultate* 8.5, does draw attention to an important puzzle. According to 8.4, sense-perception judges only its experiences (*pathê*) and not the underlying objects. The same is said at 10.1–3 (cf. 11.1), except Ptolemy here remarks that sense-perception sometimes reports falsely about the underlying objects perceived. This latter claim makes sense, however, only if the senses may sometimes report truly about these objects as well.

　　In any case, the question raised by Ptolemy's argument thus far in the *Harmonica* becomes, 'when hearing reports veridically about the occurrence of sounds and certain of their differences, does it simply report truly its experiences or does it somehow disclose true information about the physical state of affairs producing these experiences?' At issue is Ptolemy's idea of what sound and, in particular, musical sound, is (see p. 310).

36 In *De iudicandi facultate* 2.4–5, Ptolemy distinguishes *phantasia*, which is the impression and transmission to the intellect of information reached by contact through the sense-organs, and *ennoia* (conception), which is the possession and retention of these transmissions in memory. The conceptions are what may become scientific if integrated into theory (cf. 10.2–6).

37 In the *Almagest*, Ptolemy uses *hupotheseis* in reference to his planetary models: cf. Toomer 1984, 23–4.

38 Where I have 'in its so very beautiful constructions, which sorts of things the [constructions] of the more rational senses, hearing and vision, are', Barker (1989, 279) proposes 'the kinds [*sc.* constructions] that belong to the more rational of the senses, sight and hearing'. It is not clear just what these constructions belonging to sight and hearing are supposed to be. They are most likely not the objects of these senses: Ptolemy's meaning here is that the theoretician is duty-bound to maintain the reliability of sight and hearing, not the intelligibility of their objects. Cf. Düring 1934, 23.

39 Cf. Long 1988, 189. The claim made by Blumenthal, Long, *et al.* (1989, 217) that Ptolemy nowhere uses '*kritêrion*' to signify a standard is apparently mistaken.

　　If one recalls the various meanings of 'criterion' that Ptolemy lists at *De iudicandi facultate* 2.1–2, the argument of *Harmonica* i 1–2 would seem to indicate that: *harmonia* is a criterion *qua* object of judgment; hearing and reason are criteria *qua* means through which and means by which, respectively; the harmonic theorist is a criterion *qua* agent of judgment; what most people hear when the canon is set up according to theory and struck is a criterion *qua* standard; and preserving truth, that is, the concordance of the hypotheses of harmonic science with this standard, is a criterion *qua* goal.

40 Thus Ptolemy counters scepticism that harmonic science does in fact constitute knowledge, because of the acknowledged variations in hearing from person to person, and so on (cf. Düring 1930, 3.17–21).

41 There is, after all, no evidence in Ptolemy's preceding remarks that he limits this criterion to experts or *cognoscenti*.

42 Until such matters are settled, I hesitate to follow Long (1988, 194) in inferring that the *De iudicandi facultate* presents science as 'a stable and incontrovertible state of the intellect, consisting in self-evident and expert discrimination', especially since there is, so far as I can tell, nothing in this treatise that favors this view and excludes the role of third criterion I have just indicated.

43 On progress in astronomy, see *Almagest* i 1 with Toomer 1984, 37 n11. At its most general, the question is, How does Ptolemy understand the *Almagest* and its place in the history of astronomy?

BIBLIOGRAPHY

PRIMARY LITERATURE

Ancient documents

In this subsection, translations are in English unless specified otherwise.

Archimedes. *De lineis spiralibus*. See Heiberg 1910–23, ii (with Latin trans.); Mugler 1970–72, ii (with French trans.).

—— *De sphaera et cylindro*. See Heiberg 1910–23, i (with Latin trans.).

—— *Quadratura parabolae*. See Heiberg 1910–23, ii (with Latin trans.).

Aristotle. *Physica*. See Ross 1955.

Astronomical Cuneiform Texts. See Neugebauer 1955.

Autolycus. *De sphaera quae movetur*. See Mogenet 1950, Aujac 1979 (with French trans.).

Boethius. *De institutione musica*. See Friedlein 1867, 175–371 (with Latin trans.).

Euclid. *Elementa*. See Heiberg and Stamatis 1969–77. Trans. by Heath 1956.

—— *Sectio canonis*. See Menge 1916.

Geminus. *Introductio astronomiae*. See Manitius 1898 (with German trans.), Aujac 1975 (with French trans.).

Hypsicles. *Anaphoricus*. See de Falco and Krause 1966.

MUL.APIN. See Hunger and Pingree 1989 (with trans.).

P. Hibeh 27. See Grenfell and Hunt 1906, 138–57 (with trans.).

Plato. *Meno*. See Burnet 1900–7, iii; Bluck 1964. Trans. by Grube 1967.

Pliny. *Historia naturalis* ii. See Mayhoff 1906.

Proclus. *In primum Euclidis elementorum librum*. See Friedlein 1873.

Ptolemy. *Almagest*. See Heiberg 1898–1907, i–ii. Trans. by Toomer 1984.
—— *De iudicandi facultate et animi principatu*. See Blumenthal, Long, *et al.* 1989 (with trans.).
—— *Harmonica*. See Düring 1930. Trans. by Barker 1989, 270–391; Düring 1934 (German). For a Latin version of *Harmonica* i 1–2, see Boethius, *De institutione musica* v 2 with Bowen and Bowen 1997.
Saros Texts. See Aaboe, Britton, *et al.* 1991 (with trans.).

Modern editions and translations

Aaboe, A., Britton, J. P., Henderson, J. A., Neugebauer, O., and Sachs, A. J. (1991) *Saros Cycle Dates and Related Babylonian Astronomical Texts*, Transactions of the American Philosophical Society 81.6, Philadelphia: American Philosophical Society.

Aujac, G. (1975) ed. and trans. *Géminos, Introduction aux phénomènes*, Paris: Les Belles Lettres.

—— (1979) ed. and trans. *Autolycos de Pitane: La sphère en mouvement, Levers et couchers, testimonia*, Paris: Les Belles Lettres.

Barker, A. D. (1989) trans. *Greek Musical Writings: II. Harmonic and Acoustic Theory*, Cambridge/New York: Cambridge University Press.

Bluck, R. S. (1964) ed. *Plato's Meno Edited with an Introduction, Commentary and an Appendix*, Cambridge: Cambridge University Press.

Blumenthal, H., Long, A. A., *et al.* (1989) ed. and trans. 'On the Kriterion and Hegemonikon: Claudius Ptolemaeus'. See Huby and Neal 1989, 179–230.

Burnet, J. (1900–7) ed. *Platonis opera*, 5 vols, Oxford Classical Texts, Oxford: Clarendon Press.

de Falco, V. and Krause, M. K. (1966) ed. and trans. *Hypsikles, Die Aufgangszeiten der Gestirne mit einer Einführung von O. Neugebauer*, Abhandlungen der Akademie der Wissenschaften in Göttingen, philologisch-historische Klasse, dritte Folge, Nr. 62. Göttingen: Vandenhoeck and Ruprecht.

Düring, I. (1930) ed. *Die Harmonielehre des Klaudios Ptolemaios*, Göteborg Högskolas Årsskrift 36, Göteborg: Elanders Boktryckeri Aktiebolag. (Reprinted, New York and London: Garland 1980).

—— (1934) *Ptolemaios und Porphyrios über die Musik*, Göteborg Högskolas Årsskrift 40, Göteborg: Elanders Boktryckeri Aktiebolag. (Reprinted, New York and London: Garland 1980).

Friedlein, G. (1867) ed. and trans. *Anicii Manlii Torquati Severini Boetii de institutione arithmetica libri duo, de institutione musica libri quinque*, Leipzig: Teubner.

—— (1873) ed. *Procli Diadochi in primum Euclidis elementorum librum commentarii*, Leipzig: Teubner.

Grenfell, B. P. and Hunt, A. S. (1906) ed. and trans. *The Hibeh Papyri*, Part 1, London: Egypt Exploration Fund.

Grube, G. M. A. (1967) trans. *Plato's Meno*, Indianapolis: Hackett Publishing.

Heath, T. L. (1956) trans. *Euclid's Elements*, 3 vols. New York: Dover.

Heiberg, J. L. (1898–1907) ed. and trans. *Claudii Ptolemaei opera quae exstant omnia*, 3 vols, Leipzig: Teubner.

——— (1910–23) ed. and trans. *Archimedis opera omnia cum commentariis Eutocii*, 4 vols, Leipzig: Teubner.

Heiberg, J. L. and Stamatis, E. S. (1969–77) ed. *Euclides, Elementa*, 5 vols. Leipzig: Teubner.

Hunger, H. and Pingree, D. (1989) ed. and trans. *MUL.APIN: An Astronomical Compendium in Cuneiform*, Archiv für Orientforschung, Beiheft 24, Horn, Austria: Ferdinand Berger & Söhne.

Manitius, K. (1898) ed. and trans. *Geminus: Elementa astronomiae*. Leipzig: Teubner.

Mayhoff, C. (1906) ed. *C. Plinii Secundi naturalis historia* i, Leipzig: Teubner.

Menge, H. (1916) ed. *Euclidis phaenomena et scripta musica*, Leipzig: Teubner.

Mogenet, J. (1950) ed. *Autolycus de Pitane: Histoire du texte, suivie de l'édition critique des traités, De la sphère en mouvement et Des levers et couchers*, Louvain: Publications Universitaires de Louvain.

Mugler, C. (1970–72) ed. and trans. *Archimède*, 3 vols, Paris: Les Belles Lettres.

Neugebauer, O. (1955) ed. *Astronomical Cuneiform Texts: Babylonian Ephemerides of the Seleucid Period for the Motion of the Sun, the Moon, and the Planets*, London: Lund Humphries. Repr. Sources in the History of Mathematics and Physical Sciences 5, New York/Heidelberg/Berlin: Springer-Verlag.

Ross, D. (1955) *Aristotle's Physics: A Revised Text with Introduction and Commentary*, Oxford: Clarendon Press.

Toomer, G. J. (1984) trans. *Ptolemy's Almagest*, New York/Berlin: Springer-Verlag.

❧ SECONDARY LITERATURE ❧

Books

Aaboe, A. (1964) *Episodes from the Early History of Mathematics*, New Mathematical Library 13, Washington, DC: Mathematical Association of America.

Barbera, A. (1990) ed. *Music Theory and its Sources: Antiquity and the Middle Ages*, Notre Dame, IN: University of Notre Dame Press.

Bowen, A. C. (1991) ed. *Science and Philosophy in Classical Greece*, Institute for Research in Classical Philosophy and Science: Sources and Studies in the History and Philosophy of Classical Science 2, New York/London: Garland Publishing.

Dijksterhuis, E. J. (1987) *Archimedes*, trans. by C. Dikshoorn with a new bibliographic essay by W. R. Knorr, Princeton: Princeton University Press.

Dillon, J. M. and Long, A. A. (1988) eds. *The Question of 'Eclecticism': Studies in Later Greek Philosophy*, Berkeley/Los Angeles: University of California Press.

Gersh, S. and Kannengieser, C. (1992) eds. *Platonism in Late Antiquity*, Christianity and Judaism in Antiquity 8, Notre Dame, IN: University of Notre Dame Press.

Gillispie, C. C. (1970–80) ed. *Dictionary of Scientific Biography*, New York: Scribners.

Grasshoff, G. (1990) *The History of Ptolemy's Star Catalogue*, Studies in the History of Mathematics and Physical Sciences 14, New York: Springer-Verlag.

Heath, T. L. (1921) *A History of Greek Mathematics*, 2 vols, Oxford: Clarendon Press.

Huby, P. and Neal, G. (1989) eds. *The Criterion of Truth: Essays in Honour of George Kerferd*, Liverpool: Liverpool University Press.

Maniates, M. R. (1997) ed. *Music Discourse from Classical to Early Modern Times: Editing and Translating Texts*, Conference on Editorial Problems 26, Toronto/Buffalo/London: University of Toronto Press.

Neugebauer, O. (1934) *Vorlesungen über Geschichte der antiken mathematischen Wissenschaften. I: Vorgriechische Mathematik*, Berlin: Springer-Verlag.

—— (1969) *The Exact Sciences in Antiquity*, 2nd edn, New York: Dover.

—— (1975) *A History of Ancient Mathematical Astronomy*, 3 vols, Studies in the History of Mathematics and Physical Sciences 1, Berlin/ Heidelberg/New York: Springer-Verlag.

Taub, L. C. (1993) *Ptolemy's Universe: The Natural Philosophical and Ethical Foundations of Ptolemy's Astronomy*, Chicago/La Salle: Open Court.

Walbank, F. W. *et al.* (1984) eds. *The Cambridge Ancient History. VII.1: The Hellenistic World*, 2nd edn, Cambridge/London/New York: Cambridge University Press.

Wallace, R. W. and MacLachlan, B. (1991) eds. *Harmonia mundi: Musica e filosofia nell' antichità*, Biblioteca di quaderni urbinati di cultura classica 5, Rome: Edizione dell' Ateneo.

Walker, C. B. F. (1996) *Astronomy before the Telescope*, London/New York: British Museum Press/St Martin's Press.

Papers and reviews

Barker, A. D. (1991) 'Reason and Perception in Ptolemy's *Harmonics*'. See Wallace and MacLachlan 1991, 104–30.

Berggren, J. L. (1991) 'The Relation of Greek Sphaerics to Early Greek Astronomy'. See Bowen 1991, 227–48.

—— and Thomas, R. S. D. (1992) 'Mathematical Astronomy in the Fourth Century BC as Found in Euclid's *Phaenomena*', *Physis* 39: 7–33.

Blumenthal, H. (1989) 'Plotinus and Proclus on the Criterion of Truth'. See Huby and Neal 1989, 257–80.

Bowen, A. C. (1993) review of Hunger and Pingree 1989. *Ancient Philosophy* 13: 139–42.

—— (1994) review of Taub 1993. *Isis* 85: 140–1.

—— and Bowen, W. R. (1997) 'The Translator as Interpreter: Euclid's *Sectio canonis* and Ptolemy's *Harmonica* in the Latin Tradition'. See Maniates 1997, 97–148.

—— and Goldstein, B. R. (1991) 'Hipparchus' Treatment of Early Greek Astronomy: The Case of Eudoxus and the Length of Daytime', *Proceedings of the American Philosophical Society* 135: 233–54.

Britton, J. P. and Walker, C. B. F. (1996) 'Astronomy and Astrology in Mesopotamia'. See Walker 1996, 42–67.

Gersh, S. (1992) 'Porphyry's Commentary on the "Harmonics" of Ptolemy and Neoplatonic Musical Theory'. See Gersh and Kannengieser 1992, 141–55.

Lloyd, G. E. R. (1984) 'Hellenistic Science'. See Walbank *et al.* 1984, 321–52, 591–8.

—— (1994) review of Taub 1993. *Journal for the History of Astronomy* 25: 62–3.

Long, A. A. (1988) 'Ptolemy *On the Criterion*: An Epistemology for the Practicing Scientist'. See Dillon and Long 1988, 176–207.

Pingree, D. (1992) 'Hellenophilia *versus* the History of Science', *Isis* 83: 554–63.

Solomon, J. (1990) 'A Preliminary Analysis of the Organization of Ptolemy's *Harmonics*'. See Barbera 1990, 68–84.

Toomer, G. J. (1978) 'Ptolemy'. See Gillispie 1970–80, xi 186–206.

von Staden, H. (1992) 'Affinities and Elisions: Helen and Hellenocentrism', *Isis* 83: 578–95.

CHAPTER 10

Hellenistic biological sciences

R. J. Hankinson

The five centuries that separate Aristotle's death in 322 BC from Galen's ascendancy in Rome in the latter part of the second century AD were fertile ones for the biological sciences, in particular medicine. Nor is the period solely of interest to historians of science – for the methodological debates characteristic of the life sciences of the time shadow, and in some cases foreshadow, those which raged between the contemporary Sceptical and Dogmatic schools. If our knowledge of the medicine of the period is necessarily circumscribed by the fragmentary nature of almost all of our sources, and if the project of reconstructing the science is consequently all the more difficult, the enterprise is none the less a rich, fascinating, and exciting one.

EMPIRICISM AND AETIOLOGY

When Aristotle died, scientific theories, their nature and status, had already been the subject of intense debate for at least a century. The more theoretical of the Hippocratic doctors, such as the authors of *On Regimen* 1.2 (who analysed human physiology in terms of fire and water) and *Nature of Man* (who introduced the theory of the four humours: blood, phlegm, black and yellow bile), took issue with their empirically-minded colleagues, notably the writer of *On Ancient Medicine*, who eschewed such arcana, championing instead the cause of explanations grounded in experience. That debate revolved around the issue of what science properly investigates, and what sorts of explanation it should produce. Should it deal in grand theoretical structures, postulating hidden entities in terms of which the course of ordinary observable events is to be determined (and, for the practising physician, altered)? Or must it rather simply concentrate on establishing a secure body of data concerning which phenomena are observed to go along with which others? What, crucially, is the analysis and role of the notion of cause in science?

These questions were posed with unprecedented sharpness in Aristotle's theoretical works on science, most particularly in *Posterior Analytics* and *Parts of Animals* 1. Aristotle stressed that science must start from an empirical base (*Parts of Animals* 1.1, 639b3 ff., 640a14 ff.; although precisely how it should do so is obscure: *Posterior Analytics* 2.19); but it must also aspire to final exhibition in the form of a complete and rigorous deductive structure, whose theorems can be seen to flow from its fundamental axioms and definitions. Science's explanatory force resides in that dependency: a fact is explained when it is shown to follow as a deductive consequence of some causally prior and more basic facts about the domain in question (*Posterior Analytics* 1.2; cf. 1 13, 2 16–17). Aristotelian science seeks to make patent the total structure of reality, and is thus strongly realist in conception. The axioms are not merely arbitrary postulates: they are the bedrock foundational facts upon which everything else depends. Yet such realisms are, of course, notoriously prone to epistemological attack; and Aristotelian realism was no exception. It is one thing to assert that science ought to have some such form; quite another to explain how we can know when we have actually arrived at it. Such difficulties form the core of the empiricist, and later the sceptical, onslaughts upon the scientific pretensions of those they called the Dogmatists.

DIOCLES OF CARYSTUS

Let us begin, however, with Diocles of Carystus:

> Those who think that one should state a cause in every case do not appear to understand first that it is not always necessary to do so from a practical point of view, and second that many things which exist are somehow by their nature akin to principles, so that they cannot be given a causal account. Furthermore, they sometimes err in assuming what is unknown, disputed, and implausible, thinking that they have adequately given the cause. You should disregard people who aetiologize in this manner, and who think that one should state causes for everything; you should rather rely upon things which have been excogitated over a long period on the basis of experience [*empeiria*]; and you should seek a cause for contingent things when that is likely to make what you say about them more understandable and more believable.
>
> (Diocles, in Galen, *On the Powers of Foodstuffs* VI, 455–6 Kühn [10.10])[1]

Diocles was a doctor. His dates are controversial, but he is very likely a younger contemporary of Aristotle: and that text has unmistakable Aristotelian echoes, so much so that Jaeger [10.55] was moved to make Diocles a more or less orthodox Aristotelian. However, this is clearly an exaggeration: although Diocles agrees with Aristotle that not everything requires causal explanation, his reasons are not Aristotle's.

Aristotle took genuine first principles to be indemonstrable – that is what it *is* to be a first principle (*Posterior Analytics* 1 2; *Metaphysics* 4 3). Diocles however says only that some things are akin to first principles – he does not say that they *are*. Moreover, anticipating a familiar Sceptical trope (the Fourth Mode of Agrippa: Sextus Empiricus, *Outlines of Pyrrhonism* (hereafter *PH*) 1 168, 173–4), he notes that theorists frequently merely assume, without argument or justification, some hypothetical starting-point for their systems in spite of its being a matter of controversy. The physician should offer explanatory accounts only where they are pedagogically helpful, basing his actual practice firmly on *empeiria*. Indeed, Diocles does not even insist that such accounts be true – they function simply as useful heuristic and persuasive tools.

Diocles was concerned to combat what he took to be an overly simplified view of the powers of particular foodstuffs:

> those who think that things which possess similar juices [? humours] or smells or degrees of heat or anything else of this sort have identical powers [*dunameis*] are mistaken, for one may point to many cases in which dissimilar things arise from things which are similar in these ways.
>
> (*ibid.*, Fragment 112 Wellmann)

One rather needs to realize that 'their nature as a whole is the cause' of their particular powers. Diocles does not, then, reject theory or the offering of *aitiologiai*, causal accounts; and he is happy to recognize the existence of powers or faculties (quite what this involves will be of paramount importance in what follows). But he opposes what he takes to be the too naive and typological view adopted by some of his opponents (in this case probably Pleistarchus), a position which is at least compatible with the description of him (by Celsus: *On Medicine* Proem 8) as a Hippocratic.

 HEROPHILUS

This tentative attitude towards causal explanation was shared by the great Alexandrian physician, anatomist, and physiological theorist Herophilus of Chalcedon (fl. *c.* 260 BC). Herophilus was perhaps the first Greek doctor to practise systematic anatomical researches upon human beings based upon dissection (the evidence is collected in von Staden [10.15 – hereafter VS] ch.

VI, T 60–129; see also 139–53), although he was not the first systematic dissector. That honour, like so many others, belongs to Aristotle: and Herophilus was perhaps indebted to Aristotle in other respects as well.

A methodological injunction of his is preserved, in slightly different forms, in two sources:

> let the *phainomena* be said [*legesthai*: perhaps 'be stated'] first [*prôta*: perhaps 'to be primary'], even if they are not first.
> (Herophilus T 50a VS; cf. T 50b VS: the bracketed words point to the interpretative problems).[2]

This text has been compared (VS p.118) to the methodological proem to *Parts of Animals* (1. 1, 639b3–11), where Aristotle asks whether the natural scientist should ape the mathematical astronomers by first studying the *phainomena* and only then going on to state their causes. At 640a14–15 he answers his own question affirmatively; and our passage apparently echoes this (particularly if '*legesthai*' is translated as 'be stated'). If Herophilus really intends to recall Aristotle, then it is significant that his dictum makes no mention of causes or causal explanation (although as it stands it leaves room for such explanations). Rather (on what is, on balance, the most plausible interpretation) Herophilus urges us to treat the phenomena as being of primary importance, even if they may not (in the genuine metaphysical order of things) be really basic. Whatever else may be true, we need to start from the apparent facts, and only then (if at all) proceed to discover their underlying causes. This has an obvious Dioclean ring; and it appears too that Herophilus is offering a more circumspect version of Anaxagoras's celebrated dictum: 'the *phainomena* are a glimpse of the non-evident (*ta adêla*)' (Fragment 21a).

This is empiricism with a small 'e': science must start from the *phainomena*: these are what need, in the famous Greek slogan, to be saved (cf. Lloyd [10.57]), and which science, ideally, tries to explain.

Other texts attest to Herophilus's reliance on experience, *empeiria*:

> We find, however, that this Herophilus concedes no small importance to experience, nay indeed, to speak the truth, he makes experience all-important
>
> (T 52 VS)

and he is said (T 53 VS) to have given an account of pulse-rhythm based on observation and experience, rather than abstract rational theorizing.

On the other hand, he did not reject theory altogether; indeed in the immediately preceding passage (T 147 VS), Galen says that he 'surpassed the great majority of the ancients, not only in breadth of knowledge but in intellect', citing as an example his 'rational account' (*logos*) of the arterial pulse. In fact, the historian Polybius went so far as to stigmatize the 'Herophileans' (although not directly Herophilus himself) for relying purely on theory, and hence being about as much practical use as a pilot who navigated from a book (T 56 VS). And while that charge is clearly unjustified if levelled against Herophilus himself, none the less it is clear that he was perfectly prepared to countenance theoretical speculation of the type that was to become anathema to the medical Empiricists (see below, p. 33), whose stance Polybius represents.

What, then, was the relation for Herophilus between theory and experience? This question is peculiarly difficult to answer, and not only because of the fragmentary nature of our evidence; for that evidence, although incomplete, appears to ascribe to Herophilus two quite distinct and on the face of it incompatible attitudes. Let us approach them, however, by way of a brief treatment of Herophilus's anatomical achievements.

Only three actual citations from his *On Anatomy* survive (60–2 VS); but a wealth of testimonia attests to his comprehensiveness and to his influence in the field of general human anatomy. He gave a far more complete account of the structure of the brain than any of his predecessors (T 75–9 VS; cf. [10.15] 155–9), distinguishing its main ventricles, discovering the 'calamus scriptorius', and bequeathing to his modern successors the name and description of the 'torcular Herophili'.[3] His dissections of the eye were of a calibre and detail quite unparalleled by any of his forebears (T 82–9 VS): he was the first to distinguish the four membranes of the eye, as well as isolating the optic nerve. Indeed he is usually (and justifiably) credited with the discovery of the functions of the nerves in general (Solmsen [10.69]; it is disputed whether he or Erasistratus was the first to distinguish between motor and sensory nerves: T 81 VS).

Herophilus applied himself, then, to dissective anatomy with unprecedented vigour and attention to detail. However, he

> does not think that anatomical descriptions of the type which say that
> 'this part has its natural origin in that' can produce any general
> preconception relevant to theoretical knowledge . . . ; for the faculties
> [*dunameis*] which control us are discovered from other *phainomena*,
> and not simply from inspection of the part itself.

(T 57 VS)

It's no good basing your account of the functioning of the body simply on its apparent structure, presumably because (and this was to be a Galenic commonplace: see Furley and Wilkie [10.5] Introduction IV; Hankinson [10.45]) such structures, considered simply as inert constructions, tell you nothing about how they actually work. Thus we need to examine 'other *phainomena*', in this case presumably the observable effects of cutting or ligating the connections between them in a living animal (again as Galen was to do: see below, p. 349).

At this point we may introduce another controversy. Herophilus and his rough contemporary Erasistratus were both associated in an ancient tradition with the deliberate vivisection of live human beings. The most detailed (although by no means the only) evidence comes from Celsus:

> So it is necessary [sc. according to Rationalist doctors] to dissect the bodies of the dead in order to examine their viscera and intestines. And they say that Herophilus and Erasistratus did this in the best way by far, by cutting open criminals provided by kings from prison, and inspecting, while they were still alive, those parts which nature had previously hidden as to their position, colour, shape, size, arrangement, hardness, softness, smoothness, connection, and the projections and concavities of each, and whether anything is inserted into something else and whether anything receives into itself a part from some other.
>
> (T 63a VS: cf. T 63b–7)

This story has often been questioned, although not with good cause; and there is no reason not to accept it. Celsus does not say that Herophilus (and Erasistratus) vivisected in order more directly to investigate functions as such – but it is a highly plausible conjecture, since only by such experimentation on live creatures could the difference between motor and sensory nerves be discovered.

And equally obviously it is only in living creatures that faculties (*dunameis*) in this sense can be detected. T 57 VS cautions against too straightforward and unreflective a set of mechanical assumptions regarding the causal relations that hold between the parts of the body: merely observing that one is inserted into another is not enough to determine whether the two are causally related, and if so how and in what direction. Such inferences can only be made on the basis of the observation of the structures at work. Herophilus apparently posited four faculties of living creatures (131 VS), one of which was the vital faculty (T 164 VS) – but our evidence for these is exiguous in the extreme.

The 'vital faculty' may be that which is transmitted through the coats of the arteries (in Herophilus's view) to produce the pulse (which was of supreme importance in Herophilean diagnostics; he invented a water-clock for more accurate time-keeping: T 182 VS; cf. VS pp. 282–4); and if he did indeed distinguish motor and sensory nerves, that would provide a physiological basis for two more faculties (with thought as the fourth?) – but this is conjectural.

At all events, Herophilus seems to have started with a conceptual analysis of what it is that animals (perhaps particularly humans) standardly do – and then to have proceeded, on the basis of anatomical investigation, to try and isolate the media via which these faculties were transmitted. But as to precisely what the faculties consisted in, he perhaps maintained a prudent reserve.

This brings us to the issue of Herophilean scepticism. On the basis of the following reports in Galen's *On Antecedent Causes* (hereafter *CP*),[4]

Kudlien [10.56] saw Herophilus as an important figure in the history of Greek scepticism:

> Some people say that nothing exists as a cause of anything, while others, like the Empiricists, dispute whether or not there is a cause, and still others, like Herophilus, accept it on a hypothetical basis, and others again – whose leader he [sc. Erasistratus][5] was – rejected, among the causes, the antecedent . . . causes as not very plausible.
>
> (T 58 VS)

> What, then, does Herophilus say? 'Whether or not there is a cause, is by nature undiscoverable; but in my opinion[6] I believe I am chilled, warmed, and filled with food and drink.'
>
> (Herophilus T 59a VS)

Presumably, to accept causes on a hypothetical basis[7] is to accord them a merely provisional status: we may make causal ascriptions on the basis of the phenomena, but the phenomena do entail them – and hence we can never know for certain that our causal hypotheses are correct (this is reminiscent of, but more sophisticated than, Diocles' position). Thus Herophilus anticipates the second mode of Aenesidemus against the aetiologists (Sextus, *PH* 1 180–1). This picture derives modest support from T 59a, provided that we understand ablatives of agency (for example 'by the wind', 'by the sun') with 'chilled' and 'heated' to square them with the repletion example. Herophilus then does not doubt that he is being (phenomenally speaking) chilled, heated, or filled up – but he cannot be certain that the sun (or whatever) is responsible for it (hence the cause is 'undiscoverable by nature': although it is worth noting that Celsus reports that he held that all diseases have their causes in the humours: *On Medicine* Proem 14). That coherent and moderately sophisticated attitude in regard to causal ascriptions represents, I think, an improvement on Aristotle's theory of science.

Thus the sceptical Herophilus seems to be a chimaera. Yet elsewhere in the same passage, Galen accuses Herophilus of lacking the courage of his convictions:

> Having expressed doubt about every cause with many strong arguments, he is himself subsequently detected using them, by saying 'it seems this way to everyone'.
>
> (T 59a VS)

This suggests that Herophilus offered an antithetical set of considerations, both for and against causes, in a manner reminiscent of the Pyrrhonists (cf. Sextus, *PH* 3 13–30), where the majority opinion that causes exist is weighed against contrary abstract argument. Indeed immediately afterwards Galen presents as Herophilean three general arguments against the very conceivability of causes which were later to find a natural home in

Pyrrhonism (they are rehearsed by Sextus: *Adversus Mathematicos* (*M*) 9 210–36). The arguments are similar in form, so one example will suffice:

(1) If there are causes, then either (a) bodies cause bodies, or
(b) incorporeals cause incorporeals, or (c) bodies cause incorporeals,
or (d) incorporeals cause bodies;

but

(2) neither (a), nor (b), nor (c), nor (d);

so

(3) there are no causes.

That argument is sceptical both in form and content; and from it 'he drew the inference that nothing is the cause of anything'.

It is not clear what to make of these passages, but they are not obviously compatible with the earlier causal hypotheticalism – indeed, they seem clearly in conflict with it. It is one thing to have epistemological doubts about our access to the causal facts of the matter, quite another to impugn their very metaphysical coherence. I confess I can see no very satisfactory solution to this problem; but perhaps if we stress the fact that it is by nature (or perhaps 'in their nature') that causes are undiscoverable, we might attempt one along the following lines. The difficult, perhaps impossible, metaphysics of causation undermines any purely rationalistic attempt to create an aetiology: hence we can never give a satisfactory account of what causal powers and causal transmission really are. On the other hand, empirical experience and investigation provide us with clear examples of causal correlation – and we need no grand metaphysical theory in order to investigate and establish them. It is perhaps no accident that Herophilus talks neutrally of the 'powers' (*dunameis*) of the body: these are uncontroversial, empirically determined place-holders for whatever arcane, hidden facts in fact underlie them.

ERASISTRATUS

Herophilus's great contemporary (and accomplice in the charge of human vivisection), Erasistratus, probably also lived and worked for some at least of his life in Alexandria.[8] He too was an innovative theorist in anatomy (the differentiation between motor and sensory nerves is also attributed to him: Fragment 39 Garofalo [10.6] – hereafter G), and in physiology, where he introduced the theory of *triplokia*, the triple plaiting of three basic types of vessel (nerve, artery and vein), which he held to be the fundamental elements of all bodily tissue (Fragments 86–90 G. See further G, pp. 32–3).

Our main source for Erasistratus is Galen; and he is generally hostile to him (although he is much sharper with Erasistratus's latter-day followers), pouring scorn on his rejection of 'natural faculties' of attraction, repulsion, and excretion (with which Galen chose to account for the functions of the bodily organs) in favour of the principle of *horror vacui* as the agent of internal movements of material in bodies (Fragments 93–6 G).[9] But behind Galen's polemic we may discern an Erasistratean attempt to reduce the physical mechanisms needed to explain metabolism and general physiological functioning to the bare minimum required to explain those processes – and if Galen is sometimes justified in his particular criticisms, we may none the less applaud Erasistratus's reductionist zeal. Indeed we may best proceed by following the outlines of Galen's rebuttal of the Erasistratean position.

Erasistratus is lambasted by Galen for his anti-teleological belief that some organs (including the spleen and the omentum) fulfilled no function at all (*On the Natural Faculties* II 33, 91, 132, 134; Fragment 81 G). Yet Erasistratus was not opposed to teleological explanation as such – in fact, he considered it to be the proper business of the philosopher (Fragment 114 G; Fragment 83 G; cf. Fragments 77–8 G; and G pp. 45–6); his attitude seems rather to be closer to that of Aristotle,[10] for whom some structures of the body are not susceptible of direct teleological explanation. But for all that, and in spite of the relative exiguousness (and partiality) of the sources, an Erasistratus committed as far as possible to the explanation of biological functioning on mechanistic principles emerges with reasonable clarity. Erasistratus further rejected the humoural theory of human constitution (Fragment 92 G), for which once more Galen takes him to task. But even Galen is not always hostile to him, admiring his diagnostic acumen;[11] and Erasistratus was held in the highest regard in antiquity.

From our point of view, Erasistratus's most significant doctrines concern causes. First of all (from a practical perspective) he held that all fevers are caused by inflammations, which are in turn caused by transfusion (*paremptôsis*) of blood from the veins (where it naturally belongs) to the arteries, where its presence is, for Erasistratus, pathological (Fragment 109 G).

The most important Erasistratean claim, however, concerns the status of what came to be known as antecedent causes (*aitia prokatarktika*),[12] the external factors responsible (in some medical theories, Galen's included) for triggering the already-existing disposition of the patient into illness. The bulk of Galen's *On Antecedent Causes* is devoted to refuting Erasistratus's causal 'sophisms', by which he seeks to remove *aitia prokatarktika* from the causal lists. Antecedent causes of disease include, standardly, such items as overheating, refrigeration, overwork, over-indulgence in food, drink, or sex, and the like. Such factors may not affect all equally – but none the less (so at least Galen thinks) they are pathogenically relevant. This is precisely what Erasistratus denies. His greatest mistake in pathology, according to Galen's view, was to deny the importance of external heating and chilling upon the human body, which are (Galen holds) of great pathogenic moment; yet Erasistratus holds them responsible only for surface alterations in animals' conditions, having no effect on their internal dispositions (Fragment 75 G).

But Erasistratus's rejection of such antecedent causes is theoretically motivated. He contends that heat and cold cannot be the causes of illness, since they are not invariably followed by it, and do not persist at the time of the illness:[13]

> In this way sophists find reasons for their arguments that attempt to show that, even if on some occasion these things [i.e. antecedent heat, cold, etc.] harm weak bodies, not even then can they properly be called causes. For if indeed they do act because of their own internal nature, and this action derives from themselves, then they must be seen to have an effect at all times.
>
> (Galen, *CP* i 9–10)

Later, Galen quotes from Erasistratus directly:

> Most people, both now and in the past, have sought the causes of fevers, trying to ascertain and learn from the sick whether the illness has its origin in being chilled or exhausted or repletion, or some other cause of this kind; but this kind of inquiry into into the causes of diseases yields results neither true nor useful. For if cold were a cause of fever, then those who have been chilled the more should suffer the greater fever. But this is not what happens: rather there are some who have faced extreme danger from freezing, and who when rescued have remained unaffected by fever. . . . [And] many people who experience far worse exhaustion and repletion than that which coincides with fever in some others yet escape the illness.
>
> (Erasistratus, *CP* viii 102–3; cf. xi 141–4; xiii 166–8)

Similar arguments were, unsurprisingly, deployed by the Sceptics (Sextus, *M* 9 242–3). This argument has the effect of radically restricting the class of items allowable as causes: in effect, it stipulates that all causes must be *aitia sunektika*, containing causes. The notion of containing causes originated with the Stoic idea that every existent object required some internal tensile force to account for its persistence, that force being labelled its *aition sunektikon*. But the concept was soon redeployed by the doctors to cover not merely the persistence of objects, but the necessary and sufficient conditions of events and processes. Sextus defines *aitia sunektika* as 'those in the presence of which the effect is present, and with the removal of which it is removed, and with the lessening of which it is lessened' (Sextus, *PH* 3 15).

Thus, containing causes are strongly functionally-correlated with their effects (Sextus's example is of the relation between a noose and strangulation: the tighter the noose, the greater the strangulation).

In this way Erasistratus seeks to deny the status of cause to anything which does not meet these stringent requirements. It is however another matter whether he need be committed by this thesis concerning the proper application of the term 'cause' to the view that no item, unless constantly conjoined with some other, can have any causal relevance to it. Galen sometimes tries to pin this on Erasistratus – but it is by no means apparent that Erasistratus need accept this consequence. In fact Erasistratus allows that over-eating and exhaustion are implicated in the triggering of disease, although he apparently refused to grant them the title of causes.[14]

The crucial component in the Erasistratean pathology of fever was *plêthôra*. *Plêthôra* is vascular congestion caused by an influx of undigested food into the veins (Fragment 161 G). If the digestive system cannot cope with the excess of nutriment, and if evacuation does not take place by other means, the undigested food enters the veins, compressing the blood and forcing it through the valves (*anastomôseis*) between the veins and arteries (which normally contain only *pneuma*), causing inflammation and fever (Fragment 198 G). However, *plêthôra* can be treated before disease itself sets in; but once *paremptôsis* takes place, disease is unavoidable. Even so, these inflammations can be reduced by encouraging the blood to flow back through the *anastomôseis* into the veins.

Galen is concerned to emphasize the fact that external antecedent causes are causally relevant to that patient's subsequent condition. Erasistratus asks why, of a thousand people who attend the theatre on a hot afternoon (and hence who are exposed to the same external conditions) only four get overheated, and of these only one develops a full-blown fever: and infers that antecedent heating cannot be a cause of illness. Galen replies that it is not the *sole* cause (which fact accounts for the differential response to it; some people are more constitutionally susceptible than others). But even so, how can something no longer present be the cause of anything? The overheating occurs, *ex hypothesi*, several hours before the actual onset of the illness.

Erasistratus thus adopts two distinct theses:

(1) nothing can be a cause unless it is actually producing its effect;

and

(2) nothing can be a cause unless it invariably produces its effect.

Effectively, Galen rejects both of them, rightly: but Erasistratus's position is not negligible, and it requires a certain sophistication in causal analysis to rebut it.

Erasistratus held that x was a genuine cause of y only if x at least initiated a sequence which was such that, other things being equal, y was bound to result. Thus he treats *paremptôsis* as being responsible for the fever,

even though the disease can still be alleviated by the appropriate inter-
ventions, since if left to run its own course, disease inevitably results.
Plêthôra, on the other hand, cannot be a genuine (i.e. proximate) cause,
although Erasistratus allows its causal relevance. However, he clearly rejects
the notion that anything prior to the *plêthôra* can be a cause, on the basis of
thesis (2).

THE EMPIRICISTS

Thus the theoretical contributions of the Alexandrians bring into centre-
stage the preoccupation with the analysis and classification (as well as the
epistemic justification) of the causal relation that was to characterize later
Greek philosophy and science. Central to this debate were the doctors of
the medical sect known as the Empiricists. Empiricism had a long history.
The founding of the school is usually attributed to Philinus (fl. 250 BC) and
Serapion (fl. 225 BC), although, following the ancient penchant for creating
long and prestigious intellectual pedigrees, some Empiricists traced their
ancestry back to the fifth-century Sicilian doctor Acro.

Serapion was connected with Herophilus; and it is plausible to see
Empiricism proper as an outgrowth of the epistemological and explanatory
caution which we have seen evinced by Herophilus. But the Empiricists go a
good deal further. Their method simply consists in the observation and
recording of phenomenal concurrences of events: therapies (both appropriate
and inappropriate) are indicated by the past course of events. If I see that
pomegranates are efficacious in one case of diarrhoea, I shall be moved to try
them on another – and if that turns out well I shall be well on the way to
forming what the Empiricists called an experience, an *empeiria*. Crucial
to this is personal observation, *autopsia*, although the initial discoveries are
held to be the result of luck:

> The Empiricists say that the art comes about as follows: one has
> observed many affections in people. Of these some are spontaneous,
> both in the sick and the healthy (for example nose-bleeds, sweating, or
> diarrhoea, or something similar which brings harm or benefit), even
> though one cannot see what it was that produced the effect. In other
> cases, the cause is obvious, although they too occur as a result of
> chance, not choice. Thus it just so happened that someone fell, or was
> hit or wounded in some other way, and that there followed a flow of
> blood, or that somebody who was sick satisfied his appetites by
> drinking cold water or wine, or whatever, each of which had either a
> harmful or beneficial effect. The first kind of beneficial or harmful
> effect they call 'natural', the second 'chance'. But in both cases they
> called the first observation of such an event an accident, choosing this

331

name because one happens upon these things not by design. The accidental type of experience, then, is roughly like this. The extemporary kind, however, is characterized by the fact that we deliberately come to try something, led either by dreams or by something else to form an opinion as to what should be done. But there is further a third kind of experience, the imitative . . . where something which has proved to be beneficial . . . is tried out again for the same disease. This sort of experience has contributed the most to their art. For when they have imitated, not just two or three but very many times, what has turned out beneficial in the past, and when they discover that it has, for the most part, the same effect in the case of the same diseases, they call such a memory a theorem, and think it to be credible and to form part of the art. But when they had collected many such theorems, the whole collection formed the art of medicine. . . . Such collections came to be called *autopsia* by them . . . [which] consists in a certain kind of memory of what one has often perceived to happen in the same way. But they also called the same thing *empeiria*. History, however, they called the report of an *autopsia*.

(Galen, *On Sects* (*SI*) 2, 2–3 Helmreich: trans. after Frede)[15]

That sketch of the Empirical method prompts several questions which will be taken up in the next section. But its general outline is clear enough. What the Empiricists are reacting against is the tendency of the theoretically-minded physicians (whom they compendiously lump together as the 'Dogmatists' or 'Rationalists') to explain both disease and therapy in terms of hidden internal conditions of the body which they must infer on the basis of the *phainomena*, the appearances. For the Empiricists all that there is are the appearances, and the theorems that are built up as a result of them.

Thus the debate between Rationalists (among whom are standardly enrolled Diocles, Herophilus, Erasistratus, and Asclepiades) and Empiricists turns, among other things, on the possibility of our having epistemic access to a purely theoretical domain; and in turn it forms part of the central Hellenistic debate among the philosophers about the nature and acceptability of certain types of sign-inference. Here is not the place to do more than sketch that debate (reproduced most fully in Sextus: *PH* 2 97–133; *M* 8 141–299); but crucial to it is the classification of different ways in which something may be non-evident (*adêlon*):

Of matters, then, according to the Dogmatists, some are
(a) pre-evident, some (b) non-evident; and of the non-evident, some are (i) totally non-evident, some (ii) temporarily non-evident, and some (iii) naturally non-evident. Pre-evident are those which come to our knowledge from themselves, e.g. that it is day; totally non-evident are those which are not of a nature to fall under our knowledge, such as that the number of the stars is even; temporarily non-evident are

those which, although they possess an evident nature, are now not evident to us because of certain external circumstances, as the city of Athens is to me now; while the naturally non-evident are those which do not possess a nature such as to be evident to us, such as the theoretical pores.

(Sextus, *PH* 2 97–8)

Things in category (a) are unproblematic – likewise no one claims to be able to have any sort of access to the items under (b i). Moreover, all alike agree that the contents of (b ii) are accessible, by way of 'commemorative signs': I see smoke on the horizon, although I cannot now see any fire; but knowing that there's no smoke without fire, I infer that there must be a fire there, temporarily hidden from me. What distinguishes the Sceptic or the Empiricist from the Dogmatist is their attitudes towards category (biii).

The Dogmatists hold that we can legitimately infer purely theoretical entities: in the paradigm case of such an inference (which will be of importance in the next section), the fact of sweating is an indicative sign (as they called them) of the existence of invisible pores in the skin. It is the latter type of reasoning (or *analogismos*, as they call it) that the Empiricists reject. The important difference between it and the smoke–fire case is that, in the latter, we may simply perceptually verify the inference; but in the case of (biii), no direct perceptual confirmation can, by definition, be forthcoming. In a manner significantly reminiscent of the philosophical Sceptics, Empiricists chide Dogmatists for the rashness of their theorizing, for the way it outruns its evidential base. The only things they will allow are the Humean concatenations of evident events that make up the general theorems to be used in commemorative sign-inference – and even that is, in principle, defeasible.

The Dogmatists treat the indicative sign as being 'an antecedent proposition in a sound conditional, which is revelatory of the consequent' (Sextus, *PH* 2 101). The Empiricists, like the Sceptics, urge that there can be no such uniquely revelatory conditionals: there is in principle always more than one way to account for the evident facts (cf. The Eight Modes of Aenesidemus against the Aetiologists: Sextus, *PH* 1 180–5); and in any case the Dogmatists are unable to agree among themselves as to what their 'signs' are signs of:

In the case of fever patients, flushing and prominence of the vessels and a moist skin and increased temperature and quickening of the pulse and all the other signs . . . do not appear alike to all; but to Herophilus, for example, they seem to be definite signs of good blood, to Erasistratus of the transference of the blood from the veins to the arteries,[16] and to Asclepiades of the lodgement of theoretical particles in the theoretical interstices.

(Sextus, *M* 8 219–20; cf. 189)

And, again in obvious tandem with Pyrrhonian scepticism, the Empiricists point to the endemic and irresoluble disputes among the Dogmatists as proof that their 'signs' are nothing of the sort (*SI* 5, 11–12 Helmreich).

Moreover, there is no need for such theorizing: everything necessary to medical science can be discovered on the basis of experience. Thus the Empiricist accumulates collections of instances in which certain things follow upon certain others. This collection is an *empeiria*; and if it is big enough, it will constitute a general theorem. It is worth noting that, for the Empiricists, the relations that hold between the items in such theorems do not have to be universal and affirmative. They outlined a five-fold typology of connection and disjunction according to whether things were seen to go together always, for the most part, half the time, rarely, or never: all of these are valuable in determining which therapies are, and which are not, appropriate.

None the less, some Empiricists did allow another way in which therapies could be obtained, their 'transition to the similar' (*hê tou homoiou metabasis*). Transition is a form of analogical reasoning, to be used in cases of

> diseases which had not been encountered previously, or which were known, but for which there was no ready supply of medicines proven by experience. Hence they turned transition to the similar into a means for finding remedies. By its means they transfer the same remedy from one ailment to another and from one affected place to another, and they move from a previously discovered remedy to one similar to it.
>
> (Galen, *SI* 2, 3–4 Helmreich)

Similar ailments may yield to similar medicines; and what works on one part of the body may well work on another similar part. Transition, then,

> amounts to a method of discovery, but not yet to discovery itself, prior to testing. But as soon as you put what is expected to the test, it is already as credible (if the test is positive) as if it had been observed many times.
>
> (ibid. 4)

Thus transition does not itself generate theorems; but it suggests likely testable candidates for them – and the Empiricists have a high degree of confidence in successfully tested transitional solutions.

Even so, they are at pains to point out the distinctions between this limited acceptance of inference and the opposing position of the Dogmatists:

> Logical [i.e. Dogmatic] transition based on the nature of things lays hold of knowledge by means of indication [*endeixis*].[17] But the Empirical variety relies on what is discovered by experience, not because it is persuasive or plausible that the similar should be

productive of something similar, or require similar things, or undergo similar things; it is not on the basis of this, or anything else of this sort, that they think it justifiable to make the transition, but on the basis of the fact that they have discovered by experience that things behave this way.

(Galen, *Subfiguratio Empirica* 9, 70 Deichgräber)

Thus transition for the Empiricists is not, supposedly, grounded in any conviction that its past successes render it objectively probable that the procedure will deliver useful results; rather the Empiricist simply acts directly on the basis of past experience. It is plausible to assimilate their position here (as elsewhere) to that of Hume – we can provide no rational basis for our reliance on the procedures involved: but we are simply constrained by nature to behave in such a way.

But even so, transition was a source of internal controversy within the Empiricist school itself. This probably arose in the course of the debates with the Rationalists, in response to the latters' accusations that the basic Empirical practice of *autopsia* supplemented by *historia*[18] is fatally circumscribed: it is simply not rich enough to discover the whole art of medicine on its own (Galen, for example, claims that the cupping-glass could never have been discovered by Empiricist extemporaneousness alone: *On the Affected Parts* VIII 154). Thus, as a result of the on-going debate between the medical schools on the nature of allowable inference (paralleled of course in the great philosophical debates), some Empiricists come to relax their original epistemological hard line:

the question has been raised whether Serapion too believed that transition to the similar is a third constitutive part of medicine as a whole. Menodotus taught that it was not, but that the Empiricist only makes use of transition, it not being the same thing to make use of something and to treat it as a part. Cassius the Pyrrhonian even tries to show that the Empiricist does not even make use of transition of this sort. . . . Theodas did better in saying that transition constituted reasonable experience. Others still have held that transition is more like a tool.

(*Subfiguratio Empirica* 4, 49–50 Deichgräber)

Galen's caution about Serapion shows that by his day little was known for sure about the early history of Empiricism. Menodotus was the leading Empiricist of the middle of the second century AD (and hence the author of the Empiricism Galen is familiar with). The intriguing Cassius probably flourished in the middle of the first century BC; and just as Aenesidemus abandoned an Academy gone soft and Stoic in epistemology to refound Pyrrhonism, so too Cassius reacted against the increasingly watered-down nature of Empiricist epistemology in order to rediscover its pristine originality.

These debates, then, concern the acceptability of certain types of reasoning, and what attitude the Empiricist should take to them. Effectively, Menodotus refuses to enshrine transition as a proper part of the Empiricist method of discovery. He allows that Empiricists do, in the course of their practice, make use of such manoeuvres: but it is one thing to employ a procedure, quite another to endorse it.

However one interprets the complex and shadowy history of Empiricism, it is clear that the more the Empiricists are prepared to allow some form of reasoning (and perhaps hence of rational justification) into their practice, the harder it becomes to distinguish them from their Dogmatic opponents: and indeed Galen, true to his syncretist tendencies, discerned a convergence between the practices of the better Empiricists and the more reputable Dogmatists. None the less, there will remain for even the most relaxed Empiricism a sharp distinction between what entities (and hence what types of explanation) each school will allow. The Dogmatist will happily admit theoretical entities into his structures, and will use them in both physiological and therapeutic explanations: the *phainomena* are indications (*endeixeis*) of the hidden conditions of the body which are ultimately causally responsible for its funtioning well or ill. By contrast, the only indications the Empiricists allow are those afforded by commemorative sign-inference, or *epilogismos*, direct psychological suggestions of therapies that have proved appropriate in similar conditions in the past; and they will countenance no theory at all involving things by nature non-evident. A corollary of this is that all explanation for the Empiricists will be epistemic in form: an Empiricist physician can explain why he adopts a certain course of action, in the sense of saying what prompts him to do so – but he will have no views whatsoever on the metaphysical reasons (if any) why it should be effective.

Of a piece with this rejection of theory is the Empiricists' refusal to have anything to do with anatomy, which they consider to be, for the most part, entirely useless (see Galen, *On Anatomical Procedures* II 288–90). They attacked the Alexandrian practice of vivisection as being not only cruel but also pointless (Celsus, *On Medicine Pr.* 74–5; cf. 23–6, and Ts. 63b–c VS), since what if anything a physician needed to know was how the body functioned under normal circumstances – but there is nothing normal about a body undergoing vivisection.[19]

But if the Empiricists will have nothing to do with hidden causes and conditions, it appears that they are none the less prepared to admit antecedent causes, *aitia prokatarktika*: for these are indeed evident events, and hence can be put into suitable Humean correlations with further evident outcomes. Thus when Galen seeks, in *SI*, to offer a brief, thumbnail characterization of the differences between the major schools, he allows that the Empiricists (unlike the Methodists, for instance: see below, pp. 340–2) will admit antecedent causes into their account of the general set of circumstances, surrounding the illness or *sundromê* (*SI* 8, 18–20 Helmreich). Yet on the other hand Galen also reports (*CP* xiii 162) that the Empiricists refuse either to affirm or deny the existence of antecedent causes. This apparent contradiction is, I think, easily resolved. What the Empiricists refuse to allow is any theory of causal interaction – hence they will have nothing to do with the Dogmatists' theoretical accounts of how antecedent causes of the sort embraced by Galen and rejected by Erasistratus can have the effects they apparently do. But that does not mean that they cannot treat them, in sound Empiricist fashion, as signs that produce expectations of future occurrences. Why then call them causes? Simply, the Empiricists (like the Pyrrhonists) do not bother themselves with terminological disputes. Thus there is no real inconsistency in the positions ascribed to them by Galen.[20]

ASCLEPIADES

The last section situated the development of Empiricism within the context of their long-running dispute with their Dogmatist opponents that paralleled the contemporary epistemological debates of the philosophical schools. A key figure in that debate is Asclepiades of Bithynia (fl. *c.* 125 BC). Galen's early text, *On Medical Experience*, rehearses a debate between a Dogmatist and an Empiricist: the debate is fictional, but the bulk of the Dogmatic polemic is ascribable to Asclepiades (Menodotus lies behind the Empiricist reply). Asclepiades made a great reputation for himself in Rome, not least because of the pleasantness of the treatments he prescribed (a fact which earned him the scorn of Pliny: *Natural History* 26 12–15). But he was not merely a panderer to public tastes: he elaborated a theory of disease in which the main pathogenic factor was the lodgement in and blockage of invisible pores in the body of invisible corpuscles (this feature has often led people to assume that Asclepiades was an atomist of sorts: as Vallance [10.70] demonstrates, that conclusion is unfounded and premature). Moreover, as far as we can tell (the evidence is fragmentary and very difficult to assess) he accounted for motions of fluids within the body (and perhaps outside it) on the principle of 'movement towards the rarefied' (*pros to leptomeres phora*), a modification of Erasistratus's *horror vacui*.[21] Galen takes him to task both for this and for his abandonment of teleology (for example *On the Function of Parts* III 464–71), and considers him to be in the same case as Epicurus (*On the Natural Faculties* II 30–57).

But most important from our point of view is his attack on Empiricism. Pliny takes him to task for being a medical parvenu, insufficiently versed in *autopsia* and *empeiria* (*Natural History* 26 12); but it is clear from Galen's *On Medical Experience* that he was an implacable foe of Empiricism. First of all, he attacks the Empiricists' right simply to help themselves to a pre-theoretical notion of similarity, a notion he takes it that they require in order to ground their theorems. Diseases are infinitely variable: we require theory in order to determine what counts as relevant similarity between one condition and another, and what does not – but that is precisely what the Empiricists eschew (*On Medical Experience* 3–4, 88–90 Walzer):

> What is more manifold than disease? How does one discover that a
> disease is the same as another in all its characteristics? Is it by the
> number of the symptoms, or by their strength and power?
>
> (*On Medical Experience* 4, 89 Walzer)

And mere hearsay of the sort afforded by Empiricist *historia* cannot confirm that it is precisely the same condition that is being experienced (ibid.).

Moreover, even if this is allowed, how can the Empiricists pre-theoretically narrow down sufficiently the indefinitely many distinct events and factors that surround each individual case in order to make them empirically tractable? Why, in default of theory, should one be concerned about what patients ate, whether they overworked, were overheated, drank too much or had too much sex, rather than where they lived, what they had been reading and what types of clothes they wore (ibid. 6, 91–2)? The Empiricists thus require theory to sort out the relevant from the irrelevant, otherwise their syndromes will be too large to be contained even in a library (ibid. 7, 94).

Finally, even if all these difficulties can be resolved, what is it that makes the Empiricists' 'experience' 'technical', i.e. constitutive of the art of medicine? For a single instance of observed connection is not enough:

> They themselves also say that what has been observed but once does
> not amount to anything technical; so what is observed very many
> times is composed of many things each of which is non-technical. The
> argument could also be presented as follows . . . : what has been
> observed once is non-technical; hence the same is true of what has
> been observed very many times.
>
> (ibid. 7, 94 Walzer)

Finally Asclepiades asks: 'how many times is many?' Does the Empiricist have an account of how frequently some conjunction needs to be observed before it becomes theorematic, some account 'grounded in the nature of things' (ibid. 95–6)? If so, then he is a theorist of natures *malgré lui*. But if not, the Empirical 'art' is irremediably vague and without foundation. Moreover, it is vulnerable to a soritical objection: how can the addition of one single instance (which the Empiricists allow is, on its own, evidentially inadequate) make the difference between having and lacking theorematic status (ibid. 96–7)?

The Empiricists' reply, in essence, is that the Dogmatists' demands here are misplaced. They, from their own avowedly theoretical standpoint, may think it necessary to provide an account of how many instances validate a particular theorem; but the Empiricist is under no such obligation. He allows that different cases provide for different degrees of (subjective) confirmation, but that is a fact about his own psychology, having nothing necessarily to do with the way things really are. All the Empiricist does is describe a practice, in strictly psychological, associationist terms. Like Hume, he may be able to point to the mechanisms which operate in particular cases to generate certain degrees of confidence or expectation: but equally like him he will not produce any metaphysical justification of those attitudes. Thus as regards the sorites (ibid. 16–18, 114–20), the Empiricist will not say how many times makes many. The answer to the question will vary from individual to individual and case to case, since it is, at bottom, a matter of individual psychology rather than logic. Building up an experience is not a matter of inference – rather, after observing a certain number of particular cases, the Empiricist simply sees that they exhibit a general pattern. Now, that pattern may ultimately prove to be misleading and chimerical (then it will be abandoned or modified in the light of further experience): but past experience gives us (once more subjective) grounds for hoping that it will not do so. Experience, then, does not license belief – it merely causes it. That position is, I think, coherent. It may not, for a variety of reasons, be satisfying, especially to an Asclepiadean Dogmatist – but mere dissatisfaction with it cannot show it to be untenable.

ATHENAEUS OF ATTALEIA AND THE PRECEDING CAUSE

We noted above the crucial distinction insisted upon by Galen and others between antecedent and containing causes. That distinction is a venerable one (traces of it are to be found in the Hippocratics); but the terminology of antecedent and containing is usually ascribed to the Stoics. In a famous image, Chrysippus compared the relation of external stimulus and internal disposition in the case of human action to the rolling of a cylinder: it requires a shove to get it going, but thereafter contains to roll '*suapte vi et natura*' (Cicero, *On Fate* 49). The antecedent shove is necessary (although not sufficient) for the initial movement – however, the movement continues after the shove has stopped, under its own steam, as it were: for that, the nature of the cylinder is a sufficient, containing cause. Chrysippus's interests were in showing how human beings could be part of a fully deterministic causal nexus, in which their actions are conditioned by an ineluctable fate (defined as the interrelations of antecedent causes), and yet still be fit objects for moral appraisal: we can be praised and blamed for what we do because, after the initial stimulus, it is our dispositional structures (and our assent to the various presented impressions) that account for our actions.

It is often assumed that a third type of cause, the preceding (*proêgou-menon*) cause is also to be attributed to the Stoics, although this is far from clear (no text unequivocally so ascribes it). The distinction between antecedent and preceding causes is to be found in Galen, although he does not invariably avail himself of it. Roughly speaking, however, the preceding cause is an internal dispositional state which is roused into actuality by the impact of the antecedent cause, thus setting in train what is now the containing cause of the condition in question. An antecedent (*prokatarktikon*) cause is evident, open to inspection, while a preceding (*proêgoumenon*) cause is not: it is an internal state of affairs. Frede ([10.26] 242) remarks that such a distinction would have been at home in Chrysippean psychology; but the rolling drum passage does not apparently advert to it,[22] and it is not found elsewhere in surviving Stoic discussions of psychology and action. In fact, the distinction may well be medical in origin, and due to Athenaeus of Attaleia.[23]

Athenaeus (fl. ?*c*. 100 BC) founded the Pneumatist school of medicine, which accounted for proper and improper physiological functioning in terms of the states of the various internal types of *pneuma*, or dynamic gaseous fluid, in the body. What matters for us, however, is not the structure of his general physiology, but rather the causal taxonomy Galen attributes to him in *On Containing Causes* 2 (= *CMG* Supp. Or. II, 134.3–19). Galen explicitly says that Athenaeus was responsible for the tripartite division into antecedent, preceding and containing causes, where preceding causes are the internally conditioned effects of external antecedent causes, but are not yet themselves containing causes of the illness. This account is supported by Pseudo-Galen, *Medical Definitions* XIX 392; and one may readily see how such a distinction might commend itself to medical theorists. If this is right, then, an important refinement in Hellenistic causal theory is owed not to the philosophers but to the doctors – and this is by no means the only such instance of philosophically important innovations being made in the medical schools.

 THE METHODISTS

The origins of the Methodist school of medicine, which arose early in the first century AD, are obscure, but it seems to have been developed out of Asclepiadean corpuscularian physiology, first by Themison of Laodicea at the end of the first century BC (who is generally thought not himself to have been a Methodist), and completed by his pupil Thessalus, a contemporary of Nero.

They held that there were two fundamental ways in which the parts of the body could become out of balance: they could either be too loose (and hence promote too free a flow of the bodily fluids) or too costive (with the opposite effect). In line with this magnificently simple pathology, they rejected the patient's causal history as being therapeutically irrelevant, claiming that the indication [*endeixis*] as to what is beneficial, derived directly from the affections themselves, is enough for them, and not even these taken as specific particulars, but taking them to be common and universal. Thus they also call these affections which pervade all particulars 'communalities' . . . which they call restriction and relaxation, and they say that each disease is either constricted, relaxed, or a mixture of the two.

(Galen, *SI* 6, 12–13 Helmreich)

The physician's only task is to recognize the existence of these pathological states, which, on the Methodists' own account, he should be able to manage without difficulty after a little practice (medicine could be learned in six months, so they claimed), since these 'communalities' are not inferred, theoretical entities, but are in fact perfectly evident. Thus the Methodists reject antecedent causes, even in the sense in which the Empiricists accept them. In an instructive passage (ibid. 8, 18–19) Galen compares the attitudes of Empiricists and Methodists to the case of a man bitten by a rabid dog. For the former, the dog's condition will be relevant (mad dogs' bites having been observed to be far more serious than others); for the Methodists, however, all that matters is the wound itself – and that of course has nothing to do with the condition of the dog (Dogmatists will of course go further than the Empiricists, trying to specify how the dog's condition can have had the devastating effect on someone's internal constitution).

Indeed Sextus commends the Methodists for being closer to the Pyrrhonians than the Empiricists are, since

the Methodist speaks of 'communality' and 'pervade' and the like in a non-committal way. Thus also he uses the term 'indication' undogmatically to denote the guidance derived from the apparent affections or symptoms, both natural and unnatural, for the discovery of the apparently appropriate remedies.

(Sextus, *PH* 1 240)

And the Methodist, like the Sceptic, is driven by the 'compulsion of the affections' to apply countervailing remedies.

Moreover, it seems from Sextus's account that Methodism, unlike Empiricism, does not even rely on the memory. One does not, apparently, need to develop an understanding of the communalities on the basis of long experience; rather one simply sees them. And while the Methodists admit indication of sorts (cf. Galen, *SI* 6, 14 Helmreich), it involves no inferences of hidden conditions. In fact, the fifth-century AD medical writer Caelius Aurelianus[24] preserves a Methodist argument against sign-inference:

Thessalus and his sect . . . argue thus: if there were sure and inevitable signs of future events, such as the onset of phrenitis, all who

341

manifested them would necessarily develop phrenitis. But some of those who show these symptoms do not develop phrenitis.

(Caelius Aurelianus, *On Acute Diseases* 1 22)

Moreover, Caelius continues:

every sign is understood in relation to what is signified, since signs belong in the category of relations. But can anything be called a sign if the thing signified is not only not present now, but in some cases never will be?

(ibid. 1 29)

This parallels Erasistratus's claims about causes; and it is vulnerable to the same objections. But even so, there is surely something to the anti-Dogmatic doctors' claims that the endemic dispute among the Dogmatists about the relative significance of pathological signs at the very least compromises their claims to expertise.

 GALEN

Thus, by the beginning of the Imperial period, there were three major competing groups of doctors in the Greco-Roman world, of which one class, the Dogmatists, includes a wide variety of different theoretical standpoints united only by a common belief in the importance of inference to the hidden, internal conditions of the body, and of producing theoretical aetiologies for diseases. Moroever, as we have seen, Empiricism was not a monolithic orthodoxy – it came in different strengths, and evolved over time. Equally even Methodism, whose hard-line early position was sketched above, came to soften some of its rough edges over time. Soranus of Ephesus (fl. early second century AD), whose *Gynaecology* survives, allowed himself a good deal of doctrinal leeway. He was prepared to talk, against the original Thessalian orthodoxy, of causes and aetiology, and would sometimes speculate on patients' internal conditions.

This is the world upon which Galen was to make such a deep and lasting impression. Born into a well-to-do family in Pergamon in AD 129, Galen was first broadly educated in philosophy (at the feet of some of the major figures of the day), and then equally well schooled in Dogmatist medicine and anatomy. For all that, Galen never underestimated the value of empiricism: indeed his main contribution to medical theory and methodology was his largely successful attempt to supersede and render redundant the dispute between the schools by showing just what each of them had to offer to a synthetic medical method.

But, for all his eclecticism, Galen was no mere indiscriminate plunderer of the various previous traditions. Rather his aim is, in line with the general tendency of the emerging Middle Platonist orthodoxy of the time, syncretic: he seeks to show how the best elements of the various schools can not only be combined to form a coherent whole – they are, in a deep sense, equivalent. And we can trace this drive both in medicine and philosophy. Galen sought both to show how successful Empiricist and Dogmatist practice could converge into a theoretically unified whole, and to demonstrate the fundamental agreement between at least the reputable philosophical schools on all important issues of metaphysics and epistemology. But it should be stressed that this is no anodyne compendiousness – Galen is implacably hostile to Methodism (at least in its original Thessalian form), and he frequently lambasts representatives of various Dogmatic schools, including Herophilus, Erasistratus, and Asclepiades for their perceived theoretical shortcomings (we have already briefly noted some of these broadsides). Equally, he regularly attacks Chrysippus and other Stoics for what he sees as their lack of logical acumen, and insufficiency of rigour in argument. Sceptics in particular receive short shrift from him (although, significantly, he reveals that as a young man he was seduced by Scepticism's siren song, rejecting it only after discovering the a priori certainties of geometrical demonstration: *On His Own Books* XIX 49).

And Galen is consistent in his expressed view that the pinnacle of all wisdom is to be sought in Plato in philosophy and Hippocrates in medicine. Indeed, his monumental *On the Doctrines of Hippocrates and Plato* (*PHP*: V 181–805) is devoted to demonstrating the substantial agreement on all major points between his two great authorities (this is the clearest measure of Galen's syncretism). Thus both of them (he contends) support a divided soul, whose rational faculty is located, contra Aristotle and the Stoics, in the brain, while emotion and desire find their seats in heart and liver respectively. Even so, Galen will not follow Plato slavishly – he refuses to commit himself one way or the other on questions such as the eternity of the world or the soul's immortality, holding that such 'philosophical' questions are beyond the reach of human knowledge; and in general he will not treat any of his predecessors' work, no matter how exalted, as holy writ.

In fact, he considers his principal debt to the great ancients to be one of method rather than substance: they pointed the way both to the discovery and justification of true science, and it is the duty of all who follow in their footsteps to carry that programme to completion. Of course their task has been rendered immeasurably harder by the proliferation of sophists and charlatans whose only concern is with a quick and easy reputation at the ultimate expense of their duped clientele, a fact which Galen harps upon throughout his works. A passage of *On the Natural Faculties* is worth quoting at length:

> Although the statements of the ancients on these matters were
> accurate, they did not support their case with logical demonstration;

of course they did not suspect that there could be sophists so shameless as to contradict plain facts. Of the moderns, some have been taken in by their sophisms, while others who have tried to argue against them lack, for the most part, the ability of the ancients. For these reasons I have tried to construct my arguments on the lines the ancients would have adopted if they were around to take issue with those who seek to overturn the finest achievements of the science. That I will achieve but little success, however, I realise. For I find that very many things which were conclusively demonstrated by the ancients are unintelligible to most people because of their ignorance, or perhaps because of their unwillingness to come to understanding, which is due to idleness. And even if they have arrived at any knowledge, they have not properly examined the issue. It is essential that anyone who wants to understand anything better than the ordinary run of humanity must far outshine them, both in natural endowment, and in the quality of their early training. As a lad he must develop an almost erotic passion for the truth, so that day and night, like someone possessed, he will not let up in his desire to learn what was propounded by the most illustrious of the ancients. And when he has learnt these things, he must spend a great deal of time testing and justifying them, seeing what accords with the observable facts and what does not; and on the basis of this he will accept some doctrines and reject others.

(Galen, *On the Natural Faculties* II 178–80)

That passage encapsulates many of Galen's obsessions: with the necessity for rigorous and lengthy training allied to innate ability (a combination he clearly felt himself to have been blessed with); the importance of logic in general and demonstration in particular to the construction of medical science; the need empirically to test and confirm the results of any theory before accepting it (time and again Galen castigates his theoretical opponents for failing either to see or to admit that their theories clash with the evidence); and the moral degeneracy and inadequacy of the vast majority of his contemporary opponents. These themes are ubiquitous in Galen – and they are of course highly rhetorically coloured. But that fact alone should not cause us to dismiss his claims out of hand. Let us finally, then, see what they amounted to in a variety of different areas.

First of all training and logic. These things go together, Galen thinks – it is because of people's lamentable logical shortcomings that they are unable to see through the fallacies of the medical charlatans (Galen's principal, although by no means exclusive, targets here are Methodists and Erasistrateans) that surround them. Only by understanding logical consequence, and being able to expose equivocation and other similar sources of fallacy (*PHP* V 795–7), will the young hopeful be able to expose the sophistries of the medical degenerates (among which Galen classes, for example, Erasistratus's arguments against antecedent causation).

Indeed the tiro doctor should acquaint himself with both Aristotelian categorical and Stoic hypothetical syllogistic (in his syncretic manner, Galen thinks them to be but two sides of the same basic coin) in order to be able to recognize and to construct valid arguments, and to expose the invalid. Indeed, Galen wrote voluminously on logic (his fifteen-book *On Demonstration* is lost), of which only a short handbook, the *Introduction to Logic*,[25] survives. The *Introduction* briefly outlines the Aristotelian and Stoic systems, before pointing out that neither is equipped to handle the sort of relational inference to be found in mathematics and elsewhere, for which he proposes the development of a third type of argument, the relational syllogism, arguments which have their validity 'in virtue of an axiom' (*Introduction* 16–18). Galen's actual treatment of the logic of relations is limited and naive: but he deserves the credit for having seen clearly (and uniquely among the ancients) the syntactic inadequacies of the traditional logics.

But logic was not merely useful as a destructive weapon for rooting out bad argument. The proper model for science, Galen thinks, is Aristotelian, along the lines laid out in *Posterior Analytics* (upon which Galen wrote commentaries, now lost). Galen insists that all science, medicine included, is axiomatic in structure, proceeding from basic, indubitable axioms via secure principles of inference to the theorematic derived truths. The axioms will include logical laws (such as that of the excluded middle); but also comprehended are principles of mathematics ('equals subtracted from equals leave equals'), and various metaphysical principles such as 'nothing occurs causelessly', 'nothing comes to be from nothing', and 'nothing is completely annihilated'. These axioms are described as being 'evident to the understanding', and anyone who rejects them is simply not worthy of further consideration.

But in addition to the class of things evident to the understanding, there is a set of items which are equally evident to perception. Galen has no truck with scepticism, accusing sceptics of bad faith and of subverting human life (*On Distinguishing Pulses* VIII 782–6; *On the Best Method of Teaching* I 40–52). In fact, Galen thinks, it turns out upon analysis that even the Academics agreed with the undeniability of things perceptually evident, an agreement they obscured by their insistence upon talking about the 'persuasive' (*pithanon*) as opposed to the true (*PHP* V 777–8). Galen no doubt minimizes the genuine differences that existed between the Stoic and Academic epistemologies (he considers the Stoic criterion of the cataleptic impression to amount to no more than the common-sense view that what is evident to perception is true); but equally it is worth pointing out that, by the end of the two-centuries-long debate between the schools, some others (notably Antiochus and Aenesidemus, from their different perspectives) could see little difference either. Galen is surely right to stress the fact of pragmatic convergence between them.

And just as he stresses the convergence of practice between the good Empiricist and the competent Dogmatist (above, p. 336) in the realm of prescription and therapy, so here in epistemology his bent towards syncretism manifests itself. At the end of the day, when all the dust has settled, everyone who is not hopelessly ensnared in sophistry and illusion will agree that the senses, in good condition and uncorrupted by disease, are criteria of truth: for we have nothing else to go on; and in any case, nature could not have provided us with such 'natural criteria' if they were not, for the most part at least, reliable (*PHP* V 725–6). That, admittedly brief, attempt to justify his epistemological optimism serves as a convenient bridge into what is in many ways the most important feature of Galen's natural philosophy: his teleology.

Galen attributes his teleology, as so much else, to the example of Plato (of the *Timaeus*) and Hippocrates:

> even if you are one of those who through ignorance of Nature's works accuse her of lack of skill, I think you will repent with shame and change your view for the better, agreeing with Hippocrates who is continually singing the praises of Nature's righteousness and the foresight she displays in the creation of animals.
>
> (*On the Usefulness of the Parts* (*UP*) III 235)

A page or so later, he invites the reader to choose between two choruses: that surrounding Plato and Hippocrates, which exalts the purposiveness and foresight of Nature in arranging things in animals' bodies for the best; and the other, which denies Nature's skill and claims that many things are created by her to no purpose.

The invocation of Hippocrates is a trifle strained; and while Plato in the *Timaeus* clearly outlines a natural teleology, and one which does indeed in important respects anticipate Galen's own, it is clear that, insofar as the detailed working-out of his teleological conception of nature is concerned, it is the Aristotle of *Parts of Animals* to whom he is most indebted. But if the detail is Aristotelian (although Galen claims to expand upon and advance Aristotle's position), the form of the teleology is indeed Platonic: for Galen, unlike Aristotle, attributes the teleological structure of nature to a divine artificer, whose praises he sings contantly throughout *UP*, and whom he calls, in conscious recollection of the *Timaeus*, the Demiurge.

Thus there is no doubt on which side of the great ancient debate between teleology and mechanism Galen will find himself: he is particularly harsh on those who (such as Epicurus and Asclepiades) wilfully refuse, as he sees it, to recognize the providential form of Nature. His reason for ascribing nature's purposive structure to a Demiurge is a simple and familiar one (it is to be found also in the Stoics, and appealed to the young Aristotle: Cicero, *Nature of the Gods* 2 95): if one compares the construction of the natural world with the work of any human artisan, one will immediately recognize a basic similarity in design, although the former by far outshines the latter in beauty, functionality, economy, and goodness (*UP* III 238–9; IV 346–66). Thus if it is absurd to suppose that any human artefact might have come about by chance and undesigned, how much more so in the case of the natural world. That version of the Argument from Design is currently out of favour; but it is so only because we possess far more sophisticated conceptual resources (in the form of cybernetics, and Darwinian notions of natural selection) with which to explain how unplanned, mechanically produced structures can none the less mimic design. The ancient mechanists, lacking such resources, were woefully inadequately equipped to offer any such account.[26]

It is from this perspective that he takes Asclepiades to task in an instructive passage from *UP* (III 464–71), in which he endorses the Aristotelian system of Four Causes (although he assimilates the Formal Cause to the Platonic paradigm, and elsewhere in his works makes no reference to it), with the Middle Platonist addition of the Instrumental Cause, that with which something is brought about (cf. *CP* vi 54–67). Asclepiades held that the 'venous arteries' (i.e. the pulmonary veins) became thin (unlike other arteries) because of their hard work; Galen holds, conversely, that they were made that way in order to be able to work hard. Thus Asclepiades gets the primary direction of explanation the wrong way round, because he fails to allow for purposiveness in nature; and he fails to see 'that the arteries of the lung are venous and the veins arterial because it is better so' (*UP* III 469). They are made thin by the Artificer in order that they may perform the function they are supposed to; their thinness is a mere instrumental cause, 'the most insignificant of all, and which I believe anyone versed in the philosophical method would not call a proper cause at all, but one that is contingent or consequential, like a counterfeit drachma' (ibid. 466; moreover the whole debate is vitiated by the fact that the ancients, lacking a circulatory account of the vascular system, mistook the pulmonary artery for a vein and vice versa).

Elsewhere (*CP* vi 67), Galen says that the final and efficient causes are the most important, followed by the instrumental and material; but Galen does not underestimate the importance of the latter – it is precisely by appealing to material factors that he can circumvent Erasistratus's 'sophism' against antecedent causes. Thus he appropriates three at least of Aristotle's canonical tetrad; the efficient and material causes are readily further assimilable to the Stoics' active and passive principles (cf. Sextus, *PH* 3 1–2), and the Stoics too invoked purpose and design, the final cause. Moreover, Galen takes advantage of the conceptual distinctions made by the Stoics in philosophy and people such as Athenaeus in the medical tradition (see above, p. 340) in order to refine the notion of an efficient cause. The resulting structure gives him an explanatory model of great power and flexibility.

It remains to consider Galen's attitude towards the relations between theory and practice, reason and experience. We have already seen Galen's own report of how the dispute between the Dogmatists and the Empiricists played itself out in terms of an increasing convergence between the practices of at least the more reputable representatives of each tendency. Galen himself, in his own voice, underlines the need to appeal both to reason and to experience in order to arrive at a coherent and empirically adequate medical theory. On the one hand, he denies that the pure Empiricism of Cassius could ever have arrived either at complex remedies or at the discovery of such useful tools as the cupping-glass. On the other hand, theory without experience is blind: only by repeated testing of expected theoretical outcomes at the tribunal of experience (*peira*) can a theory be validated.

This is, of course, of a piece with his view that some things are evident to sense-perception; but unlike the Empiricists, Galen does not think that *peira* can be relied upon to deliver the candidates for theorematic status that are to be the subject of empirical testing – that is the role of theory, or *logos*. That is, *peira* is necessary for testing the results of logical deductions, but is on its own insufficient to discover the whole truth of science – in modern parlance, it functions in the context of justification, not that of discovery (cf. Galen, *On Hippocrates' 'Nature of Man'* XV 152–3). At MM X 29, he puts it slightly differently: *logos* serves to demonstrate the soundness of causal explanations, while *peira* assesses the results; moreover, *logos* and *peira* should be kept strictly separated and not confused, although any not thoroughly versed in the demonstrative method should restrict themselves to *peira* (ibid. 30–2). But even though the Empiricist may discover some therapies by his own method, his practice is fatally restricted – he lacks the means to progress logically from one item to another (ibid. 486; cf. 608, 628, 901).[27]

Furthermore, Galen is implacably opposed to the Empiricist line that anatomy is pointless: on the contrary, it is a vital tool in the discovery of the facts of connection and disconnection among the parts of the body that enable the competent theorist to deduce the functional relations that hold within it from facts of its structure.[28] In his treatise, *On Anatomical Procedures* (*AA*), he writes:

> anatomical study has one application for the scientist who loves knowledge for its own sake, another for him who values it only to demonstrate that Nature does nothing in vain, a third for one who provides himself from anatomy with data for investigating a physical or mental function, and a fourth for the practitioner who has to remove splinters and missiles efficiently, to excise parts properly, or to treat wounds, fistulae and abscesses.

> (*AA* II 286)

Thus anatomy has a variety of uses, theoretical and practical – but Galen is adamant that the sort of knowledge gained by the 'adventitious anatomy' that the Empiricists allow is insufficient for the purpose (*AA* II 288–9; cf. 224). 'Adventitious anatomy' is the chance observation of corpses on a battlefield, or of skeletons exposed by flooding in a graveyard, as by Galen himself (ibid. 221); and this underscores the fact that, by Galen's time, practising anatomists were in a much worse case than their Alexandrian predecessors. It had, in fact, become socially impossible even to investigate corpses on purpose; and the bulk of Galen's research was carried out on monkeys, pigs, goats and other animals (ibid. 222–4). In order for this to be productive, he had to rely on a theory of animal homology which occasionally led him astray – but for the most part, the fruits of this research were impressive and original.

One of his most remarkable results was the demonstration of the function of the recurrent laryngeal nerve in voice-production (*AA* II 675–81) upon experimental animals, in the course of a precise and brilliant sequence of experiments on neural sections in the spinal column, in which Galen showed how a ligature at a variety of different points variously affected the animal's abilities to move and to produce sounds. These experiments are important not least for the fact that they *are* experiments. It is often alleged that the ancients were innocent of anything that might be called 'the experimental method' in science and there is something to that claim. Although ancient science abounds with reports of observations from the Hippocratics onwards, there is at least in the classical period scant evidence of anything we might recognize as experimental design: the deliberate manipulation of selected variables in artificial conditions in order to determine their various relations.

But Erasistratus at least performed a recognizable experiment, by placing a bird in a sealed container, and weighing it before and after feeding, along with its droppings, in order to show that some of its body-weight had been lost by invisible emanations; and Galen in several places reports experiments he claims to have carried out. They are not, it must be admitted, uniformly well designed and performed. In *On the Use of Breathing* IV 504–5, he says that a boy was able to survive an entire day with an ox-bladder over his nose and mouth to prevent him from breathing; while in two places (IV 73 and II 645–8) he describes an experiment involving severing an artery and inserting a thin tube linking the severed parts. Galen claims, *contra* Erasistratus (whom he accuses of not having observed the phenomena), that the portion of the artery distal to the incision will exhibit no pulse, thereby proving that the faculty of pulsation is carried in the arterial walls, and does not result from the pumping of the blood itself. But as Harvey, who repeated the experiment, observed, it is extremely difficult to effect such a severance and junction neatly, and in any case, the relative absence of pulsation distal to the cut can be explained on other grounds consistent with the pulse's being caused by the blood-flow.[29] But whatever the particular shortcomings of conception and execution, it is clear that by Galen's time appeal to artificially created experimental circumstances in order to support or disconfirm a theory was an established part of scientific procedure. There is a theoretical motivation for this: this is part of the *peira* which tests and confirms the discoveries of *logos*.

This methodology can be seen at work in *On the Doctrines of Hippocrates and Plato* in Galen's rebuttal of the Stoic (and Aristotelian) doctrine that reason was located in the heart rather than in the brain. He begins by distinguishing, in Aristotelian fashion, between properly scientific premises, which are 'found in the very essence of the matter under consideration . . . we should first state the essence and definition of the thing under consideration, and then use it as a standard' (*PHP* V 219), and those which are 'superfluous and irrelevant; and this is how a premiss that is scientific differs from one that is either rhetorical or sophistical' (V 220).

We begin, then, with conceptual analysis:

> The governing part of the soul, as even [the Stoics] allow, is the source of sensation and drive. Therefore the demonstration that the heart is the location of the governing part must not start from any other premises than that it initiates every voluntary motion in the other parts of the animal's body, and every sensation is referred to it.
>
> (*PHP* V 219–20)

But to determine that the heart really is the centre of voluntary control demands empirical data:

> What can this be shown from . . . apart from anatomy? For if it supplies the power of sensation and movement to all parts of the body, then it is necessary that there be some vessel growing out of it to perform this service.
>
> (*PHP* V 220)

This vessel can be isolated on the basis of anatomical experiment: hence the importance of the neural sections, which determine both what mediates the psychic power (here as elsewhere Galen speaks in studiedly neutral terms), and its direction of flow. By tracing the neural canals backwards to their source we can establish that they originate from the brain, and hence that it is the brain and not the heart from which voluntary motion arises and to which sensation is referred. The argument is not innocent of certain controvertible causal assumptions, but it is typical of Galen's willingness to marry abstract argument to empirical investigation.[30]

Finally, a word about the notion of a power or faculty (*dunamis*). We have already noted Herophilus's deployment of the concept (see above, p. 325). Galen frequently speaks of powers: and where he does so it is precisely in order to avoid too rash a set of claims regarding the actual physical status of things. Thus he disavows knowledge of the substance of the soul (cf. *On the Formation of Foetuses* IV 700–2); but he thinks its powers can perfectly well be investigated.

In *On the Natural Faculties* he is concerned with enumerating and specifying the function of various faculties that he discerns at work in the human body: thus, for instance, the kidneys possess (so he supposes) the faculty of attracting urine (II 57–64, 74, etc.). Quite how they do so is another matter; but that they do so is, Galen thinks, clear simply from the inadequacy of purely mechanical theories such as those of Erasistratus and Asclepiades to explain how the various bodily fluids get separated out and conveyed to their various proper places.

And whatever the empirical and theoretical shortcomings of this concept, at least in these cases there is something attractive both about the caution with which Galen essays his theorizing here, and, congruently, with the weight he seeks to place upon the empirical facts. Theories, for him, must be empirically driven and answerable to the tribunal of experience. Galen thus represents the culmination of the development we have discerned throughout the period of this study.

 ABBREVIATIONS

AA	Galen, *Anatomical Procedures*
CP	Galen, *On Antecedent Causes*
DL	Diogenes Laertius, *Lives of the Philosophers*
G	Garofalo [10.6], *Erasistratus*
MM	Galen, *De methodo medendi*
PH	Sextus Empiricus, *Outlines of Pyrrhonism*
PHP	Galen, *On the Doctrines of Hippocrates and Plato*
SI	Galen, *On Sects*
UP	Galen, *On the Usefulness of the Parts*

 NOTES

1 Even where later and better texts of Galen's work are available (as they are in this case: Corpus Medicorum Graecorum V. 4.2), I generally refer to the edition of Kühn [10.10], since the later texts are (for the most part) keyed to it. Exceptions are noted where they occur.

2 The sense of this lapidary fragment is disputed: see von Staden [10.15] and Hankinson, review of this in *Phronesis* 35 (1990). VS (125) translates 'let the appearances be described first even if they are not primary': but that reading requires us to take the two occurrences of the word *'prôta'* in completely distinct senses, even thought there is no indication to that effect.

3 This structure, the confluence of the four major cranial sinuses, is more common and more visible in animals than in humans, a fact which, along with his erroneous but influential ascription of a *rete mirabile* to humans (T 121 VS), has encouraged

351

some to doubt whether Herophilus ever did in fact dissect humans; but on the whole the evidence suggests that he did: see p. 325.

4   See Hankinson [10.49] for an edition, translation and commentary of this text; it survives in a mediaeval Latin translation made by the Italian scholar Niccolò da Reggio.

5   Galen clearly refers here to Erasistratus, who was mentioned by name in the previous sentence (and who is the principal target of *CP*), and not to Herophilus, as von Staden suggests: [10.15] 136. See Hankinson [10.49] ad loc.

6   Niccolò's Latin reads: 'quid igitur ait? "causa vero, utrum sit vel non, natura quidem non est invenibile, existimatione autem puto infrigidari, estuari, cibo et potibus repleri".'

Von Staden renders '*existimatione*' as though it stands for '*ex hupotheseôs*'; but Niccolò's '*ex suppositione*' of T 58 VS clearly translates '*ex hupotheseôs*': and he was careful to render technical terms unambiguously. Thus '*doxêi*' or the like seems more probable (so Bardong in his 'Rückübersetzung': CMG Supp. II, p. 53), yielding my translation. Von Staden's sense is undeniably attractive, and perhaps the text should be emended; but as the text stands it recalls the Pyrrhonist Timon of Phlius' remark that 'I do not claim honey is sweet; but I agree it seems so' (Diogenes Laertius *Lives of the Philosophers* 9 105 (hereafter DL)); which perhaps argues against emendation.

7   Von Staden misleadingly compares the Aristotelian doctrine of hypothetical necessity (*Physics* 2: 9; *Parts of Animals* 1: 1) with Herophilus' causal hypotheticalism – but there are no significant similarities between them; see Hankinson in *Phronesis* 1990, 209, n. 30.

8   This is a matter of dispute: see Fraser [10.25] and Lloyd [10.58] for opposing views.

9   On the Erasistratean principle of *horror vacui*, see Garofalo [10.6] 33–5; and Vallance [10.70] especially ch. 2.

10 This may not be accidental: Erasistratus is said to have studied with Theophrastus in the Lyceum (DL 5.57; cf. Fragment 7 G).

11 In particular his celebrated diagnosis of love-sickness by a method Galen himself repeated: he took the woman's pulse, and reeled off an apparently random list of names. When the woman's pulse suddenly quickened, Galen inferred that she was enamoured of the man he had just mentioned: *On Prognosis* XIV 630–5; cf. Nutton [10.66] 195–6.

12 For the history of the development of the concept, see Frede [10.26]; Hankinson [10.37], [10.38] and [10.49].

13 See *CP* ii 9–10; vi 46; viii 96–114; Hankinson [10.49].

14 Garofalo ([10.6] 30) thinks that Erasistratus called them 'origins (*archai*)' of disease: Fragment 162 G; 223 G; but it seems rather that Erasistratus reserved the term *archê* for the condition of *plêthôra* consequent upon them: see further below. On these issues in general, see [10.6] 29–31.

15 I here depart from my usual practice, and refer to *SI* by way of Helmreich, 1893, since Frede's English [10.4] is keyed only to that text.

16 This is the famous *paremptôsis* of Erasistratean pathology (although Sextus uses the term '*metaptôsis*'): for Erasistratus, all fever was consequent upon inflammation caused by blood being forced through the *anastomôseis* between the veins (in which in normal circumstances the blood resides) to the arteries, where it has no business being.

17 'Indication' here is equivalent to indicative sign-inference.
18 *Historia* did not, for the Empiricists, involve an uncritical acceptance of all received testimony: on the contrary, they elaborated a complex and sophisticated system of assessment of the relative value of different testimony (according to how far it cohered with other parts of the art already discovered, and on the basis of the past reliability of the source in question).
19 On the Empiricist attitude to anatomy, see Hankinson [10.50].
20 For more on this, see Hankinson [10.38]; and on the nature of antecedent causes in general, Hankinson [10.37].
21 See Vallance [10.70] ch. 2, for a careful analysis of the (principally Galenic) evidence, and a reconstruction of the theory.
22 However, this turns on tricky issues in the interpretation of Cicero's Latin rendering of technical Greek terminology: see Sedley [10.68] and Hankinson, forthcoming [10.52].
23 See Hankinson [10.37].
24 Caelius's two treatises, *On Acute Diseases* and *On Chronic Diseases*, are Latin adaptations of lost original works of the second-century Methodist Soranus of Ephesus.
25 Not discovered until 1841, and hence not edited by Kühn; see Kalbfleisch [10.9].
26 I discuss this in Hankinson [10.41], and [10.43].
27 On all these issues, see further Barnes [10.19].
28 On the relation of structure and function in Galen, see Furley and Wilkie [10.5] and Hankinson [10.42].
29 See Furley and Wilkie [10.5] 51–3.
30 See also Galen's criticism of the Stoic argument against the view that the mind is located in the brain from the fact that voice passes through the windpipe (*PHP* V 241).

BIBLIOGRAPHY

TEXTS AND TRANSLATIONS

[*CMG* = *Corpus medicorum graecorum*]
10.1 Bardong, K., *Galeni de Causis Procatarcticis*, *CMG* Supp. II², Berlin, 1937.
10.2 Deichgräber, K., *Die griechische Empirikerschule*, Berlin, 1930.
10.3 Duckworth, W.H.L. with M.C. Lyons and B. Towers, *Galen on Anatomical Procedures: the Later Books*, Cambridge, 1962 (trans.).
10.4 Frede, M., *Galen: Three Treatises on the Nature of Science*, Indiana, 1985 (trans.).
10.5 Furley, D. and Wilkie, J.S., *Galen on Respiration and the Arteries*, Cambridge, 1984 (text and trans.).
10.6 Garofalo, I., *Erasistrato*, Pisa, 1988.
10.7 Hankinson, R.J., *Galen on the Therapeutic Method*, Books I and II, Oxford, 1991 (trans.).
10.8 Helmreich, G., *Galeni Scripta Minora*, vol. 3, Leipzig, 1893.
10.9 Kalbfleisch, K., *Galeni Institutio Logica*, Leipzig, 1896.

10.10 Kühn, C.G., *Galeni opera omnia*, Leipzig, 1821–33.

10.11 May, M.T., *Galen on the Usefulness of Parts*, Ithaca, NY, 1968 (trans.).

10.12 Nutton, V., *Galen on Prognosis*, *CMG* V, 8:1, Berlin, 1979 (text and trans.).

10.13 Simon, M., *Sieben Bücher Anatomie des Galen*, Leipzig, 1906.

10.14 Singer, C., *Galen on Anatomical Procedures*, Cambridge, 1956 (trans.).

10.15 von Staden, H., *Herophilus: The Art of Medicine in Early Alexandria*, Cambridge, 1989 (text and trans.).

10.16 Walzer, R., *Galen on Medical Experience*, Oxford, 1944 (trans.).

10.17 Wellman, M., *Die pneumatische Schule bis auf Archigenes in ihrer Entwicklung dargestellt*, Philologische Untersuchungen 14, Berlin, 1895.

❧ BOOKS AND ARTICLES ❧

10.18 Barnes, J., 'Una terceira especie de silogismo', *Analise* 1, 2, 1985.

10.19 —— 'Galen on logic and therapy', in Durling and Kudlien [10.22].

10.20 Algra, K. *et al.*, eds, *The Cambridge History of Hellenistic Philosophy* [6.16].

10.21 Brunschwig, J. and Nussbaum, M.C., eds, *Passions and Perceptions: Studies in Hellenistic Philosophy of Mind*, Cambridge, 1993 [6.9].

10.22 Durling, R. and Kudlien, F., eds, *Galen's Method of Healing*, Leiden, 1991.

10.23 Edelstein, L., *Ancient Medicine*, Baltimore, 1967.

10.24 Flashar, H., ed., *Antike Medizin*, Darmstadt, 1971.

10.25 Fraser, P.M., 'The career of Erasistratus of Ceos', *Rendiconti del' Istituto Lombardo, Let., Sci., Mor., e Stor.* 103, 1969.

10.26 Frede, M., 'The original notion of cause', in Barnes *et al.*, 1980 [6.6].

10.27 —— 'Galen's epistemology', in Nutton [10.66].

10.28 —— 'On the method of the so-called Methodical school of medicine', in Barnes *et al.*, 1982 [6.6].

10.29 —— 'Philosophy and medicine in Antiquity', in Frede [10.30].

10.30 —— *Essays in Ancient Philosophy*, Oxford 1987.

10.31 —— 'The ancient Empiricists', in Frede [10.30].

10.32 —— 'The Empiricist attitude towards reason and theory', in Hankinson [10.53].

10.33 —— 'An Empiricist view of knowledge', in Everson, S. (ed.) *Epistemology*. Companions to Ancient Thought 1, Cambridge, 1990.

10.34 Fuchs, R., 'Die Plethora bei Erasistratos', *Neue Jahrbücher für Philologie und Pädagogik* 38, 1892, 679–91.

10.35 Giannantoni, G., ed., *Lo Scetticismo Antico*, 2 vols, Naples, 1981.

10.36 Gotthelf, A., ed., *Aristotle on Nature and Living Things*, Bristol, NJ, 1985.

10.37 Hankinson, R.J., 'Evidence, externality and antecedence', *Phronesis* 32, 1987, 80–100.

10.38 —— 'Causes and empiricism', *Phronesis* 32, 1987, 329–48.

10.39 —— 'Stoicism, science and divination', in Hankinson [10.53].

10.40 —— 'Science and certainty: the central issues', in Hankinson [10.53].

10.41 —— 'Galien: la médecine et la philosophie antisceptique', *Revue de Philosophie Ancienne* 6, 229–69.

10.42 —— 'Galen explains the elephant', in Matthen and Linsky [10.64].

10.43 —— 'Galen and the best of all possible worlds', *Classical Quarterly* 39, 1989, 206–27.

10.44 —— 'Greek medical models of the mind', in Everson, S. (ed.), *Psychology*. Companions to Ancient Thought 2, Cambridge, 1991.

10.45 —— 'Galen's anatomy of the soul', *Phronesis* 36, 1991, 197–233.

10.46 —— 'Galen's philosophical eclectism', *Aufstieg und Niedergang der Römischen Welt* II, 36:5, 1992, 3427–43.

10.47 —— 'A purely verbal dispute? Galen on Stoic and Academic epistemology', *Revue de Philosophie Internationale*, 1992.

10.48 —— 'Actions and passions', in Brunschwig and Nussbaum [6.9].

10.49 —— *Galen on Antecedent Causes*, Cambridge, 1998.

10.50 —— 'Galen's anatomical procedures', *Aufstieg und Niedergang der Römischen Welt* II, 37:2, 1994.

10.51 —— 'Causation and explanation', in Algra *et al.* [6.16].

10.52 —— 'Determinism and indeterminism', in Algra *et al.* [6.16].

10.53 —— ed., *Method, Medicine, and Metaphysics, Apeiron* Supp. Vol. 21, 1988.

10.54 Hulser, K., 'Galen und die Logik', *Aufstieg und Niedergang der Römischen Welt* II 36:5, 1992.

10.55 Jaeger, W., *Diokles von Karystos: die griechischen Medizin und die Schule des Aristoteles*, Berlin, 1938.

10.56 Kudlien, F., 'Herophilus und der Beginn der medizinischen Skepsis', *Gesnerus* 21, 1964, 1–13; repr. in Flashar [10.24].

10.57 Lloyd, G.E.R., 'Saving the appearances', *Classical Quarterly* 25, 1975 , 171–92; repr. in Lloyd [10.61].

10.58 —— 'A Note on Erasistratus of Ceos', *Journal of Hellenic Studies* 95, 1975.

10.59 —— *Magic, Reason and Experience*, Cambridge, 1979.

10.60 —— *Science, Folklore and Ideology*, Cambridge, 1983.

10.61 —— *Methods and Problems in Ancient Science*, Cambridge, 1991.

10.62 Marelli, C., 'La medicina empirica ed il suo sistema epistemologico', in Giannantoni [10.35].

10.63 Matthen, M., 'Empiricism and ontology in ancient medicine', in Hankinson [10.53].

10.64 —— and Linsky, B., eds, *Philosophy and Biology, Canadian Journal of Philosophy* Supp. Vol. 14, Calgary, 1988.

10.65 Moraux, P., 'Galen and Aristotle's de Partibus Animalium', in Gotthelf [1.55].

10.66 Nutton, V., ed., *Galen: Problems and Prospects*, London, 1981.

10.67 Rawson, E., 'The life and death of Asclepiades of Bithynia', *Classical Quarterly* 32, 1982, 358–70.

10.68 Sedley, D.N., 'Chrysippus on psychophysical causality', in Brunschwig and Nussbaum [6.9].

10.69 Solmsen, F., 'Greek philosophy and the discovery of the nerves', *Museum Helveticum* 18, 1961, 150–97; repr. in Flashar [10.24].

10.70 Vallance, J., *The Lost Theory of Asclepiades of Bithynia*, Oxford, 1990.

10.71 Viano, C.A., 'Lo scetticismo antico e la medicina', in Giannantoni [10.35].

CHAPTER 11

Neo-Platonism

Eyjólfur K. Emilsson

Neo-Platonism is usually defined as the philosophy of Plotinus, who lived in the third century AD, and his followers in the pagan Graeco-Roman world in late antiquity. The most significant philosophers among these followers are Porphyry, Iamblichus and Proclus. In a more liberal sense the term 'Neo-Platonic' may be applied to all philosophers on whom these primary Neo-Platonists exerted considerable influence. It may thus be used so as to include Christian thinkers such as St Augustine, Boethius, Pseudo-Dionysius and John the Scot Erigena and of later people, Marsilio Ficino, Cusanus, Bruno and Cudworth, to name just a few.

Neo-Platonism was the dominant philosophy in the Graeco-Roman world from the third century till the sixth, when the emperor Justinian closed the pagan schools. It survived even after this in Alexandria down to the Islamic conquest in 642. Plotinus taught in Rome, but eventually Neo-Platonism spread out in the Empire, especially in the East, with major centers for a while in Rome, Syria and Pergamum, and with long lasting traditions in Athens and Alexandria. Neo-Platonism was thus an active philosophy for about 400 years. As the last phase of pagan philosophy prevalent in the early centuries of Christianity, Neo-Platonism was the school of ancient philosophy which at first opposed and soon profoundly influenced Christian thought and theology.[1] Its later stages are characterized by the Aristotelian Neo-Platonist Greek commentators, who fall outside the span of this volume. But even the period from Plotinus in the third century AD to Proclus in the fifth provides a fairly long list of Neo-Platonic philosophers. Rather than commenting on every name – our knowledge of the doctrines of most of the thinkers involved is extremely limited in any case – I shall treat Plotinus, the greatest mind of all the Neo-Platonists, most extensively. In so doing I shall point out traits that are characteristic of Neo-Platonism generally. This will be followed by shorter accounts of Porphyry, Iamblichus and Proclus.

The definition of Neo-Platonism given at the outset tells us of course nothing about philosophical content. Before attempting to give such an account, it may be helpful to have an outline of the background of Neo-Platonism in antiquity and an explanation of the term 'Neo-Platonism'.

Throughout antiquity there were thinkers, often quite different from each other, who claimed to be followers of Plato. Arguably, they were all right in maintaining such affiliation, for Plato's thought is so rich that one can develop it in many directions. Platonic tradition in antiquity can be divided into four main types that correspond, at least roughly, to different periods. First comes the Old Academy, a metaphysically inclined school of thought which dominated in Plato's Academy for the next few generations after Plato's death. In the early third century BC scepticism became the prevailing view. This tendency lasted into the first century BC, when the Academy became dogmatic again with Antiochus of Ascalon, who blended his Platonism with a good deal of Stoicism.

The period that follows till Plotinus (205–69/70) is usually called Middle Platonism.[2] Our knowledge about Platonic thinkers during this time is extremely fragmentary. Nevertheless, we know enough to affirm that there was considerable activity, by no means exclusively or even primarily in the Academy but at various places in the Hellenized world. In fact Middle Platonism is no unified school of thought, but a label put on various Platonically inspired thinkers at different places during this period. It is possible, nevertheless, to point out some general trends: Platonists have now become metaphysically oriented again, happily engaging in speculations about the ultimate principles and structure of the world. So in a way we see here a return to the kind of philosophy characteristic of the Old Academy but with important new features: the Middle Platonists generally show significant influence of other philosophical schools in terminology and even in doctrine. The Peripatetics are the most relevant here, but Stoic influence is by no means negligible. The authors Plutarch of Chaeronea and Apuleius (the author of the *Golden Ass*), who are better known for their non-philosophical writings, both wrote philosophical works and count as Middle Platonists. Among the philosophically most important of the Middle Platonists should be mentioned Albinus, author of *Introduction to Plato's Dialogues*, and Alcinous. The latter, whom some scholars wish to identify with Albinus, wrote a work called the *Didaskalikos*, which in many respects is representative of Middle Platonism. Concurrently with Middle Platonism and not easily distinguishable from it there arose a movement of Neo-Pythagoreanism represented by such figures as Moderatus and Numenius. Their doctrines paved the way for Plotinus, who was in fact accused of plagiarizing from Numenius.

Plotinus' thought, and thereby the kind of philosophy that has come to be known as Neo-Platonism, grows out of this soil. It is even questionable whether Plotinus, who on all accounts is considered the founder of

Neo-Platonism, really marks a breaking point in the history of Platonism. (As we shall see, this is not meant to downgrade his importance and originality.) For most of the supposedly characteristic elements of Neo-Platonism can be traced back to the Middle Platonists. Plotinus constitutes a historical milestone primarily because he synthesizes and in some respects carries further ideas already current. Nor should we forget that he is the first significant Platonist of his era who has left a large extant corpus. Even our meager sources suggest that a more complete picture of his Middle Platonist predecessors would reveal Plotinus as a great mind belonging to an already established mode of thought. Thus, Neo-Platonism, defined as a philosophical movement beginning with Plotinus, is a somewhat artificial notion.

As with the names of so many other movements in the history of culture, 'Neo-Platonism' is an intellectual historian's term of art, invented in modern times to describe the past. The philosophers involved surely did not think of themselves as *Neo*-Platonists. They would simply see themselves as Platonists, interpreters and followers of Plato's philosophy. But so have many others thought of themselves both before and after Plotinus and his followers in antiquity. The main reason why historians have found it expedient to put a special label, 'Neo-Platonists', on these particular Platonists is that for a long time after the study of Plato's dialogues was resumed in Europe during the Renaissance, the distinction between his thought and that of the late ancient Platonists, especially Plotinus and Proclus, tended to be blurred: Plato was generally seen from a Neo-Platonic viewpoint. Moreover, this attitude was often mixed with an effort to harmonize and even mix Platonism with Christianity. Gradually, however, it became evident that this view involved serious historical distortions. Not only did it turn out to be worth while to study Plato stripped of the outfit of the ancient Platonic tradition, not to mention Christianity, increasing historical awareness also suggested that many features foreign to Plato had infiltrated the minds of Plotinus and his successors. It was originally in a revolt against the historical errors of the total fusion of Plato and the late ancient Platonists that scholars began to distinguish sharply between the philosophy of Plato and that of Plotinus and his successors, calling the latter 'Neo-Platonists'.

Understandable as these motives are, the reaction was in some respects excessive: new historical errors and misunderstandings have separated Plato and the Neo-Platonists even further apart than is reasonable. The presence of Plato in the Neo-Platonists' writings, which today is obvious to all serious students of both, faded into the background, whereas all sorts of other elements came to the fore: the Neo-Platonists' alleged orientalism, superstition and philosophical eclecticism. Truly Platonic elements even went unnoticed in cases where they are, by hindsight, obvious. The most notorious example of this is scholarly views of the Neo-Platonic One (I shall have more to say about this shortly) about whose non-Platonic and even

non-Greek origin there had been imaginative speculations, until in 1928 E.R.
Dodds proved beyond any reasonable doubt that the One's key features
come right out of Plato's *Parmenides*.[3] The fact is that as philosophers the
Neo-Platonists are above all genuine Platonists and this must be the first
guiding principle in the interpretation of their thought.

But what sort of Platonists? It is sometimes said that Neo-Platonism is
Plato without Socrates, meaning that the ethico-political side of Plato as well
as Socratic ignorance with all its implications are largely absent in the Neo-
Platonists. Their interests lie primarily in metaphysics and in the philosophy
of nature and of Man as seen from the viewpoint of their metaphysics. In fact
there are relatively few Platonic passages on which the Neo-Platonists build.
The *Timaeus* enjoys a prominent position, presenting for the Neo-Platonists
a picture of the world as a whole and its structure. Other much cited dialogues are the *Parmenides* (the second part), which was thought to present
Plato's theology (i.e. metaphysics or ontology) – the Neo-Pythagoreans
mentioned above were the first to read the *Parmenides* in this way; the
Republic, especially books V–VII and the myth of Er. To this may be added
passages from the *Symposium* (Diotima's speech), *Phaedrus*, *Phaedo*,
Theaetetus, *Philebus*, the *Sophist*, the *Laws* and the first *Alcibiades*.

The Neo-Platonists were convinced that Plato presents a coherent and
true account of the reality. The problem is to understand him correctly, for
often he expresses himself cryptically – according to the Neo-Platonists
Plato's myths contain important philosophical truths. In addition the tradition of Plato's unwritten doctrines, i.e. Aristotle's presentation of Plato's
principles and accounts of the celebrated lecture on the Good, play a role
in the Neo-Platonists' picture of Plato. Not that the tradition of the unwritten doctrines supersedes that of the dialogues; rather the dialogues
are interpreted in the light of the 'unwritten doctrines'. An example of this is
the identification of the One and the Good as Plato's highest principle.

The Neo-Platonists could not fail to be influenced by the philosophical
developments that took place in the Graeco-Roman world during the 600
years between Plato and Plotinus as well as by the intellectual climate of their
day. In the third century AD it was impossible to talk about philosophy
without some Stoic and Aristotelian accent, which had become a part of
the language of philosophy itself. And however convinced a Platonist a late
ancient philosopher may have been, he would of course use any tools
available to him and compatible with his basic Platonic views to argue for and
state his position. Thus, the Neo-Platonists' position can be compared to that
of, say, any sensible Marxist of today who uses whatever he finds useful in
twentieth-century non-Marxist philosophy, sociology or economics, not
attempting to transform himself into a nineteenth-century mind but, on the
contrary, addressing the issues of the day. In any case, for the Neo-Platonists
Aristotle was not a complete outsider. The late ancient Platonist attitudes
towards him vary from hostility to a friendliness that would only befit a

faithful fellow Platonist. Plotinus' attitude may perhaps be expressed by saying that Aristotle was an aberrant Platonist who nevertheless is most useful. After Porphyry the dominant view came to be that in fact Plato and Aristotle were in essential agreement.

Plato belonged to Athens, a small homogeneous city-state, where active participation in politics was expected of every free man; the Neo-Platonists, by contrast, belonged to the immense and multifarious Roman Empire. The general mood of the times, not only among the Neo-Platonists themselves who in due course did much to create the intellectual climate at least among the educated, was oriented inwards and upwards rather than out to the physical world and society. The rise of Christianity and the popularity of gnosticism and other kindred trends bear witness to this. All this helps to explain the Neo-Platonists' lack of enthusiasm for Plato's worldly ethics and political philosophy and preoccupation with the speculative aspects of his thought.

How good an interpretation of Plato came out of all this? This is by no means an easy question to answer, if only because also today even fundamental aspects of Plato's philosophy are debated. The Neo-Platonists did not have a sense of a development in Plato's thought and they would give much greater weight to Plato's myths and allegorical interpretations than most scholars today are willing to do. However, given that one's task is to set forth systematic metaphysics out of the Platonic material the Neo-Platonists rely on, their results are not at all implausible, as can be seen from the fact that modern scholars who attempt to reconstruct systematic metaphysics out of Plato tend to come up with structures that have a good deal in common with Neo-Platonism, albeit admittedly not the whole thing.

Plato is in any event a central figure in ancient philosophy: he brings together many ideas from previous Greek philosophy and puts a strong mark on subsequent ancient mainstream metaphysics, i.e. on the Aristotelian and the Stoic traditions in addition to the Platonic tradition itself. So Neo-Platonism as a philosophical movement concerned with Plato's thought while being aware of and employing ideas from the other schools can be fruitfully seen as a culmination not only of Platonic but Greek metaphysical thought in general. In many cases Neo-Platonism takes to their extreme, to their logical conclusion one might even say, ideas already present in the tradition. The philosophical value of the movement lies not least in this play with the entire Greek tradition which results in a distinctive and, when at its best, quite sophisticated metaphysical thinking.

Within the history of philosophy Neo-Platonism has a rather peculiar and in some respects an uncomfortable position. It lies on the border between antiquity and the Middle Ages, which constitute two separate fields of expertise whose focal points lie far from Neo-Platonism. The Neo-Platonists' writings also tend to make difficult reading, even for philosophical works. This is not only because their works may present views that are in themselves difficult to grasp, but also and no less because the Neo-Platonists incorporate and presuppose so much of the previous Greek tradition in their writings that no Neo-Platonic text is intelligible without prior familiarity with this tradition. The result of all this is that the Neo-Platonists are usually not given much attention in the standard philosophy curriculum. Furthermore, the prevailing trends in twentieth-century philosophy, especially in the English-speaking world, have on the whole been unsympathetic towards Neo-Platonism, which is seen to exhibit many signs of corrupt philosophy: uncontrolled rationalistic metaphysical speculation combined with faith in an authority (who is moreover misunderstood); to this are added the sins of mysticism, occultism and superstition. Even if genuine progress has been made in Neo-Platonic studies in recent years, the image of the Neo-Platonist as a thinker engaged in 'wild fancy' seems to linger on. While there are certainly passages that make some of these charges understandable, the Neo-Platonists' reputation as philosophers has in general been lower than they deserve. And whatever one thinks of their philosophy, the Neo-Platonists have had an immense influence not only on the history of philosophy but also in the history of art, literature and science. Richard Wallis hardly exaggerates when he writes that 'a survey of Neo-Platonism's influence threatens to become little less than a cultural history of Europe and the Near East down to the Renaissance, and on some points far beyond'.[4] At the end of this chapter I shall briefly take up the issue of the influence of Neo-Platonism.

 PLOTINUS, THE MASTER
THINKER OF NEO-PLATONISM

LIFE AND WRITINGS

We are lucky to have a fairly reliable account of Plotinus' life and writings. His student, friend and editor, Porphyry, composed a biography, *On the Life of Plotinus and the Order of His Books* (hereafter *Life*) which prefaced his posthumous edition of Plotinus' writings. Plotinus was born in 204/5, probably in Lycopolis in Egypt, though this piece of information does not come from Porphyry. About his ethnic origin nothing is known, but he wrote in Greek. At the age of 28 Plotinus began his philosophical studies in Alexandria under a certain Ammonius (often called Ammonius Saccas), with whom he studied for about eleven years. In an attempt to acquaint himself with the philosophy of Persia and India, he joined the emperor Gordian on a campaign against the Persians. Gordian was murdered on the way and Plotinus escaped with difficulty. He settled in Rome at the age of 40, where he established a school. He stayed in Rome for the rest of his life except during his final illness, when he retired to Campania.

Few ancient philosophers have left a larger extant corpus than Plotinus and we probably possess everything he wrote. His works are treatises that vary greatly in length and scope. Some are only a few pages dealing with a specific question, while others are extensive writings. Porphyry arranged the treatises according to subject matter into six sets of nine treatises, i.e. six 'enneads'. In order to arrive at this division he had to split some treatises, for example IV.3–5, *The Problems of Soul*, which originally was a single treatise. The order is supposed to be pedagogical, starting with the easier and proceeding to the more difficult. Thus, Porphyry included in the first *Ennead* treatises that deal with ethical matters. In the second and third he put treatises dealing with the physical universe. The fourth is about soul and the fifth about intellect and the doctrine of the three principal hypostases. Porphyry does not say explicitly which subject the sixth *Ennead* is supposed to cover, but apparently it is meant to be being and the One. In any case, Porphyry's arrangement according to subject matter is an approximate one, partly because he is forcing the material to meet his principles of division, partly because many of Plotinus' treatises do not readily fall under one, or even two, headings.[5]

Plotinus' treatises grew out of discussions in his school. These discussions would often be concerned with exegesis of some text or other. Plotinus used to have commentaries on Plato and Aristotle read in the school (*Life*, 14). The object of reading these would be to arrive at a correct understanding of the relevant primary text. Thus, more often than not, Plotinus' writings are interpretations of some Platonic text or doctrine, sometimes involving refutations of rival interpretations. However, he did not follow the standard procedures of the writing of commentaries. Porphyry says that he did not speak straight out of the books that were read in his seminars 'but took a distinctive personal line in his consideration, and brought the mind of Ammonius to bear on the investigations in hand' (*Life*, 14, 14–16). Of Plotinus' manner of writing Porphyry informs us that when Plotinus wrote he did so continuously as if he was copying from a book and that owing to bad eyesight he could not bear to read over what he had written (*Life*, 8). All this suggests that the style of Plotinus' lectures and writings was quite unconventional. So far as his writings are concerned we can confirm that so they are indeed. Already in antiquity people complained that he was difficult to follow (*Life*, 17–18). He was sometimes accused of being 'a big driveller', sometimes a plagiarist (*Life*, 17). Porphyry's account of Plotinus' style and manner of philosophizing aims to show that such accusations are unjustified.

Plotinus is sometimes described as a systematic philosopher who never reveals his whole system in an organized way and that the system must be inferred from bits and pieces here and there in his writings. Another common dictum is that every one of his treatises presupposes all the rest and the whole system. Even if there is something to these claims and a more organized comprehensive view lies behind Plotinus' writings than meets the eye, Plotinus' mind is not that of the rigid system-builder. In this he is different from Proclus and even Porphyry. Plotinus has perhaps been seen as more of a system-builder than he really is because many features of later Neo-Platonists' systems can be detected by the benefit of hindsight in Plotinus' works. Plotinus' philosophical genius consists rather in the combination of sensitivity and shrewdness with which he addresses the problems inherent in his tradition. The result is that after him this tradition was transformed.

❧ PLOTINIAN METAPHYSICS ❧

A characteristic of Plotinus' philosophy and Neo-Platonism generally is a division of reality into hierarchically ordered stages or levels, so-called 'hypostases'. The following list presents the main levels of the Plotinian hierarchy, which was essentially taken over by the later Neo-Platonists though certain details may have varied.

> The One (the Good)
> Being – Intellect – Platonic Ideas
> Soul
> The World-Soul – Individual Souls
> Organisms
> Bodies
> Matter

Why should reality be structured in this way? In order to answer this question let us first point out some affinities with earlier Greek thought. From the outset Greek philosophers were engaged in explaining the world of everyday experience in terms of some underlying nature: Thales proposed water, Anaximander some indeterminate nature, Plato the Ideas and so forth. In general the Greek philosophers took a strong realist position with regard to their explanatory postulates – principles (*archai*) as they came to be called. Not only were the principles supposed to exist, but frequently they were supposed to be more real, to exist in some fuller sense, than that which they were meant to explain.

The Neo-Platonic One, Intellect, Soul are principles in this traditional sense. With certain qualifications, to be explained below, so is matter. Inorganic bodies, organisms and their functions, and human consciousness and experiences are phenomena to be accounted for in terms of the principles. We can even readily identify the sources of the Neo-Platonic principles in previous Greek thought:[6] the One (the Good) is founded on Platonic passages such as the first hypothesis of the *Parmenides* and the Idea of the Good in the *Republic*. In formulating his theory about it Plotinus also draws on Parmenides of Elea himself, the Pythagoreans, Speusippus and Xenocrates, all of whom posited a One as an ultimate principle. Intellect, as the sphere of being and the Ideas, has its source in Plato of course but also in Aristotle, especially *Metaphysics* 12, where God is described as a pure intellectual activity. Soul as a cosmological principle comes primarily from Plato's *Timaeus*. Plotinus' notion of matter is a combination of the receptacle of forms in the *Timaeus* and Aristotle's notion of matter. The three first principles, the One, Intellect and Soul, comprise together the intelligible world (though, as we shall see, the One is not strictly speaking intelligible). Like Plato, Plotinus works with a fundamental dichotomy between the intelligible and the sensible. The intelligible world is distinguished from the sensible world primarily by being non-spatial; it is also the sphere of the real (in the sense of being what it is in virtue of itself), whereas in Plotinus' view nothing in the sensible world counts as real in this sense.

So the Neo-Platonic hierarchy is a hierarchy of principles. But a host of questions remains: Why do the principles assume a hierarchical form? What are the distinguishing features of each level? Why exactly these principles? How are the levels related to one another? The answer to the first question is that once we have distinguished between what is to be accounted for and a principle that explains it, questions may arise about the principle itself: the principle itself may turn out to have features that stand in need of an explanation and a further principle must then be postulated to account for the one we encountered first. This process may go on until we come up with a principle which needs no further explanation, a principle about which no further questions can be asked. For the Neo-Platonists this ultimate principle is the One.

The Neo-Platonists generally assume that the explanatory principles themselves must have the features they explain. For instance Soul, which is the principle of life in the sensible realm, is itself alive. Moreover, the principles ideally have these features in such a way that it is pointless to ask why they have them. The principle possesses of itself what other things possess as an imposed feature and hence one that requires explanation. Plotinus frequently expresses this by saying of a principle that it is such and such in itself (*en heautôi*), whereas other things have the same feature as in another (*en allôi*). This corresponds roughly to what in modern philosophy is expressed in terms of necessary and contingent properties. The notion that the principles have of themselves the features they explain in others is of course implicit or explicit in much of previous Greek thought: for example the Platonic Ideas are themselves primary instances of what other things are in virtue of them – the Idea of beauty is beautiful *par excellence*. Let us call this assumption the Principle of the Self-Sufficiency of the Cause.

The Neo-Platonic hierarchy is above all a hierarchy of degrees of unity: each level has a characteristic kind of unity with the One on top as the absolutely simple stage which, by the Principle of the Self-Sufficiency of the

Cause, is the cause of all other unity there is and thereby, in fact, the cause of everything else whatsoever. Why should unity be such an important concept? Once again Plotinus is drawing on the previous Greek tradition and interpreting the facts in light of it. Unity had been a key concept in the tradition from the Pythagoreans and the Eleatics to Aristotle and the Old Academy: unity is what distinguishes between an entity and a non-entity. Plotinus accepts Aristotle's view that being and unity are coextensive: to be is to be one thing, to be unified, and the more 'one' something is the more of a being it is. The most striking feature of the world of everyday experience is in fact the unity of it as a whole and of individual objects, especially living things, in it. The organization, regularity and beauty that is evident in the world of everyday experience – all these may be said to express its unity – cannot be explained in terms of its constituent parts. The latter are what is unified and their unity is an imposed feature which must come from elsewhere. The unity revealed in the sensible world is far from perfect but it gives the sensible world the reality it has. The same may be said of our experiences of ourselves: introspection shows that the human soul has a more perfect kind of unity than anything pertaining to the body, although even the soul does not have unity of itself (IV.2 (4) 2; IV.7. (2) 6–7). Thus, our everyday experiences, both of the external world and our mental life, point beyond themselves to a higher level of reality which is its principle.

This process of going upwards from everyday phenomena to their principles reminds us of and in fact draws on Plato's dialectic as described for instance in the *Symposium* and the *Republic*. There are many instances of such spiritual ascent in the *Enneads*. The most famous one is Plotinus' first treatise, *On Beauty*, I.6, where he builds on Diotima's speech in the *Symposium*. This treatise has been extremely influential in art, especially during the Renaissance. The ascent from the beauty of corporeal things to the Beautiful itself is as one would expect interpreted in terms of the Plotinian hierarchy and general doctrine of spiritual ascent. Interestingly, he deviates from Plato's views of the arts as expressed in the *Republic* in that for Plotinus art does not imitate nature but operates in parallel with nature (I.6.3; V.8 (31) 1). Thus, the artist uses the intelligible world directly and expresses it in sensible form. The artist's status is thereby elevated to that of a micro-demiurge instead of being a maker of shadows of shadows. Other treatises where spiritual ascent is prominent are I.3 (20), *On Dialectic*, V.1, *On the Three Primary Hippostases* (10) and *On the Knowing Hypostaseis* V.3 (4). In IV.7 (4), *On the Soul's Immortality*, Plotinus argues against rival views on the nature of the soul and attempts to prove its independence of the body and kinship with a higher realm. This is one of Plotinus' most accessible treatises and shows how he thinks everyday natural phenomena point to transcendent causes.

Leaving the intermediate stages aside for the moment, the Principle of the Self-Sufficiency of the Cause together with the claim that everything presupposes unity, leads to the highest principle, the One. The doctrine of the One, even if foreshadowed by the tradition before Plotinus, is presumably his most significant contribution. His Aristotelizing predecessors such as Alcinous and Numenius believed in a simple first principle, but, like Aristotle, they thought that this simple principle was an intellect of some sort. As we have seen, in Plotinus the level below the One is an intellect which is characterized by a high degree of unity. Nevertheless, Plotinus maintains, any intellect involves plurality: there is plurality in thought because there is at least a conceptual distinction between the thought and its object, and what is thought is in any case varied (cf. for example V.3.10.). So the One is not an intellect.

The One is both absolutely simple and unique – i.e. there can at most be one absolutely simple principle (V.4 (7) 1) – and it involves no variation or limitation. From this it follows that the One cannot be positively described. It cannot be grasped by thought or known in its true nature, since any thought of it distorts in so far as the thought is bound to be composite. It is not even appropriate to say of the One that it *is*, or that it *is one*, since such expressions indicate something unified rather than the absolutely simple nature which gives unity to whatever is unified (VI.9.5). Nevertheless, it is possible to approach the One and even become one with it in a kind of non-cognitive union, a 'vision' which escapes all description (VI.9 (9) 8–11). On account of this doctrine of a union with the ultimate principle, a union which transcends conceptualization, Plotinus has been called a mystic. It must however be said that this 'mystical union' does not play a major role in his writings.

Even if there are precedents for a supreme formal principle in Plotinus' tradition, most of his predecessors would postulate in addition other ultimate principles. Thus, Aristotle posits both form and matter and it seems that Plato too, in the *Philebus* and according to Aristotle's account, posits in addition to a formal, unifying principle an independent principle of plurality. In Plotinus and the other Neo-Platonists this is different. Even if the lower levels in his hierarchy function in fact as principles of multiplicity – we shall see in greater detail below precisely how – all these lower levels derive from the One. In this sense Plotinus is an unwavering monist.

Intellect, the level below the One, is the realm of the Platonic Ideas and of real being – by which is meant that which is what it is in virtue of itself, not through something else. Historically the Plotinian Intellect is the unification of Aristotle's God from *Metaphysics* 12 (identified with the demiurge of Plato's *Timaeus*), the active intellect of *On the Soul* 3, 4–6 and the realm of the Platonic Ideas. The identification of the realm of the Ideas with real being is straightforward, provided that one believes in Platonic Ideas, for by definition each Idea is perfectly and of itself that which it causes in others. More problematic is the identification of the Ideas with a divine intellect. Plotinus finds historical support for such a view in Plato's *Sophist* where the Ideas are said to have intelligence and life, and in Aristotle's views of God:

God is an Intellect and at the same time the supreme being or substance, i.e. it is in virtue of being pure thought of himself that God is pure actuality, and being pure actuality God has a fuller being than anything else, is more real. But what philosophical motivation lies behind placing the Ideas within a divine Intellect?

An important question Platonists face is how to describe the relation between the demiurge and his intelligible model in the *Timaeus* in precise philosophical terms. In treatise V.5(32), *That the Ideas are not Outside the Intellect and on the One*, Plotinus discusses this question and gives several arguments for the view that the Ideas are indeed internal to the divine intellect. Of these arguments the philosophically most interesting one is an argument to the effect that if the Ideas are outside the Intellect, the latter's knowledge of them must be acquired, i.e. the Intellect will receive only an impression of the Idea, not the Idea itself; but the Ideas are the standards of judgment and if the Intellect does not possess these standards previously, it will lack the necessary means of recognizing the impression of each Idea for what it is. So, if the Intellect does not essentially contain the Ideas as its thoughts, its knowledge and wisdom become problematic: an unacceptable conclusion since it is agreed that the divine intellect has supreme knowledge.

These ideas are further developed in V.3(49) where there emerges a picture of the Intellect as really identical with, though conceptually distinct from, the objects of its thought, the Ideas. The Intellect's thought is described as self-thought and its knowledge as a kind of self-knowledge. At the same time this self-thought is the Ideas and real being. In his account of this Plotinus makes use of the Aristotelian view that God is an Intellect and also what is supremely real, a substance *par excellence*: only a self-contained thought is fully actual, pure actuality. But Plotinus goes far beyond Aristotle not only in identifying the thoughts of the Intellect with the Ideas but also in his use of this doctrine. For him, the identification of real being with a divine intellect means that there is a level of reality where knowledge and being, epistemology and ontology, coincide. This he takes to be a necessary condition of the possibility of knowledge.

We mentioned above that Intellect is characterized by a greater unity than the sensible world.[7] Intellect is non-spatial and non-temporal and hence free from the dispersion that has to do with space and time. (It follows from this that talk of 'above' and 'below', 'first' and 'after' in connection with the hypostases is of course merely metaphorical.) Secondly, the part–whole relations in Intellect are such that not only does the whole contain its parts, the whole is also implicit in each of the parts (cf. for example VI.2.20). Thirdly, as we have noted there is not a real distinction between subject and attribute on the level of Intellect. It is replaced by the notion of intellectual substance and its activity (*energeia*), which is identical with the substance. Much of this doctrine about the relationships between the items on the level of Intellect is founded on interpretations and suggestions in Plato's late dialogues. Plotinus takes the five greatest kinds of the *Sophist*, being, sameness, difference, motion and rest, as the highest genera of his ontology. Each of these is at once distinct and presupposes and is interwoven with all the others. Together they constitute the Intellect or the Intelligible substance and particular Ideas are generated from them as species from higher genera. The integrity of Intellect implies that Intellect's thought, Intellect's self-thought as we have seen, is in some ways different from ordinary thought: it employs neither inferences nor words; its objects which are at the same time its vehicles are the very things themselves, the prototypes and causes of which everything else, whether natural phenomena or lower modes of human thought, are inferior manifestations.

Soul is the level below Intellect.[8] On account of the multiplicity of its functions Soul is in some ways the most complex of the Plotinian hypostases and conceptually the least unified one. The historical sources of Plotinus' notion of soul are primarily Plato, above all the *Timaeus*, but Plotinus' psychology also reveals strong Aristotelian and Stoic influences. We shall have more to say about human psychology later in connection with Plotinus' views on Man and the remarks here are intended primarily to give an outline of the place of soul within the system.

The hypostasis Soul is the intelligible level that is directly responsible for the sensible world. Thus, everything below the level of soul is its product: matter itself, inorganic bodies, ordinary living things, including the sensible cosmos itself, which according to the Neo-Platonists as well as Plato and the Stoics is a supreme organism. Certain difficulties arise precisely on account of Soul's close relationship with the sensible. In the first place, how can soul cause the extended sensible world, administer it and, in fact, ensoul it without thereby coming to share in its extended nature? How could soul operate here and also there without being divisible into spatially distinct parts? If it is divided, its intelligible status will be lost or at least seriously threatened. This difficulty is increased by the fact that according to common and deeply ingrained opinion soul is present in the bodies it ensouls. Plato in the *Timaeus* even speaks of the soul of the world as extending throughout it. Plotinus was deeply disturbed by these and other puzzles having to do with the soul's relationship with the sensible realm as is shown by the fact that he returns to them repeatedly.

Plotinus finds it necessary to make certain distinctions within the level of soul. There is the hypostasis Soul, which remains in the intelligible realm, and there is the World-Soul and the souls of individuals, the latter two being on the same level (IV.3.1–8). Plotinus further distinguishes within the two latter types of soul between a higher and a lower soul, corresponding to a distinction between soul directly operating through a body and soul not so operating (this distinction coincides with the distinction between rational and non-rational soul). These distinctions are useful for other purposes, but surely do not solve the real philosophical difficulties about the soul's relation to the sensible realm. For if the sensible realm is caused and administered by something belonging to the intelligible realm something of the intelligible order must stain itself in the mud, as it were.

Nor does Plotinus think, at least not when he is at his best, that creating new levels will help solve this problem. One solution he frequently suggests and argues for, mainly from facts about the unity of consciousness in sensation, is that the soul is present as a whole at every point of the body it ensouls. Thereby it can be at different places without being divided. Its being so present as a whole in different parts of space shows its different ontological status from that of bodies which have numerically distinct spatial parts (see for example IV.2.2). Another account, however, presents soul as not present in body at all, but rather the reverse, body as present to soul: body is in soul somewhat as bodies may be said to be in light or in heat; they thereby become illuminated or warm without (in Plotinus' view) dividing or affecting the source of light or heat in any way. Similarly, bodies become ensouled, alive, in virtue of presence to soul (IV.3.22; IV.4.18). The treatises VI.4 and VI.5(21–2), *On the Ubiquitous Presence of Being* (which constitute a single treatise), contain what is perhaps Plotinus' subtlest account of the relation between the sensible and the intelligible along these lines.

In connection with Plotinus' views on Soul mention should be made of the strange doctrine that all souls are one, that all souls are identical with the hypostasis Soul (and by implication with one another). The Neo-Platonists after Porphyry rejected this doctrine but Plotinus maintains it consistently and attaches considerable importance to it (IV.9 (8), VI.4.4; IV.3.1–8 (27)). Plotinus is clearly aware that the doctrine sounds strange and he himself seems not altogether at ease in maintaining it. So one may wonder why he considers it necessary to do so. Such a doctrine however seems to be implied by the combination of two Plotinian doctrines that we have just mentioned: the soul's membership in the intelligible realm (or the realm of real being) and the integrity of that realm. The upshot of the treatises VI.4–5 is that if being is indivisible, and what participates in being therefore participates in it as a whole, and if the so-called presence of soul in extension is just another way of looking at such participation, then the whole of soul must presumably be present to whatever any soul is present to. In other words, the doctrine of the unity of soul can be seen as just a special case of the indivisibility of being.

Above we mentioned that Intellect is outside space and time. In III.7 (45), *On Eternity and Time*, Plotinus states his views on time. Developing his own view from the account in Plato's *Timaeus*, Plotinus offers interesting and powerful criticisms of the views of Aristotle, the Stoics and the Epicureans. He defines eternity as 'the life which belongs to that which is and is in that which is, all together and full, completely without extension or interval' (III.7.3, 36–8) and time he defines as 'the life of soul in the movement of passage from one mode of life to another' (III.7.11, 43–5). Thus, time comes in at the level of soul as the 'image of eternity'. This means that the soul, in producing the sensible world, unfolds in successive stages what is present all together and without interval at the level above. Plotinus' doctrine of time had deep impact in the West, for it influenced both St Augustine and Boethius.

The lowest level in the Plotinian hierarchy is matter.[9] Plotinian matter is like the One in that it permits no positive characterization, but for exactly the opposite reasons: the One is, one might say, so full, so perfect that it eludes any positive description; matter, on the contrary, is such on account of its utter privation, lack of being. It is the receptacle or substrate of immanent bodily forms, such as colors, shapes and sizes. Physical objects, bodies, are composites of matter and such immanent forms. Matter itself is not subject to change but underlies change: as forms come and go matter remains un-affected (III.6 (26)). It is as such imperceptible but reason convinces us of its existence as a purely negatively characterized substrate of forms. Since matter is what underlies all forms of bodies, it might be tempting to identify it with space or with mass. Plotinus considers this and rejects it. The three-dimensionality of space presupposes local determination and all mass contains form, but matter is totally indeterminate and without form (II.4 (12) 8–12). Nevertheless, matter is the principle of spatial extension in that the dispersion characteristic of space is due to matter (II.4.11–12). So matter is a principle in the sense that it is necessary to explain plurality, though it is not a principle of being in Plotinus' sense.

In this brief account of the Plotinian hierarchy every now and then mention has been made of the relationships between the stages: we have noted for instance that a given level is somehow 'produced' by one above it. It remains, however, to address this topic generally. Plotinus and the other Neo-Platonists use Plato's language of participation: a lower level participates in a higher one and thereby comes to have the character of the latter. They also use Plato's language of model, imitation and image to the same affect. What is new in Neo-Platonism in this regard is the so-called emanation – a term that has found its way into just about every survey of Neo-Platonism, however brief. Plotinus frequently uses the analogies of the sun and the light it radiates, fire and heat and the like to illustrate how a higher hypostasis generates a lower. Sometimes he uses metaphors from the language of water ('to flow out' etc.). The later Neo-Platonists speak of 'procession' from the higher to the lower. Thus, the Neo-Platonists frequently describe the production of the lower in terms of some kind of process originating in the higher. The term 'emanation' may however mislead in so far as it suggests that the cause spreads itself out. The Neo-Platonists on the contrary consistently maintain that the cause always remains unaffected and loses nothing by giving away.

In Plotinus there is sometimes an explicit and often an implicit distinction drawn between an 'internal activity' and an 'external activity' (cf. e.g V.3.12; V.4.2). This distinction runs through every Plotinian cause down to soul and is crucial for an understanding of causation in the Plotinian system. Keeping in mind what was said above about the identity of a substance with its activity (*energeia*), the internal activity will be the same as the thing itself. In terms of the light analogy the inner act is whatever the source of light, considered in itself and as a source of light, is doing. The external act is this same entity as operating in something else, causing the brightness on the wall for instance. It is illuminating to compare this with Aristotle's account of actualization.[10] When a teacher, who actually knows something, teaches a pupil what he knows, the teacher is producing an effect in another without being cut off from that other (cf. *Physics* 3, 202b7–8). The events of teaching and learning are in fact one and the same event, though different in definition. Plotinus applies and transforms these ideas: the external act, the effect in another, becomes an inferior image or expression of the original, an image which nevertheless is not cut off from its cause, because the image still depends on the activity of the cause.

It makes the matter still more complicated that the Neo-Platonists speak not only of a process from the cause but also of a reversion (*epistrophê*) of the produced towards its source. It is clear that the analogies from everyday physical phenomena mentioned above are no longer of any help here: the light on the wall surely does not have to return to the sun. In any event the Neo-Platonists thought that some kind of reversion is needed whereby the product is informed by the source in order for the product to be complete (see for example V.1, 5–7 and Proclus, *Elements of Theology* (hereafter *ET*), props. 31–9). The outward process and the reversion are not temporal processes and hence neither is temporally prior to the other. Nor does reversion mean 'reunion' – in that case nothing new would come about. Rather it seems that the Neo-Platonists thought that the outward process distinguishes the product from the original whereas the reversion establishes their identity, which however is not complete since what assumes the character of the source in the reversion is something which by proceeding is already other than the source (6, 130–5). As the Neo-Platonists do not posit any kind of pre-existent matter as the recipient of form, what gets informed must come from the informing cause. Thus, the outgoing aspect functions as a material principle, the returning aspect as the informing of the material principle.

This structure of process from a source which remains in itself unaffected and then a reversion, an inclination back towards the source, pervades the system. Only at the very lowest level, that of matter and immanent sensible forms, is there no generation, which of course is another way of saying that we have reached the bottom. So what is the external activity of the One becomes the internal activity of Intellect, which in turn has Soul as its external activity. The internal activity of a generated hypostasis consists of thought of its source, a reversion. We may visualize the system as a hierarchy where each stage below the One is an expression or a mirror image of its cause, revealing a more 'unfolded' and thereby, in the Neo-Platonists' view, causally weaker version of it – 'unfolding' is one of Plotinus' favorite metaphorical expressions. So in a way the same items exist on every level: the One is everything there is, but in such a unified form that no distinctions are to be found. Likewise, Intellect and Soul, and finally the physical world contain everything there is.

❧ PLOTINUS' VIEWS ON MAN ❧

Plotinus' attitude towards the sensible world and to human life within it is somewhat ambivalent. While constantly emphasizing its low worth as compared with the higher realms, he does not consider it totally evil or worthless. In all essentials his view is the same as Plato's in the middle dialogues. First I shall present an outline of the picture and then take up certain aspects in greater detail.

Man is identified with his higher soul, reason (I.1(53) 7, etc.). The soul is distinct from the body and survives it: it is essentially a member of the intelligible realm and has a source in Intellect on which it constantly depends. This undescended source is sometimes described as the real man and our true self. However, as a result of the communion with the body and through it with the sensible world, human beings may also identify themselves with the body and the sensible. Thus, Man stands on the border between two worlds, the sensible and the intelligible. Our existential choice is about which of the two we identify ourselves with. Philosophy is the means of purification and intellectual vision. As noted above it is possible, however, to ascend beyond the level of philosophy and arrive at a mystical reunion with the source of all, the One. In contrast with the post-Porphyrian Neo-Platonists, who maintained theurgy as an alternative, Plotinus stands firmly with classical Greek rationalism in holding that philosophical training and contemplation are the means by which we can ascend to the intelligible realm.

The most noteworthy feature of Plotinus' psychology is perhaps his use of Aristotelian machinery to defend what is unmistakably Platonic dualism (17; 21). We find him for instance using the Aristotelian distinctions between reason, sense-perception and vegetative soul much more than the tripartition of Plato's *Republic*. He employs the notions of power and act, and sense-perception is described in Aristotelian terms as the reception of the form of the object perceived. However he never slavishly follows Aristotle and one should expect some modifications even where Plotinus sounds quite Aristotelian.

Sense-perception in Plotinus is an interesting case of how he can be original while relying on tradition.[11] He sees sense-perception as the soul's internalization of something external and extended. This involves grave difficulties: on the one hand, the external physical object must evidently somehow affect the percipient, if there is to be perception of that object; on the other hand, action of a lower level on a higher is generally ruled out and a genuine affection of the soul is in any case objectionable because the soul is not subject to change. So Plotinus sees sense-perception as involving the crossing of an ontological gap between the sensible and the intelligible. In formulating this problem his dualism becomes sharper and in some respects closer to modern Cartesian dualism than anything we find in Plato or previous ancient thinkers.[12]

His solution to the problem is clever even if it is questionable whether it succeeds in all respects: what is affected from the outside is an ensouled sense-organ, not the soul itself. This affection of the sense-organ is however not the perception itself but rather something like a mere preconceptual sensation; the perception proper belongs to the soul and consists in a judgment (*krisis*) of the external object. This judgment does not constitute a genuine change in the soul for it is an actualization of a power already present. Plotinus contrasts sense-perception as a form of cognition with Intellect's thought which is the paradigm and source of all other forms of cognition. Sense-perception is in fact a mode of thought but obscure (VI.7 (38) 7). This is so apparently because the senses do not grasp the 'things themselves', the thoughts on the level of Intellect, but mere images. Since they are images they also fail to reveal the grounds of their being and necessary connections. This is Plotinus' version of the view that considered in themselves facts about the sensible world appear contingent.

In the treatise I.8 (51), *On What Are and Whence Come Evils*, Plotinus discusses at length questions concerning evil, a topic also brought up in many other treatises. The intelligible world is perfect and totally self-sufficient. The sensible world, which is imperfect and contains evil, is a reflection of the former and contains nothing which does not have its origins there. It is therefore puzzling how evil can have arisen: can it be caused by what is perfect? Plotinus argues that evil as such does exist and he identifies it with matter, understood as total formlessness. Being total formlessness matter is in a sense nothing, and hence evil; even if it exists, it is not an entity. In Plotinus' view the existence of absolute evil is required by the fact that the Good exists. Matter is to be understood as the contrary of the Good in the sense that it is that which is furthest removed from it and which thus is characterized by all the opposite features. Matter, as the negation of unity and being, is absolute evil. Other things such as bodies are evil in a relative way according to the extent of their participation in matter.

The goal of human life is the soul's liberation from the body and concerns with the sensible realm and reunion with the unchanging intelligible world. In outline this seems to be approximately the doctrine of Plato's *Phaedo*. But there are interesting elaborations. Plato affirms the soul's kinship with the Ideas on the ground that without such kinship it would be unable to know them. Plotinus agrees and presents an account of the nature of this kinship which goes beyond what can be found in Plato. As we have seen the whole realm of Ideas is for Plotinus the thought of Intellect and the human soul has a counterpart in Intellect, a partial mind which in fact is the true self on which the soul depends. This has two interesting consequences for the doctrine of spiritual ascent: first, the ascent may be correctly described as the search after oneself and, if successful, as true self-knowledge, as fully becoming what one essentially is.[13] Second, on account of Plotinus' doctrine about the interconnectedness of Intellect as a whole, this gain of self-knowledge and self-identity would also involve knowledge of the realm of Ideas as a whole.

Plotinus' views on classical Greek ethical topics such as virtue and happiness are determined by his general position that intellectual life is the true life and Man's proper goal. The treatise I.2(19) is devoted to the virtues. Plotinus' main objective here is to reconcile apparent discrepancies in Plato's teaching. In this case it is the doctrine of the four cardinal virtues in the *Republic*, the doctrine of the *Phaedo* according to which virtue is the soul's purification, and the view suggested in *Theaetetus* that the virtues assimilate us to the divine. Plotinus distinguishes between political virtues, purgative virtues and the archetypes of the virtues at the level of Intellect. These form a hierarchy of virtues. This classification is taken up and elaborated by Porphyry in the *Sententiae* (see p. 376 below). The function of the political virtues (the lowest grade) is to give order to the desires. The question arises whether the political virtues can be said to assimilate us to God (which for Plotinus is Intellect), for the divine does not have any desires that must be ordered and hence, it would seem, cannot possess the political virtues. Plotinus' answer is that although God does not possess the political virtues, there is something in God answering to them and from which they are derived. Further, the similarity that holds between a reflection and the original is not reciprocal. Thus, the political virtues may be images of something belonging to the divine without the divine possessing the political virtues as such.

The first *Ennead* contains two treatises dealing with happiness or well-being (*eudaimonia*): I.4(46), *On Happiness* and I.5(36), *On Whether Happiness Increases with Time*. In the former treatise Plotinus argues against the Epicurean view that happiness consists in pleasure, a sensation of a particular sort. One can be happy without being aware of it. He also rejects the Stoic account of happiness as rational life. His own position is that happiness applies to life as such, not to a certain sort of life. There is a supremely perfect and self-sufficient life, that of the hypostasis Intellect, upon which every other sort of life depends. Happiness pertains primarily to this perfect life, which does not depend on any external good. But as all other kinds of life are reflections of this one, all living beings are capable of at least a reflection of happiness according to the kind of life they have. On account of the human soul's ability to ascend, human beings are capable of attaining the perfect kind of life of Intellect. Plotinus holds with the Stoics that none of the so-called 'external evils' can deprive a happy man of his happiness and that none of the so-called 'goods' pertaining to the sensible world are necessary for human happiness. In the second treatise on happiness, Plotinus discusses various questions concerning the relation between happiness and time, in particular whether the length of a person's life is relevant to his happiness. His answer is that it is not, because happiness, consisting in a good life, must be the life of real being, i.e. that of Intellect. This life is not dispersed in time but is in eternity, which here means outside time, not lasting forever.

Plotinus makes several remarks on human freedom or autonomy, in particular in *On Destiny* (III.1), *On Providence* I and II (III.2–3) and in *On the Voluntary and on the Will of the One* (VI.8). He defines a voluntary act as one which is not forced and is carried out with full knowledge of everything relevant (VI.8.1). It appears that he had doubts that human beings, as agents in the sensible world, can be fully free in this sense, and hence they enjoy at best a limited autonomy. Nevertheless, in so far as the human soul is the agent of human actions, the person is responsible for them. Full autonomy belongs only to the soul that is entirely free from the body and lives on the level of Intellect. Thus, autonomy is possible, but it is questionable whether we are free to seek it and attain it.

PORPHYRY: THE DISSEMINATOR OF NEO-PLATONISM

Porphyry was an exceptionally learned man and a prolific writer, whose importance as a disseminator of Neo-Platonism can scarcely be exaggerated. Not only did he write extensively on philosophy strictly speaking but he applied his philosophical approach to other areas as well. After Porphyry Neo-Platonism became a way of thought and life having applications everywhere. During Porphyry's lifetime the Roman empire began to split into two and separate traditions began to evolve in the East and the West. Porphyry's works were known and had impact on both sides. For the West Porphyry is particularly important because some of his writings were translated into Latin and he influenced such important thinkers as St Augustine and Boethius.

Porphyry was born in Tyre in Phoenicia around AD 234. He studied first in Athens with Longinus, a learned Platonic scholar, and subsequently joined Plotinus in Rome where he stayed for six years and became a convert to Plotinus' version of Platonism. We do not have good records of his life after this, but we know that he lived in Sicily and then in Rome again, and presumably visited his native Syria. He died in c. 305. Porphyry wrote on a vast number of different subjects: commentaries on Plato, Aristotle,

Theophrastus, Ptolemy and Plotinus; philosophical and religious essays; the history of philosophy; on Homer and a work against the Christians. All in all there are some seventy-seven titles attributed to him. Only a small portion of this bulk is extant and what there is is often fragmentary. Of these writings the following are the most philosophically significant: *Aids to the Study of the Intelligibles* (best known under its Latin title *Sententiae ad intelligibilia ducentes*); *Isagoge* (introduction to Aristotle's *Categories*); *Letter to Marcella* and *On abstinence*; excerpts of the works *On the Return of the Soul* and *Miscellaneous questions* (*Symmikta zêtêmata*) are preserved by St Augustine and Nemesius, respectively. Then there is an incomplete commentary on Plato's *Parmenides* which is likely to be by Porphyry or someone close to him.

We have Porphyry's own words for his admiration of Plotinus as a philosopher in his *Life of Plotinus*. The writings we do possess and the reports of later ancient thinkers also suggest that philosophically he was essentially a follower of Plotinus, the differences consisting mainly in interests, emphasis and wording. Porphyry stresses purity of life as essential for the the soul's ascent. He is also much interested in religion and paved the way for the intermingling of philosophy and late ancient paganism in the later Neo-Platonists. Given that most of the works in which Porphyry's strictly metaphysical views are likely to have been explicitly stated are lost, it is difficult to present an accurate overall picture of his views and hence to assess to what extent he may have gone beyond Plotinus. Scholarly opinions here are also divided. The *Sententiae*, which though incomplete is the most extensive purely philosophical text we have, is essentially Plotinian. The French scholar of Neo-Platonism, Pierre Hadot, has made a strong case on Porphyry's behalf for an elaborate system of triads at the apex of the Neo-Platonic hierarchy, consisting of Existence, Life and Intelligence.[14] This however involves liberal use of the *Parmenides* commentary and other sources whose Porphyrian authenticity is not certain (cf. 36, 737–41).

Porphyry's student, Iamblichus, accuses Plotinus and Porphyry of failing to distinguish between intellect and soul (in Stobaeus, p. 365 Wachsmuth [5.81]). In the *Sententiae* Porphyry often ignores the distinction, even if he is also perfectly able to uphold it. At issue here seems to be the question of the soul's ontological status. We saw in connection with Plotinus above that he insists on the soul's status as a genuine intelligible and not merely something intermediate between the sensible and the intelligible as the most obvious reading of the celebrated passage on the constitution of the soul in the *Timaeus* would suggest. On this, together with the *Parmenides* commentary mentioned above, Anthony Lloyd founds a thesis about Porphyrian metaphysics claiming that Porphyry tends to telescope the hypostases into one another with the result that only the One is real, everything else being appearances of it.[15] The idea is this: the whole Neo-Platonic hierarchy is an ordered series (or perhaps a set of ordered series with a common first member, the One). Each member (aside from the very first) is not only a mere image of a previous one, the first cause is the only real item in the series: the real man is the intelligible man, the real soul is not the soul in union with body, but the pure soul as it is in itself without consideration of its external activities and relations. In general terms we might say that each thing should be defined in terms of the internal act constituting it. The internal act of anything below the One, however, is constituted by the external act of the level above it and thus points beyond itself. So in search of the real we are forced to climb the ladder in the hierarchy so that ultimately only the One turns out to be fully real. The evidence does not permit us to claim with confidence that Porphyry systematically taught extreme metaphysical monism of this sort. Such a trend is however present in Plotinus and Porphyry may have carried it further, though neither consistently maintains this as dogma.[16]

In this context we may raise the question of idealism: is reality mental according to the Neo-Platonism of Plotinus and Porphyry? This is a tricky question that does not permit an unqualified answer. Taking extreme metaphysical monism as just described as our standpoint, we might answer 'no' because the One, which alone exists, is beyond thinking. However, at least in Plotinus and Porphyry mental life is ascribed to the One in a special way: the One has an analog of mental life, some kind of superintellection (VI.8.16; V.1.7). Thus, it would be misleading to stress that the ultimate principle is void of mental life. Secondly, disregarding extreme monism, the realm of Intellect is also the realm of being, the realm containing the real archetypes of which things in the physical world are images. These archetypes are thoughts and hence mental. So Plotinus and Porphyry are idealists at least in the sense that ordinary non-mental things have a mental principle. We should note, however, that this idealism is not of the type which holds the physical world to be the product of our minds. Even if it is an appearance, even an illusion, it is to be seen as an appearance or illusion on analogy with a mirror image, not with a hallucination: what is seen in the mirror is of course not the real thing and if we take it for one we are under an illusion; nevertheless, the mirror image is not just *our* fancy.

One unmistakable and lasting contribution Porphyry made to philosophy is his promotion of Aristotle's logical works in the Platonic curriculum. As mentioned above, even before Plotinus there were Aristotelizing Platonists. There were even Platonists before Porphyry who dealt with Aristotle's logical treatises. Porphyry is however the one who put Aristotelian logic to positive use within Platonic teaching. Through him Aristotle's *Organon* came to serve as an introduction to philosophy – a function transmitted on to the Middle Ages and well beyond. Porphyry wrote an introduction to Aristotle's *Categories*, the so-called *Isagoge*, which was translated into Latin by Boethius and became a standard introductory text in the Middle Ages. In fact the *Isagoge* not only influenced the Latin

West but also the Greek East and was later translated into Syriac and Arabic. Porphyry also wrote extensive commentaries on Aristotle's logical treatises of which all is lost except an elementary commentary on the *Categories*.

Anybody familiar with Aristotle's *Categories* will note that it contains certain anti-Platonic doctrines, for example the doctrine of the primacy of individuals over genus and species. How could ardent Platonists like Porphyry integrate such works into their philosophy? Porphyry and the later Neo-Platonists following him believed in the essential agreement between Plato and Aristotle and were predisposed to explain apparent differences away – Porphyry is said to have written a work on their agreement and another about their differences. In the case of the logic the adoption of Aristotle was much eased by Porphyry's views on the status of the logical treatises. Plotinus, who also wrote a critical but not altogether hostile treatise on Aristotle's *Categories* (VI.1–3), took the work to be about the genera of being and thus a work in ontology, containing doctrines about the structure of the world. Plotinus comes to the conclusion that a revised version of the doctrine of Aristotle's *Categories* holds true for sensibles. Porphyry agrees that the categories apply to the sensible world, but denies that the treatise is a treatise in ontology, even the ontology of the sensible world: he adopts the view that the *Categories* (and presumably Aristotle's logic in general) is quite independent of metaphysics and is really about significative expressions for sensible phenomena (*On Aristotle's Categories*, 58). These may be primary in the order of experience, though not in the order of reality where Platonic metaphysics prevails.

❧ PROCLUS: THE SYSTEM BUILDER ❧

Proclus (*c.* 410–85) is the third Neo-Platonic thinker who was to have great impact on posterity. He came as a young man to Athens where he studied Platonic philosophy and eventually became the Head of the Academy. He was the most systematic expositor of Neo-Platonism and a prolific writer. He left systematic philosophical works such as the celebrated *Elements of Theology*, which proceeds by a strictly deductive Euclidean method such as Descartes and Spinoza were to use much later. In the *Elements* Proclus sets out from the apex of the hierarchy and proceeds downward. The work covers the three first hypostases, in which the sphere of theology coincides with metaphysics as the study of first causes. Another major work is the *Platonic Theology*, which covers the same ground as the *Elements of Theology* but is larger and more intractable. There is also a systematic work on natural philosophy, the *Elements of Physics*. He wrote extensive commentaries on Plato, a large bulk of which have survived even if much is lost. They are less interesting as a source of Proclus's philosophical views than one might expect but a mine of information about the history of Platonism, in addition to representing late Neo-Platonic reading of Plato. Proclus also wrote on mathematics and literature and composed pagan hymns.

Proclus was a pious pagan in a world were pagans were an oppressed minority, having lost all chance of victory. Proclus nevertheless had an ironic revenge against the Christians: his system is the philosophical foundation of the 'Christian theology' of Pseudo-Dionysius, a man who pretended to be the Dionysius mentioned in the Acts as a Christian convert of Paul. The whole medieval world was deceived by the fraud, which was not fully eradicated until the nineteenth century. The writings of Pseudo-Dionysius acquired an immense authority in the medieval Christian tradition.

Systematic and influential though Proclus undeniably was, there is some doubt about the originality of his views. However that may be, the very conception of such a work as the *Elements of Theology* is in itself a great achievement and, for all we know, an original one. In order to assess his contributions we must briefly consider the period between Porphyry and Proclus.

Two new Neo-Platonic movements in the East appeared after Porphyry. One is the so-called 'school' at Pergamum, whose chief representatives are Sallust and the emperor Julian (called the 'Apostate' by Christians). This brand of Neo-Platonism seems to have been more religious than philosophical. It was Neo-Platonism and its interpretation of pagan religion and culture turned against the Christians. The other is the Athenian school whose founder was Plutarch of Athens (died 432), succeeded by Proclus's teacher Syrianus. Proclus represents the culmination of the Athenian school. Both these schools or trends owe much of their distinctive traits to Porphyry's most renowned student, Iamblichus, whom many scholars regard as a second father of Neo-Platonism. We possess even less of his writings than of Porphyry's and he is credited with this honor – in some respects a questionable honor considering the content of his teaching – on the basis of others' evidence, not least remarks in Proclus himself. At any rate, Iamblichus's achievements can be summarized as follows. First, he claims theurgy as the means to union with divine intellects and as in some ways superior to philosophy. This is of course a deviation from the teaching of Plotinus but was to become the received opinion. Nevertheless Iamblichus insisted on keeping theurgy and philosophy apart. Secondly, he established a standard school curriculum and proposed the principles of interpretation of Platonic dialogues that came to prevail. According to these each dialogue has one theme (*skopos*) which determines the interpretation of all aspects of it. Thirdly, he gave the Athenian school what is distinctive in its metaphysics: pervasive use of mathematical concepts such as triads and monads. In all this Proclus is highly indebted to Iamblichus.

In outline Proclus's system resembles that of Plotinus: we find the same principal hypostases, the One, Intellect and Soul, and their relationships are described in similar terms: process or irradiation from above and the inverse relation, participation, from below. We also find the same general assumptions about the principles, often made quite explicit in Proclus: the cause is more perfect than effect, has a fuller degree of unity, contains in some manner its effect and so forth. Proclus, however, shows a tendency towards a more extreme logical realism: he likes distinctions and every distinction is liable to turn into a difference between entities with a proliferation of entities as a result: what in Plotinus has the status of aspect or relation is apt to be reified in Proclus. As an example of this we may mention time and eternity which for Plotinus are aspects of Intellect and Soul respectively but have become substances in Proclus (cf. pp. 369–70 above and *ET*, props. 52–5). Thus, even if the simple ineffable One is the root of it all, it does not take Proclus long to derive an astounding multiplicity from it. Proclus's entities frequently come in triads whose general structure is extremes connected by a middle term having affinity with both the extremes. Such triads proliferate both as reified aspects of a hypostasis and in the relations between hypostases. As concerns us, this complexity means that we must make do with mentioning a few general features and for a fuller of view of his system the reader is referred to Proclus himself and items in the bibliography.

We can get a glimpse of Proclus's system by considering the top of the hierarchy. First there is the One (the Good) itself which is entirely transcendent and unparticipated. Then, in between the transcendent One and Intellect but also belonging to the first hypostasis, is a series of unities (henads) – this doctrine of unities has no parallel in Plotinus (*ET*, props. 7 and 113–65). These unities are participated terms from which anything else receives its unity (*ET*, prop. 116; *In Platonis Parmenidem* 6, 148). What we have just seen exemplifies a structure that pervades the Proclean system: a distinction between an unparticipated term, a participated term and a participant. This triad reappears in a more familiar setting as a transcendent (unparticipated) Platonic Idea, an immanent participated form, and a sensible participant (*In Platonis Parmenidem* 3, 797). Thus there is, for example, the ideal Man, instances of Man and organic bodies that take on the human form. The doctrine of the triad of participation is of course meant to answer the question 'Is the Platonic Idea transcendent or immanent?' and the answer is that it is both, i.e. the Idea itself is transcendent but it has an immanent counterpart, the participated term.

No less fundamental is a triad consisting of rest (*monê*), process (*proodos*) and reversion (*epistrophê*) (*ET*, props. 25–39; cf. pp. 370–2 above), which is parallel or identical to another triad: limit, infinity and mixture (*ET*, props. 87–96). These latter are ingredients of the first unities and of everything else below them. Rest, process and return are operative throughout the hierarchy. At every level there is a first term (monad) which generates by procession and return subordinate entities of the same kind belonging to the same level. Each such monad, however, also simultaneously proceeds to generate incomplete products, i.e. products that are mere images and not the same sort of things as the monad: not every product of soul is itself a soul and not every product of intellect is an intellect, for soul is a product of intellect (cf. *ET*, prop. 65). In this double procession, both horizontal and vertical, as one might say, we have the analog of internal and external activity in Plotinus – the generation of the entities within each hypostasis corresponding to the internal activity.

The level of Intellect is characterized by the triad Existence, Life and Thought, a special case, it seems, of rest–procession–return. There are many other triads there but this one is especially important. Existence, Life and Intelligence are in turn each implicit in one another so that each contains a triad of Existence, Life and Intelligence, the difference being a matter of predominance (*ET*, props. 101–3). However this is to be understood in precise terms, we can note some interesting consequences: the traditional Platonic Ideas are monads containing this triad and each Idea exists in all three modes or, alternatively, a single Idea may be participated in either existentially, vitally or intellectually (*Platonic Theology*, 903–4). The concrete result of this is that for instance the Idea 'Moon' may be represented as moon-fish or moon-stone (existential), as a lunar daemon (vital) or again as a lunar angel (intellectual).

An important Proclean principle is the doctrine of the greater power of the higher causes (*ET*, props. 57, 71–2). This does not only mean that a higher level in the hierarchy causes a greater number of and more perfect effects than a lower one, but also that the higher causes extend further down. So the entities at the bottom of the hierarchy participate only in the highest levels: inanimate bodies, having only unity and minimal being, participate directly in Existence, and matter, having no properties of its own and hence no being, participates only in a corresponding unity in the first hypostasis. These principles, therefore, extend all the way down to the level of bodies, without the involvement of the intermediate stages. Souls by contrast participate in life (rational souls in thought as well) and through life in existence. This is illustrated in the diagram below taken from A. C. Lloyd ([11.6], 112). The arrows point from causes to effects.

DESCENT OF MONADS

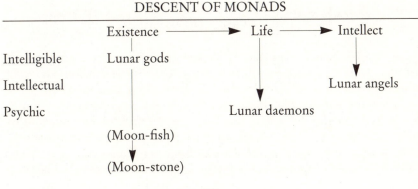

	Existence ——→ Life ——→ Intellect
Intelligible	Lunar gods
Intellectual	Lunar angels
Psychic	Lunar daemons
	(Moon-fish)
	(Moon-stone)

Even if this diagram depicts only a fraction of Proclus's world it gives us a sense of what it looks like. It is indeed as one his theorems in the *Elements of Theology* states: 'All things are in all things, but in each according to its proper nature' (prop. 103). The same intelligible item may be instantiated by different phenomena according to its mode (existential, vital or intellectual) and all the phenomena on the same level are interconnected both via the monad of that level and via the interconnectedness of everything at the top. So Proclus's world is a tightly knitted web.

This is strange philosophy by our lights. Nevertheless, it is in many ways quite successful, intellectually speaking, in harmonizing the world-view of the late Neo-Platonists and no doubt many of their contemporaries. In the words of Dodds, Proclus's ideal is 'the one comprehensive philosophy that should embrace all the garnered wisdom of the ancient world'.[17] All the pagan Gods, the old, new and even foreign, had a place in Proclus's hierarchy. The first participated unities mentioned above are in fact identical with the higher gods. Lesser divinities and intermediate beings all find their place in the intermediate stages between these and the world of the senses. Thus, we may choose different types of discourse to talk about the same phenomena according to our concerns on each occasion. Rest–process–return, substance–power–actuality and Cronos–Rhea–Zeus all express the same or parallel phenomena. We may approach these either through abstract philosophical reasoning or through religious practices. Occult phenomena, theurgy and mantic, which so preoccupied Proclus and his group, have their place and explanation as well. They are explained by the bonds that connect entities both horizontally and vertically in the system: a physical object such as a particular stone has invested in it higher powers which can be influenced through their manifestation in the stone. So everything worth speaking of had a place within the Athenian system and was to be made intelligible through it. Confusing though the Athenian system may be and incorporating the most bizarre elements, it nevertheless still is rational philosophy aiming at explanations on the basis of solid premisses.

THE LEGACY OF NEO-PLATONISM

After Proclus the Athenian school had one significant master, Damascius. He wrote a work *On Principles*, where he posits an ineffable principle above the One – a view also held by Iamblichus. During his term as Head of the Academy the emperor Justinian closed the school in 529. Platonism had been active in Alexandria for a long time – that is where Plotinus studied as we have seen (p. 361 above) – and presumably had a very long continuous history there even if there are gaps in our knowledge of it. The school flourished in the fifth century and was still active into the seventh. There was considerable communication between the Athenians and the Alexandrians, but still a very notable difference of emphasis: the Alexandrians were less bent on metaphysical speculations than the Athenians and are best known for their commentaries on Aristotle. The Alexandrians were also less ardently pagan and included Christian members, for instance the well known commentator and notable critic of Aristotle, John Philoponus.[18]

The Christian Latin West produced a thinker of great importance who stands with one leg in the tradition of late ancient Platonism, namely Anicius Manlius Severinus Boethius (480–524). Boethius was a Catholic and a highly educated Roman statesman who served under Theodoric the Ostrogoth, an Arian king of Italy. Boethius wrote extensively on a host of subjects including the mathematical disciplines, theology and philosophy. He had great ambitions about translating all works of Aristotle and Plato into Latin and elucidating them. He succeeded in translating Aristotle's *Organon* and prefaced it with a translation of Porphyry's *Isagoge*. He also wrote several commentaries and logical treatises. These works became the foundation of logical studies in medieval Europe. Boethius did not live to complete his project. Accused of treason, he was imprisoned and finally tortured and executed. While in prison he wrote his masterpiece, *On the Consolation of Philosophy*, in which philosophy personified comes to the aid of the unjustly suffering man – it is noteworthy of course that Boethius should call upon philosophy rather than his Christian faith at this difficult time of his life. Boethius's philosophy is fundamentally Neo-Platonic. His emphasis on logic and other traits suggest influence of the Alexandrian school.

Boethius's *Consolation* and his theological treatises abound in Platonic, Aristotelian and Neo-Platonic doctrines and contributed, along with the works of St Augustine and others, to rendering such ideas commonplace in medieval philosophical theology. Thus, on Boethius's account, in addition to being one and simple God is supreme being and supreme goodness and power; God is these things themselves whereas other things only have them by participation in or imitation of God. Furthermore, goodness and being are one and same, and hence evil and lack of being (*How Substances are Good in Virtue of Their Existence without Being Substantial Goods*; *Consolation* 3, 12). God is of course eternal and in a notorious passage in the *Consolation* Boethius gives an account of eternity and then distinguishes between eternity and everlastingness. Eternity is defined as 'perfect possession of endless life, all present at once' (5, 6), a definition that reflects Plotinus (see pp. 369–70 above). This is contrasted with the created universe, which even if without beginning and end unfolds in temporal succession what exists timelessly in God's mind.

The final victories of Christianity and Islam in what once was one pagan Roman empire stretching over much of Europe, the Middle East and North Africa put an end to Neo-Platonism in the strict sense of the term. But many ideas of the Neo-Platonists' and in some cases their works lived on and were absorbed by the new cultures. In the Christian world Plotinus and Porphyry influenced the Church fathers both Greek and Latin and we have mentioned Proclus's great impact through Pseudo-Dionysius. If only for these reasons the whole of Christian medieval theology was thoroughly colored by Neo-Platonism. In fact there are innumerable threads that connect Neo-Platonism with the subsequent history of Europe. To mention just one interesting example: the great medieval Islamic and Jewish philosophers, who in turn were to influence European philosophy, studied and absorbed Neo-Platonic thought. In the fifteenth century pagan Neo-Platonism had a comeback in Europe that lasted into the seventeenth. It has continued to exert influence on important thinkers such as Berkeley and Hegel, who was an admirer of Proclus, and Bergson, who admired Plotinus.

 NOTES

1 See O'Meara [11.8].
2 See Dillon [11.3].
3 See Dodds [11.20].
4 See Wallis [11.12], 160.
5 Conventionally, references to the *Enneads* are often given only in numerals: 'V. 3 (49) 2, 14–16', for instance, means '5th Ennead, 3rd treatise (which is number 49 on Porphyry's chronological list of Plotinus's writings), chapter 2, lines 14 to 16'.
6 For details see Armstrong [11.1], 15.
7 See Gurtler [11.22].
8 See Blumenthal [11.17].
9 See O'Brien [11.23].
10 That Plotinus's distinction between the internal and the external act has its roots in Aristotle's account of actualization is suggested by Lloyd [11.6], 98–103. Hadot [11.33], 228, n. 4. and others suppose that the two acts doctrine originates in a Stoic distinction between substantial qualities and their external effects. Plotinus may well be drawing on both kinds of sources.
11 See Emilsson [11.21].
12 See Dodds[11.20], 145–8.
13 See O'Daly [11.24].
14 See Hadot [11.33].
15 See Armstrong [11.1], 287–93.
16 See Smith [11.35], 5 ff.
17 See Dodds [11.41], xxv.
18 See Sorabji [11.52].

SELECTIVE BIBLIOGRAPHY

The bibliography below is mostly limited to works in English of a fairly general scope. Literature on Neo-Platonism and translations of the ancient texts in other languages, especially French and German, is abundant. In [11.5] below there are extensive bibliographies of Neo-Platonic studies to and including Porphyry. In addition to the bibliographical items [11.16], [11.19] and [11.36], item [11.5] vol. 2, 36.1 contains a bibliography on Middle Platonism by L. Deitz, 'Bibliographie du platonisme impérial antérieur à Plotin: 1926–1986'.

GENERAL

11.1 Armstrong, A. H. (ed.) *The Cambridge History of Later Greek and Early Medieval Philosophy*. Cambridge, 1970.

11.2 Baine Harris, R. (ed.) *The Significance of Neoplatonism*. Norfolk, Va, 1976.

11.3 Dillon, J. *The Middle Platonists*. London, 1977.

11.4 Goodman, L. E. (ed.) *Neoplatonism and Jewish Thought*. Albany, NY, 1992.

11.5 Haase, W. (ed.) *Aufstieg und Niedergang der römischen Welt*. Vols 2, 36, 1, and 2, 36, 2. Berlin, 1987.

11.6 Lloyd, A. C. *The Anatomy of Neoplatonism*. Oxford, 1990. A philosophically penetrating study, rewarding even if not easy reading.

11.7 Merlan, P. *From Platonism to Neoplatonism*. The Hague, 1968.

11.8 O'Meara, D. J. (ed.) *Neoplatonism and Christian Thought*. Norfolk, Va, 1982.

11.9 —— *Pythagoras Revived*. Oxford, 1989.

11.10 Sambursky, S. *The Physical World of Late Antiquity*. London, 1962.

11.11 Wallis, R. T. and J. Bregman (eds) *Neoplatonism and Gnosticism*. Albany, NY, 1992.

11.12 Wallis, R. T. *Neoplatonism*. London, 1972. This is the best general overview over the whole of Neo-Platonism.

PLOTINUS

11.13 *Plotinus* I–VII. Trans. A. H. Armstrong. Cambridge, Mass., 1966–88. This translation, accompanied by the Greek text, is based on the authoritative editions of P. Henry and H.-R. Schwyzer.

11.14 *Plotinus. The Enneads*. Trans S. MacKenna, abridged with an introduction and notes by J. Dillon. Harmondsworth, 1991.

11.15 Armstrong, A. H. *The Architecture of the Intelligible Universe in the Philosophy of Plotinus*. Cambridge, 1940.

11.16 Blumenthal, H. J. 'Plotinus in the Light of Twenty Years' Scholarship, 1951–1971'. In [11.5], 36, 1.

11.17 —— *Plotinus' Psychology*. The Hague, 1971.

11.18 Bussanich, J. *The One and Its Relation to Intellect in Plotinus*. Leiden, 1988.

11.19 Corrigan, K. and O'Cleirigh, P. 'The Course of Plotinian Scholarship from 1971 to 1986'. In [11.5], 36, 1.

11.20 Dodds, E. R. 'The Parmenides of Plato and the Origin of the Neoplatonic "One"', *Classical Quarterly*, 22 (1928), 129–43.

11.21 Emilsson, E. K. *Plotinus on Sense-Perception: A Philosophical Study.* Cambridge, 1988.

11.22 Gurtler, G. M. *Plotinus: The Experience of Unity.* New York, 1988.

11.23 O'Brien, D. *Plotinus on the Origin of Matter.* Naples, 1991.

11.24 O'Daly, G. *Plotinus' Philosophy of the Self.* Shannon, 1973.

11.25 O'Meara, D. J. 'Plotinus', in F. Cranz and P. Kristeller (eds) *Catalogus translationum et commentariorum*, vol. 7. Washington, D.C., 1992. An overview of Plotinus's impact.

11.26 —— *Plotinus: An Introduction to the Enneads.* Oxford, 1993. Highly recommendable as an introduction to Plotinus.

11.27 Rist, J. M. *Plotinus: The Road to Reality.* Cambridge, 1967.

11.28 Schroeder, F. M. *Form and Transformation: A Study in the Philosophy of Plotinus.* Montreal and Kingston, 1992.

 PORPHYRY

11.29 *Life of Plotinus.* In [11.13], vol. 1 and [11.14].

11.30 *The Sentences.* Trans. T. Davidson, *Journal of Speculative Philosophy* III (1869), 46–73.

11.31 *On Aristotle's Categories.* Trans. S. K. Strange. London, 1992.

11.32 *Isagoge.* Trans. and commentary E. W. Warren. Toronto, 1975.

11.33 Hadot, P. *Porphyre et Victorinus.* 2 vols, Paris, 1968. Text and French trans. of *Anonymous Commentary on the 'Parmenides'*, attributed to Porphyry in vol. 2.

11.34 *Porphyrios' 'Symmikta zetemata'.* German trans. and comentary by H. Dörrie. Munich, 1959.

11.35 Smith, A. *The Place of Porphyry in the Neoplatonic Tradition. A Study in Post-Plotinian Neoplatonism.* The Hague, 1974.

11.36 Smith, A. 'Porphyrian Studies since 1913'. In [11.5], 36, 1. Contains a review of the state of Porphyrian studies in addition to a bibliography.

11.37 Evangeliou, C. *Aristotle's Categories and Porphyry.* Leiden, 1987.

IAMBLICHUS, PROCLUS AND LATER NEO-PLATONISM

11.38 *Iamblichi Chalcidensis in Platonis Dialogos Commentariorum Fragmenta.* With text, trans. and comm. by J. M. Dillon. Leiden, 1973.

11.39 *Iamblichus, Les Mystères d'Égypte.* Ed. and French trans. by E. des Places. Paris, 1966.

11.40 Iamblichus, *De anima.* French trans. by A. J. Festugière. In vol. 3 of *La Révélation d'Hermès Trismégiste.* Paris, 1953.

11.41 *Proclus, The Elements of Theology.* Ed., trans and comm. E. R. Dodds. 2nd edn. Oxford, 1992. An indispensable aid both for novice as well as for the expert.

11.42 *Proclus' Commentary on Plato's Parmenides*. Trans. G. R. Morrow and J. M. Dillon with introduction and notes by J. M. Dillon. Princeton, 1987.

11.43 *Proclus, Théologie Platonicienne*. Ed. and French trans. H. D. Saffrey and L. G. Westerink. 4 vols of 6 have appeared. Paris, 1968–81.

11.44 *Proclus, Dix Problèmes concernant la Providence*. Ed. D. Isaac. Paris, 1977.

11.45 *Proclus, Providence, Fatalité, Liberté*. Ed. D. Isaac. Paris, 1979.

11.46 Boethius, *The Theological Tractates*, trans. H. F. Stewart and E. K. Rand, *The Consolation of Philosophy*, trans. S. J. Tester. Cambridge, Mass. 1973.

11.47 *Boethius's De Topicis Differentiis*. Trans. with notes and essays on the text by E. Stump. Ithaca, NY, 1978.

11.48 Dillon, J. M. 'Iamblichus of Chalcis (c. 240–325 AD)' in [11.5], 36, 2.

11.49 Blumenthal, H. J. and A. C. Lloyd (eds) *Soul and the Structure of Being in Late Neoplatonism*. Liverpool, 1982.

11.50 Rosán, L. J. *The Philosophy of Proclus*. New York, 1949.

11.51 Baierwaltes, W. *Proklos, Grundzüge seiner Metaphysik*. Frankfurt am Main, 1965.

11.52 Sorabji, R. (ed.) *Philoponus and the Rejection of Aristotelian Science*. London, 1987.

11.53 Chadwick, H. (ed.) *Boethius. The Consolations of Music, Logic, Theology, and Philosophy*. Oxford, 1981.

CHAPTER 12

Augustine

Gerard O'Daly

❧ 1 LIFE AND PHILOSOPHICAL READINGS ❧

Augustine was born in Thagaste (modern Souk Ahras in Algeria) in Roman North Africa in AD 354. He died as bishop of Hippo (now Annaba, Algeria) in 430. His education followed the standard Roman practice of the later Empire (Marrou [12.59]), in schools at Thagaste, Madauros, and Carthage, and it involved some study of philosophical texts, if only for their literary and rhetorical qualities. At the age of 18 he read Cicero's *Hortensius* as part of the syllabus at Carthage, and it affected him profoundly, introducing him to philosophy, and in particular to ethical eudemonism (*conf.* 3.7). He cites the *Hortensius* regularly in his writings.[1] But, although already a Christian catechumen (his mother Monnica was a pious believer), and inclined to think of Christ when 'wisdom' (*sapientia*) was spoken of, he found himself more attracted to the Manichees than to what he perceived as the crudities of style in the Latin translations of the Christian scriptures available to him. What attracted him to Manichaeism was its appeal to reason rather than authority (a polarity that was to dominate his mature thought: see section 3): to the modern reader confronted with the bizarre cosmic mythology of the Manichees, this seems an odd claim. But the Manichees proffered a universal system, encompassing cosmology, psychology, and a synthesis of several religions, including Christianity; and they prescribed a way of life consistent with their revealed 'knowledge'. Augustine was to be deeply influenced by their account of evil, based on the belief in an evil principle in the universe and in humans, a 'substance' at war with the good principle in the individual and the universe (*duab. an.*). It was many years before he shed this belief. Furthermore, Manichaean criticism of the Old Testament enabled him to reject what he took to be its primitive concept of God and its moral ambiguities.

As a young man at Carthage Augustine read Aristotle's *Categories* and claims not to have found them difficult (*conf.* 4.28). His other early philosophical readings are not easy to determine. Cicero, especially the *Tusculan Disputations*, the *De re publica*, the *De natura deorum*, and the *Academica* (and to a lesser extent the *De fato* and the *De officiis*), is his principal source of information about every period of Greek philosophy (he probably read Plato's *Timaeus* in Cicero's translation).[2] In his first published work, *De pulchro et apto* (not extant), on aesthetics, written in 380–1, Augustine reveals knowledge of the distinction between beauty (*kalon*) and 'appropriateness' (*prepon*), the Stoic theory of beauty as proportion of the parts of a thing, and the monad/dyad principles (*conf.* 4.20–1).

Augustine adopted the career of a *rhetor*, teaching at Carthage, Rome (from 383), and Milan (from 384), where he held the post of public orator (Milan was then the seat of the Western imperial court). At Milan (possibly in a Platonist circle including figures like the retired high public official Manlius Theodorus) he encountered Neoplatonism, reading – in the Latin translation by Marius Victorinus – works, probably by both Plotinus and Porphyry, in 386 (*conf.* 7.13–27; *beata v.* 4; *c. Acad.* 3.41).[3] His knowledge of Greek was mediocre. He expresses distaste for the way in which it was taught at school (*conf.* 1.23), and he was always to be dependent upon translations for his access to Greek philosophy, Scripture, and theological literature.[4] At Milan he also heard the sermons of Ambrose, whose Platonizing Christianity undermined the materialistic concept of God that Augustine found in both Manichaeism and Stoicism, and who initiated him into the subtleties of exegetical method, based upon the distinction, taken from Philo of Alexandria and Greek Christian theologians such as Origen, between literal and figurative readings of Scripture. He underwent a conversion experience in autumn 386, resigning his post at Milan and spending the winter of 386–7 in retreat at a country villa in nearby Cassiciacum.

From this period came his first extant works, a series of philosophical dialogues whose form is much influenced by Cicero, which includes the *Contra Academicos*, a critique of Academic scepticism (Cicero's *Academica* is Augustine's principal source), and, in the *De ordine* and the *De beata vita*, discussions of the nature of happiness and its relation to knowledge, God's nature, order in the universe, and the problem of evil. In another 'inner' dialogue between Augustine and reason, the *Soliloquia*, he explores the nature of mind, the identification of truth with being, and the problem of error. Neoplatonist influences permeate these dialogues. Augustine's characteristic theories of the will and semantics were not developed until after his baptism in 387 and his return to Thagaste in 388 (*De libero arbitrio, De Magistro*). Anti-Manichaean polemic dominated his writings at this time. The first mature synthesis of his thought, *De vera religione*, was written in 390.

From 371 to 386 Augustine had lived with a concubine: the couple had a son, Adeodatus, who stayed with Augustine after his mother was sent back to Africa in 386, at a time when Augustine was planning to marry an heiress of high social standing (Adeodatus died young, probably in 389). Augustine's conversion led to the abandonment of his marriage plans and the adoption of a life of celibacy. At Thagaste he established a religious community. In 391 he was ordained priest at Hippo, becoming bishop in 396. Several of his works at this time reveal the influence of Pauline theology upon his thought. When he wrote his autobiography, the *Confessions*, from 397 on, he was able to apply his analysis of the will and Pauline principles to his conversion experience of 386: both elements were missing from the Cassiciacum dialogues.[5]

By 397 Augustine's philosophical views were largely formed, and there is no new encounter with other thinkers or fresh ideas in his later career. But he elaborated his thought in several major works, all written over several years: the *De trinitate* (whose psychological schemes reveal much of his philosophy of mind), the *De Genesi ad litteram* (on creation, the soul, sense-perception, and imagination), the *De doctrina christiana* (on hermeneutics), and the *De civitate dei* (on ethics and social theory). In the last two decades of his life he wrote much on free will, grace, and the causes of evil, in a series of polemical works directed against Pelagius and his followers, in particular Julian of Eclanum.

Augustine's philosophical readings were eclectic and haphazard. Only Cicero was studied systematically, as part of an educational syllabus. Plato was read either in translation or in extracts (or both), the Neoplatonists likewise. The Middle Platonists were known indirectly, through the doxographical tradition (Solignac [12.61]): Apuleius was an exception, but was chiefly exploited for his demonology. Christian writers were more often targets of criticism than sources of new ideas: Tertullian's corporealist views on the soul, and Origen's theories of the soul's pre-existence, periodic reincarnation, and embodiment as punishment for previously committed sin, all invited Augustinian objections. But Augustine made a lot of his limited philosophical background, exploiting it with acuity and imagination.

❦ 2 AUGUSTINE'S CHRISTIAN PHILOSOPHY ❦

Augustine philosophizes throughout his writings. But, despite the fact that some of his earlier works concentrate on specific philosophical themes, the great majority of his writings are responses to a variety of personal, theological, and church political circumstances (Bonner [12.32]). Speculation for its own sake, although it may determine the amount of space that he devotes to analysing particular problems, is never what motivates Augustine to write in the first place. The polemical aspect cannot be neglected. The *De libero arbitrio* is directed against the Manichees, for example (*retr.* 1.9). In longer works, such as *De Genesi ad litteram*, which were not composed under pressure of time and whose subject-matter offered scope for open exploration of certain (for example cosmological) questions, Augustine speculates most freely (*Gn. litt.* 1.18.37–21.41; 2.9.20–1; 2.18.38). Augustine does not construct a philosophical system. But certain themes preoccupy him, and his treatment of them evinces a continuity of development or a coherence of treatment that allows us to describe his position with some confidence. At times he understands by 'philosophy' the Graeco-Roman tradition of rational inquiry, as opposed to Christianity; and he distinguishes between rational method in philosophy and Christian belief in religious principles that are often historical events (above all, Christ's Incarnation) (*beata v.* 4; *c. Acad.* 3.37–42; *vera rel.* 2–8, 30–3; *conf.* 7.13–27; *civ.* 8.1–12). He deprecates pagan philosophy, when he wishes to throw Christian doctrine into sharp relief. At other times, however, he does not distinguish between the philosophical and theological aspects of his thought. Christianity is the 'one true philosophy' (*c. Iul.* 4.72), and the 'true religion' of *De vera religione* is inconceivable without its Platonist components. Thus he can speak of a 'Christian philosophy' (*c. Iul.* 4.72; *c. Iul. imp.* 2.166), arguing that the love of wisdom, the search for, and discovery of, truth, and the quest for happiness all find fulfilment in the Christian religion. Augustine appropriates traditional philosophical questions, but the answers which he provides are religious ones. Thus the universal desire for happiness, which he grants to be the proper activity of the highest human faculty, the mind, is, he argues, only fully satisfied in the afterlife, and not in a disembodied mental state, but in the resurrected heavenly body of the saints.[6] At the same time, the questions which he asks are those of the Greek and Roman philosophical tradition. When he investigates problems of the soul, he inquires into its origin or source, its substance, the nature of the body–soul relationship, its immortality, its condition after death, and so on.[7] He does not pretend to answer all questions: for example, when human souls are created (see section 7).

The scope of Augustine's Christian philosophy may be appreciated when we realize that he fuses the 'wisdom' of the *Hortensius* with the 'intellect' of the Neoplatonist writings and the 'word' of the beginning of John's gospel (*conf.* 3.7–8; 7.13–27; *civ.* 10.29). He establishes several parallels between the themes of the Johannine prologue and Neoplatonist writings. Platonism enjoys a special status in his thought. 'If Plato were alive' (*vera rel.* 3), he would recognize in Christianity the realization of his striving: a monotheistic religion with a belief in immaterial principles, God, and the soul. But, despite its theoretical monism, Platonism is, Augustine believes, vitiated by polytheistic demonologies (*civ.* 8–10).

Augustine's familiarity with the doxographical tradition means that he follows the school division of philosophy into three areas of physics, ethics, and logic (*vera rel.* 30–3; *civ.* 8.4; *ep.* 118.16–21). But he employs no such division in any stringent sense in his discussion of philosophical issues. It serves chiefly to articulate his reporting of philosophical doctrines, as well as to assess the achievement of Platonism in fusing Pythagorean physics with Socratic ethics, and completing the fusion by the development of dialectic (*c. Acad.* 3.37; *civ.* 8.4).

Augustine embraces the traditional definition of philosophy as the science of things divine and human, and he sometimes distinguishes between *sapientia* as knowledge of things divine (including truth in the strict sense), and *scientia* as the knowledge of temporal things (*trin.* 14.2–3). He understands it to be the achievement of Christianity to establish the true relationship between eternal immutable truth and the beliefs that we may have about temporal things. The proportion of *Timaeus* 29c (being: becoming : : truth: belief) expresses an ontological and epistemological classification that Augustine approves (*trin.* 4.24). But he believes that the links between the temporal and the eternal are only realized in the incarnate Christ, who is both *sapientia* and *scientia*, and in the doctrines which emerge in Christianity (*Gn. litt.* 1.21.41).

Augustine knows the term *theologia* from Varro's scheme of the three kinds of 'theology' – mythical, natural, and civil – but he uses the word to refer to Christian doctrine only once (*civ.* 6.8) and in passing. Nor does he proffer a natural theology in the sense in which this is understood in medieval and modern contexts, namely, a theology that refuses to admit doctrinal propositions that are not also accessible to reason as premises. But he is arguably the founder in the Western tradition of 'philosophical theology', which does accept such doctrinal premises as assumptions, testing their coherence by analysis and argumentation, explaining them and analysing their implications and connections. Augustine's programme aims at illuminating faith, which is based on authority, by the understanding which reason provides, inasmuch as this is possible. Nor is this attempt at rational inquiry merely something in which Christians may indulge, but it is a duty incumbent upon them, for it involves use of their God-given reason, the same reason which enables them to believe in the first place (*ep.* 120.3). Augustine interprets the Latin translation of the Septuagint version of Isaiah 7:9 ('Unless you believe, you shall not understand') as an assertion of temporal conditionality (faith precedes understanding), as well as of confidence that 'God will aid us and make us understand what we believe' (*lib. arb.* 1.4; 2.6). But if 'authority is temporally prior, reason is prior in reality' (*ord.* 2.26). Augustine argues that even if Christian beliefs are initially credible only because the believer subjectively accepts divine authority, these beliefs are in principle accessible to, and explicable by, rational inquiry. And he attempts to broaden the basis of authority, stressing, for example, the role of historical evidence and wide acceptability in the tradition of Christ's life and teaching. His stand is in sharp contrast to Tertullian's anti-intellectualism, which uses the argument that the mysteries of faith are inaccessible to reason, and that their very inaccessibility constitutes their status as mysteries (*De carne Christi* 5.4; *De praescriptione haereticorum* 7.2–3). Augustine appears to claim that all mysteries may be understood, if not in this life, then in the afterlife. And some, such as the Trinity, may only be partly understood (*ep.* 120.2). Augustine's claim, he assumes, is strengthened by his observation that the same reason is operative in belief and in understanding.[8]

🙞 3 BELIEF AND KNOWLEDGE 🙜

Although he sometimes distinguishes sharply between the certainty of knowledge and the insubstantial nature of belief (*c. Acad.* 3.37, 43; *div. qu.* 9, 48; *ep.* 147.7, 10), Augustine, not least because of his Christianity, more often grants belief, if properly founded, the status of a kind of knowledge. If believing is nothing other than 'thinking with assent' (*praed. sanct.* 5), belief is rational. The validity of our beliefs depends upon the authority by which they are held, the evidence or testimony which commands assent (*c. Acad.* 3.42–3; *ord.* 2.26–7; *lib. arb.* 2.5; *util. cred.*). Different kinds of authority are in play in, for example, historical evidence and the truths of religion, but it is the same kind of mental activity which engages in belief in each case. Yet the objects of belief may differ radically. Historical evidence can only be believed: it can never be scientific knowledge (*mag.* 37; *div. qu.* 48). But religious truths may one day be understood, and so known, by believers. In fact, the progression from belief to understanding is a fundamental tenet of Augustine's views about our knowledge of truths about God, though the transformation of this kind of belief into knowledge will, he argues, occur only in the afterlife (*trin.* 9.1; *ser.* 43; *en. Ps.* 118, *ser.* 18.3). This theological postulate betrays a fundamental attitude of Augustine's, that belief is inferior to understanding. True belief may be rational, justified, and trustworthy, but it lacks the first-hand justification of knowledge, and the comprehensive synoptic overview of a complex field achieved by understanding (*mag.* 31, 39–40, 46; *ep.* 147.21; Burnyeat [12.67]). It also lacks the first-hand justification of sense-perception: properly authenticated sense-perception is a form of knowledge (*ep.* 147.38; *trin.* 12.3; *retr.* 1.14.3) in the sense that historical testimony never can be. It is only when Augustine is arguing against sceptics that he is moved to talk of our 'knowing' historical facts (*trin.* 4.21; 15.21).

Augustine's knowledge of Academic scepticism is chiefly informed by Cicero's *Academica*, and it was his disenchantment with Manichaeism that made him a temporary sceptic (*conf.* 5.19, 25). His arguments against sceptics in *Contra Academicos* are concerned with exposing inconsistencies and inadequacies in the Academic position (such as the concept of the 'persuasive' or 'probable', and the claim that there can be an Academic sage (*c. Acad.* 2.12, 19; 3.30–2)), and preparing the ground for an acceptance of the possibility of epistemic certainty in general.[9]

Augustine's premise that the sage alone is happy is tested by the sceptical argument that wisdom may be the quest for truth rather than its attainment. In his answer he argues that nobody can be happy if she cannot attain something which she desires greatly, such as the truth (*c. Acad.* 1.9). But this argument presupposes that happiness entails accomplishment of desired goals rather than the conviction that the pursuit of a worthwhile desire, even if unfulfilled, is satisfying (Kirwan [12.42] 17–20). In fact, Augustine never repudiates the premise that the unremitting search for truth may in itself be a worthy human activity, and that wisdom may consist in the path that leads towards truth and not merely the goal of truth discovered (*c. Acad.* 1.13–14).

The Academic claims that things may be credible or probable without those or other things being known. Augustine exploits the fact that Cicero translates the Greek term *pithanon* ('persuasive' or 'credible') by *verisimile*, 'like truth' (*c. Acad.* 2.16, 19, 27–8). Augustine argues that it is absurd to claim that something is like a truth when one purports not to know what the truth is, applying a version of Plato's thesis (*Phaedo* 74d–e) that comparing x with y entails previous knowledge of y. But I can say that x is like y if I know how y would seem if it existed. The Academic claim stands if the Academic knows 'how a truth would seem if there were any'.[10] Augustine's argument fails.

Augustine's critique of sceptical *epochê* or suspension of judgement – itself an intended safeguard against the risk of error – concentrates on the inevitability of risking error if one habitually assents to what one does not know (*c. Acad.* 2.11). This is a neat rejoinder. Since action and the forming of judgements are not to be avoided, as the Academic concedes, the Academic cannot claim that suspension of judgement is either possible or brings with it avoidance of error (*c. Acad.* 3. 33–6).[11]

Augustine's attack on scepticism takes the form of a defence of the Stoic criterion of truth (*c. Acad.* 2.11; 3.18, 21; cf. Cicero, *Academica priora* 18, 113). He believes that the evidence of sense-perception does not, strictly speaking, satisfy the conditions of the criterion. His search for propositions which satisfy the conditions, as he understands them, leads him to look for propositions of such a kind that they cannot be taken for false. He argues that propositions of logic (such as 'not p and q', 'if p, then not q') satisfy the conditions, as do mathematical propositions (*c. Acad.* 3.21, 23, 25, 29; cf. *doctr. chr.* 2.49–53). So do such propositions as 'I exist', 'I am alive', or even 'If I am deceived, I exist' (*beata v.* 7; *sol.* 2.1; *lib. arb.* 2.7; *vera rel.* 73; *trin.* 10.14; *civ.* 11.26). It is arguable that propositions of this last kind are intended to demonstrate the impossibility of thinking of any kind without existing, and that Augustine is inferring the certainty of our existence from the fact of consciousness. But it may be that Augustine is arguing that he cannot mistakenly believe that he exists, or is alive, etc.[12] Does Augustine anticipate Descartes's *cogito*? When Descartes's first readers suggested to him that this was so, Descartes replied that there was a difference between Augustine's use of the argument and his own.[13] But in fact Augustine puts his *cogito* argument to various uses, to argue for the immateriality of the mind, or as part of a demonstration of God's existence.

In his account of what we can indubitably know Augustine follows the Platonist tradition in asserting that knowledge is not derived from sense-perception or experience, but that truths are somehow impressed upon our minds a priori. What are these truths? They certainly include the mathematical and logical propositions alluded to above. But they also include ideas or concepts like that of 'unity' (*lib. arb.* 2.21–3, 26, 28–9, 40; *trin.* 8.4). For knowledge is not just of propositions; it is also direct acquaintance with entities that correspond to the Forms of Plato and the Platonist tradition, in which particular things in our world participate (*div. qu.* 46). Augustine contrasts the immutability of the eternal Forms with the mutability even of the human reason which apprehends them (*imm. an.* 7; *ser.* 241.2). He adopts the Middle Platonist view that the Forms are the thoughts of God, who looks into his mind in order to create the universe (*div. qu.* 46; *civ.* 12.27). In Christian terms, Augustine links the concept of the Forms to the belief that the son of God is both wisdom and 'word', in the sense of a causal creative power (*vera rel.* 66, 113; *ep.* 14.4; *civ.* 9.22; *Gn. litt* 1.18.36).

Augustine considers but rejects the Platonic doctrine of *anamnêsis* as an explanation of the presence in the human mind of knowledge that is not derived from sense-experience. Knowledge is recollection, an exercise of the memory, but in the sense that when I know I actualize what is latent in my mind, eliciting truths by a process of concentration. This sounds Plotinian, but it is combined with a reluctance to believe in the pre-existence of the soul (*c. Acad.* 1.22; *sol.* 2.35; *imm. an.* 6; *ep.* 7; *conf.* 10.16–19).[14] Nor is the human mind able to realize knowledge unaided. Augustine believes that divine illumination is required to achieve this. God is the light of the mind, and knowing is a kind of mental seeing. The divine light illumines not merely what is apprehended, but also the apprehending mind. Moreover, the light of truth is also the light in which we make judgements, whether about intelligible phenomena or sense-perceptions. But illumination's role is not just normative or formal: illumination attempts to account for the mind's access to concepts and ideas, not merely its power to judge (*sol.* 1.12, 15; *ep.* 120.10; *conf.* 9.10; *div. qu.* 46; *trin.* 4.4; 14.21; *Gn. litt.* 12.31.59).[15] Although it is obvious that the illumination theory is an aspect of the doctrine of divine grace, it is not an attempt to deny the mind its proper cognitive activity. Rather, it is a realization of the mind's natural capacity.

Knowledge of this kind is a result of introspection. Augustine powerfully reiterates the Neoplatonist themes of conversion or return to oneself, of self-knowledge as the means to all knowledge, the fulfilment of a deep desire to possess wisdom, as deep as the desire to be happy (*vera rel.* 72; *sol.* 2.1; *trin.* 9.14; 10.1–16).[16] Self-knowledge is a realization of self-love, but self-love moves beyond itself to the knowledge of truth (*beata v.* 33, 35; *ord.* 2.35; *trin.* 9.18). In a sense, God is the truth which I know. But God is not the Forms. Transcending them, he is both known and unknowable, 'touched' rather than apprehended, a vision like our seeing the Forms, but unlike our seeing them a vision that cannot be complete in our temporal condition (*conf.* 9.24; 10.35–8; *trin.* 15.2; *ser.* 117.5).

❧ 4 SEMANTICS AND HERMENEUTICS ❧

The most discussed aspect of Augustine's philosophy of language in this century is the account of language-acquisition criticized by Wittgenstein for concentrating on words as names of objects and on ostensive definition as the means by which words are understood (*Philosophical Investigations* 1–3, 32, citing *conf.* 1.13). Wittgenstein's critique is, at least in part, misplaced. Whereas Augustine tends to insist that single words are names, he does not regard ostensive definition as the sole or even principal way in which understanding of language is achieved. For Augustine, language is a system of signs conveyed in speech: every word signifies something. What words signify is not immediately obvious. They convey thoughts from speaker to hearer, but it is not clear whether Augustine maintains that they signify those thoughts, or the objects of those thoughts, or both thoughts and objects. Augustine adapts to an explicitly linguistic context Stoic discussions (themselves indebted to Aristotle) of signs as a means of inference in the acquisition of scientific knowledge.[17] Verbal signs refer to something 'beyond themselves'. But verbal signs are not the kind of sign upon which Stoic theory concentrates: these Augustine calls 'natural', whereas verbal signs are 'given' by a speaker to express something, to provide evidence of, at the very least, mental contents (*mag.* 1–31; *doctr. chr.* 1.2; 2.1–4; *dial.* 5; *conf.* 1.7, 12–13, 23).

If verbal signs are evidential, they will signify not merely specific things, but also facts, actual or purported. Thus sentences as well as individual words signify, and some individual words (conjunctions or prepositions, for example) are more readily understood as signifiers when they are considered as parts of a sentence or proposition. But Augustine also attempts to show that all individual words are names, and that every word can be used to refer to itself: every word is a sign inasmuch as it can be used to bring itself to mind (this is how Augustine deals with words like 'if' and 'because') (*mag.* 3, 13–19).

In the *De dialectica*[18] Augustine distinguishes between words and what is 'sayable' (*dicibile*), the conception of a word in the mind, what is understood by a word, the mental perception of a word (*dial.* 5). This account has something in common with the Stoic *lekta* doctrine. But there are substantial differences between the two concepts. If *lekta* are the incorporeal meanings of words, they are only 'complete' as the meanings of completed sentences. Their principal function is to be true or false, and their linguistic form is propositional. Parts of *lekta* are not meanings. Augustine's *dicibile* concept is underdeveloped. In part, it resembles his concept of the inner word, the notion that thought is a kind of inner speech in no particular language, but capable of being verbalized, even if, as in the case of God's word, it is not vocal (see section 9).[19] Language expresses the speaker's will, verbal signs signify states of mind ('if' indicates doubt, 'nothing' a perception that there is no object or real thing there (*mag.* 3, 19)). We explain words by means of other words, using signs to signify other signs (*mag.* 7–18). Likewise, gestures, whether mimic or not, function as signs that make things known (*mag.* 4–6). But we can also make things known by performance, for example of an action like walking, where no signs are used (*mag.* 29). Signs point beyond themselves to that which they signify, and cognition of what is signified is superior to perception of its sign. Augustine suggests that this is so because the sign is functionally dependent upon the thing signified, or is a means to an end, but he does not resolve satisfactorily the question of value (*mag.* 24–8). Why are words inferior to things?

The reason why Augustine raises the value-question may be that, despite his initial thesis that language teaches something, Augustine eventually adopts the position that nothing is learnt by means of signs (*mag.* 32–5).[20] Rather, it is perceptions of things that teach us the meaning of signs like words. Words do not convey their meaning unless we know that to which they refer. More precisely, words have the function of calling to mind the things of which they are signs (*mag.* 33). But 'calling to mind' or 'making known' or 'showing' is not the same as 'teaching', and having something 'made clear' is not the same as 'learning' it (*mag.* 33–5). Knowledge is direct acquaintance with what is known, signs have an instrumental function, they serve to remind us of what we know. Augustine expresses this theory in Christian terms by asserting that the one teacher is Christ, the divine 'inner teacher', the wisdom whereby we know what we know (*mag.* 2, 38–40, 46). But we only achieve knowledge because we teach ourselves, through introspection: we are no passive recipients of that which we learn. This Platonist position leads to the devaluation of signs in the learning process. Their function is auxiliary. They may prompt the direct acquaintance that is knowledge. And they also serve as vehicles for communication of thoughts and ideas. When communication occurs, something is indeed transferred from one mind to another, but once again it is not a case of communication from an active sign-giver to a passive sign-recipient. Rather, what one mind has apprehended is apprehended through the sign by another mind: it is simply another instance of cognition (*mag.* 39–46).

The focus of Augustine's semantics is epistemological rather than linguistic, although he has interesting observations to make about language and meaning. The uses of his sign-theory in theological contexts, such as its application to his views on non-literal, figurative meanings of Scripture or to the Church's sacraments, proved to be highly influential.[21] Together with his North African contemporary Tyconius, Augustine, especially in the *De doctrina christiana*, develops a hermeneutics of reading Scripture that is profoundly original, with repercussions beyond Biblical interpretation.

~ 5 ETHICS, POLITICAL THEORY, ~ AESTHETICS

Augustine appropriates the eudemonist ethics of ancient philosophy.[22] Happiness (*beatitudo*) is a universal human desire (*c. Acad.* 1.5–9; *beata v.* 10, 14; *civ.* 10.1), the goal (*finis*) of human endeavour (*civ.* 19.1): it is the highest good for humans (in one version of this thesis Augustine posits peace, rather than happiness, as the universal goal (*civ.* 19.10–13). In common with the eudemonistic tradition since Aristotle, Augustine investigates what constitutes the well-being of the human being as a rational being (*beata v.* 30–7; *lib. arb.* 2.7, 26; *Gn. c. Man.* 1.31). He does not equate happiness with pleasure or enjoyment, any more than Aristotle or the Stoics do, although he argues that the happiness appropriate to humans, if realized, is accompanied by delight and enjoyment (*doctr. chr.* 1.3–5; *trin.* 11.10). The happiest form of life is living in accordance with reason, whether this consists in the search for truth or its discovery and possession, the state of wisdom (*sapientia*) that reflects divine wisdom (see section 3). The proper end or goal for humans is to 'enjoy God' *qua* truth as an end in itself, and this teleological goal should also determine all our moral choices (*lib. arb.* 2.35–6; *civ.* 8.8; 15.7; *c. Faust.* 22.78).

In one sense, Augustine's account of happiness equates it with a form of knowledge, namely knowledge of what is best and highest: happiness consists in contemplation of stable eternal being, something that endures and, unlike other kinds of possessions, cannot be lost (*beata v.* 11; *lib. arb.* 1.32–4; *vera rel.* 86; *mor.* 1.5). But Augustine qualifies this equation of perfect virtue with knowledge by an insistence that enjoying or 'possessing' God entails doing what God wills, living well, performing virtuous actions. On the one hand, therefore, wisdom is contrasted (Stoically) with folly (*beata v.* 28–9). But Augustine also argues that being virtuous and its contrary are not merely instances of knowledge or ignorance. In this context his concepts of use and enjoyment, and his notion of the will, are crucial.

The Augustinian contrast between use and enjoyment is influenced by rhetorical and philosophical antitheses in Cicero, in particular the 'useful–good' (*utile–honestum*) contrast (*div. qu.* 30). At first sight, however, it is not so much a distinction between kinds of evaluation of temporal things as a contrast between the eternal and the temporal (*lib. arb.* 1.32–4). In order to enjoy God, who is eternal being, we may use temporal things, as means to an end, in an instrumental way. Augustine includes other human beings among the objects of use, but only by arguing that my use of them is appropriate if it involves love of them 'on God's account' (*propter deum*) (*doctr. chr.* 1.3–4, 20–1).[23] In Augustine's maturer thought the category of use is not seen in exclusively instrumental terms, but as a pointer towards the activity of willing, so that even enjoyment becomes a sub-category of use. God's love for us is not 'enjoyment', for that would imply that God needs us for his blessedness. Divine love is rather 'use' in a providential sense (*doctr. chr.* 1.34–5). If there is order and hierarchy among beings, it is an 'order of love' (*ordo amoris*) (*civ.* 15.22). A difficulty with human beings is that, whereas their relations with one another are temporal, they are not just temporal beings. Augustine's vision of the afterlife for those saved is of a heavenly community of God and the saints: thus loving (or enjoying) one another in God becomes a frequent expression in his attempts to escape from problematic consequences of the application of the use–enjoyment category to human relations (*doctr. chr.* 1.36–7; *trin.* 9.13).

Augustine appropriates the Greek philosophical principle that what is especially valuable about truth and knowledge is that they cannot be lost involuntarily (*mor.* 1.5). He understands the principle in terms of love, rather than merely of choice (*trin.* 13.7–11). This is in part because, in thinking about truth, he is thinking about a person, God, and our relation to that person. But the principal reason why he talks of love in this context is to be found in his psychology. It is commonplace in Augustine that what I do depends upon what I love, not merely in the sense of what I value, but above all in the sense that I act in accordance with a settled inclination (*conf.* 13.10; *civ.* 14.7). Acting in accordance with a settled inclination is, for him, acting voluntarily in the strict sense. He finds no place for the Aristotelian view that *enkrateia* (self-mastery) may involve acting voluntarily and morally despite inclining to the wrong things. For Augustine it is not possible to love and value the wrong things and at the same time to choose what is right (*conf.* 8.19–24). Loving the right things is a question of character, not just of rational insight.[24]

Loving something is a necessary condition of willing it: sometimes Augustine suggests that it is tantamount to willing it. Loving the right things for the right reasons is a pre-condition of acting well. Loving the wrong things, or the right things for the wrong reasons, leads to evil actions. Reacting against the Manichaean belief that evil is a substance or a nature in the universe and in ourselves, and also to some extent reacting against the Plotinian view that metaphysical evil (matter or bodies formed in matter) somehow helps to determine moral evil,[25] Augustine argues that whatever exists is, *qua* created by God, good in some degree (*civ.* 19.13). If things ceased to be good in any sense, they would cease to exist. On this principle things are relatively evil to the degree that they lack goodness. Evil is privation of good, but not in an absolute sense. This is not necessarily a moral distinction: a stone has less goodness than a mind, but I cannot speak of the stone's moral status. Evil in the moral sense is, Augustine suggests, the fact or consequence of willed evil action, chosen by a mind (angelic or human) that remains essentially good, whose nature is good (*civ.* 12.1–9). Persons are, strictly speaking, not evil: actions may be.

If love determines action and is a symptom of character, self-love is the source of sin: more specifically, the source is pride, understood as a refusal to accept subordination to God, to acquiesce in one's place in the hierarchy of beings. In Platonist terms, this is a 'turning away' from God to self-absorption (*sibi placere*), a failure to understand the relationship between God and humans. Adam's fall results from the delusion that he is an autonomous being. His sin is a 'perverse imitation of God' (*conf.* 2.12–14; *civ.* 12.6–8; 14.12–14).

Virtue is defined in terms of order (*doctr. chr.* 1.28; *civ.* 15.22). In the early *De beata vita*, Augustine understands the virtues to possess a kind of measure that is without either excess or defect (*beata v.* 30–3). In that work he suggests that the attainment of wisdom by the sage entails possession of the virtues. In his later writings he is less sanguine about the perfectibility of human nature in this life. Life is a continuing struggle with vices; virtue is not a stable, attainable state (*civ.* 19.4). The virtues control but do not extirpate emotions. Augustine recognizes the traditional four cardinal virtues (*mor.* 1.25; *div. qu.* 31). Virtue is a form of love (*mor.* 1.25, 46), primarily of God, but also of other humans. Justice is 'giving God his due' (*civ.* 19.21) as well as loving one's neighbour. The practice of the virtues expresses the inherently social nature of humans: we are naturally members of societies (*civ.* 12.22; 19.12; *ep.* 130.13). Augustine subscribes to the natural law theory (*div. qu.* 53; *spir. et litt.* 48). Our awareness of the natural law derives from self-love, or the instinct for self-preservation, and it extends (as does the Stoic concept from which it derives) to a realization of the need for justly regulated relations with others (*civ.* 19.4; *doctr. chr.* 1.27). Primarily, this realization is a form of the Golden Rule[26] in its negative version 'Do not do to others what you would not have others do to you' (*ep.* 157.15; *en. Ps.* 57.1; *Io. ev. tr.* 49.12). Augustine gives the natural, or, as he often calls it, eternal law the status of a Platonic Form inasmuch as he says of it, as he says of the Forms, that it is 'stamped on our minds' (*lib. arb.* 1.50–1; *trin.* 14.21; *ser.* 81.2). Strictly speaking, the laws of human societies should be framed in accordance with divine eternal law (*vera rel.* 58), but it is political authority, rather than strict conformity to natural law, that gives validity to positive law (*ep.* 153.16; *civ.* 19.14). Only those human laws that are explicit contraventions of divine commands may be disobeyed, and Augustine's understanding of what constitutes divine commands is specific: they are commands directly revealed in Scripture, such as the prohibition of idolatry (*doctr. chr.* 2.40, 58; *civ.* 19.17; *ser* 62.13). Augustine is otherwise reluctant to assert as a principle that individuals may decide for themselves whether an individual temporal law is just or unjust, even if promulgated by an unjust ruler or without reference to the natural law. One obvious exception is a law that might sanction something contrary to nature (Augustine's example is sodomy (*conf.* 3.15–16)). Other laws (for example, about monogamy or polygamy) merely reflect the customs of different societies (*conf.* 3.12–13; *c. Faust.* 22.47). Hence there is scope for great differences in the laws of different societies.[27]

The peace which is the highest good is also the proper aim of human societies. They should aspire to practise justice, to be stable, to be equitable in their dealings.[28] In practice, this is often only realized by coercion, punitive measures, and harsh exercise of authority: Augustine finds this appropriate to our fallen human nature, vitiated as it is by original sin. Controlling humans driven by greed, pride, ambition, and lust calls for a rule of law that, at best, contains vestiges or traces of authentic justice (*Simpl.* 1.2.16; *trin.* 14.22). Certain features of his society – private property and slavery, for instance – Augustine regards as consequences of the Fall, not, strictly speaking, natural, at least not natural to our pristine created selves (*civ.* 19.15–16; *Io. ev. tr.* 6.25–6). In general, Augustine insists that it is the proper use of wealth and possessions that counts. He proffers no moral critique of the economic or social institutions of his society. Misuse of wealth is wrongful possession of it, not in the legal sense (unless the misuse is also criminal), but in the moral sense that, in strict justice, the individual has forfeited his right to a material good (*ep.* 153.26; *ser.* 113.4; *en. Ps.* 131.25). Renunciation of property and wealth is part of the ascetic ideal, but it is the desire for unnecessary wealth, rather than the possession of wealth, that is immoral. Curbing desires is a central function of political authority, and it often has to take the form of merely restricting the harm that those who misuse the world's goods would do: Augustine takes a sanguine view of government, which will not be required in the ideal state of heaven, where the tranquillity of order that is only realized by the rule of law in earthly societies (and only infrequently) will be realized spontaneously by the community of saints (*civ.* 19.11, 13–14; 22.30).[29]

One social institution which Augustine defends is matrimony. His defence argues that it is not merely for the procreation of children but also to provide fellowship for the partners (*b. coniug.* 3). But a state of sexual abstinence is preferable. Augustine's one argument for this view revolves around his understanding of sexual arousal. He has many grounds for championing abstinence as the supreme form of ascetic renunciation,[30] but they usually reflect his attitude to sensuality in general and control of emotions in particular. The argument concerning sexual arousal is that it is involuntary, not subject to the will or consent (*civ.* 14.16, 24; *ep.* 184A.3). It seems to be an exception to the rule that other bodily organs can be activated by the will, with or without emotional stimulus, indeed require some kind of willing in order to operate. But sexual arousal happens without the will's consent, and neither can it be aroused at will. Even when desire has fired the mind after arousal (and so some kind of willing has occurred), the sex organs may fail to be responsive. Augustine considers this to be a consequence of original sin, and can envisage a pre-lapsarian form of sexual activity that is controlled by the will. His Pelagian adversary Julian of Eclanum argues that sexual desire is not merely necessary for copulation but also natural and in itself morally neutral (c. Iul. imp. 1.70–1; 3.209). But why are anarchic genitals so bad? What distinguishes sexual arousal from, say, sneezing or coughing?

Augustine seems to argue that what distinguishes it is its power over both body and mind: it overwhelms a person emotionally, physically, and mentally. This he finds sinister. There is, by implication, no emotion which cannot be brought under the control of reason, but sexual arousal is impervious to reason and to will (civ. 14.16). Augustine's other arguments – such as the sense of shame attending sexual desire and acts – cannot explain why sex is tainted. But he finds that sexual arousal occurs even in the dreams of those who, like him, have devoted themselves to a life of continence, and that in dreams he seems to consent to sexual acts that his waking self repudiates. He argues that this cannot involve any moral responsibility, but feels that such dreams are a symptom of his imperfect moral status, as well as being yet another indication that the sex instinct is beyond our conscious control (conf. 10. 41–2; Gn. litt. 12.15.31).[31]

In several areas of ethics where Augustine's ideas are not necessarily original he exerted, because of his authority and the wide dissemination of his views, a considerable influence. This is the case with what he says about the ethics of warfare, which does not advance much beyond Cicero (civ. 1.21; 4.15; 19.7; ep. 189.6; 229.2; c. Faust. 22.75),[32] or his views about suicide, which contain the arguments that we do not dispose of our lives (a Platonic argument) and that killing oneself is a kind of cowardice and of despair, the triumph of emotion over reason (civ. 1.17–27; ser. 353.8).[33]

Augustine's Platonism makes him equate the beautiful with the good. The God whom we love is the supreme beauty which we desire (conf. 7.7; 10.8, 38; sol. 1.22; trin. 1.31; civ. 8.6, 11.10; ser. 241.2; en. Ps. 44.3). Beauty consists of a numerically founded form or relation whose sensible manifestation is a reflection of a higher, immutable divine 'reason'. Beauty's structure is rational and accessible to the judging mind (ord. 1.18, 2.33–4; mus. 6.30, 38; Gn. litt. 3.16.25). But the formal beauty of the arts is to be transcended no less than natural beauty, and all perceptible beauty is an 'admonition' to mind to ascend to a spiritual plane where intelligible beauty is one with truth and wisdom (conf. 7.23; 10.9; vera rel. 101). In his creation account, Augustine uses the craftsman-analogy: God is the true artist and the universe is an artefact whose perfection is both numerical and hierarchical (civ. 11.18, 21–2; 12.24–5; Gn. c. Man. 1.25). If we could perceive the whole, we would realize that evil in the universe does not detract from its overall goodness, and that the presence of antitheses and contraries in it may enhance its beauty (*ord.* 1.18; *conf.* 7.18; *civ.* 11.18, 22; 12.4). Augustine recognizes the temptations inherent in aesthetic pleasure, as in any pleasure. He perceives, for example, that piety and fervour can be nourished by church music, but that the senses may sometimes usurp the place of reason when we delight in song (*conf.* 10.49–50). Once more, it is a question of proper use of a lesser good. To delight in the beauty of the universe for its own sake, even if the delight is intellectual rather than sensual, is to confuse reflected goodness and beauty with the truly and perfectly good and beautiful. This would be a failure to know the Good and to love God. It would also, Augustine believes, leave us dissatisfied, our potential for the perfecting of our natures unrealized.[34]

<h2>~ 6 THE WILL ~</h2>

Augustine's concept of the will[35] and defence of free will rest on the paradox that God determines our wills when we will the good, but that such willing is nonetheless free choice, for which we are responsible. This applies as much to Adam before the Fall as to humanity's postlapsarian state. Divine help for Adam in paradise was a necessary, but not sufficient condition of his free choice of the good, and neither was freedom of choice sufficient. Only divine grace and human free choice together are sufficient for attaining the good (*civ.* 14.26; *corrept.* 28–34). Augustine argues, puzzlingly, that Adam, and all created beings, have a tendency to choose evil rather than good because they are created out of nothing and are possessed of an ontological weakness that does not entail their sinning but makes it possible that they will choose evil (*civ.* 12.6; 14.13; *c. Iul. imp.* 5.3).

In an early work, the *De libero arbitrio*, Augustine describes the faculty of free will as a middle good whose activity is necessary to virtue: the neutral will can be used either rightly or wrongly, it is morally indifferent (*lib. arb.* 2.50–3). But as his thought develops, Augustine argues for the concept of a will that is morally determined, that is good or evil depending upon the value of what is willed. This is in part a reaction against Pelagian views. Pelagius describes human choice as a 'power to take either side', neither good nor evil *per se*: 'in the middle'. Augustine denies that the same will can choose good and evil. Will is either good or evil, or, more accurately, the power of free choice (*liberum arbitrium*) of the will (*voluntas*) may be exercised in a good or an evil way (*lib. arb.* 2.1). The Pelagians had a strong case when they argued that Augustine's views in *De libero arbitrio* were akin to theirs (*retr.* 1.9; *conf.* 8.19–21; *pecc. mer.* 2.18–30; *spir. et litt.* 58; *gr. et pecc. or.* 1.19–21).

Will for Augustine is a mental power or capacity, like memory, but because it is morally qualified it reflects a person's moral standing in a way that memory cannot. As well as referring to a good or bad will in the singular,

Augustine talks of two or more wills in us, where there is moral conflict: in this latter case, our wills are the range of possible courses of action open to us (*lib. arb.* 2.51; *conf.* 8.19–21; *gr. et lib. arb.* 4).

If God determines my good will, how can I be free? Augustine believes that the fact that God has foreknowledge of my will does not determine that will, for God's knowledge (strictly speaking, not foreknowledge) is timelessly eternal (*Simpl.* 2.2.2; *civ.* 5.9; 11.21; *praed. sanct.* 19). Divine omniscience is compatible with free choice of the will. Yet predestination to salvation is actively caused by God. Augustine argues that this does not make us passive recipients of divine grace. The notion of 'compulsion of the will' is to him an absurd one (*c. Iul. imp.* 1.101; *c. ep. Pel.* 2.9–12). Willing entails the power to do X through, and only through, the means of willing X. Augustine's psychology is based upon the belief (which he derives from analysis of our behaviour) in the centrality of concentration or attention (*intentio*) in all mental processes. The mind is activated by the will, not in the sense of one faculty or 'part of the soul' affecting another, but inasmuch as we cannot perceive, or imagine, or remember without concentrating or paying attention or willing to do so. Thus grace may only become operative in humans when the will is attracted to the good. For the will is always goal-directed, and will entails assent. Willing is a form of action, not a reaction to external stimuli (*gr. et lib. arb.* 32; *c. ep. Pel.* 1.5, 27). If divine grace is irresistible, this does not entail that grace compels us. People are 'acted upon that they may act' (*corrept.* 4). It is seems impossible to argue that this is not determinism. What Augustine is stressing is that consent is necessary to the *modus operandi* of the will's reception of grace.

Augustine's arguments against Pelagius' description of human choice as 'a power to take either side' is based upon the observation that it posits the same cause (the indifferent will) of opposite effects (*gr. et pecc. or.* 1.19–21). Augustine appears here to reject the so-called 'freedom of indifference' of the will. His position seems to be closer to freedom of spontaneity, where absence of force or compulsion, rather than absence of external causation, is characteristic. Will is not self-determining, yet humans are not accurately to be described as being instruments of God's will. Thus the Stoic example of the dog tied to, and dragged by, the cart (*SVF* II 975 [7.2]) cannot apply to Augustine's understanding of spontaneity. Freedom is not merely acquiescence in God's activity, but rather the exercise of a human faculty that involves both consent and power to act, or to initiate action. Both in his account of Adam's freedom in paradise and in his early version of his free-will theory in *De libero arbitrio* Augustine subscribes to the liberty of indifference account; but it is not applicable to fallen humanity. However, the fallen human being possesses both the ability and, it may be, the opportunity, to act otherwise, even though that ability is not, in fact, exercised when the will is determined by the good. Exercising the ability to commit sin is not, of course, an exercise of freedom of the will for the mature

Augustine. Rather, it is an instance of the enslavement of the will to evil, from which only divine grace can liberate it. If freedom to sin is a form of slavery, then willing and obedient slavery to the will of God is true freedom (*ench.* 30). On the other hand, sin is the price of having free will, and having free will is a necessary condition of acting rightly. Sin is the price of freedom, because freedom entails absence of compulsion. This is Augustine's version of the free will defence (*ench.* 27; *lib. arb.* 2.1–3).[36] It reveals why defence of free choice of the will seems to be so important to Augustine. Heavenly rewards (and hellish punishments) make no sense if they are not a consequence of acting rightly (or wrongly), even if God is the author of our virtuous actions. The argument does not explain satisfactorily why God tolerates sin. Augustine's characteristic strategy here is to concede that nothing happens 'apart from God's will', even those things, like sin, that happen 'against God's will' (*ench.* 100). God lets us sin, but does not cause us to do so. But it is difficult, on these premises, to avoid the consequence that God is responsible for sin, in the sense that he is responsible for states of affairs brought about voluntarily, if not intentionally, by him. The distinction between causing and permitting seems impossible to maintain.[37]

God's grace precedes (in Augustine's terminology) acts of the free will. God makes good decisions possible, but also causes them, for grace is irresistible. Prevenient grace is more than merely enabling, nor is it a form of co-operation between God and humans. Rather it is operative. Again, the question arises: can a decision caused by God be free? Augustine's answer is the one discussed above. God causes the reception of his gifts by the mechanism of human consent. But since God's will is never thwarted, it is as true to say that what happens as a consequence of divine will happens by necessity, as it is to maintain that human realization of good behaviour is an instance of human freedom. 'God cannot will in vain anything that he has willed' (*ench.* 103), and the human being whom God wills to save cannot be damned. But neither will such a human being be saved against her will.

❄ 7 SOUL ❄

Augustine's concept of soul as an immaterial, naturally good, active, inextended, and indivisible substance owes much to his Neoplatonist readings. It is also likely that Porphyry is a major source of his knowledge of the contents of Plato's *Phaedo*, *Phaedrus*, and *Timaeus*. Scripture and the Christian tradition provide Augustine less with a concept of soul's nature than with texts requiring exegetical elucidation by means of Platonist psychology, and attempts at philosophical exegesis which he rejects, such as Tertullian's corporealist theories and Origen's arguments for pre-existence, embodiment as punishment for sin, and reincarnation.[38]

Soul is the life-principle, and to various kinds of life – vegetative, sentient, intelligent – correspond degrees of soul (*civ.* 7.23, 29; *en. Ps.* 137.4). The awareness that we are alive is awareness that we are, or have, souls: Augustine argues that we are empirically conscious of the fact that we have a soul, even if we do not perceive soul with any of the senses (*beata v.* 7; *trin.* 8.9). The single soul in humans has rational and irrational faculties: the latter include the powers of impulse, sense-perception, and certain kinds of memory, and they can be disturbed by the passions. It is the function of the rational soul (and mind is a part of soul) to control the irrational element (*civ.* 5.11; 9.5; *en. Ps.* 145.5). There is an inescapable moral dimension in Augustine's accounts of the levels of soul, and it is linked to the Neoplatonist concept of soul's conversion to the Good, seen in terms of an ascent from the corporeal and percipient levels, through those of discursive reason and moral purification, to the intellection of the highest principle by a mind that is morally and mentally prepared for understanding. This conversion or return makes good the 'turning-away' from divine wisdom and interiority that characterizes sin: rejecting the distracting multiplicity of what is external, it discovers the divine within us (*imm. an.* 12, 19; *ord.* 1.3; 2.31; *conf.* 2.1; 7.23; 13.3; *trin.* 8.4; 10.7; 14.21).

Soul, the principle of movement in bodies, is itself a self-moving principle: my consciousness of my self-movement is my consciousness of my power to will (*div. qu.* 8). Soul's movement is not local, nor does it entail substantial change, but impulse and will often result in bodily movement (*ep.* 166.4; *quant. an.* 23). Rejecting all corporealist theories of the soul's substance, Augustine engages in polemic against them, be they Epicurean, Stoic, Manichaean, or Christian. Examination of the nature of soul's activities rules out even the most subtle of corporeal soul-substances. Memory and imagination are not subject to the physical law that corporeal likenesses correspond in size to the bodies in which they are reflected, like the image in the pupil of the eye. Perception, concentration, and volition are indicators of immateriality, as is the mind's power of abstraction and intellection of non-corporeal objects, such as geometrical figures (*quant. an.* 8–22; *Gn. litt.* 7.14.20; 7.19.25–20.26). Although physical and mental powers appear to develop concomitantly in growing humans, there is no strict correlation between their development, still less any evidence that soul physically grows or diminishes (*quant. an.* 26–40). Augustine is nonetheless aware that it is paradoxical to maintain that soul is present as an entirety throughout the body and is yet inextended and indivisible. It is omnipresent not in a spatial sense, but as a 'vital tension' (*vitalis intentio*), which, for example, enables it to perceive in more than one bodily part simultaneously (*imm. an.* 25; *quant. an.* 26, 41–68; *ep.* 166.4).

Soul is mutable: that makes it substantially different from God's unchangeable nature (*conf.* 7.1–4). As a Manichee, Augustine had believed that the good human soul is part of the divine, and he sees Stoic pantheism as leading to the same conclusions (*duab. an.* 16; *vera rel.* 16; *civ.* 7.13, 23). The soul is subject to various kinds of mutability. Learning, the affections, moral deterioration and progress, all effect changes in the soul (*imm. an.* 7). Soul exists in a temporal medium in which it can and must change. It is maintained in its continued existence by God's will (*div. qu.* 19; *ep.* 166.3; *trin.* 4.5, 16, 24). To characterize soul's changeability Augustine uses the Aristotelian distinction between a subject and qualitative changes in that subject which do not entail substantial change in it (Aristotle, *Categories* 2). For the soul's identity persists through change. In fact, the necessarily unchangeable nature of certain kinds of knowledge entails the substantial identity of the mind in which, as in a subject, such knowledge is present. Augustine regards this as proof of the soul's immortality (*imm. an.* 5, 7–9; *sol.* 2.22, 24). He also argues for its immortality from its equation with life. If being alive is the defining characteristic of soul, soul cannot admit the contrary of life and so cannot cease to live (*imm. an.* 4–5, 9, 12, 16; *trin.* 10.9): this is the final argument for the soul's immortality in Plato's *Phaedo* (102a–107b). Augustine believes that the irrational human soul is also immortal, and that we have both memory and feelings in the afterlife (*civ.* 21.3; *Gn. litt.* 12.32.60–34.67). The soul, like God inasmuch as it has a similar creative and rational domination over subordinate creation, cannot, in its nature, be evil. It is a corruptible good, occupying a medial position between God and bodies. Its position on the scale of being and its moral standing should coincide. Pride, a desire for self-mastery in an order where the soul is not the master, degrades it morally to animal level (*conf.* 7.18; *civ.* 19.13; *en. Ps.* 145.5; *ep.* 140.3–4; *trin.* 12.16). But this degradation can only be understood in a metaphorical sense. Augustine repudiates Manichaean and Platonist doctrines of transmigration of human souls into, or from, animal bodies, agreeing with what he takes to be Porphyry's rejection of the view that a rational soul, whose reason is not accidental but belongs to its substance, could become the essentially different irrational soul of an animal, or vice versa (*civ.* 10.29–30; 12.14, 21, 27; 13.19; *Gn. litt.* 7.10.15–11.17).

The incorporeal soul cannot be a condition of the body, such as its harmony or the proportion of its parts (*imm. an.* 2, 17; *Gn. litt.* 3.16.25; 7.19.25). Yet soul is entirely present in every part of the body, and its various activities and conditions point to a symbiosis in which body and soul influence one another (*ep.* 9.3–4). Soul is mixed with body in a way that allows each element to maintain its identity, as in the mixture of light and air (*ep.* 137.11; *Gn. litt.* 3.16.25). The 'vital tension' (*ep.* 166.4) by which soul is present to body has also a volitional dimension (*mus.* 6.9; *Gn. litt.* 8.21.42). Augustine is aware of the Platonist view that, even when not embodied, souls may inhabit a vehicle, but doubts the truth of the theory, considering pure spiritual existence to be possible, even if he also believes in the future resurrection of the body: it is natural for souls to govern bodies (*ep.* 13.2–4; *Gn. litt.* 8.25.47; 12.32.60; 12.35.68).

On two traditional problems Augustine remains agnostic: the origin of souls, and the existence of a world-soul. On origins he vacillates between the view that souls are propagated by parents, like bodies, and the theory that they are created directly by God as each individual is conceived. The former is difficult to explain, the latter seems to compromise the completeness of God's creation. Augustine considers various forms of pre-existence theory, including the view that all souls are created individually in the moment of creation, and embodied at different times. But his discussions remain inconclusive, just as he remains uncertain about the moment when the foetus is animated (*lib. arb.* 3.56–9; *Gn. litt.* 6; 7; 10).[39] He vacillates on the question of the world-soul because he finds it plausible to believe that the ordered and cohesive universe owes its continued existence to the presence of a cosmic soul. He objects to particular consequences of world-soul theories (dual good and evil cosmic principles, as in Manichaeism; Stoic views on the world as the body of a divine mind) rather than the theories as such, and is benevolent towards what he takes to be Plotinus' position, that cosmic soul is created and illuminated by a transcendent divine principle. But his tentative conclusion is that the universe is an inanimate body full of stratified soul-kinds (*imm. an.* 24; *ord.* 2.30; *civ.* 4.12, 31; 7.5–6, 23; 10.2, 29; 13.16–17).[40]

When Augustine analyses human behaviour, he recognizes that impulse or assent (*appetitus*) is the cause of action, whether it is the impulse of self-preservation, or motions of appetency or avoidance or simply the motor of a proposed course of behaviour (*div. qu.* 40; *ep.* 104.12; *civ.* 19.4; *trin.* 12.3, 17). Augustine's views on impulse and assent are crucial to his account of the will. The links between impulse, assent, will, and desire are fundamental in his psychology: to eradicate desire is impossible, and desire can be for good things – knowledge, happiness, God (*lib. arb.* 3.70; *div. qu.* 35.2; *civ.* 10.3; *conf.* 13.47). Assent is good if it results in moral behaviour, if desire is directed towards appropriate goals, and for the right reasons. It is the same with the emotions. They are expressions of the irrational faculty, and forms of intention. They should be controlled by reason and used properly. They are an inescapable feature of our condition: Augustine does not believe in the existence of a dispassionate soul (*civ.* 9.4; 14.6–10).

Augustine's insistence upon the value of introspection, both as a means of discovering the truth and as a condition of moral purification (*vera rel.* 72; *trin.* 9.4; 10.2–15), leads him to talk of senses of the soul, of inner senses, inner speaking, and – using a Pauline analogy (Romans 7:22–3, etc.) – of the 'inner man' (*ser.* 126.3; *Io. ev. tr.* 99.4; *civ.* 13.24). Augustine supposes that such locutions are about our souls or our minds, and that the phenomena which they describe entail mind–body dualism. But they do not. They may describe the contrast (or consistency) between model cases of human behaviour and how we actually behave, or they may refer to dissembling or insincere behaviour.[41]

In Christological and Trinitarian contexts Augustine speaks of the concept of a person, whether he is talking about the unity of Christ's *persona*, despite his human and divine natures, or about the relation between the three persons of the single substance that is the Trinity (*trin.* 7.7–11; *ep.* 137.11; *Io. ev. tr.* 19.15). Sometimes he equates the person with the self, as distinct from the emotional or mental powers or activities (*trin.* 15.42), or as the subject of personal attributes. But his conclusions do not lead to any concept of personality as distinct from traditional views of what it is to be human. The distinction between person and substance in his Trinitarian theology, and the relational aspect of his definition of person there, are not exploited in his account of human psychology.[42]

∾ 8 SENSE-PERCEPTION AND IMAGINATION ∾

Augustine's theory of sense-perception has a physiological bias. Like Plotinus, he exploits the discovery of the nervous system by Alexandrian medicine (Plotinus 4.3.23; see Solmsen [12.106]). The sensory nerves transmit stimuli to the brain from the various sense-organs. The nerves contain soul *pneuma* as a means of communication between brain and senses (*Gn. litt.* 7.13.20; 7.19.25). Augustine co-ordinates this belief with other traditional philosophical accounts of perceptive processes, such as the ray theory of vision (*trin.* 9.3; *ser.* 277.10). The senses are not reflexive, and awareness of their activity is a perception of the internal sense (which corresponds to Aristotle's *koinê aisthêsis*), which controls and judges sensations (*lib. arb.* 2.8–12). Sensation is a form of motion or change. Augustine believes that it is a motion running counter to the motion set up in the body by sensory stimuli (*mus.* 6.10–11, 15). Sentience is the product of the interaction of two movements of qualitative change. Most likely it is the soul *pneuma* that is set in motion in this process. Because of the presence of *pneuma* in the sensory nerves, they are themselves sentient. The perceiving subject, soul, is entirely present in them, and is not merely located in a central receptive organ with which they communicate in a non-sentient way (*imm. an.* 25; *c. ep. fund.* 16.20).

But if sensation has a physiological mechanism, perception is nonetheless a psychological process. The body–soul interaction in perception is a kind of tempering by mixture (*contemperatio*); its mental aspect is called concentration (*intentio*). In vision, for example, the visual ray is the necessary physical counterpart of mental concentration. *Intentio* is an activity, the active concentration of soul power: perception is exercised upon the sensory stimulus rather than being a passive reception of the latter (*quant. an.* 41–9; *mus.* 6.7–11; *trin.* 11.2; *Gn. litt.* 7.20.26; 12.12.25; 12.20.42). Body does not act upon soul: 'perception is something directly undergone by the body of which the soul is aware' (*quant. an.* 48). Augustine extends the notions of concentration and counter-motion to his accounts of feelings like pleasure and pain (*mus.* 6.5, 9, 23, 26, 34–58).

The awareness implicit in any perceptive process is underpinned by the instantaneous operation of memory. A series of memory-impressions is stored in the mind in the course of even the shortest perception, and this process is essential to the functioning of perception (*mus.* 6.21; *Gn. litt.* 12.11.22). Some texts of Augustine dispute that perception gives us any knowledge of the external world, suggesting that there are no characteristics of our sense-perceptions that enable us infallibly to distinguish between true and false (*c. Acad.* 3.39; *div. qu.* 9). But many other texts make claims for our ability to know the external world, the kind of knowledge that Augustine calls *scientia*, contrasting it with *sapientia*, the knowledge of eternal and immutable truths (*trin.* 12.16–17, 21; 15.21). Even optical illusions have a kind of consistency (*c. Acad.* 3.36). Augustine maintains that if our perception of an object is comprehensive and our faculties are functioning normally, reliable information may be acquired about the external world (*ep.* 147.21; *civ.* 19.18).

Sense-perception is perception of images of objects, not of the objects themselves, and these images are not corporeal. Like Aristotle (*De anima* 2.12), Augustine argues that perception is the ability to receive forms without matter (*quant. an.* 8–9). Moreover, perception is the perception of like by like. There is an affinity between the percipient's reason and the image or form of the object perceived, and it is this affinity which makes perception possible as well as reliable (*ord.* 2.32–3; *trin.* 11.2, 4, 26). Now the objects of perception are themselves formed by the Forms or Reasons or Ideas in the mind of God, to which they owe their existence (*div. qu.* 23, 46). In sense-perception these Forms function as standards (*regulae*) accessible to our minds whereby we may distinguish between the truth and falsity of the images conveyed by perception (*vera rel.* 58; *trin.* 9.9–11). When the mind errs in its evaluation of perceptions it does so because it applies itself to the phenomena in question in some deficient way: access to the Forms is no guarantee of infallibility in perception (*Gn. litt.* 12.25.52). Assembling of evidence and common sense will prevent mistakes being made: Augustine believes that we are capable of establishing working distinctions between reliable and illusory perceptions. Strictly speaking, perception does not convey certainty, but empirical processes operate on the basis of a distinction between true and false, and there is a 'truth appropriate to this class of things' (ibid.). That this is so is due to our access to the transcendent criterion, the Form, because of divine illumination of our minds (*sol.* 1.27; *trin.* 9.10–11).

The reproductive exercise of the imagination (often called *phantasia* by Augustine) depends on remembered images that are reactivated, but so does the creative activity of imagination (often called *phantasma* by him) (*mus.* 6.32; *trin.* 8.9; 9.10). Imagination may be willed and subject to our control, but not necessarily so. Creative imagination is a process of contracting and expanding the images of what we have perceived, or of combining or separating their data (*ep.* 7.6; *trin.* 11.8). In such cases concentration or will is operative (*trin.* 11.6–7). But there are imaginative processes that seem to be involuntary, such as dreams and hallucinations. Augustine adds to this category prophetic inspiration, arguing that some dreams are also prophetic. Dreaming is imagining, often on the basis of images derived from the day's preoccupations, and it is beyond rational control (*Gn. litt.* 12.18.39; 12.23.49; 12.30.58). Thus consent to sinful actions in dreams is not morally reprehensible although it is the case that our dreams reflect our moral character (see section 5). In dreams the creative imagination is more usually in operation. But not all dreams or visions are entirely dependent upon our mental powers. Augustine recognizes external agencies, divine, angelic, or demonic, and is curious to explain a wide variety of paranormal phenomena in terms of the imagination (O'Daly [12.46] 118–27). In such cases a reciprocal influence of body and soul upon one another is often discernible (*ep.* 9.3–4; *Gn. litt.* 12.13.27; 12.17.37–8).

Anticipation of intended actions is an activity of imagination, as is the prediction of future events, and both of these processes depend upon experience and the creative manipulation of images (*conf.* 10.14; 11.23–4, 26, 30, 36–8; *trin.* 15.13; *Gn. litt.* 12.23.40).

Augustine is also interested in the pathology of the imagination, where some physical disruption of the link between brain and sensory nervous system occurs. In such cases concentration takes place, but because it cannot function normally, it generates images in a wholly introspective way. Or the disturbance may be in the brain itself or in the sense-organ. The hallucinatory states which ensue have something in common with dreams (*Gn. litt.* 12.12.25; 12.20.42–4).

There is no single influence upon Augustine's accounts of sense-perception and imagination. The Stoic concept of *sunaisthêsis* lies behind his definition of perception, as it does behind Plotinus' account. There are Neoplatonist traces in his concept of internal sense. But he is not reproducing other men's doctrines.[43]

∞ 9 MEMORY ∞

Augustine argues that memory is indispensable to our perceptions of spatio-temporal continua and to the exercise of the imagination. But how are memory-images formed? The series of images stored in the mind in the course of every perception is not merely essential to the process of perception itself, but also to the recollection of perceptions (*conf.* 10.12–15; *quant. an.* 8–9; *Gn. litt.* 12.16.33). Incorporeal sense-impression leads to incorporeal memory-image, and memory depends upon and corresponds to perception in quality, quantity, and kind (*trin.* 11.13, 16; *c. ep. fund.* 16.20). But memory-images are not formed spontaneously. They are willed, a consequence of concentration. And if memory, like expectation, is a prerequisite of deliberate action, concentration is the necessary link between memory and expectation, if the moments of such action are to cohere (*imm. an.* 3–4; *trin.* 11.15).

In his account of the process of remembering Augustine applies the analogy with sense-perception. The will directs the mind towards the memory's contents, and the mind's vision is formed by memory-images. Recollecting is perceiving memory-images: it actualizes memory-traces (*mag.* 39; *trin.* 11.6). However, this model of the memory process is only fully satisfactory as an account of how we remember sense-perceptions, and, in addition, it only serves as an analogy between types of mental activity (perceiving and remembering), not between the objects of these activities. The images perceived in sense-perception are those of objects actually there and perceptible by other percipients. The truth-value of the images is verifiable. But Augustine has a difficulty with memory-images of perceptions, for they are images of things absent, no longer there in the state in which they were perceived. Augustine suggests that they must have evidential character as 'proofs [*documenta*] of previously perceived things' (*mag.* 39), but, strictly speaking, only for the percipient: their verifiability remains problematic.[44] Augustine does not offer a direct solution to this dilemma. But elements of his solution may be constructed from his account of the functional relations between words and images. That he must envisage a solution is evident, for memory is essential to every type of knowledge claim, including claims about the objects of sense-perceptions.

What we perceive is an articulated image, a rational structure which has an affinity with our minds, and is stored in our memory as a form of knowledge. When we wish to reactivate this knowledge by directing our concentration upon it, we generate an 'inner word', co-extensive with the memory-image. The image appears to be stored in the memory pre-verbally, as a word-potential (*trin.* 8.9; 15.16, 19–22). The linguistic metaphor here employed, and the reason for its employment, are clarified by Augustine's remarks about the understanding and retention of the meaning of words (*dial.* 5). The meaning (*dicibile*) grasped by the mind is also a word-potential, capable of being expressed in language. But meaning is always present to the mind in a verbal manner. Also, it may have a general semantic function: the meaning of 'city', if understood, enables me, not merely to recall or recognize known cities, but also to identify new cities and classify them, and so on. Identifying, understanding, naming, and recalling are inextricably linked. Not every perception must be accompanied by overt naming of the object perceived, but naming is usually at least implicit or expected. The metaphor of the 'inner word' recognizes this. But Augustine also feels that he can best elucidate the mechanism of perceiving, storing, and recalling by the linguistic illustration: grasping a word's meaning, storing it as a *dicibile*, and expressing it. Recalling my memory-image of an object is like actualizing the semantic content of a known word, it is like bringing its meaning to mind. What this analogy emphasizes is the coherence and objectivity of our recollected perceptions: memory claims are meaningful.[45]

Augustine does not apply this solution to the problem of the verifiability of memory-images. But the implication of his argument is that, if sense-perception leads to knowledge of the external world, memory is the storing of such knowledge. Verifying memory-claims may involve deciding whether another person's claims are worthy of credence on grounds of inherent plausibility: it involves deciding what I should believe, and for Augustine belief is a form of knowledge (see section 3).

Augustine extends the mental-image theory to one other type of memory, that of past emotions, but he does so tentatively (*conf.* 10.21–3). For recalling a past feeling need not entail re-experiencing that feeling, whereas the memory-image of a past perception conveys some distinctive quality of what is remembered. Augustine adduces his famous metaphor of memory as the mind's 'stomach' (*conf.* 10.21), taking in but transforming different emotions. But he is clearly not at ease with the application of the mental-image theory to this kind of memory, chiefly because the ideas of past feelings have not been perceived by any of the senses, but are derived from the mind's introspection of its own experiences. However, if he were to claim that they can be recalled without an image, he would be making a claim about them that is made for recalled ideal numbers, scientific principles, and Forms. Affections may be mental phenomena, but we can recall them only because we have experienced them, unlike numbers, principles, and Forms. Against the trend of his argument Augustine concludes that memories of past feelings are more like memories of past perceptions than the privileged category of remembering that does not require images.

Augustine puts forward a criterion for establishing that something is in the memory. If I can name P and recognize what the name P refers to, I remember P (*conf.* 10.23). He applies this criterion to the fact of forgetting (*conf.* 10.24–5, 27–8). But how can I actualize forgetting in my mind without, in fact, forgetting? Augustine first suggests that the image theory may solve the problem: recalling forgetting may be like recalling a past feeling, and I must not actually experience forgetting every time I recall it. But he is not satisfied with this suggestion, and embarks upon an alternative argument. When I forget the name of a person I know, both my rejection of wrong names and my recognition of the right name, when I recall or am told it, are possible only because I have not entirely forgotten it. Remembering forgetting is related to an object: it is remembering that I have forgotten something. But to remember that I have forgotten something entails that I have not entirely forgotten it. And the experience of forgetting does not entail having a mental image of forgetting. Without such an image I can recognize what 'forgetting' means and so remember forgetting something.

Augustine also suggests that I can recall the circumstances or context of something which I have forgotten, and that this can help me recollect it. There may be certain indicators (*signa*) which are contextual and remind me by association of what I have forgotten (*trin.* 11.12; 14.17).

Memory is the focal point of consciousness, in which past, present, and future are related: it appears to underwrite the continuity of mental processes and provide the subject's sense of his identity (*conf.* 1.12; 10.14, 21, 26). Mind, memory, and the self are inextricably linked, and Augustine may seem to argue that my identity is dependent upon continuity of consciousness, as does Locke (*Essay Concerning Human Understanding* 2.27.9). But Augustine is not making any such claim. He points out that areas of my past, such as infancy, are not accessible to my memory, yet nonetheless constitute my identity: my knowledge of myself, past and present, is imperfect (*conf.* 1.7–12; 2.1; 10.15). Nor is memory the mind without qualification, but rather the mind engaged in certain activities, just as understanding and will are the mind engaged in equally distinctive activities (*trin.* 10.18–19). Augustine is familiar with the Platonic theory of recollection (*anamnêsis*) as an explanation of the presence in the mind of knowledge that is not derived from sense-experience. He mentions the complementary doctrine of the soul's pre-existence as a possibility for the created human soul (*lib. arb.* 1.24; 3.56–9), but never adopts the doctrine, preferring to use Platonic language about recollection to convey active and latent states of the mind's possession of knowledge (see section 7).[46] Recollection is eliciting what is latent in the memory by a process of mental concentration and ordering (*quant. an.* 50–6). Because of the mind's intelligible nature it is 'joined . . . to intelligible object in a natural arrangement [*naturali ordine*]' (*trin.* 12.24). Such objects are known by direct acquaintance, and no mental image is required in recollecting them (*conf.* 10.16–19).

It might seem appropriate for Augustine to say that God too is in my memory, like ideas. But he is careful to stress that God cannot be in my memory before I learn of him. The reason is, that God is both knowable (as the truth and the Good) and unknowable to the human mind (*sol.* 1.15; *ord.* 2.44, 47; *ep.* 130.28; *Gn. litt.* 5.16.34), whereas Forms and scientific principles are fully known by us. Knowing God is a different matter, attainable only in a paradoxical sense, and by submission of the will. I may love God before I know him, but I can only remember God after I have, in some respect, learnt about him (*conf.* 10.8–11, 35–8).

Augustine's use of *memoria* and of terms for remembering covers a wide range of activities, not all of them self-evidently kinds of memory: self-consciousness, self-knowledge, understanding a scientific principle. In this he is influenced by Platonist *anamnêsis* theory and discussions about the rediscovery of one's true self by self-reflection. His account of memory is recognizably part of ancient philosophical discussions of the problem. But it is not possible to identify a specific influence to which he is indebted. He neither agrees with Aristotle that all memory processes depend upon the mental image, nor with Plotinus that such an image theory is unnecessary. He implicitly concurs with Stoic theory in his account of memories of sense-perceptions, and his account owes much to Stoic views on presentation and assent (*SVF* 2.83, 115 [7.2]). But he cannot accept the Stoic theory as a global account of memory. His view that in some kinds of memory the mental image is a prerequisite, whereas in others it is not, is closest to Plato's position, even if it cannot be based on extensive reading of Plato's dialogues. Several elements of Augustine's account are anticipated in Cicero (*Tusculan Disputations* 1.57–71): memory as an impressive power of the immaterial mind, and as a means of understanding the mind's self-knowledge and obtaining knowledge of God through his works and by analogy with the human mind. But if the themes are traditional, Augustine's analysis is of sustained originality.[47]

Some uses of memory-language in Augustine appear questionable or untenable. One such case is his claim that memory is essential to the performance of serial operations such as perception or speaking a sentence. These are not cases of actual reminiscence or memory performance. Not-forgetting or bearing in mind are not instances of recalling or remembering, and the concomitant concentration is neither remembering nor does it entail self-consciousness in the sense implied by Augustine.[48]

~ 10 TIME ~

Although Augustine occasionally refers to time as a trace or copy of eternity (*mus.* 6.29; *en. Ps.* 9.17; *Gn. litt. imp.* 13.38), he departs from the Platonic tradition in not attempting to analyse time with reference to eternity (*conf.* 11.17–39). The contrast between God's eternity and human temporality leads Augustine to consider time empirically, as a fact of everyday experience, a practical problem. The ensuing speculative freedom of his discussion has attracted much modern attention: for Wittgenstein (*Philosophical Investigations* 89–90) it is an example of a typical but flawed kind of discourse about time.[49]

Augustine's puzzles about the difficulty of defining something as familiar as time are traditional in ancient philosophy since Aristotle (*Physics* 4.10–14). They lead him not to a definition of time, but to an attempt to answer two questions: how do we measure time? how can stretches of time have any length? Augustine admits, if only by implication, that time may not be explicitly definable. His celebrated description of time as a *distentio animi* (*conf.* 11.33) is not so much a definition as a metaphor evoking the psychological state (more 'tension' or 'distraction' than 'extension') that accompanies the mental act of time-measurement.[50]

Augustine believes that time is an infinitely divisible continuum. There are no time-atoms. There are extended time-stretches, but at any given instant time has no actual measurable extent (*conf.* 11.20, 34). Nevertheless, Augustine erroneously asserts that the present 'is' (exists now), despite being extensionless and without duration (*conf.* 11.22–6). This is partly due to the fact that, like most ancient philosophers, he views time as a flow of events of which each instant successively constitutes a present or 'now' (Plutarch, *De communibus notitiis* 1082A).[51] But he also assumes that 'now' is a point or part of time, failing to see that the division of an extended time-stretch will always result in extended time-stretches. For Augustine, the past and the future do not exist (in the sense of existing now), but are present in memory and expectation. Past events are present in the images derived from sense-perception; the presence of the signs or causes of future events enables us to anticipate or predict them. Like the Stoics (*SVF* 2.509, 518–19 [7.2]), Augustine criticizes conventional language concerning three grammatical tenses: we should, strictly speaking, talk only of three present tenses, and of a 'present of things past' and a 'present of things future' (*conf.* 11.22–4, 26).

Time is measured in the mind, and is a measurement of duration, which may be a duration of change or motion, but need not be so. Augustine is at pains to demonstrate that our ability to make temporal measurements is prior to, and independent of, any observed physical movement. Time units like day and year are indeed derived from observation of the motion of heavenly bodies, which form an astronomical clock, but our time sense does not presuppose a clock, depending rather upon memories of time-stretches. When the sun stood still in Joshua's war against the Amorites (Joshua 10: 12–13), time *qua* duration still passed (*conf.* 11.27, 29–30).

Time is the measurement of a relation, by comparison with known (remembered) time-stretches, but we do not make direct temporal comparisons with the standard unit of measurement: measuring time is not like measuring length, for example. Nor do we measure time as it passes, for time at any given instant is extensionless. What we measure is not the time-process itself, but the impress (*affectio*) which memory retains after perceptions. In the case of future processes, we measure them by anticipation when we possess the necessary knowledge to enable us to make advance calculations (*conf.* 11.31, 33–8).

Augustine's insight that our ability to measure times depends upon the fact that durations can be remembered is vitiated by his inference that the time-impress (*affectio*) is the time-stretch itself. He is led to the inference because he believes that when a time is not present it does not exist, and that the past and the future must somehow currently exist, if they are to be the objects of currently existing memory or expectation. But the proper objects of present memories and expectations are past and future events (not times), and it is they which do not have present existence. Yet that fact does not entail that my dealing with them can take place only through present images and signs of them.[52] Elements of Augustine's analysis of time-measurement reflect Stoic views: the assumption that time is infinitely divisible; the distinction between loose and strict language about temporal phenomena, especially the criticism of grammatical tenses; the distinction between infinite duration and least perceptible times. It is likely that his analysis develops from a Stoic or Stoic-influenced discussion. But his conclusions form a personal contribution of great ingenuity to traditional questions.[53]

Augustine believes that there cannot be time before the creation, for time requires change and there was no change in God's eternity. Time, therefore, had a beginning (*conf.* 11.12–16; *civ.* 11.6; *Gn. litt.* 5.5.12). The principle that time requires change is common to Plato, Aristotle, and the Stoics, but Augustine appears to repudiate it when he argues for the primacy of time sense over measured time units. Perhaps he should have concentrated upon the argument that, since creation is a first event, there cannot be time before that event.[54]

⚬⚬ 11 GOD AND CREATION ⚬⚬

Augustine's concept of divine immutability developed gradually. Initially he seems to have accepted the Manichaean belief that there is a changeable divine principle partly immanent in nature. Later he thought of God as immanent and material, but infinite, incorruptible and immutable. His encounter with the Platonists changed his concept of God definitively: God is transcendent, immaterial, and his timelessness entails unchangeability (*duab. an.* 16; *vera rel.* 16; *conf.* 7.1–2, 26; *en. Ps.* 101). God is subject neither to decay nor death, he is perfect living being, in whom substance and qualities are identical (*trin.* 6.6, 8; 7.1–3).

The 'present' of God's existence is extensionless, like the 'present' of an infinitely divisible time continuum, but God's present is indivisible, a condition of permanent stability (*vera rel.* 97; *conf.* 11.12; *ser.* 6.4). Divine substance is mental: the eternal Forms (*rationes, ideae*) are, in Middle Platonist fashion, understood to be in the divine mind, and the second person of the Trinity is often said to be divine wisdom or truth, and hence God is truth (*div. qu.* 46.2; *mag.* 38; *trin.* 4.3). Divine perfection is perfect life, thought, and will (*conf.* 3.10; *div. qu.* 28).

God is omniscient. His knowledge necessarily embraces events in time, but he does not and cannot know these as past and future occurrences. God apprehends temporal events timelessly as present events. It is more correct to say that he has knowledge, rather than foreknowledge, of events that have not yet happened, and this knowledge is immutable (*civ.* 5.9; 11.21; *Simpl.* 2.2.2).[55] Although Augustine does not apply this notion of God's not knowing the future as future to the question whether divine foreknowledge entails determinism, he in fact argues that divine foreknowledge is compatible with free choice of the will (*lib. arb.* 3.4–9).

God the creator timelessly causes the universe to begin. The 'Why not sooner?' argument against its beginning is countered by Augustine's insistence that there was no time before the creation, since time depends on change and God is unchanging. Nor does creation entail that God's will changes: he changelessly wills to create the universe. The notions that the universe persists for ever or that worlds endlessly recur derive from the misconception that there is otherwise a time prior to creation in which God is idle (*conf.* 11.8, 12–17; 12.18, 38; *civ.* 11.4–6, 21; 12.15, 18).[56]

The Greek philosophical principle that nothing comes from nothing led some authors in the Judaeo-Christian tradition to assert that God made the world out of a pre-existing, beginningless matter. But others violated the principle by asserting that God created the world out of nothing.[57] Augustine adopts the latter viewpoint, which had become dominant by his day (*Gn. litt. imp.* 1.2; *sol.* 1.2; *mus.* 6.57; *conf.* 11.7; 12.7; 13.48; *vera rel.* 35; *c. Fel.* 2.19). But he also argues that God creates unformed matter from nothing, to be the subject of change. Matter is the necessary condition of change, but its creation does not precede that of created beings. Even created immaterial beings have a 'spiritual' matter (*conf.* 12.4–8, 38; *Gn. litt.* 1.4.9–5.11; 5.5.12–16; 7.6.9–9.12; *Gn. litt. imp.* 4.11–15; Armstrong [12.117]).

Creation is instantaneous and complete, but living organisms are produced at different times throughout the history of the world. In order to account both for the completeness of creation at the moment of creation and the gradual realization of created organisms Augustine adopts and adapts the theory of seminal *logoi* (*rationes causales, seminales*). These are immaterial causes and conditions of living organisms, potentials that are realized in the material seeds from which plants and animals develop, with all their specific differences. The *rationes* are created in the primal creation, along with the heavenly bodies, the firmament, and the elements of earth and water (*Gn. litt.* 5–7; *trin.* 3.13, 16).[58]

 ABBREVIATIONS

b. coniug.	*De bono coniugali*
beata v.	*De beata vita*
c. Acad.	*Contra Academicos*
c. ep. fund.	*Contra epistulam fundamenti*
c. ep. Pel.	*Contra duas epistulas Pelagianorum*
c. Faust.	*Contra Faustum Manichaeum*
c. Fel.	*Contra Felicem*
c. Iul.	*Contra Iulianum Pelagianum*
c. Iul. imp.	*Contra Iulianum opus imperfectum*
civ.	*De civitate Dei*
conf.	*Confessiones*

corrept.	*De correptione et gratia*
dial.	*De dialectica*
div. qu.	*De diversis quaestionibus LXXXIII*
doctr. chr.	*De doctrina christiana*
duab. an.	*De duabus animabus*
ench.	*Enchiridion ad Laurentium*
en. Ps.	*Enarrationes in Psalmos*
ep.	*Epistulae*
Gn. c. Man.	*De Genesi contra Manichaeos*
Gn. litt.	*De Genesi ad litteram*
Gn. litt. imp.	*De Genesi ad litteram imperfectus liber*
gr. et. lib. arb.	*De gratia et libero arbitrio*
gr. et pecc. or.	*De gratia Christi et de peccato originali*
imm. an.	*De immortalitate animae*
Io. ev. tr.	*Tractatus in Evangelium Iohannis*
lib. arb.	*De libero arbitrio*
mag.	*De magistro*
mor.	*De moribus ecclesiae catholicae et de moribus Manichaeorum*
mus.	*De musica*
ord.	*De ordine*
pecc. mer.	*De peccatorum meritis et remissione*
praed. sanct.	*De praedestinatione sanctorum*
quant. an.	*De quantitate animae*
retr.	*Retractationes*
ser.	*Sermones*
Simpl.	*De diversis quaestionibus ad Simplicianum*
sol.	*Soliloquia*
spir. et litt.	*De spiritu et littera*
trin.	*De trinitate*
util. cred.	*De utilitate credendi*
vera rel.	*De vera religione*

NOTES

1 Hagendahl [12.57] 79–94, 486–97.
2 Hagendahl [12.57] 52–156, 498–553.
3 Courcelle [12.56] 159–76; O'Meara [12.38] 131–55.
4 Marrou [12.59] 27–46; Courcelle [12.56] 183–94.
5 Fredriksen [12.51]; Markus [12.52].
6 Miles [12.88] 99–125.
7 O'Daly [12.46] 7–79.
8 Kretzmann [12.64].
9 Rist [12.48] 41–8, 53–6.

10 Kirwan [12.42] 22.

11 Kirwan [12.42] 22–3.

12 Matthews [12.69]; Kirwan [12.42] 30–4; Sorabji [12.120] 289; Rist [12.48] 63–7.

13 *Letter to Colvius*, Adam-Tannery 3.247; *Philosophical Letters*, tr. A. Kenny, Oxford 1970, 83–4; Matthews [12.70] 11–38.

14 O'Daly [12.104]; cf. O'Connell [12.102].

15 Nash [12.71] 94–124; O'Daly [12.46] 203–7.

16 O'Donovan [12.47] 60–92.

17 Rist [12.48] 23–40.

18 Stock [12.77] 138–45.

19 Kirwan [12.42] 55–9.

20 Stock [12.77] 145–62.

21 Markus [12.73]; Mayer [12.75].

22 Rist [12.48] 48–53.

23 O'Donovan [12.89].

24 Kirwan [12.42] 187–92.

25 Rist [12.98].

26 Dihle [12.81].

27 Deane [12.80] 78–94.

28 Rist [12.48] 203–55.

29 Deane [12.80] 94–153; Markus [12.85] 72–104.

30 Brown [12.79] 387–427.

31 Matthews [12.70] 90–106; Kirwan [12.42] 192–6.

32 Markus [12.86]; Swift [12.92].

33 Kirwan [12.42] 204–8.

34 Harrison [12.83]; Svoboda [12.91].

35 Rist [12.48] 148–202.

36 Kirwan [12.42] 78–81.

37 O'Daly [12.96] 93–7; Kirwan [12.42] 82–150.

38 O' Daly [12.46] 8–11.

39 O'Daly [12.105].

40 O'Daly [12.46] 62–70.

41 Matthews [12.101].

42 Lloyd [12.100], criticizing Henry [12.99].

43 Schwyzer [12.60]; O'Daly [12.46] 103–4.

44 Matthews [12.110]; Bubacz [12.109].

45 O'Daly [12.46] 141–5.

46 O'Daly [12.104]; O'Connell [12.103].

47 O'Daly [12.112] 44–6.

48 G. Ryle, *The Concept of Mind*, London, Hutchinson's University Library, 1949, 6.4.

49 Mundle [12.115]; McEvoy [12.114].

50 O'Daly [12.116].

51 Sorabji [12.120] 35–51.

52 Kirwan [12.42] 182–3.

53 O'Daly [12.46] 153–9; Rist [12.48] 73–85.

54 Sorabji [12.120] 232–8; Kirwan [12.42] 163–6.

55 Sorabji [12.120] 255–6, 263–4; Kirwan [12.42] 171–4.

56 Sorabji [12.120] 232–8; Kirwan [12.42] 159–63.
57 Sorabji [12.120] 193–202; May [12.118] 122–82.
58 TeSelle [12.49] 216–18; Meyer [12.119].

BIBLIOGRAPHY

Note: A full synopsis of Augustine's works and of modern editions is provided in [12.30] 1.xxvi–xli.

ORIGINAL LANGUAGE EDITIONS

12.1 *Sancti Augustini Hipponensis Episcopi Opera Omnia*, ed. J.-P. Migne, Paris, 11 vols, 1841–2 (= *Patrologia Latina* 32–47). A reprint of the Benedictine edition of St Maur, Paris, 1679–1700.

12.2 *Corpus Scriptorum Ecclesiasticorum Latinorum*, Vienna, Hoelder–Pichler–Tempsky, 1866–. Several vols devoted to Augustine (in progress).

12.3 *Corpus Christianorum. Series Latina*, Turnhout, Brepols, 1953–. Several vols devoted to Augustine (in progress).

12.4 *Bibliothèque Augustinienne. Oeuvres de Saint Augustin*, Paris, Desclée de Brouwer and Etudes Augustiniennes, 1936–. In progress. With French trans., introductions, and notes.

12.5 *S. Aureli Augustini Confessionum libri XIII*, ed. M. Skutella. Stuttgart, B.G. Teubner, 2nd edn, 1969.

12.6 *Sancti Aurelii Augustini Episcopi De Civitate Dei libri XXII*, ed. B. Dombart and A. Kalb. Leipzig, B.G. Teubner, 4th edn, 1928–9.

12.7 *Augustine, De Dialectica*, ed. B. Darrell Jackson and J. Pinborg. Dordrecht/Boston, Mass., North-Holland Publishing, 1975.

ENGLISH TRANSLATIONS

12.8 *The Works of Aurelius Augustine, Bishop of Hippo*, ed. M. Dods. Edinburgh, T. and T. Clark, 15 vols, 1871–6. Wide selection of Augustine's works.

12.9 *A Select Library of the Nicene and Post-Nicene Fathers of the Christian Church*, New York, 1887–1902. Wide selection of Augustine's works (reprinted by W.B. Eerdmans, Grand Rapids, Mich., 1979: vols 1–8 = Augustine).

12.10 *Ancient Christian Writers*, Westminster, Maryland (later New York), Newman Press, 1946–. Several vols devoted to Augustine (in progress).

12.11 *The Fathers of the Church*, Washington DC, Catholic University of America Press, 1947–. Several vols devoted to Augustine (in progress).

12.12 V. J. Bourke (ed.), *The Essential Augustine*, selection with commentary, Indianapolis, Hackett Publishing Co., 1974.

12.13 *Augustine: Confessions*, trans. H. Chadwick. Oxford, Oxford University Press, 1991.

12.14 *Augustine: City of God*, trans. H. Bettenson. Harmondsworth, Penguin Books, new edn 1984.

12.15 *Saint Augustine: On Free Choice of the Will*, trans. A.S. Benjamin and L.H. Hackstaff. Indianapolis/New York, Bobbs-Merrill, 1964.

12.16 *Saint Augustine: On Christian Teaching*, tr. R. Green, with introduction and notes. Oxford, Oxford University Press, 1997.

❧ COMMENTARIES ❧

12.17 J.J. O'Meara (ed.), *St. Augustine: Against the Academics*, Ancient Christian Writers, vol. 12 (see [12.10] above), 1951.

12.18 T. Fuhrer (ed.), *Augustin: Contra Academicos (vel De Academicis) Bücher 2 und 3*, Patristische Texte und Studien, 46. Berlin and New York, de Gruyter, 1997.

12.19 J.J. O'Donnell (ed.), *Augustine: Confessions*, introduction, text, commentary. Oxford, Oxford University Press, 3 vols, 1992.

12.20 G. Clark (ed.), *Augustine: Confessions I–IV*. Cambridge, Cambridge University Press, 1995.

12.21 E.P. Meijering (ed.), *Augustin über Schöpfung, Ewigkeit und Zeit. Das elfte Buch der Bekenntnisse*, Philosophia Patrum, 4. Leiden, E.J. Brill, 1979.

12.22 G. Watson (ed.), *Augustine: Soliloquies and Immortality of the Soul*. Warminster, Aris and Phillips, 1991.

12.23 P. Agaësse and A. Solignac (eds), *De Genesi ad Litteram*, Bibliothèque Augustinienne, vols 48–9 (see [12.4] above), 1972.

See also [12.7] and the notes in the individual vols of [12.4].

❧ BIBLIOGRAPHIES AND RESEARCH REPORTS ❧

12.24 C. Andresen, *Bibliographia Augustiniana*. Darmstadt, Wissenschaftliche Buchgesellschaft, 2nd edn, 1973.

12.25 T.J. van Bavel and F. van der Zande, *Répertoire bibliographique de saint Augustin 1950–1960*. Stenbrugge/Den Haag, M. Nijhoff, 1963.

12.26 R. Lorenz, 'Augustinliteratur seit dem Jubiläum von 1954', *Theologische Rundschau* NF 25 (1959) 1–75; id., 'Zwölf Jahre Augustinusforschung (1959–1970)', *Theologische Rundschau* NF 38 (1974) 292–333; 39 (1974) 95–138, 253–86, 331–64; 40 (1975) 1–41, 97–149, 227–61.

12.27 *Augustine Bibliography/Fichier Augustinien*, Boston, Mass., G.K. Hall, 4 vols, 1972. Supplementary vol. 1981.

12.28 *Revue des Etudes Augustiniennes* (1955–) incorporates an annual bibliographical survey (*Bulletin*).

❧ CONCORDANCE ❧

12.29 *Corpus Augustinianum Gissense*, ed. C. Mayer. Computerized concordance of all of Augustine's writings and bibliography on CD-ROM. Basle, Schwabe, 1996.

❧ ENCYCLOPAEDIA ❧

12.30 C. Mayer *et al.*, *Augustinus-Lexikon*. Basle, Schwabe, 1986– .

❧ BIOGRAPHIES AND GENERAL SURVEYS ❧

Ancient

12.31 (Possidius) M. Pellegrino (ed.), *Possidio, Vita di S. Agostino*, Alba, Edizioni Paoline, 1955.

Modern

12.32 G. Bonner, *St Augustine of Hippo: Life and Controversies*, Norwich, Canterbury Press, 2nd edn, 1986.
12.33 P. Brown, *Augustine of Hippo: A Biography*, London, Faber & Faber, 1967.
12.34 J. Burnaby, *Amor Dei: A Study of the Religion of St Augustine*, London, Hodder & Stoughton, 1938 (reprinted Norwich, Canterbury Press, 1991).
12.35 H. Chadwick, *Augustine*, Oxford, Oxford University Press, 1986.
12.36 C. Horn, *Augustinus*, Munich, C.H. Beck, 1995.
12.37 J.J. O'Donnell, *Augustine*, Boston, Mass., Twayne Publishers, 1985.
12.38 J.J. O'Meara, *The Young Augustine: The Growth of St Augustine's Mind up to his Conversion*, London, Longmans, Green, 1954.
12.39 A. Schindler, 'Augustin', *Theologische Realenzyklopädie* 4 (1979) 646–98.

❧ AUGUSTINE'S PHILOSOPHY: GENERAL STUDIES, COLLECTIONS OF ARTICLES ❧

12.40 G.R. Evans, *Augustine on Evil*, Cambridge, Cambridge University Press, 1982.
12.41 E. Gilson, *Introduction à l'étude de Saint Augustin*, Paris, J. Vrin, 4th edn, 1969 (Eng. trans. of 1st edn, *The Christian Philosophy of Saint Augustine*, New York, Random House, 1960).
12.42 C. Kirwan, *Augustine*, London and New York, Routledge, 1989.
12.43 R.A. Markus, in A.H. Armstrong (ed.), *The Cambridge History of Later Greek and Early Medieval Philosophy*, Cambridge, Cambridge University Press, 1967, 341–419.

12.44 R.A. Markus (ed.), *Augustine: A Collection of Critical Essays*, New York, Doubleday, 1972.

12.45 R.J. O'Connell, *St Augustine's Early Theory of Man, A.D. 386–391*, Cambridge, Mass., Harvard University Press, 1968.

12.46 G. O'Daly, *Augustine's Philosophy of Mind*, London, Duckworth, 1987.

12.47 O. O'Donovan, *The Problem of Self-Love in St Augustine*, New Haven/London, Yale University Press, 1980.

12.48 J.M. Rist, *Augustine: Ancient Thought Baptized*, Cambridge, Cambridge University Press, 1994.

12.49 E. TeSelle, *Augustine the Theologian*, London, Burns & Oates, 1970.

❧ AUGUSTINE AS AUTOBIOGRAPHER ❧

12.50 G. Clark, *Augustine: The Confessions*, Cambridge, Cambridge University Press, 1993.

12.51 P. Fredriksen, 'Paul and Augustine: Conversion Narratives, Orthodox Traditions, and the Retrospective Self', *Journal of Theological Studies* NS 37 (1986) 3–34.

12.52 R.A. Markus, *Conversion and Disenchantment in Augustine's Spiritual Career*, Villanova, Pa., Villanova University Press, 1989.

12.53 G. Misch, *A History of Autobiography in Antiquity*, London, Routledge and Kegan Paul, vol. 2, 1950, 625–67.

❧ AUGUSTINE'S PHILOSOPHICAL READINGS ❧

12.54 A.H. Armstrong, 'St Augustine and Christian Platonism', in [12.44] 3–37.

12.55 M. Colish, *The Stoic Tradition from Antiquity to the Early Middle Ages*, Leiden, E.J. Brill, vol. 2, 1985.

12.56 P. Courcelle, *Les Lettres grecques en Occident de Macrobe à Cassiodore*, Paris, Boccard, 2nd edn, 1948 (Eng. trans. *Late Latin Writers and their Greek Sources*, Cambridge, Mass., Harvard University Press, 1969).

12.57 H. Hagendahl, *Augustine and the Latin Classics*, Göteborg, Institute of Classical Studies of the University of Göteborg, 2 vols, 1967.

12.58 P. Henry, *Plotin et l'Occident: Firmicus Maternus, Marius Victorinus, Saint Augustin et Macrobe*, Louvain, Spicilegium Sacrum Lovaniense, 1934.

12.59 H.-I. Marrou, *Saint Augustin et la fin de la culture antique*, Paris, Boccard, 1938, and *Retractatio*, Paris, Boccard, 1949.

12.60 H.-R. Schwyzer, 'Bewußt und Unbewußt bei Plotin', *Les Sources de Plotin*, Entretiens Fondation Hardt, 5, Vandoeuvres/Geneva, 1960, 343–90.

12.61 A. Solignac, 'Doxographies et manuels dans la formation philosophique de s. Augustin', *Recherches Augustiniennes* 1 (1958) 113–48.

12.62 M. Testard, *Saint Augustin et Cicéron*, Paris, Etudes Augustiniennes, 2 vols, 1958.

12.63 W. Theiler, 'Porphyrios und Augustin', *Forschungen zum Neuplatonismus*, Berlin, de Gruyter, 1966, 160–251 (first published 1933).

❧ AUGUSTINE'S CHRISTIAN PHILOSOPHY ❧

12.64 N. Kretzmann, 'Faith Seeks, Understanding Finds: Augustine's Charter for Christian Philosophy', in T.P. Flint (ed.), *Christian Philosophy*, Notre Dame, Ind., University of Notre Dame Press, 1990, 1–36.

12.65 G. Madec, 'Augustinus', in 'Philosophie', *Historisches Wörterbuch der Philosophie* 7 (1989) 630–3.

❧ BELIEF AND KNOWLEDGE ❧

12.66 B. Bubacz, *St Augustine's Theory of Knowledge: A Contemporary Analysis*, New York/Toronto, Edwin Mellen, 1981.

12.67 M. F. Burnyeat, 'Wittgenstein and Augustine *De Magistro*', *The Aristotelian Society. Supplementary Volume* 61 (1987) 1–24.

12.68 R. Lorenz, 'Gnade und Erkenntnis bei Augustinus', *Zeitschrift für Kirchengeschichte* 75 (1964) 21–78.

12.69 G.B. Matthews, '*Si Fallor Sum*', in [12.44] 151–67.

12.70 G.B. Matthews, *Thought's Ego in Augustine and Descartes*, Ithaca, NY and London, Cornell University Press, 1992.

12.71 R.H. Nash, *The Light of the Mind: St Augustine's Theory of Knowledge*, Lexington, University of Kentucky Press, 1969.

See also [12.46] 162–216; [12.48] 41–91.

❧ SEMANTICS AND HERMENEUTICS ❧

12.72 B.D. Jackson, 'The Theory of Signs in St Augustine's *De Doctrina Christiana*', in A.H. Armstrong (ed.), *The Cambridge History of Later Greek and Early Medieval Philosophy*, Cambridge, Cambridge University Press, 1967, 92–147 (reprinted from *Revue des Etudes Augustiniennes* 15 (1969) 9–49). And in [12.44].

12.73 R.A. Markus, 'St Augustine on Signs', in [12.44] 61–91 (reprinted from *Phronesis* 2 (1957) 60–83).

12.74 R.A. Markus, *Signs and Meanings: World and Text in Ancient Christianity*, Liverpool, Liverpool University Press, 1996.

12.75 C.P. Mayer, *Die Zeichen in der geistigen Entwicklung und in der Theologie Augustins*, Würzburg, Augustinus-Verlag, 2 vols, 1969 and 1974.

12.76 K. Pollmann, *Doctrina Christiana. Untersuchungen zu den Anfängen der christlichen Hermeneutik unter besonderer Berücksichtigung von Augustinus, De doctrina christiana*, Paradosis, 41, Fribourg, Universitätsverlag Freiburg Schweiz, 1996.

12.77 B. Stock, *Augustine the Reader: Meditation, Self-Knowledge, and the Ethics of Interpretation*, Cambridge, Mass. and London, Harvard University Press, 1996.

12.78 G. Watson, 'St Augustine's Theory of Language', *Maynooth Review* 6 (1982) 4–20.

See also [12.48] 23–40.

❧ ETHICS, POLITICAL THEORY, AESTHETICS ❧

12.79 P. Brown, *The Body and Society*, London, Faber & Faber, 1989, 387–427.

12.80 H. A. Deane, *The Political and Social Ideas of St Augustine*, New York and London, Columbia University Press, 1963.

12.81 A. Dihle, *Die Goldene Regel*, Göttingen, Vandenhoeck & Ruprecht, 1962.

12.82 D.F. Donnelly (ed.), *The City of God: A Collection of Critical Essays*, New York, Peter Lang, 1995.

12.83 C. Harrison, *Beauty and Revelation in the Thought of Saint Augustine*, Oxford, Oxford University Press, 1992.

12.84 R. Holte, *Béatitude et Sagesse: Saint Augustin et le problème de la fin de l'homme dans la philosophie ancienne*, Paris and Worcester, Mass., Etudes Augustiniennes and Augustinian Studies, 1962.

12.85 R. A. Markus, *Saeculum: History and Society in the Theology of St Augustine*, Cambridge, Cambridge University Press, revised edn, 1988.

12.86 R.A. Markus, 'Saint Augustine's Views on the "Just War"', *Studies in Church History* 20 (1983) 1–13.

12.87 J. Mausbach, *Die Ethik des heiligen Augustinus*, Freiburg im Breisgau, Herder, 2 vols, 2nd edn, 1929.

12.88 M. R. Miles, *Augustine on the Body*, Missoula, Scholars Press, 1979.

12.89 O. O'Donovan, '*Usus and Fruitio* in Augustine, *De Doctrina Christiana* I', *Journal of Theological Studies* NS 33 (1982) 361–97.

12.90 O. O'Donovan, 'Augustine's *City of God XIX* and Western Political Thought', *Dionysius* 11 (1987) 89–110.

12.91 K. Svoboda, *L'Esthétique de S. Augustin et ses sources*, Paris/Brno, Philosophical Faculty of Masaryk, University of Brno, 1933.

12.92 L.J. Swift, 'Augustine on War and Killing: Another View', *Harvard Theological Review* 66 (1973) 369–83.

12.93 J. Wetzel, *Augustine and the Limits of Virtue*, Cambridge, Cambridge University Press, 1992.

See also [12.48] 203–55.

❧ WILL ❧

12.94 J.P. Burns, *The Development of Augustine's Doctrine of Operative Grace*, Paris, Etudes Augustiniennes, 1990.

12.95 A. Dihle, *The Theory of Will in Classical Antiquity*, Berkeley/Los Angeles/London, University of California Press, 1982.

12.96 G. O'Daly, 'Predestination and Freedom in Augustine's Ethics', in G. Vesey (ed.), *The Philosophy in Christianity*, Cambridge, Cambridge University Press, 1989, 85–97.

12.97 J.M. Rist, 'Augustine on Free Will and Predestination', *Journal of Theological Studies* NS 20 (1969) 420–47.

12.98 J.M. Rist, 'Plotinus and Augustine on Evil', *Plotino e il Neoplatonismo in Oriente e in Occidente*, Rome, Accademia Nazionale dei Lincei, 1974, 495–508.

See also [12.48] 148–202; [12.93].

❧ SOUL ❧

12.99   P. Henry, *Saint Augustine on Personality*, New York, Macmillan, 1960.

12.100 A.C. Lloyd, 'On Augustine's Concept of a Person', in [12.44] 191–205.

12.101 G.B. Matthews, 'The Inner Man', in [12.44] 176–90 (reprinted from *American Philosophical Quarterly* 4/2 (1967) 1–7).

12.102 R.J. O'Connell, 'Pre-existence in the Early Augustine', *Revue des Etudes Augustiniennes* 26 (1980) 176–88.

12.103 R.J. O'Connell, *The Origin of the Soul in St Augustine's Later Works*, New York, Fordham University Press, 1988.

12.104 G. O'Daly, 'Did St Augustine ever believe in the Soul's Pre-existence?', *Augustinian Studies* 5 (1974) 227–35.

12.105 G. O'Daly, 'Augustine on the Origin of Souls', in H.-D. Blume and F. Mann (eds), *Platonismus und Christentum = Jahrbuch für Antike und Christentum*, Ergänzungsband 10 (1983) 184–91.

See also [12.48] 92–147.

❧ SENSE-PERCEPTION AND IMAGINATION ❧

12.106 F. Solmsen, 'Greek Philosophy and the Discovery of the Nerves', *Museum Helveticum* 18 (1961) 150–67 and 169–97 (reprinted in *Kleine Schriften*, Hildesheim, Georg Olms Verlag, vol. 1, 536–82.

12.107 G. Verbeke, *L'Évolution de la doctrine du pneuma du Stoïcisme à S. Augustin*, Paris/Louvain, Desclée de Brouwer, 1945.

12.108 G. Watson, *Phantasia in Classical Thought*, Galway, Galway University Press, 1988.

❧ MEMORY ❧

12.109 B. Bubacz, 'Augustine's Account of Factual Memory', *Augustinian Studies* 6 (1975) 181–92.

12.110 G.B. Matthews, 'Augustine on Speaking from Memory', in [12.44] 168–75 (reprinted from *American Philosophical Quarterly* 2/2 (1965) 1–4).

12.111 J.A. Mourant, *Saint Augustine on Memory*, Villanova, Pa., Villanova University Press, 1980.

12.112 G. O'Daly, 'Remembering and Forgetting in Augustine, *Confessions X*', in *Memoria. Vergessen und Erinnern = Poetik und Hermeneutik XV*, Munich, Wilhelm Fink Verlag, 1993, 31–46.

❧ TIME ❧

12.113 H.M. Lacey, 'Empiricism and Augustine's Problems about Time', in [12.44] 280–308 (reprinted from *Review of Metaphysics* 22 (1968) 219–45).

12.114 J. McEvoy, 'St Augustine's Account of Time and Wittgenstein's Criticisms', *Review of Metaphysics* 38 (1984) 547–77.

12.115 C.W.K. Mundle, 'Augustine's Pervasive Error concerning Time', *Philosophy* 41 (1966) 165–8.

12.116 G. O'Daly, 'Time as *distentio* and St Augustine's Exegesis of *Philippians* 3, 12–14', *Revue des Etudes Augustiniennes* 23 (1977) 265–71.

❧ GOD AND CREATION ❧

12.117 A.H. Armstrong, 'Spiritual or Intelligible Matter in Plotinus and St Augustine', *Augustinus Magister*, Paris, Etudes Augustiniennes, vol. 1, 1954, 277–83.

12.118 G. May, *Schöpfung aus dem Nichts*, Berlin, de Gruyter, 1978.

12.119 H. Meyer, *Geschichte der Lehre von den Keimkräften von der Stoa bis zum Ausgang der Patristik*, Bonn, Peter Hansteins Verlagsbuchhandlung, 1914, 123–224.

12.120 R. Sorabji, *Time, Creation and the Continuum: Theories in Antiquity and the Early Middle Ages*, London, Duckworth, 1983.

Glossary

Academy: the area in the outskirts of Athens where Plato had his 'school'.

actuality: translates Greek *energeia* or *entelecheia*, the Aristotelian term for the state of really being (something), as opposed to having the potentiality to become (something).

aethêr: the Aristotelian term for the element of which the heavens are made: the fifth element.

anamnêsis: 'recollection', the Platonic doctrine (*Meno*, *Phaedo*) that human knowledge is the recollection of conceptions (Forms) instilled in the soul before birth.

ataraxia: the state of being undisturbed in mind (Epicurean technical term).

archê: a principle.

category: an ultimate class. Aristotle was the first to write a treatise on categories: see ch. 2.

cause: translates Greek *aition* or *aitia*. It is applied more widely by Greek philosophers, especially Aristotle, than in modern philosophy and science. Following Aristotle, to state the cause of something is to answer any of these four questions: what is it made of? (material cause); what brought it into being? (efficient cause); what is it? (formal cause); what is it for? (final cause).

cosmos: 'a system composed of heaven and earth and the natures contained within them' (pseudo-Aristotle, *On the cosmos*). Identified with the universe (i.e. all that there is) by Aristotle, but distinguished as a limited part of the universe by post-Aristotelians. The word also denotes the state of *order* that prevails in our or any other cosmos.

Cyrenaics: a school of philosophy associated primarily with Aristippus of Cyrene (late fourth century BC), known for an unsophisticated doctrine of hedonism. No original writings survive.

demonstration: translates Greek *apodeixis*, a valid deductive argument, with necessarily true premises. See ch. 2, pp. 48–53.

Demiurge: the divine Craftsman, creator of the cosmos according to Plato's *Timaeus*.

deontological: favouring the view that duty takes precedence over other ethical claims.

dialectic: argument between opponents.

Dogmatists: a term applied by ancient Sceptics to their philosophical opponents who claimed to have knowledge.

doxa: 'belief', 'opinion', 'judgement', often contrasted with knowledge.

eidôlon: an image (English 'idol'). An Epicurean technical term for the image (composed of atoms) received by the sense-organs in perception.

Eleatics: Parmenides of Elea (in southern Italy) and his successors, Melissus and Zeno.

elements: usually applied to the four 'primary bodies', namely earth, water, air and fire, first listed by Empedocles in the fifth century, and adopted by Plato, Aristotle, and most others.

elenchus: refutation; a type of critical examination practised by Socrates.

emanation: see '*exhalation*'.

empeiria: experience.

endoxa: an Aristotelian term meaning 'views held by most people or by those best qualified to judge'.

energeia: see 'actuality'.

entelecheia: see 'actuality'.

epideictic: rhetoric concerned to display the merits of the orator, the person praised, or both; it was contrasted with forensic rhetoric (prosecution and defence in lawcourts) and deliberative rhetoric (arguing for or against a course of action in a political context).

epistêmê: 'knowledge'. In Aristotle, specifically scientific knowledge, or 'a science'.

essence: usually translates Greek *to ti ên einai* ('what it was to be [something]'), an Aristotelian term.

eudaimonia: usually translated 'happiness'. However, it does not necessarily denote a feeling, but rather a flourishing condition of body and soul, of long duration, perhaps extending to the whole of a life. Hence, the primary goal of human life.

exhalation: in classical meteorology, a hot or cold vapour that ascends from the earth into the sky.

fifth element: see '*aethêr*'.

form: Greek *eidos* or *idea*. Originally *eidos* means 'perceptible shape'. In philosophy (Plato and after), 'form' denotes the defining character of an entity, transcendent in Plato, immanent in Aristotle.

happiness: see '*eudaimonia*'.

hêgemonikon: literally, 'that which leads', applied to the rational part or faculty of the soul.

homoiomerous: having parts similar to the whole (e.g. skin, parts of which are skin; as opposed to hand, parts of which are fingers, palm, etc.).

horror vacui: the cause that propels a body into a neighbouring empty space.

hylemorphic (or **hylomorphic**): analysed into matter and form.

hypostasis: a Neo-Platonic term for a level of reality in a hierarchical scale.

katastematic: not in motion (opposite of **kinetic**).

katharsis: literally 'cleansing' or 'religious purification'. Used by Aristotle of the effect of tragedy upon the mind. For the controversy about its meaning in that context, see ch. 3, pp. 86–90.

kinetic: of, in, or to do with motion.

lekta: 'things said', distinguished from things with physical existence or no existence. A Stoic term.

Lyceum: the public park in Athens, dedicated to Apollo Lycaeus, where Aristotle taught.

Manichees: adherents to the doctrines of Mani (third century AD), combining elements of Persian religion with Christianity.

matter: translates Greek *hylê* (literally 'wood'). A technical term in Aristotle and after, denoting the substrate (q.v.) underlying quality, quantity, shape, colour, etc.

metaphysics: literally 'what comes after physics', originally the name given by an editor, perhaps Andronicus of Rhodes in the first century BC, to the books of Aristotle now called by this name. It is debated whether the name simply means 'after' the *Physics* in some edition or list of Aristotle's work, or implies that these books express something more fundamental than physics.

meteorology: in classical antiquity the term applies to whatever goes on in the region between the heavens and the earth.

Middle Platonists: Philosophers of the Academy, beginning with Antiochus' rejection of Scepticism in the early first century BC and ending with the Neo-Platonic school of Plotinus in the third century AD. Plutarch is the only one whose writings survive.

mimêsis: imitation or representation, especially in literature or in visual art. See ch. 3, pp. 78 ff.

nous: usually translated 'mind' or 'intelligence'. Sometimes denotes specifically right understanding, distinguished from cogitation or imagination.

oikeiôsis: this Stoic term, sometimes translated 'appropriation', refers to a disposition of affectionate ownership towards oneself, said to be innate in all animals, including humans. It provides a basis for the Stoic ethical goal of 'living in accordance with nature'.

ontology: the study of being or beings.

organon: literally, a tool. Used of Aristotle's logic, to distinguish it from philosophy proper.

participation (methexis): a Platonic technical term for the relation that individual objects bear to Forms.

pathos: emotion (plural *pathê*).

Pelagian: related to Pelagius, a fourth-century Christian 'heretic'.

Peripatetic: belonging to the school of Aristotle, who taught in the *peripatos* or 'walkway' in the park in Athens named 'the Lyceum'.

phainomena: whatever can be perceived or observed to be the case.

phantasia: usually translated as 'imagination', but its meaning includes 'presentations' of sense-perception, and 'appearances' in any mode of experience.

potentiality: translates Greek *dynamis*, an Aristotelian technical term, meaning 'capability of becoming (something)'. Contrasted with actuality (Greek *energeia* or *entelecheia*).

Presocratics: a modern term for the succession of philosophers beginning with Thales and ending (usually) with Democritus, who was in fact contemporary with Socrates.

prime matter: whatever, if anything, is left of a thing when all of its properties are removed in thought.

privation (sterêsis): an Aristotelian term for the absence of a form.

prolêpsis: literally 'anticipation'. An Epicurean technical term for a concept stored in the mind.

Protagorean: pertaining to Protagoras, the fifth-century sophist, notorious for his relativism.

psuchê or **psychê:** Latin *anima*, the principle of life; usually but awkwardly translated as 'soul' in English.

Pyrrhonism: the (unwritten) doctrine of Pyrrhon of Elis (fourth/third century BC), the founder of Greek Scepticism, revived in the first century BC by Aenesidemus.

Pythagoreans: followers of Pythagoras, the almost mythical sixth-century philosopher who migrated from Samos to South Italy.

sempiternal: lasting through the whole of time (as opposed to eternal = timeless).

sôritês: from *sôros*, a heap. A paradox generated from the idea that, if one grain of sand does not make a heap, neither do two grains, nor three, nor four, nor any number generated by adding one at a time.

sublunary: 'below the moon', includes everything in the Aristotelian cosmos except the heavenly spheres and their contents.

substance: usually translates Greek *ousia*, and denotes an independent being.

substrate: Greek *hypokeimenon*, a term in logic and metaphysics for whatever 'underlies' predicates of quality, quantity, etc.

syllogism: Aristotle's ideal form of scientific argument. See ch. 2, pp. 48–53.

teleology: the doctrine that processes of nature, like intentional human actions, are goal-directed.

Topics: Aristotle's writings on the 'commonplaces' of argument.

transmigration: Greek *metempsychôsis*, the transference of the psyche from one human or animal body to another (a Pythagorean idea).

Name index

Subject index

Index locorum

Augustine